Review
of
Biblical Literature

2014

SBL Press

Review of Biblical Literature _____

Editor
Jan G. van der Watt (The Netherlands)

Managing Editor
Bob Buller (U.S.A.)

Editorial Board
Rubén R. Dupertuis (U.S.A.)
Mark W. Hamilton (U.S.A.)
James Alfred Loader (Austria)
Joseph Verheyden (Belgium)

Volume 16 (2014)
ISSN 1099-0046

SBL Press
825 Houston Mill Road, Suite 350
Atlanta, GA 30329
http://www.sbl-site.org

© 2014 SBL Press

Typesetting by Lindsay Lingo, The Project Company, Loveland, Colorado

Contents_____

Indexes

Editor's Foreword_____

The *Review of Biblical Literature* has established itself internationally as one of the leading review organs for biblical literature and related fields. It has become especially known for being comprehensive, international, timely, and authoritative.

+ *RBL* reviews a wide and comprehensive spectrum of books from publishers large and small—seventy-two different publishers over the past twelve months—across the entire range of biblical studies and its cognate disciplines. To broaden our offerings, *RBL* publishes multiple and contrasting reviews as often as possible.
+ Not only does *RBL* review books written in various languages (e.g., English, German, French, Italian, Spanish, Hebrew); it also invites scholars from a variety of language groups to review for *RBL*. Further, the editorial board overseeing this process consists of leading academics from around the world.
+ *RBL* reviews are published in a timely fashion. As a rule, we attempt to review books within two years of their publication, and we try to place the review within a few months of receiving a book. Finally, we typically publish each review within two to three months of receiving it.
+ *RBL* reviews are written by the most qualified scholars available, whether a member of the Society of Biblical Literature or the broader scholarly guild. In addition, all *RBL* reviews are vetted to ensure their quality by a member of our editorial board.

During the past twelve months, thanks to the cooperative efforts of our reviewers, editors, and staff, *RBL* published 390 reviews. With an average of 4 pages per review, the past year's output would fill 1,560 published pages. To take this a step further, the 7,510 reviews published since the beginning of *RBL* through the end of September 2013 would require over 30,000 printed pages. This is truly a monumental accomplishment, not least because it has been achieved almost entirely through the contributions of volunteers

As is well known, *RBL* announces the publication of new reviews in a weekly newsletter. That newsletter is distributed to over 9,000 subscribers, many of whom have no other contact with the Society than *RBL*. The *RBL* newsletter plays a significant role in leading scholars, students, and interested laypersons to the *RBL* website (www.bookreviews.org), where they can read the latest reviews or search for books reviewed since *RBL*'s creation fourteen years ago. The *RBL* website records over two million visits each year. Taking all these data into account, it is no stretch to conclude that *RBL* indeed leads the way in providing scholarly reviews of biblical studies publications.

But there is even more to the story than the number of reviews *RBL* publishes and the number of visitors to the website. *RBL* also leads the way in building bridges between biblical scholarship from every region of the world. Not only do we provide free access to scholarly reviews to anyone with access to the Internet, but over the last twelve months we have published reviews by scholars from twenty-seven different countries, which underscores our international scope. These countries include: Australia, Austria, Belgium, Brazil, Canada, Denmark, Finland, Germany, Greece, Hungary, Indonesia, Ireland, Israel, Italy, Malawi, New Zealand, Nigeria, Norway, Papau New Guinea, Romania, South Africa, South Korea, Sweden, Switzerland, The Netherlands, U.K., and U.S. Once again, roughly half (49.5 percent) of *RBL* reviews were authored by scholars outside of the U.S.

Obviously, our success depends not only on the publishers supplying books but also on hundreds of academics who are willing to share their time and expertise with the readership of *RBL*. We would like to thank them all. *RBL* is a group effort in the true sense of the word, with so many SBL members joining together to make it the success it is.

Thus with gratitude and pride we present this print publication, a selection of 158 reviews published on our website during the latter half of 2013 and the first half of 2014. We hope that this printed selection of reviews published electronically the past year will encourage readers to visit the *RBL* website at http://bookreviews.org/ or the RBL blog, where new reviews are announced each week, at http://rblnewsletter.blogspot.com/.

Jan van der Watt
RBL General Editor
Radboud University Nijmegen
Nijmegen, The Netherlands

Benjamin D. Sommer, ed.
Jewish Concepts of Scripture: A Comparative Introduction
New York: New York University Press, 2012. Pp. ix + 334. Paper. $26.00. ISBN:
9780814760024.

Introduction
Marc Zvi Brettler
Brandeis University

The following four papers represent revisions of presentations at the 2013 Annual
Meeting of the Society of Biblical Literature, in a session of the Theologies of
Hebrew Scriptures Section dedicated to discussing a work edited by Ben Sommer,
Jewish Concepts of Scripture. Sommer teaches Bible at the Jewish Theological
Seminary of America. As the reviewers note, this book is the first of its kind.
Many have written on Jewish biblical interpretation, but no one has assembled
a set of essays that asks the fundamental question: What are the Jewish concepts
of scripture? In its seventeen chapters, this book offers a wide variety of answers,
showing the complicated ways that Jews (including Karaites) over the ages have
understood what the Bible is. The answers are fundamentally different from those
offered by a 2006 volume edited by Justin Holcomb and published by the same
press, *Christian Theologies of Scripture: A Comparative Introduction*, and much
utility is derived from reading these two collections in tandem.

The panel at SBL was organized with the help of Tamara Eskenazi, Professor
of Bible at Hebrew Union College-Jewish Institute of Religion in Los Angeles.
The responses we elicited aimed to cover three different perspectives: a Jewish
theological perspective (Tamar Kamionkowski), a Christian theological perspective (Mary Chilton Callaway), and a perspective from the comparative study of
religion (Barbara Holdrege). As in the session, these are followed by a response
from the editor, Benjamin Sommer.

S. Tamar Kamionkowski
Reconstructionist Rabbinical College

Jewish Concepts of Scripture: A Comparative Introduction is a must read for
anyone in biblical studies who is interested either in the history of interpretation or in multifaith work. In his fine introduction Sommer lays out the project

of the volume. While there are several excellent books on the history of Jewish interpretation, Sommer indicates that the function of this collection is to ask the prior questions: "Why do they [Jews] read it, or perform rituals with it, in the first place? For what reasons have Jews turned to this anthology?" (2). He then goes on to problematize the very term "scripture," suggesting that rabbinic works are just as much "scripture" as is the written collection known as the Bible. So if the Bible is not necessarily scripture, what is the Bible for Jews?

Several years ago I participated on a panel at the SBL on Jewish biblical theology and I quoted what has now become a seminal article for Jewish biblical theology: Jon Levenson's assertion that, "[w]hereas in the church the sacred text tends to be seen as a *word* (the singular is telling) demanding to be proclaimed magisterially, in Judaism it tends to be seen as a *problem* with many facets, each of which deserves attention and debate."[1] I then asserted that "a Jewish biblical theology should not look for a unity or *Mitte*. The role of a Jewish biblical theologian is to explicate and highlight the points of the debate rather than to seek which one is earlier and which is more evolved. For Jewish scholars, the concept of dialogue and debate is not a methodological entry point that may take us to new places; dialogue is the essence of Jewish theology and is at the heart of the Jewish textual tradition. It is the spirit of debate and diversity of opinions that I believe to be most significant in a Jewish biblical theology." I assumed that this collection of essays would reaffirm this understanding; it has, rather, complicated it.

If we summarize the arguments in this collection, we might boil it down to the following: What is the Bible for Jews? It is a collection of verses. It is the body of God. It is a cultural artifact. It is text that is performed in synagogue. It is a partner to Jewish readers in dialogic relationship. It is a modern political manifesto. It is the word of God. It is a divinely inspired work. It is a document composed and redacted by humans over the course of hundreds of years.

In other words, a reading of Sommer's collection leads one to conclude that the text of the Bible is not stable, the methods of interpretation are not stable, and the understanding of the nature of the Bible is not stable. Sommer writes, "For the rabbis, the Bible is not really a book at all. It is not a scroll, and it is not a text.... Rather, the Bible is a hypertext, a database with myriad internal connections spanning the whole canon" (68). Moshe Idel writes, "the Torah serves as an intermediary between the creator and man. The letters of the Torah represent what I termed earlier the linguistic immanence of the divine within the created world. The Hasidic mystic can restrict his contemplation solely to letters of the Torah and attain the divine source" (173). Meira Polliack writes, concerning the Judeo-Arabic exegetes, that they "give voice to a scientific (secularizing) conception of biblical language, viewing it as a system of signs comparable to those of

---

1. Jon D. Levenson, "Why Jews Are Not Interested in Biblical Theology," in *Judaic Perspectives on Ancient Israel* (ed. J. Neusner, B. A. Levine and E. S. Frerichs; Philadelphia: Fortress, 1987), 55.

other languages and denying it an inherent mystical and mythological dimension" (86). Furthermore, she and Robert Harris assert that in the Jewish medieval world the Bible was analyzed as literature. Yair Zakovitch discusses the ways in which early Zionists secularized the Bible, disassociating it from rabbinic interpretation and reclaiming the Bible's focus on the land and nationalism (299–316). James Diamond explains that for Maimonides those exegetes who look to the Bible for ritual and legal law diminish the stature of the Bible; but those who penetrate its more lofty metaphysical mysteries bring honor to Scripture (130).

As I reflect on this multifaceted range, I ask myself: Is there any unified understanding of the Bible in Judaism? If there is a common core, what is it? If there is not a common core, what are the ramifications of such a conclusion? I would argue that the Bible becomes whatever each generation needs it to be, that Jewish intelligentsia have used the Bible as the clay from which Judaism is reshaped over and over again, adapting to the cultures in which it finds itself. This implies that the stable element in Jewish readings of the Bible is that the Bible is the playground through which each generation expresses its Jewishness. The Bible becomes a mirror of sorts, a reflection and a mechanism for more clearly understanding and articulating one's Judaism.

In the introduction to this book, Sommer raises up Moshe Halbertal's distinction between normative and formative canon. Normative texts are those that are obeyed, those to which a group is loyal. Formative texts are (to quote Halbertal via Sommer) "taught, read, transmitted and interpreted.… They provide a society or a profession with a shared vocabulary" (5). For Halbertal, the Bible is a normative canon, but Sommer rightly points out that a Jew goes to rabbinic literature, not biblical literature, for information about how one ought to act in specific contexts. In other words, the Bible is a formative collection; it provides Jewish exegetes throughout the generations with a shared vocabulary or, minimally, with a shared source.

The only common thread that I perceive after considering this collection of essays is that for an interpretive approach to Bible to be Jewish, it must somehow hook itself or understand itself as part of a larger tradition of Jewish textual interpretation. A reader might incorporate, co-opt, recontextualize, or even claim to reject earlier Jewish uses of the Bible—but in each of these cases there is an acknowledgement and in most cases an incorporation of the work of earlier generations. Play any game you want to, but you must play on our playground. This means that Jewish practice, belief, and identity precede and define the nature of the engagement with the text. In other words, it is the Judaism of each generation that determines the function of the Bible. Simultaneously, it is engagement with the Bible that helps those practices, beliefs and identities to flourish. The medieval exegetes began to read the Bible as literature because they were born into a world in which these reading modalities were valued. Buber's engagement with the Bible was inspired by immersion in modern philosophy. Maimonides brought Aristotelian logic into Jewish thinking via his approach to engagement with the Bible.

This point then brings me to another question: If the Bible has functioned as a divinely authored reference book from which Jewish legal practice is derived and as the body of God and as a collection of human-produced documents that may teach us something about antiquity, are there any interpretive methods that would fall beyond the pale. Where is the boundary?

I believe that the answer lies not in methodology but in sociology. As each generation has developed new uses for the Bible, there is always some kind of reference to other branches of interpretation. There is a consciousness about being a part of a larger enterprise. The new mode of interpretation must gain some measure of authority within the arena of the teacher-student relationship. Interpretation is a communal activity.

Let me bring in a specific example from the contemporary world of Jewish textual interpretation. Tamar Ross, professor of Jewish Philosophy at Bar Ilan University and author of *Expanding the Palace of Torah*,[2] advocates for an approach to revelation that she refers to as cumulative revelation (this is a model from Abraham Isaac Kook). She argues for an approach to revelation that understands Torah not as rigid and fixed but as a fluid, dynamic dialectic between original revelation and the unfolding of history (which itself is controlled by God) as a means of revealing God's unfolding will.

She argues that, just as Torah cannot be blamed for patriarchy (patriarchy having come from human culture), so too our modern sensibilities cannot be construed as foreign to Judaism. Ultimately, where the values come from is irrelevant—what is important is that as Jewish communities encounter new values they must be integrated into Torah and that this project is what God desires. She writes: "It is Torah that must absorb the world rather than the world the Torah."

There is nothing in her use of the Bible that is radically new, but when her book was first published it was deemed too radical for her intended audience (modern Orthodox Jews) because she was not recognized as an authority figure and because her use of the Bible did not conform to the Judaism of her audience. While the rhetoric surrounding Ross's work is "academic," the problem has really been a sociological one.

This brings me to my final question: To what extent is biblical criticism, as practiced by Jewish scholars, a Jewish enterprise? Can biblical criticism as practiced by Jewish scholars make a claim to be yet another visit to the same playground? If each generation of interpreters has brought the text into conversation with the world in which they lived, what cultural factors are we trying to bring into Judaism by the way we interpret the Bible?

My answer to this question is a highly personal one. Jewish life today is characterized by a range of Jewish movements whose members interact with one another perhaps more than at any other time in Jewish history. Orthodox Jews work from day to day among non-Jews and non-Orthodox Jews. Conservative, Reform, and Reconstructionist Jews are completely integrated with one another

---

2. Tamar Ross, *Expanding the Palace of Torah: Orthodoxy and Feminism* (HBI Series on Jewish Women; Waltham, MA: Brandeis, 2004).

and with the broader world in which we live. The majority of Jewish Americans see themselves as primarily citizens of the world without any particular allegiance to the Jewish people.

Amidst this reality are a small group of Jewish biblicists who have been trying to bring biblical scholarship to Jewish communities. I wonder whether the celebration of multiplicity in the Bible is a way of connecting with the realities of Jewish life today—with the multiplicity of ways in which Jews today live their lives. Are we trying to draw subtle lines of connection between contemporary Jewish life and the composition of the Bible? Are we bolstering the notion that there have always been a range of approaches to Jewish living? After all, just look at JE and D and P. To assert that the Bible is both a compilation of varied voices and a unique collection aligns in interesting ways with the challenge of Judaism today. We are one and we are many.

Upon completing Sommer's collection, a famous biblical passage came to mind from Deuteronomy: "You shall love the LORD your God with all your heart, with all your soul, and with all your might. These words that I command you today shall be upon your heart. You shall teach them to your children and speak of them when you are sitting in your home, when you walk on the road, when you lie down, and when you rise up" (Deut 6:5–7).

The collection echoes those ancient words: the Bible may represent the body of God, it may be literature, or it may be a vast database waiting for its readers to reveal its secrets—the key is *v'dibbarta bam*: speak of them.

Mary Chilton Callaway
Fordham University

In my early years after graduate school I had a jolting experience, unsettling any thought that I could bracket my Christian perspective and read Scripture simply as a scholar. One of the teachings I had absorbed was that the narrative of the people Israel that frames the laws in the center of the Torah provides the authority for the law. We keep these laws because God has done great things for us. How disorienting, then, to be challenged by a Jewish colleague who suggested that I had it backwards. The heart of Torah is not story, but law, and this law provides the frame in which to read the story, which leads the reader to Sinai. Being asked to comment on this volume from the perspective of a Christian biblical scholar brought this incident to mind, with a bit of embarrassment at the naïve assumptions of my young self. But of course we are all reading *as*, and one of the many contributions of this volume is the way that it helps us think constructively and in new ways about this reality of our *situadedness* as readers when we consider Jewish concepts of Scripture.

The collection is a pleasure to read. Each essay is elegantly crafted, so that historical and technical details that might be daunting are hospitably presented and a pleasure to savor as part of a clear argument. Even more impressive is way that the essays create a rich meta-narrative telling the story of Jewish engagements with Scripture. In my reading, two threads that run through this meta-narrative are *delight* and *struggle*. In every era exegetes play in the garden of Scripture, savoring words, characters, contradictions, even problems. From Robbie Harris on Rashi to Marc Brettler on Moshe Greenberg, the authors present exegetes address-ing problems in Scripture not as trouble but rather as opportunity. At the same time, the authors of these essays present their exegetes as aware in some way that they are outsiders to the world of Scripture. Ancient and medieval exegetes may not have been as self-consciously aware of this as Buber and Rosenzweig, yet all clearly struggled to navigate living simultaneously in the rich textual world of the Bible and in their own culture, whose worldly language was incommensurate with Hebrew. These two threads of delight and struggle are, in my reading, the highlight of the collection's meta-narrative of a Jewish concept of Scripture. It is this hallmark of Jewish engagement with Scripture that I want to explore from my Christian perspective.

The essays repeatedly illustrate the sheer joy that Torah brings, the delight in the play of language, all those colorful characters, and especially the knotty problems that stop an attentive reader. The essays gave Ps 1's phrase "delight in the Torah of the LORD" new meaning for me. Steve Fraade's explanation of the reality of Oral Torah that surrounds the written Torah like a nimbus, somehow simul-taneously prior and subsequent to written Torah, articulates one kind of delight. Ben Sommer's analysis of the rabbinic understanding of scriptural language as having *supercharged meaning* that needed to be unpacked using particular her-meneutical rules suggests to me delight in the constant movement between one particular word or verse and another, apparently unrelated one, elsewhere in Scripture. The Holy One dropped clues, and we have a lifetime to decipher them and find the treasures of supercharged meaning. Robbie Harris presents a memo-rable example in the question of eleventh-century French exegete Rashbam, who asked why God's blessing of the seventh day appears at the beginning of the Torah. It is, this grandson of Rashi proposed, the Holy One foreseeing the surprise and confusion that readers might experience at Exod 20:11, when they learn that the one who took them out of Egypt and gives them the law at Sinai is also the creator of the world! In Harris's reading, Rashbam's observation anticipates by centuries the modern literary-critical concept of prolepsis. For this Christian reader, Rash-bam's exegetical maneuver perfectly exemplifies the devout playfulness that Jews traditionally brought to reading Scripture. The essays also highlight the savoring of multiple voices, contradiction, and even, as James Diamond suggests in his essay on Maimonides, awe that finally ends in silence rather than words. This familial joy in decoding and even outwitting Scripture is distinctive to Judaism. Christians love their Bible and find comfort in it, but images of play are not typi-cally part of their vocabulary.

Yet this delight in Scripture is always complicated by conflicts that arise from reading *as*. Jonathan Cohen shows how Buber and Rosenzweig read as German intellectuals, navigating between the universal humanism of their culture and the encounter between God and humans that occurs in the particular context of Jewish observance. The essays on the challenge of biblical criticism, on Yehezkel Kaufmann, and on Moshe Greenberg all offer richly textured narratives of Jewish scholars navigating the conflicts arising from reading *as*—in this case reading as scholars grappling with historical-critical methods of the nineteenth and twentieth centuries. The ancient world is where I am most at home as a biblical scholar, yet in reading these essays I suddenly felt like an interloper, because my task is to respond as a *Christian* biblical scholar, that is, as outsider. This is a useful exercise because it exchanges the experience of usually being at the center for the view from the margin. More, the exercise highlighted for me aspects of experiencing Scripture that Jews and Christians appear to share but that on closer look turn out to foreground genuine differences.

Elsie Stern's essay highlights one such aspect, the place of Scripture in liturgy. Early Christians developed their liturgies by adapting the synagogue service that they knew, which included readings from two different parts of Scripture. This practice highlighted the nature of Scripture as dialogical and showed the skills of the rabbi/preacher as wise—and often playful—exegete, able to find hidden relationships between the texts. By the late fourth century, the Jewish practice of pairing longer Torah readings with brief prophetic texts became part of Christian worship, but with different implications. The church reversed the order. While the synagogue liturgy gave pride of place to the first reading, in the church the first reading was usually from "the Old Testament" and was often called "the prophet," even if it was not from a prophetic book. The second reading, from Christian writings, was the important one. In the late second century, Melito of Sardis had given the name "the Old Testament" to the books of the Septuagint that New Testament writers called "the Scriptures." By the fourth century the complex understanding of the Scriptures apparent in earliest Christianity was beginning to be flattened into a hermeneutic of supersessionism. The riches of what the early Christians had called "the Scriptures" became instead a theological problem, treated in part by an implicit downgrading that was played out in worship services.

Elsie Stern uses the evocative term "performed Torah" to describe the place of Scripture in Jewish liturgy; it applies also to Christian use of Scripture in worship. The choreography of the Torah scroll being carried, admired, unrolled, and read was taken up in Christian liturgy, where the Gospel book, often enclosed in a highly decorated cover, took the place of the Torah scroll. It was (and still often is) carried in procession, held up, and kissed before being read. The irony that Stern points out, that the performed Torah presented pairs of readings chosen to highlight central rabbinic ideologies, is equally true in the church. The Bible that Christians hear in church is a highly edited, theologically shaped, and quite limited set of texts. Often the lectionary shapes the relation between the two Testaments as a simple prophecy-fulfillment scheme, rather than a rich dialogical interplay provoking thought about the nature of God or what it means to be faithful. Stern's argument that the way texts are paired in the lectionary teaches worshipers how to interpret them is mirrored in ongoing contemporary Christian debates about lectionaries, which are, as Stern shows, theological constructs.

The performance of Scriptures in Christian liturgical settings has historically caused unspeakable harm, especially through lectionary pairings and their association with certain freighted holy days. Throughout the Middle Ages, readings in Holy Week paired Jeremiah with scenes from the passion narrative, making an implicit link between Jeremiah and Jesus. The pairing of Lam 1:12, known as the Reproaches, with a reading of John's passion narrative on Good Friday often inflamed anti-Jewish sentiments. The liturgical performance of Scripture became the fuel for the fires of hatred, with devastating consequences for the lives of many Jews. Even today the passion narrative in the Gospel of John is often not simply read by one reader on Palm Sunday but given a dramatic performance by assigning different readers to characters in the story. The shameful legacy of anti-Judaism began to be addressed in some Christian quarters in the second half of the twentieth century. A first step was a new theological understanding of the ways that Christians might read the Hebrew Scriptures, not as the first act or as a foreshadowing, but as the Word of God complete in itself. Another step was acknowledging the real harm caused by the Gospels, not only as used, but as written. Some churches include teaching notes in the bulletin, distinguishing the historical setting of Jesus' death in the third decade of the first century from the contentious time of those who wrote the narratives decades later. Much remains to be done as Christians wrestle with the reality of what Gadamer called the history-of-effects of their Scriptures.

At the heart of this book is the question not only of how to read but just what is being read; that is, what is meant by Scripture? Ben Sommer's observation that in Judaism Scripture and tradition have never been separate realities but were intertwined from the beginning is pertinent. His statement that "the whole concept of Scripture is more fluid than it is in Christianity" (4) accounts in part for why Jews can struggle fruitfully with the Scriptures while often for Christians the Bible is just a problem. Modernity posed unsettling questions about Scripture for Jews, yet the essays of Jonathan Cohen, Baruch Schwartz, Job Jindo, and Marc Brettler all illustrate the varied ways that tradition was an ally in developing answers that accommodated Enlightenment thinking. For some parts of Christianity, on the other hand, modernity and the development of historical-critical exegesis led directly to fundamentalism, while for others it resulted in the reading practice that Ruldolf Bultmann called "demythologizing." Protestant Christianity had lost the rich medieval approach called the fourfold sense of Scripture, which assumed that a biblical text contained literal, allegorical, moral, and mystical meanings. Like similar levels in Jewish understanding that expand the notions of *peshat* and *drash*, the medieval Christian approach implied that Scripture is multivalent, never fully understood, and designed to accommodate different levels of human intellect and education. It was, as St. Gregory wrote in the preface to his commentary on Job, shallow enough for a lamb to wade in and deep enough for an elephant to swim in. Without this flexible exegetical tradition, many Christians saw modernity as an attack on their Scriptures and retreated into literalism. The essays in this collection show the multiple ways that Jewish wrestling with Scripture throughout history remains in close conversation with tradition. Jewish exegetes as diverse as Maimonides and Moshe Greenberg successfully combine the intellectual approaches of their time with rabbinic insights, rejecting the zero sum position that the plain sense is the only truth.

The collection creatively expands the exploration of "Scriptures" with essays by Yael Feldman and Yair Zakovitch on Scripture in contemporary Israeli life and literature. Both illustrate the magnetic power of evocative names and tropes from Scripture, even when cut loose from any religious context. These studies could productively be used in a conversation about the Bible in American culture, where Americans may be religious and love their Bible but are often innocent of what it contains. One gets the impression that Americans, like Israelis, like the *idea* of Scripture more than the realities of what Northrop Frye called "this huge sprawling book [sitting] in the middle of our cultural heritage." The sentimental view of Scripture as a kind of vestigial heritage in a secular culture makes the task of dealing with the complexity of historically embedded Scriptures, and the history-of-effects of those Scriptures, a challenge. These last essays effectively address in a different key the quest at the heart of the book, which seeks the parameters of Jewish concepts (not theology!) of Scripture. This Christian reader is indebted to Sommer for asking the question and to his authors for their instructive and engaging responses. By the end of my reading, the recurrent themes of delight and struggle that I read as the meta-narrative of the book began to mirror the witness of Scripture to Israel's experiences with the living God. Perhaps this parallel between encountering God and studying Torah itself suggests a Jewish concept of Scripture.

Barbara A. Holdrege
University of California, Santa Barbara

The academic study of scripture from the nineteenth century until the 1980s was almost exclusively the domain of biblical studies scholars and orientalist scholars who focused on the content and form of particular religious texts and on questions of the history of origins, the history of causes and conditions that produced specific texts. In recent decades comparative historians of religions such as Wilfred Cantwell Smith and William A. Graham have advanced an alternative model of scriptural study that gives priority instead to the *concept* and *functions* of scripture as a cross-cultural religious category. Scripture as a concept in the history of religions is primarily a *relational category*, which refers not simply to a text but to a text in its relationship to a religious community for whom it is sacred and authoritative. In this essay I would like to reflect on the contributions of Benjamin Sommer's *Jewish Concepts of Scripture: A Comparative Introduction* to the study of scripture within biblical studies and within the history of religions. More specifically, I will comment on the ways in which this collection of essays by an international group of sixteen noted specialists breaks from the prevailing paradigms of biblical studies and exemplifies what I term the "relational approach to the study of scripture" advocated in recent years by historians of religions such as Smith, Graham, and myself.[1] In the introduction to this edited collection Sommer explicitly invokes both Smith and Graham when outlining the volume's approach to the category of scripture.[2]

SCRIPTURE AS A RELATIONAL CATEGORY

The relational approach to the study of scripture advocated by historians of religions provides an alternative model of scriptural study that challenges in significant ways the dominant paradigms employed by biblical studies scholars. Building on and adapting a framework suggested by Fernando Segovia, we can distinguish four competing paradigms of biblical criticism, each of which encompasses a variety of methods: historical criticism, literary criticism, sociocultural criticism, and ideological criticism.[3] The dominant paradigms of biblical criticism tend to be "nonscriptural" in their respective approaches in that they treat the biblical texts not as religious documents but rather as historical documents, in the case of historical criticism, or as literary creations, in the case of literary criticism, or as sociocultural products, in the case of sociocultural criticism and ideological criticism. Such approaches, as Smith has emphasized, are primarily concerned with the biblical texts in their "prescriptural phase" or "postscriptural phase" and consequently give little emphasis to the functions of the Hebrew Bible or Christian Bible as scripture (Smith 1989, 45). The relational approach to the study of scripture, in contrast, focuses on the concept and functions of scripture as a *religious* category and a *relational* category and is concerned with the question of what it means for a text such as the Hebrew Bible to be regarded as *scripture* by a

---

1. Among landmark studies, see Smith 1971, 1989, 1993; Graham 1987a, 1987b. Among other studies that have been inspired by the relational approach to the study of scripture, see Levering 1989; Holdrege 1996; Wimbush 2000.

2. Sommer invokes in particular Smith 1993; Graham 1987b.

3. In plotting recent shifts in biblical studies, Segovia distinguishes four paradigms, which he terms historical criticism, literary criticism, cultural criticism, and cultural studies. Although "historical criticism" and "literary criticism" are generally accepted designations for paradigms of biblical criticism, Segovia's use of the terms "cultural criticism" and "cultural studies" is idiosyncratic and ambiguous, as these terms are used in disciplines outside of biblical studies—including literary studies, sociology, anthropology, and social history—to encompass specific clusters of theoretical approaches in the human sciences. In lieu of Segovia's "cultural criticism" and "cultural studies," I prefer the terms "sociocultural criticism" and "ideological criticism," which accord more closely with the terminology adopted by a range of biblical scholars to describe recent shifts in the discipline. For critical appraisal of the four dominant paradigms of biblical criticism, see Segovia 1995a, 1995b.

religious community. What does it mean for religious communities to "scriptural-ize"? Graham remarks:

> From the historian's perspective, the sacrality or holiness of a book is not an a priori attribute of a text but one that is realized historically in the life of communities who respond to it as something sacred or holy. A text becomes "scripture" in active subjective relationship to persons, and as part of a cumulative communal tradition. No text, written or oral or both, is sacred or authoritative in isolation from a community.... A book is only "scripture" insofar as a group of persons perceive it to be sacred or holy, powerful and portentous, possessed of an exalted authority, and in some fashion transcendent of, and hence distinct from, all other speech and writing. (Graham 1987a, 5)

Sommer's edited collection of essays, in its focus on mapping key moments in the history of the Hebrew Bible's functions as scripture in the ongoing lives of those Jewish thinkers and communities who revere the text as sacred and authoritative, exemplifies a new model of biblical studies that is above all relational—and thereby scriptural—in its approach. I would like to reflect briefly on this collaborative volume's contributions to four specific issues that are critical components of the study of scripture as a relational category: (1) canonical authority, (2) reception histories, (3) social location, and (4) modes of appropriation.

CANONICAL AUTHORITY

Religious communities employ a variety of mechanisms by means of which they circumscribe a corpus of texts and set it apart from other texts as a sacred and authoritative canon. In discussing the category of canon in the history of religions, Jonathan Z. Smith has suggested that "canon is best seen as one form of a basic cultural process of limitation and overcoming that limitation through ingenuity" (Smith 1982, 52). He further suggests that the task of overcoming the limitation posed by a closed canon is accomplished through the exegetical enterprise, in which the task of the interpreter is "continually to extend the domain of the closed canon over everything that is known or everything that exists *without* altering the canon in the process" (1982, 48). The Jewish conception of Torah, as defined in the classical rabbinic texts discussed in a number of the essays (Sommer, Fraade, and Yadin-Israel), accords well with Smith's model of canon in that it functions within the classical rabbinic tradition as a delimited corpus of texts that is also potentially unlimited.

At the center of the rabbinic canon is a fixed corpus of written texts that has been scrupulously preserved in unaltered form by the Jewish scribal tradition: the Sefer Torah (Book of the Torah), which comprises the Five Books of Moses, or the Pentateuch. The canonical authority of the Sefer Torah is ascribed to its sacred status as the Word of God that was revealed at Mount Sinai through the agency of the prophet Moses. Every word of the Sefer Torah is held to have been directly dictated by God to Moses, who acted as a scribe and recorded the words of God verbatim in the Book of the Torah; therefore, as Sommer's essay emphasizes, the language of the Sefer Torah is invested with a unique ontological status as the divine language, which is radically different from ordinary human language.

The domain of Torah and its divinely sanctioned authority is subsequently extended to encompass the entire Hebrew Bible, the Tanak, including not only the Pentateuch but also the Nevi'im (Prophets) and the Ketuvim (Writings). While remaining delimited as the Hebrew Bible, which is designated as the Written Torah (*tôrāh še bi-ktāb*), the Torah is expanded even further to incorporate the Oral Torah (*tôrāh še bĕ-ʾal peh*), the oral tradition of interpretation of the written text. The Oral Torah functions as a fluid, open-ended category that includes the halakic and aggadic teachings contained in the Mishnah, Talmud, and Midrash, along with potentially all texts, teachings, and practices authorized by the rabbinic elite.[4] The rabbinic sages claim that the distinction between Written Torah and Oral Torah derives from the original revelation at Mount Sinai, in which God revealed to Moses two Torahs: a written text, comprising the Sefer Torah, Nevi'im, and Ketuvim; and an oral tradition of interpretation of the written text that has been preserved in the authoritative teachings of the rabbis.

The rabbinic canon of Written Torah and Oral Torah is thus simultaneously closed and open, fixed and fluid, delimited and potentially unlimited, as Fraade's essay emphasizes.[5] Although Sommer indicates in his introduction that, for practical as well as theoretical reasons, the essays in the volume limit their discussion to Jewish conceptions of the Hebrew Bible, or Written Torah, I would argue that the classical rabbinic notion of the dual Torah—Written Torah and Oral Torah—continues to haunt many of the medieval and modern responses to the question "What is scripture for the Jews?" that are addressed in the essays. Whether classical rabbinic formulations of canon are upheld or rejected, appropriated or subverted, the dual Torah remains a category invested with authoritative power that must be contended with by all those who wish to position themselves in relation to the rabbinic elite.

RECEPTION HISTORIES

This collection of essays on Jewish constructions of scripture, as an exemplum of the relational approach to the study of scripture, is concerned with excavating the reception histories of the Hebrew Bible in the lives of various Jewish thinkers and communities over the past two thousand years. This approach to history radically diverges from the "tempocentric" approach of the prevailing paradigms of biblical criticism, which tend to privilege certain time periods, focusing primarily on

---

4. The term *halakah* is used to designate any normative law, practice, or custom sanctioned by rabbinic authorities, while the term *aggadah* refers to nonlegal rabbinic teachings, including moral exhortations, theological speculations, and didactic narratives.

5. For an extended study of rabbinic constructions of Torah as an encompassing, paradigmatic symbol that is simultaneously delimited and potentially unlimited, see Holdrege 1996.

the ancient past—the biblical period—and/or on the present—the contemporary period. While historical criticism and sociocultural criticism tend to focus on the ancient past, on reconstructing the historical and sociocultural conditions that produced the biblical texts and recovering what the texts *meant* in their original contexts, the more recent trends of ideological criticism are concerned to connect the meanings of the ancient past with the meanings of the present, with a primary focus on what the biblical texts *mean* to contemporary readers in different social locations. The relational approach to the study of scripture, in contrast, is concerned with bridging the gap between past and present and reconstructing what a sacred text *has meant* to successive generations of readers—and listeners—from the inception of the text's canonization as scripture to the present day.

The history with which the relational approach is concerned is not *Entstehungsgeschichte*, a "history of origins," but rather *Wirkungsgeschichte*, a "history of effects," understood as the tradition of interpretations and appropriations of a sacred text in the cumulative histories of the various communities who revere the text as scripture. In the study of scripture *qua* scripture the primary concern is not to determine the sociohistorical conditions that produced a religious text but rather to excavate the multilayered and multivocal reception histories that the text itself has produced in the ongoing lives of religious communities. Wilfred Cantwell Smith writes with respect to the Qur'ān:

> [T]he Qur'ān, if it is to be understood in anything remotely approaching its religious significance, must be seen as not merely a seventh-century Arabian document (which has tended to be the way in which Western Orientalists, as distinct from religionists, have treated it) but also as an eighth-, and a twelfth-, and a seventeenth-, and a twentieth-century document, and one intimately intertwined in the life not only of Arabia but also of East Africa and Indonesia. For the Qur'ān has played a role—formative, dominating, liberating, spectacular—in the lives of millions of people, philosophers and peasants, politicians and merchants and housewives, saints and sinners, in Baghdad and Cordoba and Agra, in the Soviet Union since the Communist revolution, and so on. That role is worth discerning and pondering. The attempt to understand the Qur'ān is to understand how it has fired the imagination, and inspired the poetry, and formulated the inhibitions, and guided the ecstasies, and teased the intellects, and ordered the family relations and the legal chicaneries, and nurtured the piety, of hundreds of millions of people in widely diverse climes and over a series of radically divergent centuries.... What produced the Qur'ān is an interesting and legitimate question, but a secondary one. Less minor than it, less antiquarian, religiously much more significant, is the marvelous question, What has the Qur'ān produced? (Smith 1971, 20-21)

This collection of essays on Jewish constructions of scripture similarly takes as its starting-point the question, what has the Hebrew Bible produced? More specifically, what roles—"formative, dominating, liberating, spectacular"—has the Bible assumed in the lives of Jewish thinkers and communities in various historical periods, geographical regions, and sociocultural contexts from the beginning of the Common Era to the present day? The essays explore a range of questions pertaining to specific moments in this long history. How were the categories of Written Torah and Oral Torah constructed and elaborated in the classical rabbinic formulations found in the Mishnah, Palestinian Talmud, Babylonian Talmud, and Midrash collections during the first millennium CE (Fraade, Yadin-Israel, Sommer)? How were the contents of the Written Torah reshaped by the rabbinic authorities through their selection and arrangement of the pentateuchal and prophetic readings included in the synagogue liturgy (Stern)? How were the midrashic modes of interpretation of the Written Torah appropriated, reconfigured, and/or displaced in the respective approaches of the triumvirate of medieval rabbinic biblical commentators: Rashi (1040–1105), whose commentary embodies the traditionalist approach of the northern French school (Harris); Abraham Ibn Ezra (ca. 1089–1167), who was born in Muslim Spain and integrated into his Hebrew commentary the heritage of the Judeo-Arabic tradition of biblical interpretation (Polliack); and Naḥmanides (1194–1270), who was born in Christian Spain and incorporated into his biblical commentary mystical currents from the newly burgeoning kabbalistic tradition (Hughes)? How was the Torah re-visioned by thirteenth-century kabbalists as a supratextual, transhistorical reality that participates in the nature and structure of the Godhead (Idel)? Within the domain of philosophy, how was the Written Torah re-read by the acclaimed medieval philosopher Maimonides (1138–1204) in the Golden Age of Muslim Spain as a philosophical text from which metaphysical truths can be derived (Diamond)?

Within the modern period, how was the midrashic mode of reading the Written Torah further displaced by the "dialogical hermeneutics" of the German philosophers Martin Buber (1878–1965) and Franz Rosenzweig (1886–1929), who collaborated on a German translation of the Hebrew Bible (Cohen)? With the rise of the historical-critical approach to study of the Pentateuch in the nineteenth century, particularly as expressed in the Documentary Hypothesis, how did the leaders of the contending religious movements in Europe and the United States— Reform, Conservative, and Orthodox—respond by either accepting, rejecting, or accommodating some form of pentateuchal criticism (Schwartz, Carmy)? How did Jewish biblical studies scholars in the academy, such as Yehezkel Kaufmann (1889-1963) and Moshe Greenberg (1928-2010), respond by developing their own distinctly Jewish approaches to pentateuchal criticism (Schwartz, Jindo, Brettler)? Finally, what roles has the Hebrew Bible assumed in modern Israeli literature and in Israeli secular culture (Feldman, Zakovitch)?

This collection of essays, in responding to these and other questions, reconstructs a history of key moments in Jewish engagements with the Hebrew Bible, from the classical rabbinic formulations at the beginning of the Common Era to contemporary appropriations at the beginning of the third millennium, and thereby provides a critical chapter in the ongoing project of reconstructing the multivocal reception histories of the Hebrew Bible among the multifarious Jewish communities who have revered the text as scripture.

SOCIAL LOCATION

In excavating the reception histories of particular scriptures, the relational approach to the study of scripture is concerned to illuminate the interconnections among canonical authority, social location, and modes of scriptural appropriation. In contrast to the dominant paradigms of biblical criticism, which tend to give precedence to the interpretations of highly educated readers who are trained in the methods of biblical studies, the relational approach does not privilege the interpretations of any one socioreligious group but rather is concerned with delineating the various types of interpretive strategies adopted by different groups positioned at different locations in the socioreligious hierarchy to legitimate their respective sectional interests. The relational approach, of course, includes an analysis of the interpretive strategies used by various types of religious elites who position themselves at the *higher rungs* of the hierarchy. However, such an approach is equally concerned to recover the interpretations emanating from the popular power matrix, which draws its strength from so-called "common religious folk" as well as marginalized social and religious groups who have been relegated to the *lower rungs* or *margins* of the hierarchy. In addition, such an approach takes into account the countervailing interpretive strategies developed by liminal figures who stand in the *interstices* or at the *edges* of institutional structures, such as reformers and critics of the dominant culture and poets, writers, and other artists.

This volume on Jewish concepts of scripture does a masterful job of mapping the multilayered readings of the Hebrew Bible by various types of male Jewish elites: the Tannaim and Amoraim of the classical rabbinic period; medieval rabbinic biblical commentators; esoteric circles of medieval kabbalists; medieval and modern Jewish philosophers; modern Reform rabbis, Conservative rabbis, and Orthodox rabbis; and biblical studies scholars in the modern academy. Indeed, the essays on the classical rabbinic and medieval interpreters of the Hebrew Bible, when read together, provide a marvelous demonstration of the "omnisignificance" of the Written Torah—to use a term by James Kugel (1981, 103–4) that is frequently invoked in the essays—in that they point to the multileveled meanings ascribed to the text by different interpreters: (1) *děrāšāh*, the hermeneutical meaning, which is derived through the interpretive principles and methods of rabbinic Midrashim; (2) *pěšāṭ*, the plain meaning, which is the focus of the contextual exegeses of Rashi and the other medieval rabbinic commentators of the northern French school; (3) the allegorical meaning, which is the locus of the philosophical mode of interpretation adopted by Maimonides; and (4) *sôd*, the esoteric meaning, which is the focus of the kabbalistic exegeses of Naḥmanides and other medieval kabbalists. While the medieval biblical commentators may claim an allegiance to more than one interpretive mode—for example, *pěšāṭ* and *děrāšāh*, in the case of Rashi, or *pěšāṭ* and *sôd*, in the case of Naḥmanides—the medieval kabbalist Moses de Leon (ca. 1240–1305) used the acronym PaRDēS (literally, "garden" or "paradise") to reframe these four levels as a fourfold *hierarchy of meanings*, which the kabbalist exegete progressively unfolds, layer by layer, from lowest to highest: from *pěšāṭ*, the plain meaning, to *děrāšāh*, the hermeneutical meaning, to *remez*, the allegorical meaning, culminating in *sôd*, in which the kabbalist fathoms the deepest secrets of the Torah.

While this collection of essays thus provides a sophisticated and nuanced treatment of the multilayered exegetical enterprise in which various types of male elites have been engaged since the beginning of the Common Era, I would also like to see this volume break open the guild and give hermeneutical space to a more diverse array of readings—elite and popular, normative and subversive, literate and illiterate, male and female. The volume does give voice to the alternative scriptural readings of the Karaites, who rejected the Oral Torah and subverted rabbinic notions of authority based on familial background and scholarly lineage, giving precedence instead to the individual male interpreter whose authority derives from his training and expertise in the tools of biblical exegesis, regardless of socioeconomic status or scholarly class (Polliack). Beyond the Karaites, however, I long to hear at least some whisper of the suppressed voices of the various marginalized groups who were excluded from the academies of the rabbinic elite and subjected to hermeneutical forgetting by the sages—in particular, the uneducated common folk who were deemed the *ʿam hā-ʾāreṣ* (literally, "people of the land") and women. In Stern's essay about the synagogue service, we learn about rabbinic regulations that stipulate that the male reciter who reads from the Torah scroll must pause after each verse to allow the male translator to recite an Aramaic translation (*targûm*) of the verse. However, it would also be helpful to have some discussion about the role of the excluded "others" in the broader congregation who could engage the Torah aurally in the synagogue liturgy, through listening to the Torah reading and to its exposition in the homily, but who were not allowed to recite, study, or interpret the Torah themselves.

Several of the essays point to the new modes of accessing the Torah that became available to these excluded "others" in the modern period. Idel's essay about Jewish mysticism briefly mentions certain Ḥasidic masters who ascribe theurgic efficacy to the oral recitation of the Written Torah and insist that even an "unlettered but pious Jew" who does not understand the meaning of what he recites can draw down the divine presence through his oral performance. Feldman's essay about modern Israeli literature discusses several Israeli women writers who re-vision the biblical imagery of the Aqedah in their works. However, beyond these few references I would like to see a more full consideration of the strategies adopted by women and other marginalized groups to participate in the life of Torah even though they were historically excluded, prior to the modern period, from study of the Torah.

MODES OF APPROPRIATION

The relational approach to the study of scripture, in its call for a sociocultural expansion beyond the interpretations of the religious and academic elite to include a multitude of readings that are representative of all levels of the socioreligious hierarchy, also calls for a methodological expansion beyond text-bound, analytical modes of study to include a variety of cultural modes of appropriation. Although I realize that this mandate is beyond the scope of Sommer's volume on Jewish concepts of scripture, I can envision a companion volume that would focus on the lived traditions of Torah practice and performance, in which the Torah has assumed a pivotal role not only as an authoritative text to be studied and interpreted but also as a prodigious living force and as an identity-forging "world" that has shaped, nurtured, and transformed the lives of Jewish communities throughout their history. Jews have heard and received the living Word through a variety of oral-performative as well as written-analytical modes of reception. The companion volume that I envision would be concerned with the ways in which the Torah has been appropriated, engaged, experienced, embodied, and performed by various Jewish communities, transforming it from a fixed, bounded text into a fluid, open-ended language world that has found expression in a variety of cultural forms—in ritual performances and liturgies; in prayers, liturgical poems, and homilies; in music, literature, and the visual arts; in dance, drama, and film; in educational initiatives and social reforms; in political movements and ideologies; and in various forms of popular culture.

REFERENCES

Graham, William A. 1987a. *Beyond the Written Word: Oral Aspects of Scripture in the History of Religion*. New York: Cambridge University Press.
———. 1987b. "Scripture." *The Encyclopedia of Religion*. Edited by Mircea Eliade et al. New York: Macmillan.
Holdrege, Barbara A. 1996. *Veda and Torah: Transcending the Textuality of Scripture*. Albany: State University of New York Press.
Kugel, James L. 1981. *The Idea of Biblical Poetry: Parallelism and Its History*. New Haven: Yale University Press.
Levering, Miriam, ed. 1989. *Rethinking Scripture: Essays from a Comparative Perspective*. Albany: State University of New York Press.
Segovia, Fernando F. 1995a. "'And They Began to Speak in Other Tongues': Competing Modes of Discourse in Contemporary Biblical Criticism." Pages 1–32 in *Social Location and Biblical Interpretation in the United States*, vol. 1 of *Reading from This Place*. Edited by Fernando F. Segovia and Mary Ann Tolbert. Minneapolis: Fortress.
———. 1995b. "Cultural Studies and Contemporary Biblical Criticism: Ideological Criticism as Mode of Discourse." Pages 1–17 in *Social Location and Biblical Interpretation in Global Perspective*, vol. 2 of *Reading from This Place*. Edited by Fernando F. Segovia and Mary Ann Tolbert. Minneapolis: Fortress.
Smith, Jonathan Z. 1982. "Sacred Persistence: Toward a Redescription of Canon." Pages 36–52 in his *Imagining Religion: From Babylon to Jonestown*. Chicago: University of Chicago Press.
Smith, Wilfred Cantwell. 1971. "The Study of Religion and the Study of the Bible." *Journal of the American Academy of Religion* 39:131–40.
Smith, Wilfred Cantwell. 1989. "Scripture as Form and Concept: Their Emer-

gence for the Western World." Pages 29–57 in *Rethinking Scripture: Essays from a Comparative Perspective.* Edited by Miriam Levering. Albany: State University of New York Press.

———. 1993. *What Is Scripture? A Comparative Approach.* Minneapolis: Fortress.

Wimbush, Vincent L. 2000. *African Americans and the Bible: Sacred Texts and Social Textures.* New York: Continuum.

Response
Benjamin D. Sommer
Jewish Theological Seminary of America

I am pleased to thank Barbara Holdrege, Tamar Kamionkowski, and Mary Chilton Callaway for their thoughtful and perceptive discussions of *Jewish Concepts of Scripture,* as well as Marc Brettler and Tamara Eskenazi for organizing the panel at the SBL's 2013 meeting and Marc for arranging for this publication of the papers in *RBL.* The three review essays speak for themselves, and speak fairly and accurately about the anthology. These essays prompt thoughts on the nature of the volume I edited and its place in both biblical studies and religious studies, as well as some of the implications of the book for a Jewish biblical theology.

Barbara Holdrege notes that the volume raises questions regarding the contextualization of biblical studies within the academy. Biblical studies can be situated as a subdiscipline within Jewish studies and within the study of Christianity, and it is not uncommon to find scholars discussing biblical exegesis or theology in conversation with Jewish and Christian thinkers such as Franz Rosenzweig or Karl Barth. But it is surprisingly uncommon to find biblical critics referring to scholars of comparative religion who discuss the cross-cultural category of scripture, such as Wilfred Cantwell Smith, William Graham, Miriam Levering, or Barbara Holdrege herself. Thus I am very glad that Holdrege's paper focuses attention on these comparative scholars' influence on the volume I edited. Following these scholars, I hope that *Jewish Concepts of Scripture* can help to demystify or demythologize common-sense views about what scripture is and what it does. I think here of assumptions that have a very wide purchase in American culture, such as the idea of the perspicuity of scripture and the idea that scripture intends to provide specific types of information (e.g., historical or scientific information). Assumptions such as these imply that so-called literal readings of scripture are somehow more religious, more authentic, or more loyal to biblical texts and their worldview than other ways of understanding scripture. The volume I edited problematizes these assumptions by describing other views of scripture found among religious Jewish thinkers and communities through the ages. The very existence of these concepts of scripture demonstrates that the comparatively recent construction of scripture common among contemporary American fundamentalists is not the only possibility, even for religious people who have a deep and personal commitment to the Bible. The last two essays in the book, which deal with concepts of scripture among secular Israelis, show that the Tanak need not be read as sacred even among those who accept it as formative for their culture and thus further challenge popular assumptions about scripture in Western culture.

In discussing the ways this volume demythologizes concepts of scripture that are widespread but not inevitable or necessary, I am also thinking about trends within the academy, in particular of the work of Brevard Childs and his followers. Childs did great service by turning our attention to the elephant in the room: the fact that modern biblical scholars are not attending to Bible as scripture at all. In this regard Childs's work dovetails with that of W. C. Smith and with Holdrege's emphasis on scripture as a relational category. But, in part because Childs did not have the benefit of W. C. Smith's work when he began his project, he seems never to have paused to ask himself, "Is my notion of what scripture is the only possible one? Does it really have anything to do with the notions of scripture that motivated the redactors, the canonizers, the early interpreters in the church and in the synagogue?" I think that the critiques of people like James Barr and John Barton make clear that Childs's answer to the questions, "What is scripture? How does scripture expect to be read?" were at a variance with those of the ancient Jews and Christians whose answers he claimed undergirded his own. The work of Smith and those he influenced, including the volume under discussion, at once shows how important Childs's challenge to biblical criticism is and also how important it is to access models from the comparative study of religions when attempting to explain what it can mean to read the Bible as scripture.

These are questions of both academic and theological import. They are also of pedagogical import: they bear on our essential vocation as teachers in the university. (My thoughts on this issue are spurred in part by Mark Schwehn's *Exiles from Eden: Religion and the Academic Vocation in America*.) So let me relate the project implied by *Jewish Concepts of Scripture* to our teaching in university settings. In doing so, I shall speak less as a professor at a Jewish seminary than as someone who taught for a decade a half at a secular institution, Northwestern University. I think that in most cases students come to our classes in North American colleges and universities because they are interested in *scripture*, in the relational category that Holdrege speaks of. Yet, as Holdrege and Smith before her emphasize, modern biblical critics have tended not to be interested in the Bible as scripture. Rather, we biblical critics most of all to devote attention to the prescriptural documents from which the Bible was formed or to the books of the Bible as literary and historical artifacts from various ancient cultures. Indeed, as scholars such as Edward Breuer, Yaacov Shavit, Mordechai Eran, and Michael LeGaspi have emphasized, a core goal of modern biblical scholarship has been to deflate the relational category that is scripture altogether. Thus there is a basic disconnect between the perfectly legitimate intellectual project of the modern biblical critic and the no less legitimate intellectual and even spiritual or religious interests of most students who show up to the course "Introduction to Bible." But the academic study of the relational category ought not to be out of bounds. Why scholars such as myself in departments of religion have long insisted on teaching precisely the course that the students are not interested in is a question worth asking. Of course, in recent decades there have been attempts to move toward offering courses that address this relational category and to write scholarship that attends to it as well. This has been the case above all in the career of James Kugel and of scholars influenced by him, such as Gary Anderson—and the overwhelming popularity of Kugel's course at Harvard should be noted. Similarly, recent years have witnessed attempts to connect the relational category that is scripture to the ancient Near Eastern artifacts that are individual biblical texts so brilliantly recovered by modern biblical criticism. (This synthesis of scripturally oriented approaches and artifactually oriented ones is pretty much the goal of my own career.)

One can imagine a course "Introduction to the Bible as Scriptures" that might be given alongside or instead of the typical "Introduction to the Bible" of the sort that I used to give, and very much enjoyed giving, when I taught at Northwestern. This "Introduction to Bible as Scriptures" would not be a course that follows Childs's idiosyncratic approach to scriptural research, in spite of the similarity of its name to titles of several of his publications. It would not presume any faith commitment on the part of its students, nor would it inculcate one. Rather, it would examine the roles the Bible has played in Judaisms and Christianities: not only intellectual roles expressed through biblical exegesis but liturgical, ritual, magical, musical, artistic, and community-forming roles. It would be, in short, a religion course, which is precisely what many typical intro courses in our field are not, in spite of the fact that many are in fact offered within a department of religion. The volume under consideration here is designed to serve such a course.

Kamionkowski writes in her review that this volume led her to raise a crucial question: "Is there any unified understanding of the Bible in Judaism. If there is a common core, what is it? If there is not a common core, what are the ramifications of such a conclusion?" She suggests the possibility that "the Bible becomes whatever each generation needs it to be." I find this a bracing reflection on the volume. Given the extraordinary variety of Jewish answers to the question "What is scripture?" might the effect of this volume be the deflation of the very notion that there is such a thing as a Jewish concept of scripture? I would like to attempt to give a negative answer to this question: I think there are three common cores among the remarkably diverse conceptions, uses, roles, and reading strategies that Jews have associated with the Tanak.

First, both Callaway and Kamionkowski speak at length of play in Jewish approaches to scripture. There is a high seriousness in the interpretation, recitation, and use of scripture among Jews, but there is also joy and familiarity. This is the case in many periods, among many populations, and in many types of Judaism. Further, Callaway points out that this play is often accompanied by a struggle to make the ancient text contemporary, to bridge a gulf, in some cases while denying the gulf exists. These characteristics of play and struggle are, Callaway points out, to some degree distinctive, and their pairing throughout Jewish history suggests that they provide a common core in Jewish notions of scripture—not necessarily a common understanding of scripture but a common relationship to scripture. Here again we see the usefulness of Holdrege's terminology when she speaks of scripture as a relational category.

The second commonality among Jewish concepts of scripture moves in a different direction. At least until modernity, the Bible's reception among Jews, like the Bible itself, was uncompromisingly theological, more specifically monotheistic. Neither the Bible nor its reception allows any place for polytheism or atheism. To be sure, there are individual texts or verses that might, perhaps, be read as polytheistic: Gen 6:1–4, Exod 15:11 and 20:2, and Ps 82 come to mind. (Thus Mark Smith, among others, has proposed a plausible reading of Ps 82 as a polytheistic text, but Matitiahu Tsevat and Jon Levenson provide equally plausible readings of the poem as polemically monotheistic. We have empirical evidence that lines such as Exod 15:11 can be polytheistic, since nearly identical lines appear in hymns to Shamash, Nanna, Ishtar, and others; but we also know empirically that this line can be understood as monotheistic, since it appears in monotheistic contexts such as the daily liturgy of rabbinic Judaism.) These passages, in short, can be read in more than one way, but in their canonical context they are clearly monotheistic, and this is even more strongly the case in their reception in Judaism.

The third commonality relates closely to the second: at least until modernity, the Jewish Bible is consistently nomistic. As a whole, and in most of its constituent parts, it insists that a core way that Jews must relate to God is through observing certain ritual, ethical, civil, and criminal laws. Hebrew Scripture does not regard law as the only way to God, but it regards law as an essential way. Law is perhaps not sufficient, but it certainly is necessary. This is the case not only in the redacted Pentateuch but in all the blocks of material from which the Pentateuch was created; law is central not only to R but to P, to D, and to the non-P, non-D traditions. The sources disagree on many questions relating to the law: where it was given (on top of Sinai [J], on top of Horeb [E and D], or at the tabernacle [P]), how it was given, and, most of all, what the law actually is. But they agree that revelation is lawgiving. Outside the Torah, some texts focus on the importance of law more than others. Those that discuss the relationship between the nation Israel and God for the most part emphasize covenant, Israel's side of which is expressed through observance of specific laws. Even those texts that speak of the relationship without referring to covenant—I think here especially of wisdom texts—valorize behaviors entirely consonant with the Torah's law codes and condemn behaviors that they forbid. None of the texts in the Prophets and Writings rejects the law, even though some reject a specific law or, more typically, the people who practice it. (To use Franz Rosenzweig's phrasing: no text in the Hebrew Bible rejects *Gebot*, though some reject specific *Gesetze*.) Further, in the Jewish structure of the biblical canon, both of the sections outside the Torah endorse centrality of the Torah and emphasize their own second status. This is evident in their respective first chapters (Josh 1:7–8 and Ps 1), which speak of keeping the Torah in mind at all times. The same must be said of the reception of these texts in postbiblical Judaisms, at least until the mid-nineteenth century: covenant and law remain central. This is the case not only in rabbinic/Pharasaic forms of Judaism but of other forms as well; if anything, the Qumran documents, for example, are more insistently nomistic than the rabbis.

In modernity, two of these unities—monotheism and nomism—break down. This reality is addressed with great insight in Zakovitch's essay on the Bible in Israeli secular Jewish culture. One cannot deny the Jewishness of a poet such as Yehudah Amichai, and yet one cannot deny his aggressive secularity, his provocative rejection of the law, and his dismissal of theism. But the first commonality among Jewish concepts of scripture endures. The combination of play and struggle in Jewish relationships with scripture to which Callaway and Kamionkowski turn our attention could not be more abundantly clear in the biblical allusions and revisions found in Amichai's work, and in this he is representative of modern Hebrew poetry generally. Play and struggle are also hard at work in a modern Hebrew novel such as *Mar Mani* by A. B. Yehoshua or a play such as *Bereishit* by Aharon Meged. But in the case of Amichai, it is worth noting (with the literary critic Chana Kronfeld [*On the Margins of Modernism*, 139–40]), that the reception of Amichai, especially by Jews outside Israel, has been more traditionalist and less iconoclastic than Amichai intended. His antiscriptural poems have already begun to be treated in some Jewish communities in ways that I think Smith and Graham would term scriptural—for example, by being included in liturgy. לא נביא אנכי: I am not a prophet, but I will venture to state that I would not be surprised if some of the agnostic, antinomian appropriations of scripture in modern Judaism come to be appropriated in theistic, nomian ways, and those reappropriated appropriations may turn out to be the ones that endure in the canon: the secularism of poets such as Amichai may turn out to be fleeting. If so, their work will mark an exception to the second and third commonalities for only a brief time.

"The stable element in Jewish readings of the Bible," Kamionkowski writes, "is that the Bible is the playground through which each generation expresses its Jewishness.... Play any game you want to, but you must play on our playground." To this I would add that one's choice of playground affects the games that you play. Further, it determines which games you cannot play, no matter how hard you try. Expressing one's identity in the arena of the two Torahs, Oral and Written, inevitably means shaping an identity that is monotheistic and nomistic. This is the case whether that was what one intended or not. The Bible may be the modern Jew's playground, but the playground may prove more powerful than the player.

REFERENCE WORKS

Dictionary of the Old Testament: Prophets, edited by Mark J. Boda and J. Gordon McConville. Downers Grove, Ill.: InterVarsity Press, 2012. Pp. ix + 966. Cloth. $60.00. ISBN 9780830817849.

Göran Eidevall, Uppsala, Sweden

A new, comprehensive dictionary devoted to the prophetic writings in the Hebrew Bible/ Old Testament is certainly to be welcomed by all scholars within this field, as well as by a wide readership. The *Dictionary of the Old Testament Prophets,* edited by Mark Boda and Gordon McConville, represents a major achievement in more than one respect. This dictionary (henceforth *DOTP*), a volume within the series of "black dictionaries" of the Bible, contains contributions from almost one hundred authors (ninety-four, to be precise). A variety of perspectives is offered. According to the preface, *DOTP* aims at presenting "a broad picture of contemporary scholarship on the Prophets" (ix).

In a review such as this, it is not possible to discuss all contributions included in a multiauthored work of such dimensions. Instead of just picking out a few random samples, I shall focus on issues relating to general principles of selection and organization. However, in order to illustrate some important aspects, I have also selected two prophetic books, Amos and Isaiah, representing the two groups of "minor" and "major" prophetic books in the Hebrew Bible, for closer scrutiny.

Which scholarly perspectives on the prophetic literature are included? Which are missing? One way of assessing this is to study the entries devoted to specific methods or approaches. Among the traditional historical-critical methods, the following are represented in the form of substantial articles: form criticism, textual criticism, and editorial/redaction criticism. In addition, the reader can find several entries relating to the wide range of currently practiced approaches and methods (in alphabetical order): "canonical criticism," "conversation analysis," "feminist interpretation," "hermeneutics," "intertextuality and innerbiblical interpretation," "literary approaches," "performance criticism," "prophecy and psychology," "rhetorical criticism," and "social-scientific approaches." Nevertheless, there are some lacunae in this "broad picture of contemporary scholarship." A number of recent approaches within biblical studies, such as cultural criticism (or reception history), deconstruction, gender criticism, ideological criticism, and postcolonial criticism, are *not* represented.

In some respects, then, this dictionary is admirably updated, especially regarding methods designed to refine the analysis of how an oral or written prophetic message was delivered (conversation criticism, performance criticism, and rhetorical criticism). But with the notable exception of feminist criticism (which has by now become mainstream), *DOTP* tends to downplay or ignore approaches involving some kind of ideological critique of the biblical texts. This observation would seem to indicate a certain tendency: *DOTP* presents mainstream and centrist scholarship rather than radical perspectives from the margins. This reflection leads over to another question: Who are the contributors? What do they represent?

In the preface, the two editors declare that "scholars from all points of the scholarly spectrum, Jewish as well as Christian" (ix) have participated in the project. It is certainly true that several scholars with a Jewish background are among the contributors (but it is also true that *DOTP* never uses the terms Tanak or the Hebrew Bible alongside "the Old Testament"). However, in terms of gender, geography, or language, no balance has been achieved. Female scholars are underrepresented. The Anglo-American dominance is almost total. The majority within this vast array of experts come from (or hold academic positions in) North America. With the exception of the United Kingdom, European (including German) scholarship is poorly represented. Universities in Africa, Asia, and Latin America are not represented at all. There may be practical reasons for this. Nevertheless, many "points of the scholarly spectrum" are not visible in the picture presented by this dictionary.

Turning to the subject matter of the dictionary, it should first of all be noted that *DOTP* allows the reader to study the prophetic literature from many different angles. Numerous articles deal with various aspects of the history of interpretation of these writings. A number of central theological themes are discussed, as well as several types of imagery. Moreover, the dictionary is user-friendly, in the sense that it is easy to navigate and to discover how different entries are connected to each other. For instance, those who take an interest in a comparative approach will quickly find the article on "Ancient Near Eastern Prophecy" (16–24), authored by Jonathan Stökl. Thanks to the helpful cross-references at the end of the article, one will also be directed further to a number of entries of relevance, such as "Divination," "Magic," and "Writing and Prophecy." During the process of exploring the rich system of cross-references, one may observe many cases of overlaps. In my opinion, though, this adds to the value of the dictionary. Many texts and topics are thus treated by more than one scholar.

In addition to the cross-references, there is a subject index as well as an index of scriptural references. Many readers will no doubt be especially grateful for this. A quick glance in the scripture index reveals that, as might be expected, the references to passages in the book of Isaiah outnumber the references to passages in Amos. The list of Isaiah references is about seven times longer than the Amos list, which corresponds roughly to the difference in size between these two biblical books.

However, in some respects these two prophetic writings have not been treated equally. Quite naturally, the book of Amos has an entry of its own. The article "Amos, book of" (5–16), written by Karl Möller, contains an outline of the book's structure, a resumé of its argumentation, and an overview of recent research. In addition, the book of Amos is treated in some detail in the entry "Twelve, book of the" (788–806, esp. 795–97), by Marvin Sweeney. Here the reader will find a slightly different understanding of the book's structure and message.

Due to the fact that the book of Amos is discussed in two separate articles (and this is the case for the other books within "the Twelve" as well), it gets considerably more space, proportionally, than any of the three "major" prophetic books: Isaiah, Jeremiah, and Ezekiel. The entry "Isaiah: book of" (364–78), written by Hugh Williamson, is only four pages longer than the article on Amos. If Sweeney's section on Amos is added, these two books have been allotted almost the same number of columns! As a consequence, someone who takes a special interest in Isa 40–55 (often referred to as Deutero-Isaiah, a designation that occurs very sparsely in *DOTP*) will have to be content with much less than a student of Amos: only a brief summary of the contents of chapters 40–55 (covering half a column, on 368). No outline of the structure of this composition within the larger composition (chs. 1–66) is offered. It should be pointed out that Williamson's article has many merits. It is condensed and insightful, and it serves as a good introduction to major themes in the book of Isaiah as a whole, as well as to important issues discussed in previous and current scholarship (including various perspectives on Deutero-Isaiah). However, it remains a fact that the Amos student can be regarded as a winner, since she or he gets a more detailed picture of the content, structure, and possible functions of the prophetic text being studied.

Despite some critical remarks above and some *pia desideria* concerning the principles of selection and organization, I warmly recommend the *Dictionary of the Old Testament Prophets* to all serious students of the prophetic literature. This dictionary is amazingly rich and resourceful, combining large quantity with high quality, advanced research with accessibility and readability. Its users will probably not be able to find everything there; some perspectives are missing. Therefore, this dictionary should be used together with other tools. However, many scholarly perspectives are represented in an excellent way. In addition to the information provided by the articles, the reader will find a helpful bibliography at the end of each article. What the editors of this volume, Mark Boda and Gordon McConville, have accomplished is truly impressive.

The Cambridge Guide to Jewish History, Religion, and Culture, edited by Baskin Judith and Kenneth Seeskin. Cambridge: Cambridge University Press, 2010. Pp. xv + 539. Paper. $39.99. ISBN 0521689740.

Alan Avery-Peck, College of the Holy Cross, Worcester, Massachusetts

The Cambridge Guide to Jewish History, Religion, and Culture follows a familiar model of the *Handbuch,* a single volume aimed at educated but not necessarily specialist readers that systematically surveys all aspects of a chosen topic. In this case, Judaism is presented both historically, from its earliest Israelite origins until the present day, and through a series of thematic chapters that cover diverse aspects of Jewish life and thought. The essays collected here represent the best and most recent scholarship on their topics, and the overall result is an anthology that will serve readers well, both those who wish to gain a broad overview of Judaism and those interested in some specific historical period or subject.

At the same time, it bears noting that the problem of applying the *Handbuch* model to Judaism has been and remains exceptional. The difficulty is that Judaism both transcends and encompasses all of the topics, approaches, and methodologies that might singly form the focus of any anthological introduction such as this: history, theology, politics, economics, community, culture, and so on and so forth. Even given the hefty five hundred pages that make up the *Cambridge Guide*, a book such as this is by definition the product of a multitude of its editors' choices regarding what topics best define Judaism, their decisions concerning what general readers should be taught about Judaism, and their attitude regarding the methodologies and approaches that best and most accurately reveal their subject.

In their introduction and overview (1–5), volume editors Judith Baskin (University of Oregon) and Kenneth Seeskin (Northwestern University) are clear on their particular grasp of and response to this problem. If anything might unite Jews over the thousands of years of Jewish history, throughout the diverse cultures in which they have lived and which they have created, and across the varied philosophical and theological ideas about God and their own ritual life that Jews have produced, it is their enduring *sense* of peoplehood, of a distinctively shared Jewish history and destiny that spans time and space and that exists in spite of the very real differences among Jews both over time and in any given time. So, as Baskin and Seeskin explain, even as this book's twenty-one chapters point to the diversity and discontinuities in the history of Judaism and in the lives of Jews, the volume still holds together as more than an amalgam of assorted approaches and topics. Read together, these essays make it impossible for us to forget what has been shared and continues to be shared within an evolving tradition of a people who are the product of distinctive convictions about God and, for much if not all of their history, a shared sense of being scattered and of awaiting some future redemption, messianic or otherwise. *The Cambridge Guide* thus accomplishes what a *Handbuch* at its best should. The chapters stand on their own, and certainly many readers will focus only on the specific topics that interest them, but read together, the volume exhibits a synergism that results from its editors' careful decisions about what, beyond the history of where Jews lived and what books they wrote, makes up Jewish religion and culture.

The volume begins along chronological lines, covering Jewish history from biblical times and through the founding of the state of Israel and the Arab/Israeli conflict. These chapters are as follows: 1. "The Hebrew Bible and the Early History of Israel" (Mark Brettler); 2. "The Second Temple Period" (Alan Segal); 3. "The Rabbinic Movement" (Hayim Lapin); 4. "The Jewish Experience in the Muslim World" (Norman Stillman); 5. "Jewish Life in Western Christendom" (Robert Chazan); 6. "Jews and Judaism in Early Modern Europe" (Adam Shear); 7. "European Jewry: 1800–1933" (Marsha Rozenblit); 8. "Jews and Judaism in the United

States" (Pamela Nadell); 9. "The Shoah and Its Legacies" (Peter Hayes); 10. "The Founding of Modern Israel and the Arab–Israeli Conflict" (Bernard Reich).

The historical survey is followed by thematic treatments of central topics in Jewish history, particularly materials essential for comprehending modern and contemporary Jewish life, belief, and practice. These chapters are: 11. "Judaism as a Religious System" (Harvey Goldberg); 12. "The Centrality of Talmud" (Michael Berger); 13. "Jewish Worship and Liturgy" (Ruth Langer); 14. "Jewish Private Life: Gender, Marriage, and the Lives of Women" (Judith Baskin); 15. "Jewish Philosophy" (Kenneth Seeskin); 16. "Jewish Mysticism" (Hava Tirosh-Samuelson); 17. "Modern Jewish Thought" (Leora Batnitzky); 18. "Contemporary Forms of Judaism" (Dana Evan Kaplan); 19 "Jewish Popular Culture" (Jeffrey Shandler); 20. "Aspects of Israeli Society" (Judith Baskin); and 21. "The Future of World Jewish Communities" (Calvin Goldscheider).

That choices have been made is clear. The volume takes eighty pages (three chapters) to get from the dawn of Israelite existence up to the seventh century CE and fifty-five pages (two chapters) to cover medieval Jewish history. But, this accomplished, modern and contemporary times are allocated about two hundred pages (ten chapters, including the relevant topical chapters). While the treatment is in many regards unbalanced, it also means that the book focuses on topics that strengthen it, assuming an audience that is most likely particularly interested in contemporary religious ideologies, cultures, and even Israeli politics and life. Of course, the relatively brief treatment of the earlier history, especially of the rabbinic history that shaped so much of modern Jewish religious practice, means that use of the book as a text for an introductory Judaism course will require supplementation with other sources for coverage of the foundations of Judaism (this despite the engaging and valuable chapters by Lapin and Berger). But since no one book can in any event cover all that is needed for such a survey course, the additional materials would undoubtedly be required whatever the editors' choice of focus here.

At the same time, the collection's limited focus on early history and texts means that ample space can be and is dedicated to a serious treatment of nonelite (including nonrabbinic and nonmale) Jewish culture. While this important interest is reflected primarily in the chapters on the contemporary period, the collection overall allows the reader to see Judaism as a lived religion in ways in which the more usual focus on Judaism's religious elites and textual history does not. Thus, while the anthology begins by presenting the expected historical narrative, ultimately its chapters broadly cover Jewish culture as it is expressed in the lives of common people, of women, and in many of the other aspects of the Jewish experience that transcend "official" Judaism as the unfolding of elite rabbinic culture.

Baskin and Seeskin have done an excellent job both of shaping the book's content and of choosing authors who are uniformly top scholars in their particular fields. The individual chapters are gems of up-to-date scholarship presented in an accessible way. These essays are supplemented by numerous illustrations, a full glossary, timeline, a topical index, and, with each chapter, a very full bibliography.

The result is a volume that accomplishes its purpose well and that performs a true service both for classroom use and for general readers, of all levels of expertise. Whether one is interested in some specific aspect of Jewish history or experience or wishes to gain a broader perspective on what it has meant from antiquity and until today to live and believe as a Jew, this volume is an excellent place to start.

BIBLICAL THEMES

Sacred Texts and Sacred Meanings: Studies in Biblical Language and Literature, by John F. A. Sawyer. Hebrew Bible Monographs 28. Sheffield: Sheffield Phoenix, 2011. Pp. xx + 457. Hardcover. $130.00. ISBN 9781906055943.

Al Wolters, Redeemer University College, Ancaster, Ontario, Canada

This volume is a collection forty-six shorter publications on biblical topics by John F. A. Sawyer, who taught successively in Glasgow, Newcastle upon Tyne, Lancaster, and Oxford. They span a time period of almost half a century, from 1964 to 2011. Alongside the substantial list of books that Sawyer has authored or edited, this selection of his scholarly articles represents the fruit of a long and productive academic career. They are here reprinted in substantially the form in which they were first published, having been updated only with respect to the use of inclusive language. The volume concludes with a list of publications of the author, an index of biblical references, and an index of names.

The essays are grouped under four roughly thematic headings, although the fourth is simply a miscellany of short notes. They do not follow any kind of chronological order; in fact, the later essays are concentrated in the first part, and the earlier ones in the fourth.

Part 1, "The Bible and Its Readers," comprises the following pieces: (1) "The Bible and Its Readers," (2) "A Change of Emphasis in the Study of the Prophets," (3) "The Original Meaning of the Text and Other Legitimate Subjects for Semantic Description," (4) "The Place of Reception History in a Postmodern Commentary," (5) "The Contribution of Social Anthropology to Biblical Scholarship," (6) "Reading Other People's Readings of Scripture," (7) "Combating Prejudices about the Bible and Judaism," (8) "The Bible in Future Jewish-Christian Relations," (9) Reading the Book of Job," (10) "Ezekiel in the History of Christianity," (11) "Encounters with Hebrew in Mediaeval Perugia," and (12) "Biblical Alternatives to Monotheism."

Part 2, "Reading Isaiah," comprises: (13) "A Qumran Reading of Isaiah 6.13," (14) "The Meaning of the Name 'Immanuel' (7.14)," (15) "'Blessed Be Egypt, My People': A Commentary on Isaiah 19.16–25," (16) "'My Secret Is with Me' (Isaiah 24.16): Semantic Links between Isaiah 24–27 and Daniel," (17) "*Rorate coeli desuper*: Some Christian Interpretations of Isaiah 45.8," (18) "Daughter of Zion and Servant of the Lord in Isaiah," (19) "'I Have Trodden the Wine-Press Alone': Radical Images of Yhwh in Isaiah 63," (20) "The Divine 'Here I Am' (*hinneni*) in Isaiah

(52.6; 58.9 and 65.1)," (21) "Reading Isaiah in the Context of Death and Bereavement," (22) "Isaiah and the Jews: Some Reflections on the Church's Use of the Bible," (23) "Isaiah and Zionism," and (24) "The Gospel according to Isaiah."

Part 3, "Language and Imagery," includes the following pieces: (25) "Hebrew Terms for the Resurrection of the Dead," (26) "Spaciousness in Biblical Language about Salvation," (27) "Types of Prayer in the Hebrew Bible," (28) "The Terminology of the Psalm Headings," (29) "The Image of God, the Wisdom of Serpents and the Knowledge of Good and Evil," (30) "Relics of Metalworker Traditions in Genesis 4," (31) "'O Sun, Be Still at Gibeon!' Joshua 10.12–14 and the Solar Eclipse of 30 September 1131 BCE," (32) "King David's Treatment of the Ammonites (2 Samuel 12.31)," (33) "The Ruined House in Ecclesiastes 12.3-5," (34) "The Role of Folk-Linguistics in Biblical Interpretation," (35) The Place of Jewish Studies in Biblical Semantics," (36) "Root-Meanings in Hebrew," and (37) "Language and Religion."

Part 4, "Short Notes" comprises: (38) "The Language of Leviticus," (39) "Biblical 'Leprosy' and the Etymology of *sara'at*," (40) "*Barzel* in Expressions Like 'Iron Yoke' and 'Iron Chariots,'" (41) "What Was a *Moshia*?" (42) "'From Heaven Fought the Stars': A Solar Eclipse in Judges 5.20?" (43) "The Brooding Partridge in Jeremiah 17.11," (44) " 'Those Priests in Damascus': Anti-Sectarian Polemic in the Septuagint Version of Amos 3.12," (45) "Was Jeshua ben Sira a Priest?" and (46) "Why Is a Solar Eclipse Mentioned in the Passion Narrative (Luke 23.45)?Space limitations for this review do not allow a summary, however brief, of each of these essays. However, it is possible to draw attention to some pervasive themes and emphases that occur repeatedly in this rich collection of provocative and stimulating studies, each of which testifies to a penetrating mind and high standards of scholarship. Many of them also reveal a passionate and generous heart, both in combating prejudice (especially anti-Semitism) and in making room for a plurality of interpretations. Let me single out five basic emphases that run like *leitmotifs* through this collection.

The first is an emphasis on the value of interdisciplinarity. Those who work in the guild of biblical studies have much to learn from the practitioners of other academic disciplines. In the essays in this collection, Sawyer thanks colleagues in social anthropology (no. 5), metallurgy (no. 30), astronomy (nos. 31, 42, 46), French (no. 32), and medicine (no. 39). Thus astronomical calculations help him to argue that the episode of the sun standing still in Josh 10 probably refers to the solar eclipse of 30 September 1131 BCE (nos. 31 and 42) and that the eclipse mentioned in Luke 23:45 cannot be accurate (no. 46). He clearly has a high regard for science in general and also likes to refer to his own specialty as a "scientific" one.

A particular case of interdisciplinarity is prominent enough in Sawyer's work to qualify as a second major emphasis: the application of the insights of contemporary *linguistics* (especially semantics) to the interpretation of the Bible. In this Sawyer acknowledges his indebtedness to John Lyons, Barbara Strang, and Haim Rabin. He also refers frequently to the work of James Barr. One evidence of this emphasis is his rejection of etymology and Semitic cognates as a safe guide to lexical meaning, and another is his adoption of the basic rule that strict synonyms do not exist. Many of his essays are devoted to establishing more accurately how various terms in Biblical Hebrew can be more precisely discriminated from each other (e.g., nos. 14, 25, 26, 27, 28, 35, 36, 38, 39, 40).

A third emphasis that pervades this anthology is an appreciation for multiple meanings. Sawyer repeatedly stresses that the original meaning of a biblical text (to the extent that this can be recovered) should not be given priority (except in a chronological sense) over meanings that later readers have found in it. Furthermore, later readers whose understanding of the text must be valued include not only professional exegetes and theologically educated clergy but also lay readers and the artists and writers who have been inspired by the Bible in their work. In Sawyer's view, these later readings are frequently more interesting and important than any purported original meaning.

An obvious corollary of the third emphasis is a fourth: the value of consulting the history of interpretation. Indispensable to the interpretation of the Bible is its *Wirkungsgeschichte*, or reception history. Rabbinic, patristic, medieval, and early modern precritical commentaries all have their value, as does the history of art and literature. None can claim a privileged position with respect to the true meaning of the text.

Finally, the most obvious emphasis of this collection is on the value of the long history of Jewish interpretation of the Hebrew Bible. Sawyers has made himself thoroughly familiar with much of this tradition and always speaks of it with great respect and appreciation. In fact, when he compares Jewish and Christian interpretations, it is almost always to the advantage of the former. This is no doubt a direct result of his passionate rejection of all anti-Semitic Christian readings of Scripture (see especially no. 22) and the horrors to which they have given rise. It is only in this connection that he sometimes uses explicitly theological language, as when he condemns supersessionism as "heresy" (64). He also mounts a vigorous campaign against the use of the term "Old Testament" as being offensive to Jews (no. 7). (Ironically, the index of biblical references at the back of the book still uses the term.)

In a sense, the five prominent emphases I have highlighted can be reduced to two, since the second is really a special case of the first, and the last two are really special cases of the third. To oversimplify somewhat, we can say that if Sawyer's work can be compared to an ellipse, its two foci are (1) comprehensive scientific rigor that allows for fairly exact conclusions, and (2) a celebration of the multiplicity of meanings that privileges none. The first is characteristic of the modernism of the Enlightenment tradition, the second of the postmodernism of the late twentieth century. To this reviewer, this double focus raises a basic question of methodological consistency. Can the precise delimitation of meaning co-exist comfortably with a celebration of the indeterminacy of meaning? Unfortunately, this is not a question that Sawyer addresses. I have the impression that the apparent tension can be partially resolved in chronological terms: that over the half-century of his distinguished academic career Sawyer has moved from a modernist to a postmodernist approach to meaning in biblical studies.

Three Testaments: Torah, Gospel, and Quran, by Brian Arthur Brown. Lanham, Md.: Rowman & Littlefield, 2012. Pp. xvi + 635. Hardcover. $59.95. ISBN 9781442214927.

John Kaltner, Rhodes College, Memphis, Tennessee

The events of September 11, 2001, helped to kick-start a conversation that has continued unabated since that fateful day. In the intervening years, Muslims and non-Muslims have regularly attempted to engage one another in ways that have varied wildly in their methods and motivations. Some efforts have sought to denigrate or demonize the other side by highlighting its perceived flaws and shortcomings, usually in order to demonstrate the superiority of one's own perspective. At other times, the outcome has been more positive as people have learned more about the Other in order to build bridges and discover a shared humanity on the other side.

Not surprisingly, the sacred texts of the communities involved have often loomed large in these encounters. In the English language alone, dozens of books have been written since 9/11 on the relationship between the Bible and the Qur'an, with some of the biggest sellers accusing the Islamic text of being an inferior or derivative work that advocates violence and hatred toward non-Muslims. More positively, sometimes the two texts have been studied and interpreted in light of one another in ways that bring to the fore the richness and depth of both and enhance mutual understanding. The Common Word initiative, which began as a 2007 letter from Muslim leaders to their Christian counterparts about the shared message of the Qur'an and Bible, is a recent case in point (www.acommonword.com).

As valuable as reading these works can be, some of the most fruitful exchanges between Muslims and non-Muslims have occurred when they have come together in the same place to listen and learn from one another. This is so because their close physical proximity and the opportunity to interact in a more direct and immediate manner increase the possibility for meaningful and sustained dialogue. It was therefore probably only a matter a time before someone came up with the idea of doing a similar thing with their sacred books and have them share the same space and cover (or, if you are using an e-reader, the same link). In effect, a work such as Brian Arthur Brown's *Three Testaments* is the publishing equivalent of an interfaith gathering of Jews, Christians, and Muslims, and it has the potential to lead to some fascinating discussions and interaction.

Unfortunately, it does not fully realize that potential. In its foreword Amir Hussain describes the book as "revolutionary," and in a sense that descriptor is an apt one, since this is the first time the Hebrew Bible, New Testament, and Qur'an appear in the same volume. But it is revolutionary in the way that the Egyptian election of Mohammed Morsi in 2012 was revolutionary—it institutes a change and a new way of doing things, but that change is far from complete. The main drawback is that most of the nonscriptural part of *Three Testaments* is an extended argument for Zoroastrian influence on and presence in the Bible and the Qur'an. This has sometimes been claimed by others for both texts, and it is an issue that merits careful consideration, but Brown's approach and analysis ultimately leave the reader unconvinced and feeling that he has missed a golden opportunity to makes a unique and important contribution to interfaith relations.

There are three sections to the book, and they all follow the same format. A preface to the scripture treated in the section is followed by four chapters that discuss the relationship between the scripture and Zoroastrianism, and then there is an introduction to the scripture. The twelve chapters are all written by Brown, and the prefaces and introductions have other authors: Ellen Frankel and Marc Zvi Brettler for the Torah, Henry L. Carrigan Jr. and David Bruce for the Gospel, and Laleh Bakhtiar and Nevin Reda for the Qur'an. These essays are then followed by the text of the scripture in the following English translations: *The Contemporary Torah: A Gender-Sensitive Adaptation of the JPS Translation* (2006), the entire New Testament from *The Inclusive Bible* (2007), and *The Sublime Qur'an* (2011). Because Brown's twelve essays comprise the bulk of the nonscriptural part of the volume (113 of its 162 pages), and they are the primary lens through which the sacred texts should be read, the comments below are limited mainly to his contributions.

Scholars have long debated when Zoroaster lived, and Brown opts for a late date that puts his birth at around 638 BCE. He acknowledges that this chronology serves his purposes well, and it supports his view that Israelite monotheism predated Zoroastrianism and was likely an influence on it. He does not cite or discuss scholars of Zoroastrianism, but he is dependent upon the work of Mary Boyce, a prominent expert in the field whom he consulted shortly before her death in 2006. While he sees clear evidence of Zoroastrian ideas and beliefs in the biblical literature, Brown maintains that citations from the Avesta, the sacred writings of Zoroastrianism, are much more prevalent in the Qur'an. He admits in a number of places that his conclusions are speculative, but Brown nonetheless makes his argument with a level of confidence that belies the lack of evidence for it. In a number of places the contributors take positions that are opposed to or less certain than those espoused by Brown. For example, Brettler refers to the Torah's "vigorous dialogue" with Zoroastrianism, rather than Brown's direct influence of the latter on the former (63). Similarly, Reda rightly disagrees with Brown's view that the Sabians mentioned in the Qur'an are a reference to Zoroastrians (446).

In his treatment of the Hebrew Bible, Brown sometimes makes claims that put him outside the mainstream of critical scholarship. He maintains, for example, that Second Isaiah possibly knew First Isaiah personally (29), that Isa 7:14 anticipates the virgin birth of a savior (48), that the name Elihu means "God in person" (202–3), and that all of Leviticus can be read as a Zoroastrian sacrifice manual. In an attempt to demonstrate the close ties between Zoroastrianism

and Israelite religion, Brown argues that passages such as Isa 45:1–7 are praising Cyrus, when in fact they more likely are meant to demonstrate the power
of Israel's God over foreign forces. Zoroastrian beliefs undoubtedly influenced
some parts of the Hebrew Bible, particularly writings that took shape in the exile,
but Brown attempts to see direct evidence of this through his suggestion lacking
philological support that Zerubbabel's name was actually Zorobabel (42–43).

Regarding the New Testament, some of Brown's analysis is equally questionable and demonstrates lack of familiarity with the dominant views of critical
scholarship. For instance, he states that Matthew spent time in Persia spreading
the faith after he wrote his Gospel (185), that there are references to the Messiah
in every chapter of Matthew (187), and that Jesus' death is more Zoroastrian than
Jewish (203). This problem extends to the essays written by other contributors to
the volume, as when Bruce identifies Paul as the author of Colossians and Ephesians. One of the most problematic sections of the book is Brown's reconstruction
of a trip (complete with a map) that Jesus made to India, where he was exposed
to Zoroastrian and Buddhist teachings. He acknowledges the hypothetical nature
of this suggestion, and he posits an alternative whereby India came to Jesus in the
form of Buddhist missioners, but he bases it on "evidence" that is far from persuasive and ultimately undermines his attempt to establish a connection between
Jesus and Zoroastrianism.

Brown's discussion of the Qur'an is similarly problematic, and here the weaknesses of his method are most apparent. He claims that the Islamic text is full of
allusions to and citations of the Avesta, yet the Zoroastrian texts are never mentioned explicitly in it. This is in marked contrast to the Torah and the Gospel,
which are specifically referred to multiple times in the Qur'an. Brown explains this
anomaly by claiming that "these (Zoroastrian) influences are indeed addressed
in the Qur'an but in such a manner that they are so persuasive as to be almost
invisible" (411). This comes across as special pleading that is done at the service
of preserving the integrity of his proposed reading rather than a conclusion that
is based on careful consideration of the evidence at hand. Brown compiles a list
of forty linguistic markers that highlight the connection between the Qur'an and
Zoroastrian sources (437), but most of these vocabulary items (cattle, choice,
cow, creation, fire, freedom, judgment, law, rivers, seven, sun, etc.) are commonly
found in the biblical literature, so they do not necessarily indicate that the Qur'an
has drawn exclusively upon the Avesta. As with the Bible, Brown occasionally
displays a lack of familiarity with scholarship on the Qur'an. For example, there is
no scholarly basis for his statement that "the current assumption (is) that all the
Mecca chapters are written in a feminine hand" (426).

There is no doubt that Zoroastrianism has left its mark on the Bible and the
Qur'an. Jews, Christians, and Muslims are likely indebted to Zoroastrianism for
its role in shaping their beliefs about matters such as angels, heaven, hell, and life
after death. The problem is not that Brown attempts to argue for the impact of what
he calls "the Z factor" on the monotheistic faiths but that he does not offer a compelling case for the level of influence that he sees. In addition, this is the sole focus

of his interest in a book that might more accurately be subtitled *Three Testaments: Torah, Gospel, Qur'an and Their Shared Zoroastrian Roots.* This is unfortunate and somewhat misleading, because the promotional material for the book, as well as its title, give the impression that "readers can explore for themselves the connections, as well as the points of departure, between the three faiths." The only way readers can do so is by consulting the sacred texts themselves, since Brown's commentary does not address relationships among Judaism, Christianity, and Islam in any detail. What promises to be a valuable resource for interfaith dialogue and debate is marred by its limited focus and narrow scope. Nonetheless, the revolution has begun, and we await what its next phase has to offer.

Experientia, Volume 2: Linking Text and Experience, edited by Colleen Shantz and Rodney A. Werline. Early Judaism and Its Literature 35. Atlanta: Society of Biblical Literature, 2012. Pp. x + 285. Paper. $26.95. ISBN 9781589836693.

Scott D. Mackie, Venice, California

This second collection of essays from the Religious Experience in Early Judaism and Early Christianity Section of SBL opens with Colleen Shantz's review of the problems and prospects attending analysis of experiential texts ("Opening the Black Box: New Prospects for Analyzing Religious Experience"). Shantz places two equally problematic approaches to religious experience at opposing extremes: on one end, the notion that religious experiences reflect a "pure" unmediated encounter with the divine, free from any human influence, and on the other, that they are entirely shaped and determined by cultural influences. While the "essential subjectivity of experience … can never be fully overcome" (5), two approaches that occupy a fruitful middle ground between these extremes are suggested. The first recognizes the mutual influence of culture and the embodied experience of the individual and accords both transformative potential. The second enlists various aspects of the cognitive science of religion, including cognitive studies, neuroscience, evolutionary psychology, and anthropology, to help identify the biological and neurological processes that shape and mediate ecstatic states (6). Through these and other "contextually sensitive" approaches, textual accounts of religious experiences that have long been considered inaccessible may be accessed and reclaimed (14–15).[1] Experientially informed methods for coping with suffering constitute the focus of Rodney A. Werline's "The Experience of God's *Paideia* in the Psalms of Solomon." Werline contends that the authors of the psalms were probably scribes who interpreted conditions of marginalization and persecution suffered in the wake of

---

1. A more thorough consideration of these issues is offered in Shantz's landmark study, *Paul in Ecstasy: The Neurobiology of the Apostle's Life and Thought* (Cambridge: Cambridge University Press, 2009).

Pompey's invasion and Herod's rule as reflecting "God's tough love." These texts thus portray God as a "disciplinarian" whose παιδεία mirrors what they had experienced while training for scribal service (27–29, 32, 36, 40, 43–44). By redefining the source and nature of their suffering, as well as exonerating the God who is "just in his judgments" (Pss. Sol. 8:7; cf. 2:15; 8:26), the authors sought to shape and express "a proper disposition towards suffering" (33). Equally significant is the fact that God's discipline evoked an embodied, emotional response: praising God "from a glad heart" (Pss. Sol. 3:2; 15:1–4) during corporate worship "physically enacts acceptance of God's discipline" (34; cf. also 44). A holistic theodicy is promoted in the performance of the psalms, one in which "ritual action, bodily performed, unites tradition, emotion, and understanding" (37), and "suffering becomes sufferable" (44).

Theodicy also evokes a transformative experiential response in Frances Flannery's reading of the esoteric elements in 4 Ezra ("Esoteric Mystical Practice in Fourth Ezra and the Reconfiguration of Social Memory"). Though the text contains exoteric teachings that attempt to theologically comprehend the post-70 CE situation, the esoteric component documents ritual praxis "that provokes divine encounter" and affords a "wider eschatological solution" to the post-70 crisis (46; cf. 4 Ezra 14:26, 45–46). In contrast to Michael Stone's singular emphasis on the revelatory manifestation of the "heavenly city" in 10:53–57 ("The City in 4 Ezra," *JBL* 126 [2007]: 402–7), Flannery detects some seven stages in "Ezra's growing mystical prowess." Her development of these seven stages is surely one of the highlights of the volume. In each successive episode, which variously involve incubatory ritual praxis, visionary dreams, angelic encounters and revelatory interpretation, the imbibing of a "fiery cup of water," and heavenly ascent, Ezra "receives increasingly more complex revelations in progressively more awakened states in which he gains closer and closer intimacy" with and confidence toward God (57).

In "Filled with New Wine? Religious Experience and Social Dynamics in the Corinthian Church," István Czachesz asserts that 1 Corinthians represents Paul's "attempt to change the nature of religious experience in the community" (85). The community's apparent prioritization of glossolalia is perceived by Czachesz as reflecting a resonant style of religious practice, one typically induced by "rhythmic music, dance, and communal prayer," and "characterized by a decreased activation in the prefrontal cortex" (77–78). Resonant religious groups also possess porous boundaries, permitting easy ingress and egress, as well as tolerance for diverse theological views (83–84). In contrast, volitional religious practice features heightened prefrontal activity and a corresponding concern for firm boundaries and more structured forms of praxis, such as catechism and text work. In his effort "to restrain resonant religious practice and establish a volitional style in Corinth," Paul sought to eliminate the community's free-form, collective exercise of glossolalia and prophecy, instituting instead a more orderly worship format with limited participation (84–85, 89). Somewhat questionable is Czachesz's novel suggestion that the drunkenness exhibited by some during the celebration of the Eucharist was actually ecstatic glossolalia or prophecy (86–87), as well as his assumption that glossolalia is ecstatic and devoid of "intentional control" (76). Paul ascribes a fair amount of volition and self-regulation to both practices in 1 Cor 14:13–40.

John R. Levison's "Ideology and Experience in the Greek Life of Adam and Eve," focuses on the middle portion of the Greek Life of Adam and Eve, "the Testament of Eve," which conveys an ideology that is subversive to the prevalent tradition. In Eve's testament, she transfers blame to Adam, noting that, unlike Adam, she was not "guarded" by angels from the devil. Furthermore, it was Adam's failure to control the animals he had been assigned, particularly the snake, that afforded the entry of "Satan, sin, and death" into the garden (108–9). Finally, Eve alone actively resisted deception (116). Levison contends that the Greek Life of Adam and Eve reflects the religious experience of "real women" in antiquity, as evidenced in the text's foregrounding of Eve's personal agency and the sympathy elicited through psychological "inside views" of her experience (109–11, 114–15). This exemplary analysis of "flawed religious experience" may be faulted for somewhat neglecting Eve's often visceral expressions of repentance, occurring in both her account of the events and her effusive "after the fact" admissions of culpability and regret. These expressions of repentance offer a model of flawed religious experience that coheres with the paraenetic function of testamentary literature (cf. T. Reu. 4.2–4; T. Sim. 2.13; 4.2), and they are as essential to the text as its concluding exhortation to "guard yourselves" against sin and deception.

A provocative reading of the violent aspects of the life and ministry of Mark's Jesus is offered by Leif E. Vaage ("Violence as Religious Experience in the Gospel of Mark"). As a "text of trauma," the Gospel of Mark "reflects and articulates the social disruption occasioned by the first Jewish War against Rome (66–73 C.E.)." The "violent behavior" of Mark's Jesus also "belongs to the same situation of everything falling apart" (125, 134). Wracked with "survivor's guilt," Mark "aims to articulate a particular moment of early Christian religious experience," namely, "the harsh pleasure of having survived the social implosion occasioned" by the war, "the bittersweet irony of knowing retrospectively the inevitability of it all, and the vague horizon of something else lurking within the end of an age" (134–35). Vaage's seven-page compendium of conflict and violence in Mark is certainly compelling, though mention of irenic elements is conspicuously absent (124–31). While many of the episodes Vaage highlights are imbued with violence, they are often instigated by Jesus' compassion (1:41; cf. 3:4; 5:19; 6:34; 8:2; 10:16) and issue in personal and social restoration (9:30; cf. esp. the healing of the Gerasene demoniac in 5:1–20 and Vaage's analysis on 127–28).

Robin Griffith-Jones ("'Keep Up Your Transformation within the Renewal of Your Mind': Romans as a Therapeutic Letter") believes Paul's letter to the Romans was intended to harness the power of God to effect a transformation and healing of the minds of the community, "during and through" the reading of his epistle (138). Toward that end, Paul encourages an imaginative "therapeutic introspection" in which both libertines and legalists would recognize that "each group's anthropology was incomplete without the other's," while their holistic union would afford a mind "accessible to healing" (147). The eighth chapter of Romans is crucial to the effort, as it represents Paul's "re-instantiation" of the Spirit's work in transferring them from futility and death to life in Christ and the hope of glory (155–56).

In one of the finest essays in the volume, "'In Christ' and 'Christ in' as Expressions of Religious Experience: Testing the Waters in Galatians," Rollin A. Ramsaran examines what are perhaps the most important Pauline indications of early Christian "interior religious experience" (179). Appearing in all of Paul's letters, the seemingly innocuous phrases "in Christ" and "Christ in" are in fact integral to a number of conceptualizations of religious experience, including revelation, baptism, participation in Christ's death and resurrection, belonging to Christ, and the gift of the Spirit. As evidenced by Gal 3:1–5, "inward, shared, and subjective" religious experiences were considered continual occurrences in the lives of the early believers. Galatians 4:1–7 also indicates that they were instrumental in establishing an enduring communal identity, as the children of God (171, 179–80). Ramsaran's case would have been strengthened by noting that the persuasive potential of Gal 3:1–5 largely rests on the accuracy of Paul's descriptions of these recurring spiritual experiences.

Bert Jan Lietaert Peerbolte ("Paul, Baptism, and Religious Experience") contends that baptism played a preeminent role in the life of the early church, and Paul's theology represents "an attempt to formulate the life-changing implications" of the "experience of baptism" (198–99). Peerbolte considers at length the role and function of baptism as an initiation rite, as well as its close connection with mystery cults. In 1 Cor 2–3, Paul establishes a two-tier hierarchy of believers that is somewhat comparable to the two most prominent stages of the mysteries: "initiate" (μύστης) and "watcher" (ἐπόπτης). Paul similarly characterizes believers who are not baptized as "infants" (νήπιος), while those who have received the Spirit in baptism are "adults" (τέλιος). This latter group, the "fully initiated," have attained "the highest level of belief" and are capable of understanding "God's wisdom, which is hidden in a mystery" (μυστήριον, 1 Cor 2:7; 186–90). Though the direct influence of the mystery cults on Paul is "improbable," it nevertheless offers the "closest parallel" to Paul's understanding and practice of baptism as an "initiation rite" (202). However, as Peerbolte asserts, "It is exactly what it is: a parallel development" (203).

Carol A. Newsom ("Religious Experience in the Dead Sea Scrolls: Two Case Studies") attempts to reconstruct the religious experiences that may have attended the communal readings of the Hodayot and Songs of Sabbath Sacrifice. Public recitation of the Hodayot by memory and the generation of subjectivity through the recurring use of the first-person pronoun "I" together contribute to the "appropriation of the words of the text as one's own experience" (208–10). The "most distinctive religious experience that the Hodayot attempt to construct," however, is the awareness that a "powerful knowledge of transcendent reality" has been divinely given to a sinful and unworthy human (211–12). The eyes and ears of the speaker "are opened to wondrous mysteries," despite the fact that he is a self-confessed "foundation of shame and a source of impurity, an oven of iniquity and a building of sin" (1QH 9.21–22; cf. also 12.27–39; 18.1–12). These sharp polarities create an intense "vertiginous experience," and human self-consciousness is "entirely elided" as the divine perspective on sinful humanity is internalized (214–16). The Sabbath Songs resonate at an even higher pitch, placing the community within the heavenly sanctuary and construing their worship as concurrent with the angels. The primary rhetorical techniques eliciting these experiences are sensuous imagery and repetitious language, the latter of which can "induce dissociated states that facilitate a meditative state of consciousness" (218). Newsom concludes with the admission that "the rich religious experience that was cultivated at Qumran remains beyond our ability to recover" (221). Despite such reservations, this excellent essay and her lifelong work on the Scrolls have surely afforded us at least an astonishing glimpse.

The volume concludes with Angela Kim Harkins's "Religious Experience through the Lens of Critical Spatiality: A Look at Embodiment Language in Prayers and Hymns." Analyses of spatiality and the embodied experience of space inform her discussion of Nehemiah 9 and Ephrem's *Hymns on Paradise*. She convincingly argues that the "embodied performative reading" of these spatially oriented texts "can arouse sensory parts of the brain that … effectively simulate a real experience of being in the places that are described" (228). Besides offering a "portal to a world constructed by the religious imagination" (characterized as "Secondspace"), performative readings have the "potential to transform a reader into a full participant in the religious event" portrayed by the text (i.e., "Thirdspace," 228–29). The penitential prayer of Neh 9 effectively accomplishes these tasks by recalling and appropriating the "vivid religious geography" traversed in Israel's wilderness wanderings and entry into the promised land, as well as the embodied "sensations related to guilt and salvation," which were experienced by the "rhetorically constructed" Israelites. In so doing, Ezra constructs for his fellow Judeans (and subsequent readers) a "phenomenal body capable of the full range of sensory perception" and "emotional responses" (231, 236). Through comparable techniques, Ephrem's *Hymns on Paradise* similarly transport readers into a "fully participatory" experience of paradise, one in which they feel themselves "'embraced,' 'kissed,' and 'lifted-up' into its environs" (241).

This volume is as excellent as its predecessor, *Experientia, Volume 1: Inquiry into Religious Experience in Early Judaism and Christianity* (ed. Frances Flannery, Colleen Shantz, and Rodney A. Werline; SBLSymS 40; Atlanta: Society of Biblical Literature, 2008). It is therefore highly recommended to scholars who recognize the integral role played by experience in the religious texts of ancient Judaism and early Christianity.

Les Prophètes de la Bible et la fin des temps: XXIIIe congrès de l'Asssociation catholique française pour l'étude de la Bible (Lille, 24-27 août 2009), edited by JacquesVermeylen. Lectio Divina. Paris: Cerf, 2010. Pp. 412. Paper. €32.00. ISBN 9782204092517.

Daniel Timmer, Montreal, Quebec, Canada

This volume collects papers from a congress of European Catholic scholars that reflect on the various intersections between the biblical books associated with writing prophets and eschatology. The focus of these reflections is a single question (though inevitably not every contribution manages to formulate a response): What future does the biblical prophetic literature foresee for the people of the sons of Abraham and for humanity as a whole (12)? The contributions treat Isaiah, Jeremiah, Ezekiel, and the Twelve as well as Daniel, the Dead Sea Scrolls, and selected New Testament writings; they do not take up the Former Prophets. The first part of the book presents eleven of the twelve plenary addresses (15–50 pages in length), while the second part presents seven of a number of seminars (generally 10–15 pages each). The volume includes indexes of contemporary authors and biblical and other references. It is pleasantly typeset, clearly structured, and well bound.

J. Vermeylen, in "La montée ver l'accomplissement de l'ordre du monde dans le livre d'Isaïe" (17–71), follows the suggestion of Barry Webb and Ulrich Berges that Isaiah's vision of the transformation of the world is best perceived via a literary reading that connects the beginning and end of the book. Vermeylen divides the book at chapter 40, with chapters 36–39 serving as a bridge between the tripartite halves, and provides a thorough but concise running commentary on the entire book in the space of forty pages. He concludes that, until the divine project described by Isaiah is accomplished, history will continue; its accomplishment will mark the end of history.

P.-M. Bogaert compares the eschatology of the various editions of Jeremiah in "La fin des jours, catastrophe, retour d'exil ou nouveauté dans les éditions conservées du livre de Jérémie" (73–98). Bogaert dates the short redaction (the Vorlage of LXX Jeremiah) to approximately the Persian period and MT Jeremiah to the third century BCE and suggests that the reception of Jeremiah in Baruch and elsewhere shows that the book lent itself to "new fulfillments," often in connection with the seventy-year interim period for which Jeremiah is famous (25:12; 29:10). The author next studies 23:19–20 (LXX 23:19–20), 30:23–24 (LXX 37:23–24), 29:10–11 (LXX 36:10–11), 31:16–17 (LXX 38:16–17), various texts that conclude oracles against the nations, and a few other passages before turning to the reception of the seventy years in Chronicles, Zechariah, Daniel, the *Paralipomena Jeremiae*, and the New Testament books of Matthew (16:14), Hebrews (1:2; 8:8–12; 10:16–17), and Revelation (chs. 15–18).

C. Nihan, in "De la fin du jugement sur Jérusalem au jugement final des nations en Ézéchiel" (99–146), studies the eschatology of Ezek 33–39 against the background of the whole book, divided into sections that treat worldwide judgment (Ezek 1–32) and the restoration of the house of Israel (Ezek 33–48). Nihan divides chapters 33–39 into two sections, the first of which pronounces judgment against those who oppose Israel's restoration and the second of which announces this restoration to the exiled community in Babylon. These chapters' perspective is that of the imminent future rather than of eschatology (105), with the exception of the oracles against Gog and Magog in Ezek 38–39. Nihan argues that the regathering and restoration of Israel in the first edition of these chapters of Ezekiel is to be understood in terms of a return to preexilic order and institutions (113, e.g., Ezek 37:24–28), while a later redaction exchanged a simple return from exile in favor of a return of the whole Israelite diaspora (114, e.g., Ezek 34:23–24). Nihan draws on Greek papyrus codex 967 in his explanations of the arrangement of the oracle against Gog and develops elaborate arguments for its origin and insertion in Ezek 33–39 (118–40). His conclusions lead him to reject the suggestion that prophetic eschatology developed systematically in nonpriestly circles and to reaffirm the distinction between the eschatology of the prophets (including Ezekiel) from apocalyptic, the former being "deliberately horizontal, strictly monotheistic (i.e. non-dualistic) and exoteric rather than esoteric" (146).

J.-M. Macchi offers a concise but thorough overview of the last two decades' research on the unity of the Twelve before focusing the remainder of his attention on the Day of YHWH as a literary theme in that corpus ("Le thème du «jour de Yhwh» dans les XII petits prophètes," 147–81). Macchi does not favor one of the more redactionally oriented approaches over another, although he is not convinced by Beck's rejection of large-scale redaction of the corpus. Macchi's contribution focuses on linking the evolution of the corpus with that of the Day of YHWH. In the earliest books of the Twelve (e.g., Hosea), the Day of YHWH denotes divine judgment of Israel/Judah or its elite (157). Next, later additions to these books (e.g., Zeph 1–2; Zech 12–14) include in the Day both the judgment of the nations and the possible restoration of Israel/Judah (159–60). A still later distinction between just/unjust was the fruit of reflection on earlier, broad-brush approaches to the Day (164). Finally, very late texts (Mal 3; Joel 3; Zech 13) grapple with the role of prophecy before and after the Day of YHWH (168). Macchi finds all these phases present in Joel, in which earlier prophetic reflections are elaborated by later scribal exegesis, a process he avers is characteristic of Jewish scribal practice of the Hellenistic period.

Philippe Abadia, in "Du temps prophétique au temps apocalyptic dans le livre de Daniel," tackles the apparent lack of coherence in the book's chronological schema, especially the relationship between Dan 2 and 7 (183–207). Against the shared chronological span of the two sections, Abadia reviews the contributions of John J. Collins and Pierre de Martin Viviés and notes several chronological problems with the book before taking the phrase באחרית יומיא in 2:28 as his point of departure. While elsewhere (e.g., Jer 23:20) the phrase is not apocalyptic, Abadia argues that here, even if it does not refer to the end of time, it none the less "prefigures a radical change in the destiny of Israel and the nations" (194). In both chapters God's control of history is clear (Dan 2:20; 7:25), but Abadia draws out a number of significant differences between the two chapters and helpfully integrates them in a coherent reading of the book, comparing it along the way with Enoch and Jubilees.

In "À la fin des temps, quels prophètes? Recherches dans les manuscrits de la mer Morte" (209–28), C. Coulot leads the reader through selected Dead Sea Scrolls that together constitute a sketch of the eschatological prophet. He studies 1QS IX.10–11; 4Q175 1-8; 11Q13 II.9–15; 4Q521; CD VII.17–21; and 4Q558 51, concluding that the Dead Sea Scrolls "bear witness to the development of a triple tradition concerning the coming of a prophet at the end of time": a prophet like Moses (Deut 18:18–20), like Elijah (Mal 3:23–24), and like the Lord's Anointed (Isa 61:1–3) (227).

In "Marc 12,18-27 et la portée eschatologique de la prophétie" (229–56), J. Bernard reviews recent interpretations of Jesus' argument about the resurrection with the Sadducees, including his reference to the resurrection as presaged in Exod 3:6, as well as early Jewish debates on the resurrection, before offering his own interpretation. After a careful comparison of the parallel Synoptic passages, Bernard concludes that Mark and Matthew allow two views of the resurrection: either marriage is only for this life, or "marriage" in the life to come resembles the unity of husband and wife in Eden. Luke, however, permits only the latter of these two understandings (252–53). In the light of the passage's context, Bernard suggests that Jesus' "apocalyptic prophecy" sees the application to marriage of the "transfiguration offered to the world where Jesus has appeared," a transfiguration that characterizes all divine dealings with humanity in the new covenant (255).

É. Cuvillier, in "Jean de Patmos, prophète de la fin du monde" (257–72), situates his interpretation of John of Patmos within a threefold understanding of apocalyptic as a literary genre, a social movement, and a worldview. His approach to Revelation is essentially postcolonial, and he dates the work to the reign of Domitian (81–96 CE). The perspective of John is first of all other-worldly, as shown by the liturgical material in Rev 1: John remains in this world but participates in another. This shifts to a warning against the temptation to conform to or integrate oneself in the empire, which is diabolical. Revelation thus articulates an "attitude of resistance" (269) that proposes an alternative empire that encompasses the globe and all its peoples (271). Cuvillier takes for granted that John did nothing less than propose literal social revolution (271).

D. Marguerat's "Jésus le prophète" surveys Q to describe the time of the last prophet, Luke-Acts to understand the rejected prophet, and Matthew to see Jesus as the judge of the world, before considering what he terms the erasure of prophet from the christological titles accorded to Jesus. While Q terms John the Baptist a prophet in the line of Elijah, it also proposes that Jesus was subsequently rejected as was John. Both Luke and Matthew recognize John's status as an eschatological prophet, but Luke privileges Jesus the rejected prophet, while Matthew lays more emphasis on Jesus' role as the judge of the world. Near the end of the first century, however, this appreciation of Jesus as prophet declined rapidly, as shown by John 6:14–15; 7:40–52. Marguerat explains this decline as potentially motivated by concerns that the title was not sufficiently strong with respect to a high Christology, that its Jewish connotations were undesirable, and that it exposed Jesus to the accusation of having been a false prophet (297).

In the last plenary address, "L'histoire n'est pas terminée: Prophétie, accomplissement, nouveauté" (299–313), B. Van Meenen reflects on the relation between biblical prophecy and the end of the world from a philosophical angle. Beginning with Kant's argument that all human beings anticipate an end for the cosmos (be it for better or for worse), Van Meenen observes that, despite the increase of evil in the world, many current conceptions of reality fail to grasp the beginning and/or end of the cosmos and their significance for humanity. Here prophecy can make an important contribution: it "establishes a paradoxical covenant between what must happen and what does happen by means of what is done or not done in response to the prophetic message" (305). Van Meenen argues that the increasing breadth (chronological and spatial) of current scientific conceptions of reality call for another paradigm than the traditional, Christ-centered approach of Christian theologians and philosophers: "The Bible must not serve to rearticulate the future and destiny of the universe" (308). Instead, he argues (following Karl Rahner) that Christian approaches to eschatology must hold together, in paradox, two elements: "salvation is not the end of history, and salvation is fulfilled" (311). Thought-provoking, this contribution remains heavily indebted to philosophical categories and concepts that at times jar with the biblical material it tries to encompass (e.g., if God's ultimate deliverance and the fate of the cosmos can be separated, what are we to make of the prophets' frequent presentations of a new, permanent status quo that follows the Day of YHWH?).

In "Figures de la fin des temps chez Ézéchiel: Nouvelle creation ou recherché du paradis perdu?" (317–29), E. Di Pede and C. Lichtert explore Ezekiel's reuse of earlier biblical themes, especially that of Eden, in his eschatology. They argue for the presence in Ezek 37 of a new exodus and the creation of a new humanity, both of which are descriptions of how YHWH will begin again the history of salvation. In chapters 40–48 one finds another perspective on a new creation, "ordered and perfected," as in Gen 1–2. Despite its brevity, this discussion argues well that these primordial themes are more than mere allusions and that they contribute directly to several important aspects of Ezekiel's theology.

A focus on Ezekiel continues in D. Nocquet's study of Ezek 47:1–12 : "Ez 47,1–12 et la jaillissement de l'eau à la fin des temps" (331–43). Nocquet sketches the literary context of this passage and the ancient Near Eastern background of the motif of subterranean waters flowing outward before arguing for the literary integrity of the unit, contra Zimmerli and others. Nocquet suggests that the vision critiques the decision of diaspora Jews to live in Egypt by affirming that there is no salvation outside Jerusalem (342).

The contribution of J.-M. Carrière, "La menace de la fin: Point de départ de l'oracle chez Amos?" (345–51) suggests that Amos's oracles are due to the author's awareness that an end is coming, that the literary forms chosen reflect this dire situation, that the oracles of judgment in Amos are not an absolute prediction but promote hope, and that the book as a whole prompts questions about divine decisions and divine justice.

J. Asurmendi takes up a long-standing question that touches on literary genre, history, and theology in his "De l'impossiblité pour un prophète d'être apocalypticien" (353–58). Asurmendi finds the genres and especially their central claims and rhetorical functions incompatible, thus rejecting the claim of Rowley and others that the one descended from the other.

The variety of perspectives in Mal 3 attracts the attention of I. Himbaza in "L'eschatologie de Malachie 3" (359–66). He examines 3:1–5, 6–12, 13–21, 22–24 separately before distinguishing the perspective of 3:1–21 from the chapter's closing verses. In 3:1–21 the movement is from sin, condemnation, and threat in the present through repentance to blessing and tranquility while awaiting YHWH's final intervention. In 3:22–24, by contrast, there is no inner-Israel distinction and no need for purification, since the Day of YHWH brings categorical salvation for Israel. This radical difference between the two sections seems overstated for both pragmatic and literary reasons: Would not the last redactor have suppressed contradictory material in the immediate context, and are there no other diachronic solutions to this type of development beside simple dichotomization?

T. Osborne examines the interplay between prophecy and narrative (especially the continuation in Acts of various elements in Luke 21) in "Luc 21 entre prophétie eschatologique et programme narratif" (367–76). Several dozen such connections are listed (374–76), and Osborne suggests that this continual, progressive fulfillment underlines the present-and-future aspect of Lukan eschatology, which calls for radical submission to the gospel.

The final contribution, from the pen of C. Vialle, turns to Acts 8: "L'Écriture s'accomplit, le Royaume de Dieu est proche" (377–89). Vialle draws attention to the critical role of fulfillment in the theology of Luke-Acts as a whole before highlighting several contrasts between the two episodes in Acts 8:5–25, 26–40. The two passages reflect two ways of receiving the gospel: collectively after hearing apostolic preaching and witnessing apostolic signs, and individually through meditation on Scripture with the necessary hermeneutical key. Vialle suggests that, despite the inaccessibility of the first pattern for those living after the apostles, the function of the second passage is to comfort those nostalgic for the earlier period by reminding them that the same experience can be had through means that are accessible to all.

Overall this volume presents a fine selection of well-rounded, methodologically diverse (but consistently critical), fruitful readings of a number of prophetic texts from the Jewish and Christian Bibles. Even apart from the contemporary significance of their chosen theme, these contributions will be of great value to biblical scholars, not least because the volume has the rare virtue of being reasonably priced.

Experientia, Volume 2: Linking Text and Experience, edited by Colleen Shantz and Rodney A. Werline. Early Judaism and Its Literature 35. Atlanta: Society of Biblical Literature, 2012. Pp. x + 285. Paper. $26.95. ISBN 9781589836693.

Andrew R. Guffey, The University of Virginia, Charlottesville, Virginia

This volume consists of an introduction plus ten papers collected from the work of the Religious Experience in Early Judaism and Early Christianity Section in the Society of Biblical Literature. As with the first volume of collected essays from the Experientia Group,[1] this volume offers a sampling of theoretical soundings toward the rehabilitation of the analytic category "religious experience." The work of the Experientia Group, as Colleen Shantz notes in the introduction, explores religious experience—"both what it is and how we might access it in ancient texts" (1). If the first *Experientia* volume placed the emphasis on what religious experience might be, this second volume emphasizes more how it might be accessed in ancient texts.

Colleen Shantz's introduction ("Opening the Black Box: New Prospects for Analyzing Religious Experience," 1–15) lays out the main methodological difficulties that attend the category "religious experience." Acknowledging the tendentious uses of the category to insulate religious phenomena from critical scrutiny or to assert the uniqueness of supposed unmediated experiences, Shantz admits that the category has been used in problematic ways. But all hope of prying open the "black box" of religious experience is not lost: whereas the subjectivity of the author may ultimately remain inaccessible, the cultural mediation and the *habitus* (à la Pierre Bourdieu) implicated in such experiences provide handles for a critical discourse on religious experience in ancient texts. The overall goal of the volume, according to Shantz, is to demonstrate the viability of and value in talking about religious experience when analyzing ancient texts.

The ten papers collected in the volume can be neatly divided between those that treat early Jewish texts and those that treat New Testament texts (though they are not so ordered in the book itself). Five essays draw primarily on a wide array of early Jewish texts.

Drawing on the work of Clifford Geertz, Rodney Werline ("The Experience of God's *Paideia* in the Psalms of Solomon," 17–44), puts forward the hypothesis that the Psalms of Solomon "make suffering sufferable" for those who would have composed and used them. Composed during and in the wake of Pompey's march on Jerusalem down through (at least) the reign of Herod the Great, the Psalms reflect the turbulent experiences of court scribes whose fortunes were unclear. At the same time, they provided a religious and textual tool for maintaining moral direction while under suffering by framing their suffering as a pedagogical pro-

---

1. Frances Flannery, Colleen Shantz, and Rodney A. Werline, eds., *Experientia, Volume 1: Inquiry into Religious Experience* (SBLSymS 40; Atlanta: Society of Biblical Literature, 2008).

cess. This experience became embodied, as experience does, in the ritualized action of reading the Psalms.

Frances Flannery ("Esoteric Mystical Practice in Fourth Ezra and the Reconfiguration of Social Memory," 45–70) argues that 4 Ezra resolves the cognitive dissonance of post-70 CE Jewish sages in mystical experience encoded in the text. The historical situation of 4 Ezra raised many theological questions about the faithfulness of God and the future of Israel, to which the first half of 4 Ezra gives expression. Rather than answering these questions in intellectual fashion, however, the second half of 4 Ezra describes and facilitates a series of seven progressive mystical ascents in which Ezra, retrieved from social memory, portrays the "model mystic." In following Ezra's path through reading 4 Ezra, the book enabled the wise to resolve their cognitive dissonance in mystical, textual ascent.

John Levison ("Ideology and Experience in the Greek Life of Adam and Eve," 91–118) argues that a genuine hint of ancient womens' experience can be discerned in the Greek Life of Adam and Eve. Adam's testament (5:1–3, 7) represents the standard ideology surrounding Eve as the gateway for death and the devil. But Eve's testament (14:3–30:1) presents narrative sympathetic to Eve and in Eve's own voice. This testament, Levison thinks, represents Eve's experience from a more sympathetically female perspective, revising the earlier testament of Adam.

Carol Newsom's "Religious Experience in the Dead Sea Scrolls: Two Case Studies" (205–21) is a useful study of how religious experience may have been created by certain texts. Newsom argues the use of the first-person in the Qumran Hodayot may have produced the experience of a common identity—a common experience of belonging, perhaps—for the Qumran sectarians, and therefore also a sense of the coherence of the society of the sect. In their recitation, the Songs of the Sabbath Sacrifice may have generated a meditative experience that developed a sense of *communitas*, not only with the worshiping community on earth but also with the angelic ranks.

In "Religious Experience through the Lens of Critical Spatiality: A Look at Embodiment Language in Prayer and Hymns" (223–42), Angela Kim Harkins draws on critical-spatiality theory to examine the way embodiment language in Neh 9 and Ephrem the Syrian's *Hymns on Paradise* establish a new form of subjectivity. This new subjectivity allows the reader to participate in the (alternative) world and events of the text, whether that entails experiencing God's work in the world (Neh 9) or Paradise itself (Ephrem).

Of the five essays that draw on New Testament texts, only one ventures beyond the Pauline corpus. Leif Vaage ("Violence as Religious Experience in the Gospel of Mark," 119–35) focuses on violence as religious experience in the Gospel of Mark. He explores the possibility that violence could be construed as religious experience before showing that in Mark Jesus is portrayed both as a violent figure (e.g., the Beelzebul controversy in 3:20–30, the healing of the Gerasene demoniac in 5:1–20, or the "cleansing" of the temple in 11:12–25) and ultimately as the victim of violence. Vaage reads the violence of the Gospel as a reflection of the author's experience of having lived through the violence of the Jewish revolt and its violent end.

The remaining four essays focus on Paul. István Czachesz's "Filled with New Wine? Religious Experience and Social Dynamics in the Corinthian Church?" (71–90) draws on neuroimaging research to explore the experiential roots of social divisions at Corinth. The studies of Tibetan Buddhists, Franciscan nuns, and practitioners of glossolalia on which Czachesz draws suggest two basic kinds of religious experience. "Volitional" religious experience results from the practitioners' intense focus on some stimulus (e.g., a text), and it may have the effect of altering the subject's sense of space, whereas "resonant" religious experience entails a sense of a certain loss of control. Czachesz argues that social divisions discernible in 1 Corinthians—and indeed, the divide between Paul and his "opponents"—could be attributable to which form of religiosity was characteristic of each group. Paul pushes those who identified with resonant experience toward the volitional religious experience in the common meal rather than in the ecstasies of glossolalia.

Robin Griffith-Jones ("'Keep up Your Transformation within the Renewal of Your Mind': Romans as a Therapeutic Letter," 137–160) reads Paul's letter to the Romans as a letter to be "undergone," not just read (160). The work of Paul's rhetoric throughout is designed not simply to persuade but also to heal the minds of his audience. Paul particularly seeks to transform the *nous* of libertines in 6:1–23 and that of legalists in 7:1–6. By evoking the baptismal ritual experience and the construction of an "I" that is "fictive, but not fictional" (152), Paul seeks to transform the minds of these two equally erring groups.

Rollin Ramsaran's "'In Christ' and 'Christ In' as Expressions of Religious Experience: Testing the Waters in Galatians" (161–80) argues that (*pace* Krister Stendahl) "interior religious experience is a significant part of the shared worldview of Paul and his Galatian auditors" (179). Galatians 2:20 is a lynchpin in his argument. Ramsaran interprets the notion of being "in Christ," so pronounced in Paul's letters, as the converse expression of the experience of Christ's indwelling ("Christ in"). Being in Christ is fundamentally an experience of the Spirit's presence, and Paul anticipates his readers sharing this experience.

In "Paul, Baptism, and Religious Experience" (181–204), Bert Jan Lietaert Peerbolte presents a case for viewing the mystagogy of ancient mystery cults and Paul's understanding of baptism as parallel rites. Drawing on the work of ritual theorist Roy Rappaport, Peerbolte argues that baptism was for Paul an intitiatory rite of an apocalyptic cast. This latter apparently entails visionary experience, though Peerbolte is not entirely clear about the connection between visionary experience, initiatory rite, and mystery cults. The insertion of notices about apocalyptic visionary experience seem to add little to the argument that Paul's initiatory rite of baptism is analogous to, but not dependent upon, ancient mystery cults.

As with most collections of conference papers, the essays are uneven in argumentative skill and sheer persuasiveness. Vaage and Newsom strike the right tone, drawing on theory when appropriate, focusing on concrete problems, and admitting when hypothesis outruns evidence. In others, theory tends to override evidence when convenient, and the limitations of the model employed are not always admitted. Another problem with the collection is that the "link" intimated in the subtitle of the book between text and experience is not always clear. In some of the essays "experience" seems almost incidental to literary production or reception (Peerbolte). Then there are three basic models for the link between text and experience: experience behind the text (Levison, Vaage, Czachesz, Ramsaran), experience modeled in the text (Werline, Flannery), and experience produced by the text (Griffith-Jones, Newsom, Harkins).

Does this lack of focus detract from the volume's goal of reclaiming the category of religious experience? That will depend upon one's appreciation (or not) for cultural theory as a grounding discourse. Clifford Geertz (Werline), Pierre Bourdieu (Shantz), Roy Rappaport (Werline, Peerbolte, Newsom), social-memory theory (Flannery), cognitive-dissonance theory (Flannery), René Girard (Vaage), Foucault, Bakhtin, and Lefebvre on critical-spatial theory (Harkins)—all make prominent appearances. Many of the authors admit that their particular contribution is "an experiment" (Vaage, 134) or "an imaginative engagement" that "raises more questions than it answers" (Griffith-Jones, 159). That being the case, this collection will best serve as a series of provocative hypotheses rather than sober demonstrations.

But provocation can be useful. "The investigation of religious experience in communities of antiquity is one of the most elusive of academic quests," as Carol Newsom writes in her contribution, but she rightly adds, "It is not, however, an investigation that eludes inquiry entirely" (220). This volume offers an array of voices to think with, conversation partners to engage for those interested in examining ancient religious experience and the texts that reflected and elicited them. What it lacks in coherence it makes up for in verve. Experimentation may not provide the solid results we might desire, but it might just show us which paths are worth taking and which should remain untrod. Collections such as this provide hope for the ambitious scholar. In this case the hope is that "religious experience" may not be a black box after all but rather a camera obscura: its inner mechanics may be hidden from view, but the images it casts upon the screen (i.e., text) are real enough and ample evidence that there is here something worth examining.

ANCIENT NEAR EAST

Prophecy in the Ancient Near East: A Philological and Sociological Comparison, by Jonathan Stökl. Culture and History of the Ancient Near East 56. Leiden: Brill, 2012. Pp. xvi + 297. Cloth. $151.00. ISBN 9789004229921.

Lena-Sofia Tiemeyer, University of Aberdeen, Aberdeen, United Kingdom

This monograph, the author's revised doctoral thesis, takes a thorough look at the phenomena of prophets and prophecy in the ancient Near East, with focus on the prophetic personnel and their social roles: Who is a prophet, and what does she or he do?

The book falls into five main categories. The introduction contains a relatively short discussion on the methodology involved in comparative studies. Stökl then defines the boundaries of his study. He uses the term "diviner" to denote a person who receives messages from the divine. A diviner can be either a "technical diviner" or an "intuitive diviner." "Prophets" and "dreamers" form two subcategories of the latter. Stökl further notes that, from the perspective of socio-anthropology, "prophecy" can be categorized as a type of possession. Stökl also surveys key secondary literature and evaluates their suitability for discussing ancient Near Eastern prophecy. Ultimately, he decides to understand prophecy as a phenomenon whereby a deity acts through a prophet (thus emphasizing the deity's agency). Finally, Stökl discusses briefly his selection of texts—the Old Babylonian prophetic oracles from Mari, the Neo-Assyrian oracles from the imperial archives, and the biblical prophetic material—and gives compelling arguments as to why he excludes material from Greece, Egypt, the Hittites, and Ugarit, as well as the Aramaic Inscriptions from Deir 'Alla, the Ammon Citadel, and Zakkur.

The second part deals with the Old Babylonian prophetic material from Mari. After surveying the available texts, Stökl examines the different words that denote the different types of prophets, with the aim of determining the prophets' professional role as well as their role in society. In his discussion Stökl differentiates between professional prophets and lay prophets. This distinction has little to do with their significance and/or their impact in society. Instead, it serves to demarcate their diverse social roles.

Beginning with the professional prophets, Stökl discusses in depth the Akkadian term *āpilum*. He looks at its etymology, the ways in which it is spelled (phonetically or using a Sumerogram), and what these different spellings can tell us about its exact meaning. He concludes that both ^{lú}GUB.BA and A.BIL denote the Akkadian term *āpilum*. Turning to translation, Stökl follows Fronzaroli's and Merlo's lead and translates *āpilum* as "spokesperson." An *āpilum* was sent out by the deities and functioned as their emissary. As to social role, after surveying a wide range of primary and secondary literature germane to the topic, Stökl concludes that the *āpilum* was the "only real professional prophet at Mari" (43). Further, *contra* several scholars who maintain that the *āpilum* was a cult prophet, Stökl upholds that the *āpilum* was a royal agent, directly responsible to the king and at times sent out on missions to retrieve answers to queries to the gods at remote temples. There is no evidence to suggest that the *āpilum* was an ecstatic or went into a trance.

In the same way, Stökl investigates the etymology of the lay prophets' titles, as well as their social roles: the *muḫḫûm*, the *assinnu*, and the *qammatum*. Stökl demonstrates that the *muḫḫûm* was a type of ecstatic cultic official who had a relationship with a specific deity (mostly Ištar) but not with a specific temple. The *muḫḫûm*'s main social role was to go into trances, primarily in a cultic setting. As such, the *muḫḫûm* was linked primarily to the temple administration and only secondarily to the king. Although the *muḫḫûm* prophesied from time to time, this was secondary to the ecstatic function, which defined the *muḫḫûm*'s social and cultic role in the society at Mari. Stökl argues that the *assinnu* was a cult official lacking a prophetic role. In the case of the *qammatum*, the limited information about her makes it impossible to determine her social role. Stökl concludes the discussion with some brief comments on prophetic groups and the significance of gender in prophecy.

Stökl proceeds to look at the relationship between the prophets and those who transmitted their message to the king. What authority was assigned to the prophetic communication? Furthermore, in what literary form was this communication conveyed? In this context, Stökl suggests that the *āpilum*, in as a court official, may have had direct access to the king. As a result, the *āpilum*'s oracles were delivered orally and thus not preserved for posterity. He further proposes that, although it is improbable that the extant recorded prophecies were conveyed verbatim, it is likely that they are fairly close, given that they contain important information. In this context, Stökl contests the common view that the word *egerrûm* is a technical term for prophetic utterances, and he disputes that the expression *DN išpuranni* ("DN sent me") indicates that the Mari prophets were aware of "being sent" by a particular deity. As only three out of fifty texts speak of the prophet being sent by a deity, it is unwarranted to claim that the prophets in Mari in general understood themselves as being sent. Stökl also discusses the habit of sending "hair and hem" alongside the prophetic message and argues that the *message*, rather than the prophet, was being tested. The hem and the hair determined, through ritual, the *importance* of the message, not its truthfulness.

In the chapter "Further Aspects of Old Babylonian Prophecy," Stökl looks at the geographical origin of prophecy. Noting that the oldest available evidence comes from Uruk, Ešnunna, and Mari, he points out that a Western origin of prophecy is unlikely. He also presents some scholarly views as to how prophecy "worked." These discussions, as implied by the chapter heading, are only loosely connected to the preceding discussion.

The next chapter looks in the same way at prophets and prophecy in the Neo-Assyrian sources. As in the preceding section, Stökl begins by surveying the available texts and then discusses, in dialogue with the appropriate dictionaries and secondary literature, the etymology of the different terms denoting prophets. The terms *maḫḫû* appears to denote people who fulfilled the same role as the Old Babylonian *muḫḫûm*. Both appear in cultic contexts. Stökl suggests that the *maḫḫû* was a cult ecstatic who at times prophesied, what he labels a "lay prophet." In contrast, the term *raggintu* (the feminine singular participle form of the G stem *ragāmu* ["to call out"]) undoubtedly denotes a prophet. What is less clear is her exact social role in the Neo-Assyrian society. She probably held a relatively high standing in society. Stökl rejects Parpola's suggestion that the *raggintu* fulfilled the same social function in the Neo-Assyrian Empire as the aforementioned Old Babylonian *muḫḫûm*. In particular, Stökl sees no evidence to suggest that the *raggintu* was an ecstatic prophet. Rather, the *muḫḫûm/maḫḫû* and the *raggintu* were two related types of religious personnel with different social functions who co-existed in Neo-Assyrian society. Stökl offers the conjecture that the *raggintu* refers to a prophetic position akin to that of the Old Babylonian *āpilum*. Both were closely related to the court. Stökl ends with a discussion of the significance of gender in prophecy. He rejects firmly the common view that the Neo-Assyrian prophets displayed gender ambiguity, and he also discards the idea of genital self-mutilation among the prophets.

Turning to the literary form of the Neo-Assyrian prophecies, Stökl focuses his discussion on the physical shape of the tablets upon which they are recorded and how that has a bearing on our understanding of the transmission of and redaction of the prophetic oracles. He shows, for example, that oracles were sometimes transmitted in a manner different from their original setting. They may appear as parts of a collection of prophetic oracles (on so-called *Sammeltafeln*), they may be cited in a letter in order to support a certain claim, or they may appear in Esarhaddon's and Assurbanipal's royal inscriptions. These occurrences suggest that the oracles were imbued with a certain authority. They also provide important points of comparison with the production of biblical prophetic books. They represent development: from (oral) prophetic oracle to prophetic literature.

Stökl concludes with a brief discussion of the relationship between the Neo-Assyrian prophets and the cult. The *maḫḫû* was closely linked with temples and the cult. In contrast, although the *raggintu* had a temple connection, any connection with the temple worship and the cult appears to have been incidental.

The next chapter deals with prophets and prophecy in the Hebrew Bible. In contrast to the preceding chapters, this section is rather brief. Stökl restricts his study to three Hebrew terms: חזה, נביא, and ראה. In his discussion, he upholds the distinction between professional and lay prophets. For instance, he suggests that Amos may fall into the latter category.

Stökl begins by investigating the use of the term *nabī* at Ebla and at Emar and concludes that there is no evidence of prophecy at either place. Rather, the term *nabī* refers to some form of ancestor worship. Likewise, the appearance of the term *nb'* in the Lachish letters appears to denote a member of the royal administrations. Turning to the biblical evidence, Stökl outlines the various ways in which the term נביא is employed. It can be a title of an individual prophet; the plural form can denote a band of prophets; and it appears in the formula "prophet(s) of X" (e.g., prophet of YHWH, prophet of Ba'al). Stökl concludes that there were at least three different types of prophets in ancient Israel: the ecstatic groups, the technical diviners, and the writing prophets. As to how the term נביא came to denote all three groups, Stökl suggests tentatively that it originally denoted broadly a "diviner." After the destruction of Jerusalem, the roles of the diviner and the role of the ecstatic prophet were combined. This combined form appears in most of the writing prophets. At the same time, (other) ecstatic prophets metamorphosed into temple singers (cf. 1-2 Chronicles).

Stökl also discusses what historical information we can glen about the prophets of ancient Israel from the Pentateuch and the prophetic writings. In general,

Stökl doubts that these texts can tell us much about the reality in preexilic Israel. Rather, they shed more light upon the understanding of the term נביא in post-monarchic Yehud. He also argues that there were more female prophets in ancient Israel than what the biblical records account for. As to the term חזה and ראה and the social role of the bearers of these titles, Stökl concludes that the חזה was associated with the royal court. As to whether the חזה had any connection with the temple and/or the cult is more uncertain. It is furthermore likely that the חזה originally received divine communication through visions, as the name implies. Yet, the title later became a generic term for "prophecy/divine foreknowledge." Finally, Stökl highlights that the biblical evidence does not allow us to draw any conclusions concerning the meaning and social role of the ראה. It is possible that it denoted a diviner who was not employed by the royal administration.

The final chapter is brief in character. Stökl surveys areas in the study of the prophets in ancient Israel upon which his monograph sheds new light: prophetic groups, cultic prophecy, music and prophecy, intercession, female prophets, transmitting prophecy, deities of prophecy, being sent, divine council, and ecstasy.

Stökl's monograph is carefully researched and his conclusions well supported. He relates to a wide range of primary and secondary sources, all read in the original languages. I thoroughly enjoyed reading the book, and I can highly recommend it to anyone interested in prophecy in Israel and the ancient Near East. In a few cases it is possible that Stökl errs on the side of caution. In fact, his findings are on the whole more negative than positive. For instance, he demolishes Parpola's suggested distinction between horizontal tablets (reports for immediate use) and vertical tablets (archival collections) and concludes that "all we can say is that we have at least two shapes, horizontal and vertical tablets" (131). He also argues against any comparisons between the ecstatic lay prophets at Mari and in the Neo-Assyrian Empire and those mentioned in the Bible (211). Only in a few, in my view rather surprising, cases is he is more adventurous. On very slim textual support, he upholds a distinction between vision reports and dreams reports (79–81). He also states, on the basis of the absence of contradictory evidence, with uncharacteristic certainty that "more female prophets existed than the biblical texts might suggest." These minor points of critique should not, however, detract from the real value of Stökl's monograph.

Schicksalsbestimmende Kommunikation: Sprachliche, gesellschaftliche und religiöse Aspekte hethitischer Fluch-, Segens- und Eidesformeln, by Birgit Christiansen. Studien zu den Bogazkoey-Texten 55. Wiesbaden: Harrassowitz, 2012. Pp. xii + 638. Cloth. 129 €. ISBN 9783447061742.

Gary Beckman, University of Michigan, Ann Arbor, Michigan

In a world where long-distance communication and consequently the flow of military and political intelligence was extremely slow, the rulers of the Hittite Empire of the Late Bronze Age (fourteenth–early twelfth centuries BCE) depended to a large extent on para-human forces to guarantee the adherence of vassal kings and subordinate officials throughout their extensive realm to the central authority embodied in the Great King. These forces were deployed through the swearing of oaths that present an important component of the numerous inter-state treaties and internal regulations preserved on cuneiform tablets written by Hittite scribes and recovered for the most part from the archives of their capital Hattusa, modern Boğazköy in central Turkey.

The work here under review, a revision of a 2008 doctoral dissertation written at the Freie Universität Berlin under the supervision of Professors Jörg Klinger and Volkert Haas, analyzes in great detail (1,696 notes!) all of what the author calls Hittite "fate-determining communication," that is, the oaths and the curses and blessings that constitute their enforcement provisions. She seeks thereby to create a classificatory model that will allow cross-cultural comparison (19). Adding to the complexity of her task is the fact, that in addition to the Hittite language, the Hittite chancellery utilized Akkadian, the international diplomatic language of the day, for numerous diplomatic texts.

Christiansen begins with an introduction (ch. 1) that provides all the information necessary for the noninitiate in Anatolian studies to comprehend the following discussion, sketching the character of the Hittite archives (date, location, cuneiform writing system, genres) and the history of the modern study of oaths in the ancient Near East.

Chapter 2 is a rather technical discussion of communications theory, centered upon the work of two German-language writers, Gerold Ungeheuer and Niklas Luhmann. Not being well acquainted with this field of research, I can only note the most important points that Christiansen draws from this consideration: (1) The function of the curses and blessings contained in the oaths is "to create well-being or harm for a person and his or her environment [*Lebensumfeld*]" (40). (2) Particular attention should be given to the observer who interprets an event as a curse or a blessing (51). (3) Sanctions for the breaking of oaths in Hittite society were primarily imposed by gods or impersonal forces, rather than humans, and tended toward the absolute, for example, the total eradication of the offender and family (58).

In chapter 3 Christiansen examines the relevant Hittite and Akkadian lexemes for "curse" (*hurtai-*) and "to curse" (*hu[wa]rt-*) as well as the various types of blessings promised to those honoring their obligations under an oath. (There is no single Hittite word corresponding to "to bless," only constructions such as "to treat well.") She also discusses the semantic fields of *link-* "to swear" and *lingai-* "oath."

Chapters 4–9, the heart of the work, present the oaths that appear in various categories of Hittite texts, with their curses and blessings: international treaties, royal decrees issued to vassals, decrees directed to groups within Hittite society, instructions for bureaucrats and other palace servants and priests, a collection of loyalty oaths administered to military personnel, and a similar ceremony whose participants are not specified. Each text, Hittite or Akkadian, is given in transliteration and translation, and first-rate philological commentary is provided if necessary. Christiansen then explicates the function of the oath and its elements in each composition.

In constructing her model (ch. 10), Christiansen makes use of the concept of "formula" (*Formel*), which she had earlier (75 n. 76) defined for her purposes as "a linguistic utterance relatively strictly formed [*fest geprägte*] in regard to both formal structure and contents."

She proceeds to order the cited material according to a large number of criteria (418): (1) conditional versus nonconditional, (2) grammatical type of both protasis and apodosis (simple, compound, complex sentence), (3) occurrence pattern (*Ereignisschema*), (4) modality (relationship of the utterance to actual or desired circumstances), (5) presence or absence of negation, (6) aspect/*Aktionsart*, (7) temporality (assertion regarding past or present event or situation versus promise regarding future behavior), (8) imposition by one person or group upon another versus self-imposition by an individual (cf. 350), (9) presence or absence of comparison (employment of metaphor), and (10) contents (lexical constituents). Christiansen's categories of occurrence pattern (440–68) and aspect/ *Aktionsart* (479–99) are too complex and idiosyncratic to explain here. Suffice it to say that they are primarily concerned with the interplay of lexical and semantic factors.

I certainly learned a great deal by going through the massive amount of material gathered here and by following the author's exegeses of passages and the comparisons upon which she bases her categorizations. Of greatest importance is her conclusion that the focus of an oath is not on the individual who swears it but rather on "the mutual binding between the participating human and divine persons" (525). Since he is indeed a participant, this implies that the Hittite ruler is also bound to honor an agreement, even if no sanctions are explicitly directed at him (147, 190). Even the gods themselves could be penalized if they failed to enforce a treaty's provisions (171; cf. 103).

That having been said in favor of this volume's contributions to Hittite studies, I doubt that Christiansen has met her stated goal of producing a model that might be applied to other bodies of material. Not that any of her criteria of analysis are demonstrably false, but the analytical structure as a whole seems too unwieldy to extract from this work for use elsewhere. To serve that purpose, it would have to be streamlined: Which distinctions are more significant, which are trivial? Which criteria regarding curses and blessings truly reflect the values and norms of a culture (see 517), and which are superficial? For example, does differentiating between a protasis that includes a subordinate clause and one that has two main clauses really tell us anything important?

The final chapter summarizes and synthesizes Christiansen's findings. Those who are not Hittitologists might well consult this section immediately after reading chapter 3, since Christiansen thoroughly repeats the conclusions arrived at earlier, often in the same words. The noninitiate reader (rhetorician, historian of religion, specialist in Mesopotamian languages) could then dip into each generic chapter to find illustrative examples. The volume concludes with a bibliography and extensive indices.

Predicting the Past in the Ancient Near East: Mantic Historiography in Ancient Mesopotamia, Judah, and the Mediterranean World, by Matthew Neujahr. Brown Judaic Studies 354. Providence, R.I.: Brown Judaic Studies, 2012. Pp. xvi + 300. Cloth. $64.95. ISBN 9781930675803.

Lena-Sofia Tiemeyer, University of Aberdeen, Aberdeen, Scotland, United Kingdom

This monograph, the slightly rewritten version of the author's doctoral thesis, deals with the phenomenon of mantic historiography. More specifically, it looks at so-called *ex eventu* texts, that is, texts that combine the notion of foretelling with a review of history. Neujahr argues that, although there is little in terms of direct influence between the various texts, and although they cannot be categorized as one specific literary genre, it is nevertheless fruitful to study them together. As a group, these texts testify to the tendency to express a historiographically oriented message in mantic dress.

Neujahr's study is devoted to four different sets of *ex eventu* texts. The first three chapters explore five Akkadian compositions: (Prophecy) Text A, the Marduk Prophecy, the Shulgi Prophecy, the Uruk Prophecy, and the Dynastic Prophecy. Neujahr mentions their history of reconstruction, translation, identification, publication, and interpretation. He then discusses each of the five texts in more detail. He gives a brief introduction to the discovery of the tablets and their physical condition, accompanied by a short bibliography. He also offers a transliteration of the cuneiform texts, his own English translation of the Akkadian, and textual notes that discuss the chosen reading of a cuneiform sign as well as matters of grammar. He further discusses the historical references in the text: which historical events are referred to and when the text ceases to "predict" past events and begins to speak of events still in the future, seen from the author's perspective. Neujahr evaluates different scholarly proposals regarding the origin of the given text and determines the most likely circumstances of its composition. He also seeks to establish the function of the text and its intended audience. Neujahr concludes his exegetical discussion by noting the conservative nature of the five texts. They all uphold the view that kingship is given to humankind by the gods and that it resides with one king at the time. Neujahr also anticipates the conclusion of his monograph by noting the combination of historiographical and mantic concerns. These texts are interested in the progression of past events, yet they also simultaneously predict the future.

Neujahr subsequently turns to matters related to literary genre. To what extent can we really speak of an *ex eventu* genre? Neujahr surveys pertinent form-critical studies, as well as studies that discuss genre from both author-oriented and reader-oriented perspectives. He also discusses the perceived importance of genre for understanding the meaning and message of a given text, and he touches upon some of the challenges involved in adopting modern literary approaches when studying "poorly preserved texts in partially understood, extinct languages, copied in a three-dimensional written medium" (82). As a

result, Neujahr chooses to focus on elements of form and structure for his ensuing genre analysis.

Against this background, Neujahr compares the five Akkadian *ex eventu* texts
with other Mesopotamian texts in order to see whether they fall into one established genre. After surveying seven different types of cuneiform literature (the
omen literature, the so-called historical omens, Prophecy Text B, the *Fürstenspiegel*, historiographical texts, prophecies, and first-person narrative compositions),
Neujahr concludes that the *ex eventu* texts cannot be categorized in this manner.
They are not omen literature. The lack of conditionality in the *ex eventu* texts, in
the sense that history progresses steadily toward its goal and that that goal cannot
be changed, also sets them apart from the so-called historical omens and Prophecy
Text B. The *ex eventu* texts are also not easily comparable with the *Fürstenspiegel*,
which lacks their predictive elements. They are also different from the Mesopotamian historiographical traditions, in that they use the present-future tense to
describe past events. The *ex eventu* texts also differ from the prophetic texts in
both origin and aim. According to Neujahr, prophecy is a social phenomenon, not
a literary genre, and we have no reason to believe that the *ex eventu* texts are the
products of prophets. Finally, Neujahr notes that a first-person narrative voice is
unlikely to be a defining factor for determining their genre, given that only two of
the five *ex eventu* texts are written in the first person.

Neujahr proceeds to discuss whether or not the *ex eventu* texts can be categorized as "apocalypses." On the basis of the definitions of apocalypse by Carol
Newsom, John J. Collins, and Christopher Rowland, Neujahr notes that neither
definition fits the *ex eventu* texts fully. It is thus incorrect, *contra* several scholars,
to connect these texts with the literary genre of apocalypse. Ultimately, Neujahr
concludes that the *ex eventu* texts do not belong to one specific genre. What
causes them to be categorized together is neither their form nor their manner of
narration; rather, it is the very presence of an *ex eventu* prediction that allows the
reader to connect them.

The next three chapters are devoted to comparative texts. The first of these
chapters explores the *ex eventu* predictions in Daniel and 1 Enoch. Neujahr surveys the content of Dan 8 and concludes that there is little reason to assume that
this text is a modified Hebrew version of the Akkadian *ex eventu* texts. While
they share the same deterministic view of history, they share neither a common
structure nor a common literary form. The same is true for Dan 9 and 10–12,
as well as for the schematic predictions in Dan 2 and 7. The only thing that the
biblical texts share with the Akkadian *ex eventu* texts is the concept of predictions
ex eventu!

Neujahr discusses the Animal Apocalypse and the Apocalypse of Weeks in
1 Enoch in a similar manner. He again highlights the formal literary differences
between these two texts and the five Akkadian *ex eventu* texts. They share neither
a narrative framework nor mode of revelation with the Akkadian texts, and their
focus (the functioning of the cult) differs from the focus on monarchs and successive empires in the Akkadian texts. It is thus highly unlikely, Neujahr argues, that

the Akkadian *ex eventu* texts influenced the writing of Judean apocalypses. What they have in common, however, is the fact that both sets of texts seek to reveal matters of the future to their audience while, at the same time, also enumerating past events that have led up to the audience's present situation.

The next chapter looks in a similar fashion at *ex eventu* predictions in the Dead Sea Scrolls. Given the physical conditions of the Qumranic documents, Neujahr spends a lot of ink discussing their origin, composition, and translation. As a result, the discussion is often not very tightly focused on the *ex eventu* aspects of the text. Neujahr begins by looking at the material associated with the Daniel tradition: Pseudo-Daniel (4Q243–245), the Son of God Text (4Q246), and 4QFour Kingdoms (4Q552–553). Although these texts share aspects with the *ex eventu* material in both Daniel and the Akkadian texts, Neujahr concludes that the Qumranic texts should not be categorized as *ex eventu* texts. In contrast, the nonsectarian texts 4QJeremiah and Ezekiel Pseudoepigrapha (4Q383–391) contain clear examples of *ex eventu* predictions. Turning to the sectarian texts, Neujahr discusses the Damascus Document, the *pesharim*, and 11QMelchizedek (11Q13) in a similar fashion. While he notes that they cannot be called *ex eventu* texts in the strictest sense of the name, they share certain important aspects with such texts. In particular, the pesharim employ mantic techniques in order to make predictions about the future, and the authority of these predictions is tied up with claim that the pesharim have successfully predicted past events.

Finally, Neujahr discusses the *ex eventu* predictions written in Greek, with focus on books 1–4 of the Sibylline Oracles. After a fairly in-depth discussion of the concept of sibylline prophecy in the ancient world, Neujahr explores the ways in which book 3, books 1–2, and book 4 present history as a consecutive sequence of events and how they deal with future predictions. He also discusses how the structure and content of these texts agree with and differ from the earlier apocalypses in Daniel and 1 Enoch. He concludes that the earlier material, although probably known to the authors of the Sibylline Oracles, did not constitute an important source of literary influence.

The conclusion brings all the material together. Neujahr proposes that we cannot speak of any direct influence between the different texts that feature *ex eventu* prediction and that these texts furthermore do not share literary genre. Rather, they are part of a new type of mantic text that combined historiographic and mantic practices. This type of prediction emerged in the first millennium BCE and is attested in a wide variety of texts from west Asia and the eastern Mediterranean. They betray structural and thematic differences, draw from diverse literary traditions, and adhere to different ideological viewpoints. In fact, Neujahr points out that the *ex eventu* texts adhere to the literary conventions and expectations of the culture in which they originated. For example, the Akkadian *ex eventu* texts are reminiscent of the Mesopotamian omen literature, while the Judean texts are steeped in the ideologies and language of the prophetic literature. At the same time, they all share the notion that the author and his audience are situated at a crucial point in history from which they can learn from the past and predict the future.

As to why this type of literature emerged, Neujahr suggests briefly that its appearance was triggered by and connected with social factors, such as loss of native political autonomy and military defeat. These factors together led to a fatalistic view of history, which predicted that history would culminate in the ultimate redemption of the scribe and his community.

This is an interesting and well-researched book that deserves a full hearing. In a sense, its findings are negative, in that Neujahr does not detect any evidence of direct literary dependency between the various texts. Instead, he postulates a more general affinity triggered by social events. In view of this, I would have appreciated a significantly longer discussion of these social events and how they led to the creation of the various texts featuring *ex eventu* predictions (rather than the very brief note on 249). In addition, the discussions of the various texts often included material not strictly relevant for the understanding of the *ex eventu* predictions. At times this makes it difficult to follow the main thread of the arguments. For example, the discussion of the Jewish and Christian textual layers of book 3 of the Sybilline Oracles have, as far as I can tell, no direct relevance to the topic at hand. The same is true of the extended discussion of the different fragments of 4QJeremiah and Ezekiel Pseudepigrapha. These aspects, however, are minor points of critique that should not deter the reader from appreciating Neujahr's fresh approach to these texts.

Arameans, Chaldeans, and Arabs in Babylonia and Palestine in the First Millennium B.C., edited by Angelika Berlejung and Michael P. Streck. Leipziger Altorientalistische Studien 3. Wiesbaden: Harrassowitz, 2013. Pp. vii + 336. Paper. $91.00. ISBN 9783447065443.

John MacGinnis, University of Cambridge, Cambridge, United Kingdom

This volume presents the outcome of the contributions to a conference on "Arameans, Chaldeans and Arabs in Babylonia and Palestine in the First Millennium BC," organized by the editors Berlejung and Streck and held at the University of Leipzig in 2010. This is an excellent subject for investigation, and the appearance of such a volume is most welcome.

After a brief foreword by Berlejung and Streck, ten papers are presented. First of these is a contribution by Rami Arav on "Geshur: The Southwesternmost Aramean Kingdom." Occupying the Golan, Geshur is perhaps the least well known of the kingdoms, known principally from Old Testament sources, though there are in addition to this references in the Amarna correspondence. Arav reviews the archaeology of the kingdom, taking as case studies first Tell Hadar, a site used for the storage of grain (with a capacity of ca. 150 tons) as well as wine and/or oil until it met its end in a fiery destruction, then Bethsaida, which emerges as a fortified site with a palace and granaries, plausibly identified as the capital of the kingdom that flourished until its conquest by Hazael of Damascus and subsequent incorporation into Assyria.

Paul-Alain Beaulieu reviews the "Arameans, Chaldeans and Arabs in Cuneiform Sources from the Babylonian Period," presenting evidence that the Neo-Babylonian monarchy did indeed have strong connections with the Chaldeans (houses of Bit Dakuri and Bit Amukani) and Arameans (tribes of the Puqudu and Gambulu). Bel-šum-iškun, for example, the father of Neriglissar, is listed as head of the Puqudu in the *Hofkalender* of Nebuchadnezzar. Beaulieu also draws attention to data on Arabs in Seleucid diaries where they appear as marauders harassing the settled population.

In "Nachbarn, Verwandte, Feinde und Gefährten: Die Aramäer im Alten Testament," Angelika Berlejung addresses the evidence for the Arameans in the Bible, starting with the genealogies, the different tribes recorded, the relations with Israel, and the part played in the forging of the identity of that state. The historical frameworks are highlighted, in particular with regard to Aram/Damascus, and reference is also made to the archaeological evidence.

After this Grant Frame takes on "The Political and Geographical History of the Aramean, Chaldean and Arab Tribes in Babylonia in the Neo-Assyrian Period." As Frame points out, although there are many references to these people in a wide variety of texts—chronicles, royal inscriptions, extispicy requests, legal and administrative texts, and others—and although these provide rich detail, nevertheless the data stops far short from what would be adequate to write a proper history of any of these ethnic units. Even so, over forty Aramean tribes are known together with the five of the Chaldeans, each headed by a sheikh (*nāsiku*). The Arameans emerge in the Assyrian sources both as persistent enemies and marauders, as well as engaging in more regular commercial interactions with the citizens of Babylonia. Picking up the theme of the Chaldean dynasty, it is noted that at least five of the earlier Neo-Babylonian kings were from Chaldean tribes, clearly an observation of significance.

Edward Lipiński, with "The Arameans in the West (13th–8th Centuries)," offers a detailed and highly valuable summary of the history of the western Aramean states and their interaction with Assyria and other regions. This is a huge field with a vast amount of sources and information, and Lipiński's presentation of this data in a clear and succinct form is highly welcome.

Stefan Münger, with his contribution "Early Iron Age Kinneret—Early Aramean or Just Late Canaanite? Remarks on the Material Culture of a Border Site in Northern Palestine at the Turn of an Era" reviews the architecture, ceramics, and mortuary practice of this site, together with some remarks on imagery such as the impressions stamped on jar handles, which he takes to be representations of the god Reshef, coming to the conclusion that this assemblage is in fact best seen as Late Canaanite.

With "The Religion of the Arameans in the West: The Case of Samʾal," Herbert Niehr presents an excellent overview of the different gods worshiped there, both Aramean and others. Niehr comes to the conclusion that, while there was no overriding unified Aramean religion, there was a core pantheon of, in order, Hadad, El, Resep, and Šamaš, in addition to which the rulers of

Bit Gabari "appointed" various personal deities (Ba'al-Semed, Ba'al-Hammon, Rakkab'el). To these a number of foreign deities—Ištar (the medallion illustrated on 156 surely depicts Ištar of Arbail), Sin, Kubaba and others—can be added, this roll call together betraying Neo-Hittite, Assyrian, Phoenician, and Ugaritic influence.

In "Nomadisierende Stammesverbände im Babylonien der neuassyrischen und neubabylonischen Zeit: das Beispiel der Damūnu," Marco Stockhusen surveys the evidence for the Damūnu tribe and the relationships between nomadic and sedentary populations in the centuries of Assyrian rule. The sources are protracted—covering the reigns of Tiglath-pileser III, Sargon, Sennacherib, Esarhaddon, and Ashurbanipal, as well as the Neo-Babylonian Empire, and a marshalling and evaluation of these are most useful.

Cornelia Wunsch's "Glimpses on the Lives of Deportees in Rural Babylonia" comments on the archive recently come to light stemming from the community of deported Judeans located at the settlement of Al-Iahudu in the region southeast of Nippur between that city and the Tigris and attested in texts from Nebuchadnezzar 33 to early in the reign of Xerxes. The discovery and publication of this archive is an exceptionally important development in the field of Neo-Babylonian studies.

Lastly, Ran Zadok with his contribution on "Onomastics of the Chaldean, Aramean and Arabian Tribes in Babylonia during the First Millennium" deals with the ethnonyms and anthroponyms of these three groups. A particularly important result is that almost all the non-Akkadian names of the Chaldeans are explicable in Aramaic terms. Zadok rightly draws the conclusion that the relationship between Chaldeans and Arameans must be quite close. It is probably not too much to say that the Chaldeans were in fact a subset of the Arameans. This is an important conclusion, but more research—and new evidence—will be needed to elucidate this further.

In summary, the volume succeeds admirably in doing what it says on the cover, drawing together multiple expertises from a wide range of relevant scholars and bringing it to bear most effectively on the data, problems, and issues revolving around the Arameans, Chaldeans, and Arabs in the first millennium BCE. In addition to pushing the field forward, it is also a useful summary of key data and will form a very convenient reference book for students and scholars alike. As always, there are many questions left unanswered and many that cannot be answered until new data become available. But as and when this happens, the volume before us will be an invaluable guide along the way. The editors and contributors are to be congratulated on producing a most excellent volume.

LANGUAGES

Early Biblical Hebrew, Late Biblical Hebrew, and Linguistic Variability: A Sociolinguistic Evaluation of the Linguistic Dating of Biblical Texts, by Dong-Hyuk Kim. Supplements to Vetus Testamentum 156. Leiden: Brill, 2013. Pp. xviii + 184. Hardcover. $133.00. ISBN 9789004235601.

Frank H. Polak, Tel Aviv University, Ramath Aviv, Israel

The discipline of sociolinguistics, the study of the way in which language is affected by the social context of its usage, is steadily beginning to occupy the place it deserves in the study of the Hebrew Bible, but until now we did not have a book-length treatment of this important subject. Hence the publication of this monograph by Dong-Hyuk Kim, originally a PhD thesis from Yale (2011), is a feast for all Hebraists. Following a short introduction to the history of diachronic study of Biblical Hebrew, this volume presents an extensive summary of the discussion between the school of linguists favoring a diachronic approach, such as Avi Hurvitz, Frederick Dobbs-Allsopp, Mats Eskhult, Jan Joosten, and the present reviewer (wrongly labeled "traditionalists"), and the challengers of this method, Ian Young, Robert Rezetko, and Martin Ehrensvärd.

In addition, the reader will find a short introduction to the methods of sociolinguistics, in particular in its historical branch, and to the variationist approach, which centers on the use of different, linguistically equivalent forms and lexical words, such as, in American English, the use of the endings *-ing* versus *-in'* and the (non)pronunciation of final /r/. The use of such equivalents shows language usage in variety and in flux. These introductions are followed by eight short case studies of items that in diachronic research are regarded as hallmarks of the difference between Early Biblical Hebrew (EBH), the state of the Hebrew before the exile, and the postexilic stage of Late Biblical Hebrew (LBH).

According to the challengers of this approach, it is impossible to set these states apart since EBH texts (like preexilic epigraphic texts) can be shown to contain many features that are characteristic of LBH, whereas late texts reveal a mixture of EBH and LBH features. The cases studied include a few issues of grammar: the form of the suffix following the plural of the feminine noun (*-ot-am* versus *-otey-hem*); *wayhī/wĕhāyāh* with *k/b*+infinitive construct opening temporal clauses versus the nonuse of *wayhi/wĕhāyāh*; the king X versus X, the king; the construction of the preposition *beyn* (doubling versus *beyn* ... *lĕ-*). In addition, Kim discusses a few lexical issues: the indication of the temple as house of *Yhwh* versus house of God; the terms for "kingship" (*mamlākāh* versus *malkūt*), and for the "congregation" (*'ēdāh* versus *qāhāl*; in the end Kim finds, correctly in my view, that this is not an a proper lexical shift); and a phonological issue, the interchange of *ṣā'aq* versus *zā'aq*, both meaning "shouting." The work is concluded by a general evaluation.

It is the aim of this work to propose a method to settle the discussion (to "adjudicate," in Kim's terms) between the diachronic approach and the challengers.

To this purpose Kim points to some important distinctions that are well known in sociolinguistics. Fast adopters who are quick to take up a new form or lexical item are to be set apart from conservative speakers who stick to the nonshifted form and the old item. In addition, Kim urges the distinction between shifts imposed from above by innovations in the parlance of the higher classes and shifts coming from below, intruding into "standard" language from lower-class vernacular and, for example, regional dialects. The distinction between quoted discourse ("reported speech") and narration provides Kim with a possibility to discern some the import of the shifts from below, since quoted discourse may contain traces of the vernacular. The main argument is that changes from above, such as words of French origin in (Middle) English and the Akkadian borrowings in Hebrew/Aramaic, are culturally conditioned and are known as such to the speaker/writer. By contrast, changes from below are unconscious and thus are not open to the speaker's awareness.

Analysis of the eight items selected for discussion enables Kim to conclude that most changes are from below and thus not open to the writer's consciousness. Thus, the writer would not be able to stay clear from shifts of this type, whereas he would be able to consciously avoid such terms as "the house of God" or *malkūt*. In this sense Kim accepts the principles of the diachronic school versus the challengers. On the other hand, however, he argues that the biblical text does not enable us to make out conservative language users and innovative speakers. Since it is always possible that a biblical author adheres to a conservative style, we cannot know whether the use of EBH items is to be ascribed to a preexilic or to a conservative postexilic author. Moreover, the changes from below analyzed in this study are not dependent on the role of the Babylonians and the Persians. In these respects, then, Kim accepts the conclusion of the challengers. He also accepts the argument that all authors in all periods would have had access to Aramaic, which could have influenced their parlance as a prestige language (like French in Tolstoi's novels).

This methodical argumentation merits serious consideration. Unfortunately, the thesis is marred by many, too many, shortcomings in the execution. First and foremost, the collection of the data is not faultless and might be overdependent on computerized listing and counting. For instance, for the construction "the king X" Kim mentions one case in Deutero-Isaiah, which, however, is difficult to find (119; hardly Isa 41:21). Such questions arise since Kim does not provide lists for the cases counted. It is true that sociolinguistic discussions often refrain from presenting the answers given to the interviewer's questions, since that material would be too bulky. But for philological research such data are indispensable and generally not really unwieldy. Moreover, the organization of such lists makes it possible to discern patterns that previously had not been recognized. As to counting, Kim sometimes presents figures such as 3-2, with the latter representing 40 percent, or 3-4, making for 57 percent. The percentages are impressive but extremely misleading, since the change of a single item can overturn the table. If the data are dependent on such small numbers, they can only be of secondary importance and often are better disregarded.

Third, the samples are problematic, since Kim lumps all non-P together, where a distinction between various segments could have been helpful. Moreover, all the material from Joshua until 2 Kgs 25 is brought together under the heading DtrH. Given the size of this section, subdivision would have been in its place, all the more so in view of the well-known difference between redactional-parenetic and narrative language. It is true that the redaction of this corpus is late preexilic/ early exilic, but this periodization is not universally accepted for the narratives in, say, Judges and 1–2 Samuel. The distinction would have been helpful for, for example, the position of reported speech in the case of *bēyn*: in 2 Sam 19:36 and 1 Kgs 3:9 the examples for *bēyn ... lĕ-* are the only ones in quoted discourse in Samuel and Kings, respectively (128).

This brings me to matters of theory. Let me state first of all that the history of research is in need of amplification in connection with two issues. First of all, the role of Abba Bendavid, whose *Biblical and Mishnaic Hebrew* (Tel Aviv: Dvir, 1960; 2nd ed., 2 vols., 1967–1971) aims at separating the biblical strain in modern Ivrit from the "Mishnaic" (Middle Hebrew) strain and bristles with factual data and linguistic (and sociolinguistic) insights. In Israeli biblical research this book is a real lynchpin. For the understanding of Kutscher's role it is important to note that his introduction to the linguistic analysis of the Isaiah scroll, which appeared in Hebrew in 1959, provides a broad platform for the sociolinguistic discussion of the Hellenistic–early Roman period and was, already at that "early" date, much influenced by Uriel Weinreich's epoch-making *Languages in Contact* (1953).[1] These works provided the foundations for the research of Avi Hurvitz, who turned the implicit criteria and methods of his predecessors into an explicit system that was geared to answer questions concerning the place of biblical pericopes within the periodization of biblical literature. Notably, Hurvitz does not claim that linguistic analysis is the only criterion, only that it must take precedence before exegetical considerations, since it is more specific and more open to control than the theological-literary discussion.

A second problem relates to sociolinguistic literature. Kim highlights Labov's success in establishing the relationship between language stratum and social class. It is, however, worth stressing that one of Labov's particular merits relates to his insight that the speaker's way of speaking often is related to his or her attitude and to what we would today characterize as positioning vis-à-vis oneself and others. Thus the employees of the more expensive department store were found to pronounce final /r/, whereas the employees of the cheaper store did not, and the employees of the in-between store would sometimes pronounce it and sometimes

---

1. Eduard Y. Kutscher, *The Language and Linguistic Background of the Isaiah Scroll* [Hebrew] (Jerusalem: Magnes, 1959); English translation: *The Language and Linguistic Background of the Isaiah Scroll (1QIsaa)* (STDJ 6; Leiden: Brill, 1974); Uriel Weinreich, *Languages in Contact: Findings and Problems* (New York: Linguistic Circle of New York, 1953; repr. The Hague: Mouton, 1963 and often).

would not. Notably, these employees belonged to the same social class. Another issue relates to the principle that "the linguistic variations and changes of the past should be no different from the linguistic variations and changes of today," for which Kim quotes Labov and Bergs (56 n. 42). However, Bergs indeed quotes Labov's thesis to this affect but continues to argue that this principle can only be relative, since it relates in the end to human interaction, the modes of which may have changed in social history.[2]

Of particular importance is the fact that Kim does not discuss bilingualism, a phenomenon that is much studied since the second half of the twentieth century and that is of vital importance for understanding the relationship between Aramaic and Hebrew in the Neo-Babylonian and the Persian eras. A second issue that is not touched upon is the matter of the transmission of language norms from generation to generation (or within a given period), that is to say, "language maintenance," as studied in particular by Joshua Fishman. This issue is crucial for understanding the preservation of language features and language conservation. Thus the question in which framework it would have been possible to preserve all language features of EBH, by which means and to which extent, is not even raised. Kim's rhetorical assertion that the scribes always must have had access to Aramaic cannot serve as substitute for a study of the social context of the scribe's acquaintance with and mastery of Aramaic, before the exile, in the scribal chancery of the autonomous Israelite/Judean kingdom, and after the Babylonian/Persian conquest, at the service of an empire in which the language of the administration is official (or imperial) Aramaic. Nor can one separate a conservative attitude toward a certain language, in this case Hebrew, from the social environment of communication (and the issue of time span and generational gap).

Kim asserts that much work is still to be done in the field of historical sociolinguistics of biblical Hebrew. Hopefully this study, which I deem highly valuable in spite of my criticism, will stimulate more research in this area.

The Verbal System of Biblical Hebrew: A New Synthesis Elaborated on the Basis of Classical Prose, by Jan Joosten. Jerusalem Biblical Studies 10. Jerusalem: Simor, 2012. Pp. xiv + 513. Hardcover. $75.00. ISBN 96524200910.

Jerome Lund, Kviteseid, Norway

The volume under review is a must read for every student of the Hebrew Bible, serving as a valuable tool for exegetes and Bible translators alike. The author has successfully achieved his goal of providing interpreters of the Hebrew Bible with an insightful analysis of the meaning and use of Hebrew verbal forms.

---

2. Alexander Bergs, *Social Networks and Historical Sociolinguistics: Studies in Morphosyntactic Variation in the Paston Letters, 1421–1503* (Berlin: Mouton-de Gruyter, 2005), 44–45.

The volume has three major parts: "Forms and Functions," "Verbal Usage," and "Perspectives and Open Questions." At the end appear a bibliography, an index of biblical references cited, and a detailed table of contents (without detailed pagination, however). A less detailed table of contents appears in the front of the book.

The part labeled "Forms and Functions" contains a splendid presentation of the finite verbal forms plus the active participle and imperative; it does not treat the infinitive absolute, infinitive construct, or passive participle. Joosten defines his corpus as classical Hebrew prose drawn from Genesis–2 Kings. It might be useful to specify to the uninitiated that this comprises the Pentateuch and Former Prophets. His discussions and citations, however, include much material from the Latter Prophets and Writings, to judge by his list of citations, a third of which quantitatively come from the latter corpus. While his basis is the Masoretic Text (a product of medieval times), on occasion it is necessary, according to Joosten, to distinguish between the Masoretic pointing and pre-Masoretic grammar. He rightfully asserts that an analysis of the function of a given verbal form is best described in opposition to another verbal form.

With regard to tense, Joosten suggests that *wayyiqtol* be considered +tense, while all the other forms should be considered –tense. The form *wayyiqtol* expresses past tense. Although *qatal* and the predicative participle do not express tense per se, they do convey temporal relations. The reference point of the action is the key to interpreting these forms, in Joosten's view. The *qatal* expresses anteriority, while the predicative participle expresses contemporaneousness. Joosten thus describes the forms *qatal* and the predicative participle as +time reference, though -time. Further, Joosten rejects the commonly held notion that there is an opposition between *qatal* as the conveyer of perfective aspect against *yiqtol* as the conveyer of imperfective (or nonperfective) aspect (see esp. 28–29).

Joosten identifies five main categories of the verbal paradigm: *wayyiqtol*, *qatal*, predicative participle, *yiqtol-weqatal*, and volitives (= cohortative, imperative, and jussive). He distinguishes two subsystems of the verb: the indicative, consisting of *wayyiqtol*, *qatal*, and the predicative participle; and the modal, consisting of *yiqtol- weqatal* and the volitives. Within the indicative, *wayyiqtol* is the past tense form, while *qatal* and the predicative participle are nontensed forms, the former expressing anterior action and the latter contemporaneous action. Within the modal category, *yiqtol* and *qatal* are nonvolitives, in contrast to the cohortative, imperative, and jussive, which are volitives.

Part 2, "Verbal Usage," consists of separate chapters on the following forms: *wayyiqtol* (ch. 5), *qatal* (ch. 6), the predicative participle (ch. 7), *yiqtol* and *weqatal* (ch. 8), and the volitives (ch. 9).

The *wayyiqtol*, simply put, is an indicative predicate (past tense). The form is not related to the form *yiqtol* at all. While the form *yiqtol* derives from the West Semitic present-future *yaqtulu*, the form *wayyiqtol* derives from the West Semitic preterite *yaqtul*. Moreover, to describe the form *wayyiqtol* as having a "consecutive" (sequential) quality is wrong, according to Joosten (163). While *wayyiqtol* can be used in sequential contexts and appears there frequently especially in narrative, it also appears in nonsequential contexts. For example, *wayyiqtol* can express contemporaneous events in past time, as in Gen 6:11, "Now the earth was corrupt in God's sight, and the earth was filled with violence," where successive *wayyiqtol* forms appear (*wattiššāḥēṭ ... wattimmālēʾ ...*; 168), or iterative action in past time, as in 1 Sam 8:3, "His [Samuel's] sons did not follow in his ways but turned aside after gain; they took bribes and perverted justice," where the *wayyiqtol* forms imply habitual action (*wayyiṭṭû ... wayyiqḥû ... wayyaṭṭû ...*; 174).

Joosten develops his thesis that the form *qatal* expresses anteriority in respect to the reference time in chapter 6. The form's natural environment is direct discourse, in which the default reference time is the moment of speaking. However, it appears frequently in narrative due in part to the fact that it has taken over a number of uses of preterite *wayyiqtol*, which can appear only in the first position in its clause. Anteriority can carry various nuances, such as present perfect, as in "We have found (*māṣānû*) water" (Gen 26:32); simple past, as in "For with only my staff I crossed (*ʿābartî*) the Jordan" (Gen 32:11); anterior durative action, as in "With mighty wrestlings I have wrestled (*niptaltî*) with my sister" (Gen 30:8); or anterior habitual action, as in "The God before whom my ancestors walked (*hithallᵉkû*)" (Gen 48:15). The *qatal* is the normal form for expressing the performative in classical Hebrew (202–4). It might be better to render the performative as "I hereby declare" (Deut 26:3) or "I hereby lend" (1 Sam 1:28) than as "I declare" and "I have lent," respectively, as does Joosten. He further points out that the *qatal* is used to express general truths such as "A scoffer seeks (*biqqeš*) wisdom in vain" (Prov 14:6), finding an analogy in the Greek gnomic aorist, positing that the gnomic function originated in observation of past occurrences (205). All of his references to gnomic *qatal* appear outside of his defined corpus.

In chapter 7 Joosten discusses the predicative participle, which appears only in the unit composed of the active participle functioning as predicate and its subject. Because the form is a newcomer to the Hebrew verbal paradigm in Bible times, it is relatively rare in Classical Biblical Hebrew. However, it alone expresses contemporaneous action as opposed to *wayyiqtol* and *qatal*, which express past action and anterior action, respectively, and the real (actual) present in contrast to the modal forms that express the nonreal (potential). Joosten draws a distinction between the sequence subject-predicate, which presents a situation ongoing at reference time ("Eldad and Medad are prophesying"; Num 11:27), and the sequence predicate-subject, which presents a contemporaneous situation as a fact ("he is sick"; 1 Sam 19:14).

Joosten groups the forms *yiqtol* and *weqatal* together in chapter 8, since they never express functional opposition to each other, express the same meanings (futurity and modality, general present, repetition in the past), except for residual uses of *yiqtol*, and co-occur very often with the same function.

The volitive forms, namely, the cohortative, imperative, and jussive, are discussed in chapter 9. These forms are labeled volitive because they express the speaker's volition or will. In the paradigm of the volitives, the jussive appears as the negative form of the second person. While the Hebrew imperative usually implies a command, sometimes it expresses a mere wish ("may you…"). Certain imperatives function at times as interjections (332). In classical Hebrew prose, Joosten observes the preliminary stage of a gradual obliteration of the distinction between volitive and nonvolitive forms, with the nonvolitive *yiqtol* encroaching on the volitive domain.

Part 3, "Perspectives and Open Questions," explores issues related to text-linguistics (ch. 10), developments in Late Biblical Hebrew (ch. 11), and verbal usage in poetry (ch. 12). To his credit, Joosten successfully places classical biblical prose in a continuum, recognizing language development, where forms at times replace functions of other forms first gradually with overlap and then eventually fully.

To sum up, this volume represents a significant advancement in our knowledge of the classical Hebrew prose verbal system, synthesizing an enormous amount of data. While all might not agree on points here or there, the book is a stimulating read. Subsequent research must interact with the theses presented in this tome. I urge all teachers, commentators, pastors, and Bible translators to use this volume as a standard reference work. It will richly reward them.

New Testament Greek: An Introduction, by B. H. McLean. Cambridge: Cambridge University Press, 2011. Pp. x + 266. Paper. $32.99. ISBN 9780521177023.

Daniel L. Smith, Saint Louis University, St. Louis, Missouri

B. H. McLean, Professor of New Testament Language and Literature at Knox College, University of Toronto, is perhaps best known for his handbook on ancient Greek epigraphy, *An Introduction to Greek Epigraphy of the Hellenistic and Roman Periods from Alexander the Great Down to the Reign of Constantine (323 B.C.–A.D. 337)* (University of Michigan Press, 2002). With more than two decades of experience teaching New Testament Greek, McLean has condensed his expertise into a twenty-four-chapter textbook designed for a two-semester "general introduction to the grammar and syntax of Hellenistic, or New Testament, Greek" (i).

The wide-ranging introductory chapter begins with a survey of the origins and spread of "Hellenistic" Greek, a label that McLean prefers to "New Testament" or "*koine*" Greek (1). He then proceeds to encourage Christian believers to study Hellenistic Greek: "Given the fact that the New Testament is written in Hellenistic Greek, it follows that those who desire a deeper understanding of its message must strive to attain a thorough knowledge of this language" (2). For McLean, if rabbis can read Hebrew and imams can read Arabic, then Christian theologians and clergy should be able to read Greek.

After encouraging theologians and seminarians to pursue Greek study as a means of spiritual transformation, McLean launches into a passionate discourse on Greek pronunciation. After dismissing the artificiality of the Erasmian pronunciation system, McLean introduces what he calls the "*historical Greek pronunciation system*" (4, emphasis original). Shortly thereafter he admits that the historical Greek pronunciation system "is also known as the modern Greek pronunciation system." This way of pronouncing Greek will grant students "the joy of hearing the sound of the living language of early Christianity"—apparently, the Erasmian pronunciation will not yield the same delight. While McLean alludes to the "purported benefits" of the Erasmian system, he nowhere explains to his readers what these might be (e.g., the pedagogical usefulness of being able to distinguish orally and aurally between different vowel sounds).

McLean's clear preference for historical and technical accuracy over didactic expediency is a recurring feature of the textbook. For example, McLean shows a strong distaste for smooth and rough breathing marks, arguing that, because aspiration fell out of practice before the writing of the New Testament, Greek New Testaments should no longer print breathing marks. After concluding that "there is no good reason to continue using these breathing marks in modern editions of the Greek New Testament," McLean concedes that "breathing marks can be helpful in distinguishing between similar words" (21). Still, each time that he addresses breathing marks in subsequent chapters, McLean includes a reminder of their status as editorial additions (e.g., 56, 64, 72, 77, 79, 133).

Nevertheless, McLean is by no means deaf to pedagogical concerns. For example, he closes the introduction with common-sense suggestions for studying Greek, recommending more short study sessions as opposed to fewer long cramming sessions. Even better, McLean fights the tendency of many beginning language textbooks that supply only glosses instead of true definitions of words. Not only does he offer more substantial definitions of many words in the vocabulary lists, but he also makes a special effort to illuminate the well-worn vocabulary of the New Testament. McLean wants to help students better comprehend these "*stained-glass* words ... that have special prominence in Christian belief and theology but are not employed in everyday English speech" (13, emphasis original). As an example, he defines χάρις as "gratuitous service (i.e., free from contractual obligations or counter service), grace, beneficent disposition, unmerited/undeserved goodwill toward someone, sign of favor, benefaction" (125).

As further evidence of his didactic interests, McLean presents the companion workbook to *New Testament Greek* as a way for students to practice the skills taught in the textbook. Unlike most foreign-language workbooks, McLean's workbook is an online PDF document that can be downloaded by anyone free of charge. McLean and Cambridge University Press are to be commended for this student-friendly offering. The workbook provides practice exercises for each of the twenty-four chapters of the textbook. The early exercises appear to be quite useful, ranging from writing out paradigms to parsing and translation (both English to Greek and Greek to English). Then there is a distinct shift after lesson 5. From lesson 6 to lesson 14, every lesson includes a portion of John 1–4 to translate; while there are parsing exercises in each lesson, there are no supplemental translation exercises, and English-to-Greek translation disappears.

Thus for nine consecutive lessons students can practice their grasp of newly acquired concepts only on the text of John's Gospel. The advantage of this approach is obvious: from an early stage, students are directly exposed to actual Greek texts. But there are two serious drawbacks to this method. First, the student who has read the chapter on "Present Middle and Passive Indicative, Future Middle Indicative, and Future Indicative of the Verb 'to be'" is asked to learn several new verbal paradigms (99–107). The textbook offers no Greek example sentences. The workbook gives ten sample verbs to parse, asks students to practice writing the letters τ and υ, then pairs further parsing exercises with the Greek text of John 3:9–21. Unfortunately, John 3:9–21 includes only four examples of the present middle or passive indicative and not one example of the future middle indicative or of the future indicative of εἰμί.

In addition to granting students limited opportunities to practice the paradigms that they are learning, there is another downside to the workbook. John 1:1 offers a relatively simple entry point for the beginning student of Greek. However, only a few verses later, the student runs into a variety of unfamiliar constructions; thus, McLean presents John 1:6 as follows: Ἐγένετο [There was] ἄνθρωπος, ἀπεσταλμένος [who was sent] παρὰ θεοῦ, ὄνομα [name] αὐτῷ [his] (was) Ἰωάννης· (workbook p. 29). McLean helpfully glosses unfamiliar words and constructions, but he has to do so for fully half of the words in the verse. McLean is aware of the danger of Greek turning into "some kind of mysterious secret code" (5). Is the student who reads John 1:6 in this workbook translating Greek or solving a secret code by plugging in the definitions of ἄνθρωπος, παρά, θεός, and Ἰωάννης?

The workbook becomes more useful in the later lessons. In addition to supplying New Testament passages to translate, lessons 15–24 include practice Greek sentences for translation, and the number of bracketed glosses dwindles. More of these practice sentences in earlier lessons would offer students the opportunity to master their paradigms; if McLean desires to equip theologians and seminarians for a lifetime of Greek New Testament study, his training program should encourage mastery of these basics.

In sum, McLean, an experienced teacher and scholar of the Greek language, is writing a textbook for neophytes. He excels in various facets of this task. Students will surely appreciate reading actual New Testament texts rather than endless exercise sentences. His treatment of "stained-glass words" is also laudable. Furthermore, this book can also double as a sort of beginner's reference grammar: two appendices offer a listing of principal parts for forty-seven of the irregular verbs occurring in the New Testament, as well as an extensive summary of paradigms. A thorough subject index and index of Greek words discussed are also included.

This "reference grammar" function goes too far at times. For anyone wondering why πίπτω changes to πεσοῦμαι in the future, McLean is happy to explain: "It is the only verb in the GNT that forms its future with the Doric tense formative -σε" (107). But do first-year Greek students need to know about Doric tense formatives? This example—which continues with further step-by-step explanation of how πετ + σε + ο + μαι becomes πεσοῦμαι—is one of many examples where McLean appears to expect a bit too much out of his first-year Greek student.

This textbook is therefore not ideal for self-study. The descriptions of the rules for accentuation and of the formation of different paradigms and declensions are rather dauntingly detailed, and unless the would-be Hellenist is already trained in linguistics, confusion is bound to result from undefined and unexplained phrases such as "plosive aspiration" and "intentionally polysemous" (12, 59).

As it stands, this very affordable volume may appeal to advocates of the "historical" Greek pronunciation system, to students interested in more technical aspects of Greek accentuation and morphology, or to those who want to be equipped to read actual portions of the New Testament as swiftly as possible. If McLean corrected the more than three dozen typographical errors, added more Greek practice sentences, and excised some overly technical explanations, a second edition of this textbook could become an appealing choice for a much wider range of instructors and students of New Testament Greek.

An Introduction to Biblical Aramaic, by Andreas Schuele. Louisville: Westminster John Knox, 2012. Pp. xii + 145. Paper. $30.00. ISBN 9780664234249.

Ian Young, University of Sydney, Sydney, Australia

In this very useful volume, Andreas Schuele provides an introduction to Biblical Aramaic aimed at being as helpful as possible to students in the classroom. Acknowledging that most students come to Biblical Aramaic with a prior acquaintance with Biblical Hebrew, the book adds helpful side comments relating what they are learning in Aramaic to what they already may know about Hebrew. However, it does not require that students know Hebrew to use this work. My review will focus on the features of the book that are especially helpful to students, while occasionally mentioning some features that are potentially less helpful.

The first chapter, "What Is 'Biblical Aramaic'?" gives a brief introduction outlining the Aramaic sections of the Hebrew Bible, possible reasons for the use of Aramaic in Daniel and Ezra, and the context of Biblical Aramaic in the Imperial Aramaic of the Persian Empire. Schuele also mentions the one verse of Aramaic in Jeremiah (10:11) and the two words in Gen 31:47 but does not discuss why Aramaic was used in those contexts, a question that students might also have found interesting.

The second chapter—I say second, but a potentially unhelpful feature of the book is that the chapters are not numbered—is "From the Phoenician to the Aramaic Writing System." After first introducing the Northwest Semitic writing system, the chapter then has a helpful section setting out the development of different phonemes in Aramaic and Hebrew. This clearly explains relationships such as between Aramaic דהב and Hebrew זהב "gold," which allows students more easily to relate what they know in Hebrew to what they are learning in Aramaic.

The next chapter introduces "Masoretic Vowel Signs." Particularly helpful is the section "Differences between Aramaic and Hebrew Vowels," which offers three "Observations" that help relate Hebrew vowels to Aramaic vowels, to help students recognize similar words in the two languages. For example, "Observation 1" discusses the common correspondence between Hebrew *holem* with Biblical Aramaic *qames*, as in Aramaic קָל and Hebrew קוֹל "voice." From this point each chapter includes exercises on the topics covered, here beginning with the syllabic structure of Biblical Aramaic words. Answers to these exercises are provided at the end of the volume.

The next chapter, "The Noun," covers a wide range of topics, including gender, absolute and construct states, notes on particular groups of nouns (those ending in –*û*, –*î*, and with *he*), important individual nouns (e.g., אַב "father"), nouns with suffixes, adjectives, numerals, gentilics, prepositions, and pronouns. There are numerous helpful hints, especially for those students who know Hebrew, such as a table comparing the third-person masculine suffixes on singular and plural nouns in both languages, since these are the ones that are most different. In the section on suffixes, Schuele follows many Biblical Aramaic grammars by giving only the attested forms, thus omitting the second-person singular and plural feminine forms. I think it would be beneficial to include these forms (marked as unattested in Biblical Aramaic) so that, even if they are not encountered, a complete picture of the language is given (cf. the reference grammar of Franz Rosenthal, *A Grammar of Biblical Aramaic* [Wiesbaden: Harrasowitz, 1963], 26). Ideally, teachers of Aramaic hope that students will be encouraged to put Biblical Aramaic in the broader context of other varieties of ancient Aramaic (see the appendices to this volume), so the information provided should not so narrowly focus on the practicalities of translating just Biblical Aramaic texts. A further issue, which is unhelpful even to those only interested in Biblical Aramaic, is the citing of a form such as אֱלָהָיךְ as "your gods," without any mention of the constant Qere of the MT where suffixes on singular and plural nouns fall together, thus the Qere of "(to) your gods" is לֵאלָהָךְ (see, e.g., Dan 3:12).

The next chapter covers "The Verb," discussing the basic issues such as the different conjugations and stems, verbs with suffixes, and weak verbs. This section seemed to contain less helpful advice for beginners than elsewhere in the book. In sections on the weak verbs, for example, the information seemed brief and dense, and I wonder what beginners would make of it. Fortunately, students can refer to the very helpful paradigms that cover the attested forms of the verb in Biblical Aramaic in detail (120–45). Once again, second-person feminine forms are missing (see below on the various typographical errors in this section).

Next follows a good chapter on "Syntax" that covers a wide range of topics, illustrated by citation of specific Biblical Aramaic texts and references to Biblical Hebrew. Among many good points, I liked the way that Schuele discusses Aramaic word order by detailed analysis of a complex sentence (Dan 5:12; p. 72), or the way the narrative tenses are illustrated through a detailed discussion of verbal use in Dan 5:1–10 (75).

There follows a "Word List" containing "the most common verbs and nouns in Biblical Aramaic that are worth memorizing" (84) and a section on "Persian and

Greek Loanwords." Then there is a "Comparative Word List (Aramaic/Hebrew)." Here we have entries such as that Aramaic uses בעה for "search, look for, request," whereas Hebrew uses בקש. This sort of list could be very helpful for students to get an idea of some key similarities and differences between Biblical Aramaic and Biblical Hebrew. Then there is a very useful list of idiomatic expressions, such as "eating the pieces" for "slandering."

The appendices give samples of Aramaic texts outside Biblical Aramaic. Appendix 1 gives the text of the Old Aramaic Zakkur Inscription as a representative of a linguistic stage before Imperial Aramaic. It gives the Aramaic text (of part A), with comments on the orthography and language, some notes on unfamiliar words, and a translation. Appendix 2 follows the same format for three texts from Qumran, an excerpt from the Genesis Apocryphon, an excerpt from the Testament of Levi (actually from the Cairo Genizah), and the Prayer of Nabonidus. Appendix 3 presents two short excerpts from the Wisdom of Ahiqar from Elephantine. The volume closes with "Answers to Exercises" and the very detailed "Paradigms" mentioned earlier.

Because this work aims not to get bogged down in details, there are of necessity many places where major scholarly questions and complex issues must be covered very briefly. Here Schuele tries to be as accurate as possible under the circumstances, and if students need further information, their teacher will have to provide it. Schuele cleverly avoids making a statement on the date of Daniel in the first chapter (1–2). At another point the book makes broad generalizations about the development of the Masoretic vocalization that make it sound as if the vocalizations of Biblical Hebrew and Biblical Aramaic rest solely on the decisions of the Masoretes (see, e.g., 16). I was also not sure what to make of the comment that "the energic *nun* is largely insignificant for translation purposes" (53) when it is common to see it as a key distinction between imperfect and jussive verbs (e.g., Rosenthal, 54–55).

One feature of the volume that I found unhelpful was how small the Aramaic script was printed. Although I got used to it, it occurred to me that, for beginning students, this requires extra work paying attention to the differences between vowels that, while printed clearly, could look very similar to each other on casual perusal. While I do not think this is a fatal flaw by any means, it seems to go against the otherwise well-realized aim of being as helpful as possible to beginning students. Another problem related to the production of the volume is a number of typographical errors in it, which are bound to confuse students particularly when they involve the Aramaic words. In relation to the Aramaic words, I noticed a problem of word wrap on page 5, an extra preposition in the table on 12, the Qere of "Chaldeans" on 30 is wrong, many cases of wrong *dageshes* in the verb paradigms (e.g., 36, 42, 43, 45, 48, 52 [Dan 5:20 is תִּקְפַּת; correct on 121]). Also in the verb paradigms I noticed "m. pl." for "f. sg." on 47, and "Pm. Pl." for "m. pl." on 48. I liked a great many things about this book and its approach to teaching Biblical Aramaic. I hope that such problems can be addressed in subsequent printings.

Malachi: A Handbook on the Hebrew Text, by Terry W. Eddinger. Baylor Handbook on the Hebrew Bible. Waco, Texas: Baylor University Press, 2012. Pp. xiv + 160. Paper. $29.95. ISBN 9781602584273.

Buzz Brookman, North Central University, Minneapolis, Minnesota

This is the fifth volume published in the Baylor Handbook on the Hebrew Bible series. The previous volumes are *Jonah* (2006), *Amos* and *Genesis 1–11* (2008), and *Ruth* (2010). The description of the series, as stated by Baylor University Press is: "Rather than devote space to the type of theological and exegetical comments found in most commentaries, this series instead focuses on the Hebrew text and its related issues, syntactic and otherwise. The volumes in the series serve as prequels to commentary proper, providing guides to understanding the linguistic characteristics of the texts from which the messages of the texts may then be derived." Thus, this series aims for a particular niche that is narrow yet well in need of such a resource, and I would judge the series to have met, thus far, its stated aim.

The Malachi volume is very much in step with the earlier books within the series, as the distinctive focus upon the grammatical and linguistic characteristics of the text is truly the main feature of the book. It is, indeed, a handbook in its conciseness and design. That is, I perceive it to be a useful tool for students who, having completed a first-year Hebrew course, are ready to commence reading some biblical texts. For that particular audience, this is surely a very attractive and welcome type of resource. It conveniently bundles a lot of grammatical and linguistic information about a given passage that one normally would need to garner from a wide variety of sources. For that reason alone it may be especially useful for novice readers who are not yet wholly familiar with the many resources that may potentially be consulted in running down such information about the Hebrew text. In that way, this handbook can function as a one-stop location for grammatical help as one commences to translate from the text of Malachi. While there are picky faults one can find in nearly any book of this nature (I will enumerate a few later), my general impression is that this particular volume and the series, in general, is a success given the design, scope, and goal of the project.

The book consists of a list of abbreviations (xi–xiii), an introduction (1–5), an analysis of the text of Malachi (7–120), two appendices (121–37), a glossary (139–42), a bibliography (143–50), and an index in three parts: Scripture and other ancient sources, author, and subject (151–60). The general appearance of the book is pleasing, and its compact size is appealing. The Hebrew font is a nice size in comparison to the English text within which it is oftentimes embedded. This makes reading the Hebrew text on the page very easy.

The general organization of the content is clear and intuitive. Eddinger divides the complete text of Malachi into six oracles preceded by the superscription (1:1). The first oracle is 1:2–5. The second oracle is 1:6–2:9, and he divides that into four parts (1:6–8, 9–13, 14, and 2:1–9). The third oracle encompasses 2:10–16. The fourth oracle is 2:17–3:5. The fifth oracle includes 3:6–12, and the sixth oracle is made up of 3:13–21 (English = 3:13–4:3). The pattern of presentation for each pericope is: (1) English translation, (2) brief summary statement of the character of the pericope, (3) a chart of key words within the section, (4) verse-by-verse presentation of the Hebrew text that is further broken down by clauses, phrases, and sometimes individual words, (5) complete parsing of the clauses and phrases followed by a statement of grammatical/linguistic insights, information, and comment. In this way, the author packages much content in a concisely presented way.

One should address the usefulness of this volume for those among the stated audience: students who are relative beginners. Therefore, I actually used a portion of this book in an undergraduate reading class that joins second- and third-year Hebrew students together. Six students in the course had the task of reading and preparing a translation of Mal 3 by using Eddinger's text. I solicited their comments and opinions concerning the book, and I have included a few of their remarks and sentiments along with my observations below.

In places Eddinger's translation seems quite wooden to the point of yielding somewhat awkward-sounding English sentences. For example, "And this is the second thing you do, covering with tears the altar of Yahweh, weeping and groaning, because there is no one anymore looking to the offering and taking pleasure from your hand (32:13)." Not that this needs to detract from the usefulness of this book, but it just does not always present an eloquent translation.

In his discussion on "Using this Handbook" (5), Eddinger states, "The key word charts list words that have significant meaning for the text." Yet some might well argue that his selections of these key words seem somewhat arbitrary, as no rationale beyond that single sentence addresses why he sees those particular words as "significant" compared to others. That being said, the key-words charts actually are a nice feature of the presentation that students found interesting and useful. Difficulty arose for students when unfamiliar nomenclature was used without adequate definition or explanation. For example, Eddinger states (111), "The *waw* relative indicating sequence with the perfect form of הָיָה usually has a deictic temporal function." He is alluding to Waltke and O'Connor (§32.2.6), but this is not helpful to students at all. *Deictic* is not in Eddinger's glossary. Waltke and O'Connor does have a glossary entry for *deixis* but does not have the form *deictic*. Most students would not be able to make the leap between the forms *deictic* and *deixis* back to δείκνυμι in order to glean anything useful here. This is a consistent problem in that many times technical terms used by Eddinger are not given in his glossary. For example, *nun paragogicum* (23) is in the index but is absent from the glossary. Also, Eddinger cites "desidertative clause" (23), drawn from Gesenius's grammar (GKC), but the term does not appear in this glossary. These are just a few samples from a considerable list of terms that are employed within the book but nowhere defined. For instructors and, perhaps, graduate students of some experience, this may not be a substantial hurdle. However, for the intended audience, this considerable gap between use and explanation of technical terms is a weakness.

Thus, there would seem to be a tradeoff in using this book for students who are truly relative novices. First, there is the rather daunting level of linguistic and grammatical jargon consistently employed within its pages without adequate explanation. The good news is this handbook presents a good opportunity for beginning students to get their feet wet in some of the technical nomenclature that is part of the study of the Hebrew text. The bad news is that most first-year courses and textbooks do not deal with the terminology on anywhere near the level of what is presented in this book. Therefore, as a teaching resource, the instructor needs to sell the students on its usefulness and the necessity for building a vocabulary of the technical terms used in the craft of translation.

A somewhat detracting aspect of this book is the number of miscellaneous technical errors it contains. These are found predominately within the English translation sections. There are many grammatical errors, especially in the form of run-on sentences. Other types of errors occur with some regularity right from the start to the very end. For example, the first paragraph of the introduction contains the following sentence. "The purpose of this handbook is aid [sic] the student or translator in the translation process, especially to assist with grammar and syntax" (1). The English translation of 2:10–16 (54) commences, "Does [sic] not all of us have one father?" While the technical glitches occur most frequently in English, there are a few errors in the Hebrew text. For example, chart I (121), in listing all the Hebrew words occurring in Malachi, אֱדֹום is listed instead of אֱדֹום, as the form of Edom. Also, φλέξει should be φλέξει (111). While the √ symbol is usually employed to specify a true root (e.g., √כשׁף), Eddinger cites roots throughout by always giving them in *qal*, even if it is an unattested form (e.g., √כָּשַׁף). Yet, this may be a bit nitpicky in the scope of what the book does accomplish.

In conclusion, while the text is in need of some technical revisions, it certainly had some appeal to students who used it class. They found it to be handy and beneficial. The verdict from the student perspective was positive, although they found the level of technical jargon to be daunting. Overall, this book is a handy resource that serves its stated purpose quite well.

ARCHAEOLOGY AND HISTORY

Hazon Gabriel: New Readings of the Gabriel Revelation, edited by Matthias Henze. Early Judaism and Its Literature 29. Atlanta: Society of Biblical Literature, 2011. Pp. xiii + 219. Paper. $29.95. ISBN 9781589835412.

Aaron Koller, Yeshiva University, New York, New York

This volume is the first to be devoted to the "Hazon Gabriel" text, a "Dead Sea Scroll on stone" first published in 2007.[1] The stone is owned by David Jesselsohn,

---

1. "Dead Sea Scoll in Stone" was the title of the article by Ada Yardeni in *BAR* 34/1 (2008): 60–61.

who contributed an essay to this volume on the discovery and publication of the text. The text is unprovenanced, but numerous lines of evidence suggest that it came from the region around the Dead Sea, probably on the eastern side. It appears from Jesselsohn's narrative that it came into his possession around 1999, from the Jordanian antiquities dealer Ghassan Rihani. Over the next few years Jesselsohn had photographs taken by Zeev Radovan and those photographs read by Ada Yardeni. Not much happened, however, until 2005, when Yardeni, together with Binyamin Elitzur, began to work on the text in earnest, consulting with other scholars, such as Richard Steiner, and eventually publishing the text as "A Prophetic Text on Stone from the First Century BCE."[2] Israel Knohl, who in 2000 had published a book arguing that the idea of a suffering messiah was to be found in texts from the century before Jesus, immediately got to work on this text, publishing a popular article in *Haaretz* and a scholarly article in *Tarbiz* in 2007, then another article in the *Journal of Religion* in 2008.

All this scholarly attention, and some of the more dramatic claims submitted by Knohl, piqued wider interest in the text, and the *New York Times* ran an article about it in the summer of 2008. The claim that drew the most attention was Knohl's reading of line 80 in the text, said to say, לשלשת ימים חאיה "in three days, you shall live." The effect that this particular proposal had on the attention given to the text is described by Jesselsohn on pages 6–8.

This, however, was roundly criticized by other scholars, on both material and grammatical grounds. As Moshe Bar-Asher observed, nowhere in ancient Hebrew or Aramaic is an *aleph* used as a mater lectionis for a shortened *pataḥ* (/ă/), which is the expected vowel in *ḥăyē*. In the present volume, Knohl himself has abandoned the reading, and the suggestion first put forth by Ronald Hendel to read האות "the sign" has garnered significant support.[3] Ironically, then, a proposal quickly abandoned even by its originator had the longer-lasting effect of drumming up more attention for a text than it otherwise would have had. The text, in my opinion, deserves the attention anyway.

Because the volume is a record of the conference papers and the conference papers were written before the participants knew that Knohl had dropped the suggestion to read חאיה, there are a number of pages throughout the book dedicated to rejecting that view, now defended by no one. In this way, and others, the book presents scholarly work in progress, which is (as we all know) both exciting and frustrating.

The next chapter is an English version of the original Hebrew article by Yardeni and Elitzur, with only two small changes/corrections reflecting the views of

---

2. This article appeared in *Cathedra* 123 (2007): 155–66; Steiner's contributions from 2006 are mentioned on p. 24 of the current volume.

3. As noted by Henze, however (128), it is not clear what the line לשלושת ימין האות אני גבריאל "In three days [shall be?] the sign, I am Gabriel" means. Daewoong Kim has a suggestion on 166–71.

other writers inserted. Chapter 3 is an "abbreviated version" of a very important article, also published originally in Hebrew in *Cathedra*, by Elisha Qimron and Alexey (Eliyahu) Yuditsky, which improves the reading significantly.

Following the two chapters on the material readings there is a chapter by Knohl in which he discusses very insightfully a number of the important themes and ideas in the text and, in a more exact way than anyone else, attempts to situate the text historically. His idea (retained from his earliest publications on the text) is to connect the text to events that took place in 4 BCE in the wake of the death of Herod. Josephus tells of revolts that then erupted, including one led by a man named Simon, who fled to the Transjordan and was there killed. According to Knohl, this event contributed to the rise of the idea of "catastrophic messianism," the notion that the defeat of the would-be messiah is in fact part of the process of redemption. Many are the implications of this suggestion, and it is one worth considering seriously, both with regard to the philological readings of the text that it relies on and engenders and with regard to the history of ideas.

Chapter 5 is a "grammatical sketch" of the text by Gary Rendsburg that updates his earlier article in *DSD* 16; while that article had (reasonably) been based on the *editio princeps* of the text, this one takes the readings of Qimron and Yuditsky as its starting point. Rendsburg also augmented this version by incorporating discussion of a number of issues raised by Moshe Bar-Asher in his discussion of the text's language.[4] This makes the chapter a comprehensive discussion, with the caveat that the text is very incomplete. In order to discuss the grammar of the text, one needs to know what it says, and even in the lines where the text is preserved, this is not always a simple matter. How does one vocalize טבחי: as טָבְחֵי (Rendsburg) or as טַבָּחֵי (Bar-Asher)? If the scribe writes ואגיד in line 21 but ואגדה in line 12, is he distinguishing between cohortative and indicative or not? Should ואגיד be pointed וְאַגִּיד (as Qimron and Yuditsky do)? Or do we assume that the scribe has no idea what the difference is between these forms? Is קיטוט a *qittul* noun from קטט, or is it from ק(ו)ט, as in כְּמֵעַט קָט (Ezek 16:47)—again, a point on which Rendsburg and Bar-Asher are divided? No certainty is possible with regard to such issues, but Rendsburg is a reliable guide to them even when one may disagree with a particular understanding he embraces.

With the following chapter, formally a response to Knohl by Adela Yarboro Collins, the book moves into a different gear. This and the remaining chapters— "Gabriel and David: Some Reflections on an Enigmatic Text," by John J. Collins; "Some Observations on the *Hazon Gabriel*," by Henze; "Hosts, Holy Ones, and the Words of Gabriel: The Angelology of *Hazon Gabriel* in the Context of Second Temple and Late Antique Literature," by Kelley Coblentz Bautch; "The Use of Daniel in the *Gabriel Revelation*," by Daewoong Kim; and "'Jerusalem' in the

---

4. Bar-Asher, "על הלשון ב"חזון גבריאל"," *Meghillot* 7 (2009): 193–226, translated as "On the Language of 'The Vision of Gabriel,'" *Revue de Qumran* 23 (2008): 491–524.

Gabriel Revelation and the Revelation of John," by David Capes—deal more with
the ideas in and around the text than the specific readings of the text itself.

Yarboro Collins criticizes Knohl on the grounds that "most New Testament
scholars" would not agree with the idea of catastrophic messianism, because they
do not understand Jesus to have foreseen his messianic resurrection. This is true,
but of course Knohl knows this and is challenging those scholars to reexamine the
evidence. Perhaps he is wrong, but this chapter does not show it. The same is true
for Collins's reiteration of the conventional wisdom regarding the "Messiah son
of Joseph," which, it is argued, was the result of ideas developed in the wake of the
failed revolt of Simon bar Kosiba. Again, this may be true (I continue to think that
it is), but pointing out that Knohl's view disagrees with a formerly accepted view
does not actually constitute an argument.

Henze's chapter is probably the best introduction to the text as a whole, since
it surveys what is known of the contents of the text, section by section, highlighting important or controversial points along the way. Coblentz Bautch's article on
angelology is a valuable discussion, taking the various beings mentioned in the
text, such as צבאות, מלאך, and מרכבות, as starting points and surveying what is
known of their beings within Second Temple and late antique Jewish literature.
Also surveyed are the uses of the figures of Michael and Gabriel himself. All of this
is interesting and valuable in itself but, as Coblentz Bautch says in her conclusion,
"does not shed more light on the provenance or use of this composition, the way it
was read or by whom," or even, one might add, on what it *means*.

Kim's chapter on the use of Daniel is interesting, although I am not entirely
convinced that all of the "reactivations of original texts" described here were
indeed intended by the author. This is, at least, a good discussion of some of the
many biblical allusions in the text. Finally, Capes takes on the topic of "Jerusalem"
in the text and compares it to the use of the image of the city in the book of Revelation. As it turns out, these books have in common "a great eschatological battle in
which the nations of the world march against Jerusalem" and numerous smaller
details, but the uses of the city are fundamentally different, in that Hazon Gabriel
describes the real, earthly Jerusalem, whereas Revelation looks to victory and salvation only in a heavenly Jerusalem. Whether this difference is due to the century
that elapsed between the two works, during which the temple and Jerusalem were
destroyed, or whether divergent views regarding this question were to be found
among Jews while the Second Temple yet stood, is worthy of further attention.

In sum, this volume is a very useful—one might even say indispensable—
collection of articles relating to an exciting and tantalizing text. The Society of
Biblical Literature is to be commended for publishing it, and especially for keeping the price at an eminently attainable level. The book captures much of the
excitement around an important textual find and also shares with its readers some
of the frustrations of dealing with the novelty of such a find. It is not desirable to
simply read the text in light of what was previously thought, since that strips it
of its power to make us rethink and revisit. But it is also not possible to overturn
everything, especially on the basis of a text that is, after all, highly fragmentary.

Finding those balances is the task of the text's interpreters, and this volume allows
the reader to take part in this ongoing enterprise.

*Corpus der Stempelsiegel-Amulette aus Palästina/ Israel: Von den Anfängen bis zur
Perserzeit: Katalog Band IV: Von Tel Gamma bis Chirbet Husche,* by Othmar Keel.
Orbis Biblicaus et Orientalis Series Archaeologica 33. Fribourg: Academic Press;
Göttingen: Vandenhoeck & Ruprecht, 2013. Pp. xvi + 715. Cloth. €200.00. ISBN
9783727817328.

Brent A. Strawn, Emory University, Atlanta, Georgia

Othmar Keel is best known in the English-speaking world for two pioneering
volumes. The first, *The Symbolism of the Biblical World: Ancient Near Eastern
Iconography and the Psalms* (hereafter *Symbolism*), was published in 1972 (Neukirchen-Vluyn) and then in 1978 in English translation (Seabury). Thanks to
Eisenbrauns, the English edition is still available (reprinted in 1997); the 5th
German version is also still in print (1996; note also the existence of Spanish
and Japanese translations). The second breakthrough work was co-authored
with Christoph Uehlinger: *Gods, Goddesses, and Images of God in Ancient Israel*
(hereafter *GGG*), published in German in 1992 (presently in a 6th edition,
2010) and released in English translation in 1998 (Fortress). As important as
these two works are, they are the proverbial tip of the iceberg in Keel's oeuvre,
the vast majority of which has appeared in German (with some works, especially his commentary on the Song of Songs, also available in French, English,
and Polish). Indeed, his vast scholarly accomplishments were recognized by his
winning of the Marcel Benoist Prize in 2005, the most prestigious prize granted
by the Swiss government for outstanding scientific achievement. At that time,
Keel was only the third or fourth scholar of the humanities to win this celebrated award.

In *Symbolism*, Keel brought the world of ancient Near Eastern iconography
to biblical studies in a new way. There had always been ancient art historians, of
course, including those who specialized in the ancient Near East, and there had
also always been archeologists who paid attention to artifacts. But never before
had these areas been combined and brought to bear in a systematic way on biblical studies—especially the importance of the visual data for the interpretation of
a particular book of the Bible—not, at any rate, with the care, range, and command that Keel demonstrated in *Symbolism*. This book inaugurated a subfield
and was the first publication in a massive body of work that Keel has been producing ever since. Still further, *Symbolism* and its author inaugurated a veritable
school, the Fribourg School, comprising Keel and the many talented students
he has advised at the University of Fribourg over the past forty years (including, among others, C. Uehlinger, S. Schroer, T. Staubli, J. Eggler, U. Winter, H.
Steymans), as well as some honorable mentions from beyond the borders of
Switzerland proper (I. Cornelius, M. Klingbeil, T. Ornan, C. Frevel, I. de Hulster,

J. M. LeMon; the present reviewer would also like to be numbered among the latter).

In *GGG* (reviewed in *RBL* by Raz Kletter; http://www.bookreviews.org/pdf/70_384.pdf]), Keel and Uehlinger refined the approach Keel first pursued in *Symbolism*. Instead of focusing on a specific biblical book and taking a wide-angle, phenomenological approach to the intersection of iconography and text, *GGG* focused on the history of Canaanite/Israelite religion, from the Middle Bronze Age IIB through Iron Age III, intentionally privileging the artistic remains from ancient Israel/Palestine in contrast to approaches that depended (in their view) overmuch on textual, especially biblical, evidence.

The methodological shift from *Symbolism* to *GGG* was a major development in Keel's thinking and the later Fribourg School. This development was predicated in no small way on Keel and Uehlinger's breakthrough insight that minor art (i.e., seals, scarabs, ivories, etc.) served in antiquity in a way akin to mass communication now: they were highly mobile and therefore able to disseminate information widely and easily—in some cases, even cheaply. The Biblical Institute of the University of Fribourg had been amassing a collection of minor art for some time, even prior to *GGG*, but this became a major focus of acquisition and, more importantly, research thereafter.

Keel's monumental *Corpus der Stempelsiegel-Amulettte aus Palästina/Israel: Von den Anfängen bis zur Perserzeit* is the latest step in this methodological development and the research of the Fribourg School more generally. The volume under review is *Band IV*, but it is really the sixth to date. The first volume, *Einleitung* (OBOSA 10) was published in 1995 (reviewed by Mark W. Chavalas: http://www.bookreviews.org/pdf/2677_1883.pdf). The *Katalog Band 1: Von Tell Abu Farağ bis 'Atlit* (OBOSA 13) followed in 1997; which was followed in 2010 by two further volumes: *Katalog Band 2: Von Bahan bis Tel Eton* (OBOSA 29) and *Katalog Band III: Von Tell el-Far'a Nord bis Tell el-Fir* (OBOSA 31). Also to be considered as part of this work (and the *Corpus* project proper), but numbered independently as it concerns Transjordan, is Jürg Eggler and Othmar Keel, *Corpus der Siegel-Amulette aus Jordanien: Von Neolithikum bis zur Perserzeit* (OBOSA 25), published in 2006.

The size and scope of Keel's *Corpus* is remarkable: Volume 1 published 2,139 objects from twenty-two sites beginning with the letter A; volume 2 published 1,224 items from forty-five sites starting with the letters B–E; and volume 3 offered 1,009 more items from four sites starting with the letter F. The latest volume (*Band IV*) catalogues 1,439 more objects from thirty sites (letters G–H), bringing the total number to 5,811 items. The co-authored volume on Transjordanian sites presents 716 more seals, bringing the total number of items catalogued to 6,527—a staggering number and an unbelievably rich repository of information, whether the concern is biblical studies proper (as in *Symbolism*) or the history of Canaanite/Israelite religion (as in *GGG*) or both. Or neither, as the *Corpus* stands on its own as an amazing accomplishment presenting these data in their own right for purposes of archaeological research or art historical analysis with little or no recourse to biblical studies or the history of religion. In this regard, the enormous chronological span of the *Corpus* should be kept in mind: it runs the Chalcolithic to the Persian period.

Katalog Band IV covers the following sites, with the numbers in parentheses indicating the number of items catalogued from each:

(Tel) Gamma (nos. 1–213)
Gat (der Philister) (nos. 1–60)
Gat Karmel (nos. 1–8)
Gaza (nos. 1–9)
Gedor (no. 1)
Gerar (nos. 1–2)
(Tel) Gerisa (nos. 1–54)
Geser (nos. 1–692)
Gibeon (nos. 1–58)
Ginnosar (nos. 1–10)
(El-) Ǧisr (nos. 1–4)
(Tell el-) Ǧudede (nos. 1–17)
(El-) Ǧurn (no. 1)
(Tel) Hadar (nos. 1–2)
(Tel) Hadid (nos. 1–5)
Ha-Goscherim (nos. 1–38)
(Tel) Halif (nos. 1–24)
(Tel) Hamid (nos. 1–2)
(Tell el-) Hammah (nos. 1–5)
Hanita (nos. 1–2)
Har Adar (no. 1)
(Tel) Harasim (nos. 1–40)
(Tel) Haror (nos. 1–12)
Hazor (nos. 1–118)
Hebron [also known as Ǧebel Nimra] (nos. 1–16)
(Tel) Hefer (no. 1)
Herzlija [also known as Gelilot] (nos. 1–2)
(Tell el-) Hesi (nos. 1–24)
Huǧ (nos. 1–3)
(Tell el-) Hulefi (nos. 1–14)
(Chirbet) Husche (no. 1)

While some of these sites offer only a few objects, several are especially rich: Tel Gamma (213), Gezer (692), and Hazor (118), for example, which thereby allow for geographical comparisons (south, central, north, respectively) as well as extensive material for analysis within one and the same site.

Each catalogued object is numbered within each site and is presented on the left page with a detailed description that includes information about the object proper (*Objekt*), the inscribed base (*Basis*), its date (*Datierung*), present collection

(*Sammlung*), find spot if known (*Fundkontext*), and bibliography (*Bibliographie*). Especially important, and not found in the much briefer treatments of the seals in *Symbolism* and *GGG*—which, however, include only a tiny fraction of the *Corpus*—is the discussion of parallels to the imagery on the object in question with others in the *Corpus* and beyond (this is found under *Basis*). The facing, right-hand page then presents photographs (top, side, and bottom) of each item and line drawings of the same. This format pertains to all volumes in the *Corpus*.

Also not to be missed are the front and end papers, which present a map of the sites catalogued in this particular volume (as also in the others). Using these maps one can see at a glance where the objects originate. Finally, the volume concludes with an extensive bibliography (672–714), inclusive of the previous volumes save only that of the *Einleitung* (which already contained close to 2,000 items).

Despite the importance of *Symbolism* and *GGG*, it is lamentable that more of Keel's work is not known among Anglophones. One suspects the issue is that so little of his corpus has been translated into English. That is changing with several projects underway that will bring more of his work to English-only readers (one is mentioned below). Yet even English-only readers should, with little effort, be able to access and benefit from the *Corpus*. The descriptions of the seals, while detailed, are nevertheless relatively circumscribed such that even novices in German can easily make their way through them with a bit of practice and a decent dictionary. Parts of the entries are completely transparent (e.g., the date information), and much of the bibliography refers to English publications. Note, too, that in a few select sites, the material is written in English by a contributor; this is the case with (Tel) Haror by Baruch Brandl in *Band IV* (572–81), for example.

More to the point, the data collected here are just too important to neglect. Scholars of ancient Israel/Palestine ignore Keel's work and especially this *Corpus* to their own peril. As Keel and Uehlinger put it in *GGG*, in a passage that bears repeating, "Anyone who systematically ignores the pictorial evidence that a culture has produced can hardly expect to recreate even a minimally adequate description of the culture itself. Such a person will certainly not be able to describe the nature of the religious symbols by which such a culture oriented itself" (xi). Keel's *Corpus* is a crucial tool that enables all of us who have followed him (and the Fribourg School) to attend to this "pictorial evidence." If our descriptions of ancient Israelite culture are better, this is due in no small part to the labors of Keel. Indeed, the *Corpus* can be seen as a kind of text edition, laying a foundation on which generations of scholars can and will profitably build.

(For scholars who work in German, the following important volumes should also be mentioned: Keel's massive 1,384 page history of Jerusalem, *Die Geschichte Jerusalems und die Entstehung des Monotheismus* [2 vols.; Orte und Landschaften der Bibel 4.1; Göttingen: Vandenhoeck & Ruprecht 2007], which appeared in a much abbreviated, one-volume edition as *Jerusalem und der eine Gott: Eine Religionsgeschichte* [Göttingen: Vandenhoeck & Ruprecht, 2011], an English translation of which is forthcoming with Fortress; and Silvia Schroer's *Die Iknographie Palästinas/Israels und der Alte Orient: Eine Religionsgeschichte in*

Bildern [3 vols. to date; Fribourg: Academic Press, 2005– (vol. 1 in conjunction with Keel)].)

The development from *Symbolism* to *GGG* to the *Corpus* could be seen as retrogressive in some way. Should not the foundations (i.e., the *Corpus*) be laid first before moving on to the big syntheses? Ideally, yes. The success and endurance of both *Symbolism* and *GGG*, in this light, are just further testimony to the brilliance of their author(s). It is clear, though, that early on Keel realized the importance of this kind of cataloguing work; it is equally clear that this work is even better and more helpful than it might have been earlier, given Keel's command of the whole field and the fact that this foundational work, often done by those new to the subject or with less fertile minds, is now being executed by the most mature of scholars, a veritable master of his trade—indeed, the pioneer in his self-propagated field!

In sum, Keel (and those who have assisted him, not only in *Band IV*, but the others as well) is to be heartily congratulated for this work. It is a monumental achievement, the scope of which is hard to grasp. Both of the presses involved, Academic Press and Vandenhoeck & Ruprecht, should also be congratulated for taking on what is surely an expensive but vitally important research project. It is be to hoped that the many who might assist with future volumes—including museums, collectors, and excavators who hold access to the seals—will do everything in their power to enable the timely completion of the entire project. When that happens, we will be even further in Keel's debt than we already are, as this *Corpus* will, in the end, be simply unsurpassable. Indeed, it already is.

Temples and Sanctuaries from the Early Iron Age Levant: Recovery After Collapse, by William E. Mierse. Winona Lake, Ind.: Eisenbrauns, 2012. Pp. xiv + 480. Hardcover. $59.50. ISBN 9781575062464.

Jonathan S. Greer, Grand Rapids Theological Seminary, Grand Rapids, Michigan

William Mierse's *Temples and Sanctuaries from the Early Iron Age Levant* offers a comparative study of architectural features of early Iron Age temples in the Levant dating to the historical period following the collapse of the Late Bronze Age interregional system, highlighting both continuity with Late Bronze Age designs and innovative departures from traditional forms. As an art and architectural historian and self-proclaimed ancient Near Eastern studies "outsider" (x, though on the basis of the breadth and depth exhibited in this volume, one may respectfully beg to differ), he emphasizes formal characteristics of continuity and discontinuity and provides a fresh take on the political and social forces related to his observations.

In chapter 1 Mierse spells out his ambitious aim of providing an overall synthesis of Levantine architectural forms of "temples" (or related terms, as designated by their excavators) dating to the Iron Age I–II (1200–700 BCE). After a brief review of previous research, he explains his "formalist" approach augmented by elements gleaned from the postprocessual school of archaeology. He also describes his incorporation and cautious use of textual sources, especially the "highly problematic" (8) texts of the Hebrew Bible, with which he interacts specifically in regard to the temple of Solomon. On this matter, he finds the proportional relationship between the tabernacle and the temple (which is not without its problems) to be more of a literary construct than a formal reality, though he finds the form itself to resonate with a standard Levantine temple plan. Ultimately he concludes that, while the temple of Solomon cannot be ignored in his study, its "shadowy existence renders it useless for trying to understand actual buildings" (16; cf. 107, 306).

Chapter 2 provides the backdrop for the temples discussed, with a special emphasis on the physical and human diversity of the Levant, in contrast to Egypt and Mesopotamia, and a brief mention of cosmic geography. Mierse addresses the role of climate change in regard to the Late Bronze Age collapse and the way temple builders exploited the local environment for materials as well as the importance of trade routes and water sources for temple placement. He also outlines the history of the collapse, noting major destructions and people movements as well as areas of continuity. Following a discussion of various Levantine people groups, including Canaanites, Arameans, Neo-Hittites, and Sea Peoples, Mierse provides a nuanced discussion of ethnicity based on epigraphic and material remains, unfortunately excluding any mention of the role faunal material can play in these discussions (46–53; cf. 307).

The core of Mierse's study is the archaeological survey of temple remains found in chapter 3. Following brief comments regarding the chronology of the Iron Age Levant, Mierse provides a detailed discussion (with corresponding graphics in a lengthy appendix) of thirty-eight sanctuaries with an eye toward assessing continuity and discontinuity in architectural features. He categorizes the discussion chronologically and regionally, addressing first sanctuaries from the Iron Age I, including those associated with the Sea Peoples, Arameans, Neo-Hittites, "revived" Canaanites, and Proto-Israelites. For the Iron IIA, Mierse surveys a smaller group (touching on the high versus low chronology debates), before turning to the larger corpus of diverse Iron IIB remains from Phoenician, Israelite and Judahite, Philistine, and Ammonite sites, as well as Moabite and Edomite sites of the Iron IIC, among others. Mierse closes with a critique of postcolonial "national revival" notions, finding such explanations "unjustified" (144).

Chapters 4 and 5 follow with a formal analysis of building techniques and plans. In chapter 4 continuity is emphasized in construction on preexistent sacred space, in similarities in materials and techniques (often dictated by environmental factors), and in the use of major traditional forms, including long-room, broad-room, and bent-axis types. In chapter 5 Mierse argues less for *de novo* forms and more for innovative adaptations of Late Bronze Age forms, highlighting the use of ashlar masonry, the *bīt ḫilani* plan, columns, inset windows, and ambulatories, as well as iconographic elements such as carved orthostats and reliefs.

In chapter 6 Mierse explores the potential reasons Iron Age architects built as they did. He draws a strong connection with royal ideology and emphasizes the creative and intellectual aspects of temple building from a number of angles. He highlights the role of skilled craftsmen and builders, often exchanged among rulers, and interaction (even potential disagreement) between the architects and their patrons. Mierse notes three potential sponsors for temple projects (individuals, communities, and monarchs) and the difficulty of differentiating among them. Ultimately, he argues, sacred spaces were tailored for the particular rituals (including processions and musical enactments) of the people involved.

Mierse expands his study in chapter 7 to address the western expansion of Levantine cultic architecture from the ninth century BCE on, a particular area of his expertise. In discussing locales of Greek and Phoenician interaction, he suggests that, even though later Greek temple forms relied most heavily on local Mycenaean prototypes, some influence from contact with Phoenician architectural forms should be assumed. After distinguishing a second wave of Phoenician colonization, Mierse affirms the influence of a number of different factors on local temple styles in the far West and notes that it was not the royal temple type that was meaningful in the colonies but a more varied vernacular form carried by the merchants that took hold.

In the conclusion of chapter 8, Mierse reiterates his main arguments. He sees no fundamental change between Late Bronze Age and Iron Age temples as far as structure and importance. He does, however, see Late Bronze Age forms as "prestigious buildings" characterized by an urban context, solid construction, and sacred pedigree (300). Iron Age temples often maintained these characteristics, likely intending to emulate and identify with the previous power, but also developed a "vernacular" temple type that was more modest in size, with features that may hint at wider community involvement. In the Iron Age, prestige was also indicated by associating temples with palace complexes, so that kings would have direct access to the divine, and by creating spaces for processions and large scale corporate worship. Mierse suggests that the continuity and discontinuity observed parallels the history of the period in that different regions of the Levant were affected by the collapse to varying degrees. In regard to ethnicity, he concludes that no architectural form may be tied to any particular people but that various peoples interacted with a broader temple-building *koine*. The spread of vernacular Levantine temple types may be attributed to both commercial and demographic shifts, though little influence was noted in areas that had a prior history of shrine building (i.e., Aegean) compared to the far West, largely devoid of temple traditions.

On the whole, Mierse certainly succeeds in providing an up-to-date, detailed survey of major temples and sanctuaries from the Iron Age Levant, and his work will serve as an important reference point for any future discussions of this topic. His conclusions are well argued, appropriately nuanced, and convincing. In fact, many of his conclusions, such as the shift from the "prestigious" long-room temple type of the Late Bronze Age to the diverse and innovative types of the Iron Age, are independently affirmed in the concomitantly published *Temple Building and Temple Cult*.[1] A unique strength of Mierse's volume is his consideration of the Levantine types in a broader Mediterranean context and his well-developed explanation of diffusion. Another strength of the work is the appendix: ninety pages of photos, drawings, plans, and maps essential for a study such as this. This section, however, would be significantly enhanced by more detail in many of the plans and by a better quality map with more accurate locations for the sites mentioned (cf., e.g., the locations of Kuntillet ʿAjrud and Sarepta [374]).

While affirming Mierse's broad conclusions, in a work as far-reaching as this, particular readers may quibble with his classification of certain structures. For example, I would distance myself from classifying Tel Dan's Area T as a "high place," as Mierse describes it (193–94), and resonate more with his "temple" designation applied to the complex elsewhere (123, 226); notably, Meirse recognizes the special status and high quality of construction techniques employed at Dan compared to other shrines in his "high place" category (194). Such in no way detracts from his greater contributions and, in fact, highlights that this work provides fodder for further discussion.

Indeed, this work will be appreciated by many in the various subfields related to biblical studies: biblicists will applaud the attention given to the literary descriptions of the temple of Solomon (in both MT and LXX text traditions); ancient Near Eastern historians will welcome the incorporation of ancient sources and the larger (often Braudelian) approach to historical change; art historians will resonate with the detailed descriptions of various motifs and the classification of architectural forms; and archaeologists will value the useful survey and meaningful synthesis. Mierse's volume, along with the massive *Temple Building and Temple Cult* mentioned above and *Tempel und Kultplätze der Philister und der Völker des Ostjordanlande*[2] mentioned in Mierse's chapter 1 (though appearing too late to be incorporated), among others, demonstrate that even as the interest in the cult of "household archaeology" rises (a welcome development), research on larger temples is by no means waning, and this volume will play an important role in ensuing explorations.

---

1. Jens Kamlah with Henrike Michelau, eds., *Temple Building and Temple Cult: Architecture and Cultic Paraphernalia of Temples in the Levant (2.–1. Mill. B.C.E.)* (ADPV 41; Harrassowitz: Wiesbaden, 2012).

2. Dominik Elkowicz, *Tempel und Kultplätze der Philister und der Völker des Ostjordanlande: Eine Untersuchung zur Bau- und zur Kultgeschichte während der Eisenzeit I–II* (AOAT 378. Münster: Ugarit-Verlag, 2012).

The Philistines and Other "Sea Peoples" in Text and Archaeology, edited by
Ann E. Killebrew and Gunnar Lehmann. Archaeology and Biblical Studies 15.
Atlanta: Society of Biblical Literature, 2013. Pp. xx + 751. Paper. $88.95. ISBN
9781589831292.

Ralph K. Hawkins, Averett University, Danville, Virginia

The Philistines, one of ancient Israel's most notorious enemies, have been the
subject of both popular interest and scholarly debate for many years. The ethni-
con appears about 250 times in the Hebrew Bible, and, while the preponderance
of these occurences is in the Deuteronomistic History (DtrH), it also appears
in the Pentateuch (e.g., Exod 13:17), begging the question of their origins
and identity. It is now well-known that the Philistines were one of a number
of so-called "Sea Peoples" who were key players in the transition from the
Late Bronze Age to the Iron Age I in the eastern Mediterranean world. In the
past, studies of the Sea Peoples have tended to focus on the Philistines and the
southern Levant. A much more complex and multivariate picture is emerging,
however, and this volume examines pertinent data from the northern Levant,
Cyprus, and the eastern Aegean. The editors note that "It is … increasingly clear
that, contrary to earlier treatments of the topic, the Sea Peoples were hardly a
homogenous population of destitute refugees fleeing the west Aegean eastwards
as a result of the breakdown of a politically and economically centralized palace
system" but were instead "most likely well acquainted with the eastern littoral of
the Mediterranean long before the end of the Bronze Age" (17). The textual and
archaeological evidence for these population groups, however, is still largely
ambiguous and their study is ongoing. The essays collected in this volume provide the latest archaeological, biblical, and historical examination of the origins,
identity, material culture, and impact of these peoples on those of the eastern
Mediterranean.

The volume opens with a chapter by Neil Asher Silberman entitled "When
the Past Was New: Moshe Dothan (1919–1999), An Appreciation (ix–xiv). This
chapter is a tribute to the late Moshe Dothan (1919–1999), who was the excavator
of Ashdod and a pioneer in the study of the Philistines and the other Sea Peoples. This is followed by an introductory chapter, "The World of the Philistines
and Other 'Sea Peoples,'" in which Ann Killebrew and Gunnar Lehmann explain
that the volume grew out of a workshop that Killebrew and Lehmann, along with
Michal Artzy and Rahchel Hachlili, organized with the sponsorship of the Universities of Haifa and Ben Gurion of the Negev in 2001. The workshop was an attempt
to address the "unidirectional and overly simplistic interpretations of the Philistine phenomenon that has dominated scholarship during the twentieth century"
(1). They note the application of the term "Sea Peoples" to nine different groups,
including the Lukka, Sherden, Shekelesh, Teresh, Eqwesh, Denyen, Sikil/Tjekker,
Weshesh, and Peleset (Philistines). They note that these groups are "often considered either a catalyst or a consequence resulting from the crisis that struck the
eastern Mediterranean at the end of the Late Bronze and early Iron Ages" and that,

on this basis, "archaeologists composed a twentieth-century Sea People narrative of migrating populations originating from the west Aegean who had been displaced by the collapse of the Mycenaean palace system and the aftermath of the Trojan War" (1–2). This approach has been marked by a tendency to focus on classical sites in Greece and biblical locales in the southern Levant, which has produced "a distorted and uneven archaeological record for the thirteenth and twelfth centuries B.C.E." (5). The essays collected in the current volume seek to redress the situation by addressing questions of identity, origins, material culture, and political, socioeconomic and cultural process associated with these groups.

The chapters that make up the body of *The Philistines and Other "Sea Peoples"* are grouped into three sections. The first section, "The Philistines in Text and Archaeology," contains: Itamar Singer, "The Philistines in the Bible: A Short Rejoinder to a New Perspective" (19–27); Trude Dothan and David Ben-Shlomo, "Mycenaean IIIC:1 Pottery in Philistia: Four Decades of Research" (29–35); Tristan J. Barako, "Philistines and Egyptians in Southern Coastal Canaan during the Early Iron Age" (37–51); Penelope A. Mountjoy, "The Mycenaean IIIC Pottery at Tel Miqne-Ekron" (53–75); Ann E. Killebrew, "Early Philistine Pottery Technology at Tel Miqne-Ekron: Implications for the Late Bronze-Early Iron Age Transition in the Eastern Mediterranean" (77–129); Linda Meiberg, "Philistine Lion-Headed Cups: Aegean or Anatonlian?" (131–44); Sabine Laemmel, "A Few Tomb Groups fromm Tell el-Far'ah South" (145–89); Aren M. Maeir, "Philistia Transforming: Fresh Evidence from Tell eṣ-Ṣafi/Gath on the Transformational Trajectory of the Philistine Culture" (191–242); and Hermann Michael Niemann, "Neighbors and Foes, Rivals and Kin: Philistines, Shepheleans, Judeans between Geography and Economy, History and Theology (243–64).

The second section, "The Other 'Sea Peoples' in the Levant," includes: Gunnar Lehmann, "Aegean-Style Pottery in Syria and Lebanon during Iron Age I" (265–328); Michal Artzy, "On the Other 'Sea Peoples'" (329–44); Elizabeth French, "The Origin and Date of Aegean-Type Pottery in the Levant" (345–47); Susan Sherratt and Amihai Mazar, with an appendix by Anat Cohen-Weinberger, "'Mycenaean IIIC' and Related Pottery from Beth Shean" (349–92); and Ilan Sharon and Ayelet Gilboa, "The *SKL* Town: Dor in the Early Iron Age" (393–468).

The final section, "Anatolia, the Aegean, and Cyprus," contains the following chapters: "Hermann Genz, "'No Land Could Stand Before Their Arms, from Hatti … on …'? New Light on the End of the Hittite Empire and the Early Iron Age in Central Anatolia" (469–77); Elizabeth French, "Cilicia" (479–83); Marie-Henriette Gates, "Early Iron Age Newcomers at Kinet Höyük, Eastern Cilicia (485–508); Mario Benzi, "The Southeast Aegean in the Age of the Sea Peoples" (509–42); Jeremy B. Rutter, "Aegean Elements in the Earliest Philistine Ceramic Assemblage: A View from the West" (543–61); Penelope A. Mountjoy, "The Late LH IIIB and LH IIIC Early Pottery of the East Aegean-West Anatolian Interface" (563–84); Maria Iacovou, "Aegean-Style Material Culture in Late Cypriot III: Minimal Evidence, Maximal Interpretation" (585–618); and Susan Sherratt, "The Ceramic Phenomenon of the 'Sea Peoples': An Overview" (619–44).

An appendix includes a single chapter by Matthew J. Adams and Marga-ret E. Cohen, "The 'Sea Peoples' in Primary Sources" (645–64), which collects textual references to the "Sea Peoples" found in Egyptian, Ugaritic, Hittite, and other Late Bronze Age to early Iron Age sources. This chapter provides a helpful comprehensive listing of the mentions of these peoples, with references that point researchers to translations, transcriptions, and/or transliterations that are, in most cases, easily available.

Virtually every chapter in this volume makes an important contribution to the study of the Philistines and the other Sea Peoples, but I will single out only a few in order to illustrate the importance of the volume as a whole. In the first section on "The Philistines in Text and Archaeology," the late Itamar Singer responds to Israel Finkelstein, who sweepingly states that "the biblical references to the Philistines do not contain any memory of early Iron I events or cultural behavior" ("The Philistines in the Bible: A Late-Monarchic Perspective," *JSOT* 27 [2002]: 131) and asserts that they reflect late-monarchic times instead. Singer argues that the Deuteronomistic history (Dtr) "preserves a relatively accurate memory of the distant past, of a time when the Philistines expanded from their five city-kingdoms northwards and eastwards to the central highlands, or in other words, of the Iron I" (26–27). Tristan Barako likewise addresses the issue of the early appearance of the Philistines in the southern Levant, and he utilizes a com-parison of the stratigraphic sequences at two sites: Tel Mor, a minor Egyptian military outpost; and Ashdod, a neighboring Philistine center. Barako shows that the stratigraphical sequences at both sites match up, with the critical stata of Ashdod XIII and Tel Mor V both dating to the first half of the twelfth century BCE and thereby affirming the traditional Iron I chronological sequence, which places the arrival of the Philistines during the reign of Ramesses III (1186–1155 BCE). Three of the chapters in this section—those by Dothan and Ben-Shlomo, Mountjoy, and Killebrew—deal with Mycenaean IIIC pottery, which is critical for our knowledge of the identity, dating, and diffusion of Philistine technology and style. Drawing on the entire body of data now available from Philistia, Dothan and Ben-Shlomo study the development of LH IIIC/Mycenaean IIIC:1 pottery in the southern Levant in the twelfth century BCE. Mountjoy illustrates the hybrid style of the Mycenaean IIIC pottery at Ekron and demonstrates that it was the result of a number of influences. Killebrew undertakes a comparative study of the Canaanite-style Late Bronze and Aegean-style Iron I pottery assemblages from Tel Miqne-Ekron, which reveals the dynamics at work during the final decades of the Bronze Age that led to the emergence of new regional and ethnic configura-tions during the twelfth century. She demonstrates the clear break from previous Late Bronze Age ceramic traditions in "a case study par excellence of the material manifestation of immigration in the archaeological record" (119).

The essays in the second section, "The Other 'Sea Peoples' in the Levant," each contribute to the study of the other Sea Peoples besides the Philistines. Artzy's paper is of particular interest because she deals with questions raised by the absence of the other "Sea Peoples" in biblical texts. She asks: "Why are the Sikila or the Shardana not mentioned in biblical texts? Is it because they were not in direct contact with those who left us the scriptures or is it that by the seventh century B.C.E., during the time of the Deuteronomistic compilation, the biblical texts reflect a later reality?" (329). Artzy utilizes evidence from her own excavations at Tel Nami, Tell Abu Hawam, and Tel Akko, as well as data from other sites in the vicinity, which is all different from that unearthed in Philistia, to highlight the importance of this region for our understanding of the Sea Peoples phenomenon. When one considers the data, a picture of the thirteenth century comes into focus in which they are "serving the palaces, acting as economic mercenaries, secondary and tertiary contractors, and intermediaries" (344), along with many other capacities. Unfortunately, Artzy rules out el-Ahwat as a possible Shardana site without making use of the final site report, in which Zertal makes a case for the identification of el-Ahwat as a citadel governed by the Shardana but built and populated by other autochtonic ethnic groups. He postulates that the site may have been founded "as a forward citadel opposite the many Israelite settlements east and south of it" "to defend the coastal plain against a possible Israelite invasion."[1] If this interpretation of the site is correct, it could contribute to reconstructing the history of the Shardana as well as the settlement dynamics of the region in general.

In section 3 the archaeology of the Sea Peoples is broadened out from its traditional focus on the southern Levant to Anatolia, the Aegean, and Cyprus. Several essays may be of special interest to readers of *RBL*. Genz reconsiders the end of the Hittite Empire, which has conventionally been thought of as having been caused by invasion. He postulates that foreign invasions or migrations were at best only one factor involved, while its real causes were internal (477). The idea of invasions as a source of historical change was very popular in the late nineteenth and early twentieth century, when colonization was seen in a positive light. In today's climate of anticolonialism, however, few regard invasion positively. Consequently, the Sea Peoples have come to be seen as having played less of a role as agents of historical change. An incursion of Sea Peoples may have contributed to the demise of the Hittite Empire, but Genz is probably right that it should no longer be regarded as the sole factor that led to its end. The essays of Rutter and Sherratt are both important in that they confirm the close connections between southern Levantine and Cypriot Aegean-style material culture. Rutter concludes that the LH IIIC pottery of Philistia was derived from Cyprus rather than the Aegean. Killebrew and Lehmann draw out the important implications of Rutter's conclusions:

> If the imported Mycenaean IIIC pottery at Beth Shean and the locally produced LH IIIC Early ceramics at Philistine sites are closely related to similar LH IIIC assemblages on Cyprus, which clearly predate 1130 B.C.E., this would tend to

---

1. A. Zertal, ed., *El-Ahwat, A Fortified Site from the Early Iron Age Near Nahal ʿIron, Israel: Excavations 1993–2000* (CHANE 24; Leiden: Brill, 2012), 434–35.

refute Finkelstein and Ussishkin's low chronology date (post-1130 B.C.E.) for the
Philistine migration to Palestine. (15)

The Philistines and Other "Sea Peoples" is far more than an introduction to the
study of the Sea Peoples. This volume also provides a comprehensive examination
of virtually every aspect of the quest for the biblical Philistines and the other Sea
Peoples. As noted above, the textual and archaeological evidence for the Sea Peoples is still somewhat ambiguous with regard to the identity of these peoples, yet
the study of these people groups has led to surprising insights into the termination
of the Late Bronze Age and the cultural and political fragmentation of the eastern
Mediterranean region that followed in its wake. The Sea Peoples as a whole

> should be understood as enterprising communities that also included displaced
> or migrating populations, who took advantage of the power vacuum resulting
> from imperial breakdown and decline during the crisis years. Groups associated
> with the Sea Peoples were among the "winners" to emerge from the ruins of the
> Late Bronze Age. (17)

This volume will be a "must have" for anyone concerned with the study of these
"winners." It may be more useful to those with some training in archaeology
due to the specialized nature of many of its chapters (on archaeology, ceramics, stratigraphy, etc.), though it also contains extensive treatments of historical
data—including biblical texts. *The Philistines and Other "Sea Peoples"* provides the
most up-to-date study of these important people groups and will be an essential
reference volume for graduate-school and seminary libraries.

*The Legacy of Israel in Judah's Bible: History, Politics, and the Reinscribing of Tradi-
tion,* by Daniel E. Fleming. Cambridge: Cambridge University Press, 2012. Pp.
xxii + 385. Paper. $32.99. ISBN 9781107669994.

Frank H. Polak, Tel Aviv University, Ramath Aviv, Israel

At the present juncture, the discussion of Israelite history is dominated by archeological data and their interpretation, however hotly debated they be. The impact
of biblical narrative is in steady retreat since the role of the Judahite redactors
implies that the transmitted texts are extremely remote from the events attributable to the eleventh and tenth centuries. Still, a narrative account does exist and
"would make a fascinating historical source, if we could only make out how to
use it as such," as Daniel Fleming proclaims in the sentence opening his important study, which is much informed by his research in the polities of Emar and
the kingdoms of upper Mesopotamia in the Mari era but also utilizes the findings
and multiple interpretation of archeology.

The point of departure for Fleming's study is the recognition that Israel and
Judah, the southern and the northern kingdoms, form different polities (rejecting

the terms and concepts of ethnicity) that originally were not connected one to another and were only united under the rule of David and Solomon. The picture of an all-Israelite unity is viewed as the creation of the Judahite redaction that created an encompassing history by belated identification with Israel following the fall of the northern kingdom and the appropriation of fragmented Israelite historical narrative (often designated as "lore"). Thus it is Fleming's main undertaking to retrieve the northern "lore" underlying the Judahite picture. At first the author sets forth the differences between Israel and Judah in political structure and historical background. Whereas Judah is always represented as a unified, highly homogeneous kingdom (and is not represented as a coherent collective before David's kingship), the northern kingdom, Israel proper, is represented as lacking centralization. In Fleming's view, these differences aggravate the problems inherent to the structure of biblical history as a Judahite composition that portrays the people(s) of the southern and the northern kingdoms as a unified ethnic body and thus represents both southern and northern history as a continuum. In this representation narratives concerning the people of the northern kingdom necessarily are presented through a southern prism, lacking proper understanding for the institutions of the neighboring kingdom.

Thus Fleming attempts to reconstruct the northern Israelite experience by a number of different methods. The book of Judges (Wolfgang Richter's *Retterbuch*) provides him with a series of narratives in which Judah does not play any role (the tales of Ehud, Barak, Gideon-Jerubbaal, Abimelech, and in particular the *shiboleth* tale that concerns only Ephraim and the Gilead, Judg 12:1–6). In this framework Judah remains an outsider. Like the song of Deborah, these tales indicate collaboration and competition between the various groups of the northern population, which is, in its diversity, viewed as a "tribal association," much like the aligned tribal groups found in the kingdom of Mari.

The marginal position of Judah is likewise shown by a tradition-historical analysis of the tale of the birth of Jacob's sons, in which the "ancestors" of the various groups constituting the northern population take a place of pride. Fleming concludes that the northern kingdom consisted of a number of groups of different origin that cooperated in various circumstances, in particular in war, but without sociopolitical obligation and with no participation of Judah. One of the indications that the Jacob tale includes residues of an authentic northern tradition is the mention of the god of Nahor as one of the guarantors of the treaty of Jacob and Laban (Gen 31:53). In Fleming's view the term Galeed (31:47) originally included the term *'ad* "accord" (as in Akkadian *adû*, Old Aramaic *'dy'*, "treaty"). In these narratives, then, the Jacob tales preserve clear northern reminiscences that persisted in spite of the Judahite tradition. Fleming highlights the role of herding in these tales, as in the Moses narrative, and much unlike the Judahite experience, in which herding was second to agriculture. An additional residue of the non-Judahite vista is the prominent position of locations to the east of the Jordan. The particular position of this region likewise stands out in the tale of the Israelite conquests of the kingdoms of Sihon and Og, in which

Fleming senses an authentic northern tradition that was used by the historical introduction to Deuteronomy.

The Judahite vista is of particular importance for the history of the inception of the monarchy. The perspective of these tales is Judahite, and accordingly Saul is represented as David's predecessor, to be rejected, in accordance with David's role, but to be recognized as king for the sake of royal authority and legitimacy. In Fleming's view, however, the very fact of Saul's depiction as king is indicative of the Davidic perspective. An authentic northern perspective is discerned in the tale of the Ammonite war and the rescue of Jabesh-gilead (with its Transjordan connections) with Saul as leader in war rather than as king. Fleming links this tale to the narrative of the Benjaminite war in Judg 20–21. Although this tale in its present form constitutes a Judahite, anti-Saulide propaganda piece, he senses Benjaminite sympathies in the praise of the martial capabilities of this tribe that dared to wage an all-out war against the Israelite tribes. Fleming views the traditions of this war as an indication of a different origin of the tribe of Benjamin and thus returns to its construction as a descendant from the *Binū Yamina* tribal collective in upper Mesopotamia of the nineteenth and eighteenth centuries BCE (the time of the kingdom of Mari).

The associated tribal groups of upper Mesopotamia (the "Amorites") and the kingdom of Mari provide Fleming with many data of importance for a better understanding of the Israelite polity and, most importantly, a polity that is based on the collaborative politics of a decentralized society rather on the power of centralized authority, as in the great Mesopotamian empire and in the Judahite kingdom. Collaborative politics is an anthropological and historical model for the cooperation between various groups themselves or between such groups and the central authorities. One of the important points is the role of associated tribal groups, *Binū Yamina* and *Binū Sim'al*, partly herding and transhumant and partly settled, in different regions in upper Mesopotamia. Fleming points to the alliance between the *Binū Yamina* toward the war against the new king of Mari, Zimri-Lim, around 1775 BCE. He discerns similar processes for the sociopolitical structure of the ancient northern kingdom and its predecessors. Further, he proposes to view ancient Israel against the backdrop of the Amoritic society, culture, and language. In his view, at present the data at hand enable a better view of the situation than at the time these issues were discussed by Thomas L. Thompson and John Van Seters.

In the last part of this study Fleming attempts to use the data thus gained for a reconstruction of the history of ancient Israel, taking for a point of departure Merneptah's mention of Israel, which thus already formed a sociopolitical group, ill-defined as it may have been. He proposes to view the *'apīrū* as successors of the Amorite groups and as predecessors for the Israelites, and he studies the Israelite polity in the light of collaborative politics. His depiction of language and writing in Israel highlights the literary and intellectual continuity between the northern and the southern kingdom. In Fleming's view, literary activity is to be regarded as evolving in various different centers, not exclusively in the royal sphere or in temple circles. Special attention is paid to the role of Bethel and to the question of "invented" versus "authentic" tradition.

In my opinion, Fleming's study is important for the way in which it succeeds in recognizing the recent archeological findings and their interpretation without losing sight of basic features of the biblical account. In this respect Fleming makes full use of the data from Mari and Emar and recent anthropological insights. To be sure, some of the proposed reconstructions are weak. The account of the conquest regions to the east of the Jordan hardly suits the archeological findings (and is largely dependent on Van Seters's analysis). The assumption that the term 'apīrū relates to a specific tribal group disregards the possibility this term is used as invective to designate various different groups. The analysis of the account of the rebellion against David could have taken into account that the Judahite (?) narrator has much to hide, to cover, and to camouflage. The comparison of Benjamin to the Binū Yamina remains unconvincing, in particular because of the weakness of the analysis of the narrative of the war against the Benjaminites: praise of the enemy hardly entails that the narrative conceals an enemy narrative, but rather serves as explanation for difficulties encountered and as self-praise for the heroes who vanquished such a dangerous foe. I also would question the validity of tradition-historical analysis of the tale Jacob's sons. On the other hand, the analysis of the tales of the saviors-judges seems entirely valid to me and could be supported by the treacherous role of Judah in the Samson tale and the narrative of the Danite conquest of Laish.

What seems more difficult is the position of Judah. If one recognizes, with Fleming's important insight, that the northern Israelite polity unites different groups of varying origin under the umbrella of a hegemonial identity, a different origin for Judah does not preclude its association with the polity of its northern neighbors, all the more so in view of the role of the Benjaminites in the kingdom of Judah. Judah itself was, as Wellhausen saw long ago, less unified than the court perspective might suggest, and, for instance, in the narrative world of the David tales "Calebite" was not a compliment (1 Sam 25:3), and these tales the Judahites are not always viewed with sympathy.

These are some of the musings raised by Fleming's study. But these reflections do not detract from the importance of the suggested synthesis that, indeed, brings us back to Alt, but with a better comprehension of the linguistic, cultural, and archeological context.

Israel in the Persian Period: The Fifth and Fourth Centuries B.C.E., by Erhard S. Gerstenberger. Translated by Siegfried S. Schatzmann. Biblical Encyclopedia 8. Atlanta: Society of Biblical Literature, 2011. Pp. xv + 575. Paper. $65.95. ISBN 1589832655.

Jason Silverman, Leiden University, Leiden, The Netherlands

This volume is an English translation of the 2005 contribution to the Biblische Enzyklopädie series *Israel in der Perserzeit*, the fourth such translation offered by the

Society of Biblical Literature. Other than the occasional subsequent English translations of German citations, the book does not appear to have been updated from the
original publication. It follows the format of the previous Biblische Enzyklopädie
volumes, structured in four sections: "The Biblical Portrait of the Period"; "The
Known History"; "Biblical Literature of the Period"; "Theological Contribution."

Gerstenberger has taken the unenviable task of summarizing and presenting
current research on the Persian period, an era for which one would struggle to
find even minimum consensus on anything except for maybe its importance. Each
section is prefaced with a useful sample bibliography, containing more German
scholarship than often included in English-language bibliographies. Moreover, he
has attempted to take the Achaemenid Empire seriously within his analyses, frequently prefacing his discussion of typical issues in the biblical literature with a
discussion of similar Persian topics.

The tome's 535 pages belie the opening statement (3) that only 5.39 percent of
the Hebrew Bible is directly related to the Persian period. Gerstenberger's subsequent claim that "practically all of the canonical writings (except for Ecclesiastes
and Daniel), whether intentionally or unintentionally, express something about
the situation of the Judaic communities in the Persian period" (35) better represents his approach. As such, most of the present Hebrew Bible is discussed within
the course of the volume for its contribution to the Persian period, under the headings "Original Writings" (142–273) and "Revisions of Older Writings" (274–426).

Section 1 begins with a discussion of Ezra-Nehemiah, arguing for its concern
with the reconstitution of the community and temple rather than with history.
Gerstenberger follows this with the memory of the Persians in Hellenistic texts
(Daniel, Esther, and Josephus), concluding that the main biblical portrait of the
period is one of strengthening Judaean identity.

In the first part of section 2 Gerstenberger discusses the history of the empire
under the rubrics of "Literary Traditions," "Artifacts and Architecture," "Imperial
Structures," "The Course of History," "Religion in Ancient Persia," and "Everyday
Life and Culture." In this discussion Gerstenberger notes a variety of sources from
the Avesta and the Persepolis Tablets to the Greek historians. He includes translations of the Cyrus Cylinder and XPh (48, 51) and a table of events (60–61) that is,
unfortunately, not aligned by dates, making misleading impressions of synchronic-
ity. In the next part Gerstenberger moves to Yehud. He discusses the relationship
of Yehud and Samaria, favoring Alt's hypothesis that Yehud was originally part
of Samaria; he briefly describes Jerusalem's "rise as holy city" and discusses the
persons of Nehemiah, Ezra, Sheshbazzar, Zerubbabel, and the elders. In the latter
section Gerstenberger dismisses the historicity of the so-called Nehemiah Memoir
and thus Nehemiah's position as cupbearer (91), the existence of Ezra (95), and
any knowledge of Sheshbazzar or Zerubbabel (100). Gerstenberger concludes
his discussion of Yehud under the rubrics of "social and community structures,"
"economy," "technology and culture," and "folk religion and temple." Within these
rubrics are discussed the size of the community, family structure, the centralization
of the cult, urbanization, use of incense, nontemple ritual, festivals, and psalms;

he also includes a discussion of debt in the ancient Near East. The second section ends with the Babylonian and Egyptian diasporas. He mentions the appearance of Yahwistic names in Babylonia but bases the depiction of the Babylonian groups on biblical portrayals. For Egypt, the discussion is based on Elephantine. He includes translations of a marriage contract (B28) and correspondence over the temple (AP 30/31 and AP 35). He concludes by evaluating the Elephantine community's relationship with Jerusalem, taking it as evidence that scriptural authority was being accepted within Yehud and Babylonia but not yet within other communities.

Section 3 discusses biblical literature directly, divided into texts Gerstenberger considers Persian-period creations and those edited in the Persian period. Included within this section are five excurses on various topics. The majority of the former category would receive wide assent (Chronicles, Ezra-Nehemiah, P, Haggai, Zechariah, Malachi, Trito-Isaiah). However, Gerstenberger's inclusion of the psalms, poetry, and wisdom writings within this category is perhaps more controversial. He also suggests that almost all prophecy is purely postexilic (197) and appends a discussion of the Megilloth (Esther, Qoheleth, Ruth, Song of Songs, Lamentations, 270–74), even though noting some of them are Hellenistic. Prominent in these analyses are the themes of pilgrimage, appearance of sacred texts, and hints that Gerstenberger finds evocative of the era. The second part describes the remainder of the Hebrew Bible (Deuteronomist, the compilation of the Latter Prophets, the Writings, and Torah). Gerstenberger's analysis highlights theologies that he finds to be reflective of the Persian period (and thus justifies their discussion here): what he calls "the community of Yahweh and its theology" (308), the appearance of increased liturgical use, and eschatology.

The end of section 3 thus leads directly into the final section and its discussion of theology. Gerstenberger opens with "Babylonian and Persian Spirituality," in which he characterizes Persian religion as essentially based on personal choice and contrasts Persia from Babylon as dualist and monistic, respectively. Gerstenberger then credits the Persian era with the elevation of the laity and the creation of the rituals and festivals of Judaism, monotheism, eschatology and apocalypticism, new concepts of purity, and the formation of normative monogamy. Gerstenberger concludes with musings for the relevance for contemporary theology, in which he ranges from intertextuality to modern physics, ethics, and pluralism. The volume closes with two indices.

The book is thus quite wide-ranging, and the number of topics discussed with their prefaced citations will make it a useful tool for English speakers, even if the translation is sometimes a little infelicitous. Nevertheless, there are several aspects of the volume with which this reviewer must take issue.

The dating of the entire Hebrew Bible to the Persian period (or later) is nothing new. Yet, while Gerstenberger's thoroughgoing late dating of texts has significant precedence, it decreases the usability of this book for nonbiblical scholars and for students, since it gives the mistaken impression of a consensus for such dating for all of these texts, and it is not given a thorough methodological defense in this book. The comments in which Gerstenberger defends Persian dating are often circular arguments: the intellectual horizon is somehow congruent with the Persian period, so the text must be Persian period (e.g., lack of familial concern in the Joseph cycle, 189).

One thing that stands out in this volume is the prominence of psalms, liturgy, and festivals for Gerstenberger's understanding of the period (e.g., 125–26, 148, 213, 216–52, 270–73, 328, 458–68). Given the notorious difficulty of dating poetry in general, the psalms in particular, and our general ignorance of the development of early Jewish liturgy, this is quite remarkable. Gerstenberger is aware of this difficulty (24) but uses it as an excuse to treat the psalms by default as Persian period (218). Even more problematically, he quickly and easily moves from the content of such material to assumptions of their sociological and historical context, in the present context inevitably the Persian period. This is especially evident where he thinks the psalms' language of social injustice demonstrate that Qumran-like "fragmentation" started with the temple's restoration (236). Much firmer evidence would be required for such a claim. The above two points imply that, even when Gerstenberger has valuable insights into texts, these insights may not have much secure relevance to the Persian period per se.

I applaud how seriously Gerstenberger takes the Persians and their traditions for the historical contextualization of Judaean traditions within their empire. He frequently attempts to bring the empire to bear on the topics discussed and in this models a procedure more biblical scholars ought to follow. That said, however, his particular interpretations and presentations of Iranian material ought to be used with care, representing either uncertain interpretations or inaccuracies. An example appears right at the front (xvi). The map labeled "The empire of the Medes and Persians" is misleading. It is a map of the previous Median federation, something not otherwise discussed in the book, rather than the Achaemenid Empire, and it contains a peculiar mix of toponyms from various eras. Much more important are inaccurate details that affect the analyses, such as Gerstenberger's depiction of Zoroaster as a reforming (Protestant?) monotheist (71–72, 75, 82, 247, 350–53, 430) or the assertion of Avestan "cultic communities"(438). Be that as it may, the citations are wide-ranging, and one hopes the precedent will spur deeper engagement with the empire.

Overall, Gerstenberger's work represents a new synthesis of the period, one that should stimulate further research that takes the Persian Empire seriously for its subject Judeans.

HEBREW BIBLE/OLD TESTAMENT: GENERAL

Hearing the Old Testament: Listening for God's Address, edited by David J. H. Beldmanand and Craig G. Bartholomew. Grand Rapids: Eerdmans, 2012. Pp. xviii + 475. Paper. $32.00. ISBN 9780802865618.

Jeanette Mathews, Charles Sturt University, Canberra, Australia

This multiauthored volume edited by Craig G. Bartholomew and David J. H. Beldman is a recent addition to the growing literature in the "theological interpretation" movement in biblical studies centered in the Scripture and Hermeneutics Seminar begun late last century. Inspired especially by Brevard Childs's canonical approach, theological interpretation seeks, in the words of this volume, to "listen for God's address" (the subtitle of the book and a phrase oft repeated throughout) in recognition that the Scriptures are distinctive among literary works by being the word of the living God that continues to speak in every context. Theological interpretation aims to bring ancient, premodern, modern, and contemporary hermeneutical approaches together with newer methods of critical study, always conscious of the need for biblical studies to serve the contemporary Christian church. Together with an overtly evangelical stance that emphasizes the supreme authority of the Scriptures, the authors claim that their approach retains the "utmost rigor in Old Testament studies" (xvi) and remains open to other perspectives.

The editors preface the volume with a short introduction that picturesquely describes their intention to provide a "spoon" by which to access the "feast" of Old Testament riches. Their advice that, "while collections of essays have a reputation for being more of less random assortments of chapters, readers should note that this is definitely *not* the case here" (xvi), is well supported by the ensuing volume, in which virtually every essay refers back to Bartholomew's essay that alone forms part 1, "The God Who Speaks."

Subtitled "A *Mere* Trinitarian Hermeneutic for the Old Testament," the opening essay argues for a trinitarian foundation for reading the Old Testament. The overriding message (which I think explains the emphasized "mere" in the title) is that Christian interpreters of any part of the Christian Scriptures must take seriously the doctrine of the Trinity, that is, that the God of the Old Testament is the God and Father of Jesus Christ and that Jesus' mission is continued in the work of the Spirit. Despite the differences in the Testaments (well articulated in Mark J. Boda's essay on biblical theology), the present essay argues that there is an underlying unity that enables us "to listen to the Old Testament on its own terms, trusting that the voice of the Father will be found to be in concord with that of the Son and the Spirit" (13). In my view, this affirmation does not sit comfortably with the principle that "we do not read the Old Testament truthfully unless we read it as 'fulfilled' in the New" (11). The implication of progressive revelation underlies many of the essays and is explicitly stated in Boda's essay just mentioned: "The Bible also bears witness to a God who has revealed himself [*sic*] in progressive ways throughout history. Thus, as the biblical witness unfolds, readers are given more and more details about the character of this God" (150).

Part 2, entitled "Learning to Listen," offers methodological approaches, with Old Testament interpretation being matched with the following foci: a history of approaches (Al Wolters), philosophy (Craig G. Bartholomew), literary approaches (David J. H. Beldman), history (Tremper Longman III), biblical theology (Mark J. Boda), canon (Stephen G. Dempster), mission (Christopher J. H. Wright), and ethics (M. Daniel Carroll R.). The strength of these methodological essays are their concise recounting of the history of each subdiscipline, so that they would serve as excellent secondary readings for undergraduate Old Testament courses where foundational issues such as interpretation, canon, historiography, and ethics need to be introduced to beginning students. Each essay returns to the project of the combined volume, with an emphasis on listening for God's address via trinitarian hermeneutics. Beldman's essay, for example, after succinctly setting out characteristics of Hebrew narrative and poetry, concludes: "By giving attention to the literary dimension of the Old Testament we affirm that *our* Creator and *our* Redeemer speaks *to us* through these literary forms" (95). Similarly, Wright's survey of the major pillars of Old Testament faith that support Christian mission is followed by the comment, "I trust it is sufficiently clear from the above survey that a missional approach can provide a fruitful way of 'hearing the Old Testament'... the great pillars of the faith of Old Testament Israel not only supported their identity as a people of memory and hope, but also continue to support the mission of God's people" (203).

The authors of part 3, "Hearing the Old Testament," give brief surveys of major blocks of books. The contributions cover the Pentateuch (Gordon J. Wenham), the Historical Books (Iain Provan), the Psalter (J. Clinton McCann Jr.), the Wisdom Literature (Craig. G. Bartholomew), the Major Prophets (Richard Schultz), and the Minor Prophets (Heath Thomas). Several authors have undertaken this task in a more focussed way by reading individual books in the light of theological interpretation in Kevin J. Vanhoozer, ed., *Dictionary for Theological Interpretation of the Bible* (Baker, 2005).[1] Like the *DTIB*, the books are presented in the order of the English Old Testament rather than the Hebrew Bible, so that Daniel is included among the Major Prophets and Ezra, Nehemiah, and Chronicles in the Historical Books. Thomas's essay on the Minor Prophets, however, includes discussion of implications for reading the books as a unity (the Book of the Twelve), reflecting more recent scholarship in this area that recognizes the Twelve "in some way coherently as a *book*" (359). As we would expect, the distinctive feature of these essays is to read the books in the light of a trinitarian hermeneutic. Discussions of prophetic literature, for example, emphasize a christocentric interpretation. Most of the essays have a section that specifically discusses the relationship between the books in focus and the New Testament, and all evince a canonical perspective that takes the final form and intertextual connections seriously. Once again, the survey character of the essays in this section, discussing as they do the respective books and major interpretive issues surrounding them, make these useful essays for beginning students in Old Testament Studies.

Part 4, "Hearing and Proclaiming the Old Testament," consists of one essay by Aubrey Spears with a homiletic focus. This is a logical conclusion to a volume on "Hearing the Old Testament" and indeed concentrates on ways in which we might hear the "voice of the living God" (388, 393, 402). The section on recovering the

---

1. Republished as Kevin J. Vanhoozer, ed., *Theological Interpretation of the Old Testament* (Baker, 2008).

four senses of Scripture in preaching was a helpful reminder of Wolters's essay that advocated retrieval of historical exegetical methods.

The final sixty-five pages of the book include a full bibliography of works referred to by each of the essays, followed by indices of authors, subjects, and scripture references.

This volume includes high-quality essays from a range of authors who are well known in Old Testament scholarship, particularly within evangelical circles. I like many aspects of the volume and intend to use several essays in teaching undergraduate Old Testament classes. My enthusiasm is tempered, however, by two concerns. First, I was put off by an arrogant tone that permeated a number of essays when contrasting theological interpretation with academic historical-critical scholarship. Negative comments come across as invective and detract from the claim that the trinitarian approach critically builds on earlier progress in Old Testament studies. I think particularly of comments such as "an individualistic and often narcissistic academy" (18), "a consistent historical-critical reading and a literary, final-form, theological reading are incommensurate paradigms" (304), "Historical criticism ... arises from a set of presuppositions that are in conflict with a Christian worldview" (102), and the quotation that concludes the first essay: "prodigal academics feed starving students on the dry husks of their clever unbelief" (19). I am sure that readers, like myself, who were taught by enthusiastic advocates of historical-critical methodology nonetheless found many of their teachers to be exemplary Christian and Jewish scholars committed to their faith communities. Related to this is the second of my concerns: despite affirming that different approaches to reading the Old Testament are welcomed, there is a strong implication that a trinitarian reading of Scripture is the only valid reading for Christian scholars. Where does this leave an appreciation and honoring of Jewish scholarship, and how does it remain open for "real dialogue" (xvii)?

The metaphor of the feast at the outset of the book reminds me of the story of heaven as a place where a desirable pot of stew is surrounded by a multitude whose spoons have handles so long that they can only enjoy the feast if willing to feed others. This volume would be far more palatable and inspirational for new generations of Old Testament scholars (xvii) if characterized by a greater willingness to share interpretive perspectives.

Truth Speaks to Power: The Countercultural Nature of Scripture, by Walter Brueggemann. Louisville: Westminster John Knox, 2013. Pp. viii + 167. Paper. $17.00. ISBN 9780664239145.

Gerrie Snyman, University of South Africa, Pretoria, South Africa

I enjoyed reading Brueggemann's *Truth Speaks to Power* and found it quite relevant in the light of Edward Snowden's revelations of the USA's National Security Agency's ability to monitor phone conversations, text messages, and the public's participation in interactive sites such as Facebook and Google. In contrast to the

USA, where the NSA is supposedly expressly prohibited from spying on US citizens, South African law provides for such actions by the government. After the initial revelations, Snowden is reported to have said the following: "I will never feel safe. Things are very difficult for me in all terms, but *speaking truth to power* is never without risk." This remark gives the book a very particular meaning and life within the world of academia.

There are a few biblical characters who experienced that risk, and some of them did not survive to tell their story. One of them is Shimei. Shimei was a blood relative of Saul who held David accountable for all the slayings of the sons and grandsons of Saul. To him, David could not distance himself from these killings, since it benefited him directly. In the books of Samuel, nothing happens to Shimei. It is only at David's deathbed in 1 Kings that David advised Solomon to deal with Shimei in "wisdom," that is, to kill him.

Brueggemann's book is thick on the various manifestations of power in the biblical text (Moses, Solomon, Elisha, and Josiah) but rather thin when it accounts for the political power of the context in which it originates (the last chapter). I say the latter cautiously, since I am an outsider to the USA. Being an outsider, my inclination was to expect Brueggemann to engage with American power much deeper than he did. Of course, I am also influenced by the *The Africana Bible: Reading Israel's Scriptures from Africa and the African Diaspora* (ed. Hugh R. Page; Minneapolis: Fortress, 2009). This anthology heaps argument upon argument against what the authors perceive as Western power and its hermeneutics to be and have become.

I also wondered if the norm (white Western wealthy heterosexual Christian male) of Bible reading as defined by Cheryl Anderson (*Ancient Laws and Contemporary Controversies: The Need for Inclusive Biblical Interpretation* [Oxford: Oxford University Press, 2009], 135) would be unmasked by Brueggemann's arguments. His eventual reticence to directly engage with examples of the exercise of American power made me think about the link Anderson draws between the norm of Bible reading and Brueggemann's own reading of the biblical text.

With these two books in mind, I interpret Brueggemann's book as providing a response to the exercise of power of which he is wittingly or unwittingly a part. In other words, he writes about power from the position of power itself in the American society. Bishop Thomas Breidenthal says, in his foreword, that this book is the "boldest exploration to date of the radical and subversive political implications of the Bible" (vi), and that "[t]his viewpoint comes down to a suspicion of truth claims that support vested power interests and an irrepressible conviction that God's truth stands on the side of the weak, the poor, and the excluded" (vi).

This book comprises the lectures Brueggemann delivered at a summer conference sponsored by some Episcopal dioceses in Ohio. It is easy reading and a successful transmission of academic ideas to people who are not necessarily schooled in the intricacies Old Testament studies. It is offered, in the words of Breidenthal, as a book in which "Brueggemann pulls no punches in naming the habitual collusion of government; the corporate world; the media; the academia; and, yes, the church to control the definition of truth and shut out (or co-opt) any narrative voices that object."

The book consists of an introduction (1–10); four chapters on power and specific characters in the biblical text: "Truth Speaks to Power: Moses" (11–42); "Visible Power, Truth Cunningly Subversive: Solomon" (43–80); "Truth Has Its Day: Elisha" (81–112); and "Truth Transforms Power: Josiah" (113–48). Brueggemann concludes his book with a chapter on "Truth and Power among Us" (149–67).

Brueggemann provides some theoretical background to this project in the introduction. His point of departure is a distinction similar to the distinction James C. Scott makes in *Domination and the Arts of Resistance: Hidden Transcripts* (New Haven: Yale University Press, 1990): a public power that enlists public resources to maintain itself and a hidden transcript that is close to lived reality and hidden from the public power displays. He sees public power as "a network of influence and leverage that may be channeled through the state apparatus or, as is the case in our society, through the private sector with its huge corporate combines" (2). It boils down to the one with the gold being the one who makes the rules. Over against this official public transcript Brueggemann poses the hidden transcript, a discourse that is subversive in the face of the official truth: "an incontrovertible bodily reality that continues to speak against flat claims of thin reason" (4). Taking his cue from Marx, Nietzsche, Freud, and Foucault (discussed in the briefest way possible), Brueggemann wants to "protest against reasonable truth that is featured by established power and to insist that there is another more elemental, more bodily truth that hovers beneath what is acceptable and that continues to haunt social reality" (6). For this reason Brueggemann assumes that there is in the biblical text already a contestation of the officially accepted truth, giving Scripture a subversive voice: "Thus the Bible itself is a sustained contestation over truth in which conventional modes of power do not always prevail" (6).

In the Old Testament, Brueggemann sees the public transcript being maintained by the urban elites of the dynasty and temple and the scribal class. In the New Testament, the public transcript is maintained by the scribal community that has become allied to different interest groups. Over against them he surmises in the Old Testament a truth that is carried by song, oracle, narrative and that subverts the official truth in the public transcript. In the New Testament, the counter-truth is carried by Jesus and his followers.

For example, in chapter 3 Brueggemann argues that 1–2 Kings offers the normative history of ancient Israel during the monarchical period (82):

> There is no doubt that this sequence of royal rulers identifies the visible, recognized, and legitimate power players in Israelite history. These are the ones who have occupied office, made decisions, managed the economy, waged wars, and built the temple, all the ingredients of public, visible power. And at least in the South of Jerusalem, it is understood to be power legitimated by YHWH's prom-

ise to the house of David and YHWH's residence in the Jerusalem temple (see 2 Sam. 7:11–16; 1 Kgs 8:12–13).

He argues that the material is not intended to be looked at suspiciously. This is the official view on the past that links those in exile with those before the exile. But then Brueggemann sees every now and then in the story something that interrupts the official transcript. In the story of Moses, Pharaoh is the metaphor for raw, absolute, worldly power (17), as can be seen in his use of food as a weapon with the help of Joseph, called by Brueggemann "his food czar," advancing the claims of the state against its own people. It is the latter in the form of the Israelites that will subvert Pharaoh's power by constructing a "subversive liturgy directed to an alternative God" in the desert that will become an immediate threat to established power (31). In the end, it is Pharaoh's absolute power that will lie in tatters at the Red Sea.

The way Solomon secured his kingship by, inter alia, killing Shimei in order to ensure there was no contestation to the crown by a Saulide already suggests early in the narrative that Solomon's power should be treated with suspicion. Brueggemann comes to a similar conclusion, claiming that any new world order is never innocent or disinterested: "it is always, to some important extent, a front for self-interest perpetrated through violence" (47). A discerning reader, according to Brueggemann, will not take any report of power at face value. The reader needs to look for hints of truth that jeopardize blanket claims of power, and Solomon's rise to power is full of them. Solomon achieves great power through deception and consolidates it through violence (52). Disturbingly, violence is linked to wisdom: "Now wisdom is the will to do what is necessary to secure the throne, thus the necessity of violence" (53).

The question, then, is how beneficent the reader regards the text and how suspicious one is in the act of reading. For example, is the description of Solomon's accumulation of wealth gloating about his success, or is there an ironical exposition of self-indulgence over against the hardships of the peasantry (58)? Brueggemann reads it as an exposé of extravagant self-indulgence, a rule of absolute power that cannot be sustained. In the end, Solomon's regime fails with the emergence of two kingdoms (73):

> The failure of Solomonic power has theological roots. His power cannot be sustained in the face of Torah truth and prophetic implementation. But such truthfulness is not a religious fantasy; it receives public enactment through Solomon's subjects who refuse absolute power.

It comes as no surprise, then, that Brueggemann argues in the next chapter (ch. 3) that in the subsequent royal history the key players are no longer the kings but those "who refused to be credentialed or curbed by traditional modes of power" (86). The occupants of royal power are no longer the definitive players but Elijah and Elisha as outsiders to this power. As Brueggemann puts it, "The kings turn out to be, in this telling, simply window dressing for the carriers of truth who exhibit and enact transformative power" (87). But Elisha's narrative starts with the two bears he sent to devour the children that mocked him. Brueggemann reads this story as an enactment of Elisha's power where those who do not wish to follow him will not be safe (110). But what does this story say about the social acceptance of children in Israelite society? Are they that easily dismissible? Or is Elisha perhaps not doing what people in power do, using it absolutely? No matter what the story may signify in the end regarding Elisha's power, there is a dark side to its enactment, which Brueggemann does not bring into play in his discussion of power. Power and its enactment are never innocent. Someone will bear the marks.

The main thrust of the book is the claim of speaking truth to power in a radical way. As the current speaking truth to power shows, it is never without risk. But I am not sure what Brueggemann is risking in his speaking truth to power in the book. This aspect of the book, namely, its own validity as truth speaking to power, does not come strongly forward. Brueggemann claims: "I hope, mainly, to exhibit the thick complexity of the interface of truth and power in which we ourselves are always engaged, and to insist that we are, as readers and interpreters, always contestants, whether we recognize ourselves as such or not" (8). How one is always a contestant in the current configurations of power is not spelled out. Perhaps it is unfair of me to have expected that, because Brueggemann is an Old Testament scholar and not something else, and I am not part of the power plays in the USA; in fact, what I know is what I read on the *New York Times* website and Huffington Post.

It is only in the last ten pages (158–67) that Brueggemann gives the reader an inkling of how to deal with power in the current context. He argues that there are no easy connections between the Old Testament and the current context. He labels his context as a "totalizing environment" in which he finds it difficult to "sustain action outside of that totality." But he has no wish "to draw too close an analogue to our own time or to overstate the totalizing aspects of the present American system" (160). Yet he is left with a sense of "wonderment" "that there are agents of truth who find daring, risky ways out beyond the totalism" (160). In the end, I find him hiding behind a general discipleship and a vague challenge to governmental power.

I am left with a suspicion that if Brueggemann did draw that analogue, his book would indeed have spoken truth to current political power in the USA. However, the book explores successfully the issue of speaking truth to power in the biblical text (Old Testament), and Brueggemann is to be commended for it. As can be seen in my reception, it generated a lot of ideas and concerns, and it became a mirror for my own (in)activity in a political context that is becoming more and more totalizing.

In Scripture: The First Stories of Jewish Sexual Identities, by Lori Hope Lefkovitz. New York: Rowman & Littlefield, 2010. Pp. vii + 191. Paper. $19.95. ISBN
9780742547056.

Deborah Rooke, University of Oxford, Oxford, United Kingdom

Like the scriptural narratives it discusses, Lefkovitz's volume is the result of many
years of reflection on the facts of biblical life. It is based around nine episodes
or episodic clusters in the Hebrew Scriptures. Each episode or cluster is used as
a focal point to thematize a series of investigations into Jewish constructions of
gendered identity; these investigations encompass both ancient and modern stereotypes and use a variety of postmodern theories.

   In the introduction, Lefkovitz sets out her aims in collecting her writings
on the Hebrew Bible from the last twenty-five years and describes her readings
as "a sustained response to the challenge, posed by Judith Butler at the end of
Gender Trouble, to 'denaturalize gender'" (7). Not surprisingly, given such a frame
of reference, she begins with an examination of the Eden narrative (ch. 1). Her
point is that, although the text is designed to define and fix gender identities, it
undermines the very identities that it is struggling to establish. Though woman
is the birthing sex, here man gives birth to woman; though woman tempts man,
she is first tempted by an erect snake, representing disembodied male sexuality.
Despite the text's reverence for the creative acts of God and Adam, Eve's child-
bearing function is her punishment for disobedience, thereby reversing the value
attached to procreation and betraying either fear or envy of female sexuality. The
text creates an association between death, sex, and knowledge: eating the forbidden fruit leads to knowledge of nakedness, read as sexuality; and heterosexual
sex results in male life-fluid (semen) being transferred to females, which weakens
males but empowers females. Thus the text establishes two sexes, with the male
as primary but also threatened with (sexual) knowledge and death by the woman's interaction with the (his?) snake. The story as it stands shows woman as the
temptress whose desirability undermines male reason and so must be controlled,
but this is challenged by the sexually loaded symbol of the snake as tempter. The
split between the two aspects of woman as seductress and mother is subsequently
mythologized in the figure of Lilith, Adam's disobedient first wife, who becomes a
demonic sexual predator by contrast with the submissive and maternal Eve. Rabbinic commentary (Genesis Rabbah) on God's unsuccessful attempt to prevent
the woman from being sinful by creating her from a chaste part of Adam's body
indicates an unconscious conviction that women are beyond even God's control.

   In the second chapter Lefkovitz examines the tautologous figure of the barren
mother. Biblical heroes are born of barren mothers, a trope that serves to undermine the masculinity of the biblical patriarch and results in the forming of a special
bond between mother and God, as well as strong maternal influence on the son's
early development. The resultant image of the overpowering Jewish mother and the
often weedy and introverted mama's boy is one that has persisted into modern stereotypes, together with that of the husband's compromised masculinity. The classic

biblical doublet of fertile and barren co-wives in competition with each other splits the figure of woman along the mother/lover line, betraying a fear of women's intimacy and privileging fertility as the key to female self-esteem; nevertheless, the text always vindicates the barren heroine.

Chapter 3 uses Jacob's impersonation of Esau (Gen 27) as the basis for reflection on narratives where biblical figures pass as something that they are not. In Jacob's case he passes as having the virility suitable for him to become the next patriarch by imitating Esau, the hairy outdooorsman with strong sexual appetites who is his father's favored son, and this feat of passing is engineered by and accomplished with the help of Jacob's mother Rebecca. The narrative thereby undermines the very concept of patriarchy as masculinity even as it establishes it: both the patriarch Isaac and the patriarch-to-be Jacob are feminized by Rebecca's maternal manipulations. In his gender pretense Jacob represents a prototype of modern ideas of the Jewish "not-quite-man," who shares the physical and emotional constitution of a woman. Viewed as queer parody, Jacob's passing challenges notions of an abiding self, substituting instead a concept of self as a series of improvised performances; it also functions as a carnival performance that both challenges the notion that gender binaries are inevitable and reinforces the need for their observance. Narratives of Jews passing as imperial foreigners (Joseph, Moses, Esther) add another dimension to the "passing" phenomenon, whereby gender mimicry can lead to acquiring political power that would be otherwise out of reach. These narratives underline the ultimate instability of all identity boundaries.

Chapter 4 shows how the biblical tradition omits narratives of daughters and sisters except insofar as they become wives for the male characters. In the narrative of Jacob's marriage to the sisters Leah and Rachel, there is no sense of any positive relationship between the two women; rather, they are shown competing with each other to bear his sons, thus increasing his virility and desirability in the eyes of the reader. Lefkovitz reviews how subsequent rereading of the narrative treat the sisters' relationship and how biographers have read the complex relationships of both Charles Dickens and Sigmund Freud with their wives' sisters from the same perspective of competition over the male rather than loyalty between sisters. The Woody Allen film *Hannah and Her Sisters* is a modern version of the same plot. The message is that men's needs are more important to women than their own—a "divide and rule" way of dealing with threatening female relationships.

Chapter 5 examines the Joseph narrative. The combination of beauty and chastity that appears in the biblical account of Joseph is variously problematized in the midrashic tradition into effeminacy, preternatural self-restraint, or impotence. The Qur'an, by contrast, presents Joseph's beauty as inciting lust in every woman who sees him and depicts Joseph himself with normal masculine urges. As masculine sexuality comes to be refigured over time in more vigorous, animalistic terms, Joseph's beauty and chastity is read by later interpreters as effeminacy, thereby detracting from his appeal as a role model. Joseph is like his sister Dinah in that he attracts unwelcome Gentile sexual attraction, and the rabbinic commentary on both of these figures indicates a profound insecurity about Jewish masculinity: Dinah has to be dragged away from Shechem's house because Jewish women find Gentile men irresistible, and Joseph's failure to respond to Potiphar's wife is due to impotence.

Chapter 6 moves on to Miriam. She appears to have a particular association with water. Her name can be etymologized to mean either "bitter sea" or "beloved sea"; she is one of a group of women who save Hebrew boys in general and Moses in particular from death in the Nile; she leads other Hebrew women in a song of triumph after the crossing of the Red Sea; she is punished by God with leprosy for insubordination but retains the people's loyalty; she later dies and is buried, after which the people face a water shortage. Talmudic tradition speaks of the well of Miriam that accompanied the Israelites in the wilderness, provided by God because of Miriam's merit. Miriam in the Hebrew Bible perhaps reflects an earlier water priestess or water goddess, possibly Isis. Notably, she is not defined at all by her own sexuality, but in the Midrash she encourages her father and mother to have another baby despite Pharaoh's decree, thus contributing to fertility.

Chapter 7 explores narratives of female seduction: Jael and Sisera, Samson and Delilah, Esther and Ahasuerus, Judith and Holofernes, and the modern-day stereotype of the Jewish American Princess (JAP). In all four biblical narratives, the bedroom is the battlefield where women are victorious; they have pretended to desire the man, but what they really desire is access to his power, and they use their feigned sexual desire to get it. In the JAP stereotype, the lust for power has been transformed into a lust for money, but it is nevertheless achieved by the same means: feigned sexual desire and overacting the role of woman. In this way the exaggerated enacting of femininity functions as an appropriation of masculine power.

Chapter 8 examines the role of the body in representing the body politic and sexual polity. The world order is disrupted by wine and illicit sex, both of which figure together in a number of narratives from Eden onward. The story of Balaam and Balak, read as a carnivalesque, queer narrative, disrupts the normal boundaries of identity with its talking donkey, invisible sexless angel, powerlessly tyrannical king, and God-controlled Gentile prophet, reminding the reader of the improvized nature of the Self. The story of the Levite's concubine in Judg 19 is an inscription of the chaos in the body politic onto the woman's body, in a narrative that undermines many established oppositions such as light/dark, safety/danger, friend/stranger, wife/harlot. In fact, the book of Judges as a whole is characterized by anarchic sexual reversals, a situation to which the book of Ruth, considered in Lefkovitz's ninth and final chapter, provides the antidote. Here again the narrative challenges boundaries, but in a positive way: Ruth is both mother and seductress; Naomi, Ruth, and Boaz form an unconventional family in which the women cooperate rather than compete; and the heroine from whom redemption for the entire nation will come is a Moabite. The plot is a variation on the eleventh-hour survival theme; as an origin myth for the Davidic dynasty, in its allusions and motifs it also encompasses the entirety of Jewish scripture. It is a story about long ago with implications for the far future, and it gives a foretaste of the peace and harmony of the messianic age, reiterating and refuting as arbitrary the boundaries of gender, family, and ethnicity that the foregoing narratives have set up.

This is an extremely rich book that takes time to digest. The internal structure of its chapters is not obviously linear but based on associations or clusters of ideas, and this makes it less straightforward to read and assimilate than a more sequential presentation. Having said that, there are a wealth of insightful observations that amply repay the investment of time taken to read the book. Perhaps inevitably, I found some analyses less compelling than others; in particular, the material in chapter 8 about the body makes a less coherent chapter than some of the others in the book. There also seemed to be a certain amount of overdrawing for the sake of the argument; the association of Dinah and Joseph, for example, seemed forced in some respects, although the point that the rabbinic commentary on both characters can be taken to represent anxieties about Jewish male sexuality is well made. In addition, I found myself uneasy about the allegorical readings that diminish the horror of stories of violence against women, such as the rape of Dinah or the attack on the Levite's concubine, without some kind of recognition of the damaging nature of the imagery that is being used. Nevertheless, many of Lefkovitz's readings are stunningly multitextured and perceptive, showing that new treasures can indeed be drawn from these old—indeed, ancient—texts by the skilful interpreter of Torah. In sum, what this book does not give is a straightforward or simplistic reading of its chosen texts. Rather, it is a treasury of trenchant observations effortlessly linking the then of the texts with the now of (post) modernity in a fascinating tapestry of gender and identity.

The Violence of Scripture: Overcoming the Old Testament's Troubling Legacy, by Eric A. Seibert. Minneapolis: Fortress, 2012. Pp. x + 220. Paper. $23.00. ISBN 9780800698256.

Ralph K. Hawkins, Averett University, Danville, Virginia

Eric Seibert's new volume, *The Violence of Scripture,* examines texts of violence in the Old Testament. The book is divided into three parts, including an introduction and: (1) "Exploring the Old Testament's Troubling Legacy"; (2) "Proposing a Way of Reading the Old Testament Nonviolently"; and (3) "Applying Nonviolent Strategies to Violent Texts." The book includes ten chapters that are followed by an appendix that treats the issue of biblical authority.

Chapter 1 serves as an introduction, entitled "The Bible Should Never Be Used to Harm Others" (1–12). Seibert begins by recounting the story of the Mystic River Massacre, which occurred on May 26, 1637, during which New England settlers ransacked a Pequot village and massacred its populace, including numerous women and children. The massacre was justified by appealing to the attack on the tribe of Benjamin in Judg 20 and David's war with the Ammonites in 2 Sam 12. After recounting this incident, Seibert explains: "The premise of this book is simple and straightforward: the Bible should never be used to inspire, promote, or justify acts of violence" (2). He explains that he has written the book with two particular objectives in mind. First, he advocates reading the Old Testament nonviolently, in a way that "values all people, promotes justice, and facilitates liberation," which "requires reading in an ethically responsible manner, one that utilizes various strategies for critiquing, rather than perpetuating, the Old Testament's portrayals of violence" (3). At the outset, he clarifies that "reading nonviolently means resisting all readings that … sanction killing" (3–4). Seibert lets readers know about his faith commitments up front, identifying himself as a committed Christian (5) and a lifelong member of the Brethren in Christ Church, a denomination rooted in the Anabaptist, Pietist, and Wesleyan traditions that has a strong commitment to nonviolence, peacemaking, and reconciliation. He clarifies that, "Personally, I regard all forms of violence as inappropriate for Christians, and I cannot condone the use of violence in any situation" (6).

Part 1, "Exploring the Old Testament's Troubling Legacy," consists of three chapters. In chapter 2, "The Old Testament's Troubling Legacy" (15–26), Seibert explores some of the ways the Old Testament has been used to rationalize various kinds of violence against others. He includes a discussion of how some texts have been used to justify war (16–18), legitimate colonialism (18–19), support slavery (19–20), encourage violence against women (20–21), harm children (21–22), condemn gays and lesbians (22–23), and generally distort the character of God (23–25). These examples are not meant to be exhaustive but are intended to be "representative of the harmful effects certain Old Testament texts have had over the years" (16). Seibert concludes this chapter with a brief discussion of the question of whether these cases of violence against others are the fault of Bible readers alone or whether the Bible itself is partly to blame. He concludes that the Bible is complicit in the negative effects the various violent texts have had on its readers. "The texts themselves," he explains, "*are* problematic" (26). He concludes that "the problem is much bigger than just a matter of interpretation" and that "the Old Testament *itself* is part of the problem" (26).

In chapter 3 Seibert discusses "The Pervasive Presence of 'Virtuous' Violence in the Old Testament" (27–43). He notes that violence appears early and often in the Old Testament (27), and he suggests that, at the risk of oversimplifying, the vast amount of violence in the Old Testament is portrayed either positively or negatively (28). For the sake of discussion, he refers to violence that is portrayed positively as "virtuous" violence, while he calls violence that is portrayed negatively "wrongful" violence (28). Stories of wrongful violence would include, for example, those of Cain and Abel and the story of David and Bathsheba (29), while accounts of virtuous violence would include that of David and Goliath (30–32). Seibert notes that there are many Old Testament narratives of virtuous violence in which God either commits or commands the violence (32–33). He considers cases where there is no direct criticism of violent behavior and asks whether such stories are intended to evoke the readers' approval or disapproval. Seibert considers Judg 11, in which Jephthah sacrifices his own daughter, and concludes that, "In the absence of any specific condemnation of Jephthah's behavior, it is possible to regard the sacrifice of Jephthah's daughter as an example of 'virtuous' violence, and this is precisely how some have interpreted it over the years" (39). He also looks at cases where violence is regarded as virtuous because of who carries it out (39—41), and he notes how pervasive the virtuously violent texts are in the Old Testament (41). Seibert concludes the chapter by discussing ways that faith communities fail "to reflect on the violent destruction of Egyptians [in the exodus account] or to consider their plight" or "to feel sympathy for them" (42), sanitizes violent texts such as the flood story (Gen 6–9), and "condones violence it ought to condemn" (43) and thus contributes to the Old Testament's troubling legacy.

In chapter 4, the final chapter in part 1, Seibert discusses "The Danger of Reading the Bible" (45–57). Reading the Bible can have "some rather nasty side effects," and, as noted in earlier chapters, "People have used the Bible to sanction all kinds of awful behavior" (46). Seibert discusses the influence the Bible has on its readers and argues that "violence-friendly" texts "provide all the necessary ingredients for those wishing to find religious justification for their own violent behavior" and generally make violence "acceptable" (49). He notes that there are two kinds of Bible readers, compliant and conversant readers, and he calls on all readers to be conversant in the sense of being willing to be "contentious and confrontational" with regard to the text rather than always agreeing with it (56).

Part 2, "Proposing a Way of Reading the Old Testament Nonviolently," consists of two chapters in which Seibert sets forth hermeneutical strategies for reading texts that contain violence. Chapter 5, "Developing Good Reading Habits: Becoming Ethically Responsible Readers" (61–72), calls on Bible readers to read actively, to question the text, and to engage in an ethical critique of violent ideologies (62). With regard to critiquing passages that seem to contain violent ideologies, Seibert provides three guidelines (67–69), including the rule of love (love of God and neighbor), a commitment to justice, and an ethic of life that values all people. He concludes by giving readers permission "to read differently" (70–72). In chapter 6, "Reading the Old Testament Nonviolently" (73–92), Seibert proposes five strategies for helping readers read the text nonviolently. These include: (1) naming the violence; (2) analyzing the violence; (3) critiquing the violence; (4) using textual violence constructively; and (5) transcending the violence.

Part 3 consists of three chapters in which Seibert applies his nonviolent strategies to several groups of texts. In chapter 7, "Confronting Canaanite Genocide and Its Toxic Afterlife" (95–112), he considers the accounts of the Israelite conquest of Canaan in Josh 6–11. Seibert begins by noting that, "By any standard of measure, the narrative describing the conquest of Canaan in Joshua 6–11 is one of the most troubling texts in the entire Old Testament" because of the way it portrays God as a "merciless, genocidal God" (95). He argues that, in reading Josh 6–11, readers need to "call a spade a spade" and acknowledge that what is happening in these texts is "genocide" (96). He discusses the issue of the historicity of the conquest and relies on the work of William G. Dever to conclude that the conquest "simply did not happen" (97; see W. G. Dever, *Who Were the Early Israelites and Where Did They Come From?* [Grand Rapids: Eerdmans, 2003], 227–28; for a more nuanced view, see Ralph K. Hawkins, *How Israel Became a People* [Nashville: Abingdon, 2013). Even so, the ideology of genocide is sanctioned in the text, and readers must deal with it. Seibert advises readers to look for internal critiques, read with the Canaanites, read from the margins, and deconstruct any divinely sanctioned violence (98–105). He questions the Old Testament's rationale for Canaanite genocide (105–7) and makes a plea to biblical scholars to "stop justifying genocide!" (107). He brings this chapter to a close by identifying ways that modern readers can still find value in the conquest narratives (109–10) and discussing the question of whether the conquest narratives ought to be spiritualized (110–12).

In chapter 8, "Keeping the Old Testament from Being Used to Justify War" (113–28), Seibert makes a case for how to prevent the Old Testament from being used to justify war. He argues that Old Testament passages that portray God as involved in warfare are limited in what they can reveal about God's character (117) because they are biased (119–21). He urges readers to develop compassion for Israel's enemies (121–22), put a human face on war (122–25), and emphasize Old Testament texts that critique conventional views of war (125–28). Chapter 9, "Preventing Violence against Women" (129–46), explores the important topic of patriarchy in the Old Testament and proposes reading strategies for texts that involve violence against women. In chapter 10, "The Necessity and Urgency of Reading the Old Testament Nonviolently: Some Conclusions" (147–57), Seibert provides final reflections. He reiterates the need to overcome the Old Testament's troubling legacy of being used to harm others (148–49), to be honest about the Bible's moral and theological limitations (149–50), to avoid being negatively influenced by harmful ideologies in those texts (150–51), to remove obstacles that hinder people from reading the Old Testament and coming to faith (151–52), and to help children develop good morals and Christian values (152–54). He closes with a special appeal to biblical scholars and interpreters to take the lead in helping nonspecialists deal with these difficult texts (154–56) and encourages readers to explore nonviolent alternatives for resolving conflict (156–57). In an appendix, Seibert provides "A Brief Word about Biblical Authority" (159–62), in which he suggests that the best way of talking about biblical authority is not focused on its divine inspiration, historical reliability, or theological veracity. Instead, he argues that "the Bible is authoritative—or, perhaps better said, functions authoritatively—when people take it seriously and allow their lives to be transformed by it in faith-affirming ways and God honoring ways (161). He writes:

> To put it another way, we might say that affirming the authority of Scripture has less to do with what we say about it and more to do with how we live in light of it. Affirming the authority of Scripture is not primarily about giving cognitive assent to comprehensive statements about the Bible's trustworthiness and reliability. Rather, it is about giving ourselves to the God who speaks through its pages and calls us to live lives of faithfulness and obedience. We affirm the authority of Scripture by demonstrating our willingness to be shaped by these texts even as we enter into a critical dialogue with them. (161)

The Violence of Scripture is a well-written and engaging book that will be effective in renewing conversations, both in the academy and in the church, about issues of violence both in the text and among people. I would offer three criticisms, however. First, Seibert's definition of violence itself is too broad. He defines violence as "physical, emotional, or psychological harm done to a person by an individual (or individuals), institution, or structure that results in injury, oppression, or death" (9). This definition seems to preclude the moral critique of any behavior or lifestyle choice, since such a critique would be defined, under this rubric, as violent. This is a limitation that some readers may find unacceptable. Second, Seibert's premise that all killing is wrong is an a priori assumption. He explains that "obeying God and killing people are mutually exclusive" (112). This statement implies that every character who fought and killed at God's direction, including Abraham, Joshua, Samuel, Elijah, and many, many others, were wrong on every count. In my opinion, Seibert does not effectively defend this premise, on which so much of the remaining arguments in the book rest. Third, the reading strategies for dealing with positive portrayals of violence in biblical texts seem to me to be too limited. Seibert argues that readers will either critique or perpetuate the violence of the text (3). If readers do not reject the morality of a given violent text, does this mean they are destined to go out and perpetuate the violence portrayed therein? Surely there must be additional strategies for reading, understanding, and responding to texts that seem to endorse violence.

Aside from these criticisms, however, *The Violence of Scripture* makes an important contribution in that it raises issues of grave importance to both the church and the academy. Seibert's volume will be of interest to scholars and students alike, as well as pastors and laypersons, who are concerned with the violence in our world and the ways that perpetrators of violence sometimes seek to justify their behavior on the basis of Scripture.

Introduction to the Bible, by Christine Hayes. Open Yale Courses. New Haven: Yale University Press, 2012. Pp. xiv + 430. Paper. $18.00. ISBN 9780300181791,

James Bos, University of Mississippi, University, Mississippi

This textbook on the Hebrew Bible, containing twenty-four chapters, is an adaptation of, and complement to, the twenty-four lectures that constitute Professor Hayes's course RLST 145: Introduction to the Old Testament (Hebrew Bible), which is available online to the public through the Yale Open Courses Project (http://oyc.yale.edu/). The book begins with a preface and first chapter that lay out the scope and goals of the textbook. Hayes proceeds to discuss the topic of biblical monotheism in chapter 2, then progresses to providing an introduction to each of the biblical texts in the remaining chapters (Obadiah and Chronicles excepted, the latter being relegated to a footnote in the chapter covering Ezra-Nehemiah). The order in which the texts are discussed roughly follows the order of the Tanak—Torah, Prophets, and Writings. In the section on the prophets, however, Hayes treats the literary prophets in chronological order: eighth-century figures such as Amos, followed by the seventh- and then sixth-century prophets. The postmonarchic prophets and Jonah are addressed nearer the end of the book, intermixed with discussions about the books contained in the Writings, which are grouped topically.

The following review will be from a pedagogical perspective; that is, I will evaluate this textbook's value as a primary required text in an introductory undergraduate course on the Hebrew Bible. I will begin with a discussion of those aspects of the book that I consider to be the book's strengths before addressing the book's weaknesses. First, Hayes's writing style is very accessible. In a written survey of my students (who had read through chapter 9 at the time of the survey), only a few indicated having difficulty understanding the text. Technical terminology is usually explained concisely but clearly. Second, Hayes's literary analysis of the texts, in most instances, is quite well done. Her reading of the Abram cycle (specifically the analysis of the many detours taken before the promise of an heir is fulfilled) is particularly excellent, as is her reading of Job. Her presentations of Esther, Jonah, Ruth, and Ecclesiastes are also interesting and informative. Third, her selection of quotations from, and interpretations of, the literature from the wider Near East successfully sheds the desired light on the biblical text under discussion. This is especially true for the literature, such as Enuma Elish and the Gilgamesh Epic, that is comparable to the literature in the Primeval History. The number of quotations from extrabiblical texts is significantly reduced, however, in the treatment of the prophetic books and the Writings. Finally, Hayes successfully defamiliarizes the god of the Hebrew Bible, explicitly making a distinction between Yahweh/El/Elohim and the God of Western theology. This process of defamiliarization is a crucial component in any biblical studies course offered in a public institution or secular private institution.

Other aspects of this textbook, however, are not so strong. One very prominent weakness, one that will preclude my using the book in future classes, is that Hayes almost never interacts with recent biblical scholarship (and by recent, I mean anything from the last two or three decades); as a result, when she employs a historical-critical or source-critical approach, the overarching interpretative framework and general conclusions are significantly dated. Several examples are worth mentioning in this regard. First, the discussion of Israelite monotheism in chapter 2 is limited to two outdated theories: the evolutionary model from the nineteenth century that considered the Israelites' superior monotheism to have gradually developed out of an inferior polytheism, and the revolutionary model promoted by Yehezkel Kaufmann in the early twentieth century that posited an early, radical monotheism wholly different from the surrounding paganism marked by empty magic and mythology. Neither of these positions can be sustained today, but Hayes interprets many texts through the lens of Kaufmann's dated views on monotheism. It should be mentioned that she does include a very brief discussion of Mark Smith's research on Israelite religion in a later chapter, but his conclusions should have figured much more prominently in her initial discussion of monotheism. A second example of outdated material is that the only source-critical approach to the Pentateuch that is discussed in any detail is Wellhausen's Documentary Hypothesis. Hayes does mention that scholars have criticized aspects of the theory, and she herself does a fine job discussing the anti-Judaic bias in his theory, but there is no discussion of plausible alternatives. John Van Seters is mentioned briefly, only to be dismissed as an "extreme skeptic" (73). J and E are thus very early and then combined in the eighth century; D originated in the north and was brought to Judah after Israel was destroyed, eventually being found in the temple during the reign of Josiah (and potentially updated at a later time); and P is exilic. Unfortunately, not many scholars today find this model compelling. Finally, the discussion of the prophetic books is also very traditional, betraying almost no familiarity with current research (in the six chapters devoted to the prophetic books, only Kaufmann is cited more than once). First Isaiah (minus chapters 24–27) can be attributed to a historical Isaiah in the eighth century. Amos was literate and thus the author of the book named after him (although the final oracle in the book was probably added by a later redactor, perhaps also the oracle against Judah in the first series of oracles against the nations). There is virtually no distance between book and prophet. In contrast, most contemporary scholarship on the prophetic books would posit significantly more distance between the two, the books being much later scribal elaborations that continued to expand in some cases for centuries and that thus provide no direct access to the actual words or actions of the ostensibly historical prophets. Overall, then, a sizable portion of Hayes's presentation mirrors those found in introductions to the Hebrew Bible from the mid-twentieth century, with only a hint here and there that scholarship has advanced beyond Wellhausen and Kaufmann. This situation has created some difficulties for the students in class, since my presentation of the material differs markedly in places. That said, it may also be beneficial for the students to be exposed to these differences of opinion.

A second criticism is related to Hayes's overreliance on Kaufmann's view of Israelite monotheism. In far too many places she privileges the Israelite cult over neighboring peoples' cults in ways that I think are unwarranted. For example, she writes, "In P, the cult has no actual value for Yahweh and does not affect his vitality *as in other cultures*" (256, emphasis added). In other words, Yahweh did not need the Israelites' sacrifices, while all the other gods needed theirs. This is not possible to substantiate. Another example is that in chapter 9, on biblical law, Hayes makes an extended argument that, as a whole, the biblical legal corpus is more humanitarian than its nonbiblical counterparts. This is due to the principle of divine authorship inherent in the biblical authors' presentation of the legal material. While some of the comparisons she puts forward do indeed point in that direction, other examples could be cited that point in the opposite direction. Surely the Mesopotamian law collections that make no attempt to regulate religious behavior, and thus do not condemn anyone to death for perceived religious offenses, could be considered significantly more humanitarian than the biblical legal collections that frequently mandate the death penalty for individuals who do not follow Yahweh's commands. A final example of the privilege afforded Israelite religion is that Israelite prophecy is termed "apostolic prophecy" (237). Now, it may be that Hayes means nothing more than that the prophets are sent by Yahweh to Israel or Judah with a message, but the (unintended) consequence of using this term is that it "Christianizes" this portion of the Hebrew Bible and lends the Israelite prophets more credibility than their Near Eastern counterparts. It would have been better to simply explain that the Israelite and Judahite prophets were viewed as messengers of Yahweh, just as the Neo-Assyrian prophets were viewed as messengers of Ishtar or one of the other deities in Assyria.

A final point of criticism, due more to my own idiosyncratic preferences than anything else, is that far too frequently, in my view, Hayes employs language such as this: "the Bible rejects" (53), "the Bible makes it clear" (78), "the Bible states" (98), or "the Bible mandates" (143). Part of the defamiliarization process that I consider so essential to studying the biblical texts in an institution of higher learning requires that students stop thinking about the Bible as a single Book (often presupposed to be written by a single Author) and instead think about it as a collection of writings representing (at times, widely) divergent worldviews. Hayes is fully aware of this, and she stresses this very point in the preface, chapter 1, and the epilogue. But writing "the Bible states…" only serves to reinforce the familiar. I would much prefer "the Yahwist [or non-Priestly author] states…."

A few miscellaneous points will conclude this review. Text-critical issues are only rarely brought forward in the textbook (e.g., a few sentences about the two editions of Jeremiah). Second, there is only incidental discussion of the process of canonization. Next, for an inexpensive book, it does have quite a few charts and pictures (in black-and-white). However, it has no excurses, sidebars, discussion questions, or other features often included in textbooks. The index is relatively thorough. Finally, there are a few typographical errors: "James 7" should be "Jude 7" (88); "Jud 4–7" should be "1 Samuel 4–7" (204); "1 Kgs 17" should be "2 Kgs 17" (231); and the suggested reading for chapter 20 includes the non-existent Proverbs 32 (perhaps 31 or 23 was intended).

Plotted, Shot, and Painted: Cultural Representations of Biblical Women, by, J. Cheryl Exum. 2nd edition. Classic Reprints. Sheffield: Sheffield Phoenix, 2012. Pp. 306. Paper. $39.50. ISBN 9781907534676.

Ginny Brewer-Boydston, Baylor University, Waco, Texas

J. Cheryl Exum's *Plotted, Shot, and Painted: Cultural Representations of Biblical Women* was originally published in 1996. The 2012 publication is a revised second edition but is not a rewrite or an updating, as Exum notes in the new preface. Instead, she has expanded the footnotes to include more recent sources, added a section to the chapter on Delilah to include a movie in production at the time of the first edition, and added a chapter on Lot's daughters.

Plotted, Shot, and Painted discusses portrayals of biblical women in popular culture, including literature, art, film, and music. The title refers to the medium of these depictions—"plotted" by the narrative of the biblical text, "shot" by the filmmaker, and "painted" by the artist. The main concern of the work is with "what happens to biblical women in their various cultural afterlives" (14). Exum's methods are as varied as the women she discusses (Bathsheba, Michal, the women of Exod 1:8–2:10, the wayward wife in prophetic literature, Lot and his daughters, Naomi and Ruth, and Delilah). With nearly every chapter she uses a different method to investigate the portrayal of these biblical characters. Despite the diverse use of inquiry, Exum acknowledges that feminist biblical criticism lies at the heart of the essays, yet she is moving beyond this method to cultural criticism of biblical women. The focus, then, is on how their stories have changed and how gender ideology is reinforced or challenged by the medium. Gender bias is clear in Scripture, especially in the Hebrew Bible, but now Exum is critiquing gender bias in interpretation.

The first chapter, titled "Bathsheba Plotted, Shot and Painted," stands as the model for the remaining essays. In what is arguably the best of the seven chapters, Exum critiques the theatrical representations of Bathsheba in *David and Bathsheba* (1951) and *King David* (1985) through a feminist lens. The paintings to which she responds are Rembrandt's *Bathsheba at Her Bath*, Memling's *Bathseba im Bade*, Haarlem's *Het toilet van Bathseba*, Maratti's *David and Bathsheba*, and Aachen's *David und Bathseba*.

Exum introduces the brief appearances of Bathsheba in Scripture before showing how the artistic media has interpreted those passage. David is often portrayed as less guilty in his "request" for Bathsheba. She, therefore, is not bathing in private but in such a way as to draw his attention, as if she is purposeful in wishing to catch the king's eye. The viewers of both film and painting are assumed to be men, as the focal point is a woman bathing with the viewer standing in David's place rather than viewing a man watching a woman bathe. At times Bathsheba's posture insinuates that she knows the viewers are watching and fantasizing about her. Bathsheba's nakedness is not necessarily for David alone but also for the viewer—the male viewer. He imagines himself as David, one who observes her beauty but also will be her rescuer. Uriah's character must suffer ignominy in casting him as less caring or even abusive toward Bathsheba. David is less than an adulterer; he seeks what he finds is a beautiful offering to him, then rescues her from her horrible marriage, although the insinuation is that Bathsheba lures him in.

The main difference between paintings and film is that only one scene must make the case for innocence and guilt for all those involved in the biblical story. The methods for doing so include either removing David from the bathing scene or depicting him as he looks on from afar. Just as the film shifts the viewer's gaze from both David and Bathsheba to just Bathsheba, the paintings present her nudity as the focal point of the work of art. No wonder David could not help himself when such a beautiful woman presents herself in this manner to him! She is naked—just for the viewer, seductive, vain, alluring, self-aware of her attributes. The viewers are given a "moral high ground" by showing the viewers what David sees; therefore, they can "gaze upon the naked woman without embarrassment, or at least without feeling guilty about it" (58).

Exum notes that female readers and viewers have little choice but to assume the male perspective and read it against their "own interests: to accept the concept of woman as a source of temptation that can bring about a man's downfall" (35). To resist these interpretations, readers recognize the gendered nature of the artistic media. We also recognize that the media influences how readers interpret biblical texts rather than allowing the biblical text to stand on its own. To resist, we recognize "what is at stake personally and culturally, and (take) responsibility for our interpretations" (59).

Exum's second chapter, "Michal at the Window, Michal in the Movies," uses the same method as the first chapter regarding Bathsheba. Again, Exum critiques theatrical representations of Michal in *David and Bathsheba* (1951) and *King David* (1985) and analyzes the ancient Near Eastern "Woman at the Window" ivory plaques (eighth century BCE) and de Bray's *David Dances before the Ark of the Covenant*. The twist on this chapter is that Michal is presented as the opposite of Bathsheba in character, presentation, and even dress; Michal is a "nagging, spiteful shrew" (63). She is a villain in the film presentations, and it is not David's fault she is so unhappy, despite the insinuation in the biblical text. In *David and Bathsheba* she incites David into arguing with her, and, in the moment he walks away from the fight, he spies Bathsheba bathing. Her proper place is at the window from where she gazes at David as he dances when escorting the ark into Jerusalem. The readers sympathize with David, and, from the gaze of the typical male viewer, he can hardly be blamed for turning to the passionate, loving, and beautiful Bathsheba.

The third chapter, "The Hand That Rocks the Cradle," deals with the women of Exod 1:8–2:10. Rather than investigating artistic media, Exum instead investigates her own bias in her past interpretation of the overall passage through new criticism. Rather than Exum coming to a satisfactory conclusion in the past, she had no answer to the fact that five women are lauded for their actions (in typical female roles from the patriarchal point of view) to save a male child who would be the deliverer of the Hebrews. Thus, she has reinscribed the gender ideology of the biblical text. Although Exum does not come to a satisfactory conclusion through this method, she acknowledges the patriarchal ideology of the text and recognizes how the narrator must diffuse women's power to subvert by "domesticating" and "confining" it (99).

Exum tackles the problem of a sexually violent God in prophetic literature through deconstruction in the fourth chapter, "Prophetic Pornography." These biblical passages are skilled rhetoric to make the reader sympathize with the Husband-God and support the sexually abusive actions against the Wife-Israel. Through discussion of the pertinent passages, Exum teases out how the interpretation of male commentators plays into the patriarchal argument. These commentators are quick to justify God's actions, with one commentator even noting sardonically that the images are just metaphors. Exum's response is a four-fold interpretive strategy: (1) "Attention to the differing claims these texts make upon their male and female readers" (125); (2) "Exposing prophetic pornography for what it is" (127); (3) "Looking for competing discourse(s)" (128); and (4) "A systematic deconstructive reading of the texts in question" (130).

The subject of the fifth chapter is the title itself, "Lot and his Daughters." Here Exum's approach is psycho-analytic, and she critiques the biblical text as well as Steen's *Lot und seine Töchter*, Furini's *Lot and His Daughters*, Goltzius' *Lot en zijn dochters*, and Vouet's *Loth et ses filles*. The narrative unconscious describes the sexual fantasy Lot has for his daughters, which represents the collective andro-centric desire for their own daughters. Lot cannot carry out his fantasy until all barriers, such as sons-in-laws, are removed. He finds privacy in the hills where his actions cannot be condemned. He is exempt from his actions, like David, in that his daughters are the instigators and that his lineage must continue. These paintings invite the viewers to become a voyeur, viewing the naked daughters and their clearly sexual suggestions. In the Aldrich film *The Last Days of Sodom and Gomorrah* (1962), Lot's incestuous actions are not included. Instead, his daughters are freely open to a display of their sexuality with other Sodomites. Lot is offended by them and especially by both daughters having sexual intercourse with the same Sodomite prince, whom he kills for taking his daughters' virginity. Exum argues that, despite the lack of overt incest, the father's jealousy of the daughters' sexual escapades and killing of their lover insinuate that he would rather be the object of their sexual affection.

The sixth chapter is titled "Is This Naomi?" which is in reference to Calderon's ambiguous portrayal of Ruth and Naomi's relationship in his painting *Ruth and Naomi*. Exum uses this portrait as a springboard into analysis of other paintings (Lastman's *Ruth Swears Loyalty to Naomi*, Drost's *Ruth and Naomi*, and de Morgan's *Ruth and Naomi*), literature (poems by Victor Hugo, Else Lasker-Schüler, and Maureen Duffy, and Hardy's *Far from the Madding Crowd* and Flagg's *Fried Green Tomatoes at the Whistle Stop Cafe*), and film (*The Story of Ruth* [1960]) through queer theory. For Exum, only Calderon's painting and the fictional works do justice to Ruth and Naomi's relationship through the lens of queer theory. These works sometimes allow the gaps in the text to stand and give voice to the possibility of Ruth and Naomi's same-sex relationship. With the exception of de Morgan, the remainder of the artistic media reinforce heterosexist views. For example, Naomi is an elderly woman, hardly a sexual object for Ruth, but Boaz is attractive and closer to Ruth's age. The media depict the relationship between the two as mother and daughter and the relationship between Ruth and Boaz as romantic love.

In the final chapter, titled "Why, Why, Why, Delilah?" Exum discusses a wide variety of artistic media: DeMille's film *Samson and Delilah* (1949), Turner Pictures' movie *Samson and Delilah* (1996), Tom Jones's song "Delilah," operatic works *Samson Angonistes* by Milton and *Samson* by Handel, and multiple paintings—Moreau's *Delilah* and *Samson and Delilah*, Rubens's *Samson and Delilah* and *Gefangennahme Simsons*, and Solomon's *Samson*. Here Delilah is a *femme fatale*. The vast majority of these works portray her as a Philistine, a prostitute, and motivated by money and/or patriotism to enact revenge upon the unsuspecting Samson. Unfortunately, these aspects are missing from the biblical text (Delilah may accept money from the Philistines, but it is not clear that the money is her motivation or why she accepts it). Just as with Bathsheba, the nude Delilah is for the male viewer's eyes and fantasy. Because the biblical text lacks closure with regard to Delilah, many of these works create consequences for her actions—she repents, she commits suicide, she is killed at the temple with the Philistines, she continues as a miserable prostitute. Through psychoanalytic theory, Exum describes Delilah the *femme fatale* as a male construct, demonstrating how woman is "seductive, fickle, untrustworthy, and deceptive" (273).

This book is more a collection of essays about cultural reincarnations of Hebrew Bible (despite the book's title "… of Biblical Women"). Each chapter can stand on its own as a single work, but the chapters are bound by the theme of the influence of misinterpretation in popular culture. The book's main strength is that Exum displays a variety of approaches that yield similar conclusions about male constructs placed upon biblical women in both the biblical text and in our (artistic) interpretations of them. These methods were nascent when the first edition was published and are finally making their way into mainstream scholarship fifteen years later. This edition will certainly bolster such methods as psychoanalytic critique, queer theory, and cultural biblical criticism.

The variety of methods also serve to highlight the multiplicity of artistic media and the way it is used today. Each essay is a fascinating look at how artists shape their paintings, films, songs, poems, novels, and operas to answer questions of the gaps in the biblical text. Unfortunately, these works usually either misread the text or reinforce patriarchal gender ideology. The most alarming aspect of these essays is the complicity of these artists with that gender ideology and how resistant we as readers and viewers have been to transcend the male constructs and read against the grain with viewers like Exum.

A few overall weaknesses were evident in this work. Exum chose works that only reinforced the argument of misinterpretation and patriarchal reinforcement. She remained mostly within the Golden Age of film. She did not offer a wide range of artists with regards to eras. She is not clear that her choice pieces are representative of the works of those eras or throughout the history of film and art. It seems possible that there are films, songs, paintings, and novels that read against the grain, but they simply do not fit into her belief system of gender bias. She uncovers a few of these works but uses them as more modern examples of reading against the grain. Resistance reading in general is given short shrift. Exum mostly identifies the problem and then dedicates, for example, one paragraph to resistance reading at the end of Bathsheba's chapter. She develops a far more systematic method of resistance reading in the fourth chapter on prophetic pornography. Such a method would have been helpful as a conclusion or employed throughout the essay.

The main weakness of the book also stems from it being a collection of essays. The chapters were not written as a way of advancing an argument but were written for other purposes and then massaged lightly into a book with similar themes. The book desperately needed a concluding chapter to offer overall criticism of cultural reinterpretation of biblical figures as well as ways to move forward, especially now that the nascent methods are more mainstream. Such a conclusion would have been another excellent way of outlining or sketching a method of resistance reading, such as what Exum does with prophetic pornography. Just as filmmakers and artists are dissatisfied with the biblical end of Delilah's story, this viewer of *Plotted, Shot, and Painted* is dissatisfied with a lack of closure.

'The Unconquered Land' and Other Old Testament Essays: Selected Studies by Rudolf Smend, edited by Edward Ball and Margaret Barker. Translated by Margaret Kohl. Society for Old Testament Study Monographs. Farnham, UK: Ashgate, 2013. Pp. xviii + 277. Hardcover. $104.95. ISBN 9781409429456.

David J. Reimer, University of Edinburgh, Edinburgh, United Kingdom

In spite of Rudolf Smend's significant and distinguished monographs on the Hebrew Bible and its study, the range and depth of his contribution to the field can only be adequately gauged when his voluminous essay output is taken into account. Perhaps best known in an Anglophone context for his distinctive understanding of the development of the Deuteronomistic History, Smend's writing extends well beyond this horizon to engage three broad areas of research within the field: the history of "biblical" Israel; the theology of the Hebrew Bible; and the history of its interpretation. Fragments of any one of these three areas would give enough scope for a satisfying career, but Professor Smend has worked expertly and creatively in wide explorations of each of them.

Several volumes collecting Smend's essays in German are available. In English, a selection of his contributions on the history of research on the Hebrew Bible was published in translation (also by Margaret Kohl) as *From Astruc to Zimmerli: Old Testament Scholarship in Three Centuries* (Tübingen: Mohr Siebeck, 2007). The principle of selection for the present volume, as well as its genesis, are less easy to discern. The project appears to have been initiated by Ed Ball to mark the occasion of Smend's eightieth birthday, which was celebrated in 2012. With Ed's sad and untimely death (the volume is dedicated to his memory), the work was carried forward by Margaret Barker. One might have assumed, then, that the editors were responsible for choosing the essays gathered here. However, in John Barton's engaging and illuminating introductory chapter, the selection is described as Smend's own.

Each of the fifteen articles included appears in English for the first time (although at least one of them, "Lowth in Germany," was delivered as a lecture in English prior to its initial publication in German). Some seminal articles that might have been included are thus omitted, having appeared in English elsewhere. Putting these factors together, it becomes clear that the volume is a very welcome "sampler" of Smend's wide-ranging work rather than a "greatest hits" collection. Like any good sampler, the essays cover almost the entire range of Professor Smend's career. The oldest essay is on de Wette, published originally in 1958, which goes back to the subject of Smend's doctoral work completed that same year. The most recent essay also ends the collection. From the year 2000, it is a retrospective of trends in Old Testament scholarship the twentieth century. The remainder are sprinkled fairly evenly through the intervening forty years, with four from the 1960s, and three each from the 1970s, 1980s, and 1990s.

The principle of organization for the selected essays seems more clear, and it is broadly chronological, beginning with Moses and ending with contemporary biblical scholarship. Following Barton's introduction, the first ten essays are rooted in the Old Testament text itself. A thematic study of "eating and drinking" provides a transition to the closing four essays, which have aspects the history of scholarship as their focus.

Both "Moses as a Historical Figure" (13–27) and "The Ten Commandments" (29–40) are ostensibly studies related to the exodus period. However, the former treats the problem posed in the title via the history of scholarship, plotting and analyzing the move from a perception of Moses as historical to legendary and carrying forward these reflections in a theological trajectory. Even the study of the Decalogue, which begins with observations most comfortably described as "exegetical," concludes with reflections on the nature of authorship informed by post-Enlightenment analogues. This loose association with the exodus could extend to the next essay, "The Covenant Formula" (41–71, and the longest in this collection), with its focal point in Deut 26. Set in the context of a wider survey, the essay accounts for the development of a biblical motif, with Wellhausen providing inspiration. Originally published in 1963, it neatly anticipates the contours of Ernest Nicholson's *God and His People: Covenant and Theology in the Old Testament* (Oxford: Clarendon, 1988).

In "Elements of Historical Thinking in the Old Testament" (73–98), the development of scholarly perceptions of "history" in the Old Testament provides the vehicle for a sustained probe into the nature of "historiographical" traditions, their value and significance, with the conquest narratives occupying a prominent place in Smend's analysis. This biblical moment provides the connection to a consideration of "The Unconquered Land" (99–110). Here the tension between the "ideal" of a complete conquest and the "reality" is analyzed in conjunction with the tension in the explanations offered by Albrecht Alt and his student Martin Noth. Smend's own account arises out of his distinctive understanding of the Deuteronomistic History and relates the conquest themes to concerns of later tradents. Having brought considerations to the point of the inception of a national entity (or, perhaps, "entities"), the essay on "The Place of the State in the Old Testament" (111–124) investigates the appropriateness of the language of "statehood" in the Old Testament, especially in light of interactions between kings and prophets.

The next four essays pick up the prophetic theme, with Elijah as the focus for "The Biblical and the Historical Elijah" (125–39) and "The Word of Yahweh to Elijah: Thoughts on the Composition of 1 Kings 17–19" (141–55). The first of these shares some contours with the essay on Moses that began the collection: the assessment of the "historical Elijah" proceeds step by step with a consideration of previous historiographical scholarship, accompanied by probes into the literary evidence. Smend concludes by drawing some explicit parallels between Moses and Elijah in history and tradition. The study of 1 Kings 17–19 is, as the title suggests, much more focused, examining the literary-critical contours of this pericope, both in terms of its internal development and as it relates to its wider context.

Two essays related to Amos continue the prophetic theme. Smend's exposition of "Amos's No" (157–75) comes close to being an exercise in practical theology, as the prophet's voice raised in divine opposition to the social and religious life of his people is refracted through his relationship to his contemporaries, as well as through varied scholarly assessments, both of these explicitly being brought to bear on Christian appropriation of this intransigent prophet. "'The End Has Come': An Amos Saying in the Priestly Code" (177–82) proposes a solution to a difficulty in the clause קֵץ כָּל־בָּשָׂר בָּא לְפָנַי in Gen 6:13 by appeal to Amos 8:2.[1] This not only tips Smend's hand on the nature of the "Priestly Code," but the essay also neatly exemplifies (over the course of only six pages) how close attention to the Hebrew text can open up a world of meaning.

New Testament connections provide the starting point for an exploration of "Eating and Drinking: A Piece of Worldliness in the Old Testament" (183–94), as Smend elucidates the particular shape this pairing—ubiquitous in human experience—takes in the Hebrew Bible, especially its connection to the notion of "covenant."

The attention to the history of scholarship, which flavors most if not all of the preceding essays, now comes to the forefront as the collection moves toward its conclusion. Set in the eighteenth century, "Lowth in Germany" (195–214) not only narrates a moment in the relationship between English (the term is used deliberately) and German scholarship, in which the creativity of the former inspired the latter, but also a friendship (with Michaelis) through which Lowth's ideas were mediated to a receptive but critical audience. "De Wette and the Relationship between Historical Biblical Criticism and Philosophical System in the Nineteenth Century" (215–24) is a chip off Smend's doctoral research workbench. It is fascinating to see the ways in which his concerns with the philosophy of history retain their relevance for current methodological grappling in the interpretation of Scripture, "theological interpretation" in particular. This sense of prescience is also seen in the 1966 "Post-critical Scriptural Interpretation" (225–44), an

---

1. Unfortunately, translation obscures the point of Smend's comparing the translations of Buber, de Wette, and Luther in the second paragraph.

extended methodological reflection on handling the Old Testament taking a cue from Barth, with frequent forays into nineteenth-century antecedents. These two articles together provide much food for thought in negotiating the fraught connections between "history" and "truth."

Finally, and fittingly, in "Trends. Old Testament Scholarship in the Twentieth Century: A Retrospect" (245–59) we have Smend's recent, deliberate, and lingering backward glance at the century through which he labored as a conclusion to the volume. Smend adopts three categories or "trends" used by Rudolf Kittel in 1921 to plot a possible future for Old Testament studies for his survey: literary criticism (of a pronounced historical flavor); history of religions; and what might loosely be described as traditional and theological. While these showed a tendency toward convergence mid-century, this phase has now passed. Other than emphasizing the desirability that all three should continue in some form, Smend now finds the nature of their interrelationship to be far from clear.

At one level, a collection like this from so significant and seminal a scholar as Professor Smend hardly needs justification. However, the brief and potted summaries in this review cannot begin to convey the depth of erudition, care, and level of clarity that each contribution contains. Their rootedness in the history of scholarship, combined with Smend's perceptive handling of the biblical data, results in a sequence of studies that retain their value in an academic context that has moved on from that in which Smend produced much of this work. If there is one study that I would have liked to see included here, it is his substantial piece on "Die Mitte des Alten Testaments" (1970), which I am confident would find an eager audience in English. Perhaps, however, this collection will impel some readers to explore the further riches in Smend's œuvre that still await in German, and that would be a welcome outcome.

Social Theory and the Study of Israelite Religion: Essays in Retrospect and Prospects, edited by Saul M. Olyan. Society of Biblical Literature Resources for Biblical Study 71. Atlanta: Society of Biblical Literature, 2012. Pp. x + 219. Paper. $29.95. ISBN 9781589836884.

Bob Becking, Utrecht University, Utrecht, The Netherlands

In the last fifty years or so, social theory has gained ground in biblical studies. The use of theories, hypotheses, and methods from the social sciences—mainly from sociology, anthropology, and ethnography—is, however, very haphazard and sometimes arbitrary. In reading publications from the crossroad of the two disciplines, one often has the idea that the biblical scholar went out on a blind date with a social scientist or just picked a theory or method that seemed to fit the goals. A volume like the one under consideration, therefore, is more than welcome to clear the grounds and offer perspectives for future research. Saul Olyan must be praised for convening the Ruth and Joseph Moskow Symposium in 2010 and for editing the proceedings of that meeting.

After an introduction by the editor (1–6), the volume opens with a review by Robert R. Wilson, "Social Theory and the Study of Israelite Religion" (7–17). In this well-written essay he makes clear that, after a first wave of biblical studies informed by social sciences in the first decades of the twentieth century, a "second" wave emerged between 1965 and 1980. In this wave two focal points can be indicated: a more sociological approach that starts in theory and uses the data derived from the Hebrew Bible and "Israelite" archaeology to test a thesis and a more anthropological or ethnographic approach that starts in the evidence and looks for patterns. These two tracks are still present in more contemporary studies, with Rainer Albertz and Richard Horsley as the polar ends. Correctly, Wilson warns against a haphazard use of theories and models from the social sciences. He ends his paper with a comment to biblical scholars to *consciously* choose and apply these theories. His final remark that we—biblical scholars—have to look for the correct "match" between problem and model is, unfortunately, quite necessary.

Susan Ackerman offers a lengthy essay: "Cult Centralization, the Erosion[1] of Kin-Based Communities, and the Implications for Women's Religious Practice" (19–40), in which she studies the effects for participation of women in cult(s) of the Josianic reforms. She is applying Weberian concepts on nation, community, and sib, or clan. She summarizes the works of Baruch Halpern and Joseph Blenkinsopp, who both argue that women's roles in the cult were marginalized as a result of the concentration of the cult in Jerusalem. Ackerman reads three stories from the book of Samuel that are seen as informative on pre-Josianic annual festivals of the clan. Of these stories, only 1 Sam 20 can be construed as referring to such a festival. The other two examples (1 Sam 1; 9) have more national and political traits. In 1 Sam 20, women already play a very marginal role. Next Ackerman analyses the data on the participation of women in ancestor veneration. Here she arrives at the conclusion that women were never involved in this veneration, on both ends: there is no mention of deified women ancestors of women venerating the (male) ancestors. All this leads to her view that the Josianic reform had no effect on the participation of women, since that participation already was marginal. Ackerman's argument is not completely convincing at this point. She fails to explain why Leah and Rachel were hiding the *teraphim*, to be seen as ancestor icons. She overlooks the role of Rachel in Jer 31. More important, Francesca Stavrakopoulou has argued that in the famous vow of Ruth to Naomi the *'elohim* should be construed as ancestors.[2] In my view, the book of Ruth indicates the role of women's participation in the ancestor cult.

---

1. Ironically spelled "Erosian" in the table of contents, creating an unexpected link to a character from the land of Star Wars fiction.

2. Francesca Stavrakopoulou, *Land of Our Fathers: The Roles of Ancestor Veneration in Biblical Land Claims* (LHBOTS 473; New York: T&T Clark, 2010).

In his contribution, "The Levites and Socio-cultural Change in Ancient Israel" (41–58), Stephen Cook applies the insight of the sociologist Gerhard Lenski[3] for a reconstruction of the history of the Levites. Lenski operates with an evolutionary scheme in which ongoing development leads to internal tensions. Cook makes clear that ancient Israel went through a process from an agrarian society to a more stratified advanced agrarian society during the Iron Age. This development inevitably led to tensions within the society of ancient Israel. On the basis of what Cook classifies as data, he constructs a movement in which the Levites were torn between center and periphery after the Josianic reform. This implies that the Levites at times voiced criticism against the views of the elite around court and temple but on other occasions were entangled in power positions. This is an interesting view that is based, however, on cast-iron evidence. What Cook presents as "data" is often the view of another scholar to whom he stands sympathetic.

Ronald Hendel's "Away from Ritual: The Prophetic Critique" (59–79) explores the prophetic critique of the traditional cult as voiced, for instance, in Amos 5:21–24. He makes clear that well-intentioned endeavors to smooth the dichotomy between "cultic practice" and "religious morality"—although having a positive effect on post–WW II ecumenical debates—miss the point. The prophetic critique should be construed as contesting religious identities. He underscores this view by bringing in Bourdieu's concept of *doxa*.[4] The cultic rituals of ancient Israel are to be seen as examples of unquestionable assumptions and practices of everyday life. The prophets are seen by Hendel as individual antiritualists who in their negative response to the *doxa* of their days made clear that this *doxa* had run aground and was no longer self-evident.[5] Therefore, they proposed to replace it by new forms.

T. M. Lemos, "'They Have Become Women': Judean Diaspora and Postcolonial Theories of Gender and Migration" (81–109), relates in lengthy sentences and meandering arguments that biblical scholars have an inclination to either ignore anthropological theory and ethnographic data or make only an arbitrary and theory-laden use of them. She then presents a selection of postcolonial theories of empire, migration, and gender that could, in her opinion, be helpful in understanding the Judean (forced) migration to Babylon. She applies these insights in a reading of passages from the books of Ezekiel and Daniel. To my surprise, she seems to have overlooked the work of John Ahn.[6]

Recent years have shown a growing interest in the development of writing

---

3. See Gerhard Lenski, *Power and Privilege: A Theory of Stratification* (New York: McGraw-Hill, 1966); idem, *Human Societies: An Introduction to Macrosociology* (New York: McGraw-Hill, 1970).

4. Pierre Bourdieu, *Outline of a Theory of Practice* (Cambridge: Cambridge University Press, 1977).

5. See also Mary Douglas, *Implict Meanings: Essays in Anthroplogy* (London: Routledge & Keegan Paul, 1975).

6. See John J. Ahn, *Exile as Forced Migrations: A Sociological, Literary, and Theological*

and literacy in ancient Israel. The emerging picture is quite static: text production is construed as part of a process of stabilization and conservation. In "Text Production and Destruction in Ancient Israel: Ritual and Political Dimensions" (111–39), Nathaniel Levtow opts for a quite different position. He argues for the view that text production was a function of cultural production and change. He underscores this view with a surprising argument, since he is looking at the processes that accompanied text *destruction*. In the Hebrew Bible three narratives on destruction are found: the cutting and burning of a scroll (Jer 36); the smashing of tablets (Exod 32); and the sinking of a scroll (Jer 51). Levtow adds to that the warning against destroying of the tablet in the vassal treaties (or loyalty oaths) of Esarhaddon. If I understand him correctly, he seems to argue that the fear for losing a power position that is present in and around these four texts is revealing about the composition of texts: the served the interests of a changing society. I am not immediately convinced by his "mirror" argument.

In a well-written contribution entitled "The Function of Feasts: An Anthropological Perspective on Israelite Religious Festivals" (141–68), Carol Meyers engages recent research in ethnography and anthropological archaeology on the functions of feasts and festivals. After a short introduction, she presents the views of biblical scholars on this topic, making clear that even in the excellent work of Nathan MacDonald still much is left unstudied.[7] Next she argues that regular and calendrical festivals in ancient Israel—although with local variations—have remained their character over the ages. I would add only that, since ancient Israel from the Iron Age II up to Hellenistic times was a slowly developing agrarian society, the yearly festivals also were part of the *longue durée*. Meyers correctly remarks that the participation of women in these festivals would have been marginal. Finally, she describes the various functions of these festivals using the windows of economy, culture, community, and identity.

In his own contribution, "Theorizing Violence in Biblical Ritual Contexts: The Case of Mourning Rites" (169–80), Saul Olyan discusses four passages from the Hebrew Bible that contain elements of violence in the context of mourning rites. In 2 Sam 10 David's emissaries to the mourning court in Ammon meet violence from the Ammonites who want to end the treaty relationship; 2 Sam 16 narrates acts of violent revenge by the Saulide Shimei; Neh 13 makes clear that violence played an important role in the new network of affiliations constructed by Nehemiah; in Isa 50 the victimizers seek to force their opponent into a penitential mourning posture. All four texts fit the pattern of recent cross-cultural theorizing on violence, with one exception: the biblical stress that violence is not rational but rather based on impulsive, irrational, and meaningless behavior.

Approach on the Displacement and Resettlement of the Southern Kingdom of Judah (BZAW 417; Berlin: de Gruyter, 2011).

7. Nathan MacDonald, *Not Bread Alone: The Uses of Food in the Old Testament* (Oxford: Oxford University Press, 2008).

Rüdiger Schmitt, in "Theories Regarding Witchcraft Accusations and the Hebrew Bible" (181–94), pays attention to the phenomenon of witchcraft accusation from a cross-cultural perspective. He concentrates on the ideas of Riekje Pelgrim and Peter Geschiere.[8] In his view such theories have some potential for understanding ancient Near Eastern materials. He is fully aware of the distinctiveness of each case. He considers texts such as Nah 3, Isa 47, and 2 Kgs 9 as presenting literary tales on witchcraft accusation. Ezekiel 13 is more reality-related. In this text the witch is to be seen as a representative of a rival faction. Am I old-fashioned when I observe the absence of the ideas of René Girard in this respect?[9]

David Wright's "Ritual Theory, Ritual Texts, and the Priestly-Holiness writings of the Pentateuch" (195–216) rounds off the volume with a learned essay on the interrelation between ritual theories and the descriptions of rituals in the P-H "source." His conclusion contains a disillusion: there is no formal fit between the two. He therefore invites biblical scholars to acts of creativity to bring them together in order to better understand the Priestly-Holiness material on ritual.

What is the harvest of this volume? That cannot be phrased in one sentence. As for future research, I would very much propose interdisciplinary projects. We as biblical scholars need to be aware of the limits of our knowledge and competences. Rather than going out on a blind date by picking at random theories, methods, and hypotheses from this adjacent field, we should tempt the social scientists at our institutions to cooperate. Nevertheless, the present volume is a real mind-opener and could be used as a valuable textbook in a postgraduate course on ritual, religion, and social sciences.

Levites and Priests in Biblical History and Tradition, edited by Mark Leuchter and Jeremy M. Hutton. Ancient Israel and Its Literature 9. Atlanta: Society of Biblical Literature, 2011. Pp. x + 257. Paper. $31.95. ISBN 1589836065.

Ralph K. Hawkins, Averett University, Danville, Virginia

This volume developed out of papers presented at the Annual Meetings of the Society of Biblical Literature in New Orleans (2009) and Atlanta (2010) in the program unit on "Priests and Levites in History and Tradition." This program

---

8. Peter Geschiere, *The Modernity of Witchcraft: Politics and the Occult in Postcolonial Africa* (Charlottesville: Univeristy Press of Virgina, 1976); Riekje Pelgrim, *Witchcraft and Policing: South Africa Police Service Attitudes towards Witchcraft and Witchcraft-Related Crime in the Northern Province* (African Studies Centre Research Report 72; Leiden: African Studies Centre, 2003).

9. See René Girard, *La violence et le sacré* (Paris: Grasset, 1972); idem, *Le bouc émissaire* (Paris: Grasset, 1982); William M. Swartley, ed., *Violence Renounced: Rene Girard, Biblical Studies and Peacemaking* (Telford: Pandora Press, 2000).

unit was, at the time, newly formed in order to address unresolved issues in the study of ancient Israel's priestly functionaries as they are presented in the Hebrew Bible. In an introduction (1–7), Mark Leuchter and Jeremy Hutton provide some background for the formation of the program unit and how it gave rise to the present volume.

Since the time of Wellhausen, the antiquity and authenticity of the textual sources concerned with priests and Levites have been the focus of meticulous analysis. Still, the editors note, even after a century of critical research, "many problems continue to stand in the way of our understanding of the diversity, function, origins, influence, and legacy of priests and Levites as depicted in the Hebrew Bible" (2). They review the manifold challenges involved in the study of priests and Levites, including the "presuppositions and related limitations in defining the very terms 'priest' and 'Levite'"; the idea of priests representing a common ancient Near Eastern social typology; and the fact that priestly function is evident in one form or another among individuals who appear to be lay figures. The editors summarize the problem thus:

> Religious life in ancient Israel was not simply left in the charge of priests—Levite, Aaronide, or otherwise—but was a far more textured and complicated phenomenon in which priests played an important but by no means exclusive role. Where, in this network of cultic interaction, may one situate a dedicated and priestly caste? How do the textual sources regarding the caste evidence awareness, acceptance, or repudiation of these features? (4)

Leuchter and Hutton finally note the ongoing issue of literacy and scribal authority and the role that Aaronide priests and Levites played in the production of Israel's literature. These and many other issues that remain unresolved led to the formation of the new program unit on Priests and Levites in History and Tradition, with a view to making a contribution to the study of these issues. The present volume contains a number of papers presented at sessions within this program unit, "with the aim of defining fruitful trajectories for further research" (5).

The volume is divided into three parts. Part 1, "Priests and Levites in Social Context," contains four chapters that study the historical and social aspects of religious specialists in ancient Israel. Ada Taggar-Cohen carries out a comparative study of biblical and Hittite priesthood (11–24). In addition to pointing out the functional and ideological parallels between the two, her essay significantly demonstrates that priesthood as an institution has ancient precedent in the Near East. Susan Ackerman examines the ritual dynamics of ancient Israel's sanctuaries with a view to answering the question "Who Is Sacrificing at Shiloh?" (25–43). She postulates that it was the common folk rather than the priests who were carrying out the sacrifices and suggests that women may have had an important role in such local ceremonies. Her argument hinges, in part, on silence, though it is cogently made and warrants further consideration. Jeremy Hutton conducts a review of the available scholarship on Levitical cities (45–81) and argues that, while scholars tend to focus on the textual study of Josh 21 and 1 Chr 6 as the "established lines of inquiry" for this subject, additional methodologies will need to be incorporated in the study of this topic, especially that of anthropology. Hutton points to an anthropological parallel in the Ahansal tribe of the Moroccan Atlas Mountains that suggests that lineages tend to settle precisely along tribal boundaries. This leads him to postulate that "it was the observed overlap between the historically remembered Levitical system and the tribal boundaries described in Josh 13–19 that occasioned the author's fleshing out of the list with cities from the boundary descriptions in a kind of 'pious fiction'" (81). In the final essay in this section, Sarah Shectman discusses the complex position of women descended from and married to priests and other members of the tribe of Levi (83–99). Based on her study of the Priestly legislation regarding marriage, mourning, and access to the tithe and sacred foods, she proposes that "women in priestly and Levitical families were subject to unique social standards and restrictions while also having rights of access to restricted people and foods" (98). She infers that these rules suggest "a high degree of social stratification" between women who belonged to various priestly, Levite, and lay groups in ancient Israelite society and suggests that "we can imagine, then, that the wife or the mother of a priest, and especially of a high priest, could have enjoyed a status well above that of other women and perhaps even of certain men" (99). Shectman's chapter will be of special interest to those with an interest in gender studies in the Old Testament.

Part 2 comprises four essays that examine "Priests and Levites in Scriptural Context." In this section's lead essay, Joel Baden uses traditional source-critical theories to study the early Levites. He examines four texts and argues that the common factor underlying all of them is "the violence of the Levites as a determining factor in their tribal and social status" (116). He concludes that violence was a "salient feature of the status of the Levites in Israelite society" (116). Cory Crawford compares and contrasts the literary memories of the Jerusalem temple and the wilderness tabernacle, with a view to elucidating the relationship between the two constructions. In the end, he suggests that the First Temple "came to constitute a visual testimony to earlier traditions, much the way the menorah and the bronze serpent housed the cultural memories of desert theophany and the wilderness wanderings" (133). Peter Altmann considers the similarities and differences between North American and European approaches to the study of priests and Levites, after which he turns to the textual analysis of a single text, Deut 18:1–8. He concludes that each "school" has special emphases and that each should be able to learn from the other in order to enhance scholarly study overall. Stephen Cook's essay epitomizes Altmann's "American approach," with its emphasis on social-scientific approaches to the study of the biblical text. He proposes that Deuteronomy "appears to have mounted a multipronged plan for overcoming Levitical disenfranchisement," which included "rotating country Levites into the capital to serve as interpreters of the covenant at the palace, to hear legal cases within appeals courts, and to serve as altar priests at the temple" (169). The purpose of such a plan was to temper monarchic power and guarantee justice and holiness throughout the land, particularly in the extensive rural area. Cook provides interesting correlations between Deuteronomy with Jeremiah and the Josianic reform.

In part 3, three papers consider "Priests and Levites in Exegetical Context." All three of these papers are concerned with how the Levitical and priestly traditions are appropriated in the Persian and Hellenistic periods. Mark Christian studies three passages—Neh 8; Lev 17–26; Deut 16:18–18:22—and makes the case that much of the pentateuchal material dealing with priests and Levites was actually formulated in the postexilic period with a focus on the concerns of a "new breed of citizen" that inhabits "a 'middle ground' between proletariat and elite, benefiting from at least rudimentary religious education" (195). Jeffrey Stackert examines the prerequisites for the Levites in select passages from Deuteronomy (especially Deut 18:1–8) and in their parallel passages in the Temple Scroll. He observes that the Temple Scroll makes several improvements to the Deuteronomic requirements that enhance the Levites' prestige. The final essay, by Mark Leuchter, provides some fascinating insights into cultural developments revealed in the book of Daniel, which portrays Israel's move away from engaging its religion through Levitical means (i.e., the temple) to scribal means. In the book of Daniel, the Levite gives way to the *maśkîl*. Leuchter explains that "it is not priests and Levites associated with the Jerusalem temple who secure divine blessing, but scribes who liberate Levitical modes of exegesis from cultic moorings and extend them to the masses" (230). This is a revolutionary development in which piety is sustained, sin and guilt are expiated, and the community is maintained through the exegesis of texts by sage-scribes, not by priests or Levites. Leuchter explores the fascinating implications of this change at some length.

In assessing the state of research into Levites and priests in biblical history and tradition, new paths of investigation are certainly needed. As new inroads are made into the study of archaeology, anthropology, sociology, the study of law, hermeneutics, literary criticism and other fields, these should all be brought to bear on the study of the sacerdotal culture of ancient Israel. Leuchter and Hutton summarize their expectations for the volume.

> In the end, it is our hope that this volume provides not only a representative look at the state of the field regarding the study of priests and Levites but also a point of departure for future research into the place of Israel's priestly caste within the miasma of ancient Near Eastern religion, the role that these figures played in their own socio-cultural universe, and the impact they had on subsequent authors and audiences. (7)

In my view, *Levites and Priests in Biblical History and Tradition* meets these expectations in that it brings together a series of essays that engage in conversation with disparate methods and new approaches. It includes multiple perspectives that will stimulate fresh thinking, and it includes extensive bibliographies for further research. I recommend this volume for Hebrew Bible scholars and graduate students interested in the sacerdotal culture of ancient Israel.

PENTATEUCH

Exodus and Deuteronomy, edited by Athalya Brenner and Gale A. Yee. Texts @ Contexts. Minneapolis: Fortress, 2012. Pp. xxxii + 351. Hardcover. $40.00. ISBN 9780800698942.

Susanne Scholz, Perkins School of Theology, Dallas, Texas

This volume is part of the Texts @ Contexts series that the general editors, Athalya Brenner for the Hebrew Bible and Nicole Wilkinson Duran for the New Testament, are in the process of publishing. Each general editor collaborates with discipline-specific co-editors. In the case of this volume, Brenner collaborates with Gale A. Yee, with whom she also co-edited the volume on Genesis and the volume on Joshua and Judges. The general editors explain in the series preface that each book is organized by clusters of contexts, issues, and themes as they emerge from the contributions. Central are the contexts because, so the series editors, "no one is native to the biblical text, no one reads only in the interests of the text itself" (viii). Everyone, and this includes "the Euro-American male voice," is a reader, and hence Brenner and Duran demand that "we must acknowledge that our own voice's particular pitch and timbre and inflection affect the meaning that emerges" (ix).

In light of these convictions, Brenner and Yee asked contributors to foreground their contexts when they interpreted the selected biblical text from Exodus and Deuteronomy, to dialogue with "'classical' informed biblical scholarship" (xi), and to assess the value of the contextualized interpretations for the specified contexts. Nineteen chapters introduce a wide spectrum of contexts, themes, and issues that selectively illustrate how exegesis benefits from serious engagement with geographical, religious, racial, postcolonial, gendered, and ecological contexts. The result is a lively potpourri of perspectives and positions held together by the biblical texts under consideration.

Following Brenner's introduction, the book is divided into three sections. The first part of the book, "Between Egypt and Canaan: To's and Fro's," focuses on the interpreters' geographical-ethnic contexts; with nine contributions, it is the longest section. Cheryl A. Kirk-Duggan presents a literary-cultural exploration of what the Exodus themes of slavery and liberation mean from her womanist perspective. Athalya Brenner, grounded in her personal-professional experience of leading a bi-local life in the Netherlands and Israel, explores the significance of exile and diaspora in the biblical imagination of identity formation. Roland Boer ruminates on the fact that the exodus motif was absent in early Australian settler stories. Magdi S. Gendi reads the story about Pharaoh in Exod 1–2 from his Christian Egyptian context, highlighting how narrative and readers sympathize against the imperial leader. David Tuesday Adamo is intrigued by the "mixed multitude" escaping from Egyptian oppression according to Exod 12:38 and proposes that the Israelites were really African-Israelites and ancient Israel a "melting pot of people from different places" (78). In light of the contemporary

Scandinavian debate on the human rights of children, Mikael Larsson investigates
how children are regarded as subjects of vision, speech, and action in the book of
Exodus. In a personal-biographical essay, Diana Lipton explains why in her view
the book of Exodus is "a document of resistance to an internal threat instead of
the record of liberation from an external one" (95). Solomon Olusola Ademiluka
reflects on the possibilities for an African Christian appreciation of the Passover
report in Exod 12, suggesting that, just as the Jewish Passover holiday bound Jews
together historically and culturally, so African annual festivals should be celebrated by African Christians in honor of their historical and cultural identity.
Finally, Matthew J. M. Coomber recounts the flexible use of the exodus narrative
in the African American abolitionist, pre–civil rights, and civil rights movements.

The second part of the book, "Leadership: Moses and Miriam," features four
essays on the two central characters in the exodus tales. Sonia Kwok Wong corre-
lates Exod 2:1–4:18 with the "post-handover" setting of Hong Kong since 1997 to
interrogate the idea of Moses' "primordial identity" (140) and the fiction of ethnic
and cultural authenticity advanced in readings of biblical texts. Naomi Graetz
recounts her work on Miriam in a personal-autobiographical essay that includes
important references to rabbinic midrashim and meta-reflections on her midrash
about this important female figure. Angelina M. G. Song presents a Singaporean
autobiographical-literary reading of Moses and Miriam through a "hermeneutics
of empathy" (170), especially in regard to Exod 2:1–22, as this passage chronicles
the characters' beginnings. Joseph Ryan Kelly focuses on the ecological crises of
our time and relates it to Deut 18 and other biblical passages, wondering how contemporary society ought to navigate "between conflicting oracles of well-being
and doom" (186) and offering repentance as a possible attitude for all of humanity.

The third part of the book, "Law," features six contributions that center on
various legislative sections in Exodus and Deuteronomy. Athalya Brenner's reflection on the gender-exclusive language of the Decalogue in Exod 20 and Deut 5
exposes androcentric and sexist practices in interpretation and translation to this
very day. Fernando Candido da Silva proposes a reading of Deuteronomy that
includes "queer subjects" in the Latin American hermeneutical agenda (212).
Sandra Jacobs examines Deut 21:10–14, the law on the "female captive," as an
example of biblical traditions that stand in contrast to rabbinic Judaism, "if not
also the ethical paradigms embedded in the Hebrew Bible itself" (239). Cheryl
Kirk-Duggan traces the internationally widespread crimes of domestic and sexual
violence in Deuteronomic legislation, such as Deut 21:10–14; 21:18–21; 22:13–29;
25:5–10, from a womanist hermeneutics, inviting us "to reread Deuteronomy
with victims and perpetrators of domestic violence, to note how they hear and
what we can newly discover" (288). Kari Latvus contextualizes his analysis of the
central debt texts in Exod 22:24–26; Deut 15:1–11; and Lev 25:1–12.35–55 within
Finnish law about indebted persons. Presented as an interview, the conversation
between Mende Nazer and Bernadette Brooten about the ongoing practice of
slavery makes clear that scholars have "to find solutions to these texts' toleration
of slavery" (316) and "to find ways to stop slavery and to overcome its legacy"

(317) because "[s]lavery is not moral, ever" (316). A bibliography and indexes on authors, scripture, and ancient nonbiblical sources conclude the volume.

This is an important book and series. We need many more such volumes, perhaps not only organized by biblical books but also by contexts, topics, and issues so that the various readings can be systematized, compared, and contrasted. What we are getting in this book is pure enjoyment in multiperspectival interpretations from diverse contexts producing ever-changing and ever-expansive meanings of biblical texts. This and the other books of the series present collections of interpretations held together by the selected biblical books. The focus on the biblical books is helpful and necessary, but we also must have coherent and systematic analyses of contextualized meanings to gain depth and understanding in the ethics and politics of contextualized readings. In light of the considerable corporate-institutional pressures put on biblical, theological-religious, and liberal arts education, such analyses are urgently needed. Perhaps contextualized biblical interpretations will succeed in convincing corporate-educational powers that the field of biblical studies is not an academic discipline of luxury. In any case, I join the editors in the conviction that contextualized approaches enrich our appreciation of biblical meanings and the wide range of the Bible's history of interpretation. The volume demonstrates that biblical readings are always polyphonic and coming from somewhere, producing countless and often utterly unexpected biblical meanings. Yet the open question remains how to evaluate, assess, and talk about the ethics and politics implied in contextualized interpretations that sometimes challenge and sometimes endorse the exegetical, theological, or societal status quo.

The Birth, the Curse and the Greening of Earth: An Ecological Reading of Genesis 1–11, by Norman Habel. Earth Bible Commentary 1. Sheffield: Sheffield Phoenix, 2011. Pp. xii + 140. Hardcover. $80.00. ISBN 9781907534195.

Terence E. Fretheim, Luther Seminary, St. Paul, Minnesota

For many years Norman Habel has been associated with issues of ecojustice, including detailed biblical exegesis, ethical-theological reflection, the Earth Bible Project, and the production of liturgical resources. This commentary on Gen 1–11 is designed for the reader who is interested in the problems and possibilities that this text presents regarding issues of ecojustice: "if we read Genesis employing an ecological hermeneutics, we discover new dimensions of meaning" (ix). This volume stands in the tradition of Habel's earlier work on these issues, including: *An Inconvenient Text: Is a Green Reading of the Bible Possible?* (Adelaide: ATF Press, 2009).

This volume is the first in the Earth Bible Commentary series, which is an extension of the multivolume The Earth Bible series published in 2000–2002. Earth is understood to be the central character of Gen 1–11, and it is primarily from Earth's point of view that Habel moves through this story. Habel defines

Earth as "the total ecosystem, the web of life, the domain of nature with which we are familiar, of which we are an integral part and in which we face the future" (3).

The opening chapter is a general introduction to this series and articulates key principles associated with recent ecological hermeneutics (1–16). At the same time, Habel seeks

> to move beyond a focus on ecological themes to a process of listening to, and identifying with, Earth as a presence or voice in the text. Our task is to take up the cause of Earth and the non-human members of the Earth community by sensing their presence in the text—whether their presence is suppressed, oppressed or celebrated. We seek to move beyond identifying ecological themes in creation theology to identifying with Earth in its ecojustice struggles (2).

Habel understands that such a "radical ecological approach to the text involves a basic hermeneutic of suspicion, identification and retrieval" (8). Regarding suspicion, "the text is likely to be inherently anthropocentric and/or has traditionally been read from an anthropocentric perspective" (8). Regarding identification, "our aim is to read in solidarity with Earth. We are Earth beings reading in empathy with Earth. … The most obvious dimension of this step is to identify with non-human figures in the narrative, empathizing with their roles, characters and treatment, and discerning their voices" (11). Regarding retrieval, "The task before us is to re-read the text to discern where Earth or members of the Earth community may have suffered, resisted or been excluded by attitudes within the text or in the history of its interpretation. … The aim is to read as Earth beings in tune with Earth, the very source of our being" (13). Generally, "Special attention will be paid to how the natural world is depicted and whether subjects from that world emerge as components that deserve special consideration in terms of the habitat reflected in the textual world" (18).

At the same time, Habel makes clear that "the task before us is not an exploration of what a given text may say *about* creation, *about* nature, or *about* Earth. In this context, Earth is not a *topos* or theme for analysis. We are not focusing on ecology *and* creation, or ecology *and* theology. … An ecological hermeneutic demands a radical change of posture both in relation to Earth as a subject in the text and also our relation to Earth as readers" (3, emphasis original).

To that end, each of the eight major sections of Gen 1–11 that Habel identifies are (usually) approached in terms of (1) Design; (2) Analysis; and (3) Retrieval. While he specifically distinguishes his approach from traditional source and form-critical analysis, his discussions of textual design and his identification of layers in the text, even sharply disagreeing layers, echo such approaches. What he calls the *Erets* myth and the *Adamah* myth bear a strong resemblance to major portions of the traditional Priestly and Yahwistic sources. Moreover, these sources are discussed in terms of "origin myth" and "catastrophe myth," with the understanding that the "recognized laws of nature and relationships do not necessarily apply in the primordial" (19). The interpreter's "task is to free these myths from their anthropocentric literary framework, and discern their intention as origin or catastrophic myths" (22).

Habel's sharpest exception to traditional source analysis is his separating out of the image of God texts (Gen 1:26–28; 5:1–2; 9:1–7) into a third basic source, which he calls the *Tselem* myth. Besides these three myths, the genealogies are identified as a "framework," giving shape to an anthropocentric orientation, while "fragments" such as Gen 6:1–4; 9:20–27; and 11:1–9 are included among "a handful of transitional legends" (21).

Special attention should be given to Habel's assessment of the *Tselem* myth, which is understood to stand in sharp contrast to the content of the other two myths, especially with its anthropocentric emphasis. Habel considers the text of the creation of *'adam* to be a "deviation or rupture" within Gen 1:1–2:4a, interrupting the focus on the nonhuman world. Two quotations suggest his perspective. Genesis 1:26–28 is "a violation of the role of the central character of the story. Earth is no longer a partner; Earth is an object of subjugation. Living creatures are no longer the celebrated progeny of Earth, but creatures to be dominated by humans" (26). In a "Retrieval" section, Habel represents the voice of *Erets* speaking as follows: "these image creatures were given a mandate from Elohim to 'subdue' me as if I were a wild beast, an enemy, or a violent force to be controlled. By so doing Elohim discarded me as a partner and handed me over for humans to abuse" (45).

Habel makes no special effort to understand the Genesis text in its present form or to offer the perspective of the final redactor (though the genealogies give signs of that with their anthropocentric perspective). Highlighting the tensions among the various myths is a more basic concern. For example, Gen 2:15 and 1:26–28 are "diametric opposites." The latter's "mandate to dominate incorporates verbs that are ecologically destructive, while the verbs in 2:15 are ecologically positive; the two traditions are mutually exclusive" (53). One wonders what interpretation might have emerged if questions like the following had been asked: What voice, and what status, does the work of the final redactor have? Or, more specifically, how would the final redactor have understood the place of Gen 1:26–28 within Gen 1–2?

The language Habel uses to speak of Gen 1:26–28 seems to this reader to be insufficiently grounded and studies of this text that would cut against the language of "domination" insufficiently considered. For example, *kabash* is used in Gen 1:28 in a pre-sin context. Does that affect our interpretation of its meaning compared to later usage? From another angle, one thinks of destructive actions by nature itself (earthquakes, volcanoes, etc.). The world that God created included natural disasters, integral to the world's becoming. Also, the high levels of violence among living nonhuman creatures in God's good but not perfect *prehuman* (and hence pre-sin) creation could be more recognized. Earth has forever lived with the effects of a divine decision to create such a messy world—in the interests of maximal creativity. As such, positively, the natural order is a major participant in the becoming of the world (adding to Habel's point about Earth's creativity). Why would not the word "subdue" be appropriate for relating to such a violent, creative natural order, indeed, finally, be in the best interests of Earth?

Built into the God-created orders of Earth, much potential exists for suffering and damage (human sin intensifies that potential). Do we know whether other creational options for God would have been better for Earth? One might wish for more recognition that Earth, created by God, is a *dangerous* place for human and nonhuman creatures alike. One thinks of water or the law of gravity. That creation also includes floods, though not at the depth and breadth of the flood depicted in Gen 1–11. More attention could have been given to this intensified flood as a morally grounded disaster, understanding its severity in terms of the consequences of sin that are *intrinsic* to the deed (Gen 6:11–13).

God cannot be let off the hook, for such effects are a manifestation of the natural moral order that God established for Earth. Moreover, God certainly mediates the judgment, using agents, agents who are not controlled by God. At the same time, is the oft-used language of "punishment" ever appropriate with God as the subject?[1] Habel repeatedly makes reference to the flood as a divine "overreaction," indeed an "unjustified divine overreaction" (83–85). At the same time, "the flood is a failure" (104), in view of which God makes changes, including the reversal of the curse and the greening of the earth (8:21–22). Regarding another judgment text (Gen 3:14–19), Habel speaks of "the cruelty of God's punishment" (61). He claims that "the enlightenment of humans is translated by God into the devaluation of nature" (62). At the same time, interestingly, Gen 3:19 is not a part of the curse, "but a homecoming." *Adamah* welcomes human beings "into her arms in death" (62).

Among many details worth pondering, Earth is a "co-agent with God" and "God's partner in the creation of all life on Earth" (51). Or, in view of Gen 2:1–3, "God is in, with, and under time as God is in, with, and under the rest of creation" (42). Or, a positive view of the snake is presented: "To declare the snake devious in any way is to devalue one of the children of *Adamah*.... The snake does not lie" (57–58). Such provocative comments are manifold.

In conclusion, I am pleased with the way Habel addresses many issues. He exhibits an honesty that is refreshing, showing that the biblical texts are more troubling ecologically than commonly recognized. He addresses ethical-theological issues directly, and his work will generate valuable conversations across disciplines. Whatever one might think of the earth-orientation of Habel's commentary, his work brings an important issue before readers and will occasion many a reflection from an angle of vision different from the usual approach. This volume is imaginative both in its proposal and in its expression.

---

1. See, e.g., Gerhard von Rad, *Old Testament Theology* (trans. D. M. G. Stalker; New York: Harper & Row, 1962), 1:385, for a contrary claim.

The Fantastic in Religious Narrative from Exodus to Elisha, by Laura Feldt. BibleWorld. Sheffield: Equinox, 2012. Pp. viii + 293. Cloth. $99.95. ISBN 9781845539429.

Michael B. Hundley, Princeton, New Jersey

In a field where it is becoming increasingly difficult to say something new, Laura Feldt's *The Fantastic in Religious Narrative from Exodus to Elisha* offers the reader a truly novel interpretation of religious narratives in the Hebrew Bible. Despite the proliferation of fantastic events, few biblical interpreters have interacted with fantasy theory. Feldt steps into the breach and applies the insights of fantasy theory to the exodus and select national epic narratives.

In a brief introduction (1–9), Feldt outlines her task. Rather than turn to the text's compositeness as an interpretive lens and as a window into ancient religious practice, she adopts a synchronic approach in order "to better understand religious narrative as a medium" (5). While others have marginalized the fantastic elements and stressed the unifying, orienting, and laudatory nature of religious narrative, Feldt highlights the centrality of the fantastic, particularly in the exodus narrative, and its tendency to generate "ambiguity, indeterminacy and uncertainty" (3), which leads to disorientation and confusion and offers the opportunity for reflection and transformation.

Chapter 1 (10–42) follows with an analysis of previous assessments of the relationship between religion and fantasy and a survey of common approaches to the exodus's fantastic elements among biblical scholars. The field of fantasy and religion can be subdivided into two primary strands: religion in fantasy and fantasy in religion. Feldt's work clearly falls into and finds its precedent in the second category. Turning to the fantastic in Exodus, she notes four interpretive trends: scholars tend to view the fantastic as premodern interpretations of natural phenomena; accept the fantastic as signs of supernatural intervention; avoid the question of the nature of the fantastic by appealing to ancient Near Eastern and folkloric parallels; and apportion them to different literary sources and strands that diminish their literary effect.

Chapter 2 (43–76) offers Feldt's methodology. It begins with an introduction of fantasy theory and argues for a broad, mode-based approach that builds on the work of Renate Lachmann (*Erzählte Phantastik: Zu Phantasiegeschichte und Semantik phantastischer Texte*). For Feldt, fantasy is an element that "may form part of any kind of literature and be articulated in historically variable ways" (46). As such, rather than characterizing the exodus as fantasy literature, she chooses to apply the insights of fantasy theory to the fantastic elements in the religious narrative of Exodus. Such an approach addresses not the veracity of the fantastic but rather the literary strategies employed in expressing it, thereby rendering it appropriate for religious narrative. Since the fantastic may be identified as an element that "does not exist or occur in 'normal' experience" (50), Feldt notes the need for "distinguishing the fantastic from the possible, the everyday, the normal and the natural, of which it represents a violation" (53). Building on advances in the cognitive sciences, she contends that humans, even members of ancient societies, share affective responses to their world and can identify the counterintuitive, the elements in their world that defy expectations of how the world should work. Feldt then offers her "strategy of analysis" (57), which emerges more fully and clearly in her analysis itself. The chapter concludes with a discussion of the interpretive complexities of reading the Hebrew Bible.

Chapter 3 (77–132) offers an analysis of the fantastic in Exod 1–18 through a select sequential, close reading of the text through the lens of fantasy theory with a view toward identifying how fantastic strategies function, how the fantastic effect is elicited, which fantastic elements are verbalized, and how they relate to alterity and identity construction.

Chapter 4 (133–55) investigates the cumulative effect of the fantastic in Exod 1–18. Feldt subdivides her analysis into five fantastic strategies (briefly identified on 59–62). Metamorphosis refers to violations of the normal that the text presents as "disturbances of order, inversions of existing assumptions about phenomena" (133). Category metamorphoses refer to the change of basic ontological categories (e.g., a staff to a snake), while kind metamorphoses refer to the change from one state to another (e.g., bitter to fresh water). Adynata both violate "universal, intuitive cognitive categories" and are represented as "strange or inexplicable" (135). For example, a bush burns without being consumed, and a voice speaks from within the bush. Adynata fall into three categories: alimentary, "the systematic inversion of what constitutes ordinary food" (e.g., manna) (136); atmospheric/natural, the transfer of expectations from one category to another (e.g., clouds and fire that guide like people and form columns like objects); the anthropological/personal, involving the violation of expectations of the category of person (e.g., YHWH and the destroyer killing so many people in such a short time). Hyperbole refers to the element of exaggeration that cumulatively points beyond the improbable to the impossible (e.g., the Israelites' extreme fertility). Coincidence refers to events that may be either identified as happenstance or as the product of divine intervention (e.g., Pharaoh's daughter finding baby Moses). In Feldt's analysis, paradox refers mostly to textual inconsistencies and contradictions (e.g., Pharaoh pursues the Israelites on horses when they have presumably been killed in the plague). Feldt contends that "by means of these elements, the narrative points self-reflectively toward its own artifice" (140). Rather than exclusively expressing belief and offering praise, the people also respond to the fantastic with "hesitation, doubt, disbelief and suspicion" (142) and find themselves "in a pendulous motion between belief and disbelief" (143). This human equivocation clashes with the perspective presented by the narrator and the deity himself as well as the explicit purposes of the fantastic, which promote belief and the formation of Israelite identity, such that YHWH's phantasms fail to ultimately achieve their purpose. Instead of simply producing belief, the fantastic elements serve as points of mediation between Israel and YHWH (and Israel and Egypt) and repeatedly transgress the boundaries of the known and the familiar, producing reactions that are both positive and negative. Israel then, Feldt argues, is "suspended between what it is and what it ought to be" (151), as an as-yet-unrealized ideal. She concludes that the fantastic strategies are central, and their cumulative effect emphasizes mutability, ambiguity, and uncertainty and indicates that the exodus narrative is a time of reflection and transformation.

Chapter 5 (156–78) addresses how the fantastic contributes to memory formation and what sorts of memory are promoted. Feldt suggests that, since none of the eyewitnesses enter the promised land, "the memory of the founding events must be transformed from a biographical to a cultural memory" (159). The majority of the mnemonic techniques are linked with the Passover ritual, which provides the link between memory and the fantastic events. Those who participate in the ritual serve as vicarious eyewitnesses and, when presented with the narrator's interpretation, possess and transmit the authoritative interpretation. Feldt argues that, while at first blush the divine purposes fail, as the people's direct experience leads to doubt and disorientation, narration looks to the future, providing distance and promoting belief. Thus, she suggests that "the fantastic strategies are used to create an origin, which may alter the future" (167).

In chapter 6 (179–234) Feldt extends her analysis to other the narratives in the national epic (Num 11–4; Judg 6–9; 1 Kgs 17–9; 2 Kgs 4–7), in much the same fashion as she addressed the exodus in chapters 3–5. Ambiguity and uncertainty remain as demonstrated by the discrepancy between YHWH's fantastic deeds and Israel's continuing lack of trust, yet the setting of the fantastic changes, turning to the issue of divine presence in everyday life. In the national epic, "the context of the fantastic event changes from the collective, ethnic scene to the private or individual, from large to small scale, from international to local, from ethnogenesis to everyday life" (217). In addition, Feldt notes that, while Exodus focused on divine instigation and control, the other narratives in the national epic focus much more "on human cooperation and reciprocity, and on the relationship between fantastic event and everyday life" (217). The fantastic elements are embedded in "process stories and ambiguity and uncertainty are irreducible parts of them" (224).

Chapter 7 (235–58) concludes the study by addressing more generally the potential contribution of fantasy theory to the study of religious narrative. Feldt argues that "in the foregrounding of a fantastic effect (mutability, ambiguity and uncertainty), the Hebrew Bible religious narratives remain relatively 'open' to multiple, variant interpretations and uses" (235). "Israel ends up poised between what it is and what it ought to be, and the identity of Israel comes to consist not primarily in a difference from others, from Egypt, but in this internal tension between is and ought" (236). The fantastic elements fail to achieve their stated purpose of inducing belief and thus do not solely exist to celebrate the divine power. Instead, they function as "mediating points between YHWH and Israel, heaven and earth, points of dynamic exchange" (237). She concludes by suggesting that the fantasy-theoretical perspective can be profitably applied to other religious narratives.

Feldt is to be commended for applying fantasy theory to the interpretation of narratives in the Hebrew Bible and for offering various new insights that take scholarship in fruitful new directions. The reader will benefit from her close and

insightful reading of the passages under investigation, and especially her syntheses. She rightly stresses the centrality of the fantastic in theophanic narratives and
the uncertainty that comes with a collision of worlds, an irruption of the divine
into normal human life. She offers various other promising observations, such as
the disconnect between the stated purpose of the phantasms and the reaction of
the characters, the role of the fantastic as a point of mediation, and the use of the
fantastic as a site of reflection, transformation, cultural memory formation, and
an appeal to the future to become Israel, the as-yet unrealized ideal.

As with any groundbreaking work, Feldt's analysis is not without limitations.
Rather than mention all of my quibbles, I will note a few before turning to avenues
for future exploration. Feldt at times tries too hard to convince the reader of the
novelty and usefulness of her approach. Her analysis breaks new ground in several
places and in several ways. However, rather than further delving into the complexities of the texts and the implications of these complexities, her analysis often
stops short to reiterate the importance and uniqueness of her approach. Like most
scholars, she is also occasionally too beholden to her approach, following it and
reading the data through that lens rather than following the text where it leads. In
addition, her assertion that "the narrative points self-reflectively toward its own
artifice" (140 and passim) is questionable. Thanks to modern biblical criticism,
scholars are trained to note the inconsistencies in the text. However, biblical criticism is a modern phenomenon, and many educated readers continue to read the
stories without being distracted by the textual "artifice." Thus, rather than consciously flouting its own artifice, the inconsistencies are a byproduct of the text's
compositeness, one that ancient and many modern readers overlook as they are
caught up in the story itself.

As an initial foray into fantasy-theoretical analysis there is also much more
ground to be covered. While Feldt is right to notice the uncertainty generated
by phantasms, scholars would be well-served to further examine what about the
phantasms promotes uncertainty, why and for whom. For example, the characters in the fantastic episodes rarely express doubt that YHWH is the source of
the phantasms. Rather, they doubt whether the deity can be trusted, whether
following him even with all the phantasms is profitable, whether becoming the
Israel that he and the narrator urge will be profitable for them. In addition, the
authoritative statements of the narrator and deity are also selective in what they
assert. They ascribe the fantastic to the deity, promote trust in him, and champion
national transformation. However, they rarely attempt to explain the phantasms
themselves (e.g., how a bush burns without being consumed or the precise relationship between YHWH and his angels). In other words, while the deity and
his fantastic intervention must remain mysterious as humans bump against their
perceptual and imaginative limits, the divine message (and that of the narrator)
remains clear.

Scholars may further examine the differing role of the fantastic (and memory)
in origin stories and all other types of narratives, including the national epic.
Scholars may also benefit from attending more to the text's rhetoric. For example,

precisely because they break from normal human experience, such phantasms are hard to believe in the past, harder still to see as plausible in the present. Recognizing this, the exodus text preempts readers' doubts. The eyewitnesses respond inappropriately with doubt and fleeting trust, which the narrator and deity are quick to authoritatively indicate. Rather than doubt the fantastic itself, the people doubt YHWH. The people's response thereby reinforces the veracity of the fantastic, while urging the audience to remember these "true" events that they did not experience and respond to them with trust. The people's doubt in the story also helps to explain the audience's present condition and offers a tantalizing future possibility. Because of the failure of their ancestors, they are neither experiencing the promised benefits nor the fantastic. However, the text suggests that if YHWH persistently interceded for disobedient Israel, how much more will he intercede for an obedient Israel.

All in all, Feldt's book is to be highly recommended both as a source of insights and as an impetus for exciting new research.

Interpreting Deuteronomy: Issues and Approaches, edited by David G. Firth and Philip S. Johnston. Downers Grove, Ill.: InterVarsity Press, 2012. Pp. 280. Paper. $28.00. ISBN 9780830839896.

Nathan MacDonald, St. John's College, University of Cambridge, Cambridge, United Kingdom

Interpreting Deuteronomy, the third volume to originate from the Tyndale Old Testament Study Group, follows the format of the earlier volumes on Isaiah (2009) and Psalms (2005). It collects about a dozen papers that were given at an annual Tyndale Conference. The essays assume more than a basic knowledge of the Old Testament and are written mostly for more advanced undergraduate students or for ministers who wish to keep up on Old Testament scholarship. With such an audience in view, the essays seek both to broker more advanced scholarship to this audience and to contribute to scholarship on Deuteronomy. The essays in the volume have been divided into three groups. The first section has essays that provide an overview of recent scholarship. The essays in the second section discuss particular themes within Deuteronomy. The third section is concerned with the contemporary relevance of Deuteronomy. Most of the essays are about twenty pages each, but the review essays are considerably longer.

James Robson's opening essay, "The Literary Composition of Deuteronomy," is the longest in the book and mostly concerned with the date of composition. Robson considers explicit and implicit testimony about authorship from within Deuteronomy, testimony from elsewhere in the Old Testament, and evidence from the ancient Near East. Intellectually the essay is rather unsatisfactory, since Robson is frequently evasive under the guise of balancing arguments. Additionally, he frequently disavows leading his readers to careful historical judgments himself and places the responsibility upon his readers. Thus, he concludes one part of his discussion with the assertion that "interpreting these statements historically is essential" (33), though this commendable sentiment should really open and guide the analysis. On the other hand, when Robson tries to make more definitive statements, his prose can become rather torturous. Thus, he concludes that, "evidence of material from a later date sits less comfortably with an overall early dating than vice versa" (57). Simply stated, Robson thinks the present form of the text is late, but Deuteronomy has Mosaic origins. A plausible account for how the book might have been transmitted if this is the case is never offered.

Some aspects of Robson's discussion of Deuteronomy are rather surprising. The statement that "many scholars regard all, or almost all, of Deuteronomy 5–26 as from the same hand" (31; but cf. 42!) is not how I would characterize recent literature on the book. Nor is it evident to me that Deuteronomy has significant links with creation theologies (33–34). The book of Deuteronomy famously mentions creation only once, somewhat *en passant*, in Deut 4:32. But perhaps the most puzzling feature of Robson's essay is the absence of a discussion of centralization, since this has been viewed as one of the most important indicators of the book's date (relative to other biblical texts and absolutely). The issue is mentioned in passing, but its significance is not perceived (36–37). Possibly Robson passed over it because of Vogt's essay on the subject later in the volume, though the omission still seems rather odd.

Paul Barker surveys theological interpretation of Deuteronomy since 1995 in his essay, "Contemporary Theological Interpretation of Deuteronomy." He tackles a number of subjects, each of which gets between two and seven pages: mission, election, war (*herem*), politics, community, monotheism, name theology, and grace. Reading Barker's essay, I was struck by how many of the theological interpreters he cited had some association with the United Kingdom: McConville, Moberly, Goldingay, Wright. Perhaps this reveals how restricted the interest in Deuteronomy's theology has become in recent years, but it does overlook contributions by Brueggemann, Miller, Chapman, and Levinson. More importantly, German contributions are noticeably absent, as are the theological and ethical issues raised by feminist or liberationist readings.

Barker's survey is a form of advocacy rather than an even-handed account of different positions. The primacy he gives to C. J. H. Wright's emphasis on mission is unlikely to convince many (though many of the other essayists in the volume seem persuaded by it!). This rather too easily reads Deuteronomy in light of a particular interpretation of Gen 12:3 and a certain "metanarrative" that supposedly derives from the Bible's primary history. As a result of this missiological hermeneutic, H. H. Rowley's "election for service" makes an unexpected comeback (66).

John Walton's "The Decalogue Structure of the Deuteronomic Law" returns to that hoary chestnut of whether the Ten Commandments have provided the structure of Deut 11–25. This is a personal return: Walton studied with Kaufman, who propounded the idea in an early fascicle of *MAARAV* in 1978–1979, and Walton offered his own variation a decade later in *Grace Theological Journal*. Walton seeks to bolster his earlier convictions by appeal to Near Eastern law and speech-act theory. Both help the interpreter identify connections between the Ten Commandments and the specific laws in the following law code.

Despite Walton's best efforts, so much of the similarity seems to be in the eye of the beholder and at points leads to an unhelpful flattening of the biblical text. Two examples of the latter problem will suffice. First, the attempt to see Deut 14:22–16:17 as an exposition of the Sabbath commandment only works by reading Deuteronomy in light of the festival and tithing legislation of the Holiness Code. In the Holiness Code, the Sabbath principle becomes a *Leitmotif* that it never is in Deuteronomy. As a form of pentateuchal harmonization, this is perhaps tempting, but it encounters numerous historical-critical problems. Second, Walton compares the Deuteronomic lawcode with the Exodus version of the Decalogue, whose division of the commandments differs from the Deuteronomy version. In particular, this would require Walton to identify two different sorts of laws at the end of the Deuteronomic lawcode concerning with coveting. Walton is not unaware of some of the difficulties with his proposal. He highlights those passages that he has not been able to integrate into his schema: Deut 14:1–21; 16:1–17; 21:10–22:12; and 23:1–18. This circumspection is commendable.

Peter Vogt tackles the issue of centralization in "Centralization and Decentralization in Deuteronomy." He helpfully questions whether the restriction of sacrificial worship to the chosen place should be understood as "secularization." This point was already pressed by Milgrom in an incisive article on Weinfeld's *Deuteronomy and the Deuteronomic School*. We find a particular concern with the virulent pollution caused by shed blood in Deuteronomy, and the pouring out of animal blood reflects that worldview. Secularization fails to capture this perspective. But I am not convinced by Vogt's claim that the slaughtering of animals away from the altar should be regarded as "worship." What Vogt has in mind seems much closer to Paul in Rom 12 than anything that would make sense centuries earlier in the world of ancient Israel.

Philip Johnston's "Civil Leadership in Deuteronomy" considers the laws concerning public offices in 16:18–18:22, as well as other references to civil leadership in the Deuteronomic law and in the framework (e.g., 1:9–18). Johnston excludes religious leadership from his analysis. In some texts a civil-religious distinction can be made, but this distinction is not as clinical as one would like. After all, the difficult cases are taken to Levitical priests and the judge, according to Deut 17:9. Similarly, the unsolved murder requires the actions of elders and priests. Johnston concludes his essay with historical-critical reflections. He critiques the idea that Deuteronomy reflects a reform of the judiciary by Jehoshaphat or Josiah. Instead, he proposes that the Deuteronomic law preserves ancient material only lightly modified in later periods. He attempts to draw parallels with some texts from Judges and 1 Samuel. Johnston's application of historical criticism is rather unevenly applied: the incisive critiques for a reform under Jehoshaphat or Josiah are not paralleled in the discussion of his own proposal.

David Firth's "Passing on the Faith in Deuteronomy" demonstrates how central the issues of teaching and passing on the law are in every part of the book of

Deuteronomy. Moses himself is presented as a model teacher of Torah, and the Israelites are commanded to pass on the Deuteronomic law to their children in a similar way. What animates Firth's essay is K. Noll's assertion that "Deuteronomy's meagre provisions for public dissemination are predestined to fail." For Firth, this focuses too narrowly on the public reading of Torah at the Feast of Tabernacles. Instead, "Deuteronomy employs a variety of strategies to ensure that the faith is passed on" (175). I am not sure that Noll would disagree. His point seems to be that for an earlier period the audience of Deuteronomy was limited to the elites, and it was only in the Hellenistic period that we have a communal program of catechesis that included everyone. Firth's careful discussion of Deuteronomy's theology of learning does not really touch upon these sociohistorical issues. Overall, then, this is a careful, if unadventurous, synchronic reading of Deuteronomy. It might have been even more incisive if use had been made of Karin Finsterbusch's *Weisung für Israel: Studien zu religiösem Lehren und Lernen im Deuteronomium und in seinem Umfeld*, which unfortunately has been overlooked.

Heath Thomas's "Life and Death in Deuteronomy" is also a synchronic investigation of a theological theme. "He will be your life" (Deut 30:20) provides Thomas's launch point for an account of how Deuteronomy presents Yhwh as the sovereign lord who brings life to those who obey him. As with so many other essays in this volume, Thomas rather too quickly moves to harmonize Deuteronomy with Gen 1–11, though this does allow him to show the integral connection between life and land. Thomas's exposition of his theme brings him back round to Deut 30 as a climax to the book, forcing the hearer of the book to the place of decision. But there is death as much as life in Deuteronomy, Thomas reminds us. In particular, Moses's impending death hovers over the book and provides a visible reminder of the perils of disobedience. Mostly Thomas concentrates on the framework, and it is interesting to speculate how his analysis would change if life and death in the lawcode were incorporated.

Csilla Saysell concentrates on one of the earliest applications of the book of Deuteronomy in "Deuteronomy in the Intermarriage Crises in Ezra-Nehemiah." Already there is a distance between the book and the circumstances of the returning exiles that requires some interpretation. Saysell shows how Ezra 9 draws on both Deut 7 and 23, while also going beyond them. Though neither text handles how to deal with marriages that have been contracted, the exiles are portrayed as obedient to Torah. Saysell shows how *herem* has been reinterpreted with hints from the Torah to mean the confiscation of property. Saysell also gives some attention to Neh 13, although her discussion of this passage is rather briefer. In Nehemiah, divorce does not seem to be in view. Overall, Saysell provides a useful reading of Ezra-Nehemiah attentive to the phenomena of inner-biblical interpretation. She suggests reading Ezra-Nehemiah as having no single view on intermarriage and attributes to it a more open-ended perspective than usually the case.

Greg Goswell's essay is entitled "The Paratext of Deuteronomy." By *paratext* Goswell means the various features that accompany the text and influence the reading of the text: the placement adjacent to other books; the name of the book;

its internal divisions. Goswell describes how these differ between the various reading traditions and some of the difference it makes for the understanding of the book. Goswell usefully introduces aspects of the text that are often forgotten by readers, especially those who work with an English translation only. The uninspiring title of the essay is in danger of turning readers away from what is the highlight of this collection.

Jenny Corcoran offers the shortest contribution, "The Alien in Deuteronomy 29 and Today." The incorporation of the *ger* into the covenant in Deut 29 is applied to contemporary ecclesiology. Like many of the other essayists, Corcoran finds that C. J. H. Wright offers her a useful hermeneutic. In fact, it is Deuteronomy's occasional appeal to *imitatio dei* that provides the hermeneutical perspective. The *ger* is a reminder to Israel that Yhwh has a concern for vulnerable Israel, and it, too, is to reflect that to the aliens in Israel. This provides a paradigm for the church. None of this seems particularly earth-shattering, but it is refreshing to see an interpreter taking that extra step toward application.

Christian Hofreiter addresses the subject of "Genocide in Deuteronomy and Christian Interpretation." He provides some useful sketches from the early history of interpretation as Christian writers struggled with the difficult problem of *herem*. Christian interpreters of the past were forced to abandon belief in God's goodness or belief in the faithful witness of scripture to God or moral revulsion at the command to kill. Hofreiter rightly observes that many recent interpreters have sought to avoid this invidious choice by adopting nonliteral readings of Deuteronomy. He helpfully distinguishes between allegorical, mythical, metaphorical, and hyperbolic interpretations. Such typologizing makes a fairly modest contribution to the discussion, and thus it is a little disappointing that Hofreiter declines to identify himself with one position or offer a new approach of his own.

Despite a degree of diversity, the essays in this volume are relatively homogenous. They are characterized by a conservative approach to critical issues: a number of them want to keep open a premonarchic date for some or most of the book. This often appears as no more than an aside. Walton claims that his argument about the structure of the Deuteronomic Law, "demonstrates that the Decalogue suffused Israelite life ... from earliest times" (117). Similarly, Johnston argues that the "portrayal of leadership reflects the pre- and early monarchy periods better than later eras" (155). The essays also show an instinct to harmonize biblical texts, as when Vogt insists that Exod 20 and Deut 12 are not far apart (122–23), Barker's reading of Deuteronomy in the light of Gen 1 and 12, Johnston's insistence that the appointment of elders in Exodus and Deuteronomy may be complementary (141), or Thomas's harmonization of the different accounts of Moses's punishment with death (191–192). A number of the essays make claims about Deuteronomy as the center of Old Testament theology. With Deuteronomy's theology interesting only a small group in English-speaking scholarship as we have seen, it is rather stirring to see such assertions. Nevertheless, there are reasons why such sentiments are rarely expressed today: they do not do justice to the place of wisdom literature or the influence of priestly thought. Old Testament theology needs to have a number of foci, rather than a single center. Finally, in common with much recent English-language scholarship on Deuteronomy they each take almost no notice of the numerous studies on Deuteronomy that have appeared in German in recent years.

To summarize, this volume may have value for evangelical students and pastors, and these are probably its envisaged audience. It brokers a limited selection of recent scholarship and may act as an encouragement to read more deeply within scholarship on Deuteronomy. If it achieves this, it is to be welcomed. Those undertaking more advanced work, even of evangelical persuasion, will encounter the volume's limitations fairly quickly. As teaching resources, many of the essays have significant deficiencies: they harmonize rather too easily and apply historical-critical analysis somewhat unevenly.

Gottes Volk im Deuteronomium, by Dominik Markl. Beihefte zur Zeitschrift für Altorientalische und Biblische Rechtsgeschichte 18. Wiesbaden: Harrassowitz, 2012. Pp. xiv + 363. Hardcover. €84.00. ISBN 9783447067638.

Simone Paganini, RWTH-University Aachen, Aachen, Germany

Dass bereits der Titel der Arbeit von Markl an die Dissertationsschrift von Gerhard von Rad aus dem Jahre 1929 erinnert, ist sicherlich kein Zufall. Die Untersuchung des Deuteronomiums unter dem Gesichtspunkt seiner Bedeutung als volksstiftender Text ist zunächst einmal nichts Neues. Dem jungen Jesuit Dominik Markl, seit kurzen Dozent am Päpstlichen Bibelinstitut in Rom, gelingt jedoch eine Untersuchung, die nicht nur Bekanntes in ein neues Licht führt, sondern sowohl inhaltlich als auch methodisch entscheidende Weichen stellt.

Die identitätsstiftende Kraft von Religionen und religiösen Texten ist heutzutage nämlich nicht weniger brisant als vor 100 Jahre. In diesem Sinn ist die Untersuchung von Markl, als Versuch das fünfte Buch der Torah in seiner Endgestalt zu deuten, ein höchst interessanter Beitrag und zwar für die soziologische und theologische Auswertung des Buches, ebenso wie im Hinblick auf den zur Anwendung kommenden methodischen Ansatz.

Daher sind die einleitenden Paragraphen zur Forschungsgeschichte (1.1) und zur Hermeneutik der Endgestalt (1.2) wesentliche Beiträge für die Verortung der Studie innerhalb einer breiten—nicht immer akzeptierten, sehr oft missverstandenen und nicht minder häufig als „naiv" gebrandmarkten—wissenschaftlichen Forschungstradition zu verorten.

Die theologische Relevanz der Arbeit besteht darin aufzuzeigen, inwiefern die Endgestalt des Deuteronomiums das Ziel verfolgt, Israel als „Volk Gottes" zu formieren. Markl arbeitet dabei auf einer doppelten Ebene: textintern, wenn es darum geht, innerhalb der deuteronomischen Erzählung die Merkmale der Mose-Reden an die Israeliten in Moab zu identifizieren, und textextern, wenn Markl an die realen Adressaten gerichtete Botschaft des Buches in der nachexilischen

Gesellschaft darstellt. In drei inhaltlichen aufeinander aufbauenden Kapiteln gelingt es ihm zu explizieren, wie diese dynamische Bewegung zustande kommt. Im Schlusskapitel werden die Ergebnisse noch einmal zusammengefasst und systematisiert dargestellt.

Kapitel 2 untersucht die funktionale Struktur, politische Rhetorik, Didaktik und Adressatenkommunikation. All diese Elemente dienen dazu, Idee und Konkretheit des Gottesvolkes zu formieren und zu untermauern. Die wichtigste Erkenntnis besteht dabei in der Beobachtung, dass die Identität des Volkes durch die in der Mose-Rede grundgelegte Beziehung mit Jhwh hervorgerufen wird.

Das Gesamtkonstrukt dieses systematischen Teils ist durchaus überzeugend. Zahlreiche Detailbeobachtungen sind außerdem geeignet, neue Erkenntnisse für die Deuteronomium-Forschung zu evozieren.

Es seien hier nur einige wenige, dabei aber bemerkenswerte Beispiele genannt:

1.) Die Diskussion über das „Vierüberschriftensystem" des Deuteronomiums und die Darstellung der systematischen Verbindungen zwischen Dtn 5–11 und Dtn 12–18 sprechen Themen an, die in der Forschung äußerst kontrovers diskutiert werden. In beiden Fällen schlägt Markl Lösungen vor, die nicht nur gut akzeptabel sind, sondern neue Wege in der Textauslegung bahnen.

2.) Die präzise Wahrnehmung von Mikro- und Makrostrukturen innerhalb des Buches zeigt auf eindrucksvoller Weise—durch zahlreiche Diagrammen und Tabellen gekonnt dargestellt—die interne Zusammengehörigkeit des Buches und seine dynamische Entwicklung.

3.) Das Erkennen der Bedeutung von Bekenntnistexten (Dtn 6,20–25 und 26,1–15) legt entscheidende Weichen für den Verständnishorizont der gesamten Komposition.

4.) Die Untersuchung der pädagogischen und didaktischen Mittel in der politischen Rhetorik des Deuteronomiums ist ein Thema, das in den vergangenen Jahren große Beliebtheit erfahren hat. Mit der Beschreibung der meta–pragmatischen Vorgänge thematisiert Markl jedoch ganz neue Aspekte, die nicht zuletzt für die Welt der impliziten Adressaten des Buches von großer Signifikanz sind.

5.) Ganz besonders gelungen und aufschlussreich ist die Untersuchung des semantischen Wortfeldes des Lexems „heute", welches—wie Markl überzeugend zeigt—immer wieder als Brücke zwischen den fiktiven Adressaten der Erzählung und den realen Lesern der nachexilischen Zeit fungiert.

Aus diesen Beobachtungen lässt sich die Erkenntnis gewinnen, dass die Formierung des Gottesvolkes das Programm des Deuteronomium-Buches schlechthin darstellt. Anschließend konzentriert sich Markl in einer intensiven Vers-für-Vers-Analyse paradigmatisch auf zwei wichtige Gruppen von Texten. Innerhalb dieser Texte kommen nämlich die wesentlichen rhetorischen und literarischen Dynamiken des Buches zu ihrem Ziel. In Kap. 3 konzentriert sich Markl auf die Schlusskapitel des Buches (Dtn 31–34) und in Kap. 4 auf die Texte, welche sich besonders mit dem Moabbund beschäftigen.

Mit fast 200 Seiten stellt Kap. 3 einen klaren Schwerpunkt dar und ist auch im Hinblick auf den Inhalt betrifft Zentrum der Untersuchung.

Auch in diesem Fall seien lediglich einige wesentliche Aspekte der Untersuchung hervorgehoben:

1.) Die positive Wahrnehmung von Dtn 31–34 als zweifacher Abschluss sowohl des Deuteronomiums als auch des gesamten Pentateuchs. Dies erlaubt einen Schlussstrich unter die gegensätzlichen diachronen Theorien zu ziehen, die entweder den einen oder den anderen Aspekt als entscheidend dargestellt haben.

2.) Die detaillierte Analyse nimmt Spannungen und Brüche wahr, kann sie aber innerhalb der Entwicklung der Erzählung kohärent deuten.

3.) Der Paragraph zum Moselied bildet m. E. den absoluten Höhepunkt der Arbeit, wobei die Einzelheiten im Rahmen dieses Gutachtens nicht ausführlich diskutiert werden können. Markl gelingt es, eine der schwierigsten Passagen des gesamten Alten Testamentes klar darzustellen, ohne dabei die Feinheiten des Textes übergehen zu müssen. Die ausführliche Diskussion der Bedeutung dieses Textes in Zusammenhang mit den Hinteren Propheten, dem Psalter und den übrigen Ketubim stellt Dtn 32 in eine gesamtbiblische Perspektive, die Markl als erster in dieser Breite und Ausführlichkeit wahrnimmt.

Das vierte Kapitel konzentriert sich auf Texte, die den Moabbund in den Blick nehmen, insbesondere auf Dtn 29–30. Auch diese beiden Kapitel sind in den vergangenen Jahren vermehrt Objekt einzelner Untersuchungen geworden. Markl rezipiert sie und ist dennoch innovativ. Vor allem in der Analyse der rhetorischen Dynamik des Textes—in der zweifachen Perspektive der Adressaten der Erzählung (die Moab-Generation) und der impliziten Adressaten des Textes (die nachexilische Leserschaft)—schlägt er einen ganz neuen und äußerst interessanten hermeneutischen Weg vor. Ob der Moabbund wirklich eine überbietende Transformation des Sinaibundes darstellt oder ob Dtn 28,69 doch als Überschrift verstanden werden soll, sind Fragestellungen, die auch weiterhin diskutiert werden können. Das Thema des Moabbundes ist jedenfalls sauber ausgearbeitet, die vielen hervorgehobenen Einzelaspekte und Details sind eine wahre „Fundgrube", aus der Anschlussforschung Gewinn schöpfen wird können.

Das abschließende fünfte Kapitel ist nicht eine Zusammenfassung, sondern eine unter vier Gesichtspunkten erfolgende Auswertung der Beobachtungen zur Formierung des Gottesvolkes im Deuteronomium, wie die vorigen Kapitel sie präsentiert haben,.

Hervorzuheben ist insbesondere der Paragraph zur Rechtshermeneutik des Deuteronomiums innerhalb des Pentateuchs: Die sich ergebende Dialektik zwischen einer durch Mose fixierten Torah im Deuteronomium und dem Inhalt des Deuteronomiums selbst, welches de facto eine Rechtsrevision ist, erlaubt es, die Hermeneutik der juridischen Valenz der deuteronomischen Legislation wahrzunehmen. Markl bietet dabei vor allem Impulse für die weitere wissenschaftliche Reflexion und weitet den Blick zu Recht auf den kanonischen Zusammenhang des Alten Testamentes.

Markl diskutiert seine Grundthese nicht nur präzis und ausführlich. Und er scheut nicht zu provozieren, wenn er mehrere Fragen offen lässt. In diesem Sinne liefert seine Habilitationsschrift nicht nur einen souveränen Beweis der wissenschaftlichen Qualifikation des Antragstellers, sondern stellt entscheidende Weichen dar für zukünftige Deuteronomium-Forschung wie für die Untersuchung des synchron gelesenen Pentateuchs.

The Rhetoric of Remembrance: An Investigation of the "Fathers" in Deuteronomy, by Jerry Hwang. Siphrut: Literature and Theology of the Hebrew Scriptures 8. Winona Lake, Ind.: Eisenbrauns, 2012. Pp. xiv + 290. Hardcover. $39.50. ISBN 9781575062389.

Joel Barker, Heritage College and Seminary, Cambridge, Ontario, Canada

This monograph is a revision of the author's 2009 Wheaton College dissertation in which he undertakes a detailed examination of the references to "fathers" in Deuteronomy. He highlights the varied nature of these references, noting that in different places they refer to specific patriarchs, Israel's ancestors in general, and even the exodus generation. Hwang's intention is to address this ambiguity from a rhetorical, synchronic perspective. He suggests that this allows him to move beyond impasses in redactional studies of these texts exemplified in the competing perspectives of Römer, who suggests that the exodus generation is the original referent of the "fathers," and Lohfink, who identifies Abraham, Isaac, and Jacob as the default interpretation (4–5). Hwang suggests that this sets up a false dichotomy that he can circumvent by appealing to the rhetorical function of such references. He provides three reasons for adopting a rhetorical approach, suggesting that (1) it can explain Deteronomy's repeated use of the "fathers" as a device to inculcate the audience with memory of its past experiences; (2) it can explore how shaping this memory contributes to Deuteronomy's paraenesis for the present generation; and (3) it suits Deuteronomy's sermon-like tone, emphasized in Deut 1:1, which presents the book as the "words that Moses spoke" (6–7). The introduction concludes with an extremely brief discussion of rhetorical-critical methodology in which Hwang makes a cursory connection between his approach and that of Muilenburg.

Hwang divides the body of his work into three parts, each of which has two chapters. These parts emphasize different elements of the references to "fathers" in Deuteronomy. Part 1 discusses the promises of land to the "fathers," part 2 analyzes the references to the "God of the fathers," and part 3 discusses the "fathers" in conversation with covenantal language in Deuteronomy. The first chapter of each part addresses general issues and positions the discussion that follows within the context of previous research. The second chapter of each part delves into a detailed examination of the key texts. In each part, the summary chapters focus on diachronic issues, in which Hwang details the impasses reached by previous scholarship before offering his rhetorical analysis as a means of advancing the conversation. In the chapters focused on textual analysis, Hwang considers the references to the "fathers" in its immediate literary context before drawing out broader implications for the passages in which these verses are located.

Part 1 consists of chapters 2–3, in which Hwang discusses the promises of land given to the "fathers." In chapter 2 Hwang details variations in vocabulary related to the promises of land before discussing how redaction critics use these variations to identify primary and secondary material. He highlights the work of Römer and Diepold, who come to opposing conclusions on the priority of land promises that refer the land as a "gift" (נתן) versus the land as the result of a divine oath (נשׁבע). Hwang, however, suggests that these variations are part of the intentional compositional strategy and merit study as they stand. His first case study is Deut 1:8, where he argues that the reference to YHWH's gift of the land to "your fathers, to Abraham, to Isaac, and to Jacob" relates to the broader context of Deut 1 by enhancing the continuity between Moses' audience on the plains of Moab, the generation that left Horeb, and the patriarchs. In this instance, the promise of land suggests corporate solidarity between those three generations, rooted in the continuing nature of their relationship with YHWH (39). He sees the presence of this solidarity throughout Deuteronomy's reference to the "fathers" and the promise of land, including notably Deut 30:20, where the promise of the land given to the patriarchs is the reward if the present generation of Israel faithfully obeys the commands of Moses.

In part 2 Hwang shifts to discussing the identity of the "fathers" in the context of the phrase "the God of the fathers." In chapter 4 he surveys research that mostly views the examples of this epithet as intrusive. Contrary to the consensus, Hwang suggests that Deuteronomy's use of this epithet deliberately connects it back to the Tetrateuch and indicates that YHWH is a personal deity who also possesses cosmic authority. In chapter 5 he divides the eight uses of this epithet into three categories: multiplication (Deut 1:1; 6:3); land (Deut 1:21; 4:1; 12:1; 27:3); and covenant (Deut 26:7; 29:24 [25]). Of particular interest are the covenant references, since these provide evidence of Deuteronomy's concern to connect multiple generations of Israelites. Hwang suggests that Deut 26:7 continues the look backward begun in Deut 26:5 and links the "God of the fathers" to the time of Israel's patriarchs, Israel's sojourn in Egypt, and the exodus. Deuteronomy 29:24 [25] looks forward and suggests that, if a future generation of Israel were to go into exile, it would be because it broke covenant with "the God of their fathers." This epithet thus has implications for Israel's past, present, and future, drawing multiple generations together through their shared commitment to YHWH.

In part 3 Hwang addresses the divine-human covenant in Deuteronomy through references to the "fathers." In chapter 6 he argues that Deuteronomy does more than reflect a "conditional" covenant given to Israel, which scholars often set in contrast to the "unconditional" covenant language associated with Abraham (156). He draws upon insights from speech-act theory to suggest that Deuteronomy's narrative discussions of Israel's history can be considered "imaginative speech-acts." Their purpose is to invite the immediate audience and subsequent generations to place themselves upon the plains of Moab to reaffirm their covenant commitment to YHWH. Hwang explores this assertion in chapter 7, with reference to passages where Deuteronomy speaks of an oath or covenant with the "fathers" (Deut 4:31; 7:8, 12; 8:18; 29:11 [12], 13 [14], 24 [25]). Hwang revisits Deut 29, focusing this time on the idea that Moses connects the call to keep the covenant to YHWH's dealings with past, present, and future genera- tions of Israel. This is evident in Moses' retelling of Israel's story of exodus from Egypt, which bore witness to YHWH's provision. Hwang notes that this speech conflates the generation on the plains of Moab with the previous generation that experienced the escape from Egypt. This generational solidarity then extends back even to the patriarchs (Deut 29:13 [14]) and to future generations who may experience exile if they disobey the covenant (Deut 29:24 [25]). Both Deut 29:13 [14] and 24 [25] mention the "God of the fathers," though the first reference does identify them as Abraham, Isaac, and Jacob. Hwang suggests that this creative use of chronology effectively consolidates Israel's generations and calls on them to affirm YHWH's covenant.

Hwang concludes with a brief discussion of his results and prospects for future research in chapter 8. In this chapter he gives his strongest statement con- cerning the usefulness of synchronic study in a field dominated by diachronic, redactional studies. He suggests that the creative ambiguity of the references to the "fathers" indicates that these references are much more than redactional seams. Rather, they can be read as reflecting a deliberate rhetorical strategy to consolidate Israel's generations around its relationship with YHWH. This may require a reevaluation of proposed theories of redactional and textual growth in Deuteronomy. Hwang's analysis may suggest to some the infamous "trick of the disappearing redactor," but at the very least he has demonstrated a plausible case for seeing continuity in Deuteronomy's thought and message, rooted in its refer- ences to the "fathers."

In summary, Hwang's work makes a solid contribution to the study of Deu- teronomy. He is conversant with the current state of the discussion and offers an approach that holds out some promise of moving beyond endless layers of redactional minutiae that separate the text from its meaning. It would be help- ful if he developed a more refined rhetorical methodology that pushes beyond Muilenburg, but his synchronic reading and his use of speech-act theory yields useful results. The weakness of this book is that the relationship between the three parts is difficult to sustain, especially when Hwang uses the same chapter for multiple case studies (notably, Deut 26 and 29). While the author highlights different aspects of these texts in each case study, it is awkward to split analysis of key texts in this fashion. Further, it is a challenge to follow the movements from micro to macro analysis. Hwang's attention to detail effectively draws the reader deeply into each passage and its issues, but occasionally he struggles to bring these discussions back to the broader themes of land, divine epithet, and covenant. On balance, however, the strengths of this monograph make it a worthwhile read for scholars who are seeking to uncover the message of Deuteronomy.

Fremdlinge im eigenen Land: Zur Entstehung und Intention der priesterlichen Passagen der Vätergeschichte, by Jakob Wöhrle. Forschungen zur Religion und Literatur des Alten und Neuen Testaments 246. Göttingen: Vandenhoeck & Ruprecht, 2012. Pp. 245. Hardcover. €79.99. ISBN 9783525535462.

Marc Vervenne, Katholieke Universiteit Leuven, Leuven, Belgium

Understanding the formation process of the biblical texts in their historical context remains a key for a decent interpretation of the Hebrew Bible. Since the emergence of pentateuchal criticism, the book of Genesis has been the sample composition upon which a variety of literary-historical hypotheses have been developed and redirected. However, in the past three decades scholarship has radically retreated from the classical "documentary" pattern, which has served for almost two centuries to offer valuable but definitely inadequate explanations of the origins of the Pentateuch. Nowadays Pentateuch studies increasingly rely on encompassing redaction/composition-critical models instead of splitting the ancient texts into what has often been conceived to be originally self-contained "documents." A consensus has grown that the corpus Genesis–Kings patently reveals two main competing written traditions: the Deuteronomic (D) tradition and the Priestly (P) tradition. Scholars agree that both literary layers are intertwined with each other but also contain non-D and non-P materials. However, they are divided on the following issues: (1) the scope of P, (2) the identification of material that is seemingly neither P nor D, (3) the original sequence of the various traditions and their chronological settings, (4) the intra-textual stratification of D and P, and (5) the definition of the nature of the P "story" as either an independent source text or a redaction in relation to an existing composition.

The question about the nature of the P tradition is the central topic in this study by Jakob Wöhrle. The author is *Privatdozent* at the Protestant Faculty of Theology of the Westfälische Wilhelms-Universität in Münster and also Heisenberg Fellow of the Deutsche Forschungsgemeinschaft. His book has resulted from a research project within the framework of the Cluster of Excellence "Religion and Politics" at WWU, directed by Wöhrle and Rainer Albertz.

The introductory chapter (11–24) starts from the position that the Priestly sections and elements in the Pentateuch are the only remaining benchmarks for sound literary-historical research. However, the consensus stops here. Wöhrle then clearly outlines four main problems on which scholars currently debate with respect to P: the literary character of the P texts (either source or redaction); the delimitation of the P version of the Pentateuch and, more particularly, its end (either the Sinai, Moses' death, or the settlement traditions); the historical setting of P (either preexilic, exilic, or postexilic); and the intention of P (either the cult at Mount Sinai or the promise of the land). According to Wöhrle, these fundamental problems can be thoroughly studied only on the basis of coherent tradition units in which Priestly textual portions are embedded. To that end, instead of selecting a small pericope he opts for a larger complex: the "Patriarchal

History" in Gen 11–50. He argues that until today the P portions of this literary complex have not been studied in detail from the perspective of the questions mentioned above.

Following on the methodological introduction, Wöhrle successively deals with the origin (ch. 2) and the intention (ch. 3) of the Priestly passages in the patriarchal narrative. Chapter 2 (25–164) contains a detailed analysis of twenty textual units that scholars by and large characterize as reflecting in whole or in part the P tradition: (Abraham narratives) Gen 11:27–32; 12–13; 16; 17; 19; 21:1–7; 23; 25:1–18; (Jacob narratives) Gen 25:19–26; 26:34–28:9; 29–33; 35; 36; (history of Joseph) Gen 37; 38–45; 46; 47; 48; 49; 50:1–Exod 1:7. Each passage is systematically studied according to an established pattern: description of the contents, succinct presentation of the classical literary-historical characterization of the text, identification of problems relating to this characterization, and resolving the problems by means of the redaction-historical method, focusing on the literary nature of the P passage under concern.

Wöhrle writes perspicuously, building up a solid line of reasoning. His analysis results in a number of conclusions. First, the P portions in the so-called Patriarchal History comprise the following passages, or textual elements: Gen 11:27–32; 12:4b, 5; 13:6, 11b, 12aba; 16:3, 16; 17:1–8, 15–22; 19:29; 21:5; 23:1–2; 25:7–8, 9*, 11–17, 18a, 19–20, 26b; 26:34–35; 27:46–28:9; 31:18*; 33:18*; 35:6*, 9–13, 22b, 23–29; 36:1–8; 37:1, 2aa; 41:46a; 46:6–7; 47:7–11, 27b, 28; 48:3–7; 49:1a, 29a, 33aab; 50:22; Exod 1:6a, 7 (163). Second, besides some extensive compositional units, the P strand in the Patriarchal History mostly consists of small narrative notes such as dates, short references to the belongings of the patriarchs, their dwelling places, deaths, and burials. Wöhrle is of the opinion that the P portions that have been identified do not shape a continuous story in this tradition complex. On the contrary, these passages, or elements, are apparently written with a view to the non-P context in which they are embedded. In sum, the P portions in the Patriarchal History are not part of an originally independent source but rather redactional texts and fragments that have been composed as if it were in dialogue with an existing non-P patriarchal tradition. Moreover, the P redactors have put together independently transmitted non-P narrative compositions in order to shape for the first time a coherent and comprehensive tradition complex, running from the Primeval History up to and including the narrative of the exodus out of Egypt. However, contrary to the complex Gen 11–Exod 1, which according to Wöhrle clearly is a redactional layer (*Bearbeitungsschicht*) that was consciously shaped to be integrated in the non-P context, the P portions in Gen 1:1–11:26 and Exod 6ff. are to be considered as self-contained source texts in which existing non-P traditions have been inserted. Finally, Wöhrle argues that this comprehensive P tradition came into being in the land of Israel at the beginning of the Persian era, shortly after 520 BCE, when the first groups of exiles returned to the land.

Departing from the preceding redaction-historical study, Wöhrle finally aims at defining the intention of the P re-editing of the Patriarchal History. In this respect, chapter 3 (165–222) offers a synthetic description of the "theology" of the P narrative in Gen 11:27–Exod 1:7 within the broader context of the comprehensive P tradition, in which the Patriarchal History is sandwiched between the "universally oriented" Primeval History and the "particularly oriented" exodus narrative (168). Wöhrle distinguishes the intention of the P redaction of the Patriarchal History into four main themes. First, the patriarchal tradition is conceived from the perspective of the exilic community that considers itself the true people of God. The patriarchs are pictured as exemplary exiles moving from Mesopotamian regions into the land. In addition, P emphasizes that the people of Israel was constituted outside the land, since the patriarchs were born abroad, where YHWH revealed himself to them. According to Wöhrle, it is obvious that the Patriarchal History in its P form reflects the late exilic discussion about the conditions to belong to the people of Israel. The second them concerns life in the land. This land is consequently described as "the land of Canaan," which means that its inhabitants are seen as foreigners, whereas the patriarchs are strangers in their new country. Moreover, the land is considered a gift that must be acquired by each generation. This view matches well with the Priestly conviction that the land can be acquired again by the returning exiles. The third thematic intention affects the relationship between the patriarchs and their relatives in the neighboring countries. P makes clear that the land is meant exclusively for the patriarchs and their offspring and that the relationship with surrounding peoples is of a peaceful and coexisting nature. A fourth and last thematic line regards the relationship with the people of Canaan who live in the land. The P redaction clarifies that the patriarchs and their descendants cannot commit themselves to the Canaanites. On the other hand, their living together in the land is also characterized by peaceful cohabitation.

In the concluding chapter (223–26) Wöhrle summarizes the results of his study according to his typical clear style, which repeats the key issues that have been investigated. The book ends with a list of scholarly literature in different languages.

This book is a challenging study that is most welcome for present-day research into the Hebrew Bible. Today a majority of biblical scholars are rather indifferent to the issue of the literary history of the Pentateuch, although they may appreciate that some continue to be involved in this area of research. However, as already stated, the redaction-historical study of the biblical texts remains of vital importance. There is still a lot of work to do. Wöhrle's thesis of a mixed literary origin of the P tradition as redaction and source is debatable. By way of example, I am not convinced that the compositional unit Gen 1:1–2:4 was shaped as an originally self-contained narrative. In-depth study reveals that this composition might have come into existence by a theological "opposition" of P against the non-P Eden story (Gen 2:5–3:24). The same phenomenon occurs in the sea narrative in Exod 13:17–14:31, where a P redactor seems to have reworked an existing non-P story that bears close resemblance to the D-tradition, or at least might marks the beginnings of D.

FORMER PROPHETS

Say It Again, Sam: A Literary and Filmic Study of Narrative Repetition in 1 Samuel 28, by Grenville J. R. Kent. Cambridge: Lutterworth, 2011. Pp. xvi + 251. Paper. £19.50. ISBN 9780718892715.

Andrew E. Steinmann, Concordia University Chicago, Chicago, Illinois

Can the theoretical discussions of repetition in modern films bring fresh insight for those who seek to interpret biblical texts? The media used by ancient writers to produce textual narration—pen and parchment—are far different from the flashing frames of film and its accompanying soundtrack that narrate by action, lighting, sound, and sometimes text. Grenville Kent believes that, while there are obvious differences in the two media that often make direct comparisons difficult, because scholars of film discuss the effects of repetition and not simply its forms, film theory has much to contribute to biblical exegesis.

Say It Again, Sam is a study of narrative repetition based on Kent's PhD thesis submitted to the University of Manchester. It looks at verbal repetition as a narrative tactic used by authors for its adaptability and versatility in highlighting themes and creating intratexual and intertextual connections. Organized much like a dissertation, the study is divided into seven chapters. The short first chapter introduces a general discussion of repetition, its definition, and the methodology to be followed in the remainder of the book.

Chapter 2 surveys various studies by biblical scholars during the last half-century that make some attempt to note the use and effect of repetition in the Bible, concentrating on studies of the Old Testament from James Muilenberg in 1968 to David Firth in 2002. Here the reader begins to see that repetition as defined in this study casts a wide net: redundancy of sound, exact words, phrases, semantic domains, themes, and concepts are just some of the modes of repetition in narrative texts. Kent concludes that, while some attention has been paid to repetition by biblical scholars, the investigation of the rhetorical purposes of repetition has been haphazard. He believes that the theoretical basis for studying repetition needs to be expanded.

The next two chapters examine repetition in literary theory and film theory. Especially important for Kent is Barbara Johnstone's work on repetition in literature, though he also surveys other late twentieth and early twenty-first-century literary studies and notes that some have begun to classify not only the forms of repetition but their functions in conveying meaning and leading (or misleading) readers. When turning to film theory Kent cautiously notes: "While film theory is not totally and unproblematically transferable to ancient narratives written on very different media, it does at least offer analogies and insights which can be adapted and applied across the constraints of either medium" (89).

Kent first acknowledges that a select few biblical scholars such as Serge Frolov and Eric Christianson have used analogies from cinema to inform their investigations of the biblical text. However, he concludes that their method is primarily intuitive and not a systematic application of film theory. Next he turns to film scholars to note their theoretical work on repetition in narrative cinema. The most important of these for Kent is Bruce Kawin. As he examines the various functions of repetition in film documented by these theorists, Kent also notes analogous examples in 1 Samuel. He concludes that

> Film theorists have tended to focus on the effects of repetition, while literary theorists and biblical scholars have concentrated more on forms of repetition. Film theory has been shown to cast light from a range of angles and sources on textual details so as to reveal their art and ideology. This continues the case that repetition is a useful and flexible narrative tactic in Samuel. (130)

As Kent works through these chapters, he also begins to construct a taxonomy that seeks to classify the various purposes of repetition noted by theorists, arriving at fifty-nine distinct functions.

A short fifth chapter examines previous biblical studies of 1 Sam 28, concentrating especially on more recent literary examinations, especially those of J. P. Fokkelman and Robert Polzin. While showing appreciation for these literary studies, he also notes that they make little use of literary theory and no use of film theory.

The longest chapter is Kent's exegesis of 1 Sam 28. He explains his choice of this chapter:

> 1 Samuel 28, being near the middle of the books of Samuel, is able to point back to previous choices made by Saul and show the consequences that are now overtaking him, yet also to point forward to future consequences. As such, it can illustrate structures of repetition pointing both forwards and backwards. (137)

After offering a translation and philological notes, Kent spends the rest of this chapter noting various kinds of repetition in 1 Sam 28, both within the chapter itself and repetitions of material elsewhere in Samuel. His application of film theory and his taxonomy often proves useful in providing insight into this chapter. For instance, in his examination of the predictions given to Saul by the Samuel figure conjured up by the witch at En Dor, he notes that repetition from prediction to fulfillment in 1 Samuel portrays Samuel as a sure prophet of Yahweh whose predictions "never fall to the ground." Yet the figure who appears to Saul gives predictions that seem to fall short of the reliability of the prophecies pronounced by Samuel during his lifetime. Thus, the use of repetition in 1 Sam 28 tends to create doubt in the reader's mind as to whether the woman at En Dor actually brought the prophet up from the dead. At other times, however, it appeared to me that Kent's treatment and explanation of the function of repetition was less convincing, as when he treats the meal that is provided for Saul before he leaves En Dor. Here there is some valuable insight as to the pagan connections of the meal and Saul's indulgence in them as a further alienation from Yahweh, but the discussion of repetition highlighting this appears to me to be more muddled and strained.

Overall, what are we to make of Kent's work? In a number of cases he demonstrates quite well that paying attention to repetition and applying film theory—and, to a lesser extent, literary theory—can bring fresh exegetical insights. There are any number of such insights in this book that make it well worth reading and consulting. However, Kent's definition of repetition can also be seen as very broad, almost to the point that nearly everything can be seen as repetition on some level. It seems to me that there needs to be some theoretical basis for separating out meaningful repetitions from those that may be more mundane. For instance, at one point Kent sees repetition between 1 Sam 9:24 and 28:21–22 with the verbal root שׂים. While the references to setting food before someone might be a link between these verses (1 Sam 9:24 and 28:22), I am more dubious about the use of this root as a parallel when the woman of En Dor says "I have set my life in your hands" (28:21). When is repetition meaningful, and when is it simply a consequence of having only so many ways to express a concept? Kent never explores this, and it leaves the impression that *nearly every* perceived repetition is meaningful.

Another interesting consequence of Kent's work on repetition, one to which he only occasionally alludes, is that it calls into question one important methodological assumption behind earlier source-critical analyses of the book of Samuel: that repetitions often mark different sources behind the text. Kent repeatedly demonstrates that these repetitions point more toward authorial or editorial unity than to diverse sources. He several times demonstrates that what was seen by the source critics as glaringly inept repetition can actually be seen as purposeful repetition to guide the reader and add meaning and depth to the narrative. These repetitions, then, are either authorially intended or purposefully preserved from the underlying source by a later editor. Either way, Kent's analysis calls into question whether repetitions can be reliably used as indicators of the seams in the narrative that make apparent where disparate source texts were joined together by later redactors.

Despite the few reservations expressed above, I would endorse Kent's study of repetition in 1 Samuel and his effort to supply a theoretical basis for examining repetition as an exegetical tool to open up the meaning contained in the biblical text. While film theory certainly is not completely transferrable to biblical studies, Kent has made a good case that it can provide insight for biblical scholars examining narrative texts of the Bible.

Reconciling Violence and Kingship: A Study of Judges and 1 Samuel, by Marty Alan Michelson. Cambridge: James Clarke, 2012. Pp. x + 230. Paper. £20.00. ISBN 9780227680131.

Gregory Mobley, Andover Newton Theological School, Newton Centre, Massachusetts

Michelson's revised dissertation from the University of Manchester applies the theory of René Girard to three sections of Judges and 1 Samuel—Judg 9, which

tells of the rise and fall of Abimelech; Judg 17–21, with its mini-epic of lawless-
ness, including the horrific mob murder of the Levite's concubine; and 1 Sam
9–11, which details the ascent of Saul—in order to argue that the latter, Israel's
first king, succeeded where previous warlords had failed because, in Girardian
fashion, Saul sacrificed a yoke of oxen, thus enacting the atoning benefits of the
scapegoat mechanism.

> Our reading of these texts [i.e., Judg 9, 17–21; 1 Sam 9–11] has … allowed us to
> construct an understanding of the emergence of kingship … in Israel's culture.…
> Using Girard we have seen that … there may be a concrete past, now hidden in
> the myth of these stories, that harkens back to an originary sacrifice [i.e., Saul's
> dismemberment of a yoke of oxen in 1 Sam 11:5–7] that quells violence and
> heralds sacred kingship. (198)

> The emergence and inauguration of Saul here is a new event for Israel based out
> of violence that is used to unite the brothers of Israel around sacrifice. (149)

The thesis, based on an application of Girard's ideas about scapegoating to certain texts in Judges and 1 Samuel, is that societally sponsored violence, that is,
"ordered violence," expressed through rituals of animal sacrifice such as that
depicted in 1 Sam 11:5–7, prevent widespread, that is, "chaotic," violence such as
depicted in Judges. Michelson arranges three texts to advance his argument. In
Judg 9, Israel's first attempt at kingship is unsuccessful because Abimelech's violence—the sociopathic "sacrifice" of his brothers on a stone butchering block—is
unsanctioned and disordered. The next text in the sequence, Judg 17–21 demonstrates what happens when there is "no king in the land," leading to unrestrained
violence and utter chaos. The sequence reaches its climax with the account of
Saul's rise to kingship in 1 Sam 9–11: Saul solves the Girardian knot because he
successfully redirects the malevolent, self-destructive energies conjured through
the virulent vibrations of mimetic desire and rivalry toward the pair of bovines he
quarters and distributes as a call to arms throughout the territory of Israel.

> Emergent rivalries (particularly featuring characters like Abimelech) rise to the
> point of dissolution and chaotic sacrifice (the dismembered concubine [in Judg
> 19]) where kingship emerges to resolve the conflict (even when Saul enacts the
> same kinds of violence by dismembering a yoke of oxen. (9)

Michelson makes an additional move, by contending that the ambivalence
toward kingship in 1 Samuel emerges from cultural uneasiness about the entire
scapegoating mechanism. Organized violence ameliorates disorganized violence—"institutionalized violence leads to social stability" (8)—but the virus
survives, ready to break out anew. Paradoxically, the antidote to violence is
produced from and preserves the toxin. This complicated dynamic leads to the
juxtaposition of texts with rival points of view: the portrait of Saul's rise to kingship in 1 Sam 9–11 is framed by Samuel's speeches condemning kingship in 1

Sam 8 and 12. Finally, then, Michelson contends that the institution of kingship itself functions as a scapegoat. That is, Samuel's criticism of kingship is a form of scapegoating.

Michelson initially insists that his is a literary study, but early on (4) he edges toward historical reconstruction from literary analysis, making "proposals regarding the historical reality of the start of kingship in Israel." Unfortunately, his foundation for historical reconstruction of this pivotal period rests solely on biblical texts. But as a comparison of the narrative of Ruth with that of Judges demonstrates, the era when "the judges judged" can be depicted by later tradents either as bucolic or vitriolic, depending on the aims of the storyteller. Nowhere does Michelson acknowledge that it served monarchic interests writing "after" to exaggerate the evils of the time "before," in the same way that weight-loss advertisements contrast images of slouching corpulence with svelte elegance.

After an introduction (ch. 1, "Thesis and Scope of Study," 1–14), Michelson devotes chapter 2, "Composition and Kingship in the Deuteronomistic History" (15–40) to sketching the range of ideas about how central the theme of kingship is to the books of Joshua through 2 Kings. In chapter 3, "Abimelech," the narrative in Judg 9 is subjected to a "close reading" keen to uncover entries from the lexicon of Girardian theory such as "rivalry," "violence," and "desire." The same can be said of chapters 4, "Micah, the Levite, and the Concubine" (71–112), and 5, "Saul and Kingship" (113–52). The concluding chapters 6 ("Assessing a Girardian Hermeneutic within This Study," 153–97) and 7 ("Summary and Conclusions," 198–201) hammer away at the joins of his shaky structure of argumentation.

I took no pleasure in reading this book, nor do I take any in cataloguing its flaws. The title itself with its initial, indecisive participle hamstrings progress toward coherence. (Note: all italics below are mine.) The publication history page, with its reference to the "british Library" damages the credibility before we even reach page i. There is frequent subject-verb disagreement ("The speech-complex ... *point* out to us," 114; "But *none* of the characters *are* named for us," 199). There is careless editing ("If we had not been told enough that *is* [it?] had been night," 97, "Mar*k* Brettler," 151 n. 101). There is clumsy sentence construction ("Since the woman [in Judg 19] leaves the Levite 'not in order to live with another man in either a marital or sexual sense, as we might expect if sexual fidelity was the issue' but rather returns to her father's house in Bethlehem it is odd," 86), inanely repetitive diction ("This [i.e., 'king'] is a new title *for* our narrative *for* the tribes of Israel," 114; "*focal* attention," 113, and "*narrative story*," 118), faulty punctuation ranging from using semicolons as functional colons to mismatched single- and double-quotation marks (seen where n. 80 appears in the main text on 99), to unnecessarily dramatic exclamations (in the same paragraph on 117: "[A] sympathetic reading of Saul will not be our focus!" builds toward the climax of "[I]t is with Saul that kingship begins!"), and inconsistent management of tense ("Saul was inaugurated as king, they celebrate, and we have record of his kingship," 150). These lapses render the book virtually unreadable.

Who is to blame for what constitutes the most poorly written work of published "scholarship" I have ever read? The author, for sure, but what of the publisher and of the dissertation committee that granted a Doctor of Philosophy from the University of Manchester on the basis of an earlier form of this "work"? We should not blame Professor Girard for this tortured misapplication of his ideas.

The logic of Michelson's argument is tortured: Since Girard has argued that ritualized violence expressed through animal sacrifice creates social unity, and since there is a biblical narrative that depicts Saul performing such an act, the historicity of Saul's reign is more likely. Saul ben Kish should be honored for inaugurating kingship in Israel and for proleptically confirming the brilliance of a prominent contemporary French philosopher.

Unfortunately, I cannot recommend this book to anyone. Neither its ideas nor its writing meet any standard I recognize for publishable biblical scholarship.

Joshua and Judges, edited by Athalya Brenner and Gale A. Yee. Texts @ Contexts. Minneapolis: Fortress, 2013. Pp. xxii + 333. Cloth. $49.00. ISBN 9780800699376.

Ginny Brewer-Boydston, Baylor University, Waco, Texas

Joshua and Judges, edited by Athalya Brenner and Gale A. Yee, is the fourth installment of the Hebrew Bible portion of the Texts @ Contexts series. This series approaches reading the biblical text contextually, decentering biblical scholarship from its predominantly Western (masculine) viewpoint. This point of view is not denigrated, as it is a social location rather than *the* social location of choice for biblical scholarship. *Joshua and Judges* is a collection of fifteen essays that explores ancient Israel's claim to divine chosenness and subsequent conquest of the land of Canaan. As a whole, these individual chapters challenge ancient Israel's collective memory and approach the narratives that retell those memories from the view of the "Other," the native inhabitants of the land. The collection is divided into two parts. "What Do We Do, What Can We Do, about Joshua and Judges?" focuses on the biblical books, more so upon Joshua, and methods as a whole, investigating and letting stand the tension of the divine chosenness and the violent conquest of those who held original, valid claim to the land. The second part, "Case Studies in Judges," focuses upon particular stories and ideological readings of those passages.

In the first essay, "The God of Joshua: An Ambivalent Field of Negotiation," Walter Brueggemann discusses three "probes" in seeking understanding of passages that depict a violent God who destroys the "Other" as well as consideration for responsible interpretation that is still faithful to the text. The first probe recognizes that the capture of the land is a function of chosenness. The second probe addresses how chosenness leads to the destruction of the Other. The third probe acknowledges little to no dissenting voices counteracting the violent seizure and destruction of Canaan. Brueggemann argues that traditional criticism can offer that voice of dissent so as to recognize the violence of the text and negation of the

Other and yet be a critique to it rather than attempting to ameliorate the chosenness of the land and Israel.

In "Joshua–Judges and Postcolonial Criticism," Trent C. Butler acknowledges that he is an "outsider" among postcolonial critics, as he traditionally has not experienced being an Other. Butler than employs questions representative of postcolonial criticism in regard to Joshua and Judges and concludes that a postcolonial reader cannot automatically assume Israel is the colonizer and non-Israelites are the colonized. The identification of Other will fluctuate depending on the circumstance, even at times traversing both polarities; it is "a static category, for the same group may well fit different categories at different places in the literature, and at different times and context" (32).

zCheryl Kirk-Duggan reflects on American and world history that parallels the violence of the conquest of Canaan in "Inside, Outside, or in Between: Feminist/Womanist Hermeneutical Challenges for Joshua and Judges." Given the underlying causes of systemic violence, Kirk-Duggan encourages reading Joshua and Judges from a womanist perspective in the hope of transforming this violence and empowerment for all rather than black women alone. Emphasizing the female characters, both those who rise to leadership over men and those against whom great violence is done, allows for transcending literal readings or readings from the Israelite perspective, which in turn reveals "new insights into connections around systems, power, and culture" (87).

Employing reception analysis in "The Finns' Holy War against the Soviet Union: The Use of War Rhetoric in Finnish History during the Second World War," Kari Latvus explores the Finnish newspaper *Kotimaa* and the Finnish journal *Teologinen Aikakauskirja* in 1941 at the beginning of Finland's Continuation War against the Soviet Union. What Latvus finds is parallel thematic clusters of divine chosenness and promise of land as described in Joshua and Judges. The chosen media present a view of Finland as God's instrument, protection of Finland as God's will, and the need for individual repentance and piety. Latvus ends with compelling questions regarding Finland's and future usage of biblical concepts for "holy war" and "crusade."

L. Daniel Hawk's "Indigenous Helpers and Invader Homelands" explores the folklore of the Indian Maid that inspired a statue at Fort Ball in Tiffin, Ohio, and her parallel, Rahab, in Joshua. The two women served as indigenous helpers who aided foreign invaders in their conquest and occupation of the land. The indigenous helper is "the pivot upon which the land turns away from the indigenous nations and toward the immigrant people" (121). Rahab the Canaanite welcomes the Israelite spies and assumes their religious and political worldview. After the destruction of Jericho, symbolizing the conquering of the Other and the cleansing of the land, she assimilates with the Israelites in a land that has been "re-created in (Israel's) own image" (121).

Athalya Brenner's "Women Frame the Book of Judges—How and Why?" introduces the second section of case studies in Judges. Brenner seeks to answer the question of why women, specifically daughters, frame the book of Judges and appear at critical junctions, such as the center. Brenner first presents a survey of the principal characteristics of these women and then an additional survey of scholarship's multiplicity of answers to the question of framing. Her conclusion refutes the belief that Judg 17–21 are later additions, as these chapters complete the structure of the entire book with their focus on the daughters who appear in them.

Ora Brison's "Jael, *'eshet heber* the Kenite: A Diviner?" offers a unique reading of Judg 4–5 that counters the traditional view of Sisera seeking shelter with Jael. Instead, she argues that Sisera is "seeking an audience with a (female) cultic intermediary/diviner in order to learn about his future fate" (141). Sisera's patronizing of Jael shares characteristics with Saul's patronizing of the medium of En-dor. The encounter between Sisera the military commander and Jael the medium is not maternal or sexual (consensual or forced), but these maternal and sexual overtones are best explained as cultic practices associated with divination.

Ryan P. Bonfiglio explains the inconsistencies between the two narratives of Judg 4–5 with regard to Sisera's and Jael's encounter through prose and then poetry in "Choosing Sides in Judges 4–5: Rethinking Representations of Jael." In Judg 4 Jael, clearly an outsider living on Israelite land, must choose between her Kenite ties or Israelite ideology when Sisera enters her tent; she becomes Israel's deliverer when she chooses to kill him rather than uphold the Kenite-Canaanite peace. In Judg 5 the text presents Yahweh as Israel's deliverer, and Jael kills Sisera in self-defense in the face of rape rather than choosing one side over another. Employing postcolonial mimetic and model minorities theories, Bonfiglio demonstrates how in Judg 4 Jael is a model minority who is faithful to Israel and serves their interests as an "Israelite" heroine but in Judg 5 is a "model of agency and resistance for women—both ancient and modern—who likewise face sexual violence," a heroine "among women" (171).

As a Chinese American female, Gale A. Yee explores the parallels between Jael (Judg 4–5) and the legend of Mulan, both of whom are female warriors entering the male world of warfare, in "The Woman Warrior Revisited, Jael, Fa Mulan, and American Orientalism." Both women cross gender boundaries and contribute to gender destabilization. Their reception history is often contradictory in terms of their representations from the text and legend. Through a closer look at the Disney film *Mulan*, Yee prods the reader to consider gender and racial formation based on such representations of boundary-crossing women.

In "This Season You'll be Wearing God: On the Manning of Gideon and the Undressing of the Israelites (Judges 6:1–8:32)," Meir Bar Mymon describes the masculinization process of the Israeli army and parallels it with God's masculinization of Gideon and ancient Israel. Israelite masculinity suffers and, thus, God's masculinity is reduced in the opening of Judg 6. Yahweh "recruit(s) the weak Gideon and transform(s) him into a *Man*, thus changing the matrix into a new equation: strong leader = strong nation = one strong God" (195). Through the masculinization of Gideon, Yahweh is masculinized, so much so that Gideon puts on God's spirit and the deity and Gideon co-exist in the figure of Gideon the soldier. Once the campaign is won, Gideon refuses to continue in the way God has masculinized him and "takes off" Yahweh by creating an ephod and retiring to civilian life. Through Gideon's rejection, he shapes another model of *Man*, one who refuses to participate in ancient Israel's warfare.

Pamela J. Milne's "From the Margins to the Margins: Jephthah's Daughter and Her Father" asks the question of whether feminist biblical scholarship is extending outside of its own community into the nonacademic arena of the average biblical reader. She developed a project that interviews these nonspecialists about their own interpretation of Judg 11 and concludes that her interview subjects had no direct knowledge of feminist biblical studies nor did the readers apply a feminist critique of the passage, although there were some promising responses in the issues of the text the interviewees found problematic.

Royce M. Victor "revisits" Delilah and reads her story though a Philistine perspective in "Delilah—A Forgotten Hero (Judges 16:4–21): A Cross-Cultural Narrative Reading." Victor describes Delilah as a Philistine hero who endangers her life to save her people and their land and possibly the whole of Canaan, as Samson is a threat to society. Her heroic exploits have either been forgotten or co-opted by ancient Israelite memory, and she is transformed from a great heroine into a seductive, foreign betrayer. Victor then compares Delilah to a nearly forgotten, unnamed heroine in the Indian epics of *Ramayana* and *Mahabharata*.

In "Narrative Loss, the (Important) Role of Women, and Community in Judges 19," Brad Embry ponders a view of the church without the violent text of Judg 19. The unified, conquering Israel of Joshua disintegrates and wars with one another in the extended family of Israel in Judges. While Judg 19 is an example of that deterioration, it is also a "typology" of society in which the concubine represents the fate of Israel. More so, the violent, murderous fate of the concubine spurs Israel to evaluate its disintegration. For the community of faith, the reading and incorporation of this passage in the life of faith "reawakens" the community and spurs "reflection on its own potential and capacity for evil" (269) and upon the choosing of a "canon within a canon" and why.

Janelle Stanley approaches Judg 19 through a psychological lens and labels it a text of trauma in "Judges 19: Text of Trauma." The passage displays three typical symptoms of trauma—dissociation (lack of personal names and of the description of the rape), repetition compulsion (repetition of speech by the old man and of particular features of Gen 19), and fragmentation (dismemberment of the concubine). More important, this text of trauma performs the healing function of "constructing the narrative [so that] the trauma memory [is] recovered, told, and retold" (288). Identification as a text of trauma allows trauma victims to identify with it and begin their own healing process by reconstructing their narrative.

Joshua and Judges clearly demonstrates the difficulties for both scholars and instructors in interpreting Joshua and Judges. While the first essay may leave the reader with the feeling that interpretation of the two books leaves academia with nothing but tension, the remaining essays serve as an answer to the probes Brueggemann laid out. This volume is not apologetic of the conquest stories of

Joshua and Judges, does not attempt to ameliorate these passages, and does not attempt to answer the historical issues of the conquest. For those academics who acknowledge interpretational difficulties, *Joshua and Judges* offers more than just a shrug of the shoulders in response to the violent texts. The book offers readings, methods, conclusions, and teaching strategies to those who do not know what to do beyond letting the tension stand.

Indicative of the Texts @ Contexts series, this collection offers an abundance of diversity with regard to the social location of its authors. There is a multiplicity of ethnicities, nationalities (although the vast majority are American or have close ties to the US), junior scholars, and senior scholars. Exactly half of the authors are male, and half are female. Such volumes as this tend to favor female academics, but *Joshua and Judges* recognizes an Othering of men when ideological criticism is perceived as a female discipline. Indeed, feminist biblical studies are featured the most. The list of authors, however, includes the perspectives of white Anglo-Saxon men in recognition that such readings do have validity, although they are not the only valid readings or contexts with which to approach the text. Mymon even offers a study in masculinity and Judges. Although it may seem as if this book is for anyone but white males, the essays serve as excellent studies for all readers, minorities and majorities alike, with regard to how individual social location colors and changes a reading.

The diversity and method is somewhat of a drawback. Each author identifies her or his social location before delving into the essay, an excellent avenue for showing how social location and interpretation interacts. However, this identification feels as if authors must show their qualifications for being a contextual critic, or, for those who have little experience as an Other, they must justify why their works are included in this volume. These particular non-Others also lean toward being apologetic for employing contextual criticism, as if they are overstepping their bounds or right to add their viewpoints. Speaking of the Other, those authors who heavily identify with the Other or attempt such identification gravitate toward particular topics and passages, which is a drawback for this volume. Judges 4–5 (particularly the character of Jael) and 19 are heavily featured. The volume favors Judges as whole—the second portion of the book is titled "Case Studies in Judges." Case studies in both Joshua and Judges would have helped keep the volume evenly distributed across the two books.

Another issue with diversity and method is that these essays on the whole employ large amounts of "I" language despite a focus on the Other. While there are a multiplicity of benefits of authors offering their social locations, some of these interpretations can become very individualistic. At times, an author appears to be saying "This is how *I* read this text," rather than offering an additional perspective. Due to this individualistic method of interpretation, the volume does not always offer application that one can extract and duplicate unless that particular person shares the same social location. This method also lends itself toward problems with argument or twisting of the interpretation to produce the desired outcome. The advantage of such individualistic readings and even the twisting of readings is that the reader must still think beyond her or his social location and be aware of the influence of others' social locations upon texts and the validity of such readings. What would have been helpful to note in the preface or introduction is the danger of ideological methods and reader-response criticism rather than stressing the benefits alone.

Women at Work in the Deuteronomistic History, by Mercedes L. García Bachmann. International Voices in Biblical Studies 4. Atlanta: Society of Biblical Literature, 2013. Pp. xvi + 413. Paper. $54.95. ISBN 9781589837553.

Ralph K. Hawkins, Averett University, Danville, Virginia

Women at Work in the Deuteronomistic History began as Bachmann's dissertation, which she completed at the Lutheran School of Theology in Chicago in 1999. She resumed research on the subject over a decade later in order to turn the dissertation into a book, now published as volume 4 in the Society of Biblical Literature's International Voices in Biblical Studies series. Bachmann's interest in female labor grew out of her impression that most scholarly descriptions of ancient Israelite women were too uniform and seemed to see them as too similar to today's middle class. Furthermore, conventional scholarship has supposed that the ancient biblical world was operated on the basis of a system of honor and shame, in which the ascription of honor and shame were social instruments used by the dominant culture to reward the compliant and censure the noncompliant. Bachmann contends, however, that "there are also sub-cultures of the peasants and other poor who uphold other values, such as working hard, being upright, cooperative with the poor, and shrewd with those in power and, in the case of women, taking as much control of their reproductive capability as possible" (3). Her goal is to substantiate this contention in order that a more nuanced model might be adopted.

In a short introduction, Bachmann notes some of the challenges involved in studying her particular subject matter. For example, the semantic field of the very common verb *'bd*, "work," "toil," "serve," does not differentiate between the general connotations of "do" or "make," nor are there feminine nouns or verbal forms derived from it. Similarly, another verb, *šrt*, "to minister," can have either a secular or a cultic meaning. Everyone, except perhaps the very rich families, worked, from the father of the household to the lowest of the slaves, and a number of terms attest to the variety of tasks that women were engaged in, apart from daily household chores. Bachmann notes that "women appear working for their own households and at other peoples' households, both for private ones (especially in Genesis) and for the great institutions; but most of the time they are only very generally located" (9), and the terms for their work are semantically unclear. These and other semantic challenges make it clear that "there is much to disentangle before we can have a fairly complete view of such an important item in life as work" (7). She notes her intention to focus on the host of women who appear behind the scenes of Dtr's history engaged in such tasks as harvesting and gleaning, grinding and cooking, fetching water and preparing baths, spinning and weaving, healing the sick and washing the dirty, consulting with spirits and preventing the evil omens from affecting their beloved ones, recording events, burying the dead and keeping their memory alive. These people are taken for granted rather than recognized, because the writers' interests lie elsewhere, and because the elite class was accustomed to being served. These mostly anonymous women ... who worked for others, who are sometimes mentioned in only one verse, and who have gone unrecognized in DtrH and in modern scholarship, despite their contribution to the socio-economic system (and as secondary characters to narratives): these women constitute our focus. (15)

Bachmann suggests that, now that society is beginning to recognize that women have been marginalized historically, theology has an obligation to take up their cause.

In chapter 1 Bachmann explains the assumptions on which her work is based, as well as the methodology she utilizes in her study. Her work is an exegetical study from a liberation feminist perspective. She incorporates the tools of the sociohistorical approach, which means that, instead of looking at history focused around great names or the "winners," she intends to undertake a historiography of everyday life, with a focus on the "little people" (17–18). She notes again the limitations imposed by the sources, especially the lack of information in the Hebrew Bible about women in general and the social location of lower-class women in particular. Bachmann spells out the advantages of using the DtrH for her study. In contrast to the Torah, which is too narrow to provide enough data about women and occupations in general, the DtrH contains narrative material, which makes it possible to examine a sample of terms appearing in historical accounts, speeches, laws, formulae, and fables. Special challenges include Dtr's tendency to value women for their virginity or sex appeal, and Bachmann is especially interested in assessing instead their socioeconomic, political, and cultural contribution to society, especially of those who are the forgotten laborers, whose lives were left unrecorded, the "unknown" women. Her interest is in recovering the contributions of these women.

Chapter 2 provides a review of the literature, with a focus on major contributions to the understanding of lower-class women. She includes sources from other disciplines, especially ancient Near Eastern history and archaeology, and also seeks to incorporate insights from anthropology and sociology.

Chapter 3 examines the conditions in which women worked in ancient Israel. These conditions were generally very similar to those in Egypt and the wider Levant. Bachmann describes them as "peasantry," "agrarian society," and "slave" or "unfree." Land ownership may have been the ideal in ancient Israel, but people often had to undertake other strategies to survive. Women often became "economically dependent" on others in all kinds of ways, a term Bachmann uses for the status of those who had to work due to financial or social pressures and engaged in various types of work, from hiring themselves out as harvesters to those who were carried away as spoils of war to work in another society altogether. She concludes that "the picture concerning women is, if anything, worse than that of men, because of the high imbalance in the use of power and of the added sexual discrimination—facts which, incidentally, still apply" (114).

In chapters 4–7 Bachmann examines different clusters of terms. In chapter 4 she examines all the texts in the DtrH in which any of the words for "female slave" or "dependent" play a role. Chapter 5 concentrates on the "hidden workers" who appear especially in passages dealing with midwifery, nourishing tasks, tools, textiles, and commercial activity. In chapter 6 Bachmann studies occupations related to the royal household, noting the focus of the DtrH on androcentric historiography, including especially Yahwist-religious and political concerns. When household occupations are mentioned, they are overwhelmingly in the royal household or connected with prominent leaders. There is a lack of recognition of any occupation that would serve exclusively female needs. "Dtr's interest in these women goes only so far as they are part of important males' lives, so their record is left empty after the events the narrator recounts" (265), with only a few exceptions.

Chapter 7, one of the longest in the book, is focused on the sex worker, broadly defined. Bachmann proposes a number of conceptual difficulties involved with studying sex workers in the ancient Near East, including: (1) the wide range of meanings of the stem *znh*, from the exercise of prostitution to idolatry; (2) biased translations that have found prostitutes in virtually every passage in which a woman is unaccounted for; (3) the fact that even marriage involved the exchange of gifts for sex; and (4) disagreement about which of today's categories would apply to each of the ancient cases. Bachmann carefully defines prostitution and concludes that, if prostitution is defined as occurring outside the cultural bounds of controlled sexuality, then sex within the sacred sphere does not qualify as prostitution, since it would have been controlled. She reasons that, "even though the terms [traditionally understood as referring to sacred prostitution] designate some occupation or office involving 'controlled sexuality' they would belong to the religious realm together with the prophetess, the priestess, the singer, and others" and should not be included in an assessment of the sex worker in ancient Israel (271). In her study of the sex worker, Bachmann notes that the verb *znh* and the noun *zōnâ* have a wide range of meanings and can refer not only to the professional sex worker but also to fornication, illicit religious practice, and unattached life outside the patriarchal household. Harlots clearly belong to the lower echelons of society and are more or less despised by their society (328).

In chapter 8, her concluding chapter, Bachmann reassesses the social location of female labor in the DtrH. She reiterates the fact that the DtrH is a product of the exile and, as such, was concerned primarily with YHWH's plans and promises, the collapse of the monarchy, and the apparent defeat of YHWH. With such interests as the royal household and the king's political and religious behavior, the stories of peasants and accounts of the experiences of workers are neglected. Bachmann reviews the contents of her study and concludes that all the data surveyed "indicate that the number of female workers was percentagewise higher than one tends to think" and that vast areas of the socioeconomic and political life of Israel influenced women's lives. Distribution of land, increasing pauperization of peasants and of debt-slaves, consolidation of the state bureaucracy and of a wealthy elite, remission of debts, natural phenomena, and warfare are some of the socioeconomic factors pervasive in biblical Israel as well as in today's world (336).

Working women came from several situations, including free Israelites in economic duress, corvée service, indentured slaves working for their families' creditors, abducted people, members of the temple and court staff, and Canaanites taken into service as permanent slaves of the state (336). Bachmann resists the idea that the values of honor and shame comprise a universal system that could regulate behavior on the grounds that it is too general to account for poor women and poor families, and she notes that "we have demonstrated that several texts evaluate women by very different standards than sexual faithfulness to a husband or restriction to their home" (337). This is part of Bachmann's objective, to see how various lower-class women were viewed by their peers. In the end, for the reasons noted above, the evidence is sparse. Still, Bachmann concludes that

> Meager as this evidence is for a history of women, it deserves to be evaluated upon its own merit, as witness from a world largely ignored or depreciated. To recognize these women in their own merit would at least imply a recognition of their contribution to society, not only as women whose sexuality belonged to a man and had to be fiercely protected against improper advances, but as persons recognized for their contribution to society, most noticeably in social and economic terms. (344)

Bachmann's volume does an admirable job of scouring the DtrH for terms that would identify women's involvement in the social and economic realms of ancient Israelite society. The evidence, as she noted repeatedly, is somewhat meager, though this does not diminish her contribution.

I would, however, offer one criticism. Bachmann does consult some of the recent archaeological studies to compensate for the limitation of Dtr's focus on the royal household and the king's political and religious behavior, and this allows her to emphasize that women did indeed have a larger role in the social and economic life of ancient Israel. However, she overlooks a revolutionary essay by Carol Meyers that calls into question the whole hierarchy model in which ancient Israelite society was completely patriarchal and in which she postulates a heterarchy model in its place.[1] The gist of Meyers's argument is that examining women's

---

1. Carol Meyers, "Hierarchy or Heterarchy? Archaeology and the Theorizing of Israelite Society," in *Confronting the Past: Archaeological and Historical Essays on Ancient Israel in Honor of William G. Dever* (ed. S. Gitin, J. E. Wright, and J. P. Dessel; Winona Lake, IN: Eisenbrauns, 2006), 245–54.

social, economic, and religious roles, along with the attendant power dynamics in ancient Israel, in light of ethnographic data and models suggests the existence of women's organizational structures that would have cut across household and clan structures. This calls the patriarchal model into question. This has been overlooked because many of the women's organizational structures functioned on informal levels typically not recognized in discussions of Israelite society and political organization, which tend to focus on associations formed by men for military, economic, political, or religious purposes. Meyers proposes that these networks of professional women would have existed in relation to at least five different skills, including: (1) musical traditions; (2) prophetic roles; (3) funerary services; (4) psychological care, counseling, and conflict resolution provided by wise women; and (5) midwifery and other forms of health care (Meyers, 248). Each of these guilds would have had its own hierarchies, with women holding positions of knowledge, expertise, and authority. Meyers is not arguing for the complete elimination of the hierarchy model, only that different social units, including individuals, households, guilds of professionals, kinship groups, and villages were involved in multiple vertical and lateral relationships. Men held authority in some of these, while women held authority in others. According to this heterarchical model, an individual can simultaneously rank high in one modality and low in another (Meyers, 249–51). While women may have had little influence in certain areas, therefore, they would have been regarded as experts and authoritative figures in other areas—and not just by other women. In my view, Meyers's heterarchy model is groundbreaking and must be considered in any future study of women's roles in the ancient biblical world.

Aside from this omission, Bachmann's volume provides an excellent compendium that analyzes virtually every term related to women's work in the DtrH. Her volume does not solve all the conundrums associated with several of these terms, nor does it claim to. It does, however, introduce the issues associated with the study of these terms, and it will serve as an important springboard for future research. For students and scholars with an interest in gender studies as it relates to the Old Testament, *Women at Work in the Deuteronomistic History* will provide a valuable reference work worthy of repeated consultation.

LATTER PROPHETS

Zechariah 9–14, by Paul L. Redditt. International Exegetical Commentary on the Old Testament. Stuttgart: Kohlhammer, 2012. Pp. 167. Hardcover. €54.00. ISBN 9783170216518.

Lena-Sofia Tiemeyer, University of Aberdeen, Aberdeen, Scotland, U.K.

This is a relatively slim, yet ultimately satisfying commentary. It is the first volume of the new international commentary series IECOT (International Exegetical Commentary on the Old Testament). It seeks to bring together scholars from diverse religious backgrounds and perspectives working in North America, Europe, and Israel. Both the editorial board and the list of planned authors of the forthcoming commentaries in the series consist of a broad and diverse group of international biblical scholars. In addition, Kohlhammer's website promises that "all volumes will appear in both English and German." So far, however, no German translation of Redditt's commentary has been published.

The series also seeks to bridge the perceived gap between synchronic and diachronic readings of the text. Each volume will therefore look at not only how the given text can be read (synchronic) but also how that given text is the end result of a long process of development (diachronic). At the same time, each volume will be defined by its contributor's own strengths: while some contributors may emphasize gender-critical or liberation-theological aspects of a text, others may highlight its reception history or its social-historical background. The aim of the commentary series is to serve a broad audience (pastors, scholars, and laypeople).

The commentary opens with an introduction in which Redditt discusses briefly the relationship of Zech 9–14 with Zech 1–8. He outlines and explains a representative selection of key views: some uphold shared authorship but postulate a changed social location; some maintain that the extant book of Zechariah invites the reader to find a way to understand the book as a coherent whole; and some understand the function of the later chapters 9–14 as an explanation of issues in the earlier chapters 1–8. Redditt himself emphasizes the literary and thematic differences between the two parts and postulates that Zech 9–14 constitutes a set of additions to Zech 1–8.

Redditt then offers a synchronic analysis of Zech 9–14. He outlines the key themes of each of the six chapters. In particular, he highlights the change from positive hopes in 9–10 to a more negative evaluation of the situation in 11. Further, while 9–10 speak of Judah and Ephraim, 12–14 focus solely on Jerusalem and Judah. Redditt also notes the changing role of the Davidic king throughout the six chapters and the emergence of the theme of holy war in 12 and 14.

Turning to the literary structure of Zech 9–14, the (redactional) heading מַשָּׂא (9:1; 12:1) implies a break between chapters 9–11 and 12–14. Redditt discusses four alternative theories (by Ernst Sellin, Danielle Ellul, David J. Clark, and Byran Curtis), then proposes his own theory, that the so-called "shepherd sign-enactment report" in Zech 11:4–16 forms the centerpiece of the six chapters. It stands between the hope for a reunited Israel and Judah (chs. 9–10) and the depiction of future wars against Jerusalem and Judah (chs. 12; 14).

Redditt subsequently looks at the diachronic development of Zech 9–14. He approaches the subject by way of the expressed hope for a future king in 9:9–10. Redditt notes that such pro-Davidic sentiments are present in the so-called Book of the Four (Amos, Hosea, Micah, and Habakkuk), which, according to Redditt, was compiled shortly after the fall of Jerusalem. Redditt postulates that texts from the early postmonarchic period express the hope of a new David (e.g., 2 Kgs 25:26–30; Jer 33:15–26; Ezek 37:24–25; Hag 2:20–23; Zech 4:6ab–10a). In contrast, the later material in Ezra and Nehemiah sees the Persian monarch as the king of Yehud. In view of these two factors, Redditt suggests a date for Zech 9:9–10 prior to 500 BCE. He further postulates that the hope for the reunification of Israel and Judah, expressed throughout Zech 9–10 (9:10, 13, 14–15; 10:6ab–12), is a sign of their relatively early date of composition. At the same time, chapters 9–10 contain signs of redactional activity. According to Redditt, the oracle of judgement in Zech 10:2–3a is redactional in character, added in order to bring Zech 9–10 closer to the (negative) message of the following Zech 11–14.

Redditt's discussion of the gradual composition of Zech 12–14 is less lucid. Redditt isolates 12:1–9; 12:10–13:6; and 14:1–21 as three sections. He further suggests that the material about the shepherds (10:2–3a; 11:1–3, 17; 13:7–9) was composed at a subsequent date to hold Zech 9–14 together. In addition, Redditt postulates additional redactional "bridges" that bind together the various textual units. At this point I would have appreciated a chart outlining the various textual strands. Redditt explains the diachronic development of Zech 9–14 in more detail in the ensuing commentary.

Looking more specifically at the date of Zech 9–14, Redditt reviews a selection of existing models. He concludes, following in rough brush strokes the theories by Walter Harrelson and by Carol and Eric Meyers, that Zech 9 fits the late sixth century, that Zech 10 was written slightly later in the early fifth century, and that the rest of Zech 11–14 was composed during the later years of the fifth century BCE.

The last part of the introduction looks briefly at the identity of the "shepherds" and the "merchant" in Zech 10:2–3a; 11:3, 4–17; and 13:7. Redditt maintains that the former are the Jerusalem clergy while the latter are their Persian-backed overlords. In a few words, Redditt also discusses the location of Zech 9–14 within the Book of the Twelve and postulates that it may have been the last piece to have been added.

Turning to the actual commentary, the division of the text of Zech 9–14 into sections follows the structure determined in the introduction. The discussion of each section falls into five parts: (1) "A New Translation of the Text"; (2) "Notes on Texts and Translation"; (3) "Synchronic Analysis"; (4) "Diachronic Analysis"; and (5) "Concluding Remarks."

The "Notes on Texts and Translation" are easy to follow, as they actually explain in complete sentences what the different interpretative options are and how various scholars have sought to emend the text. The Hebrew is written in Hebrew characters. There is little interaction with the ancient versions. The LXX is consulted when relevant, but the actual text is not cited. There are frequent references to modern translations, in particular to the NRSV (possibly as a result of Redditt's earlier commentary in the NCBC series, which is based on the text of RSV). Redditt also interacts frequently with Carol and Eric Meyers's commentary (AB 25C).

"Synchronic Analysis" is by far the most extensive part. Redditt discusses the content and plot progression of the extant text. Redditt goes through the text systematically, explains key concepts, and elucidates its message.

In the significantly shorter "Diachronic Analysis" Redditt discusses the likeliest historical background of the textual section in question. His lead questions are: When was the message of the text relevant? Where else in the Bible do we encounter similar thoughts or literary motifs. What is the chronological relationship between these texts and the section in Zech 9–14 under scrutiny?

In "Concluding Remarks" Redditt discusses the message of the section as a whole, how it fits in with the message of the other sections in Zech 9–14, and how it, when relevant, reworks and reinterprets some of those earlier sections. Redditt concludes with some brief remarks as to how select verses of the text were reused and transformed in the later New Testament.

The commentary ends with a conclusion that sums up the findings. Redditt also briefly looks at the issue of the growth of the book of Zechariah and of the Book of the Twelve. He suggests that the first text to become attached to Zech 1–8 was Zech 9:9–10, due to its expressed hope for a new king. Next, material about Jerusalem, Judah, and Ephraim was added, thus creating Zech 9 and Zech 10*. Later the rest of the material was added to the growing textual corpus, as were minor redactional additions that served to facilitate the incorporation of Zech 9–14* into the Book of the Twelve. As to the group responsible for composing Zech 9–14, Redditt suggests a group of scribes living in the vicinity of Jerusalem who were critical of the postexilic, priestly leadership. The volume ends with a bibliography and four indices (Hebrew words, key words, citations, and other sources).

The presentation of the commentary is commendable in its clarity. Redditt is able to elucidate the text and to bring its message to the forefront. I also find its layout, reminiscent of that of the Herder's commentary series (Herders Theologischer Kommentar zum Alten Testament), user-friendly. Both series use brief subject indicators in the margin, which are helpful when navigating the commentary. I furthermore like the existence of footnotes for two reasons. (1) It enables readers to locate and consult the opposing views, something that the reader of a commentary in a series such as Biblischer Kommentar Altes Testament cannot do. (2) It leaves the text of the commentary uncluttered, in contrast to the custom of the Anchor Bible commentary, where bibliographic information appear in the main text.

More negatively, the volume contains misprints such as missing commas and full stops, as well as several typos. Let us hope that forthcoming volumes will be better proofread. In addition, given the explicit aims of the commentary series to be truly international, I missed serious interaction with non-English material. Although Redditt refers to French and German scholarly works (e.g., the commentaries by Rudolph, Reventlow, and Willi-Plein and the articles by Caquot and Delcor) from time to time, the overwhelming majority of the footnotes cite books and articles in the English language.

Paul Redditt wrote a commentary on Haggai, Zechariah, and Malachi in 1995 (New Century Bible Commentary). This raises the question as to how this new commentary compares with his earlier one. It also touches on the wider issue as to whether one exegete should be asked to write more than one commentary on the same text. On the one hand, a reader should not expect an exegete to change his or her mind over time in any drastic manner. On the other hand, a reader should be able to assume that the new commentary supplements the earlier one to such a degree that it is worthwhile consulting both.

Redditt himself makes clear that his views on the milieu from which Zech 9–14 emerged, first expressed in an article in 1989, have not changed. What has developed, however, is his understanding of the literary location of Zech 9–14 within the Book of the Twelve. In particular, Redditt's approach is indebted to, among others, the works of Nogalski and Schart. I am, however, surprised that Redditt does not refer to Wöhrle's two major volumes about the development of the Book of the Twelve (BZAW 360 and 389). Redditt further interacts with a number of recent monographs on Zechariah (e.g., Curtis, *Up the Steep and Stony Road*; Petterson, *Behold Your King*), as well as recent commentaries (e.g., Nogalski, *Micah–Malachi*). As to the structure of Zech 9–14, Redditt declares that his understanding of the narrative of the six chapters depends to a large degree on his former work, yet also incorporates the insights of especially Curtis.

Given the different layouts of Redditt's two commentaries, as well as the different aims of the two series, it is in my view worthwhile to consult both. Although there is a significant degree of overlap, this is, after all, what can be expected.

Isaiah: The Prophet and His Book, by Ulrich F. Berges. Translated by Philip Sumpter. Classic Reprints. Sheffield: Sheffield Phoenix, 2012. Pp. xii + 159. Paper. $35.00. ISBN 9781907534577.

Marvin A. Sweeney, Claremont Lincoln University and Claremont School of Theology, Claremont, California

Berges's volume is apparently a translation of Ulrich Berges, *Jesaja: Das Buch und der Prophet* (Biblische Gestalten 22; Leipzig: Evangelische Verlaganstalt, 2010). Although the preface of the English volume notes the earlier publication in the Biblische Gestalten series (xi), the details of the original German publication do not appear anywhere in the volume. This volume presupposes Berges's earlier work, *Das Buch Jesaja: Komposition und Endgestalt* (Herders biblische Studien 16; Freiburg: Herder, 1998; see my review in *RBL* 04/15/2002), but it has developed further as Berges has published a commentary on Isa 40–48 (*Jesaja 40–48* [HThKAT; Freiburg: Herders, 2008]) as well as other works cited in the bibliography. Although the bibliography and discussion account for works published through the late 2000s, there is a decided emphasis on European scholarship on Isaiah, with relatively little representation of the extensive English-language discussion of the book. Major commentaries, with the exceptions of Duhm's classic commentary on the entire book of Isaiah, W. A. M. Beuken on Isa 1–39, and Berges's own work on Isa 40–48, are absent. Missing commentaries include works on the whole of Isaiah, such as those by Blenkinsopp and Childs; those on Isa

1–39 by Clements, Kaiser, the present reviewer, Wildberger, and Williamson; and those on Isa 40–66 (or major portions thereof) by Bonnard, Elliger, Goldingay, Hermission, Koole, Seitz, Westermann, and Whybray, among others. Likewise, influential studies by Ackroyd, Clements, Gitay, Melugin, Rendtorff, Sommer, Willey (Tull), and others are missing. Such absences represent serious lacunae in Berges's discussion of Isaiah. Readers should at least have reference to these works so that they might know where to turn for further and often alternative discussion.

Berges's work appropriately employs a combination of synchronic and diachronic literary analysis that pays attention to both the literary features of the book, the historical process of its composition, and the views of the writers who produced Isaiah. In order to illustrate these perspectives, he employs the metaphor of the medieval cathedral. The great cathedrals of the Middle Ages were built over the course of centuries, and one may detect the influence of the various individual architects and stonemasons who contributed to the whole. So it is with the individual authors and editors who contributed to Isaiah over the course of time to produce the present form of the book. Such a metaphor illustrates the motto of his work, "If you want to grasp the prophet, you cannot bypass the book" (xi). He further clarifies that "this is the manner in which the word of G-d [my spelling] in human words echoes throughout these literary masterpieces, impacting anew each generation of readers, including those of our own day and age" (xi). Such an approach well represents in principle the current state of modern critical research on Isaiah.

Berges's "cathedral"-like view for the composition of the book informs his first chapter on "Historical Background and Literary Development" (1–22). He focuses here especially on the superscription of the book in Isa 1:1, which emphasizes the visionary role of Isaiah ben Amoz in the days of the Judean kings Uzziah, Jotham, Ahaz, and Hezekiah. The superscription functions to identify Isaiah not as the author of the book but rather as the authority who stands behind the book insofar as everything that appears in the sixty-six chapters of Isaiah is connected with this man of G-d. Isaiah is only one of many figures who appear within its pages; the others, however, remain anonymous as they hide behind the figure of Isaiah, the implied author who guides his readers through the historical vision that has now become a book. Berges argues that the superscription was added after a 450-year process of development, a figure that corresponds roughly to the current state of discussion, although some scholars incorrectly trace the development of the book well into the Hellenistic age. Unfortunately, Berges dismisses the significance of the superscriptions in Isa 2:1 and 13:1, passing them off only as introductions to visions in their respective immediate literary contexts, thereby losing important insights into the synchronic form of the book and clues to its diachronic composition.

Berges's historical work is very questionable. He argues that Isaiah's activity may be divided into four periods: (1) the early period from around 740 BCE, (2) the Syro-Ephraimitic War, (3) the period of the Philistine revolts, and (4)

Sennacherib's invasion. The first period presupposes a medieval argument put forward by R. David Kimchi (1160–1235 CE) and introduced to critical scholarship by Jacob Milgrom (*VT* 14 [1964]: 164–82) that Isa 1–5 presupposes Isaiah's prophecies from the period of Uzziah's reign, since Isa 6:1 refers to Uzziah's death. Neither is cited here, although Berges's earlier work cites Milgrom's article. This view is generally not accepted in modern scholarship, especially since so much of Isa 1 and 2–4 appear to presuppose Sennacherib's invasion in which Judah was besieged and Jerusalem left alone like "a sukkah in a vineyard" (Isa 1:9), and its men (3:1–15) and women (3:16–4:1) are left to suffer the consequences of Hezekiah's revolt. Berges inexplicably dismisses the historicity of the Syro-Ephraimitic War in which northern Israel and Aram allied to resist Assyria and unsuccessfully attempted to force Judah into their coalition. He presumes that maybe Aram alone invaded, but he offers no clue as to why they would do so without Israel. If Berges was better versed in historical research, he would recognize that the reigns of the last six monarchs of northern Israel, in which four were assassinated, represented a period of conflict in which the northern kingdom ultimately abandoned its alliance with Assyria to ally instead with Aram. The result was a disaster for both Aram and the northern kingdom based on their political miscalculation and their failure to line up their allies, including Judah, in time. Berges's conclusion that Sennacherib's treatment of Hezekiah was relatively "mild" because he left Hezekiah on the throne misses two important points: (1) the devastation of the land of Judah, demonstrated by archeology, that left the kingdom decimated for nearly a century; and (2) the need to cut a deal with Hezekiah so that Sennacherib could confront Hezekiah's ally, Merodach Baladan of Babylonia, whom Sennacherib never subdued. The consequences of that failure were felt in 652–648 BCE and again in 627 BCE, when Babylon revolted against Assyria.

On the other hand, Berges is correct to emphasize the process of *Fortschreibung*, here translated as "literary extension" (13), as later writers continued to reflect upon and develop the book. Noting the prevalence of liturgical forms throughout the book, he posits that it was developed in part by liturgical singers, whom he finally identifies as Levitical singers, although he is unable to posit a convincing setting for such work. One might consider the building of the Second Temple in the late sixth century and again the reforms of Nehemiah and Ezra in the fifth–fourth centuries BCE in which the temple was reinstitutionalized at the center of Jerusalemite and Judean life as potential candidates for such a liturgically oriented prophetic composition. This is especially so because the book of Isaiah calls upon its audience to return to Jerusalem so that YHWH's sovereignty might be recognized throughout all creation. Perhaps he is hindered by his view that Nehemiah and Ezra represented a repressive and antisocial regime, despite that fact that Koch long ago demonstrated that Ezra acted in an attempt to fulfill the prophecies of Isaiah (*JSS* 19 [1974]: 173–97) and that Judaism affirms both temple and Torah as the foundations for its religious worldview and practice. Are there threats against the wicked in Isa 56–66? Yes, but there is no evidence that either Nehemiah or Ezra attempted to kill their opponents. Such fates would be left to G-d, in keeping with the biblical and Jewish view that G-d is the ultimate arbitrator of such matters, especially under Persian rule, when Judah had little coercive power.

Berges's literary-theological work likewise raises questions, particularly since he lacks a coherent critical methodology for assessing the final form of a prophetic book and its various components. He instead relies on traditional divisions that go back to Duhm's long-outmoded early-collection hypotheses that have been rejected in much of American scholarship. He defines the book as a series of "Acts," which seem to stand in for Duhm's former "collections" insofar as he defines them as "compositional units" (24). The Acts include the usual groupings of Isa 1–12; 13–27; 28–35; 36–39; 40–48; 49–55; and 56–66. Berges completely misses Ackroyd's pioneering work concerning the parallels between the portrayal of Ahaz in Isa 7–9 and Hezekiah in Isa 36–39 (now published in *Studies in the Religious Tradition of the Old Testament* [London: SCM, 1987]). His work led ultimately to the recognition of a two-part structure for the book in Isa 1–33 and 34–66 that pointed to Ahaz's failures leading to judgment in the first part of the book and to Hezekiah's faithfulness in the second part of the book that readers were asked to emulate (see my *Isaiah 1–39, with an Introduction to Prophetic Literature* [FOTL 16; Grand Rapids: Eerdmans, 1996]). Although Berges's exegesis is aware of intertextual connections between the various parts of the book, he seems unaware of its rhetorical dimensions, particularly its interest in calling upon the people to join in the recognition of YHWH as the true sovereign of the universe as demonstrated by YHWH's actions in exiling and restoring Jerusalem. Of course, he also misses the theological difficulties presented by such a view: Why should generations of Jerusalemites and Judeans be sacrificed by YHWH's commission to the prophet in Isa 6 to render the people blind, deaf, and dumb so that YHWH's purposes might be realized? The argument works only if one is at the tail end of the process, not in its midst.

Finally, Berges presents a history of research from antiquity up to modern times. It is relatively complete in its treatment of Hellenistic sources, Qumran, the New Testament, patristic literature, and visual arts and music. It is inadequate in its treatment of rabbinic literature. Berges is not aware that the Talmud considers Isaiah an edited book written by "Hezekiah and his colleagues" (b. Baba Batra 15a), and he provides no discussion of the medieval interpreters, such as Rashi and David Kimchi. Abraham Ibn Ezra is briefly mentioned elsewhere in the book only because he recognized that Isa 40 and following might be the work of a different author.

In sum, this volume attempts to be comprehensive in scope, presumably to serve as an introduction to students and perhaps also to scholars. Unfortunately, its shortcomings prevent it from fully achieving this goal.

The Role of Zion/Jerusalem in Isaiah 40–55: A Corpus-Linguistic Approach, by Reinoud Oosting. Studia Semitica Neerlandica 59. Leiden: Brill, 2013. Pp. xiv + 314. Cloth. $182.00. ISBN 9789004232983.

Marvin A. Sweeney, Claremont Lincoln University and Claremont School of Theology, Claremont, California

The volume under review is a revised version of a VU University Amsterdam Ph.D. dissertation defended in February 2011. The author does not mention the name of his doctoral advisor. The study presents a corpus-linguistic analysis of Isa 40–55 in an attempt to trace the linguistic regularities that underlie the structures of these texts. Such an approach provides an important aid in analyzing the linguistic structure of a given text and therefore in interpreting that text. It makes use of the Werkgroep Informatica at the Faculty of Theology, VU University Amsterdam, which employs computers to build up a database of the Masoretic Text of the Hebrew Bible to facilitate searches for specific linguistic features. The database takes the MT at face value, even in cases where the MT is unclear or assumed to be wrong, insofar as the project assumes the MT to be legible. The database was employed to create the *Stuttgart Electronic Study Bible* (*SESB*, 3rd ed., 2009) as a basis for study.

Oosting chose Isa 40–55 as the basis for his study because these chapters are widely recognized as a distinct corpus. An earlier study by M. Rosenbaum, *Word Order Variation in Isaiah 40–55: A Functional Perspective* (SSN 36; Assen: Van Gorcum, 1997), employed a "functional perspective" to analyze these chapters in an effort to determine whether verbal patterns in Isa 40–55 employ the basis functional pattern verb—subject—object. Rosenbaum observed that Isa 40–55 does not consistently employ this basic pattern, and he argues that the poetic character of the text is the main reason for this deviation insofar as the author sought to avoid familiarization and triteness. Oosting questions whether the text of Isa 40–55 is defamiliarized, insofar as Rosenbaum presupposed the normative character of his basic model. Oosting proposes instead that analysis must proceed on the basis of the text at hand, without such presuppositions, especially since Rosenbaum privileged literary and text-critical phenomena in his analysis. Oosting therefore calls for a linguistic approach that gives due attention to the semantic features of the text at hand and the contextual function of semantic elements in the text rather than their genesis. Such an approach constitutes Oosting's corpus-linguistic approach that is not confined to the recurrence of particular semantic terms.

Oosting claims that a corpus-linguistic approach begins with the linguistic signals that are found within the text. By comparing the linguistic features of the text under study with those of other texts, it is possible to detect the linguistic regularities that underlie the text of Isa 40–55. Such features include the synaptic features of the text; its discourse structure; and an analysis of its participants, in this case understood as the characters found within the text, such as Zion/Jerusalem. Oosting finally tells his readers that a main goal of his study is to investigate the role of Zion/Jerusalem in Isa 40–55, whether the text presents a coherent concept of Zion/Jerusalem.

Oosting then turns to valency patterns in Isa 40–55. Valency patterns refer to the syntactic potential of a verb. Insofar as the verb is the basis for Hebrew syntax, study of valency patterns determines the capacity of a verb to combine with other sentence constituents to produce intelligible syntactic patterns. Oosting considers nominal clauses, verbless clauses, and clauses in which the verb has elided as well.

Finally, Oosting turns to the syntactic features of Isa 40–55. Here he considers the syntactic patterns of nominal and verbal clauses, nonrelevant clause constituents, recursive valency patterns, ellipsis, Ketiv and Qere readings, and Masoretic accents. All of these features are relevant to determining the regularity of the linguistic features of this text.

The heart of the study is a linguistic analysis of twelve pericopes in which the participant, Zion/Jerusalem, plays a role, including Isa 40:1–11; 41:21–29; 44:24–28; 45:9–13; 46:1–13; 48:1–11; 49:13–26; 50:1–3; 51:1–16; 57:17–23; 52:1–12; and 54:1–17. For each passage, Oosting examines textual hierarchy, syntax, discourse analysis, and the characterization of the participant, Zion/Jerusalem. He expects that the portrayal of Zion/Jerusalem in the first half of Isa 40–55 sets the terms for her depiction in the second half. His analysis of Isa 40:1–11, for example, demonstrates that an anonymous plural audience is called upon to comfort Zion, but by the end of Isa 40–55 this task has not been accomplished. Based upon the portrayal of Zion as a barren woman in Isa 49:13–26, Oosting argues that the reference to "your mother" in Isa 50:1–3 cannot refer to Zion. Instead, "your mother" must refer to another female figure, Jerusalem. This distinction is crucial to Oosting's analysis, insofar as he will ultimately distinguish Zion as the place to which the exiles return, whereas Jerusalem refers to the city that is to be rebuilt. Oosting makes a similar distinction in his analysis of Isa 54:1–17 when he distinguishes verses 1–10, in which Zion is depicted as a barren woman, and verses 11–17, in which Jerusalem is depicted as a city to whom children have returned.

Oosting's discussion of the participant, Zion/Jerusalem, continues to distinguish between Zion, the place of return, and Jerusalem, the city. As he continues his linguistic and contextual examination of these terms and their roles, he concludes that Zion refers to the captive daughter Zion whose future children will return to Jerusalem, whereas Jerusalem refers to the rebuilt Holy City to which the exiles return. Oosting observes that in Trito-Isaiah Zion appears as a mother giving birth to children in Isa 66:7–9, whereas Jerusalem appears as a wet nurse for the children of Zion in Isa 66:10–11.

Oosting's study has some very attractive dimensions, particularly its attention to a synchronic linguistic analysis that attempts to establish the final form of the text as a basis for examining the characters, his "participants," within it. Likewise, his attempt to distinguish the identities and roles of (Bat) Zion and Jerusalem is attractive, given the attention that previous scholars have paid to this question. But Oosting's distinction between Zion and Jerusalem is based on tenuous grounds, specifically, his claim that the abandonment of Zion in Isa

49:14 means both Zion's abandonment by her husband (YHWH) and her consequent inability to have children until her husband returns. But such a claim reads
too much into the text insofar as the context indicates that Zion is abandoned
both by her husband, YHWH, and her children. Do the references to Zion's bar-
renness and her failure to bear children indicate that she was barren and childless
from the outset or only after her husband abandoned her? Did YHWH abandon
her because she was childless? Did she not have children before she was exiled,
when her husband was presumably present? If so, what happened to them? Were
they slain as their mother was taken off into exile? Oosting's distinction between
the barren, captive Zion and the Holy City, Jerusalem, to whom the children will
return, leaves many questions open, most importantly, her prehistory prior to
her exile.

Oosting's exegetical discussions oftentimes fail to convince. Nevertheless,
Oosting has put forward a stimulating and potentially cogent methodological
model that deserves further study.

The Book of Isaiah: Its Composition and Final Form, by Ulrich F. Berges. Translated by Millard C. Lind. Hebrew Bible Monographs 46. Sheffield: Sheffield Phoenix, 2012. Pp. xviii + 601. Hardcover. $70.00. ISBN 9781907534591.

Bo H. Lim, Seattle Pacific University, Seattle, Washington

The translation of Ulrich Berges's *Das Buch Jesaja: Komposition und Endgestalt*
(Freiburg: Herder, 1998) into English by Millard Lind is a timely contribution,
given the current climate in Isaianic studies. The divide between Continental and
Anglophone scholarship is ever-increasing, as evidenced by the fact that separate sessions on the same topic, one devoted to the perspective of Anglophone
scholarship and the other to Continental works, have been held at SBL's Annual
Meeting. Berges's habilitation thesis, *The Book of Isaiah*, helps to bridge this gap.
The work is a synchronic and diachronic reading of the entire book of Isaiah that
interacts with current research on both sides of the Atlantic. The project is massive in scope, as evidenced by the fact that the English edition runs 601 pages
long, including bibliography and indices. Berges's primary conversation partners
are other German scholars, yet he also engages Anglophone scholars devoted to
the study of Isaiah as a book. This review will primarily consider the contribution
of Berges's work to Isaianic studies written in English.

Chapter 1 is Berges's attempt to introduce to his German audience the
importance of reading Isaiah synchronically and diachronically at the level of
the book. He admits that, even though Rendtorff and Steck raised this issue,
it has not garnered significant attention in Germany. He believes the question
why such voluminous prophetic literature such as the vision of Isaiah became
associated with a prophet who factors so little in the prophecy itself deserves the
same amount of attention in Germany that it has received in the U.K. and North
America. The remainder of the chapter is a survey of one-book interpretations

organized under the headings of the search for a holistic structure, close readings, theme-oriented interpretations, canon criticism, ideological criticism, and
redaction-critical approaches. Berges concludes his survey with a summary of his
own methodology. He believes that what is needed is a "diachronically-reflected
synchrony" (34) where the interpreter exposes the literary seams without destroying the final product. The book must be understood first at the synchronic level,
but from then on the text's historicity and strata ought to be unearthed. He finds
that the best paradigm to understand the book is not one of a final redaction or
composition but rather to view it as sectional compositions, each supplementing the other and the latter respecting the earlier. For Berges, in its final form
Isaiah contains a "frozen dialogue" between various Jewish groups in the postexilic period over the meaning of Zion and the nations.

Berges goes on to treat the book of Isaiah according to sectional compositions, so that chapters 2-7 each address a major unit of Isaiah. Each of these
chapters provides a detailed synchronic and diachronic interpretation of the passage ending with a summation of Berges's main argument. Chapter 2 addresses
Isa 1-12, which he considers to be the book of Isaiah *en miniature*. Berges ascribes
Isa 1:21-25; 2:12-17; and 6:1-8:18 to Isaiah ben Amoz, with the exception of
6:9-11 and 7:10-14a, 17a. He believes the royal and Immanuel promises 7:14;
9:1-6; and 11:1-9 democratize the notion of kingship such that the righteous
postexilic community of Zion viewed themselves as the successors of the Davidic
kingship. The priorities of Isa 1-12 reflect the interests of the entire book with its
message of the purification of Zion as the prerequisite for the eschatological pilgrimage of the nations to Zion. Berges believes that these texts may have served
as a counterargument to exclusionary policies of Ezra and Nehemiah's from the
community in Jerusalem.

Chapter 3 covers Isa 13-27, and here Berges assigns 14:28-22* to the prophet
Isaiah but dates the final form of the chapters 13-27 to the Persian period. Viewed
in this manner, the redaction of this section follows that of Isa 40-48. Berges
observes a "Babylonizing" of the oracles against the nations as well as a "Zion-
izing" of the oracles concerning the nations and assumes Xerxes' attack against
Babylon in 482 served as a catalytic event for the redactors. Berges finds Kaiser's
categories of eschatological, proto-apocalyptic, and apocalyptic texts helpful, yet
he does not wish to separate chapters 24-27 from 13-23. Therefore he designates
the so-called apocalypse as late prophecy and chapter 24 as a conclusion to the
oracles to the nations in chapters 13-23.

In chapter 4 Berges covers Isa 28-35 and assigns some material within chapters 28-31 to Isaiah ben Amoz from the period of 705-701, yet he dates much of
this unit's material, particularly chapters 33-35, to a later date. Berges considers
Isa 33 as the first bridge text of the book of Isaiah, since it was written with the
intention to conjoin the two distinct prophecies, Isa 1-32* and Isa 40-52*. Late in
the fifth century after the fall of Edom, Isa 34 was written in response to the Edom
oracle in 63:1-6 and added to the collection after Isa 33. Berges acknowledges
that Isa 34 and 35 on a synchronic level function as a diptych, yet he believes Isa

35 was added in a separate redaction to serve as an additional bridge text within the book of Isaiah.

Chapter 5 covers Isa 36–39, and in this chapter Berges interacts in a substantial manner with Anglophone scholars, since many of them have argued against what was previously the consensus, that much of the material in these chapters was borrowed from 2 Kgs 18–19. He observes that within the book of Isaiah these narratives serve to fulfill the prophetic word of Isa 1–35 concerning the exaltation of Zion and destruction of Zion's enemies, and chapter 39 prepares the readers for chapters 40–55. Berges observes that this unit emphasizes Yhwh's protection of Zion against the movements of the nations against Zion, so he dates the insertion of this unit to the last stages of the book's formation.

Chapter 6 covers Isa 40–55, which Berges divides synchronically and diachronically into the "Jacob-Babylonian-Liberation" (chs. 40–48) and "Zion-Restoration" (chs. 49–55) segments. He seeks to liberate Isa 40–55 from its "exilic imprisonment" and situate these texts in Palestine rather than Babylon, as reflected in his decision to assign Isa 40–48 to the disciples of an anonymous prophet urging the *golah* to return to Jerusalem. It worth noting that, since the publication of the original work in German, Berges has abandoned the search to identify an exilic prophet named Deutero-Isaiah or a postexilic prophet designated Trito-Isaiah. While these texts urge the audience to accept Cyrus's liberation as act of Yhwh, Berges does not associate the Persian king with the "new things" but instead believes this language refers to the formation of the *golah* as the Servant of Yhwh to the nations. To the initial Babylonian section was added an initial Jerusalem redaction (chs. 49–52*) after 521, a second Jerusalem redaction (chs. 54–55*) in the middle of the fifth century, and a subsequent insertion of the fourth Servant song (52:13–53:12). Berges acknowledges the parallelisms between the motifs of Daughter Zion and the Servant throughout chapters 49–53 and concludes that they are the one and the same figure in the fourth song. Isaiah 53 is then about the transformed attitudes of Diaspora Jews to the destruction of Jerusalem and its subsequent unbelievable restoration and exaltation.

Chapter 7 covers Isa 56–66, and chapter 8 provides a summary of Berges's conclusions. He believes this last unit is structured in a chiastic or concentric arrangement with Isa 60–62 at its core and assigns these chapters to Trito-Isaiah, an anonymous prophet who ministered in the years after 480 and deliberately crafted his message in dependence upon Proto- and Deutero-Isaianic texts. Berges believes disciples of Trito-Isaiah later added a "Repentance Redaction" consisting of 56:9–59:21* in the latter half of the fifth century to conjoin Isa 60–62* with 40–55, while also creating the first bridge to the Proto-Isaianic texts with the addition of 1:27–28. At the turn of the fifth to fourth century the "Redaction of the Servant Community" (56:1–8; 63:1–66:24*) was added to address the bleak situation in Jerusalem following the exile. No longer is ethnicity determinative whether one finds entrance into the servant community but rather ethics. Following on the heels of Israel, the nations are included among Yhwh's servants, and together they form a new Jerusalem, that is, a new society that is none other than Isaiah's vision for a new creation.

Lind is to be congratulated for translating Berges's work into English, which should help bridge the gap between Anglophone and Continental scholars. While the prose is somewhat stilted at times, that is understandable given the technical nature of the work. In addition to the main text, the footnotes have been translated into English, with the exception of non-German texts. Berges is to be commended for interacting with scholarship written in not only German, French, and English but also in Spanish, Dutch, and Italian. With the exception of commentaries, no other work attempts to provide a diachronic and synchronic reading of the entire book of Isaiah. In this manner, this book will serve as a valuable reference for scholars working in Isaiah, by providing a critical introduction to each major literary unit of Isaiah as well as the book as a whole. Berges's thesis that the book of Isaiah consistently provides a Zion-centered message of hope for the nations because of their inclusion as servants of Yhwh is compelling and rigorously defended.

Unfortunately, this translation appears fourteen years after the publication of Berges's original German edition, so the work is somewhat dated. Significant commentaries written by Blenkinsopp, Childs, Goldingay and Payne, Paul, Seitz, and other works have been published since the 1998 German edition. Yet even for works written prior to 1998, noticeably absent from Berges's discussion are Scandinavian and Jewish voices. Scandinavian scholars such as Antti Laato have made significant contributions to synchronic and diachronic readings of Isaiah, and Jewish scholars such as Kaufmann and Haran, and more recently Sommer and Paul, have argued for the unity of Isa 40–66. In addition, Berges fails to engage the argument for a Josianic redaction to Isa 1–39*, as defended by Barth and Sweeney.

The question remains whether Berges genuinely engages the question of why the Isaianic material became associated with Isaiah ben Amoz when the prophet is so absent within the text. Although he claims to engage in synchronic analysis, diachronic concerns dominate. In his chapter on Isa 56–66, Berges does not even offer a synchronic reading of the unit and instead launches immediately into a discussion of its diachronic development. If Berges attends to the same research question with the same methodology as his Anglophone counterparts, why do his conclusions differ so markedly from them? In addition, while Berges highlights Isaiah's message of inclusion for Gentiles within the Zion community based upon ethical living, he minimizes texts that emphasize Torah obedience (e.g., 48:18–19; 56:6–7). Rather than view Isaiah, particularly chapters 56–66, as a protest against Ezra and Nehemiah's religious reforms, as Berges argues, the authors of Ezra-Neh viewed the postexilic community in Jerusalem as a fulfillment, albeit a partial one, of the promises of Isa 40–55, as argued by Koch, McConville, Williamson, Baltzer, and, more recently, Goldingay and Payne.

Ulrich Berges's *The Book of Isaiah* takes its place along with Albert's *Israel in Exile* and Steck's *The Prophetic Books and Their Theological Witness* as the most significant German works on Isaiah and prophetic literature to be translated into

English in recent years. Even if one does not share Berges's diachronic and theological conclusions, the work is a must read for its summaries of research and
synchronic readings of the major units of Isaiah.

Zeichen und Sinnbilder: Die Kinder der Propheten Jesaja und Hosea, by Kay Weißflog. Arbeiten zur Bibel und ihrer Geschichte 36. Leipzig: Evangelische Verlagsanstalt, 2011. Pp. 577. Hardcover. €68.00. ISBN 9783374028528.

Mark W. Hamilton, Abilene Christian University, Abilene, Texas

Even casual readers of the Hebrew prophets find the odd names of Isaiah's and
Hosea's children tantalizing or amusing. Their very oddness, however, makes
them useful as signals of the prophetic books' methods of composition (with
Hosea, for example, turning them alternatively into symbols of doom and restoration, in keeping with its overall pattern of doom and then hope) and their
overall intent (with both books looking forward to restoration after catastrophe). The name-giving thus functions as more than a "prophetic sign act," as
older scholars argued. *Nomen est omen* (at least *fortasse*), if not for the bearer
of the name, then for an entire people (and not for magical reasons but because
of a divine choice now concretized by creators of a prophetic text). They are
literary devices, appropriate to a work of literature, and must be understood as
such.

In this massive study of the names and their literary contexts, a revision of
his PhD dissertation at Leipzig, Kay Weißflog has sought to do just that. After a
detailed introduction to the problem (11–45), he offers a line-by-line text-critical
analysis (37–85), then a detailed commentary (entitled simply "Textanalyse")
on Isa 7–8 and Hos 1–3 (87–457). This latter, core chapter itself deserves a place
alongside full-scale commentaries on Isaiah because Weißflog considers a wide
range of issues beyond the key problem of the names and their signification, often
drawing judicious conclusions that steer a course between the textual realism too
common in Anglophone scholarship and the extreme speculation on redaction-
critical grounds arguably too abundant in the German world. The book concludes
with four chapters comparing the two conceptions of the names present in the
Isaiah and Hosea scrolls and helpful summary of this rather (perhaps overly) long
book (459–531).

Reading Weißflog's study reveals several things long suspected but insufficiently comprehended. Both Isa 7–8 (or better, Isa 6–8, the so-called Isaianic
Denkschrift, which Weißflog rightly attributes to the late Assyrian period) and
Hos 1–3 shows signs of literary reworking. Sometimes this reworking seems close
to a process of compilation of preexisting literary units (which Weißflog compares
to the compilation of prophetic oracles at Deir 'Alla and elsewhere [244]), and at
others a more redaction-critical approach seems to be illuminating. The point is
that the texts are just that: *literary* creations and not simply reports of events in
the life of the prophets, thus not susceptible to facile psychological readings. Since

the prophets themselves are now literary characters, the names of their children function as part of a literary world (e.g., 528).

True, the act of name-giving for symbolic purposes has several ancient Near Eastern antecedents, especially in the royal court, as Weißflog points out. But the prophetic texts at hand go their own ways, and with skill. As Weißflog puts it with reference to the use of the names of Isaiah's children, "Die Charakterisierung der Namen als Warnungen vor drohendem, aber nicht unausweichlichem Unheil, die die Alternative von Heils- oder Unheilsverkündigung aufbricht, wird zum einen dem literarischen Befund gerecht, der retrospektiv die Möglichkeiten einer Verhinderung des Unheils als geeben erkennen last (vgl. Jes 7), und stimmt insofern mit den zu beobachtenden heilsprophetischen Zügen des Jesajabildes überein" (244–45). The suppleness of the books' use of the names is part and parcel of its overall artistry. The best explanation for this literary virtuosity would be that it reflects the work of skilled authors who were of several minds about their understanding of the fate of their people and the work of its God. Weißflog's study helps make this fact more clear.

The second realization is that the two prophetic books use the literary device of name-giving in different ways because they reflect different historical settings, but more importantly, different conceptions of the role of the northern and southern Israelite kingdoms and of the agency of Yhwh. For Isa 7–8, the names שאר ישוב and מהר שלל חש בז are "Drohwörter" concerning Judah's tragic fate after the Assyrian intervention in the region. Because the names are themselves ambiguous—does the *remnant* return or the remnant *return*?—their interpretation can alter with the combination of the more hopeful (?) name עמנו אל (Weißflog thus takes the opposite view of Sweeney in his FOTL volume). Hosea, on the other hand, exploits the multivalence of its names, first by announcing through them Yhwh's implacable rejection of Israel, then by reversing field and undoing their negative function, this time with reference solely (?) to the north. (But even this "solely" invites further study of the book's reference to "Judah," which seems to be other than a redactional addition, as in Wolff's major treatment.) In short, literary, theological, and historical concerns thus intertwine in both cases in highly complex ways.

In reading this book, then, one finds many things with which to agree and others about which further thinking is required. Certainly the problem Weißflog raises is significant, not so much in itself but for its ability to show how prophetic works use the same literary device in different ways to address a common problem (i.e., the terrible tragedies of the late eighth century and the theological challenges raised by foreign domination). Since it has become increasingly clear that the various prophetic books (especially those named for eighth-century BCE prophets) share an interconnected literary history, the problem at hand offers a case study for considering larger issues: How did Israel come to create prophetic books on a scale unprecedented in their environment? How did various Israelite thinkers deal with the experience of Assyrian domination (compare the multilayered presentation of the end of the northern kingdom in 2 Kgs 17)? How did the creators of prophetic texts intend for their juxtaposition of hope and doom oracles to be interpreted coherently by their audiences? How do the *Kindernamen* fit in with the prophetic books' overall use of names (Isa 7–8 and Hos 1–3 contain others, after all), not to mention the use of names, often in large constellations, in other prophetic texts. There are other questions as well.

Weißflog's work leaves such questions unanswered, of course, but offers potential resources for their address. In part, this study is limited by its own self-chosen scope and in part by its method, for the kind of close reading Weißflog practices does some things well, while for others, the deployment of more recent approaches to semiotics or textual analysis would have proven illuminating. Still, all scholars must make choices, and a reviewer should not fault a book for not doing what it did not set out to do. One may hope that Weißflog will continue his studies in the shaping of the prophetic works in days . This volume evidences a willingness to take a fresh look at old problems, surely a commendable thing for all scholars of the exciting world of the biblical prophets. Weißflog thus deserves our thanks for this comprehensive, yet clear and inviting, work.

Sworn Enemies: The Divine Oath, the Book of Ezekiel, and the Polemics of Exile, by C. A. Strine. Beihefte zur Zeitschrift für die alttestamentliche Wissenschaft 436. Berlin: de Gruyter, 2013. Pp. xvi + 343. Hardcover. $140.00. ISBN 9783110290530.

John T. Strong, Missouri State University, Springfield, Missouri

This work presents the published version of Strine's D.Phil. thesis (2011, Oxford). It is a careful and exhaustive piece of sustained research into two motifs found in the text of Ezekiel: "as I live" and the "lifted hand" formula. The results of Strine's research are bold, bringing the interesting theory of public and hidden transcripts to bear on Ezekiel's oracles. Although suspect at points, Strine's argument makes significant additions to the current discussions over this enigmatic prophet and ancient Israel's traditions.

Strine argues a twofold thesis. First, Ezekiel took the "as I live" formula from the Deuteronomistic traditions but used it to announce punishment against the "nonexiles" (i.e., those Judahites left in the land after 597 BCE). Second, he concludes that the "lifted hand" formula is not an oath formula at all but rather either a transfer of land formula or a judgment formula. Both formulae serve the public transcript of the (formerly) intellectual elite of Jerusalem, challenging the nonexiles' claims to the land, which they based on a combined Abraham-Jacob tradition and a hidden transcript intended to subvert Marduk's claims as the powerful deity who controls Chaos, subtly placing Yahweh in that role.

Strine's introductory chapter asks: Why does Ezekiel not condemn the Babylonians, especially given other oracles against the nations? (1). To satisfy his curiosity, Strine turns to the authenticating elements in the "as I live" and the "lifted hand" formulae (6–10). Strine then surveys the secondary literature

(10–16), a strength of this work throughout. His method of study includes the ancient Near Eastern context and form criticism, but he also brings in the discourse model of James C. Scott (26–39), which highlights the concepts of "public transcript" (the self-portrait of the ruling class; 26–28) and "hidden transcripts" (the offstage speech by a dominated class; 29–33), an interesting and important contribution to Ezekiel studies.

Chapter 2 examines the ancient Near Eastern context for divine oaths. Strine finds only eight instances in the ancient Near Eastern corpus where deities make oaths using the authenticating formula "as I live" (44–71), compared to the Hebrew Bible, which contains conservatively six times the number (70). Strine's "Excursus 1," at the end of this chapter, is an extensive discussion of the "lifted hand" formula. First, Strine argues that there is no ancient Near Eastern gesture that parallels the authenticating element "lifted hand" (dismissing a touching the throat gesture that is found with oath taking; 73). Second, and central to Strine's argument, the "lifted hand" formula in the Hebrew Bible is not an oath formula at all, citing Ps 10:12; Isa 49:22, but most critically, Deut 32:40. I have serious reservations about Strine's interpretation of this verse. The most natural reading of the Hebrew would be to read the "lifted hand" in Deut 32:40a in synthetic parallelism with the "as I live" formula in 32:40b, hence both formulae denoting oath taking. Strine, however, separates these two lines on the basis of a line break found in 4QDeut^{q} and argues that the "lifted hand" formula closes out a strophe dealing with judgment and has nothing to do with the oath formula, "as I live" in Deut 32:40b (75–80). Next, Strine argues that the "lifted hand" formula does have a parallel Akkadian formula *našâ-nadānu* ("to take/give"), by which an authority figure takes land from one party and gives it to another. Strine then defines the "lifted hand" formula as a land-transfer formula, a definition that he nuances a little later in his book. His argument here bears much of the weight of his analysis of the "lifted hand" formula in his study, and it is curious that he placed this analysis in an excursus rather than as a part of the main body of his thesis.

Strine's third chapter examines the two formulae form-critically. In regard to the "as I live" formula, Strine argues that it announces punishment in prophetic speeches (103–6), frequently in disputation speeches (107–12; hence the title of his book, *Sworn Enemies*). The "lifted hand" formula Strine separates into two conventions. The first (נשׂא יד + ל with infinitive construct; Exod 6:8; Num 14:30; Ezek 20:5b, 6, 15, 23, 28, 42; 47:14; Ps 106:26; Neh 9:15) deals with the transfer of land (118–23). One may ask, however, whether Exod 6:8 and Ezek 20:5b are so narrowly focused on land transfer, or, perhaps better, whether they deal with the creation of a people. Strine's earlier conclusion regarding its parallel with the Akkadian "take/give" formula as land-transfer formula tips the scales for Strine. The second (נשׂא יד + preposition with finite verb; Deut 32:40a; Ezek 20:5a; 36:7; and 44:12) is the assignment of punishment in an oracle of salvation to God's people (123–27). Note that Strine has peeled off the "lifted hand" formula that appears in Ezek 20:5b from the one immediately above in Ezek 20:5a, explaining that verse 5a is secondary. This allows him to maintain that the form in Deut 32:40a is about judgment and that the "lifted hand" formula is not an oath formula.

The fourth chapter identifies the social and literary setting, by which Strine means the theological traditions associated with the different formulae. Strine identifies the "as I live" formula (134–53) as an adaptation of the Deuterono-mist's "as Yahweh lives," an insightful identification (134–42). Next he associates the "lifted hand" land-transfer formula with the Holiness Code (154–64). While adapted from Deuteronomistic literature and influenced by P and H, Ezekiel created something new ("the Ezekiel tradition," 169) with the third formula, the "lifted hand" punishment formula (165–66).

In part 2 Strine turns to the function of the two formulae, and he begins this examination in chapter 5 by looking at Ezekiel's use of the "as I live" and "lifted hand—punishment" formulae as they were applied against the inhabitants who remained in Jerusalem after 597 and 587. Perhaps his most important contributions are found here, where he applies Scott's theory of "public transcript" to the text, presenting a picture of Ezekiel as the creator of a polemic against the non-exiles in order to preserve his and his fellow exiles' claim on the land (221–26). Strine concludes that the prophet's use of the "as I live" formula found in 5:5–17 (v. 11; 178–81), 33:24–29 (v. 27; by which he also draws in 11:14–21; 182–90), and 20:1–44 (190–93) all work to deny the nonexiles' claim on the land on the basis of Abraham (cf. 33:24).

Strine turns next to a discussion of 35:1–36:15, which is an oracle against Edom and a salvation oracle for the mountains of Israel. Strine argues here that Ezekiel challenges the Jacob tradition, which he then claims is a cipher for the Jerusalemites remaining after the exile (193–211). It is unclear why Strine feels compelled to make this argument. First, there are good reasons to read the text quite directly as an oracle against Mount Seir, which may have had an ancient connection with the worship of Yahweh (see Isa 34–35), and so, with the destruction of the temple, may have seemed to some to hold a claim as Yahweh's throne room. Second, according to Strine, Jacob never actually appears in Ezekiel's oracles, for Strine regards all mentions of Jacob as secondary (see 20:5a; 28:25; 37:25; and 39:25; 196). I remain dubious on this point, but still it begs the question: If Jacob was never mentioned by Ezekiel, why does Strine feel the need to pit Ezekiel against a combined Abraham-Jacob tradition by which the nonexiles made a land claim?

In chapter 6 Strine returns to the initial research question with which he began his book: Why Babylon? (228–30). In this chapter he applies Scott's theoretical model of "hidden transcripts" (see especially 262–67), arguing that Ezekiel appropriated for Yahweh language and imagery used in Babylonian materials for Marduk and thereby set Yahweh in the role of the divine warrior calming chaos. In regard to Ezek 17, Ezekiel describes Yahweh as using a net, a tool used by Marduk in the Enuma Elish, and he raises high the humble and brings low the mighty (but see also 1 Sam 2:6–7; Ps 107:39–43). Second, Strine examines Ezek 34:1–16 and 20:32–44, arguing that the depiction of Yahweh as a shepherd and gatherer subverts a similar image of Marduk (243–58). Strine suggests at this point that Ezekiel may have been every bit as much involved in the development of monotheism as Deutero-Isaiah but that his contribution is obscured by his hidden transcript (258–62). He does not, however, work with Ezek 21:23–28 (Eng. 21:18–23), which is an oracle about (not against) Nebuchadnezzar, depicting him as Yahweh's tool, though there is no hidden transcript in this instance. At this point Strine concludes his work, chapter 7, summarizing his argument and discussing the prophet's role in defining the identity and significance of the exiles.

Strine's thesis is bold, though as can be seen from the comments above, it may be too bold at important points. Nevertheless, Strine engages with the text and the secondary literature in great detail and sustained energy. He has arranged his argument logically and clearly, moving from point to point. Furthermore, Strine's application of Scott's model of public and hidden transcript requires scholarship to once again pause and consider how Ezekiel's exilic community of educated elites reacted to their situation. In the end, Strine has made a substantive contribution to the scholarly dialogue about this often enigmatic, displaced priestly prophet.

Rejoice, Dear Zion! Hebrew Construct Phrases with "Daughter" and "Virgin" as Nomen Regens, by Magnar Kartveit. Beihefte zur Zeitschrift für die alttestamentliche Wissenschaft 447. Berlin: de Gruyter, 2013. Pp. viii + 200. Cloth. $112.00. ISBN 9783110309157.

Peter Bekins, Wright State University, Cincinnati, Ohio

Rejoice, Dear Zion! discusses the construct phrase בַּת־צִיּוֹן "Daughter (of) Zion" and similar phrases of the form בַּת + geographic name (GN) in the Hebrew Bible. These phrases are widely understood as feminine personifications of the GN, but there is disagreement concerning how this is achieved and what effect it is intended to produce. Magnar Kartveit adapts the argument of W. F. Stinespring ("No Daughter of Zion: A Study of the Appositional Genitive in Hebrew Grammar," *Encounter* 26 [1965]) that בַּת־צִיּוֹן is best described as an appositional genitive. Zion does not *have* a daughter; she *is* the daughter. Stinespring further suggested that בַּת functions as a term of endearment like "dear" or "poor" rather than as a kinship term. This view enjoys wide acceptance (see Adele Berlin, *Lamentations: A Commentary*, 2004, 12), but Kartveit adds the twist that the term בַּת is a metaphor applied directly to צִיּוֹן. Consequently, the phrase "Dear Zion" does not introduce or refer to a daughter at all.

Kartveit's reading is intended to counter the tendency to treat "Daughter Zion" as a feminine literary figure. In chapter 1 he is particularly critical of Carleen Mandolfo's *Daughter Zion Talks Back to the Prophets* (2007) and the subsequent collection of response essays in *Daughter Zion: Her Portrait, Her Response* (2012), the result of a 2008 special session at the Society of Biblical Literature's Annual Meeting. Kartveit objects that "The literary figure of Daughter Zion is mostly assumed, and on this assumption the authors discuss the violence, oppression, and abuse of female figures, but also Daughter Zion's salvation and joy" (6–7). In contrast to these literary studies, he calls for a more rigorous linguistic approach to the issue.

Chapters 2 and 3 survey the commentaries, grammars, and dictionaries before moving to several prominent views of בַּת־צִיּוֹן in the literature. Kartviet sees tension between the interpretation that "Daughter Zion" refers to the inhabitants of the city as a collective and the grammatical analysis of בַּת־צִיּוֹן as a genitive construction that refers to a daughter (25). He finds the ubiquitous explanation that "Daughter Zion" relates to "Zion" through personification to be imprecise, and he devotes the final portion of chapter 3 to discussions of personification, metaphor, and irony. Kartveit emphasizes that a GN may refer to its population through metonymy; therefore, characterization of the GN as animate is not necessarily evidence of personification (57). For this reason, metaphor provides a more promising framework for understanding בַּת־צִיּוֹן. These final sections are brief, however, and they are organized as literature review without presenting a coherent theory of metaphor to guide the study.

Chapter 4 examines the Biblical Hebrew construct state in relation to the genitive, and Kartveit appeals to a synchronic approach that resists the imposition of categories from outside languages. This seems irrelevant to the thesis, since appositional genitives are found in Greek, Latin, Akkadian, and Classical Arabic, among others. While Kartveit tenuously describes the relationship between בַת and צִיּוֹן as appositional, however, he rejects the use of the term *genitive*. The argument is difficult to follow, but Kartveit's concern seems to be the dependency relationship indicated by the genitive case. In the Akkadian *šarrat mātim* "the queen of the land," for instance, *mātim* is inflected as a genitive, indicating its dependence on *šarrat* "queen," which stands in the construct state and is the head of the phrase. This underlying dependency relation is also understood to be present in the Biblical Hebrew construct phrase, but Kartveit argues that the loss of case inflection has actually allowed the construct state to develop independently from the genitive so that it "had an existence of its own" (103). The construct state simply signals "connection to something that follows" (108). Most importantly, since the *nomen rectum* is no longer inflected as a genitive, Kartveit argues that this connection can go in either direction. Neither the *nomen regens* nor *nomen rectum* can be considered the "important part" of the construct phrase, apparently to the point that the *nomen regens* is not necessarily the head of the phrase. "On the other hand, it will be an exaggeration on my point of view to see the construct state word(s) as the governing word(s)" (110).

Chapter 5 turns from the grammar of the construct phrase to the semantics of בַּת־צִיּוֹן. To strengthen the claim that "Daughter Zion" refers simply to "Zion," Kartveit argues for a basic semantic equivalence between the two phrases in the prophetic literature. For instance, בַּת־צִיּוֹן can be associated with characteristics of a city rather than a daughter, such as a "wall" (Lam 2:8), "gates" (Ps 9:15), or "elders" (Lam 2:10). Further, צִיּוֹן alone can refer to the population of the city (Isa 1:27) or be personified (Isa 66:8). Therefore, the presence of בַּת־צִיּוֹן in a similar context (Jer 4:31) does not demonstrate that בַת introduces personification, since "The 'personification' of 'Zion' has already taken place through the metonymic use of 'Zion' alone, and no new element of reference seems to be provided by the use of 'daughter'" (147). Following Stinespring, Kartveit understands בַת to be a term of endearment, and the use of a בַת + GN phrase to refer to a foreign city or state, such as בַת־בָּבֶל "Dear Babylon," is ironic.

Chapter 6 asks, "Can Nomen Regens in Biblical Hebrew be a Metaphor Applied (in Apposition?) to Nomen Rectum?" This chapter returns to the problem anticipated in chapter 4 related to the dependency relation underlying the construct phrase. Kartveit begins by noting that it is common for the *nomen rectum* to have an attributive relation to the *nomen regens*, such as הַר־קָדְשׁוֹ "his holy mountain" (Ps 24:7). Following the argument in chapter 4, Kartveit suggests that this could be reversed, with the *nomen regens* an attribute of *nomen rectum*. He provides supporting examples from outside the בַת + GN corpus, such as תּוֹלַעַת יַעֲקֹב "worm Jacob" (Isa 41:14). Kartveit explains, "the nomen regens is a metaphor that describes the nomen rectum: Jacob is described in terms of a worm, where e.g. the smallness and pitifulness is transferred to Jacob" (166). After further examples, however, the chapter ends indecisively, "In בַת־צִיּוֹן nomen regens *may be* attributive and a metaphor applied to nomen rectum" (178, emphasis original).

The problem with this analysis derives from a misunderstanding of the nature of headedness and its importance to grammar and discourse. The issue is obscured in the phrase בַת־צִיּוֹן by the fact that both בַת and צִיּוֹן are considered feminine singular nouns. In contrast, the comparable phrases בְּתוּלַת יִשְׂרָאֵל "virgin (of) Israel," בַת־עַמִּי "daughter (of) my people," and תּוֹלַעַת יַעֲקֹב "worm (of) Jacob," involve a gender mismatch, and the example תּוֹלַעַת יַעֲקֹב (Isa 41:14) is particularly interesting. Like בַת־צִיּוֹן and צִיּוֹן, the phrases תּוֹלַעַת יַעֲקֹב and יַעֲקֹב occur in parallel contexts in Isa 41. For instance, Jacob is told אַל־תִּירָא "Do not fear" (Isa 41:13) and worm Jacob is told אַל־תִּירְאִי "Do not fear" (Isa 41:14). Further, Jacob is promised אֲנִי עֲזַרְתִּיךָ "I will help you" (Isa 41:13) and worm Jacob is promised אֲנִי עֲזַרְתִּיךְ "I will help you" (Isa 41:14). Nonetheless, the agreement of תּוֹלַעַת יַעֲקֹב with the feminine verb אַל־תִּירְאִי "Do not fear" and the use of the feminine pronoun for anaphoric reference in the clause אֲנִי עֲזַרְתִּיךְ "I will help you" clearly indicate that the feminine תּוֹלַעַת is the head of the phrase and establishes its referent. This poses a significant problem for the argument that תּוֹלַעַת is a metaphor applied to יַעֲקֹב in a manner in which a referent for תּוֹלַעַת is either not introduced or subsequently drops from the discourse. Rather, the poet allows the semantic frames evoked by "worm" and "Jacob" to coexist and interact until the metaphor is switched to the masculine מוֹרַג חָרוּץ "threshing sledge" in Isa 41:15. The phrases בְּתוּלַת יִשְׂרָאֵל and בַת־עַמִּי likewise occur as the subject of feminine rather than masculine verbs.

Kartveit's analysis of the great extent to which בַת־צִיּוֹן and צִיּוֹן are functioning as equivalents in the prophetic literature is persuasive and cautions against overemphasizing the degree to which "Daughter Zion" may have persisted beyond the text in the Israelite imagination. The argument that this equivalence is achieved by applying בַּת to צִיּוֹן as a metaphor within the grammar of the construct phrase has significant weaknesses, however, and it is more likely that the בַּת + GN formula has become idiomatic or conventionalized in the prophetic vocabulary (see H. G. C. Williamson, *Isaiah 1–5* [ICC], 2006, 69).

Zechariah 9–14, by Paul L. Redditt. International Exegetical Commentary on the Old Testament. Stuttgart: Kohlhammer, 2012. Pp. 167. Hardcover. €54.00. ISBN 9783170216518.

Ralph K. Hawkins, Averett University, Danville, Virginia

This volume is the first installment in the International Exegetical Commentary on the Old Testament (IECOT), which intends to offer interpretations that represent multiple perspectives on the books of the Old Testament to a wide, international audience that includes scholars, laypeople, and pastors. The series editors note that "biblical commentaries too often reflect the fragmented character of contemporary biblical scholarship, where different geographical or methodological sub-groups of scholars pursue specific methodologies and/or theories with little engagement of alternative approaches" (9). The IECOT will attempt to address this fragmentation by bringing together editors and authors from North America, Europe, and Israel with a variety of exegetical and religious perspectives, both Christian and Jewish, and will also include commentaries on books recognized as canonical by diverse Christian confessions, including the deuterocanonical Old Testament books. In accordance with the IECOT's desire to bring together European and English-speaking scholars, the series will be published in both English and German. The promotional literature promises that the delay between the publication of the original and its translation will not exceed two years.

One of the ways that the IECOT seeks to be contemporary is by bringing together synchronic and diachronic perspectives. A "synchronic" study of scripture focuses on the study of a biblical text in a particular stage of its development, often the final, canonized form of the text. This approach includes narratological study, reader-response criticism, historically informed exegesis of a particular text, as well as other methods. The "diachronic" approach studies a biblical text over time. The diachronic approach developed in Europe, while synchronic study burgeoned in North America and Israel, and the two have often been thought of as unsuited for a single study. The IECOT aims "to bring synchronic and diachronic methods into closer alignment, allowing these approaches to work in a complementary and mutually-informative rather than antagonistic manner" (9). Another way that the IECOT will be contemporary is that each author will highlight his or her own specific contemporary methodological and hermeneutical perspectives, such as gender-critical, liberation-theological, and so on. The editors express the hope that a series with the foregoing features "will be a series of volumes that display a range of ways that various methodologies and discourses can be integrated into the interpretation of the diverse books of the Old Testament" (10).

In an introduction, Redditt begins with a brief overview of the relationship between Zech 9–14 and 1–8 (13–15), noting some of the main scholarly views on the relationship between these sections. Some traditional scholars continue to argue for authorship by Zechariah, and some critical scholars have even recently adopted the view that the entire book may have been written in a single generation by one author, Zechariah himself. Others see chapters 9–14 as later additions that seek to explain the issues set forth in Zech 1–8. Redditt himself argues that there are "obvious differences" between Zech 1–8 and 9–14, including genre, date, and the use of superscriptions in Zechariah that "follow the same pattern" as a number of occurrences in Haggai and Malachi and, therefore for Redditt, point toward more continuity with Malachi than with Haggai and Zech 1–8. For these reasons, Redditt adopts the position that Zech 9–14 constitutes one or more additions to Zech 1–8, though he notes that "one can and should discern connections between Zechariah 1–8 and 9–14" (15).

After discussing the relationship between Zech 9–14 with 1–8, Redditt provides an overview of synchronic and diachronic readings of these chapters (15–17, 20–26). In his synchronic analysis, he outlines key themes in these chapters, especially the growing pessimism as one moves from chapters 9–10 into chapter 11; the change in focus from Judah and Ephraim in chapters 9–10 to Jerusalem and Judah alone in chapters 12–14; the evolving role of the Davidic king; and the surfacing in chapters 12 and 14 of the holy-war theme. Redditt examines the literary structure of Zech 9–14 (18–19), postulating that the heading repeated before 9:1 and 12:1 indicate a division between chapters 9–11 and 12–14. He notes alternative theories before conjecturing that Zech 11:4–16 constitutes a "sign-enactment report" that shapes the focus of Zech 9–14. His study of the diachronic development of Zech 9–14 focuses on the expression of hope for a future king in 9:9–10, which he discusses in relation to pro-Davidic sentiments in other parts of Scripture and concludes must have been written prior to 500 BCE. In discussing the gradual composition of 12–14, Redditt identifies 12:1–9, 12:10–13:6, and 14:1–21 as three distinct sections, proposes that the shepherd material (10:2–3a; 11:1–3, 17; 13:7–9) was added later to bring coherence to chapters 9–14, and suggests that further redactional "bridges" bound the different textual units together.

The final issues that Redditt addresses in his introduction are those of date and historical background, the identities of the mysterious "shepherds" and "merchants" who feature so prominently in chapter 11, the structure of Zech 9–14, and the relationship of these chapters to the Book of the Twelve. As for the date, Redditt reviews the current positions held by other scholars and concludes that Zech 9 accords well with the late sixth century BCE, Zech 10 was written at the beginning of the fifth century, and the remainder was compiled in the latter part of the fifth century (26–29). He identifies the "shepherds" as the Jerusalem clergy and the "merchant" as their Persian-sponsored overlords (30). As for the relationship of Zech 9–14 to the Book of the Twelve, Redditt postulates that it may have been added after the narrative of Jonah, making it the latest piece to be added to this collection (30–31).

In the commentary itself Redditt follows the fivefold division of the text he outlined in the introduction. These include: "Zechariah 9. God's Future Kingdom and Earthly King" (33–56); "Zechariah 10. Judah, Ephraim, and the Exiles" (57–73); "Zechariah 11. The Shepherd Narrative" (75–92); "Zechariah 12–13. The Future of Jerusalem and Judah, 1" (93–124); and "Zechariah 14. The Future of Jerusalem and Judah, 2" (125–46). Redditt discusses each of these sections in five divisions, including: (1) his own translation of the text; (2) "Notes on Texts and Translation"; (3) "Synchronic Analysis"; (4) "Diachronic Analysis"; and (5) "Concluding Remarks." His notes on texts and translation are easy to use, though Hebrew words are not transliterated, which may prevent some readers from being able to take full advantage of them. The section on synchronic analysis, in which Redditt works thoroughly through the text, amplifying significant concepts and explicating the message of the text, tends to be the longest. His diachronic analysis is typically brief and consists of the examination of the original setting of the text under study, the occurrence of similar ideas elsewhere in Scripture, the chronological relationships between the respective texts, and other such issues.

In a conclusion (147–52), a summary of findings provides the basis for asking four additional questions. First, Redditt asks how Zech 9–14 came to be attached to Zech 1–8, and he briefly proposes a redactional process that began in the late sixth or early fifth century and concluded by the end of the fifth century BCE. Second, he queries about who would benefit from the kind of future anticipated in Zech 9–14, and he postulates a scribe or a group of scribes who "spoke to and for other like-minded people that held a dim view of post-exilic leadership" (149). Third, Redditt asks whether the program envisioned in Zech 9–14 was viable and notes that the vision outlined in Zechariah has "no obvious political agenda to implement," but one that is much more nuanced. He writes:

> Perhaps the contribution of Zechariah 9–14 is that it does not try to solve such issues by naming a future winner. It seems to distrust all people who make power plays. Perhaps in leaving open the issue of legitimacy, it stood as a critique against *any* party that tried to advance its agenda by oppressive means. If so, that is no small achievement. If force results only in counterforce, no human agency that achieves its goals by force can be trusted. The wiser option for people living in communities formed by force and ruled by foreign empires would be not to trust any such government to obey God and care for its subjects, and not to give ultimate allegiance to such a government either. (150)

The fourth and final question Redditt asks here is whether Zech 9–14 is an apocalypse, either in whole or in part. In seeking to answer this question, Redditt provides a brief discussion of apocalyptic, on the basis of which he concludes that, while Zech 14 clearly contains idyllic material, it is not necessarily apocalyptic. He concludes that Zech 14 is "a work on the path toward the development of apocalypses, but not itself an apocalypse or fully apocalyptic in thought" (152). The volume concludes with a bibliography (153–57) and indexes of Hebrew words (158–59), key words (159–60), citations (160–64), and other sources (164).

I would note what seem to me to be a few weaknesses in this volume. First, Redditt's commentary seems to interact primarily with modern commentators. It would seem to me that, for a study to be truly diachronic, it should include some discussion of ancient and medieval interpretation. For example, Redditt takes a nonmessianic view of Zech 13:7–9 but does not discuss messianic interpretations of the passage, such as those of Rabbi Dosa, whom the Babylonian Talmud reports identified the pierced one as Messiah ben Joseph (*Sukkah* 52a), who he said would fall in battle in the war against Gog and Magog, or of Rashi (1040–1105), who adopted this view. I am not suggesting that the passage must be interpreted messianically, only that a diachronic study should review and interact with such interpretations. Second, based on the fact that the series is marketed as a major effort to bridge the gap between international scholarly communities, one would assume that the commentary would interact more with non-English material. While there is some interaction with a few French and German works, most of the sources cited are in English. A significant omission in the discussion of the Book of the Twelve, for example, are the two volumes on their development by Jakob Wöhrle, *Die frühen Sammlungen des Zwölfprophetenbuches: Untersuchungen zu ihrer Entstehung und Komposition* (BZAW 360; Berlin: de Gruyter, 2006) and *Der Abschluss des Zwölfprophetenbuches: Buchübergreifende Redaktionsprozesse in den späten Sammlungen* (BZAW 389; Berlin: de Gruyter, 2008). In Redditt's defense, however, he does note that his understanding of the place of Zechariah in the Book of the Twelve is heavily influenced by the work of James Nogalski and Aaron Schart, and he also interacts with a number of recent commentaries and monographs on Zechariah.

Aside from these shortcomings, Redditt's commentary has several strengths. First, it is clear in its explication of the text. Second, it has a design that makes for ease of use, including subject indicators that appear in the margins. These are helpful in scanning different portions of the volume. Third, the volume uses footnotes, which is helpful in locating sources for further consultation. Fourth, the volume is particularly successful in bringing synchronic and diachronic methods into closer alignment and allowing these approaches to work in a complementary and mutually informative way. Since this is identified as "one central distinguishing feature" of the IECOT, I would say that, overall, the volume achieves its purpose and charts the direction for future volumes. I would recommend Paul Redditt's IECOT volume on Zech 9–14 for scholars, graduate students, and even pastors, particularly those who are interested in gaining an international, ecumenical, and contemporary perspective on the interpretation of the Old Testament (including the deuterocanonical books), as well as those with a special interest in the synchronic and diachronic study of these texts. Furthermore, I would suggest that the importance of this series will make the IECOT a necessary addition to graduate-school and seminary libraries.

WRITINGS

The Politics of Pessimism in Ecclesiastes: A Social-Science Perspective, by Mark R. Sneed. Society of Biblical Literature Ancient Israel and Its Literature 12. Atlanta: Society of Biblical Literature, 2012. Pp. xvi + 341. Paper. $41.95. ISBN 9781589836105.

Martin A. Shields, University of Sydney, Sydney, Australia

Mark Sneed is Professor of Bible at Lubbock Christian University. *The Politics of Pessimism in Ecclesiastes* is a heavily revised version of his 1990 Ph.D. dissertation from Drew University, finally published in 2012. Sneed explains his aim as follows: "I will offer an interpretation of Ecclesiastes that both acknowledges the unorthodox nature of Qohelet's words and manages to account for its acceptance among the canonical books of the Hebrew Bible" (10).

A substantial part of Sneed's book is given over to reviewing previous scholarly attempts to account for Qohelet's heterodox character. Sneed begins examining non-social-scientific approaches, discussing in particular the notion that Qohelet's pessimism and skepticism arise out of the national crisis associated with catastrophic historical events. Sneed dismisses such attempts and concludes that "the problem of evil is a universal and perennial phenomenon that is not necessarily connected with social upheaval or anarchy" (34).

Sneed also examines the claim that Qohelet's pessimism reflects the influence of ancient Greek philosophical thought—a notion that has recently been regaining favor. Sneed concludes that "there is no definitive evidence that Qohelet has drunk deeply from the well of Hellenism" (46). He demonstrates that there are adequate antecedents for Qohelet's thought from throughout the ancient Near East (44–46).

Sneed's second chapter presents a comprehensive review of social-science approaches to Qohelet, which serves as background to his own contribution (which he describes as a "reconfiguration" of the data accumulated in his analysis of the work of others). Sneed's summary and critique of virtually all the work done in the area provides an invaluable resource for scholars and students seeking to engage with social-scientific approaches to Qohelet.

Having summarized the data, Sneed proceeds to examine Qohelet's sociohistorical context by presenting a social history (he designates it "*the* social history"; however, the number of uncertainties that appear would seem to make that inappropriate) and class analysis of Ptolemaic Judah. Although Sneed does not emphasize it, it is quickly apparent just how little definitive knowledge is available about Judah at this time: Sneed notes that "primary sources are few" (85); "there is a lot of uncertainty about whether there was a royal governor in the city or a garrison" (90); he is forced to appeal to principles that operated in Egypt that are then applied to Judah because "they seem to fit the circumstances of Jerusalem" (90). Information derived from Josephus also needs to be treated carefully because of the probable bias inherent in the data (95).

Sneed proceeds to examine the social roles of various groups (priests, secular aristocracy, temple scribes and singers, merchants, and the lower class[es]).
He argues that Ptolemaic Judah was a hierocracy (i.e., governed primarily by the
priests, 102–7) that demonstrated no significant hellenization (120–23).

Sneed next turns to consider the social location of Qohelet and his audience. He examines proposed historical allusions within Qohelet's words (the royal
experiment of Qoh 1–2; references to injustice and oppression; the tale of the old
foolish king and the youth who rises from prison to take his place in Qoh 4:13–16,
together with a number of other passages). In the end, Sneed concurs with many
others that Qohelet is not specific enough to allow us to clearly identify any specific historical information. Even in the broadest possible terms, Sneed notes that
"it is easy to see that Qohelet observes oppression and corruption in the land, but
whether it is the Ptolemaic period or some other is impossible to demonstrate"
(131). Curiously, Sneed never follows up on this expression of uncertainty over
the date of Qohelet, which, although it represents the majority opinion, is not
without significant detractors.

Sneed discusses at length Qohelet's social location, concluding that he (and
his fellow sages) occupied the "lowest rung of the indigenous aristocracy" (143)—
the "retainer class." This location introduces numerous complexities into the social
position of Qohelet and his status group. "Qohelet's ambivalence about wealth and
power is partially attributable to this social location. His class feels intellectually
superior to the governing elite but does not consider itself among the truly poor"
(154). Sneed concludes that Qohelet was an intellectual, a scribal scholar who
taught apprentices, but he held no political power.

The fifth chapter of Sneed's book focuses primarily on determining the meaning of the term הבל, which "is better translated as 'futility' or 'illusion' and not
in the sense of protest but resignation to the fact that life does not operate as
one might expect or wish" (162). He singles out Michael Fox's understanding of
הבל as "absurd" for criticism, yet Sneed's preferred glosses do not seem to convey
the ideas he seeks to invest them with, and indeed "absurd" or "senseless" more
closely approach his idea than "futility" or "illusion"! Furthermore, his critique of
Fox's position is not particularly compelling. Given that Qohelet repeatedly seeks
the answer to questions and, when he fails to find an answer, declares it to be הבל,
the idea that the world makes no sense seems eminently appropriate. That Fox
then interprets this as a protest against God does not ultimately alter the viability
of this understanding of the term. It is also difficult not to detect some amount of
protest in Qohelet's use of הבל, particularly when he describes events he so designates as, among other things, "a sickening evil" (חלי רע, Qoh 6:2).

For Sneed, the "carpe diem ethic" (e.g., Qoh 2:24–26) is an antidote to הבל
168)). Sneed argues that Qohelet does not describe this as הבל, but his case is
not convincing because the frame narrator summarizes Qohelet's argument as
everything is הבל, and those days to be seized are just as much beyond Qohelet's
ken as were all other matters. Moreover, the epilogue moves beyond Qohelet's
advice, which rests only on the concession that wisdom has provided no mean-

ingful answer in affirming religious piety. Sneed claims too much in affirming Matthew Schwartz's view that "Koheleth's world is neither meaningless nor absurd, and man may work, learn and be happy" such that "[h]e finds meaning in life" (169).[1] Qohelet never denies that there is meaning in the world; he only denies the possibility of learning that meaning in accord with the repeated theme of the wisdom literature that there is some knowledge concealed by God (Job 28; Qoh 3:11). Sneed has recourse to appeal to the supposition that Qohelet's "under the sun" perspective leaves open a possibility of finding meaning "beyond this world" (169), yet Qohelet never hints at this; it appears to be a construction of modern interpreters seeking to find some rationale for Qohelet's presence in the canon, which otherwise faces the problem noted by Sneed that, "if that were Qohelet's message, the book would have never been canonized. Such a position would not have helped anyone in Qohelet's time adjust to difficult circumstances" (170).

The significant omission in Sneed's reasoning here, however, is that he fails to account for the significance of the frame and treats Qohelet's words in isolation.[2] The frame, and in particular the epilogue, set Qohelet's words in a particular context that also distances the narrator from Qohelet. Read within that frame, other possible readings open up that allow the book of Ecclesiastes to attain a more significant relevance to an ancient audience.

For example, Sneed's earlier dismissal of my argument that the epilogist employs Qohelet's words with polemical intent ("[w]hile this is a possibility, it does not explain why one would go to the trouble to do that when a direct confrontation would have been more effective," 11 n. 38) obscures one possible explanation. Sneed does not explain how he knows that a direct confrontation would be more effective. I argue that Qohelet's words are used to draw in an audience who finds his query and methodology compelling, only to show them that the quest is pointless. By creating a sympathetic link between the audience and the character Qohelet, the author has cleverly avoided immediately alienating the audience by simply telling them that they are wrong. The leaking of the "Climategate" emails in 2009 illustrate the power of such an approach, doing far more damage to the credibility of climate science than did the direct confrontation of numerous "climate change deniers" over many years. Similarly, the honest words of the most highly regarded sage do more to undermine the legitimacy of specula-

---

1. Matthew J. Schwartz, "Koheleth and Camus: Two Views of Achievement," *Judaism* 35 (1986): 30–31.

2. Sneed only briefly engages with the epilogue in his work. On page 174 he argues that Qohelet's "pleasing words" must refer to aesthetics and not the meaning of the words. Had this been the meaning the epilogist sought to convey, however, it would have made better sense to have written "Qohelet found pleasing words." To say he "sought" following the record of Qohelet's words implies that he did not find pleasing words; see Martin A. Shields, *The End of Wisdom* (Winona Lake, Ind.: Eisenbrauns, 2006), 64–66.

tive wisdom than any direct confrontation. Thus while Sneed (following Douglas Miller and others, 170–74) is correct to find Qohelet destabilizing his audience, it is the frame narrator's words in the epilogue that restabilize them, not Qohelet's carpe diem ethic.

Sneed moves next to examine theodicial strategies employed by Qohelet. He identifies the primary strategy as a tacit denial of God's justice, a solution that fits with Qohelet's overall theme, concluding that "Qohelet no longer has to defend God's justice since it cannot be comprehended" (185). Sneed makes the important observation that Qohelet does not always use language in the same way that it is used elsewhere in the Hebrew Bible (particularly language about "fearing God," 186–87). Qohelet's God, argues Sneed, is largely impersonal and remote (189). Sneed connects Qohelet's theodicy with the social location of the retainer class as well as the oppressed condition of the Jews under Ptolemaic rule (190).

Finally, Sneed appeals to the notion of cognitive dissonance in an attempt to explain how Qohelet functioned "positively and creatively to help its audience deal with the troubling times of the Ptolemaic period" (197). The result, according to Sneed, is that the problem of theodicy is ultimately dissolved by Qohelet, whose emphasis on the sovereignty of God results in a "whatever will be, will be" attitude and an impersonal deity. Sneed thus accurately depicts Qohelet's understanding on these matters and also correctly notes that "the impersonal God that Qohelet portrays was unlikely to have been very appealing to most religious persons of his day" (201–2).

Sneed next argues that Qohelet's polemic against the overly rational traditional wisdom serves to resolve the problems raised by the doctrine of retribution around the time of the exile by making it more flexible (224). There is little doubt that Sneed is correct about Qohelet's depiction of God, although his sociohistorical rationale for Qohelet's presentation of God in these terms is perhaps less compelling.

The remainder of Sneed's work concentrates on demonstrating how Qohelet's pessimism did not serve as an impediment to the book's inclusion in the canon. He argues that Qohelet uses pessimism to lower his audience's expectations of the wisdom tradition as part of his polemic (240). This involves skepticism about human cognitive ability, about the value of a wise lifestyle, and about the doctrine of retribution. "His skepticism undermines wisdom's legitimacy and value" (242). Sneed explains that

> Qohelet does a service for his audience by questioning most of the traditional values of olden times, and he brings Judaism into a new era where new values were needed and new strategies developed. Instead of exclusive emphasis on religious piety, wisdom, and industriousness, which are possible only with social stability and predictability, Qohelet emphasizes the precariousness of his culture and society. Caution, fatalism, resignation, enjoyment of the present, and moderation are the new virtues and strategic outlooks that are more likely to succeed. (251)

In the end, Sneed argues that the final two verses (which he asserts are a gloss made by a later, Pharisaic editor, 273) of the book (Qoh 12:13–14) played a vital role in ensuring the work's acceptance.

Sneed's analysis is informed and thorough, although lacking at a number of critical points. First, he offers little justification for Ptolemaic dating but depends upon it for establishing the social context of the work. Even during this period it is clear from Sneed's work that there is a paucity of specific data, so any social reconstruction is necessarily contingent. While Sneed is successful in constructing a social setting that could fit much of what Qohelet records, it is far from clear whether Qohelet's words would not equally well fit other historical and social settings were there sufficient information available from prior to the Ptolemaic period.

Second, he fails to engage in any significant way with the epilogue, essentially dismissing the last part without adequate justification. Even without this, he fails to investigate the role the distance the epilogue places between the book's narrator and the words of Qohelet would play in the minds of the book's audience.

Third, while Sneed does identify Qohelet with pessimistic literature from the ancient Near East, his analysis of genre falls short in not investigating connections with royal autobiographies and the impact that genre has on the generation of meaning in the text.

These criticisms should not overshadow the importance of Sneed's work as both an invaluable introduction to social-scientific perspectives on Qohelet as well as an important contribution to the this area of study in its own right. For anyone interested in the area, Sneed's work is essential reading. His work reflects a solid understanding of Qohelet's message that the sages could offer no conclusive answers to the discrepancies observed in the just operation of the universe and provides a plausible sociohistorical context for the words of Qohelet.

Ruth, by Judy Fentress-Williams. Abingdon Old Testament Commentaries. Nashville: Abingdon, 2012. Pp. 152. Paper. $21.99. ISBN 9781426746253.

Peter H. W. Lau, Malaysian Theological Seminary, Seremban, Malaysia

Fentress-Williams teaches Old Testament at Virginia Theological Seminary. As part of the Abingdon Old Testament Commentary Series, her volume is primarily aimed at theological students and pastors, but also at upper-level college, university and theological students (9). The aim of the series is to "aid in the study of Scripture and provoke a deeper understanding of the Bible" (9). This volume achieves this aim and would sit well with its target audience. The commentary contains an introduction (21 pages), a commentary on the biblical text in four chapters (98 pages), and a conclusion (13 pages). One chapter is devoted to each of the chapters in the book of Ruth and is organized according to literary units. Each literary unit is discussed in three parts: (1) literary analysis; (2) exegetical analysis; and (3) theological analysis. There are no footnotes or endnotes, although there are references to works listed in the bibliography. The bibliography is meant to include "major commentaries" (11), but a number of these are missing.[1] A subject index, but no Scripture index, completes the book.

The introduction discusses the literary aspects of the book of Ruth and its themes. Fentress-Williams reads the text as a "dialogic comedy." The dialogue is between texts and between the reader and the text. Following Northrop Frye, she notes that a comedy's structure moves from harmony to chaos to resolution (17). According to Fentress-Williams, the goal of a dialogic comedy is to challenge the established reality of both ancient and modern communities (18). In regard to the dating of the book, Fentress-Williams discusses early and late provenances and leaves the question open (21–23). She rightly argues that identity is an over-looked theme in Ruth studies and discusses identity as related to family, ethnicity, gender, and levirate marriage (25–30). Fentress-Williams concludes her introduc-tion with Israel's "theology of identity" (31–34). Theologically, reading a comedy is equivalent to living life with a trust in a God who will "make things right" (34).

The tone of the commentary proper is more suggestive than definitive. The following summary aims to highlight some of Fentress-Williams's more distinct readings and to illustrate the manner of commenting.

In her discussion of Ruth 1, Fentress-Williams views Elimelech's migration to Moab in a negative light and finds a parallel with the experience of the exile and separation from God (43). She makes an interesting connection between the taking of wives from the tribe of Benjamin (Judg 21) and Mahlon and Chilion taking Moabite wives, with the use of *nasa'* instead of *lakah* hinting that either the women married against their will or the Moabite customs were not considered (40–41). She also suggests an intertextual connection between Mahlon and Chil-ion's ten years of childless marriage and Deut 23:3, where Moab is excluded from the Israelite assembly until the tenth generation (43). Fentress-Williams identifies Ruth's vow to Naomi as the center of not just chapter 1 but the whole narrative, and she views the vow as a covenant (43). The concept of *hesed* is then discussed, with "faithfulness" the translation adopted. The return to Bethlehem is compared with the return from exile. To conclude the chapter, Fentress-Williams compares Naomi's situation with those who returned home after Hurricane Katrina and the questions of identity that arose then (62–63).

In her discussion of chapter 2, Fentress-Williams highlights Ruth's changing identity. Boaz's address of Ruth as "my daughter" functions to place him in the role of relative and provider, counting her among his kin (72–73). Fentress-Wil-liams draws a connection between YHWH and Israel and Boaz and Ruth through the concept of treaty. A relationship is initiated, and then expectations are spelled

---

1. E.g., Daniel I. Block, *Judges, Ruth* (NAC 6; Nashville: Broadman & Holman, 1999); Frederic W. Bush, *Ruth, Esther* (WBC 9; Dallas: Word, 1996); Robert L. Hubbard, *The Book of Ruth* (NICOT; Grand Rapids: Eerdmans, 1988).

out. Boaz's seven commands are presented to Ruth in verses 8–9 (73–74). As the chapter progresses, the Moabite is seen as accepted into God's family on the basis of her faithfulness (79). Fentress-Williams interprets YHWH as the referent for the pronoun in 2:20 (82–83).

Fentress-Williams draws in the intertextual allusions with Ruth 3. The similarities with the Judah and Tamar narrative (Gen 38) are discussed (87–89). She notes the "confused pronouns" of Ruth 3:3–4, with Naomi's instructions to Ruth switching between first and second person. Fentress-Williams provides a solution from a literary perspective: it reminds the reader of Lot and his daughters (Gen 19). The contrast is that Ruth goes down to the threshing floor for both women (cf. Lot's two daughters). The dialogue with Gen 38 and 19 brings out the idea of redemption—the redemption of Judah, Lot, Moab, and Ammon (89–91). Ruth's preparation for meeting Boaz is then understood within this context. Just as Israel needed to be consecrated before meeting YHWH at Mount Sinai (Exod 19), so Ruth needs to be at her "best" when seeking redemption (92). In the encounter with Boaz, Fentress-Williams notes the continued development of Ruth's identity, from foreigner to maidservant to handmaid (97–98). Perhaps reflecting the ambiguous nature of the narrative, Fentress-Williams leaves open the question of what happens on the threshing floor: Boaz's request for Ruth to "stay the night" may be for her protection, or it "may be less selfless in nature" (99). Theologically, Boaz's cloak is compared with the covenant, the "covering" that God offers to his people (102). Ruth's encounter with Boaz is also compared with Moses' encounter with YHWH on Mount Sinai. Words are given both times, but they are not meant to be the last word in the relationship; rather, they are the first (105).

Fentress-Williams's designation of the Ruth narrative as a comedy comes to the fore in her discussion of chapter 4. Here we find the resolution where loose ends are tied, identities are revealed, and the tension resolved (107). Fentress-Williams draws another comparison between Boaz's disclosure of information to the nearer kinsman and Tamar. They both have information the other party does not, and they both position themselves to create an encounter. Both disclose to manipulate (112). The events are viewed within a levirate framework (Deut 25:5–10), similar to Tamar and Judah (113). Fentress-Williams suggests that Rachel is mentioned first (4:11) because: Boaz is already married; Boaz loves Ruth; to highlight the theme of reversal (115). Boaz's situation is then compared to the ancestral narratives and so look forward to Boaz receiving the same threefold blessing (117–18). In the marriage of Boaz and Ruth, she is redeemed along with the plot, as the tensions of chapter 1 are resolved (119). For instance, the emptiness motif is reversed. "El Shaddai, 'the God of the breast,'" withholds nourishment in chapter 1, but Naomi "nurses" the baby in chapter 4 (123–24).

The final chapter concludes with reflections on comedy and identity. Fentress-Williams discusses the important aspects of the Ruth narrative for hearers in the ninth century BCE (139) and after the return to the land (140–41). There is also a brief mention of reading Ruth in dialogue with Matthew 1 (141). The chapter concludes with two contemporary readings of Ruth: one from the perspective of ethnicity and race, drawing on American colonial history (141–43); the other from the perspective of gender (143–45). The conclusion ends with some theological reflections.

As a commentary targeting pastors and teachers in congregational settings, more ethical implications would have been welcomed. A consideration of the difference Jesus and the New Testament make to interpretation and application would also have been welcome for Christian readers.

The suggestive tone of this commentary reminds me of dappled moonlight. It is hard to capture the style of the book, and indeed, any summary would mar it. At many points it engages in dialogue with parts of the Old Testament, then moves on. The glancing nature of some the exchanges can be explained by the book's target audience and the limited space. Yet at times I was left longing for more detail, more description, and more substantiation for lines of interpretation. I was looking for shafts of clear light. But perhaps my experience as a reader was Fentress-Williams's intention. It certainly engages a reader in the conversation, then leaves one to probe topics by oneself. Productive, ongoing conversation would require interaction with a more detailed, more decisive commentary. Nonetheless, as a commentary that inspires readers to explore Scripture more deeply and to research further, it achieves the series' stated aim of "provok[ing] a deeper understanding of the Bible."

Gregory of Nyssa: Homilies on the Song of Songs, translated by Richard A. Norris Jr. Writings from the Greco-Roman World 13. Atlanta: Society of Biblical Literature, 2012. Pp. liv + 517. Paper. $59.95. ISBN 9781589831056.

Mark DelCogliano, University of St. Thomas, St. Paul, Minnesota

When Richard Norris died in 2005, many of us in the field of patristics and late antique Christianity wondered if the translation of Gregory of Nyssa's *Homilies on the Song of Songs* he was known to be working on would see the light of day. At long last it has appeared, thanks to the meticulous work of a team of editors who oversaw the turning of Norris's manuscript into a finished book (see vii–viii for their various contributions). The result, a bilingual edition with an extensive introduction, is a worthy epitaph to such a distinguished career.

Gregory of Nyssa's fifteen homilies on the Song of Songs, covering Song 1:1–6:8, have long been considered, along with his *Life of Moses,* a classic example of early Christian allegorical exegesis as well as the mature expression of Gregory's spiritual or mystical doctrine. Norris's introduction focuses on these two perspectives. He begins with a brief account of Gregory's life and writings. The various contested points of Gregory's biography, such as his marriage and the dates of certain works, are treated with judiciousness. Obviously, Norris could not avail himself of the 2007 translation of Gregory's letters published by Anna Silvas, which contains what many consider to be the best short biography of the bishop of Nyssa currently available (*Gregory of Nyssa: The Letters* [Leiden: Brill, 2007]).

At any event, Norris follows Jean Daniélou in dating the *Homilies on the Song of Songs* to the last years of Gregory's life (he died around 395, about sixty years old). As for their origin, Norris argues that they were preached to the regular congregation at Nyssa during Lent and later dedicated to Olympias, a rich widow devoted to asceticism who later corresponded with John Chrysostom during his exile. Here Norris departs from Daniélou, who held that the homilies were written with Olympias's community of ascetic women in mind. Hence, Gregory intended these homilies to interpret the Song of Songs not for elite ascetics but for all serious Christians. Thus, Norris contests the traditional view, popularized by Daniélou, that these homilies contain "mysticism" for a select few.

The bulk of the introduction is a discussion of Gregory's allegorical method of interpreting the Song of Songs. Norris first explores the presuppositions held by Gregory regarding how a biblical text is meant to function, specifically in its mediation of a transformative relationship between God and the reader. Norris highlights Gregory's belief that God is beyond the perceptible and intelligible created order and so must be mediated to humanity. But this mediation takes place primarily within the human being who has been created in the image of God. Since this divine likeness was lost through the fall, the more the divine image is restored in a person, the more one knows the archetype of that image. So, knowing (or seeing) God amounts to the same thing as being like God. In other words, progress in either virtue (being like God) or knowledge (seeing God) entails progress in the other. Norris also points to Gregory's appropriation of typical Greco-Roman grammatical reading techniques, particularly the identification of a work's aim or purpose (*skopos*). Gregory thinks that the biblical text at its literal level encodes intelligible mysteries that can be accessed only through allegorical interpretation. The *skopos* of the Song of Songs revealed by allegorical interpretation is the way of salvation through love and desire that causes people to the seek "marriage" with the Word of God. With regard to these presuppositions, Gregory is not being particularly innovative, as other Christians before him, such as Origen, held similar views and took similar approaches. The uniqueness of Gregory here is found in his idea that there is no final, static perfection; rather, perfection in the marriage with the Word consists in unending transformation in the presence of God who is never fully attained.

Also characteristic of Gregory is the centrality of the idea of the coherent sequence (*akolouthia*) of the scriptural text. For Gregory allegory includes the idea that the secondary level revealed by allegorical interpretation has a logical and coherent sequence of its own, which may be different from the coherent sequence of the literal text. "Gregory's allegory, then," writes Norris, "is meant, like Origen's, to elicit from the text a portrayal of the 'mysteries' of Christian faith. In his case, however, the mysteries in question are explicitly treated as forming an *akolouthia*—an extended, logically connected sequence.... In the Song, however, he understands himself to be dealing with a work that concerns the human self—'soul'—in its relation to God. Its *skopos* is precisely ... an account of how 'the soul is in a certain manner led as a bride toward an incorporeal and spiritual and undefiled marriage with God' (Hom. 1) and that *skopos* specifies the 'what' of which the Song's *akolouthia* delineates the 'how'" (xlix). Thus, the way to union with God presented by the Song (i.e., its *skopos*) is comprehended only if the Song is interpreted allegorically in such a way to discern the *akolouthia* that outlines the details, or the sequence, or the logic, of that path to union with God.

The Greek original and English translation are printed on facing pages. The Greek text is the one prepared by Hermann Langerbeck and published in the sixth volume of Gregorii Nysseni Opera in 1960, but without the critical apparatus. The pagination of the Langerbeck edition is indicated in the right margin. The translation of Norris reflects his knack for translating Greek into clear, idiomatic English prose. It is mostly free of translationese and wholly lucid. The translation is accompanied by many helpful notes explaining Gregory's teaching, providing philological information, giving cross-references, and so forth.

One oddity of the volume, however, is the complete lack of reference to the previous English translation of the same set of *Homilies on the Song of Songs* published by Casimir McCambley in 1987 (*Saint Gregory of Nyssa: Commentary on the Song of Songs* [Brookline: Hellenic College Press, 1987]). Was Norris unaware of this earlier work? McCambley's translation has the distinction of being the first in English, but there is nothing in Norris's volume to suggest that he benefited from it—or even knew about it—in any way. A brief comparison will show the relative merits of each translation. What follows is a famous passage from the first homily (Langerbeck p. 34) in which Gregory describes the so-called "spiritual senses." Here is the Greek:

Μανθάνομεν δέ τι κατὰ πάροδον καὶ ἕτερον δόγμα διὰ τῆς τοῦ βιβλίου τούτου φιλοσοφίας, ὅτι διπλῆ τίς ἐστιν ἐν ἡμῖν ἡ αἴσθησις, ἡ μὲν σωματικὴ ἡ δὲ θειοτέρα, καθὼς φησί που τῆς Παροιμίας ὁ λόγος ὅτι αἴσθησιν θείαν εὑρήσεις· ἀναλογία γάρ τίς ἐστιν ἐν τοῖς ψυχικοῖς ἐνεργήμασι πρὸς τὰ τοῦ σώματος αἰσθητήρια. καὶ τοῦτο ἐκ τῶν παρόντων <ῥημάτων> μανθάνομεν· ὁ μὲν γὰρ οἶνός τε καὶ τὸ γάλα τῇ γεύσει κρίνεται, νοητῶν δὲ ὄντων ἐκείνων νοητὴ πάντως καὶ ἡ ἀντιληπτικὴ τούτων τῆς ψυχῆς ἐστι δύναμις. τὸ δὲ φίλημα διὰ τῆς ἁπτικῆς αἰσθήσεως ἐνεργεῖται· ἐφάπτεται γὰρ ἀλλήλων τὰ χείλη ἐν τῷ φιλήματι. ἔστι δέ τις καὶ ἁφὴ τῆς ψυχῆς ἡ ἁπτομένη τοῦ λόγου διά τινος ἀσωμάτου καὶ νοητῆς ἐπαφήσεως ἐνεργουμένη, καθὼς εἶπεν ὁ εἰπὼν ὅτι Αἱ χεῖρες ἡμῶν ἐψηλάφησαν περὶ τοῦ λόγου τῆς ζωῆς. ὡσαύτως δὲ καὶ ἡ τῶν θείων μύρων ὀσμὴ οὐ μυκτήρων ἐστὶν ὀσμή, ἀλλά τινος νοητῆς καὶ ἀΰλου δυνάμεως τῇ τοῦ πνεύματος ὁλκῇ τὴν τοῦ Χριστοῦ συνεφελκομένης εὐωδίαν.

In McCambley's translation, this reads:

We are indirectly taught another lesson through the philosophy of this book, namely that perception within us is twofold—bodily and divine. As the Word says in Proverbs, "You will find perception of God" [Pr 2.5]. A certain analogy exists between the activities of the soul and the sense organs of the body. This we learn from the present text. Wine and milk are distinguished by taste, while the intellectual and apprehending capacity of the soul grasps spiritual realities. A kiss is effected through the sense of touch; the lips of two persons make contact in a kiss. On the other hand, there is a certain sense of touch in the soul which takes hold of the Word and works in an incorporeal, spiritual way. As John says: "Our hands have handled the word of life" [1 Jn 1.1]. Similarly, the scent of the divine perfumes is not perceived by the nose, but by a certain spiritual and immaterial power drawing in the good odor of Christ by an inhalation of the Spirit.

Norris renders the Greek in this way:

> We also learn, in an incidental way, another truth through the philosophical wisdom of this book, that there is in us a dual activity of perception, the one bodily, the other more divine—just as Proverbs somewhere says, "You will find a divine mode of perception." For there is a certain analogy between the sense organs of the body and the operations of the soul. And it is this that we learn from the words before us. For both wine and milk are discerned by the sense of taste, but when they are intelligible things, the power of the soul that grasps them is an intellectual power. And a kiss comes about through the sense of touch, for in a kiss lips touch each other. There is also, though, a "touch" that belongs to the soul, one that makes contact with the Word and is actuated by an incorporeal and intelligible touching, just as someone said, "Our hands have touched concerning the Word of life" (1 John 1:1). In the same way, too, the scent of the divine perfumes is not a scent in the nostrils but pertains to a certain intelligible and immaterial faculty that inhales the sweet smell of Christ by sucking in the Spirit.

Both translations are for the most part clear and understandable, but we see several slight differences between them that are indicative of the differences between their translations in general. McCambley tends to be more literal, translating single words with another single word, whereas Norris is more idiomatic, willing use a phrase to translate a single word (e.g., "philosophy" versus "philosophical wisdom," "perception" versus "activity of perception," "taste" versus "sense of taste"). While in making such choices both translators accurately render the Greek, Norris's version tends, in my opinion, to be a bit easier to read and understand. However, some may feel that Norris takes too many liberties with the text, that he is not literal enough.

More seriously, McCambley is more prone to inaccuracies than Norris is. In the passage quoted above there are several mistakes. First, the clause νοητῶν δὲ ὄντων ἐκείνων νοητὴ πάντως καὶ ἡ ἀντιληπτικὴ τούτων τῆς ψυχῆς ἐστι δύναμις is misinterpreted by McCambley as "while the intellectual and apprehending capacity of the soul grasps spiritual realities." But Norris gets it right, recognizing νοητῶν δὲ ὄντων ἐκείνων as a genitive absolute, not as a genitive modifying δύναμις (the presence of the ὄντων tips the balance in favor of Norris's interpretation): "but when they are intelligible things, the power of the soul that grasps them is an intellectual power" (the καὶ is emphatic, not conjunctive). But both McCambley and Norris inexplicably neglect to translate πάντως: "is a wholly intellectual power." Second, McCambley also mangles ἔστι δέ τις καὶ ἀφὴ τῆς ψυχῆς ἡ ἁπτομένη τοῦ λόγου διά τινος ἀσωμάτου καὶ νοητῆς ἐπαφήσεως ἐνεργουμένη with: "On the other hand, there is a certain sense of touch in the soul which takes hold of the Word and works in an incorporeal, spiritual way." Norris again gets this right: "There is also, though, a 'touch' that belongs to the soul, one that makes contact with the Word and is actuated by an incorporeal and intelligible touching." McCambley overtranslates ἀπτομένη as "takes hold of" (Norris correctly has "makes contact with") and also takes ἐνεργουμένη as active instead of passive ("works" versus "is actuated"). The idiomatic way Norris translates ἔστι δέ τις καὶ, "There is also, though," is more felicitous than McCambley's accurate but plodding "On the other hand, there is…," yet Norris does nod a bit when translates τῇ τοῦ πνεύματος ὀλκῇ as "by sucking in the Spirit," which McCambley more fittingly renders "by an inhalation of the Spirit." We can inhale with the nose, but it seems that sucking is an activity proper to the mouth. Third, McCambley omits the που referring to "somewhere" in Proverbs and identifies the scriptural reference for the passage quoted from Proverbs as verse 2.5. But Gregory's citation is not an exact match, since the scriptural verse reads ἐπίγνωσιν θεοῦ εὑρήσεις, not, as Gregory has it, αἴσθησιν θείαν εὑρήσεις. Langerbeck was not as precise as McCambley, annotating the line with "cf Prov 2, 3-5; 10," thereby signaling that Gregory is not quoting precisely but conflating several verses ("perception" is spoken about in verses 2:3 and 2:10). Oddly, McCambley's translation seems to conflate Prov 2:5 and Gregory's text: "You will find perception of God" (unless the adjective θείαν is rendered as a genitive). Norris translates the που and renders the Gregory's version of Proverbs text in his typically idiomatic way and in a note on this verse comments: "There is no such text to be found in the LXX book of Proverbs." Technically, this is correct, but perhaps he goes overboard in failing to note the allusions to Prov 2:2–3 and 2:10 as Langerbeck did. One wonders if by using the που Gregory meant to suggest that he was not quoting scripture exactly but approximating its sense, that is, "just as Proverbs more or less says…" In any event, the translation of Norris is far more reliable than McCambley's and thus should supersede it.

As for errors, page 517, the index of modern authors, has been printed twice, on the front and back of a single physical page.

Hiob: Im Räderwerk des Bösen, by Rüdiger Lux. Biblische Gestalten 25. Leipzig: Evangelische Verlagsanstalt, 2012. Pp. 320. Paper. €18.80. ISBN 9783374028788.

Urmas Nommik, University of Tartu, Tartu, Estonia

Rüdiger Lux, the recently retired professor of the University of Leipzig, has dedicated a great deal of time to this mature monograph on one of the most complicated and debated biblical figures. As the author writes in his foreword, this book has emerged from the whole of his twenty-five-year teaching activity (7–8). His long experience dealing with puzzling biblical theological problems reveals itself not only in the scholarly breadth of the discussion involving numerous German theologians, philosophers, and biblical exegetes but also in his use of language, which should be particularly emphasized here. A German-language audience will find this work a pleasure to read. Its title, "Job: (Caught) in the Machinery of Evil," sets the standard maintained throughout the work.

As its twenty-fifth volume, this monograph belongs to the noteworthy book series "Biblical Figures" (Biblische Gestalten) from Leipzig publisher Evangelische Verlagsanstalt. Together with Christfried Böttrich, Lux is also the editor of a series oriented toward a broader audience but that still takes into account the scholarly discourse on its topic.

The aim of Lux's monograph is to address Job, but not in isolation: char-acteristically for Lux, the figure of Job is treated within the framework of his relationships with other characters in the drama. Lux has done this in three chapters, with the "Introduction" (9–27), an "Exposure" (28–282), and a section named "Impact" (283–312). Lists of relevant literature and illustrations (313–20) round out the book.

The introductory chapter discusses, first, the philosophical-theological dilemma of "resistance and resignation" in the situation of suffering (9–14), as Dietrich Bonhoeffer has worded it. The second section (14–22) polemicizes on suffering and evil as a "rock of atheism," and the third section (22–27) poses the Tertullian question "*unde malum*—from whence the evil?" sharpening it by underscoring the monotheistic context of the book of Job. In this way, again char-acteristically of Lux's rhetoric, many questions emerging from the book of Job as well as from the modern-day mind are formulated.

The body of the monograph is divided into seven sections. The first (28–52) recalls that the "Joban" question is older than the Hebrew Bible and focuses on two examples: the Akkadian poem Ludlul bēl nēmeqi and the Egyptian composi-tion Dispute between a Man and His Ba. In comparison with the book of Job, their common points and basic differences, particularly concerning the cultic dimen-sion in the first case and the earthly existence as the limit of life in the second, are delineated. Lux does not support direct literary dependence of the book of Job on either of them.

In the short second section (52–57), Lux discusses some biblical passages (Genesis, Ezekiel), more or less considering "Job outside the nook of Job." Besides introducing the structure of the whole composition, the third section (57–65) gives an outline of its literary development. Lux does this skillfully: taking into consideration a stratification that can be called minimal from the point of view of critical scholarship, while maximizing what can be explained fairly in the given context. He presupposes a three-stage development starting with the poem in three parts (Job's initial lament and the dialogue with friends in chs. 3–27; Job's oath of purgation in chs. 29–31, and God's speeches with Job's answers in 38:1–42:6), continuing with the addition of the later prose frame story (1–2 + 42:7–17), and refining the book with the most recent parts: the hymn to wisdom (ch. 28) and Elihu's speeches (chs. 32–37). Lux dates the beginnings of the book with some caution to the postexilic time. If anyone from German literary- and redaction-critical scholarship has influenced Lux more than others, it is certainly

Raik Heckl with his monograph *Hiob—vom Gottesfürchtigen zum Repräsentanten Israels* (FAT 70, Tübingen, 2010).

An astonishingly coherent handling of the final form of the book of Job follows in four sections: the prologue (66–139), the dialogue-poem (139–265), the assessment of the friends in 42:7–9 (265–71), and the epilogue (271–82). The balance between the analyses of the prologue and the poem seems somewhat disproportionate, but Lux does not mask his fascination with the theological deepness of the prose frame story: it is a narrative theology that is not susceptible to systematization; the narrator approaches the boundaries of what can be thought and said about God (113–14). God is understood not as an absolute power but as a powerful person in a network of relationships—thus, Satan is not evil in himself but struggles for power and loses while bearing false witness against both Job and God (88, 91, 113, etc.). For a human relationship with God, it is the full freedom of decision against evil that matters (79, 94). Because of the generally careful composition of earthly and heavenly scenes, Lux is not in favor of the model of any literary growth in the prologue (esp. 83 n. 86). It is noteworthy that, based on Heckl's view, Lux takes the figure of Job as Yahweh's servant seriously and understands him as a "prepatriarch" (71), as a symbol for the supra-individual destiny of Israel, its suffering and salvation, and at the end (42:7–9) also as a representative (Israel) of the world (all nations) before God (270).

Job's opening lament is handled more thoroughly than the other speeches, as anti-*mythos* (144) and as an inevitable step in order for pastoral care to be enabled at all (151). Other speeches are theologically analyzed in an exemplary manner, so that representative passages are considered. Larger literary problems, particularly concerning the third round of speeches (except ch. 28) are for obvious reasons almost wholly disregarded. In general, Lux does not condemn any statement in the book of Job, as is often done by exegetes (e.g., with regard to the friends' speeches), but he carefully and consequentially observes who the speaker is and in which exact situation the speech occurs: if Job is speaking, he is in extreme suffering and lacks the contact with God capable of changing his destiny; if the three friends or Elihu are speaking, they do so always facing a sufferer and not before a learned audience, hence they act in a situation of pastoral care; if God is speaking, actual contact with Job is realized; what exactly is said is almost of secondary value.

The Job of the dialogue contradicts in many ways the Job of the prologue, but Lux explains this in terms of the complex process of working through suffering, which is psychologically obvious (143). Friends fail with their help: they believe themselves to be on God's side (164, 185, etc.), but their pastoral care "ends up—figuratively speaking—in cannibalism" (175). On the other hand, the friends help Job to come closer to God (190). Elihu comes too late and basically announces only that all theology is doxology (230). Lux considers chapter 28 with its "realism of confidence" to be an interface between two significant parts of the book and in accordance with the frame story (191–96). He sees Job's final monologue (chs. 29–31) as a meditation on the loss of Job's earlier prosperous and exemplary life and on the desire for the righteous weighing of his fate, with the Egyptian conception of the judgment of the dead as the background (196–212). God's speeches are the culmination of the dialogue addressed to all readers, not just Job. God is revealed as life-giving and preserving: God has the power to limit evil (231–58). Job gains a new perspective on his relationship with God; Lux emphasizes that he does not need to submit to God but simply sees reason beyond his own suffering (264).

Four masterful excurses flavor the analysis of the book: a very unusual exegesis of the words of Job's wife in 2:9 (122–28) and reflections on the boundaries of the discourse on the origin of evil (156–62), on one of the most difficult passages, 19:23–27 (174–81), and on how much power the Almighty has (252–58).

The third chapter, on the later "Impact" of the book of Job, admits the impossibility of considering the entire history of its reception. This is why Lux chooses to discuss four representative interpretations: Søren Kierkegaard as an admirer of Job's freedom in suffering (284–89); Rudolf Otto, who has acknowledged the significance of the irrational (290–93); Carl Gustav Jung and his thesis of the humanization of God (294–97); and Ernst Bloch with his atheistic challenge to Job's God (298–303). Lux's sermon on the "comfort of music"—since in the Middle Ages the figure of Job functioned as patron saint of musicians and other traveling people—ends his book (303–12).

Lux's book is a first-class discussion on the theological and philosophical questions that we—the moderns—pose to the book of Job. His monograph is slightly weaker concerning the traditions of the ancients behind the book of Job, particularly the impact of several traditional forms and genres employed. Additionally, for a more plastic view of the "literature of Job," one must still address many kinds of redaction-critical issues, whether possible or not in such a small monograph. In particular, the evaluation of some possible earlier literary stages of the book could add important facets to the overall picture. But as a matter of fact, Rüdiger Lux is a master of formulating questions, and in this way he demonstrates that the exegesis of the book of Job is open to much further interpretation.

New Perspectives on Ezra-Nehemiah: History and Historiography, Text, Literature, and Interpretation, edited by Isaac Kalimi. Winona Lake, Ind.: Eisenbrauns, 2012. Pp. xvi + 296. Hardcover. $49.50. ISBN 9781575062334.

Andrew E. Steinmann, Concordia University Chicago, River Forest, Illinois

Isaac Kalimi has gathered thirteen recent essays probing various aspects of Ezra-Nehemiah in this volume. They are arranged in two sections, the first presenting eight studies relating to these postexilic works as history and historiography and the second containing five articles under the heading "Text, Literature, and Interpretation."

"Ezra's Use of Documents in the Context of Hellenistic Rules of Rhetoric," by Lisbeth Fried, argues that Ezra 1–6 is written in the style of Greek historiography and intended to be persuasive by following the canons laid down by Aristotle. According to Fried, this section was the last portion of Ezra-Nehemiah written, dating sometime after the reign of Darius III and therefore in the Hellenistic period under either Alexander or the Ptolemies at the end of the fourth century. Aristotle's *Rhetoric* calls for such a work to contain a prologue (Ezra 1–3, according to Fried), a narration (4:1–3), proofs (the Aramaic letters of 4:4–6:12), and an epilogue (6:13–22). Fried makes an interesting case that this section of Ezra was a Hellenistic work written according to Hellenistic literary and historiographical conventions, yet her essay leaves some unanswered questions that deposit a lingering doubt in my mind: If the Aramaic letters provide the proof of the narration, then why is the connecting narrative between the letters also in Aramaic? More important, why is the epilogue partly in Aramaic and partly in Hebrew?

Lester Grabbe ("What Was Nehemiah Up To?") examines the claims of some scholars (e.g., E. Yamauchi, H. Kippenberg, M. Smith, J. Blenkinsopp) that Nehemiah's reforms were parallel to those in ancient Athens carried out by Solon or Pericles. He finds, however, that the reforms of Solon have only one facet in common—the cancellation of debts—and that there is no real parallel between Nehemiah's reforms and those by Pericles. However, in a brief survey of reforms from the ancient Near East under Hammurabi and Keret in Mesopotamia and the Egyptian Vizier Rekmire (mid-fifteenth century BCE), Grabbe finds more close parallels with Nehemiah's reforms. This leads him to conclude that Nehemiah follows earlier models of the righteous king or ruler in the Near East. Grabbe's thesis is interesting, but his essay is too cursory to explore the actual source texts for the Greek or Near Eastern reforms, making it difficult for the reader to conclude whether Grabbe's argument is well-supported.

In the first of two essays to explore Nehemiah's dual loyalties as a servant of the Persian court and as a Jew, Don Polaski argues that in his memoirs Nehemiah privileges oral communication over written documents ("Nehemiah: Subject of the Empire, Subject of Writing"). He does not assert his authority on the basis of the letters given him by Artaxerxes, nor does he produce written documents when corresponding with his adversaries, even when they write to him. Even when making his reforms in Neh 13, Nehemiah does not make explicit appeal even to Israel's most important written text, the Torah. While his memoir may allude to pentateuchal legislation, he accomplishes his reforms mainly on the basis of his personal authority. In this way Nehemiah can serve the Persians without succumbing to them and their essential technology, writing.

A second essay, "Nehemiah as a 'Court Jew,'" compares Nehemiah's service to the imperial court with the service of court Jews (*Hofjuden*) in Europe from the Middle Ages through the Enlightenment. Klaas Smelik notes that these court Jews often had great influence in various royal circles as successful businessmen, advisors, and financiers. However, they also faced rapid falls from grace due to false charges lodged against them by envious European subjects or even other ambitious Jews. Some faced persecution, imprisonment, and even death when they could not negotiate a way between their service to a Christian court and their identities as Jews. In a similar way, Nehemiah had to navigate between his identity as a Jew and his loyalty to the Persian crown. While he was able summarily to dismiss accusations that he was rebelling against Artaxerxes and seeking to become king in Jerusalem, he also adhered to the limits placed on him as an imperial office holder. When some Judeans complained about their debt, brought about in large part because of Persian taxation, Nehemiah effected a temporary solution by persuading richer Jews to dismiss the debts. However, he did not seek to change the taxation imposed by his Persian overlords.

Both of these essays seek to explain Nehemiah's dual loyalties and his balancing of their very different demands. Ultimately, however, I found them lacking because they appeal more to Nehemiah's ethnic identity as a Jew than to his explicit statements that he was seeking to remain loyal to Artaxerxes and also serve his fellow Judeans not simply out of ethnic loyalty but out of his faith and loyalty to Israel's God, as expressed, for instance, in his frequent inclusion of short prayers in his memoir.

In the first of a trio of articles on Nehemiah's rebuilding of Jerusalem's walls ("Nehemiah 3: Sources, Composition and Purpose"), Oded Lipschits mainly argues that the verbal root חזק used frequently in the *hiphil* stem in Neh 3 signifies financial support for the rebuilding of sections of the wall by prominent groups of Judeans. I found his argument for understanding this verb as "give financial support" weak. He argues from 1 Chr 26:27 that this must be a meaning for the verb in Late Biblical Hebrew. However, it appears to me that in that verse the verb denotes the giving of an offering to support the rebuilding (i.e., maintenance) the yet-to-be-rebuilt temple. By context it *entails* financial support, but the verb itself does not *denote* financial support by repair or rebuilding. I find his argument that Neh 5:16 uses the verb to mean *finance* also lacking. Even if one accepts Lipschits's arguments, the evidence does not indicate that חזק used in the *hiphil* stem can mean *finance* but that it carries a much more restrictive meaning: *finance a building project,* making is a technical term, which I find highly unlikely. In addition, Lipschits fails to explain why Neh 3:2 uses the root בנה for the rebuilding of the wall. However, from the description of the fall of Jerusalem in 2 Kgs 25, it appears that the northern part of the wall whose rebuilding is described at Neh 3:2 was probably the portion breached by the Babylonian army. It was the most heavily damaged, which is why it was "built" (root בנה), whereas the rest of the wall may have been less damaged and could be described as repaired (root חזק in the *hiphil* stem).

In "On Nehemiah's City Wall and the Size of Jerusalem during the Persian Period: An Archaeologist's View," David Ussishkin presents a revised version of a previous study.[1] He argues for the maximalist position that the walls rebuilt

---

1. Ussishkin, "The Borders and *de Facto* Size of Jerusalem in the Persian Period," in *Judah and the Judeans in the Persian Period* (ed. O. Lipschits and M. Oeming; Winona Lake, Ind.: Eisenbrauns, 2006), 147–66.

by Nehemiah encompassed not only the Temple Mount and City of David but also the southwest hill of Jerusalem. Ussishkin makes a formidable argument. However, his conclusions are tempered by his own admission that there is no archaeological evidence for occupation of the southwest hill of Jerusalem during the Persian period. Ussishkin's argument is also based upon his assertion that archaeological evidence ought to take precedence over the written text of Nehemiah. This is understandable, coming from an archaeologist. However, while written texts are certainly subject to various interpretations and hermeneutical questions, archaeological finds are also subject to interpretation, and archaeologists' conclusions are in some measure provisional, given that not every piece of evidence from the past has survived for the archaeologist to discover, and most excavations do not explore the complete area under investigation. (This, of course, is especially true for Jerusalem.) I think it better to say that the evidence from both the text and from archaeology needs to be used with an eye to their limitations.

Manfred Oeming's "The Real History: The Theological Ideas behind Nehemiah's Walls" is subtitled "Why the Dominance of Archaeology and the Underestimation of Theology Are a Problem When Reconstructing History." Oeming notes that there has been much discussion of the location and the historicity of the account of its construction. However, he laments that the ideological and theological importance of the wall is often overlooked. In attempting to explain the reason Nehemiah wished to build Jerusalem's wall, scholars have often looked to political or economic currents in Achaeminid Yehud. Some scholars dismiss the theological assertions of the text as secondary. Oeming states that this separating secular from religious thought is a modern artifice and out of place when examining events from the ancient Near East. Instead, he explores the theological motivations behind Nehemiah's work, noting that Hebrew prophetic texts and the Psalms also see the wall of Jerusalem as theologically significant in enclosing an area in which God could dwell with his people. Thus, while there may have been political and economic reasons for rebuilding Jerusalem's walls, these were also joined with theological motivations. Oeming's essay contains a nice corrective of recent studies of Nehemiah because it reminds us that there is almost never a single cause for a historical movement or event but that human actions often are motivated by a confluence of several factors.

Ran Zadok's "Some Issues in Ezra-Nehemiah" rounds out the first section of this volume. He discusses "Sources and Background," "Nehemiah," and "Ezra in the Shadow of Nehemiah" and presents his opinions of a number of issues relating to these books as well as citing the works of others going back to Wellhausen.

The second section opens with David Marcus's "Hidden Treasure: The Unpublished Doublet Catchwords in Ezra-Nehemiah." He presents an explanation and analysis of the catchwords that the Masoretes used when marking doublets: words that occur only twice in the MT. The catchwords reference the other verse in which the doublet occurs. For instance, for the doublet לְבְהֵמָה at Neh 2:14, the catchword is מצמיח, which occurs at Ps 104:14, the other verse that contains this doublet. Marcus discusses the relationship of the catchwords to the Masorah Magna notes, catchwords in manuscripts other than L, previous publication of catchwords, and the purpose of the catchwords. In a very interesting final section he suggests exegetical use of the catchwords, providing three interesting examples.

In "Where did the Judahites, Benjaminites, and Levites Settle? Revisiting the Text of Nehemiah 11:25–36 MT and LXX," Deirdre Fulton explores the question of which text, the MT or LXX, is the older. Using careful text-critical methodology, she determines that the shorter LXX text in this case is the older tradition and that the MT is a later expansion. She compares the settlement list to other lists in Joshua and Ezra and notes instances that may have led to the expansion of the MT. She believes the expansions present in the MT likely date to the later part of the Hellenistic period.

Paul Redditt offers an interesting and creative solution to a conundrum in "The Census List in Ezra 2 and Nehemiah 7: A Suggestion." Assuming that a common redactor of Ezra and Nehemiah placed the same list at Ezra 2:1–3:1 and Neh 7:6–72, Redditt then proceeds to compare the two versions. Noting that both list the same number of returnees: 42,360 plus 7,337 servants and 240/5 singers[2] but that the totals of the family lists are far smaller (29,818 in Ezra; 31,089 in Neh), he produces a number of interesting arguments to support his theory that the difference is ideological: the larger number represents a supposed total Israel in the land, whereas the smaller numbers represent the ideal Israel. Thus, not all members of the postexilic community belong to the true Israel envisioned by the redactor. This is an interesting solution to this problem, and Redditt presents a number of well-reasoned supporting arguments in its favor. However, like all previous proposed solutions to this puzzle, it must remain speculative, since it is based on assumptions about the redaction of Ezra-Nehemiah and on specific exegetical decisions for a number of passages in Ezra and Nehemiah.

In "Nehemiah's Request on Behalf of Jerusalem," Joseph Fleishman argues that, when Nehemiah requests permission from Artaxerxes to return to Jerusalem and rebuild its wall, the cupbearer astutely uses his knowledge of Zoroastrianism to persuade the king. After a brief survey of the evidence demonstrating that the Achaemenid kings were Zoroastrians, Fleishman explores how Nehemiah skillfully wove Zoroastrian themes into his request in order to gain the king's approval. Most important, he notes the mention of ancestral graves and the use of fire (Neh 2:3, 5). Fleishman's essay is persuasive and may well illuminate the sagaciousness demonstrated in Nehemiah's request as well as explaining why Artaxerxes permitted the rebuilding of Jerusalem's wall after having stopped it sometime earlier (Ezra 4:21–22).

---

2. Ezra 2:65 has 240; Neh 7:67 has 245. Redditt believes that the final word (וחמשה) has fallen out at Ezra 2:65.

The final essay, Mark Boda's "Prayer as Rhetoric in the Book of Nehemiah," looks at the author's purpose for including prayers within the narrative of the book. He notes that they accomplish many of the purposes often associated with direct discourse in ancient literature: internal characterization, dramatic effect, rhetorical structure, plot advancement, and ideological interpretation. In addition, he finds that the prayers demonstrate that there is an ideological unity to the book of Nehemiah in that they express the same themes throughout the book. Most helpfully, he also explores the implications of this study, noting that it emphasizes the book's view of piety, community, and worship instead of wall building. It may also bring into question the necessity or validity of reading the book in light of Ezra 1–10.

Invitation to the Psalms: A Reader's Guide for Discovery and Engagement, by Rolf A. Jacobson and Karl N. Jacobson. Grand Rapids: Baker Academic, 2013. Pp. viii + 184. Paper. $17.99. ISBN 9780801036446.

David Firth, St John's College, Nottingham, U.K.

It is always a delight to come to the end of a book and feel that it has done what is suggested by the title. In this engaging, and often entertaining, invitation to the Psalms, Rolf and Karl Jacobson have done just that. Both the main title and the subtitle are important here. This is not an *introduction* to the Psalms, the kind of work that sets out its task as guiding students into the nuances of current Psalms studies, though it covers many areas of relevance to such a task. Rather, it is an *invitation*, a work that has as its first goal the task of encouraging readers to explore these poems. So, we do not find endless footnotes and bibliographies that demonstrate the authors' acquaintance with the main lines of Psalms research, though it is clear that they are both well-informed about it. There are short bibliographies at the end of each chapter, but these are by and large also invitations to explore the Psalms further. Likewise, although there are points where other authors are appropriately referenced, the Jacobsons are not concerned to introduce their readers to all the debates about the Psalms. Rather, the references are brief points where they acknowledge their own scholarly debts. So, this is not an introduction; it is an invitation. But it is an invitation with a purpose, and that is clearly indicated in the subtitle. Having invited readers to come to the Psalms, they want them both to discover for themselves what the Psalms are and also how they might engage with them, drawing on them in their own processes of reading. It is apparent that their goal is to help such readers interact more fully and faithfully with the Psalms, so that the effect of the invitation is not just to take up and read, but to take up and read well. None of this would prevent this book being used as a textbook in an introductory course on the Psalms, and its goal of encouraging informed reading of the Psalms is surely a worthy goal for this, but it does mean that anyone doing so would need to supplement what is here. The book would also be of use in a parish setting, where it might also be employed to encourage congregations to explore the depths of the Psalms in a more informed way.

The Jacobsons open their invitation by outlining their approach as one where the Psalms are not only meant to be read; they are meant to be experienced. To demonstrate this, they draw on Billy Collins's poem "Introduction to Poetry," which rebels against the sort of analysis of poetry that tortures a confession out of it by endless analysis rather than "water-ski" across its surface. Of course, the Jacobsons know only too well that there is analysis to be done, but their aim is to let their readers read psalms more effectively so that they can water-ski across their surface. The use of Collins's poem here also points to another important aspect of the book, which is the way they use relatively contemporary Western poems and songs as a means of guiding readers into the psalms themselves. Collins's poem is clearly different in form from the psalms, but contemporary readers will recognize its form and style (whether or not they can analyze it) and can then use it as an entry point to the psalms themselves. So, various songs and poems (including *The Star Spangled Banner*) are used to illustrate the issues under discussion, taking what is familiar as the point of entry for what is unfamiliar in the biblical psalms. Questions for reflection and exploration along with a short reading list are also provided for each chapter.

This approach is then applied to a number of issues. The Jacobsons begin with the nature of Hebrew poetry, focusing particularly on the nature of parallelism. In the nature of a work such as this, they are not about to take readers through the maze of different types of parallelism, opting instead to see parallelism as a means by which subsequent sections echo or extend what has gone before. In spite of the simplicity of their presentation, it never becomes simplistic, as they are well aware of the different levels at which parallelism can occur, covering everything from parallelism within a line through to parallelism between poems. Focusing on parallelism is necessary if readers are to appreciate how the psalms work as poetry, though leaving the other aspects of poetry (metaphors, imagery, and symbolism) until chapter 5 seems odd, as it divorces the poetic form of the psalms from their poetic content, and how they work as poetry is surely found in the interchange between these elements. That said, their treatment of such matters is helpful, pointing readers to the ways these elements occur in contemporary literature and speech as a means for looking at such language in various psalms, looking especially at the "rock" metaphor.

Having considered the poetic form of psalms, the Jacobsons then take readers through the main psalm types. Although the word *Gattung* never appears, this is what they are discussing. They recognize that one of the sticking points in form-critical study has been the fact that some types are designated on the basis of their form and others on the basis of their content and that there is inevitable cross-over between types as a result. Clearly aware of this, they opt to devote one chapter to psalms that are recognizable from their form (laments, hymns, songs of trust, thanksgivings) and one to those recognizable from their content (royal, enthronement, wisdom, creation, historical, along with less-defined groups such as penitential, imprecatory, Zion, liturgical). This solution will not satisfy everyone, but it does at least open up some of the ways in which understanding genre can enable better interpretation of the biblical psalms.

After the treatment of metaphor and so on, a closing chapter then looks at the theology of the Psalms. The Jacobsons take the view that it is better to see the Psalms as a mosaic rather than a single oil painting, since a mosaic is something made up of preexisting pieces. Such an approach allows for some diversity but still permits them to argue that the faithfulness of God is central to the theology of the Psalms. As poems, many of which are also prayers, psalms are truly faith seeking understanding, though not in an abstract way. They are about lived experience where God's faithfulness can be expounded, challenged, expressed, or understood afresh from the perspective of thanksgiving, but understood within the framework of a God committed to creation. What is particularly helpful here is the way the earlier discussions about genre and poetry come together to show how the psalms are ultimately a lived theology.

All of this is very helpful, and any criticisms I have are minor because the Jacobsons have done a wonderful job in inviting readers both to discover the Psalms and also to continue their engagement with them through the resources provided. However, in a work that wears its learning lightly and yet is clearly well-informed about current discussion, I found it odd that so little was said about the ways in which Psalms may (or may not!) work as a book. There are hints of the Jacobsons' view on this: the possibility of parallelism across psalms or the fact that (within the metaphor of the mosaic) a broadly coherent theology can be discerned. But given that this has been such a major area of debate in recent decades, it is surprising that some attention is not given to this, as it does impact on the ways readers encounter the Psalms. For example, does it matter that many reading schemes for the Psalms do not follow the canonical order, or is there something important about reading Psalms from 1 to 150? I hope that in any subsequent editions they will take the opportunity address this gap, but in the meantime we should acknowledge their achievement and hope that their invitation is widely accepted in colleges and parishes so that readers not only take up and read the Psalms but take them up and read them well.

King and Temple in Chronicles: A Contextual Approach to Their Relations, by Jozef Tiňo. Forschungen zur Religion und Literatur des Alten und Neuen Testaments 234. Göttingen: Vandenhoeck & Ruprecht, 2010. Pp. 183. Hardcover. €79.00. ISBN 9783525530962.

César Melgar, Graduate Theological Union, Berkeley, California

In recent years there has been an increased interest in Chronicles resulting in new scholarly publications. The present work by Jozef Tiňo, associate professor at the Faculty of Theology at the University of Trnava in Slovakia, represents the revised version of his doctoral dissertation written at the University of Cambridge

under the supervision of William Horbury. In this monograph Tiño channels his
efforts to elaborate on the ideology embedded within exilic and postexilic texts
that aspires for a renewal of the Davidic monarchy. He seeks with this analysis to
answer the fundamental question of how this ideology deals with the issue of the
"new David's" relation with the temple (12).

    In the introduction Tiño lays out a fruitful discussion about his assumptions
and methodological approach. First, he assumes that Chronicles is the work of
a single author and postulates that the genealogies (1 Chr 1–9) and the temple
personnel (1 Chr 23–27) represent the original accounts of this composition. He
supports his assertion by relying on important works that deal with the genealogies written by M. D. Johnson (*The Purpose of the Biblical Genealogies* [SNTSMS
8; Cambridge: University Press,1969]); H. G. M. Williamson (*1 and 2 Chronicles*
[NCBC; London: Marshall, Morgan & Scott, 1982]); M. Oeming (*Das wahre
Israel: Die 'genealogische Vorhalle' 1 Chronik 1–9* [BWANT 128; Stuttgart: Kohlhammer,1990]); and G. N. Knoppers ("Greek Historiography and the Chronicler's
History: A Reexamination," *JBL* 122 [2003]: 627–50). As for the relation between
Chronicles and other historical sources, Tiño sides with the majority view that the
Chronicler made use of Samuel–Kings. However, he carefully points out that the
discovery of 4QSam[a] provides evidence that the Chronicler's *Vorlage* is not identical to the MT but that it could potentially be connected to an Old Palestinian text
type (22–29). In terms of his methodology, Tiño explains that the intrinsic relation between secular and religious matters within the Davidic dynasty constitutes
the backbone of his interpretive work (30–34).

    Chapter 2 ("The Composition of Chronicles: The History of Israel's Mon-
archy Examined through Ruler-Sanctuary Relations") contains the gist of Tiño's
argument regarding the Davidic dynasty. He proposes that the sequence of events
from the turning of the kingdom from Saul to David (סבב; 1 Chr 10:14b), the
promise of a dynasty (בית; 1 Chr 17:10), and the ratification of this eternal promise in Solomon's reign (1 Chr 17:12) points to a fresh beginning for Israel (36).
Thus, Tiño interprets the reigns of David and Solomon as a seamless unit, a
divinely sanctioned institution that stands at the axis of Israel's history in which
each of the kings partakes of secular and cultic roles (48–49). However, Tiño
stresses that this intimate link between secular and cultic functions ceases when
Solomon dies and the kingdom splits. As a consequence of this schism, the place
of each Davidic king within the dynastic promise becomes conditioned by the
king's faithful observance of the law (55). Tiño ends this important chapter with
a detailed survey of each of the Davidic kings after Solomon and their relation to
the notions of "dynasty-temple-land-Torah" (57–73).

    Chapter 3 ("Law of the King in Deuteronomy and Chronicles") deals with
the role of the "law of the king" (Deut 16:18–20; 17:8–13) in Chronicles. Initially,
Tiño shows the differences between 2 Chr 19:4–11 and the "law of the king" and
proposes that these have to do with the change that happens after the break of
the monarchy (76–83). Afterward he illustrates the way Chronicles represents the
united monarchy as the golden age of Israel's history with universalistic images

reminiscent of the Sumerian king lists and the Akkadian cosmologies, where monarchies are apotheosized and temples are seen as the centers of the universe (89–93). Tiño ends by pairing the descriptions of David and Solomon in Chronicles with the messianic expectations within Isaiah and Micah (Isa 2; 8:23b–9:6; 11:1–10; Mic 5:1–5) and proposes that these sources share the view of a future Davidic king that will be the mediator between Yahweh and the people (95–105).

Chapter 4 ("The Book of Chronicles' King-Temple Relations in the Context of the Shaping of the Psalter") constitutes Tiño's thesis that the Chronicler was somehow connected to the circles that at one point edited the Psalter. Tiño establishes that the Chronicler made use of specific psalms in his description of the united monarchy, and he sees that the creative editing of the psalmic material implies that the Chronicler was connected to the aforementioned groups (108–11). He adds that, aside from an allusion during Jehoshaphat's reign, the psalms do not appear elsewhere in the narratives of the divided monarchy, which further emphasizes the significance of the united monarchy to the Chronicler's theology. Tiño then compares and contrasts the Chronicler's perspective of kingship with that of Deutero-Isaiah and books 4 and 5 of the Psalter, where both the suzerainty of Yahweh and the earthly king are at odds (112–17). He concedes that ideological differences between them demonstrate the variety of perspectives among the temple scribes during the Persian period (119).

Chapter 5 ("The Exilic and Post-exilic Messianic Prophecy Related to the Theology of Chronicles") evaluates Chronicles with four postexilic prophecies (Jer 33:14–26; Ezek 37:14–28; Zech 9:9–10; 12:8). Tiño states that the Chronicler was familiar with the prophecies of Jer 33 and Ezek 37 and was influenced by them in his depiction of the future salvific age. But Tiño also recognizes that the Chronicler's use of these traditions is not without some divergence. For instance, Jer 33 restricts the direct involvement of a secular figure in functions of the temple (120–29). In the same manner, the use of נשיא instead of a מלך in Ezek 37 demonstrates a separation of secular and cultic roles (130–36). As for the prophecies of Zechariah, Tiño indicates that they share with Chronicles the view of David as a new type of Moses (137–45).

Chapter 6 ("Conclusion") wraps up this investigation. Here Tiño is not content with simply reiterating his findings but instead sets them in conversation with the theological context contemporary to the Chronicler. By doing this, he proceeds to answer some of the lingering questions regarding the Chronicler's ultimate goal in composing this historiographic work. Tiño holds that the Chronicler is not merely elaborating on Samuel-Kings but with the use of the genealogies and the Priestly material (P) is illustrating a broader perspective of the history of Israel that reaches as far back from Genesis to Kings (147). In addition, Tiño posits that the lack of eschatological language suggests that the Chronicler's hope for the renewal of the monarchy was not a utopian vision but rather an "achievable future" (151). Therefore, by editing these traditions and presenting David as a new type of Moses, the Chronicler stands opposite to Samuel-Kings in terms of the centrality of the Davidic kingship. Moreover, the Chronicler's vision for the future of Israel significantly differs from other postexilic texts such as Ezra-Nehemiah, where there is no unified Israel but rather a segregated community that only includes Judah or the exile returnees (160–61).

Tiňo convincingly demonstrates that David and Solomon constitute the focal point of the Chronicler's account, as they both are the high point of Israel's history and the hope for the immediate future. He is also right in pointing out that the dynastic promise endures with the Davidic monarchs as they remain faithful to Yahweh through the law. Finally, his analysis of some of the messianic prophecies provides interesting evidence of the shared aspiration for a renewal of the golden days of Israel when David, as a new type of Moses, will mediate between Yahweh and the people. Despite these persuasive points, Tiňo's argument about the Chronicler's connection to the guild that edited the Psalter is hypothetical at best. Instead, Tiňo would make a much more compelling case by focusing not just on the references to psalms but also on other descriptions and allusions to matters of worship and how worship as a communal experience emanates from the palace-temple sphere. On the role of worship for Chronicles, see John Endres, "Theology of Worship in Chronicles," in *The Chronicler as Theologian: Essays in Honor of Ralph W. Klein* (ed. M. Patrick Graham, Steven L. McKenzie, and Gary N. Knoppers; New York: T&T Clark, 2003). Lastly, this work demonstrates thorough research and sophisticated analysis, but it also evinces a lack of careful editorial attention, as there are several spelling errors and awkward grammatical constructions. Also, at $110 per copy, this monograph may be within the budget of a research library, but it might be too high of a price to pay by an individual scholar. Tiňo's final product is a good contribution that provides a manageable yet thorough description of the key motifs of monarchy and temple, and with it Tiňo has highlighted the significance of Chronicles for understanding the ideology and aspirations of postexilic Judah.

Power and Responsibility in Biblical Interpretation: Reading the Book of Job with Edward Said, by Alissa Jones Nelson. BibleWorld. Sheffield: Equinox, 2012. Pp. x + 259. Cloth. $99.95. ISBN 9781845538897.

Peter-Ben Smit, Vrije Universiteit Amsterdam, Amsterdam, The Netherlands

Power and Responsibility in Biblical Interpretation is the published version of the author's doctoral dissertation (2009, St. Andrew's University; supervisor: Mario I Aguilar). The work takes its starting point in the observation that there is a(n institutionalized) distance between "academic" and "vernacular" approaches to and interpretations of Scripture, which is also characterized by the (self-)marginalization of the latter, which raises "important ethical, praxiological, and theological questions" regarding the interpretation of Scripture and the appertaining pedagogy (1–3, see the examples on 3–11). Nelson intends to seek a way forward, that is, "the project of closing the gap between academic and vernacular hermeneutics" (11). Key to this project is the hermeneutics of Edward Said, specifically his concept of "contrapuntal reading," which is both outlined in Nelson's book and also applied in a number of ways to the book of Job. This is done as follows.

Chapters 1–3 present the "conceptual bases upon which [the book's] project will be founded" (12). In chapter 1 this takes the shape of an insightful discussion of the main characteristics of Edward Said's interpretative concerns and concepts, focusing specifically on his understanding of subjectivity, power, intellectual responsibility, and the secular (19–52). Helpfully, Nelson also gives an interpretation of Said's rather misleading (and strongly biographically colored) notion of the "religious" in this context, which for him "represents the anti-intellectual, the uncritical acceptance and veneration of the devoted individual. It typifies a propensity to accept and uphold a system or status quo; a religious critic is one whose critical position is necessarily restrained by belief or by adherence." (41) Indeed, as Nelson notes, the "religious need not be religious" (52), given that Said is not arguing against devotion as such but (only) uncritical devotion; even his own "secular" approach to interpretation can become "religious" in the pejorative sense of the word that he employs. The discussion of Said's work continues in chapter 2 (53–86), which focuses on Said's method of "contrapuntal reading," the process of reading and rereading of (especially influential or classical) texts from different (previously marginalized) contexts in order to expand their interpretation and to prevent the hegemony of single or dominant and potentially oppressing interpretations. "The point of contrapuntal reading is not to distil a single, agreed-upon meaning from a given text, but to allow different streams of meaning to coexist, to recognize that difference does not necessarily entail conflict, and that 'truth can be opposed to truth.' This does not mean that all interpretations are legitimate, but rather defends the possibility of multiple legitimate interpretations that cannot, or should not, be systematized, harmonized, or forced into continuity" (85; quite rightly, Said's musical point of reference is not so much the harmony but the atonal composition). When having to choose what does and does not constitute a legitimate interpretation, Nelson notes that Said refers to ethical criteria, in which she follows him, noting that "[t]he recognition of the ethical implications of the work of biblical scholars … is still manifestly inadequate to the needs of the contemporary world. Intellectual curiosity and professional advancement too often take precedence over issue of ethical responsibility in the realm of academic hermeneutics" (86). Next, in chapter 3 (87–119), Nelson reviews a number of attempts to bridge the gap between academic and vernacular approaches to Scripture, covering the work of Kwok Pui-lan, Elsa Tamez, Gerald O. West, Justin Ukpong, Fernando F. Segovia, and R. S. Sugirtharajah. She finds them all lacking either in practice (no real dialogue is achieved) or because the self-marginalization of vernacular approaches remains in place (118): "Although these scholars have proposed a variety of approaches in an attempt to *bridge* [the] gap, what has yet to be taken is the *elimination* of the gap through the creation of a mutual space for hermeneutical interaction" (118). This, the elimination of the gap, is, however, precisely what Nelson intends and for which she seeks to employ Said's contrapuntal hermeneutics, given that it

> allows us to view biblical interpretation from a frame of entry that does not resort to binary oppositions between trained and untrained readers, between academic and popular readers, between West and Rest, or between centre and margin. It provides a shared space between academic and vernacular hermeneutics which eliminates the opposition, although not the differences, between the two. It also indicates an approach to questions of idea versus experience which views such questions not linearly but contapuntally, as the result of a cyclical relationship rather than of a simple hierarchy or historical progression. This involves the recognition that idea and circumstantial reality mutually shape, expand, limit and exchange each other. (118)

Having outlined her approach, Nelson turns to the book of Job, which is particularly suitable to test contrapuntal hermeneutics on, given the different voices in the text itself, the broad variety of interpretative voices that have addressed the text, and the topics that are touched upon in the text that are "demonstrably resonant across a wide variety of contexts and disciplines as well as across the gap between academic and vernacular hermeneutics." (124) These considerations lead into chapter 4 of the book, in which the interpretations of Gerhard von Rad and Gustavo Gutiérrez of Job 38:1–42:6 are brought into dialogue (125–65), that is to say, a contrapuntal relationship with one another (with minor roles for the voices of David J. A. Clines, Elsa Tamez, and Enrique Dussel, 146–56). While each of these authors takes as his or her starting point the Joban text, his or her own theological concerns, and the interpretation of others, and no consensus is reached, reading them as standing in a contrapuntal relationship to one another and as interacting "across the boundaries that separate them" leads to a situation in which "the text takes on a depth and dimensionality that far exceeds any of these interpretations taken individually.… Ultimately none of [the] interpreters is able to definitively overcome the challenges posed by the opposite perspective, but the very existence of a counterchallenge is what makes hermeneutics possible" (164). In fact, Nelson seems to agree with Clines that "the book of Job was intended to subvert closure," which would make contrapuntal hermeneutics an approach that agrees well with the *intention operis* (164–65) as well. In other words, "like wisdom literature at its best, the juxtaposition of critical voices demonstrates that 'truth can be opposed to truth' and that this dissonant opposition can be a positive rather than a negative factor in biblical interpretation." In the subsequent chapter 5 Nelson addresses a next set of interpretations, placing them in contrapuntal relations to one another: "Pschology, Physiology, Society, and Spirituality: Interpreting Job with Insight from Psychological and HIV-Positive Perspectives" (166; 166–200). Having surveyed both a number of psychological approaches and of interpretations determined by the HIV pandemia, Nelson concludes that "[t]he process of boundary crossing entailed in this contrapuntal conversation leaves us with an interpretative voice which insists that the answer to this question [What is the person of faith to do when faced with the reality of suffering?] is not prescriptive but prohibitive. The book of Job does not tell the reader how one should talk about God in contexts of suffering, but it does inform the reader how *not* to talk of God" (199). Again, Nelson considers this conclusion, which can have a liberating and healing effect on those afflicted by suffering, as both positive and as a vindication of contrapuntal hermeneutics (200). The sixth and final chapter of the book then treats "The Integration of Chaos and Order: Exploring Asian Interpretations of the Book of Job" (201–27). These Asian interpretations are seen by Nelson as providing "unique interpretative insight from which academic voices can learn. We have seen that both academic and vernacular voices in Asian contexts ... find evidence in the book of Job for the necessary balance between chaos and order in God's creation." (226) Though not explored by these Asian voices, nor by her, Nelson notes that this particular exercise in contrapuntal hermeneutics also points to further interpretative horizons, particularly when placing the book of Job in relation to yin-yang hermeneutical perspectives (226).

Having both laid out her research question and theoretical framework and worked her way through three exercises in contrapuntal hermeneutics, Nelson focuses in her conclusions on the pedagogy of biblical studies in particular (229–34). A first conclusion is that "the pedagogical structure of courses in biblical interpretation must be adapted to contemporary contexts" (231); second, "vernacular" approaches to Scripture must be fully integrated into the "standard curriculum" and not be treated any longer as optional extras (232); third, such changes "should not be permitted to harden into a new pedagogical canon," but "re-evaluation and adaptation should be continual" (233). Nelson looks forward to seeing the effect on all of this in the perceptions of students (234).

Power and Responsibility in Biblical Interpretation is, for various reasons, a valuable book. First of all, it offers a good introduction to the work of Edward Said and the notion of contrapuntal hermeneutics, as well as to the functioning of this approach. I could well imagine that students from a variety of disciplines—transcending biblical studies as such—could benefit from reading this study in the context of their explorations in critical theory and hermeneutics. Also, the book is valuable because it brings together and takes seriously a very broad range of interpretations of one key biblical text, which raises the reader's awareness of the broad reception of Scripture and the productivity of canonical texts. In that context, I would underline Nelson's suggestion that a contrapuntal hermeneutics in fact continues the hermeneutics inscribed into the biblical texts themselves (not unlike James A. Sanders's notion of canonical hermeneutics). Criticism, of course, is also possible, though not along the lines of other reviews that have argued that Nelson has little original to offer concerning the interpretation of Job, which, as far as I can see, is not the main point of the book; rather, I would challenge the author to further develop the notion of the ethical responsibility of the interpreter and to lay out her own ethical framework for the interpretation of Scripture (including her positive reception contrapuntal hermeneutics);

this would complete the exercise in contrapuntal hermeneutics that *Power and Responsibility in Biblical Interpretation* constitutes even further, as it would allow her to take full responsibility for her work and approach.

The Book of Job in Form: A Literary Translation with Commentary, by Jan P. Fokkelman. Studia Semitica Neerlandica 58. Leiden: Brill, 2012. Pp. x + 335. Hardcover. $179.00. ISBN 9789004231580.

Roger Marcel Wanke, Faculdade Luterana de Teologia, São Bento do Sul, Brazil

Das Hiobbuch ist ein Werk *sui generis* nicht nur der alttestamentlichen Überlieferung, sondern auch der Weltliteratur. In der Tat ist das Hiobbuch eine schöne literarische Kombination von Prosa und Poesie. Dabei gehören Form und Inhalt im ihm eng zusammen. Sie führen die Leser des Buches zur Spannung und zum Staunen. In den letzten Jahren sind viele Studien über das Hiobbuch entstanden, die von unterschiedlichen Methoden und Fragestellungen ausgehen und die Hiobexegese fruchtbar machen. Unter anderen sind in der Hiobforschung zwei wichtigen Tendenzen zu beobachten: Besonders im deutschsprachigen Raum sind redaktionsgeschichtlichen Untersuchungen zu finden. In diesem Kontext sind ebenso die Studien zu nennen, die das Hiobbuch als Exemplar der innerbiblischen Schriftauslegung und als intertextuelles Werk untersuchen. Im englischsprachigen Raum hingegen sind zahlreichen Untersuchungen veröffentlicht, die von einer kanonischen Schriftauslegung ausgehen. Für sie ist die Betonung des Endtextes charakteristisch. Ein wichtiges Motiv für die Entstehung dieser Methode ist wiederum die Kritik an der historisch-kritischen Methode.

Die vorliegende Untersuchung gehört zu dieser zweiten Tendenz der Hiobforschung und ist eine dezidierte synchrone Analyse des Hiobbuches. Methodisch geht der Verfasser den Weg einer Kombination der Poetologie und der Narratologie. Seiner These nach kann das Hiobbuch besser verstanden werden, wenn man am Textebene bleibt und seine poetische Dimension ernst nimmt. Ausgehend von seinen anderen Werken—*Reading Biblical Poetry* (2001) und *The Psalms in Form* (2002)—führt der Verfasser seine Forschung weiter, indem er nun das Hiobbuch in seiner poetischen Form wahrnimmt und eine literarische, in Strophenform aufgebaute Übersetzung darstellt. Der Vorteil dieses Modells für die Interpretation des Hiobbuches und insgesamt alttestamentlicher Texte besteht für den Verfasser aus zwei wichtigen Aspekten: "regarding the text itself and the reader" (4).

Inhaltlich ist die Arbeit in drei Teilen gegliedert. Beim ersten Teil (3–29) geht es einführend um zwei methodischen Ansätze der Arbeit, die nach dem Verfasser für die Auslegung des Hiobbuches unentbehrlich sind: das Hiobbuch als wichtiges poetisches Werk und die kompetente Rolle der Leser. Seine Argumentation beginnt mit einer Darstellung von sechs Gründen, die inhaltlich und literarisch erklären, wie und warum das Hiobbuch ein "exceptional text" ist: Erstens gehört das Hiobbuch als Exemplar der klassisch-hebräischen Literatur zu den großen poetischen Werken in der Hebräischen Bibel, die schönkomponiert sind. Zweitens hat der Autor des Hiobbuches die grundlegenden Fragestellungen der menschlichen Existenz inhaltlich in seiner Komposition aufgegriffen, und zwar zum ungerechten Leid. Damit bietet der Autor des Hiobbuches eine Diskussion zur richtigen Vorstellung von Mensch und Gott. Der dritte Grund besteht aus der Ähnlichkeit zwischen dem Hiobbuch und Platos Dialogen. Beiden diskutieren zentralen Themen in poetischer Form. Viertens betont der Verfasser, dass das Hiobbuch seine Überzeugungskraft gerade in seiner Verbindung zwischen Prosa und Poesie findet: "the author remains, in his capacity as narrator, the first and the last person responsible for the long series of poems" (4). Als fünfter Grund geht der Verfasser auf die literarische Gattung des Hiobbuches ein. Als Exemplar der weisheitlichen Literatur ist das Hiobbuch zum Beispiel vom Sprüchebuch zu differenzieren, indem das Hiobbuch aufgrund der Fusion von Prosa und Poesie eine Art Dramatik darstellt. Nach diesem kurzen Überblick erklärt der Verfasser unterschiedlichen Begriffe der Poetik, wie z.B. "Vers", "Kolon", "Strophe" und "Prosodie" (5–9), die für das Verständnis seiner Übersetzung vorausgesetzt werden. Damit zeigt der Verfasser überzeugend, dass das Hiobbuch im Bezug auf Strophen ausgehend von einer "*numerical perfection*" aufgebaut wurde. Diese "*numerical perfection*" dient der Struktur der Dichtung. Nach dem Verfasser "they help us find the heart of the message" (9). Als literarisches Beispiel dieser Verbindung zwischen Qualität der poetischen Form und der Quantität dieser "numerical perfection" erwähnt der Verfasser den Psalm 33 und Hiob 9 (10–14). Obwohl die Analyse des Verfassers und seine Feststellung einer "numerical perfection" im Hiobbuch überzeugend scheint, bleibt als eine kritische Rückfrage das Verhältnis von diachroner und synchroner Interpretation besonders bezüglich der Ergebnisse der Textkritik. Die Rekonstruktion des Endtextes des Hiobbuches ist nicht problemlos und könnte die sogenannte "numerical perfection" gefährden. Dass der Verfasser von der kanonischen Schriftauslegung ausgeht, ist legitim und notwendig. Dass er sich von historisch-kritischen Ansätzen und Ergebnissen zu schnell und ironisch verabschiedet, bleibt doch fraglich. Der Verfasser hat in seiner Analyse leider nicht bewiesen, wie gefährlich und verheerend die historisch-kritische Methode für die Interpretation des Hiobbuches sein könnte: "With these reflections I say goodbye to the disastrous operation which historical criticism performed on the Book of Job when it maintained that its prose must be by a different author and date from a different time than its body of verse" (14–15). Interessant hingegen ist das Verständnis des Verfassers, dass der Autor des Hiobbuches als "*omniscient narrator*" verstanden werden muss. Diese Vorstellung ist nicht nur Privileg einer kanonischen Interpretation, sondern auch von den jüngsten redaktionsgeschichtlichen Studien her zu sehen. Leider sind diese im Literaturverzeichnis nicht zu finden. Dem Verfasser zufolge ist diese Qualifikation des Autors als "omniscient narrator" nicht theologisch, sondern als "narratological statement" zu verstehen (15). Exemplarisch dazu erwähnt der Verfasser die Funktion der Himmelszenen im Hiobbuch: "In his capacity as omniscient narrator the author has decided that he wants to give us a look into the heavenly council [...]" (17). Was in den Himmelszenen geschieht, bestimmt die Rolle des Autors als "omniscient narrator" und die Interpretation des Hiobbuches insgesamt. Dabei werden der Platz des Hiobbuches in der hebräischen Bibel, Gattungsfragen, das historische Profil der Hiobfigur undl die Entstehungszeit des Buches kurz dargestellt (19–21). Zum Schluss wird auf Beobachtungen zu seiner Übersetzung hingewiesen (22–24).

Im zweiten Teil der Arbeit, dem Zentrum der Untersuchung (35–193), steht die Übersetzung des Textes des Hiobbuches. Es gelingt dem Verfasser, den Text mit Hilfe seiner Analyse in Strophenform zu präsentieren. Die Darstellung nimmt sowohl die prosaische als auch die poetische Form des Hiobbuches wahr. Didaktisch, praktisch und sehr hilfreich ist der hebräische Text neben seiner englischen Übersetzung auch in Strophenform gboten. Der Verfasser folgt für seine Übersetzung teilweise der klassischen Gliederung des Hiobbuches: Prolog und Klage werden als ein Block präsentiert (Hi 1–3). Die Gespräche mit den Freunden werden klassisch in drei Gänge dargestellt: der erste Redegang (Hi 4–14), der zweite Redegang (Hi 15–21), der dritte Redegang (Hi 22–28). Als "Climax I" bezeichnet der Verfasser in seiner Übersetzung die Hiobs Monologen (Hi 29–31). Die Elihureden versteht der Verfasser als "Intervention of a fourth friend" (Hi 32–38). Die Gottesreden werden als "Climax II" genannt (Hi 38–41). Schließlich wird die Antwort Hiobs in 42,1–6 als letzte Strophe und 42,7–17 (Epilog) als Abschluss des narrativen Prosatextes dargestellt.

In Bezug auf die Übersetzung muss die folgenden kurzen Bemerkungen gemacht: Im Prolog gibt der Verfasser den Namen Satan zwei Mal als "Adversary" [Feind] (1,6 und 2,1), an anderen Stellen aber als "Prosecutor" [Ankläger] wieder. Doch es bleibt fraglich, warum der Name Satan unterschiedlich wiedergegeben wird. Diese Unterscheidung scheint neu in der Forschung zu sein, bleibt aber leider ohne Erklärung. Besonders wichtig ist aber seine Übersetzung von Hi 42,6. Der Verfasser schlägt eine andere Übersetzung vor: "Therefore I quit, and I am consoled over dust and dirt" (193). Diese Übersetzungsform von V. 6 ist nicht neu in der Hiobexegese. Im Gegenteil, dazu wird sie in der Forschung im deutschsprachigen Raum zunehmend angenommen. Die Wiedergabe der hebräischen Würzel נחם trägt im Hiobbuch immer die Bedeutung "trösten" (cf. 2,11; 6,10; 7,13; 16,2; 21,34; 29,25; 30,28; 42,11). Außerdem bleibt die Bedeutung "bereuen", wie klassisch übersetzt wird, nach der Meinung vieler Exegeten in Bezug auf dem Inhalt des Buches unverständlich. Eine überzeugende Erklärung des Verfassers für seine Übersetzung von V. 6 findet sich am Ende seiner Untersuchung (317–19). Für ihn ist die Übersetzung "I am consoled" in V. 6 das Schlüsselwort für das Verständnis des Hiobbuches: "The keyword functions as beginning and ending of the whole trajectory, thus giving a slender but identifiable frame to the whole book" (319).

Schließlich, im dritten Teil, stellt der Verfasser einen kurzen Kommentar als Leserhilfe, mit Bemerkungen und poetischen Maßstäben seiner Analyse dar (199–327). Der Verfasser greift auf seine Übersetzung und Gliederung zurück, indem er sie nun theologisch, inhaltlich und poetisch erklärt. Kapitel für Kapitel werden sowohl der Inhalt als auch die poetischen Maße und gegliederten Strophen kommentiert und ausgelegt. Neben der Wahrnehmung narrativer und poetischer Bemerkungen zeichnet sich die Untersuchung aber vor allem durch eine Vielzahl weiterführender Beobachtungen zum theologischen Inhalt des Buches aus. Insgesamt versucht der Verfasser die Rolle der Leser immer wieder zu betonen. Der Leser bleibt im konstanten Gespräch mit dem *"omniscient narrator"*. Zunächst sei auf einige Aspekte kurz hingewiesen: In der Auslegung des Prologs erwähnt der Verfasser die Begriffe "bless" und "curse". Es ist in der Hiobexegese gut bekannt, dass die hebräische Wurzel ברך manchmal als Euphemismus interpretiert wird, weil sie an verschiedenen Stellen verwendet wird, wo eigentlich *"fluchen"* (to curse) gemeint ist. Es ist aber bedauerlich, dass der Verfasser darauf nicht reagiert. Er versteht diese Verwendung als Ironie (200–201), aber er diskutiert die Forschungsgeschichte hinter dieser Übersetzung leider nicht. Auch merkwürdig ist seine Auslegung des dritten Redegangs (Hi 22–28). Da der Verfasser sich von historisch–kritischen Methode verabschiedet hat, greift er die literarischen Probleme des so gennanten dritten Redegangs nicht auf. Nach einer zusammenfassenden Pause zwischen den Kapiteln 22–24 und 25–28 legt der Verfasser die dritte Rede Bildads in Kap. 25 als *"an ironic device in the hands of the poet"* aus (260). Kap. 27,13–23 versteht er als *"Zophar-like language"* und deshalb wieder als ironisch. Als Abschluss des dritten Redegangs, aber auch als Atempause in der Diskussion mit den Freunden und Verbindung zwischen Prolog und Dichtung bleibt für ihn das Kap. 28 (265–71). Die klassische Bezeichnung von Hi 28 als *"Lied der Weisheit"* wird von ihm völlig abgelehnt, da der Text zumal gattungsgemäß kein Lied ist. Vielmehr versucht der Text Gott und die Weisheit zu beschreiben und die Argumentation des Gedichtes bleibt mit Recht vor allem kritisch und nicht hymnisch. Ein weiterer Grund für seine Ablehnung ist das Thema der Dichtung in Hi 28. Wenn die Weisheit nicht im Land der Lebenden gefunden wird (V.13), kann sie nicht das Thema dieser Dichtung sein. Die drei monologischen Kapitel 29–31 werden als *"climax"* nach den Gesprächen mit den Freunden und als *"survey in three poems"* verstanden (273–88). Der Verfasser interpretiert diese drei Kapitel als Kompendium, indem Hiob sein Leben vor dem Leid als These, seine aktuelle Situation als Antithese beschreibt und seine Prinzipien als Synthese darstellt. Am Ende bleibt endgültig festgestellt, dass *"it is for nothing that Job fears a God"* (288). Damit zeigt der Verfasser die Verbindung der Dichtung mit der Frage des Satans im Prolog und zugleich die Textstrategie des *"omniscient narrator"* deutlich wieder. Eine wichtige Rolle für die Poetik des Hiobbuches spielen die Elihureden. Nach dem Verfasser gibt es eine Ähnlichkeit zwischen den Elihureden, die aus sechs Gedichten bestehen, und Hiobs Monologen (Hi 26–31), die ebenso aus sechs Gedichten bestehen. Hier nimmt Elihu die Rolle des Erzählers auf (Hi 32) und seine Reden werden als *intermezzo* verstanden. In den Gottesreden ist die *"numerical perfection"* deutlich zu sehen. Nach dem Verfasser werden die Gottesreden zwei Mal in zwei Gedichten gegliedert. Der erste Gottesredegang ist in Kap. 38–39 und der zweite in Kap. 40–41 (jeder mit 176 Worten) zu finden. Dazwischen, als neues *intermezzo*, ist die Antwort Hiobs in 40,1–5 zu verstehen. Zum Schluss kommt die Auslegung von Kap. 42. Zuerst zeigt der Verfasser die letzte Antwort Hiobs auf die Gottesreden. Daran liegt die Betonung des ganzen Hiobbuches, dass V. 6 als "conclusion of the conclusion" verstanden wird. Zuletzt hat der Autor des Hiobbuches in seiner Rolle als Erzähler das letzte Wort dieses poetischen Werkes. Dazu liefert Fokkelman immer wieder Einzelbeobachtungen, aufs Ganze gesehen bleiben hier aber Argumentations-lücken. Trotzdem bietet der Verfasser eine Art poetischer Theologie des Hiobbuches an, die empfehlenswert bleibt.

Am Ende der Arbeit bietet der Verfasser ein kleines Literaturverzeichnis, ein Glossar mit wichtigen literarischen Begriffen und ein Sachregister. Die Noten und Bemerkungen am Ende jedes Kapitels wären besser und hilfreicher als Fußnoten gewesen. Trotz diesen kritischen Bemerkungen liegt mit dieser Arbeit ein in mehrfacher Hinsicht weiterführender Beitrag und wesentliche Bereicherung zur Forschung am Hiobbuch vor.

APOCRYPHAL/DEUTEROCANONICAL AND OTHER JEWISH WRITINGS

The Subversion of the Apocalypses in the Book of Jubilees, by Todd R. Hanneken. Early Judaism and Its Literature 34. Atlanta: Society of Biblical Literature, 2012. Pp. xiv + 331. Paper. $42.95. ISBN 9781589836426.

Robert Foster, Madonna University, Livonia, Mississippi

According to a significant body of scholarly opinion, a more or less direct route runs from the early Enochic literature, passes through Jubilees, and terminates at Qumran. Todd R. Hanneken dissents from Jubilees's placement on this trajectory. His monograph, originally a University of Notre Dame dissertation directed by James C. VanderKam, sets Jubilees in opposition to this apocalyptic tradition even while acknowledging, and accounting for, their shared literary elements.

The introductory chapter presents the problem, offers a method to address it, states a thesis, and previews the argument to come. Hanneken asks, How does Jubilees relate on the literary and ideological levels to contemporary apocalyptic writings? The study is thus a comparative examination of the early Enochic books, Daniel, and Jubilees. Relying on the formal criteria presented in *Semeia* 14, he argues that Jubilees counts as *apocalyptic literature* in terms of its generic features, especially due to elements in chapters 1, 23, and 50. However, once one abstracts its substantive ideas and compares them to contemporary apocalyptic writings, significant differences emerge. To explain the discord between Jubilees's apocalyptic genre and antiapocalyptic worldview, Hanneken proposes the category of *subversion*: Jubilees appropriates the literary characteristics of an apocalypse in order to raise and then frustrate readerly expectations, replacing those failed anticipations with its own covenantal and halakic-focused theology.

The second chapter deals with relevant literary motifs that coincide with *Semeia* 14's spatial axis, predominantly the issues of evil's origin in the cosmos, angelic/demonic involvement in history, and the division of humanity into opposing moral categories. According to Jubilees, Hanneken argues, evil begins in human transgression: there is no cosmic origin in either the miscegenation of the Watchers nor in the sin of Adam and Eve. Demons do not hamper God's justice, angels do not administer his governance over Israel, and nothing delays judgment against the wicked or on behalf of the righteous. Moving from the angelic to the human dimension, Jubilees insists on the ontological and primordial unity of all Israel: it countenances no morally elitist remnant. This indivisible nation, though it may engage in military self-defense, does not raise the sword in retributive or eschatological judgment against its foes. In all of these areas, Jubilees departs significantly from the standard viewpoint expressed in contemporary apocalyptic works.

Hanneken shifts to the apocalyptic motifs occurring on the temporal axis in chapter 3: the decline of history, the eschatological woes, the final judgment, and the restoration of Israel. In every case, Jubilees again articulates a position distinct from that typically found in the apocalypses. History is in decline, agrees Jubilees, but one that is gradual, prolonged, and already in reverse—a far cry from the catastrophic urgency typical of 1 Enoch and Daniel. Israel suffers the covenantal chastisements sent by God, not demonically inspired assaults that the righteous must endure. Because God's justice is operative already and always in history, there is no final judgment. The nations will be expelled, not annihilated, upon Israel's restoration, itself a gradual stabilization of God's original purposes for creation, not a radically new reordering of the cosmos.

The mode and function of revelation concern chapter 4. Here Hanneken contrasts the mysterious symbolism and elite wisdom typical of apocalyptic literature with the straightforward, unambiguous demonstration of God's will for all Israel found in Jubilees. The apocalypses posit new revelations that supersede the old, relying heavily on dreams, arcane imagery, and angelic interpreters. Jubilees distances itself from all this. Its downplays revelatory dreams, requires that angelic guides adhere strictly to the content of heavenly tablets, and identifies this content with the Mosaic deposit later vouchsafed to all Israel at Sinai.

The final chapter is less unified than previous ones, but its title, "Explanation," provides the overarching rubric. It explores the issues of authorial strategy, audience expectations, historical context, and social conflict over cultural symbols. Hanneken draws on Bakhtin to argue that Jubilees exploits the apocalyptic genre to critique its typical ideas rather than mounting a direct assault. The effect is rhetorically potent, since the audience encounters the discord between expectation and content in a moment of dramatic recognition. A series of historical allusions and literary correlations make a date of 159–152 BCE most likely: Jubilees was written to condemn all participants in the recent civil war, Hellenists and Hasmoneans alike, and to provide its own program for reform. Finally, the cultural symbols of revelation, heroes from the past, temple and priesthood, and Israelite identity were sharply disputed at this moment in Jewish history. In every case Jubilees advances claims that oppose the positions current in apocalyptic writing.

The value of this study is manifold. It demonstrates high competence in ancient languages, broad knowledge of the secondary literature, and deep respect for the texts under investigation. Hanneken's analyses are always illuminating. He is especially good at recognizing the distinct emphasis in individual documents even while abstracting common religious ideas. He explicates the overarching tension between the covenantal theology undergirding Jubilees and the catastrophic apocalypticism typical of 1 Enoch and Daniel without ever losing sight of textual specifics. In my judgment, he avoids the extremes of atomization and harmonization, both frequent temptations in the study of Second Temple literature.

Haneken's style gives no ground for complaint. His prose is lucid, even when the argument is dense, and does not place impediments before the reader. He makes clear to his audience at all times where the discussion is headed. There is a slight problem of repetition, especially in the preview of chapter 1, but it does not become tedious. Typographical errors are few (though the format of the section headings are frequently inconsistent).

In one area the argument leaves me unsatisfied: Hanneken's treatment of religious violence. He does convincingly distinguish Jubilees from the apocalypses in the matter of eschatological warfare. Its end-time scenario involves no punitive slaughter of the wicked, be they renegade Israelites or unjust Gentiles. Consistent with this, he argues further, is Jubilees's portrayal of Jacob's reluctance to engage Esau in armed combat. Nevertheless, the war between their two clans is a massive departure from Genesis and a clear topic of interest to the author. Contrary to Hanneken's assertion, Esau's initial reluctance to follow the aggressive advice of his sons does not bespeak a sympathetic portrayal of Esau or his contemporary descendants (115). Rather, it serves to highlight his vacillating character and the irrevocability of his final descent into murderous rage. The entire episode has a narrative counterpart in the earlier slaughter of the Shechemites. There also Jubilees diverged from Genesis precisely to give free rein to its vicious xenophobia. Moreover, despite Jubilees's avowal of Israel's inviolability, there is the possibility that it subtly aligns "apostate" Jews with Jacob's foolhardy and traitorous brother, a strategy parallel to Ezra-Nehemiah's monopolization of the label *Israel* on behalf of the returnees and its assimilation of "nonkosher" Jews to the disreputable *people of the land.* Hanneken, I think, underplays the justification of violence embedded in Jubilees. The point is important, since later in the study he makes this opposition to bloodshed in general and the pre-Maccabean civil war in particular the fundamental issue that generates Jubilees's overall antiapocalypticism (284).

In addition, I wonder about the nature of the contrast Hanneken draws between Jubilees and contemporary apocalyptic writings. He demonstrates that Jubilees, in issue after issue, presents itself as an apocalypse only to subsume the stock literary features to its very different covenantal theology. He categorizes this difference as *subversion*: Jubilees adopts generic conventions in order to flout them and raises readerly expectations in order to frustrate them. Yet I cannot help wondering how different these conclusions might be if one began from the covenantal ideology of, say, Deuteronomy, or Ezra-Nehemiah, and examined from this starting point Jubilees's introduction of apocalyptic themes. The basic framework would remain intact, but the nature of the relationship might look very different. In this case, Jubilees would reflect the positive influence of apocalyptic writings as they made their effect known on a previously alien worldview. Other than the scholarly predilection for all things subversive, why categorize Jubilees's literary and theological strategy as Hanneken does?

Hanneken is actually aware of this question and addresses it periodically. He answers in the negative and presents strong arguments, especially in chapter 5, "Explanation." But the issue, for me at least, is not settled. Hanneken himself acknowledges that difference does not itself mean polemic or even subversion, and he also notes that, in the aftermath of Jubilees, later apocalypses such as 4 Ezra and 2 Baruch are capable of utilizing the genre to express ideas unprecedented in pre-Jubilean apocalyptic writings (267 n. 19). Could it not be the case that Jubilees pointed the way forward for later apocalypses precisely because it felt compelled to move traditional covenantal theology in an apocalyptic direction?

This *is* a question, though, and not a substantive criticism. The book presents a persuasive and methodologically sound comparison between Jubilees and the apocalypses. It deserves wide reading among those currently engaged in the study of Second Temple Judaism and its internal conflicts.

Abraham in the Book of Jubilees: The Rewriting of Genesis 11:26–25:10 in the Book of Jubilees 11:14–23:8, by Jacques T. A. G. M. van Ruiten. Supplements to the Journal for the Study of Judaism 161. Leiden: Brill, 2012. Pp. xii + 383. Cloth. $189.00. ISBN 9789004234666.

John C. Endres, S.J., Jesuit School of Theology of Santa Clara University, Berkeley, California

Jacques van Ruiten is one of the most prolific scholars of the book of Jubilees. In addition to many published articles on specific aspects of this book, the present work constitutes his follow-up to an earlier volume *Primaeval History Interpreted: The Rewriting of Genesis 1–11 in the Book of Jubilees* (Leiden: Brill, 2000). This study also demonstrates encyclopedic knowledge of Jubilees, the text, textual traditions, history of interpretation, and the secondary literature. The book contains a succinct introduction (1–18), ten chapters covering the distinct sections of the Abraham text that he has discerned, and a conclusion (331–44) that contains a masterful summary of the discoveries he has made in this study. The volume contains an extensive bibliography (345–58) and an index of ancient sources (359–83).

The introduction situates Jubilees in the context of Jewish works that exhibit clear relationship between older and newer texts, wherein the older text can be seen by a careful reading of the newer text. Older texts often find responses in the rewriting process that led to newer texts. This phenomenon occurs already in the Hebrew Bible (e.g., 1–2 Chronicles rereading and rewriting of many traditions in

Samuel–Kings) and occurs more frequently in much of the Jewish literature of the Second Temple era (e.g., Temple Scroll, Genesis Apocryphon, *Biblical Antiquities* of Pseudo-Philo). Van Ruiten introduces the reader to recent conversations about the appropriate terminology for this phenomenon (Rewritten Bible, Rewritten Scripture, parabiblical texts, paratextual literature [3–5]) but ultimately speaks of "the rewriting of scriptural material in the rewritten scriptures from Chronicles to Pseudo-Philo's *Biblical Antiquities*" (8).

Van Ruiten presents a succinct but thorough introduction to Jubilees (8–18) in which he describes the authorial scheme (revelation to Moses on Mount Sinai the day after the making of the covenant); its contents (much of the material in Genesis through Exod 19; 24); and its process of interpreting the scriptural text by repetition, omission, and additions of materials that are both narrative and halakic in nature. Regarding the date of composition he notes "somewhere in the second century BCE, possibly preceding the foundation of the community of Qumran" (8 n. 23). Concerning the book he mentions the "dominant position in research … the book is in one way or another a unity" (12), though he mentions recent challenges to that notion by Menahem Kister, Michael Segal, and James Kugel. His language is precise but eminently clear, and the footnotes to these few pages provide an excellent introduction to the scholarly study of Jubilees, including the most recent challenges to the notion of a single author. Van Ruiten describes their theories and briefly analyzes them, suggesting his points of disagreement; in later chapters he discusses how these theories of composition would alter the view of the interpretation of Jubilees.

The real fruit of his labor appears in the ten chapters summarized here because they inform the reader of the contents of the book: (1) Early Abram (Gen 11:26–12:3; Jub. 11:14–12:31); (2) Abram's travels (Gen 12:4–14:24; Jub. 13); (3) land and covenant (Gen 15–16; Jub.14); (4) Abraham, Israel, and the nations (Gen 17; Jub. 15); (5) Isaac's birth (Gen 18:1–21:1; Jub.16:1–17:14); (6) Isaac's binding (Gen 22:1–19; Jub. 17:15–18:19); (7) Sarah's death to Jacob's blessing by Abraham (Gen 22:20–25:4; 25:21–28; Jub. 19); (8) Abraham's testament to his children and grandchildren (Jub. 20:1–13); (9) Abraham's testament to Isaac (Jub. 21:1–26); (10) Abraham's last day (Gen 25:7–10; Jub. 22:1–23:8).

Most chapters contain an introduction (overview of the materials), a look at the macro-structure (overall comparison between the texts in Genesis and Jubilees), comments on the literary structures and features of Jubilees (complete with very helpful charts of the materials), a closer comparison of the micro-structure: a verse-by-verse treatment where the text of Genesis (NRSV) is presented synoptically with the Jubilees text (VanderKam translation). Van Ruiten employs a fairly consistent set of visual markers (uppercase letters, italics, bold, etc.; see 17–18 for explanation of the layout) to demonstrate the relation he sees between the texts. Abundant text-critical information is found in the notes, with particular attention to readings in Dillmann, Charles, and (usually decisive) VanderKam's edition of the text; where applicable, van Ruiten cites and discusses the Latin witness and texts from Qumran. Most chapters end with concluding remarks (2, 3) or a conclusion (4, 5, 7, 8, 10) that recap a presentation that is very detailed (and most useful to specialists in Second Temple literature) with a lucid summary of discoveries in the preceding pages. Chapter 1 contains a summary paragraph (e.g., 64). Chapters 6 and 9 lack synthetic conclusions. Chapter 6, on the binding of Isaac, concludes by commenting on the halakic addition (Jub. 18:18–19) and its tension with the preceding narrative (a difference of viewpoint important for the positions of Segal and Kugel); after analyzing these positions, van Ruiten proposes that the festival referred to in the addition might be unleavened bread. Chapter 9, Abraham's testament for Isaac, concludes a bit abruptly with comments on the significance of eating blood (comments both precede and follow prescriptions about offerings, Jub. 21:6, 17b–20); a synthetic conclusion to this chapter would be a welcome addition.

Van Ruiten has clearly shown that "most passages from Abraham's story in Genesis have a parallel in the book of *Jubilees*" (237). He shows how this author sometimes abbreviates the scriptural story and text, occasionally amplifies it with narrative and (often) halakah, and sometimes makes an important transposition. Perhaps the most significant transposition occurs when the report of the birth of Abraham's grandsons, Jacob and Esau, are born before his death; the observation is not new, but van Ruiten works out the implications of Abraham's relationship with his grandsons (especially Jacob) more thoroughly than other commentators have done.

Sprinkled throughout his text are very helpful expositions of the prayer-texts that Jubilees has added to the narrative (e.g., Jub. 12 [40–45]) and an enlightening comparison with Noah's prayer (Jub. 10:1–14 [49–51]). These prayers refer to God in terms that focus on creation activity more than many other texts, and some additional reflection on this point would be welcomed.

Discussing chapter 2, Abram's travels (including events about Sarai in Egypt), van Ruiten includes a lengthy and very helpful presentation of parallels between Jub. 13 and Genesis and also adds a helpful comparison with a parallel text in the Genesis Apocryphon (93–116). Although the transition to the Genesis Apocryphon (93–94) is surprising, his meticulous comparison of these two texts proves immensely helpful: he demonstrates relationships between Jubilees and the Genesis Apocryphon that others have discussed. He doubts that either could have functioned as source text for the other; rather, he opines that both texts might draw on "yet another tradition" (118).

If there is any abiding impression given by this book, it is the mass of information it contains: bibliographic, word studies, history of particular terms, character presentations in the Bible and in other interpretive (including masses of Second Temple Jewish literature) texts, textual issues, literary issues of the text, differences with other interpreters (including myself!), interpretation of the text of Genesis, characterization (especially of Abraham, Sarai, Hagar, Isaac, Jacob), relationship to the Genesis Apocryphon (1QapGen), the notion of (one) covenant in Jubilees, halakah about important cultic celebrations (First Fruits, Tabernacles, Passover/ Unleavened Bread), demons (especially Mastema), angels, writing in the ancient world, Hebrew language, idolatry and "the nations." The reader will seldom feel a need to look up such terms in other books in order to understand van Ruiten's presentation (at times his word studies almost replace recourse to a concordance); when the issue arises he explains it, usually in beautifully clear language and with substantive documentation. As I mention this listing of terms I am reminded of one slight disappointment with the volume: while it includes an exhaustive index of ancient sources, it lacks an index of subjects/terms and an index of modern authors.

While the review has mentioned some areas for further clarification and discussion, it needs to be noted that they arise because this monograph so thoroughly addresses the question it has raised, the relationship of Jubilees with Genesis. One who reads only the introduction and conclusion will learn a great deal about Jubilees; one who engages the entire text will also learn how to study such a text, how to engage its parallel texts, how to ask the questions and how to pursue them with thoroughness, patience, and open-mindedness. Serious scholars of the rewriting of Second Temple scriptural texts need to know well this book; scholars of Jubilees need to wrestle with it, struggle with it, and learn from it. I am very grateful for van Ruiten's work.

Joseph and Aseneth: A Christian Book, by Rivka Nir. Hebrew Bible Monographs 42. Sheffield: Sheffield Phoenix, 2012. Pp. xii + 218. Cloth. $90.00. ISBN 9781907534355.

Thomas J. Kraus, Neumarkt, Federal Republic of Germany

Joseph and Aseneth is a fascinating novel from the group of Old Testament pseudepigrapha. All in all, it is an expansion of Gen 41:45, where we are told that, as an expression of honor, Joseph was given Aseneth, the daughter of the Egyptian priest Potiphera (LXX: Pentephres) from On, as his wife, and of Gen 41:50–52, where we learn about the birth of their two sons, Manasseh and Ephraim. Usually the novel is regarded as a Jewish text written in the first century CE focusing on Aseneth's conversion to the one and only God of Israel, that is, from polytheism or idolatry to monotheism, an assumption that is widely accepted among scholars. Besides, the narration is taken as "a testimony to a Hellenistic diaspora Judaism that neither observed the rules of conversion of Judaism (*giyyur*) nor cared much for the laws of the Torah" (from the text on the back of the cover).

That leads to one aspect that makes Rivka Nir's monograph so important for a better understanding of this love story in twenty-nine chapters: having examined the reasons provided for them, she doubts that these assumptions are correct. To her, Joseph and Aseneth is a Christian book embedded into a Christian context and based on the symbolic and typological nature of its two main characters. Thus, the novel has nothing in common and nothing to do with Second Temple Judaism. Consequently, Nir challenges well-established positions in research on Joseph and Aseneth and offers substantial insights in the text itself by close and scrutinizing analyses of ideas, language (above all, vocabulary), symbols, and structure. She sees the key in understanding the text "against the background of Syriac Christianity of the third and fourth century" (back of hardcover).

In her preface and acknowledgments (vii–x) Nir introduces how it came that she studied Joseph and Aseneth in detail. Basically, two main questions guided her work: Why does the text not contain anything about the observation of the Torah if it was written "by a Jew in the Jewish Hellenistic Diaspora of the Second Temple period"? Should Aseneth's conversion be regarded as *giyyur* (conversion to Judaism) or as becoming a Christian? Then Nir introduces readers to the story, its main motifs, ideas, and issues, and the history of research (1–19), before she provides her own research method (20–21), which is a historical-critical one. For filling gaps in the story, Nir discusses socioreligious sources elsewhere.

The first chapter, "Aseneth—Jewish Proselyte or Christian Convert?" (23–66), exactly highlights one of the salient questions of the book and Nir's thesis. Nir examines Jewish sources (above all, the Talmud, Josephus, and Philo) before she turns to Christian texts on conversion. Her proofs for Aseneth being a Christian convert are convincing, and she succeeds in pointing out that "the conversion in *Joseph and Aseneth* occupies a central place in the discussion of the existence of laws of conversion in Second Temple Judaism" (65). In addition, she shows that in Hellenistic Diaspora Judaism the rules of *giyyur* were not followed everywhere. At the same time, Nir demonstrates that the conversion of Aseneth does not teach us anything about the Torah but has similarities and even parallels with Christian conversion.

It is this last aspect that Nir deepens in the next two chapters: "Aseneth as the 'Type of the Church of the Gentiles'" (67–115) and "Joseph as the Prototype of Christ" (116–135). We must wait to see if the ideas, parallels, and conclusions Nir offers are accepted by scholars, but her suggestions are based on sound reasoning and arguments. Nir highlights the motifs "the city of refuge" and "the bees/the honeycomb" for Aseneth and "the Sun God Helios," "the olive tree," and "the man of God" for Joseph.

Then she turns to the parallelism between Aseneth being Joseph's bride and the marriage of Christ and the church in chapter 4 (136–58), for which she addresses the description of the bridal garment, the kiss between the two lovers, and their actual marriage. Again Nir successfully demonstrates that there are clear similarities and plausible parallels between Joseph and Aseneth and the Christian setting so that the lovers function as symbols for Christ and the church.

The fifth chapter, on "Christian Ethics in *Joseph and Aseneth*" (159–74), is rather short, but Nir mostly avoids repeating what she has already written about previously. Thus the chapter is partly a summary, partly a more in-depth treatment of Christian features in the love story. Six pages of conclusions follow, which Nir intends as a summary of the whole book. Here again she parallels central motifs in Joseph and Aseneth with Christian motifs and realities. For her the honeycomb represents the Eucharist and therefore stands for immortality. In addition, Aseneth is baptized, a fact often neglected in scholarly discussions. Leaving aside further parallels in this review, essential is Nir's notion that "*Joseph and Aseneth* is indeed a product of the Syrian church"; consequently, symbols and metaphors may originate from a Hellenistic background, and it is natural to assume that the text was originally written in Greek.

The book comes with a comprehensive bibliography (180–202) and two indices (references and authors, 203–18) in order to help readers find their way through the volume and to locate the discussion of individual passages.

Rivka Nir is to be both congratulated and thanked for writing down her stimulating analyses of Joseph and Aseneth. Her findings might provoke specialists of this text and challenge the traditional mainstream ideas about the novel and its historical background. Only the future, when her own theses are challenged, discussed, and disputed, will tell if Nir's suggestions finally change the picture most scholars have of this love story and its protagonists. Be that as it may, this book is a substantial contribution to the study of this work and relevant for everyone interested in that sort of text.

En marge du canon: Études sur les écrits apocryphes juifs et chrétiens, edited by André Gagné and Jean-François Racine. L'Écriture de la Bible 2. Paris: Cerf, 2012. Pp. 290. Cloth. €26.00. ISBN 9782204096096.

Boris Paschke, Faculté de Théologie Évangélique (ETF), Brussels, Belgium

Ce recueil présente les versions écrites des neuf exposés françaises du 65e congrès annuel de l' «Association catholique des études bibliques au Canada» (ACÉBAC), qui avait lieu en mai 2008 au Manoir d'Youville, île Saint-Bernard, à Châteauguay, Québec, Canada. Les contributions sont rédigées par sept professeurs et deux étudiants au doctorat dont la plupart sont liés aux universités canadiennes. Le recueil traite des écrits apocryphes juifs et chrétiens.

Dans l' «Introduction» (7–11) les éditeurs expliquent le but du livre: «Les œuvres explorées dans ce volume font partie de ce que Jean-Claude Picard appelait le 'continent apocryphe', un vaste champ d'études en plein essor. Ce volume ne propose pas une visite approfondie de tout ce continent, mais des excursions dans quelques-unes de ses régions» (7). Après avoir présenté des résumés des contributions (7–10) les éditeurs affirment: «Nous espérons que les lecteurs apprécieront ces neuf excursions sur le 'continent apocryphe'» (10).

Je voudrais déjà dire au début de ma critique que j'apprécie les articles du recueil parce qu'ils offrent des points de vu très instructifs par rapport au «continent apocryphe». Dans ce qui suit, les contributions sont évaluées séparément. Le fait que je les considère d'un œil critique n'enlève rien à mon appréciation positive du recueil.

Sous le titre «Écrits canoniques et écrits apocryphes: un couple bien assorti» (13–31) Jean-François Racine explique tout d'abord l'étymologie, la terminologie, le développement et les différents conceptions des canons juif et chrétien (14–17). Ensuite, il explique les problèmes par rapport à la terminologie et aux définitions des écrits apocryphes chrétiens (17–23). Enfin, Racine parle des relations entre écrits canoniques et apocryphes chrétiens (23–31). Après avoir résumé deux modèles déjà existants (ceux de compétition et d'interdépendance) Racine présente son propre modèle dont il écrit: «l'originalité de cet essai réside en la métaphore utilisée pour décrire la relation entre écrits canoniques et apocryphes: Je propose d'utiliser l'image d'un couple bien assorti» (14). Partant des deux récits de la création du premier couple en *Genèse* 1 et 2, Racine constate: «L'utilisation de ces deux récits comme métaphores pour exprimer les relations entre écrits canoniques et apocryphes nous permet également de percevoir des aspects différents de cette relation: d'une part subordination et postériorité, jouant le rôle ambigu du supplément; d'autre part, simultanéité et complémentarité. Chaque modèle représente toutefois un couple bien assorti où le décès de l'un entraînera nécessairement la disparition de l'autre» (30–31). Or, je trouve la métaphore du «couple bien assorti» assez forcée. De plus, elle ne mène à rien parce que les conclusions que Racine en tire, restent trop vagues.

Dans sa contribution «Jésus de l'histoire et écrits apocryphes chrétiens» (33–84) Jean-Paul Michaud étudie la valeur de cinq documents apocryphes pour ce qui est de la quête du Jésus de l'histoire: l'Évangile selon Thomas; le papyrus Egerton 2; l'Évangile de Pierre; l'Évangile secret de Marc; et—assez particulier—la source Q. Il en tire la conclusion que «ces écrits … n'ajoutent guère … de traits nouveaux à la figure de Jésus» (84). Au même instant (84 note 167) Michaud indique que des chercheurs précédents (A. Gregory, C. Tuckett et T. Nicklas) en sont arrivés aux conclusions identiques. Il avoue donc que son étude n'est pas innovatrice, un fait assez regrettable, au regard de sa longueur considérable.

Dans son excellent article «Vers une redéfinition du champ apocryphe: Aperçus de la recherche récente consacrée aux apocryphes chrétiens» (85–106) Paul-Hubert Poirier fait un résumé très instructif des études sur les apocryphes. Il aborde la situation jusqu'à la fin des années 1970, le changement de paradigme survenu au cours des années 1980, et les discussions qui s'en sont suivies (83). Poirier fixe son attention sur la deuxième période que l'«Association pour l'étude de la littérature apocryphe chrétienne» (AÉLAC), fondée en 1981, a marquée de son empreinte. Grâce à l'AÉLAC, la recherche des «apocryphes du Nouveau Testament» est devenue celle des «apocryphes chrétiens» (93). En vue de ce «changement de paradigme» Poirier parle d'«une sorte de révolution copernicienne» (93). Poirier liste tous les travaux et publications de l'AÉLAC en détail. Etant donné qu'ils sont connus il n'est pas nécessaire de les exposer ici. Mais il est bien convenable de souligner que feu François Bovon (1938–2013), cité par Poirier en détail (95–96), a joué un rôle très méritoire dans l'AÉLAC.

Dans sa bonne contribution «Mémoire et histoire des persécutions dans la littérature apocryphe juive et chrétienne» (107–19) Marie-Françoise Baslez étudie «l'interaction entre littérature apocryphe, martyre et pèlerinage» (114). Selon l'historienne les apocryphes associent leur héros (et parfois aussi ses morts, martyres et tombes) à un certain lieu. Ainsi invitent-ils à la mémoire et au pèlerinage. Pour ce qui est des apocryphes juifs, Baslez cite le *quatrième livre des Maccabées* et *Les vies des prophètes* comme exemples (110–14). En ce qui concerne la littérature apocryphe chrétienne Baslez renvoie aux *actes apocryphes de Paul*, de *Pierre* et de *Jean à Rome* qui localisent tous leurs héros à Rome et qui sont donc importants «pour ériger Rome en centre consensuel de la chrétienté» (118). Parfois la terminologie de Baslez est un peu confuse parce qu'elle utilise «Actes de Jean à Rome» (117) et «Actes de Jean» (117) pour le même récit. Comme Éric Junod et Jean-Daniel Kaestli le disent, «les deux textes doivent être clairement distingués» (*Acta Iohannis*, CChr.SA 1–2, Turnhout: Brepols, 1983, 835).

Dans l'article «Le cours du temps selon l'Apocalypse syriaque de Daniel: Essai de compréhension fondée sur la structure du texte» (121–57) Pierre Cardinal étudie l'Apocalypse syriaque de Daniel à partir de sa structure. Tandis que Cardinal présente les éditions du texte syriaque (121 n. 1), il n'aborde le texte syriaque que dans un seul passage où il parle du «verbe *hw*' conjugué à la troisième personne de l'imparfait du pe'al» (127 n. 25). Pour le reste, ce longue article ne fait aucune référence à des mots syriaques, ni en caractères syriaques ni en transcription.

Malheureusement la longue contribution «Le récit de la Passion dans les Oracles sibyllins» (159–200) par Jean-Michel Roessli n'offre pas de vues nouvelles, puisqu'elle a déjà été publiée en anglais dans un autre recueil (159 n. 1; voir: «The Passion Narrative in the Sibylline Oracles», dans: *Gelitten—Gestorben—Auferstanden: Passions- und Ostertraditionen im antiken Christentum*, WUNT II/273, Tübingen: Mohr Siebeck, 2010, 299–327). Il n'est donc pas nécessaire de la passer en revue ici.

Avec «L'Évangile de Judas cinq and après sa (re)découverte: Mise à jour et perspectives» (201–24), Serge Cazelais a écrit un des meilleurs articles du recueil. Il explique que bien que l'édition critique de l'*Évangile de Judas* (*EvJudas*) ait été publiée en 2007, des nouveaux fragments—les soi-disant «Ohio Fragments»—ont fait surface et sont disponibles sur l'internet depuis 2009 (202–3). Sur la base de ces nouveaux fragments et de sa compréhension de la syntaxe copte, Cazelais est en mesure d'améliorer l'édition critique de l'*EvJudas*. Il réussit à montrer que l'*EvJudas* ne présente pas une image positive mais au contraire une image négative de la figure de Judas. L'article de Cazelais est très innovateur, instructif et louable parce qu'il présente des travaux indépendants et des hypothèses ouvrant la vue à de nouvelles perspectives.

André Gagné, dans son article «Lire un apocryphe en synchronie: Analyse structurelle et intratextuelle [*sic*] du *logion* 22 de l'*Évangile selon Thomas*» (225–49), présente une interprétation intéressante du *logion* 22 de l'*Évangile selon Thomas* (*EvTh*): Il suggère que les petits enfants qui tètent «représentent ceux qui ont 'soif' des paroles de Jésus» et qu'ils «symbolisent tous ceux qui s'alimentent des paroles de Jésus» (248). Gagné en arrive à cette conclusion en utilisant l'interprétation narrative-critique (voir p. ex 246 et 249 n. 71: l'auteur et le lecteur «implicites»; 248: «monde du texte»). Or, étant donne que l'*EvTh* n'est pas un récit proprement dit mais plutôt une «collection de 114 paroles de Jésus» (226), il est douteux que la critique narrative soit une approche convenable de l'*EvTh*.

Sous le titre «L'Enoch Seminar: Quelques considérations rétrospectives et prospectives de la part d'un 'vétéran'» (251–78) Pierluigi Piovanelli, en tant que «vétéran» (selon moi Piovanelli aurait dû éviter ce langage militaire), donne un résumé très instructif de l'histoire, des colloques, des publications et des résultats de recherche de l'«Enoch Seminar» qui a été fondé en 2000 par Gabriele Boccaccini. Après avoir donné une liste de participants (278 n. 71), Piovanelli regrette qu'il n'y eût pas beaucoup de participants francophones aux colloques de l'«Enoch Seminar», constatant «que la grande majorité des douze spécialistes canadiens présents était constituée de chercheurs anglophones; que seuls cinq chercheurs français ont fait une ou deux fois seulement le voyage; que les trois participants suisses ne sont pas tout à fait francophones et que les universités belges n'ont, à ce jour, envoyé aucun spécialiste» (278). Puis il invite des chercheurs francophones à y participer. Par la présente, cette invitation est propagée en supposant que les chercheurs belges *néerlandophones* sont, eux aussi, bienvenus dans l'«Enoch Seminar».

Apres avoir évalué les contributions du livre séparément, je voudrais faire quelques remarques par rapport au recueil en général. Le livre contient beaucoup de tableaux qui fonctionnent comme des cartes géographiques du «continent apocryphe», ce qui simplifie la compréhension. Les présentations des contributeurs (279–81) et l'index onomastique (283–88) sont aussi très utiles. Tandis que le texte français est presque sans défauts, les citations allemandes et les titres allemands des œuvres citées sont truffés de fautes d'orthographe (p. ex. «Gnostiche Evangelien» [91]). Parfois le style est quelque peu populaire (p. ex. 9: «Pierre Cardinal … s'aventure dans le monde de l'apocalypse syriaque de Daniel»). Les mentions de Dan Brown (26 note 41) et d'*Indiana Jones* (65) conviendraient dans un livre populaire plutôt que dans un recueil scientifique. La rédaction du texte aurait dû être davantage soignée: des (pré)noms des chercheurs, même des explorateurs éminents du «continent apocryphe», sont parfois injuste, parfois traduits dans une autre langue (p. ex. 101: «Werner Schneemelcher»; 87 n. 12: «Edgard Hennecke»). Le livre célèbre *Le continent apocryphe* par Jean-Claude Picard est cité quatre fois (7 n. 2; 98 n. 47; 107 n. 1; 266 note 38), chaque fois les informations bibliographiques sont présentées de manière différente.

Malgré ces quelques remarques critiques, mon opinion générale sur ce beau recueil que l'ACÉBAC nous offre, est tout à fait positive. Voici une contribution très importante, et un guide compétent pour ceux qui souhaitent explorer le «continent apocryphe».

SEPTUAGINT

Law, Prophets, and Wisdom: On the Provenance of Translators and Their Books in the Septuagint Version, by Johann Cook and Arie van der Kooij. Contributions to Biblical Exegesis and Theology 68. Leuven: Peeters, 2012. Pp. xiv + 249. Paper. €46.00. ISBN 9789042927032.

Sean A. Adams, University of Edinburgh, Edinburgh, United Kingdom

This co-authored book seeks to challenge the consensus of an assumed Alexandrian provenance for the all of the translation units of the LXX. Moreover, it seeks to undermine the assumption that an Alexandrian origin naturally requires the provenance of the translator(s) to be Alexandrian as well. This is an important issue for LXX studies and is worthy of a monograph-length investigation. The title, however, is somewhat generous, as the authors claim to look at only LXX Pentateuch, Isaiah, Proverbs, and Job. Cook and van der Kooij, however, recognize the limitations of their sample group and hope that these case examples will be sufficient for proving their point.

The argument proper beings in chapter 2, "The Septuagint of the Pentateuch," in which van der Kooij addresses the question of the provenance of the LXX Pentateuch translators. However, prior to discussing this issue, van der Kooij takes the time to provide an extended discuss of a recent proposal on the original setting of the LXX translation by Sylvie Honigman. In her monograph, *The Septuagint and Homeric Scholarship in Alexandria* (Routledge, 2003), Honigman argues that, based on the Letter of Aristeas, "the early history of the LXX should be read against the background of the history of the editing of the Homeric epics in Alexandria" (120). In light of the grammatical context in Alexandria, Honigman claims that the Jews sought royal patronage to fund the editorial activity in order to have a translation of the Law placed in the library. As a result, the Law of the Jews can be seen to be a translation, "not for pragmatic needs, but for the sake of prestige" (120). This overview by van der Kooij is followed by a substantial critique and a counterproposal in which he argues that the LXX is best understood in light of a "philosophical" paradigm (34). Support for this view is found internally within the Letter of Aristeas but also externally in the comments by Demetrius of Phalerum, Theophrastus, and Aristobulus (34–38). In this he appears to suggest that the impetus for the translation was almost entirely of Greek origin.

Following this discussion van der Kooij begins to return to the chapter's original focus by asking the question: "Would it be reasonable to assume that the high priest of Jerusalem was involved in the translation project, or not?" (39). To this question he provides the answer "most likely." Building on the previous discussion of the role of the high priest in Jewish polity, van der Kooij looks at specific passages in LXX Pentateuch (Exod 19:6; 23:20–23; Deut 1:16–17; 17:14–20) that, according to him, reflect an interest in legitimizing Jewish leadership in Jerusalem. This is followed by a brief discussion on the (likely) knowledge of the Greek language by Jewish leaders at the suggested time of translation. Overall, van der Kooij claims that "the translators were Jewish scholars from Jerusalem who stayed for some time in Alexandria" (62). Van der Kooij's argument is intriguing and will no doubt be engaged with by LXX scholars. In this chapter, however, it took a long time to get to his main argument. Moreover, it would have been beneficial (since it was brought up) to evaluate the possible Greek linguistic differences between Egypt and Judea to determine if there was any further internal support for a Jerusalem origin.

In chapter 3 van der Kooij challenges the assumed Alexandrian origin of the translation of Isaiah and argues instead that it derives from Heliopolis. As evidence for this position van der Kooij cites three passages in Isaiah (10:24; 11:16;

19:18–19) where the Greek translation differs from the MT text to include a positive reference to Jews living in Egypt. The motivation for these changes, according to van der Kooij, can be found in the historical context of Egyptian Jews in the second century BCE, namely, the founding of the rival temple in Heliopolis. Josephus's accounts (*War* 7.420–432; *Ant.* 13.62468), especially Onias's letter, provide sufficient evidence for van der Kooij to posit that the changes in Isaiah were a result of a member of the Oniad group translating Isaiah so that it both reflected and spoke specifically to current events. As a result, van der Kooij claims that Isaiah was translated in Heliopolis by a scholar (or scholars) who belonged to the priestly group that fled Jerusalem in the 160s BCE and afterward lived in Egypt (85).

The fourth chapter, which is divided into six parts and is written by Cook, investigates the provenance of Proverbs. In the first two sections (87–92, 93–133) Cook summarizes his previous research on the provenance, translation technique, and ideology of LXX Proverbs. In parts 3–5 Cook looks at the role of wisdom and law in Sirach, Letter of Aristeas, and the work of Aristobulus, respectively. In these sections Cook does not substantially deal with the issue of provenance, although it is mentioned, but rather focuses on the works' perspective on the law and their pro- or anti-Hellenistic perspective(s). In the conclusion of chapter 4 (i.e., part 6) Cook brings together his discussion. He asserts that the translator of Proverbs was a conservative Jew with a wide knowledge of Greek literary conventions, but one that "evaded the idea world of Greek thought" (168). In regard to provenance, though a definitive conclusion is not possible, Cook deems Jerusalem in the second century BCE to be the likely historical context for the Proverbs translation (172). The rationale for this decision hinges on its anti-Hellenistic stance (131–32). This resistant attitude, according to Cook, would have been most likely to arise in Palestine following the Antiochian crisis than any other time in both Jerusalem and Egypt (169). Though Cook may be correct in his determination of anti-Greek attitudes, it is unfortunate that he is not able to provide any additional linguistic or content arguments to support his claim.

Chapter 5 evaluates the provenance of Job and is again divided into six parts. These divisions look at specific chapters of Job (1, 2, 14, 19, and 42), the findings of which are compiled in part 6. Cook primarily focuses in this chapter on the pluses in LXX Job and the possible references to resurrection and the afterlife. Of greatest importance for Cook is the colophon appended to the LXX (Job 42:17a–e), its comment on the resurrection, and its exposition of Job's lineage. After this entire discussion, Cook affirms the established position: "it does not seem to me as if the general consensus about Alexandria as the place of origin of LXX Job is in jeopardy" (220). This, I must admit, was surprising, given the stated intention of the book to challenge theories of Alexandrian provenance. Despite this conclusion, Cook asserts that the translator was likely a Sadducee based on his avoidance of resurrection language in his translation.

The final chapter consists of a four-page synopsis of work and accurately summarizes the conclusions of each chapter. Following this are indices of selected

Greek and Hebrew words, modern authors, and ancient sources. It would have been helpful to have a full bibliography for easier referencing.

Evaluating the book as a whole, it is clear that Cook and van der Kooij address a significant topic in LXX studies. That the monograph only interacts with LXX Pentateuch, Isaiah, Job, and Proverbs is somewhat understandable in light of the interpretive issues but disappointing in light of the expectations created by the title. This work, then, acts as a first step in returning scholarly attention to this issue. The chapters function as (near) discrete units with little attempt to form a cumulative argument. Moreover, there are noticeable differences in approaches and writing styles between the two authors that erode some of the unity of the work.

One question that I would have liked to have seen covered in more detail is: What specifically counts as evidence? I recognize that van der Kooij and Cook have debated this topic elsewhere (and Cook did so limitedly here [89]), but it would have been a real contribution to provide a comprehensive perspective on how one should go about identifying the provenance of the text and its translator(s). Along this line, the role of language and dialect was insufficiently addressed. The authors sidestepped the issue by suggesting that "Greek language was the same all over the place" (60), so there is no difference between the Greek used in Egypt and in Judea. Such a position is contested, and additional support would have been helpful. This, however, does not address the issue of second-language acquisition and the potential influence of the native language on rendering a translation into a target language. That this criterion has been employed by other scholars to assess the provenance of the translators (so Joosten) suggests that this may provide a further check on the authors' findings (or not, depending on their reasoning).

Despite these critiques, I think Cook and van der Kooij succeed in their intended goal to reopen the discussion of LXX provenance. I agree with them that situating LXX books in their historical and cultural settings is a fruitful avenue of research, and I look forward to further endeavors in this vein.

When God Spoke Greek: The Septuagint and the Making of the Christian Bible, by Timothy Michael Law. Oxford: Oxford University Press, 2013. Pp. xii + 216. Paper. $24.95. ISBN 9780199781720.

Martin Rösel, Universität Rostock, Rostock, Deutschland

Das anzuzeigende Buch ist eine sehr verständlich geschriebene Einführung in die Entstehungs- und Rezeptionsgeschichte der Septuaginta von den mutmaßlichen Anfängen bis zum Konflikt zwischen Augustin und Hieronymus über die Geltung der LXX in der Kirche. Es richtet sich an Leserinnen und Leser mit geringen Vorkenntnissen, die vom Autor direkt angesprochen werden; ein etwas ungewöhnliches Stilmittel in einem wissenschaftlichen Buch.

Im ersten Kapitel „Why This book?" (1–8) werden vier Gründe für die Bedeutung der Septuaginta genannt: Sie ermöglicht Einblicke in das jüdisch-hellenistische Denken ab dem 3. Jh. BCE; sie war die Bibel der neutestamentlichen Schriftsteller und der Alten Kirche; sie war die Grundlage für die Theologiebildung der Christen und sie belegt eine Fülle von abweichenden Lesarten des hebräischen Bibeltextes. Für die Gesamtausrichtung des Buches ist bezeichnend, dass die textkritische Bedeutung der LXX zuletzt genannt wird und im weiteren Verlauf fast keine Rolle spielt.

Im zweiten Kapitel „When the World Became Greek" (9–18) wird kurz und konzise die Geschichte Israels vom 7. Jh. bis in die hellenistische Zeit dargestellt, um den kulturellen Hintergrund der Übersetzung der hebräisch-aramäischen Bibel ins Griechische zu erhellen. Kapitel 3 „Was There a Bible before the Bible?" (19–32) stellt dann die Vielgestaltigkeit der biblischen Schriften zur Zeit der Übersetzung dar. Es führt in unterschiedliche Problembereiche wie Vokalisationsdifferenzen, die Unterschiede zwischen samaritanischer und *mainstream*-Textüberlieferung, die Bedeutung der Textfunde aus Qumran oder die unterschiedlichen Editionen biblischer Bücher am Beispiel des Jeremia-Buches ein. Hier finden sich eine Vielzahl von Beispielen dafür, dass die Textgrundlage zur Zeit der Übersetzung nicht einheitlich war. Der Abschnitt ist gründlich gearbeitet, hätte aber m.E. übersichtlicher strukturiert sein können.

In Kapitel 4 „The First Bible translators" (33–42) kommt die Septuaginta in den Blick. Nach einer kurzen Einführung in den Aristeas-Brief kommt Vf. dann auf die Übersetzer des Pentateuch zu sprechen, die er in Alexandria verortet und als „moderately educated" (40) bezeichnet, ohne dass deutlich wird, wie er zu dieser Bewertung kommt. Die vorgeschlagene Datierung des Pentateuch „at the very latest in the second century BCE" (35) entspricht nicht dem Forschungskonsens und erscheint mir zu spät zu sein. Danach werden mutmaßliche Gründe für den Anlass zur Übersetzung vorgestellt und u.a. das Interlinearitäts-Paradigma abgelehnt. Allerdings bleibt offen, welche Erklärung für die Entstehung der Übersetzung der Vf. favorisiert.

Kapitel 5 „Gog and His Not-So-Merry Grasshoppers" (43–57) trägt wie das nächste eine sehr kryptische Überschrift, die vielleicht das intendierte Zielpublikum interessieren soll, m.E. aber einen Nebenaspekt überhöht und am Kern des Gesagten vorüber geht. In diesem Abschnitt werden die einzelnen Bücher— zunächst die des hebräischen Kanons (warum das?)—in ihrer griechischen Textform vorgestellt. Dabei werden je Schrift nur einige Beispiele herausgegriffen; oft bleibt unklar, ob abweichende Vorlagentexte oder Interpretationsbemühungen der Übersetzer für die Differenzen verantwortlich gemacht werden. Datierungen der Übersetzungen oder auch nur relative Chronologien bleiben offen. Dieses Kapitel hätte klarer strukturiert werden können und vor allem mit mehr Material versehen werden sollen. Viele in der LXX-Forschung intensiv diskutierte Einzelstellen werden nicht genannt (Jes 7,10–17; 9,1–6), bei manchen der genannten Beispiele ist die Bedeutung nicht nachvollziehbar: Warum wird die Versumstellung in Num 10,33–36 erwähnt, nicht aber die wichtigere bei der Segensformel in Num 6,23/27?

In Kapitel 6 „Bird Droppings, Stoned Elephants, and Exploding Dragons" (58–74) werden die Bücher vorgestellt, die üblicherweise in griechischen Bibeln über den Umfang des hebräischen Kanons hinaus enthalten sind. Nach einer Erklärung und Problematisierung des Begriffs „Apokryphen" werden die einzelnen Schriften sehr knapp und m.E. nicht immer treffend charakterisiert. Ein kurzer Ausblick weist dann darauf hin, dass auf der Ebene der hebräischen Textüberlieferung eine Tendenz zur Harmonisierung der Textformen eingesetzt hat; dies leitet zum nächsten Kapitel über.

Kapitel 7 „E Pluribus Unum" (75–84) zeigt, dass bereits vor Abschluss der Übersetzung aller Schriften ins Griechische Revisionen hin zur protomasoretischen Textform eingesetzt haben. Allerdings stand am Ende des Prozesses keine Uniformität, sondern eine Vielfalt von Kanonsgestalten. In diesem Abschnitt wird nicht immer klar, ob Vf. über die hebräische oder die griechischen Textgestalten spricht, so ist die S. 84 gemachte Aussage, dass die Vielfalt biblischer Texte, die es am Beginn des 2. Jh. gegeben habe, zu einem Ende gekommen sei, für die griechische Überlieferung nicht sinnvoll.

Kapitel 8 „The Septuagint behind the New Testament" (85–98) widmet sich dem Problem der Abweichungen zwischen den Zitaten des NT und dem hebräischen Bibeltext. Ausführlich wird diskutiert, ob es Testimoniensammlungen gegeben hat, im Endergebnis kommt Vf. zu dem Eindruck, dass es mehrere Wege gegeben hat, auf welche Weise die Autoren des NT ihre Schriftkenntnis erworben haben, u.a. auch durch liturgischen Gebrauch. Am Ende wird kurz dargestellt, wie sehr der neutestamentliche Sprachgebrauch durch LXX-Vokabular geprägt ist.

In Kapitel 9 „The Septuagint in the New Testament" (99–116) wird sehr detailliert begründet, dass im NT vor allem die LXX zitiert wurde, mit welcher theologischen Zielrichtung dies geschah und welche Konsequenzen dieser Umstand hatte. So wird als Resultat festgehalten, dass das NT anders aussähe, wenn es die LXX nicht gegeben hätte. In diesen beiden Kapiteln liegt der Schwerpunkt des Buches; es geht um den Aufweis, dass die Verwendung der vom Hebräischen abweichenden griechischen Texte historisch verständlich und theologisch sachgerecht ist. Diese Perspektive kann man nur begrüßen, allerdings halte ich die Darstellung für wenig ausgewogen, wenn Kap. 9 länger ist als Kap. 5, in dem die Schriften der LXX vorgestellt werden.

Kapitel 10 „The New Old Testament" beschäftigt sich mit der Rezeptions- und Kanonsgeschichte des AT; in der alten Kirche wurde nun durchgängig mit dem LXX-Text gearbeitet, die Benutzung des Codex wurde zum Unterscheidungsmerkmal. Es wird dargestellt, dass der Umfang des Kanons an den Rändern lange nicht eindeutig geregelt war, hierzu werden verschiedene altkirchliche Positionen zur Kanonsfrage zitiert. Das Kapitel hätte z.B. durch Tabellen oder eine Synopse mit dem MT-Kanon an Übersichtlichkeit gewonnen; die Unterschiede in der Anordnung der Schriften werden nicht deutlich. S. 126 findet sich die etwas fragwürdige Aussage, dass durch die Arbeiten des Hieronymus eine Abwertung der Apokryphen in der westlichen Tradition begonnen habe. Sachlich falsch ist S.127 der Satz, Luther und die Reformatoren hätten den breiteren Kanon (mit Apokryphen) aufgegeben; ein Blick in die Luther-Bibel von 1534 genügt, um dies zu widerlegen.

Kapitel 11 „God's Word for the Church" (128–39) zeigt zum einen die Entwicklung von lateinischen Tochterübersetzungen, dann wird (erst hier!) dargestellt, wie die Aristeaslegende u.a. bei Philo oder Josephus weiterentwickelt wurde, um die Inspiration der LXX zu begründen; sie wurde nun in der Kirche als Wort Gottes verstanden. Hier hätte man sich vor allem eine Darstellung der Diskussionen mit dem Judentum um Textabweichungen und Kanonsfragen gewünscht. Kapitel 12 trägt erneut eine sehr kryptische Überschrift: The man of steel and the man who worshipped the sun" (140–50). Hier wird Origenes gewürdigt, u.a. durch eine viel zu ausführliche Darstellung seiner Lebensumstände. Knapp und ohne Beispiele wird dann die Hexapla erklärt und dargestellt, wie sich hexaplarische Lesarten verbreiteten.

Kapitel 13 „The Man with the Burning Hand versus the Man with the Honeyed Sword" (151–66) widmet sich dann den Diskussionen zwischen Augustin und Hieronymus um die Frage nach der Inspiriertheit der LXX und dem hebräischen Text als Grundlage der Bibel. In einem „Postscript" (167–71) kommt T.M. Law dann zu dem Ergebnis, dass die griechische Bibel eine andere Theologie als die hebräische hat und dass diese auch und gerade für die christliche Kirche lesenswert ist. Damit schließt er sich der Position des Kopenhagener Neutestamentlers M. Müller an und wehrt ein weiteres Mal die Position ab, dass die LXX keine eigenen Aussageinteressen habe. Auf einen theologischen Ausblick (den man durch den Titel des Buches erwarten konnte) wird am Ende leider verzichtet; Law versteht sich explizit als Historiker, der mit seiner Arbeit dem Theologen die Tür geöffnet habe (171).

Die Darstellungen des Buches werden durch eine Fülle von Textbeispielen illustriert und begründet. Umso unverständlicher ist, dass es kein Bibelstellenregister gibt, durch das man diesen Reichtum erschließen könnte, stattdessen wird im Schlagwortregister pauschal auf biblische Bücher wie „Genesis" oder „Isaiah" hingewiesen. Auf andere als englischsprachige Literatur wird leider im nach Themen gegliederten Literaturverzeichnis kaum verwiesen, auch sonst kommt die intensive französisch- und deutschsprachige LXX-Forschung kaum zu Wort.

Aus der Sicht eines LXX-Forschers ist etwas bedauerlich, dass der Schwerpunkt des Buches bei der Nachgeschichte des Buches im NT und der Alten Kirche liegt und daher die Darstellung der Übersetzung und ihrer vielfältigen Probleme sehr kurz kommt. An manchen Stellen wird m.E. unangemessen salopp formuliert, etwa S. 148 zu Maxentius oder die Aktualisierung S. 89, wo von einer „Palestine Bible Society" die Rede ist. Doch das sind Geschmacksfragen, außer Frage steht, dass es sich um eine nützliche und lesenswerte Einführung in die Septuaginta-Forschung handelt.

Hebrew Bible/Old Testament Theology, by Georg Fischer. Theologien des Alten Testaments. Neuer Stuttgarter Kommentar: Altes Testament 31. Stuttgart: Katholisches Bibelwerk, 2012. Pp. 328. Paper. €29.95. ISBN 9783460073111.

Martin Leuenberger, Eberhard-Karls-Universität Tübingen, Tübingen, Germany

Georg Fischer, Professor für Altes Testament an der Universität Innsbruck, legt mit seinem neuen Buch ›Theologien des Alten Testaments‹ eine erste Gesamt-schau seiner jahrelangen Beschäftigung mit der »Vielfalt des biblischen Redens von Gott« vor (9, dort kursiv).

Damit folgt er mit Recht dem breiten neueren Trend, von Theologie*n* der alttestamentlichen bzw. (hebräisch-)biblischen Schriften zu sprechen (s.a. 14ff.): Der Fokus liegt auf »ihren je eigenen Weisen des Redens von Gott« (9, dort zum Teil kursiv), ohne dabei die biblisch implizierte Bezogenheit auf den einen Gott auszublenden, wie das artikellose »von Gott« (s.a. 19–20 u.a.) oder die Rede von einer »komplexe[n] Einheit« der biblischen Gottesaussagen (18) andeutet.

Das Buch ist aus drei Hauptteilen aufgebaut: Es umfasst eine kurze Einlei-tung, den eigentlichen Hauptteil zu den Theologien der atl. Bücher sowie eine abschließenden Zusammenschau.

Die *Einleitung* (13–20) expliziert einige wichtige Grundentscheidungen des vorliegenden Entwurfs: Nach einer Erinnerung an die Dominanz des Redens von Gott in der Bibel folgt eine kurze forschungsgeschichtliche Verortung, die sich auf die Wahrnehmung pluralischer Theologien in der HB konzentriert. Im Anschluss daran legt Fischer sein Augenmerk besonders auf die spezifischen und prägnanten Redeweisen von Gott in den unterschiedlichen Büchern, wobei er aus Raumgründen die religions- und theologiegeschichtlichen Aspekte ausklammern muss (17–18). Diese vielfältigen Theologien sind, wie Fischer eigens betont, sowohl kontext- als auch gegenstandsbedingt (19–20), welche Thematik im Schlussteil aufgegriffen wird. Abschließend wird die grundsätzlich der kanonischen Anordnung folgende Behandlung der Bücher der Tora, der (vorderen und hinteren) Propheten sowie der Ketubim (näher unterteilt in spätere Geschichtsbücher und Schriften/Weisheitsli-teratur) benannt, aber auch einige Umstellungen im Bereich der Ketubim (unter Einschluss griechisch erhaltener Werke wie Baruch, Brief Jeremias, Sirach, Weisheit u.a.) erläutert, die thematisch und historisch bedingt sind (20). Hier stößt eine Ori-entierung an ›vorgegebenen‹ kanonischen Abfolgen und Umgrenzungen deutlich an Grenzen und es zeigt sich, dass der Einbezug theologie- und kanongeschichtli-cher Entwicklungen sachlich unabdingbar ist, auch wenn sie aus Raumgründen im vorliegenden Buch weitestgehend übergangen werden (müssen).

Der eigentliche *Hauptteil* (21–248) widmet dementsprechend in fünf Kapi-teln—jeweils mit kurzer Hinführung und summierendem Schluss, wo Fischer auch auf Aspekte der gegenwärtigen Relevanz hinweist (vgl. z.B. 22ff. für Gen und 29ff. für Ex)—jedem atl. Buch einen eigenen Abschnitt; dabei wird jeweils ziemlich strikt auf die Gottesaussagen im engeren Sinn fokussiert.

Um dies anhand der Schriftprophetie kurz zu umreißen: Für das Jesajabuch wählt Fischer ausgehend von Jes 6,3 die Heiligkeit Jhwhs als Leitmotiv, das er kurz

umreißt, um danach im lockeren Buchdurchgang weitere Topoi wie Rettung oder
Belehrung durch Jhwh und anderes mehr zu behandeln, die jeweils anhand von
zentralen Bezugsstellen exemplarisch eingeführt und anschließend durch allge-
meinere Überlegungen beschrieben werden.

Oder für das kleine Buch Haggai (128–29) wählt Fischer mit Recht das Motto
des mit dem Tempelbau einsetzenden göttlichen Segens (2,19), dessen komposi-
tionelle Schlüsselstellung jedoch nicht weiter ausgeführt wird; vielmehr referiert
ein kurzer Durchgang etwas additiv die wichtigsten Aussagen des Buches.

Zum Abschluss, der sich auf die Einleitung zurück bezieht, unterstreicht
Fischer die Verschiedenheit der schriftprophetischen Theologien, deren diskursi-
ven Charakter (auch gegenüber Gott selbst) und die sich gleichwohl durchhaltende
Ausrichtung auf Gottes Recht, Loyalität und Geradheit (138–39).

Das Verfahren besteht also jeweils darin, entlang den Teilbereichen der
biblischen Bücher knapp auf die wichtigsten Gottesvorstellungen einzugehen.
Aufgrund des geringen Umfanges fehlt dabei jedoch die kontextuelle Einbindung
weitgehend, sodass einerseits eine durchgängige Begleitlektüre der Bibel und
andererseits eine Konsultation von Einleitungen und Kommentaren in Bezug auf
die historischen und literaturgeschichtlichen Sachverhalte unbedingt erforder-
lich ist; dies dürfte für Studierende als wesentlich anvisierte Leser einigermaßen
anspruchsvoll sein, birgt jedoch auch zahlreiche Chancen zur Entwicklung exe-
getischer Kompetenz.

Die abschließende *Zusammenschau* (249–300) wendet sich übergreifenden
Gemeinsamkeiten zu. Vorab erinnert Fischer an den konstruktiven Aspekt aller
Gottesaussagen und an die prägende Perspektive offizieller Jerusalemer Religion.
(1) Für den biblischen Gott Jhwh charakteristisch sind dabei nicht nur recht kon-
stante Wesenszüge (251ff.) wie etwa Gottes Sprechen, Erschaffen, Zuwendung,
Barmherzigkeit usf. (wobei jeweils im Gefolge von Brueggemanns countertes-
timony auch Gegenaussagen berücksichtigt werden), sondern auch eine breite
Palette nur gelegentlich auftretender Aussagen über Gott, die in Auswahl zur
Sprache kommen (273ff.); darüber hinaus vermag es Jhwh aber sogar, Gegen-
sätze zu umfangen (277ff.). (2) Unter der Überschrift ›Diskussion und Reflexion‹
wird dies anschließend bedacht, wobei es zunächst um den Theologiebegriff,
um Entwicklungen der Gottesvorstellungen bzw. Gottes selbst sowie um einige
Grundprobleme (Gewalt, Erwählung, Alleinverehrung) geht, bevor die Spannung
von Offenbarung und Ideologie anhand einiger prägnanter Beispiele zur Sprache kommt und ausgehend von Dtn 4 Jhwhs Unvergleichlichkeit erörtert wird.
(3) Schließlich werden gesamtbiblische Perspektiven in den Blick genommen, die
einerseits auf die Selbigkeit Gottes und andererseits auf die Auszeichnung Jesu
durch wesentliche Züge Jhwhs abheben.

Diese Synthese bündelt den vorangehenden Einzeldurchgang durch das
AT auf konzise und durchaus ausgewogene Weise, nimmt jedoch die konkrete
Gewichtung und Verhältnisbestimmung der einzelnen Topoi weitgehend impli-
zit vor, ohne die literaturgeschichtlich meist komplexen und hypothetischen
Kontextualisierungsvorgänge im Einzelnen zu entfalten. Hier wären wenigs-

tens exemplarische Konkretisierungen, z.B. anhand der Gnadenformel bzw. der ›Gnadenrede‹ (35) Ex 34,6–7, die ohne weitere Begründung als »innerster Kern der gesamten Heiligen Schrift und Schlüsselaussage über den biblischen Gott« bewertet wird (35), für das Verständnis sicherlich äußerst aufschlussreich gewesen.

Ein *Literaturverzeichnis, ein Stellen- und ein Sachregister* (301–28) schließen den Band ab und erleichtern die vom Autor durchaus vorgesehene punktuelle Benutzung des Buches (s. 10). Dazu trägt auch die übersichtliche Gliederung und der gut lesbare Duktus wesentlich bei, auch wenn sich der Verfasser aus Platzgründen oft sehr knapp zu fassen hat.

Insgesamt bietet das Buch insbesondere Studierenden einen leicht zugänglichen, durch die Kürze aber auch dichten Einblick in die Vielfalt biblischer Gottesvorstellungen und in die gegenwärtige Diskussionslage zu der/den Theologie(n) der Hebräischen Bibel bzw. dem Alten Testament, der das gewichtige evangelische Werk von H. Spieckermann und R. Feldmeier, Der Gott der Lebendigen. Eine biblische Gotteslehre (TOBIT 1, Tübingen 2011) auf seine Weise ergänzt und wohl am besten in Kombination mit einer Einleitung in das AT und einer Geschichte Israels benutzt wird. Im Anschluss an die von Fischer mit vollem Recht betonte Vielfalt biblischer Gottesaussagen stellt m.E. aber auch das sukzessive »Zusammen-Denken« (M. Sæbø) ein dringendes Desiderat dar, das im Zug aktueller redaktions-, theologie- und kanongeschichtlicher Einsichten sehr wohl noch neue, weiter führende Perspektiven zu eröffnen vermag. Angesichts der bewussten Ausklammerung dieser Fragestellungen (s.a. 17) darf man auf weitere einschlägige Ausarbeitungen durch Fischer gespannt sein, nachdem sich zunächst mit Hilfe des vorliegenden Buchs die Vielfalt des biblischen Redens von Gott in ihrer ganzen kanonischen Breite sorgfältig wahrnehmen lässt.

Der Mensch, das Bild Gottes? Zum Gedanken einer Sonderstellung des Menschen im Alten Testament und in weiteren altorientalischen Quellen, by Annette Schellenberg. Abhandlungen zur Theologie des Alten und Neuen Testaments 101. Zurich: Theologischer Verlag Zürich, 2011. Pp. 474. Cloth. €64.80. ISBN 9783290176068.

Bob Becking, Utrecht University, Utrecht, The Netherlands

The idea that humanity is part of creation but at the same time stands apart from creation (so James Barr) was constantly on my mind when reading Schellenberg's Habilitationsschrift. In this book she studies the triangular relations between God, humankind and the animal kingdom as presented in a set of biblical texts that she evaluates in the context of ancient Near Eastern anthropology.

She starts with a set of introductory remarks (13–28). Here she discusses the design of her book and makes explanatory remarks on the terminology applied. Interesting is her plea not to use the concept *Gottebenbildlichkeit*. She prefers the term *Bild-Gottes-Haftigkeit* for the enigmatic idea that humankind in some way is the representative or likeness of the Divine. Strikingly, she does not make many remarks on method. Thus it is not clear, at least to me, what reading strategy or narrative concept she will apply to the pertinent texts. In the rest of the book, this lack of clarity at times turns out to be a weakness. The main body of her book is a detailed analysis of the three "Krontexte" in the Hebrew Bible concerning anthropology. She reads the P primeval history, Ps 8, and the Garden narrative with the question mind: What view do these texts contain of the special status (*Sonderstellung*) of humankind in relation to the divine and the animal kingdom?

Chapter 2 (29–142) is dedicated to the P material in the early chapters of Genesis. The many remarks made here are not easily summarized. Interesting is Schellenberg's observation on a shift in the human-animal relation provoked by the flood. After the narrative on this primordial catastrophe, domination and control changed into competition and respect. Meanwhile, humans lost their role as mediators between God and the animals. The animals now are included in the covenant. In comparison with the views expressed in other ancient Near Eastern texts, in P the connection between God and human is relatively tight and close. Schellenberg correctly observes that the human is not the image of God *sui generis*. Using an anachronistic metaphor, being like God is not part of the human DNA. The secret of the human in Gen 1 is that the human became the image of God as s result of God's address to the human. The anthropology of P is not optimistic in all respects. By reading Gen 1* in context with P's flood narrative, it becomes clear that the human failed in the assignment to rule the animal kingdom. This failure, however, did not wash away the concept of being created in the image of God. When it comes to the view on the interrelations among humans, Schellenberg observes a tendency in this P material that all humans are created equal. No human as such stands apart from other humans.

Chapter 3 discusses Ps 8 (143–77). As for the human-animal relation, Schellenberg makes some very interesting remarks. In the psalm that underscores the special position of humankind, the relation of humans with animals is not a specific theme. The human dominion over the animals is only uttered as an expression of the marvelous role humans have to play. I see her view and can follow her argument, but I wonder why so much space is dedicated to the animal kingdom in Ps 8. In my view, this space is filled with almost mythological language. Schellenberg's playing down of the relations does not answer that. I agree with her view that not much is said in Ps 8 on inter-human relationships. Her discussion of the enigmatic phrase "You have made him a little lower than God" (Ps 8:5) is somewhat bleak. She could have helped herself here by considering the word *ʾĕlōhîm* as a plural referring to heavenly beings.

After everything that has been written on the Garden narrative, it is not easy to say something new on Gen 2–3. In chapter 4 (179–230) Schellenberg presents the results of her reading of these two chapters. In Gen 2 the human has a dominant position over the animal kingdom, as shown by the naming of the various species. This position is only loosely related to the human *Sonder-stellung*. After the incident with the fruit, things change dramatically, however. In the "postparadisiacal world" human dominion over the animals is contested. In Gen 2 humans stand in a very special position in relation to God. Through the eating of the forbidden fruit, the woman and the man became on a par with God. This nearness, however, was turned into distance and alienation by God. In Schellenberg's view, the *Bild-Gottes-Haftigkeit* of humans is retribution for misconduct, not a gift from God. Here, too, I am surprised that Schellenberg does not take *'elohîm* as a reference to the celestial beings but as a noun for the Creator God. In doing so, she passes by some subtleties in biblical anthropology. As for the relations between humans, she only notes the equality of Adam and Eve.

In chapter 5 (231–300), Schellenberg seeks a systematic framework for her results. Here she brings in several ancient Near Eastern texts, especially the Atrahasis Epic and the Wisdom of Merikare and a set of visual images. She arrives at the conclusion that the concept of the special status of humans was widely present in the ancient Near East. This concept, however, was seldom elaborated in an explicit way. Text and images assume the *Sonderstellung* but do not offer systematization let alone a theology. It is only texts such as P, Ps 8, and Merikare that offer reflections on the special state. The biblical and ancient Near Eastern views on the animal kingdom function in a twofold way, comparable to the phrase coined by Barr. Although the human is seen as part of the ecosystem, humanity exceeds this system. The specifics of humanity are to be found in our cognitive brain and our ability to build civilizations. Since Schellenberg focuses on those texts that *expressis verbis* mention the relation between God and human as well as the special status of humankind, her observations could be seen as slightly one-sided. The general image in the Bible as well as in the ancient Near East is that of divine devotion—although this care could take the form of fierce criticism and judgment. Interesting is the final theme of this chapter, which is connected to inner-human relations. Many ancient Near eastern texts make a sharp differentiation between king and people or the ruling elite and the ordinary community in which the upper layers of society are seen as having a special status. This concept is almost absent in the Hebrew Bible, and where it is present, it is contested and criticized. On the other hand, the Hebrew Bible contains the concept of Israel being elected to a special status. The wise and the pious are often seen as having a special status. In my view, Schellenberg constructs too fierce a dichotomy between Israel and its neighbors. The evidence is not as black and white as she seems to assume. There are more than a few Mesopotamian and Egyptian texts that give expression to the view that "the others" were not created equal.

The final chapter (371–97) argues that the Priestly concept of the special status of the human being is a unique view. The book closes with carefully designed indices.

JUDAISM: GENERAL

Defining Jewish Difference: From Antiquity to the Present, by Beth A. Berkowitz. Cambridge: Cambridge University Press, 2012. Pp. viii + 280. Cloth. £55.00. ISBN 9781107013711.

Joshua Schwartz, Bar-Ilan University, Ramat-Gan, Israel

While working on her previous book, *Execution and Invention: Death Penalty Discourse in Early Rabbinic and Christian Cultures* (New York: Oxford University Press: 2006), Beth Berkowitz came upon a passage dealing with the rabbinic execution method of decapitation (t. Sanhedrin 9:11). In this passage the second-century sage Rabbi Judah states that the preferred rabbinic means for decapitation was an axe despite its being more gruesome than decapitation by a sword. The axe was preferred because the sword was the Roman means of decapitation, and using it would be a transgression of the rabbinic prohibition against "their (= non-Jews') laws" based on Lev 18:3: "and in their laws you should not go."

Rabbi Judah's use of the verse for issues of execution did not necessarily follow from the plain meaning of the verse: "Like the practice of the land of Canaan to which I am bringing you, you should not practice, and in their laws you should not go," which is part of a general catalog of incest and other sex taboos. What could this have to do with a Roman means of execution? The author "wondered how often this verse had been read in this way, as a directive to Israel to turn itself into an 'upside-down people' … and at what cost to Israel's moral integrity." The verse, the subsequent question, and sundry answers became the author's study on "Jewish difference," the topic of the present book.

The scope of the work is amazing. After a theoretical introduction, which begins with U.S. constitutional law, the author goes through the relevant biblical traditions, Philo, the church fathers and particularly Clement of Alexandria, rabbinic literature, medieval commentators on the Talmud and Jewish law (in particular, the Tosafists), Rabbi Nissim Gerondi, and Rabbi Joseph Colon. This material serves as the basis for Berkowitz's chapter on two modern giants of the rabbinic world of the twentieth century: the late Rabbi Moses Feinstein in the United States and Rabbi Ovadiah Yosef in Israel. I cannot think of another scholar who in a single work showed such an extensive mastery of a topic, although there are of course scholars who might be proficient in the literatures of numerous areas and periods. In spite of the above, the author herself is aware that her treatment is not complete and that she or future scholars might seek references to Lev 18:3 in, for example qur'anic literature and in the commentaries of medieval Jewish and Christian exegetes. It is hard to fault her with making do, though, with the scope and studies presented in the present work, and it serves as a model for tracing the interpretive career of a verse from ancient until modern times and indeed in showing how it might serve as a backdrop for present-day conversations on such matters as Jewish assimilation and minority identity and even the story of Jewishness in general.

The book has ten chapters, eight of which, minus the introduction and conclusion, trace the "reception history"—a term Berkowitz is not entirely comfortable using—and development of Lev 18:3. Of these eight chapters, five have appeared, or will appear, somewhat anticlimatically, in other publications. What first attracted me to this book was to follow up on Berkowitz's excellent earlier version of chapter 5 (*Jewish Quarterly Review* 99 [2009]: 121–57), in which, *inter alia*, she had discussed hairstyles in terms of Jewish law and "their law," a matter of particular interest to me.

The book begins, after the introduction ("Introduction: Law, Identity, and Leviticus 18:3) with a chapter on the biblical verse that serves as the core of the study ("The Question of Israelite Distinctiveness: Paradigms of Separatism in Leviticus 18:3"). Berkowitz shows that the meaning of Israel's distinctiveness in Lev 18:3 is dependent to a great extent on context. In its "local" context (Lev 18:1–5), Egypt's and Canaan's practices are prohibited because they are Egypt's and Canaan's practices; there are no inherent flaws in these practices. In the context of the entire chapter (Lev 18), the prohibition against "their laws" refers primarily to sexual practices and accuses the nations who previously inhabited Canaan of these practices. Leviticus 18 must also be understood in terms of other legal corpora in the Pentateuch that demand Israelite distinctiveness. These sources (Exod 23:23–25; Deut 12: 29–13:1; 18:9–14) see Israel's distinctiveness in terms of worship of other gods, methods and sites of worship, and mediators of worship. The author sees Leviticus as the final stage in biblical development, building on the earlier verses and particularly appropriate for the reality of the Persian period.

The next chapter ("Allegory and Ambiguity: Jewish Identity in Philo's *De congessu*"), is the Second Temple period representative and seeks to study Philo's Jewish identity against the collective backdrop of his many other identities—Egyptian, Greek, and Roman—and based on his long treatment of Lev 18:1–5 in *De congessu* ("On Mating"). Egypt is the land of passions representing the period of childhood when people cannot control their emotions. Canaan is the period of adolescence when vice beckons and the soul has not yet learned how to resist it. To shun those practices is to "grow up." Is this purely a philosophical discussion, or is it a discourse of Israel and the other nations, or did Philo perhaps employ a method of strategic ambiguity allowing for different interpretations, that is, cultural integration for loyalist Jews but seemingly protecting the scriptural heritage of social separatism while for less-attached Jews a more apt philosophical inclusive vision?

From Philo Berkowitz moves on not to rabbinic writings, or at least not directly, but rather to the church father Clement of Alexandria (150–215 CE), a contemporary of Mishnah-period sages, apparently chosen because he was heavily influenced by Hellenistic philosophy and thus a logical continuation from Philo ("Rethinking Universalism and Particularism in Patristic and Rabbinic Writings"). Berkowitz, however, will juxtapose his explication of Lev 18:1–5 with that found in the rabbinic midrash halakah collection Sifra. Clement proves to be an excellent choice for the focus of the chapter, proving surprisingly to be an offshoot of Jewish interpretation, seeing Lev 18:1–5 in an ethnic sense while maintaining also Christian views. All of this will require us to rethink both rabbinic and Christian "universalist" and "particularist" tendencies.

The next three chapters ("The Limits of 'Their Laws' in Midrash Halakhah"; "A Short History of the People Israel from the Patriarchs to the Messiah: Constructions of Jewish Difference in Leviticus Rabbah"; and "Syncretism and Anti-syncretism in the Babylonian Talmud") are the core of the work of Berkowitz as a scholar of rabbinic literature. They also show how different types of this literature seem to reflect the development of different rabbinic strategies in dealing with Jewish difference.

How did the rabbis deal with "assimilationist" tendencies, and how "tolerant" were they to Gentiles? These are important issues to Berkowitz, but she goes beyond them to seek to understand how the rabbis saw themselves, their claims to authority, and the scope of Torah. Bearing in mind that it is not clear how much influence the rabbis really had on society, making how they dealt with others perhaps sometimes not entirely relevant, one cannot doubt that they certainly influenced one another.

The first chapter ("The Limits of 'Their Laws'") deals with the Tannaitic material. The rabbis in the halakic midrash Sifra had two opposing strategies for dealing with Lev 18:3. The first Berkowitz defines as a "neutralization strategy" in which rabbinic leaders carve out basically for the Jewish male elite a cultural space in which Jews can function in the context of the Roman imperial world. This strategy relates to a core group of practices. The second reading of Lev 18:3 in Sifra relates to a wide array of habits; a Jew who observes Lev 18:3 must reject much that is non-Jewish, even though seemingly innocuous and far-removed from idolatry. Context and Roman behavioral norms might be instrumental in determining whether a practice is permitted or not. The context might also change.

The second chapter on the rabbinic material ("A Short History") deals with the reality in Amoraic Palestine. How did the rabbis deal with the distinctiveness of being Jewish when local Jewish and Christian communities were now organized around Jewish synagogues and Christian churches? The text examined is the fifth-century Leviticus Rabbah, which offers on Lev 18:3 a wide range of paradigms on Jewishness that incorporate moral difference, physical difference, difference in attitudes regarding obedience to God, difference as ritual competence, difference in politics and economics, difference as demography, and difference in sexual practice.

The last of the three chapters on rabbinic literature ("Syncretism and Anti-syncretism") deals with two pericopes in the Babylonian Talmud. The pericope Berkowitz discusses in b. Sanhedrin 52b offers a strategy of what Berkowitz calls "nativization" or "biblicization," which turns a Gentile practice into one that is supposedly originally Jewish. This paradoxically allows for some degree of Jewish syncretism while at the same time claiming that it is chimerical. In b. Avodah Zarah 11a there is once again a strategy of neutralization. A Gentile practice is deemed incidental to Gentile religion and thus permitted. The discussions in the

Babylonian Talmud seem to take for granted that the prohibitions in Lev 18:3 should be restricted.

The last two chapters ("The Judaization of Reason in the Tosafists, Nissim Gerondi, and Joseph Colon"; "Women's Wear and Men's Suits: Ovadiah Yosef's and Moshe Feinstein's Discourses of Jewishness") continue Berkowitz's odyssey, treating influential medieval halakic authors from the twelfth to the fifteenth centuries and then jumping to the twentieth century to discuss responsa of two of the leading rabbis of modern times with regard to Lev 18:3 and Jewish distinctiveness.

Berkowitz sees rationality as the central theme for the medieval rabbis' treatment of "their laws," which also allowed them to engage in interreligious polemics, to construct political theory, and to analyze the Jewish psyche. Questions of Jewish morality and psychology also play a role, in particular regarding the question of whether a Jew might wear the physician's robe called the *cappa*. This issue will serve as the basis for a good deal of future discussion on Jewish and non-Jewish clothing.

Finally Berkowitz reaches modern times. The relationships between Jews and non-Jews changed, whether in the Diaspora or in the State of Israel, and while new issues seemingly arose, the parameters of the legal discussion regarding these issues had not changed, at least for those operating within the framework of modern Orthodox halakic Judaism. How was one to remain distinct yet be able to function in the modern world? In Israel, Rabbi Ovadiah Yosef dealt with such questions as placing a flower on a coffin, a clearly non-Jewish custom. He also dealt with matters of women's dress such as miniskirts and whether pants might be preferable or whether married women might cover their hair with wigs, thus fulfilling laws of modesty, but by doing so and by appearing stylish perhaps ironically seeming not to observe the laws of modesty. In America, Rabbi Moshe Feinstein had to deal with "minhag America," American custom in such matters as men's clothing and with issues of "secular" religion, as it were, such as whether an observant Jew might celebrate Thanksgiving. Ironically, in modern times "their laws" were no longer confined to issues of Jews versus Gentiles but rather also related to issues of Jews versus Jews, be it Ashkenazi versus Sepharadi or Orthodox versus Conservative or Reform.

This is an absolutely outstanding work. While the scope and extent of the material studied are amazing, the sharpness and depth of Berkowitz's individual and collective analyses are brilliant. True, as the author herself admits, and pointed out above, she did not study all of the relevant material on Lev 18:3 (or Lev 18:1–5), and perhaps her conclusions might have changed if additional or different traditions had been studied. It might have also been interesting occasionally to see if the theoretical legal views that she studies jibed with the realities of material culture. The work as it is, though, makes an important contribution to the study of Jewish identity and should be read by just about anyone interested in Jewish studies in any form. It also serves as a model for future work on reception history or on the history of ideas in Jewish society.

Jewish Interpretation of the Bible: Ancient and Contemporary, by Karin Hedner Zetterholm. Minneapolis: Fortress, 2012. Pp. xiv + 210. Paper. $32.00. ISBN 9780800697983.

Marianne Grohmann, University of Vienna, Vienna, Austria

Karin Hedner Zetterholm, Centre for Theology and Religious Studies at Lund University, Sweden, presents an introduction to Jewish interpretation of the Hebrew Bible. She delineates mainly rabbinic exegesis and provides an outlook to reading strategies in contemporary Judaism.

The first three chapters of the book give basic information about the classical rabbinic ways of interpreting the Hebrew Bible in Mishnah, Talmuds, and midrash. The author focuses on the tension between the commitment to tradition and the rabbinic freedom in adopting it to the present. She describes the "essence of Jewish tradition ... as an ongoing dialectical process between divine revelation and human creative interpretation" (7). Zetterholm outlines basic concepts of rabbinic interpretation of the Bible: the revelation at Sinai as the foundation event and starting point for written and oral Torah; the tension and connection between divine revelation and human interpretation; Jewish law and divine truth; the famous seventy faces of the Torah; and the centrality of study as fellowship with God. She chooses well-known examples from biblical and rabbinic literature—for example, the classical story about rabbinic authority in b. B. Meṣiʿa 59b or the binding of Isaac in Gen 22 and Genesis Rabbah—to illustrate the basic methods and hermeneutical presuppositions of early Jewish interpretation of the Hebrew Bible.

Regarding the Talmud, Zetterholm presents main lines of the discussion of what rabbinic literature can contribute to Jewish history. She outlines the position of Jacob Neusner and others who see the rabbinic texts mainly as a source for the time and context of their redactors. She describes the tension between possible historical information provided by rabbinic texts and a reading of these texts mainly as literary artefacts—represented, for example, by Jonah Fraenkel—in a balanced way. Her own conclusions are rather cautious, as Zetterholm sums up the discussions about rabbinic literature as a source for historical reconstruction in the following way: "A general scepticism to rabbinic traditions, an awareness of the role of redactors in reworking earlier material, and the recognition that rabbinic narratives are literary artefacts have thoroughly changed the prospect of using rabbinic literature as a source for historical reconstruction" (61).

The part about basics of rabbinic interpretation of the Hebrew Bible is followed by one chapter about "The Jewish Character of the Early Jesus Movement." Jesus and Paul are presented as first-century Jewish Torah teachers. The parable about the wicked tenants (Matt 21:33–46; Mark 12:1–12; Luke 20:9–19) is compared to rabbinic parables and serves as an example of the Jewish nature of the Jesus movement. Zetterholm sums up the "new perspective on Paul" as follows: "The idea that Paul was concerned primarily with non-Jews, whom he wanted to include in the covenant with the God of Israel without first turning them into Jews, is becoming more common, and his negative statements about the law are being explained, at least in part, by his desire to prevent non-Jews from keeping commandments that were given to the Jewish people" (130). This chapter ends with the position of non-Jews in early rabbinic Judaism. The New Testament serves as the only example of Jewish literature of the Second Temple period.

From there the author jumps to "Continuity and Change in Contemporary Judaism," skipping over, for example, Rashi completely. As indicated by the subtitle, the book tries to consider both ancient and contemporary Jewish interpretation of the Bible. Still, the gap between these different periods and contexts is rather big. Zetterholm starts this chapter with an overview of movements within contemporary Judaism, which has few connections to the questions of Bible interpretation but can serve as basic background information. Zetterholm chooses two examples to illustrate the conflicts between moral values and biblical laws in contemporary Jewish interpretation of the Bible: same-sex relations and questions of medical ethics—both of which would fill books by themselves. In order to bridge the gap between rabbinic and contemporary Judaism, Zetterholm ends with rather general considerations about "the legacy of classical rabbinic Judaism": "The notion that human interpretation is part of divine revelation allows for adaption and change, and that notion, shared by the rabbis of the rabbinic period and most contemporary Jews, is itself evidence of the continuity with the past" (187).

The strength of the book lies in its presentation of basic information. It outlines the main scholarly debates in a very balanced way, without stressing a specific thesis of the author. The book gives an overview of main lines and a first orientation about rabbinic interpretation of the Bible on an elementary level. With its clear language, glossary, bibliography, illustrations, and study questions after each chapter, it can serve as a useful resource for teaching. It is based on the English language only—both in translations of biblical and rabbinic texts and in the bibliography. For more detailed knowledge, further reading, both of the original sources and secondary literature, is essential.

Between Cooperation and Hostility: Multiple Identities in Ancient Judaism and the Interaction with Foreign Powers, edited by Rainer Albertz and Jakob Wöhrle. Journal of Ancient Judaism Supplements 11. Göttingen: Vandenhoeck & Ruprecht, 2013. Pp. 280. Cloth. €89.99. ISBN 9783525550519.

Michael L. Satlow, Brown University, Providence, Rhode Island

This volume contains the twelve collected essays of a conference held at the University of Münster in 2011. According to the one-page preface, the essays show that "the contrasting Jewish attitudes towards foreign powers were not only dependent on specific political circumstances" but were "also interrelated with the emergence of multiple early Jewish identities." After very briefly summarizing the essays in this volume I will return to the question of whether the essays really do show this interrelationship.

Daniel R. Schwartz's "Judeans, Jews, and their Neighbors: Jewish Identity in the Second Temple Period" explores the question of whether "Jew" (with its religious overtones) or "Judean" (with its regional or perhaps ethnic overtones) is the best translation for the ancient Greek *ioudaios* (and its cognates) using two cases, that of 1 and 2 Maccabees and Josephus. Whereas 1 Maccabees is oriented to those who dwell in Judea (and thus a translation of "Judean" for *ioudaios* is most appropriate), the religious orientation of 2 Maccabees suggests that "Jew" is most often the better translation. This same distinction maps onto Josephus himself, whose *War* really is about Judeans and whose *Antiquities* has a more religious orientation and deals more broadly with "Jews."

Thomas Römer, in "Conflicting Models of Identity and the Publication of the Torah in the Persian Period," argues that the Hebrew Bible's different evaluations of Persian rule emerge from the authors' differing social classes. Applying a theoretical model derived from Max Weber, Römer sees traces of prophetic, priestly, and mandarin reactions to the Persians. Although intriguing, the essay is sketchy and difficult to follow.

Jakob Wöhrle argues in "Joseph in Egypt: Living under Foreign Rule according to the Joseph Story and its Early Intra- and Extra-biblical Reception" that beginning with the redaction of the biblical Joseph story itself, Israelites and Jews used the story of Joseph to reflect on their relationship with outside powers. While the biblical redactor, living "probably in the time of the exile" (59), made a neutral story about Joseph into a tale of life in the diaspora, the later writers of Ben Sira, 1 Maccabees, and the Testaments of the Twelve Patriarchs use this story to advance both hostile (in Ben Sira and 1 Maccabees) and favorable (Testaments of the Twelve Patriarchs) attitudes toward the possibility of Jewish life in a Gentile world.

Sebastian Grätz's "The Adversaries of Ezra/Nehemiah—Fictitious or Real: A Case Study on Creting Identity in Late Persian and Hellenistic Times" argues that, whether or not Ezra/Nehemiah's accounts of adversaries (particularly Geshem, Tobiah, and Sanballat) have some historical grounding, they have been shaped in order to solidify the notion of a distinct and new Judean identity.

Reinhard Achenbach, in "'Genocide' in the Book of Esther," argues that Esther "is a narrative statement about the right of the Jewish people to defend their fundamental right to ethnic, cultural, and religious integrity even when holding the status of an ethnic entity under foreign domination" (91). The highlighting of this issue suggests that it was composed in a Hellenistic (rather than Persian) milieu, when such a right was debated. More precisely, Achenbach argues that Esther was written between the times of 1 and 2 Maccabees.

Rainer Albertz suggests in "Are Foreign Rulers Allowed to Enter and Sacrifice in the Jerusalem Temple?" that behind the decision by Jerusalem priests in 66 CE to stop sacrificing at the temple on behalf of the emperor and Rome was a developed theological debate that drew on the ancient biblical tension between universalism and particularism. In Albertz's reading, this theological dimension made the gap between different priestly parties unbridgeable and "the outbreak of religiously motivated violence became unavoidable" (131).

In "The Construction of Samari(t)an Identity from the Inside and from the Outside," Stefan Schorch asks when and why Samaritans created an identity separate from the Judeans. He argues that the process of forming this distinct identity began with tensions between the (then) Samarians and Judeans in the fourth to third centuries BCE that ultimately created the rupture and establishment of a distinct Samaritan identity in the (late) second century BCE. The catalyst behind this rupture was the worshipers on Mount Gerizim's difficult position between the disapproving Judeans and their need to articulate an identity to the local foreign powers.

Andrea M. Berlin's "Manifest Identity: From *Ioudaios* to Jew; Household Judaism as Anti-Hellenization in the Late Hasmonean Era" puts her previous argument for the existence of a "household Judaism" into a diachronic context.[1] Berlin argues that beginning in the first century BCE the Judeans of the Hasmonean kingdom began to use simple and undecorated vessels. This was a deliberate break with both their past and their neighbors, whose pottery was more decorative and demonstrates contact with the wider Hellenistic world. Berlin concludes that these Judeans were using material objects to establish an increasingly religious (as opposed to territorial or ethnic) identity. Perhaps, to adopt Schwartz's earlier distinction, they were moving from Judeans to Jews.

The next two essays deal with themes in 1 and 2 Maccabees. Doron Mendels, in "Honor and Humiliation as a Factor in Hasmonean Politics according to the Narrator of 1 Maccabees," argues that "our narrator [in 1 Maccabees] believes that friction within Jewish society and with the outside world happened sometimes as a result of differing concepts of honor that could not be accommodated to each other" (180). Johannes Achnooks's "From the 'Master of the Elephants' to the 'Most Ungracious Wretch': The Image of Foreign Commanders in the Second Book of Maccabees" claims that the author of 2 Maccabees patterned his narrative on the psalms of Asaph. This knowledge then helps in disentangling historical material from its literary presentation in the book.

Catherine Hezser, in "Seduced by the Enemy or Wise Strategy? The Presentation of Non-violence and Accommodation with Foreign Powers in Ancient Jewish Literary Sources," clearly articulates what has emerged to this point as the central issue of this volume: "Ancient Jews vacillated between hostility and cooperation, between military (re)action and accommodation with foreign rulers" (222). Given the binary option of war or peace, though, "both Jews and Christians seem to have preferred non-violent conflict resolutions whenever they were possible" (246).

---

1. A. M. Berlin, "Jewish Life before the Revolt: The Archaeological Evidence," *JSJ* 36 (2005): 417–70.

In "The High Priests and Rome: Why Cooperation Failed," Kai Trampedach argues that Rome sought to treat the Judean priests as they did other provincial aristocracies, appropriating them into their bureaucratic structure. He argues, along lines similar to Albertz, that this cooperation was doomed from the start due to the priests' theological commitments.

While it would have been nice to have a more substantive introduction in which the editors tell us what they see as the central issues of the volume and the logic behind their order (I could discern none), all of the essays do touch on the issue of how Judeans (and Jews) from the exilic period to late antiquity responded to living under non-Jewish rule. The answer, predictably, is that it depended; our extant evidence demonstrates a diverse range of responses. While the title and preface of the volume gesture toward explaining this variety as rooted in the issue of identity, the essays and the volume as a whole do not, at least to my mind, clearly articulate this connection. What exactly does "identity" (however defined) have to do with a stance toward a hegemonic power or majority population?

Here I felt that some integration of theoretical models (especially postcolonialism) might have helped. Most of the essays in this volume attempt to slot Israelite or Jewish stances to their exilic or subjugated status into one of three categories: negative, neutral, or positive. Yet the interaction between a colonized population and its colonizer is not only varied but also significantly more complex than allowed for by these three categories.

The use of some theoretical perspective might also have helped to problematize the methodological assumption made in many of these essays that attributes apparent differences within a text toward foreign power to later textual editing by different authors in different historical circumstances. While this might well have been the case in some of these texts, it is also possible that an author was in fact ambivalent or had a more nuanced reaction to his situation.

This, however, is a strength of this volume. It joins a lively and growing scholarly discussion that invites us to consider more deeply and seriously the role that power played in Israelite and Jewish life in antiquity.

JUDAISM: DEAD SEA SCROLLS

Rethinking Rewritten Scripture: Composition and Exegesis in the 4QReworked Pentateuch Manuscripts, by Molly M. Zahn. Studies on the Texts of the Desert of Judah 95. Leiden: Brill, 2011. Pp. xiv + 280. Hardcover. $153.00. ISBN 9789004193901.

Martin G. Abegg Jr., Trinity Western University, Langley, British Columbia, Canada

Molly M. Zahn's *Rethinking Rewritten Scripture: Composition and Exegesis in the 4QReworked Pentateuch Manuscripts,* a revision of her PhD dissertation at the University of Notre Dame (2009), is a welcome addition to the discussion of what

John Strugnell at one time called the "Wild Torah." From this untamed beginning, to the current more subdued nomenclature ("Reworked Pentateuch") in the official publication by Emanuel Tov and Sidnie White Crawford (DJD 13, 1994), the debate has grown regarding the nature of the beast: Are these texts to be considered Scripture or are they not? Along the way, 4Q158—published in DJD 5 (1968) and virtually ignored for nearly thirty years—was recognized as a very important member of the group. Zahn has listened to the voices in the ongoing conversation (E. Tov, S. White Crawford, M. Bernstein, M. Segal, G. Brooke, E. Ulrich) and here returns to a detailed examination of the text of 4Q158 and 4Q364–367 to determine whether the answer regarding status might be forthcoming from an examination of the nature of the reworking.

After a literature review, the introduction (ch. 1) lays out the ground rules for the study. Zahn has chosen to categorize variations to her base text (the MT) as "additions, omissions, and alterations" (17). These categories are combined with observations concerning the size and frequency of the variations. "Charting along these various 'axes' (compositional technique [i.e. additions, omissions, and alterations], size, frequency) allows for a fairly nuanced description of the reworking in each particular text, while also allowing for easy comparison" (19).

Chapter 2 takes on 4Q158 (4Q Reworked Pentateuch[a]), which is also evidently the initial motivation for the study. Zahn offers a new transcription and translation of the document in appendix 1 (246–58) along with a list of unique variants in appendix 2 (259–60) for this text alone. The overarching purpose for the variations in 4Q158, which Zahn attributes to one single redactor/scribe, are to "strengthen or create connections between related texts" (73).

Chapter 3 discusses the remaining Reworked Pentateuch manuscripts, 4Q364–367. Here Zahn stands against the conclusions of Tov and Crawford (DJD 13) in two important aspects. First, on the basis of the physical makeup of 4Q365 and 4Q365A—handwriting, leather, and margins—Zahn once again combines these two groups of fragments into one manuscript. Second, on the basis of the compositional evidence richly detailed in the chapter, she concludes that the five Cave 4 manuscripts are related compositions and not five copies of the same composition. Again, the overriding concern reflected in the multitude of variations is "for the coherence of the scriptural text" (133), although she cannot locate any one redactional concern that would argue for a single editor.

Chapter 4 carries forward what we have gained from chapters 2–3 and compares the recent discoveries (4Q158 and 4Q364–367) to the Reworked Pentateuch we have known: the Samaritan Pentateuch. Although Zahn discovers that "all the compositional techniques identified in the 4QRP MSS are also attested in SP, except for paraphrase," nevertheless, "*quantitatively* there are major differences" (172). She details the lack of sizeable additions of new material, absence of paraphrase, and infrequent sequence changes to conclude that "SP represents … a more conservative reworking of the Pentateuch" (173). SP, more clearly than the 4QRP, has a prevalent redactional goal (harmonization) that gives evidence of a single foundational redaction.

Chapter 5 compares 4QRP to the Temple Scroll, a composition that clearly represents itself as revelation while reworking the Pentateuch to do so. But while 4Q158 sought to strengthen or create connections within the biblical text, 4QRP emphasized coherence, and SP intended to harmonize, TS is "for the most part ... organized spatially, proceeding outwards from the Temple" (227). Thus it could not have evolved from the Pentateuch but rather clearly evidences an authorial intent.

Finally, Zahn presents a detailed conclusion that should satisfy any reader looking to move past the details to get to the bottom line. Providing a review of compositional techniques and ideological purposes, it is here that we meet with that which is, for many, the main motivating factor for engaging in such a study: what is "the status or nature of the composition (in the eyes of its author or its audience)" (233). Zahn admits that a straight line cannot be drawn between particular compositional techniques and the status of 4Q158, 4Q364–367, although she "would incline to regarding them as copies of the Pentateuch" (236). How readers or hearers construed a text is at the heart of the status issue, and this will continue to be debated.

There is one additional chapter and an appendix that I could have hoped that Zahn had included in her study. The appendix has, thankfully, been provided in an article by Andrew Perrin: "The Variants of 4Q (Reworked) Pentateuch: A Comprehensive List of the Textual Variants in 4Q158, 4Q364–7 in Biblical Sequence" (*JJS* 43 [2012]: 127–57). Perrin has added to and corrected the variants listed in the DJD editions. The additional chapter is mentioned by Zahn herself as she writes, "a fuller analysis of exegetical variants identifiable in the biblical versions ... is also necessary" (241–42). I might suggest that the often maligned orthographic and morphological variants should also be included in such a study. This may of necessity be a multivolume work containing a nuanced description of the patterns of the smaller variations in 4Q158, 4Q364–367 as compared to the variants in the "biblical" manuscripts from the Judean Desert. Perrin's list coupled with the experience gained while preparing the *Dead Sea Scrolls Concordance iii: The Biblical Texts from the Judean Desert* (Brill, 2010) brought several such patterns of variation to my attention that may help inform a more focused profile of the "Reworked Pentateuch" manuscripts. Given the limited space and purpose of a review, one suggestive example will suffice. Elisha Qimron gives a detailed description of the morphology of the manuscripts available to him before 1986 in chapter 3 of his *The Hebrew of the Dead Sea Scrolls* (Scholars Press, 1986). In paragraph 311.13g he describes the *yiqotleni* forms with the comment that they "have no parallel in any other Hebrew tradition, and Hebraists disagree as to their origin." Now that the initial phase of publication is complete, we can make a global accounting of the occurrences of these unique forms. Of first importance for this present discussion is the fact that they occur at 4Q365 2 7 and 7 i 3. In the "nonbiblical" manuscripts from the Qumran caves they are found at 1QS 6:14; 10:13; 1QSb 3:20; 1QSb 5:28; 1QpHab 12:5; 1QHa 12:7, 25; 14:24; 1Q27 1 i 10; 4Q161 8–10 18; 4Q423 9 2; 4Q437 2 i 10; 4Q475 1 2; 4Q525 2 ii+3 5; 11QPs^a 21:12

(Sir 51:14); and 11QT^a 52:12. It is noteworthy that all of the manuscripts represented in this list are either generally recognized as sectarian documents or copied within the "Qumran Scribal School," except perhaps for 4Q525. Turning to the more than two hundred biblical manuscripts from the Judean Desert, it is of note that only three give evidence of *yiqotleni* forms: 4QDeut^n (Deut 5:22), 11QPs^a (Ps 119:2, 175; 121:7; 144:3), and 1QIsa^a (Isa 35:8), the last in a supralinear correction made by second hand. It may be important that both 4QDeut^n and 11QPs^a are themselves the objects of debates that are similar in nature to that which has been focused on the "Reworked Pentateuch." Some researchers have described the former as an "excerpted" text while the latter has often been designated a "liturgical collection." More studies such as this could be helpful in filling in some of the holes still remaining in the portrait of 4Q158, 4Q364–367.

Molly Zahn's *Rethinking Rewritten Scripture* is a critical next step forward in the study of these important manuscripts. In the end she alerts us to the fact that perhaps the most important benefit of such a study is not the elusive status of such texts but instead an appreciation for the "remarkable period in the history of exegesis" (242) from which they come.

The Dead Sea Scrolls: A Biography, by John J. Collins. Lives of Great Religious Books. Princeton: Princeton University Press, 2013. Pp. xvi + 272. Cloth. $24.95. ISBN 9780691143675.

Eileen Schuller, McMaster University, Hamilton, Ontario, Canada

The series Lives of Great Religious Books is described as "short volumes that recount the complex and fascinating histories of important religious texts from around the world." In the eight volumes now published and another fifteen in preparation, the series covers individual biblical books (Genesis, Exodus), well-known liturgical collections (The Book of Common Prayer), and more exotic compilations (Tibetan Book of the Dead). Each volume is a relatively short (admittedly, the volume under consideration is 272 pages, but the pages are only 5 by 8 inches, with rather large type). The series is geared to a general readership, not to specialists or academics.

At one level *The Dead Sea Scrolls: A Biography* is yet another introduction to the Scrolls, another in a genre that has appeared with unrelenting regularity since the early 1950s and shows no sign of abating. Going back only for four years, I can pluck off my office shelves books by Joseph Fitzmyer, *The Impact of the Dead Sea Scrolls* (Paulist, 2009); James VanderKam, *The Dead Sea Scrolls Today* (2nd ed.; Eerdmans, 2010); Geza Vermes, *The Story of the Scrolls* (Penguin Books, 2010); Craig Evans, *Holman Quick Source Guide to the Dead Sea Scrolls* (Holman, 2010); Philipp Callaway, *The Dead Sea Scrolls for A New Millennium* (Cascade Books, 2011); Peter Flint, *The Dead Sea Scrolls* (Abingdon, 2013)—and there would be others if I had more shelf space and a bigger book budget. As is standard in all of these, *mutatis mutandis,* the volume under consideration works its way chapter by chapter through the basic topics: the discovery of the Scrolls, their publication, the archaeology of the site, links with the Essenes, the Scrolls and the Bible, the Scrolls and Christianity, the Scrolls and Judaism. Each of these is handled with skill, erudition, and the sure touch that only a scholar like Collins could bring after years of researching, publishing, teaching, and lecturing on these texts and topics.

But this is not just another standard introduction. The reader will need to look elsewhere for many topics expected in an introduction, such as full lists of all of Scrolls and outlines of their content or a detailed presentation of what biblical manuscripts were found in the caves. In keeping with the specific focus of the series: "to recount the ... histories of important religious texts ... and trace how their reception, interpretation and influence have changed—often radically—over time," the book is more a history of scholarship than an introduction to the Scrolls per se.

In his first sentence Collins candidly admits that "the Dead Sea Scrolls may seem to be an unlikely candidate for inclusion in a series on 'biographies' of books" (vii). The Scrolls are not a single book but a miscellaneous—yet not entirely random—collection of manuscripts, and instead of being able to recover a linear progression of interpretation Collins must deal with a "post-resurrection afterlife" (viii) after a Rip van Winkle–like sleep of almost two millennia. While making the claim that the Scrolls now exist as a distinct corpus, Collins says surprisingly little about how he understands "corpus" and what is required for a "corpus," particularly given that he repeatedly emphasizes the diversity of the Scrolls and the dangers of reading them too homogeneously. More important, I am not sure if he thinks that the fact that this corpus comes "with a life of its own" is a good thing and a permanent condition or just a historical fluke. Many scholars today, from quite different perspectives, seem to be questioning whether there might not be better ways to conceptualize and to integrate the literature that is traditionally labeled Apocrypha, Pseudepigrapha, Hebrew Bible, New Testament, Christian Apocrypha—and Dead Sea Scrolls. In another fifty years, or even in the next scholarly generation, will we still be thinking in terms of a "corpus" of Dead Sea Scrolls?

Even though this is a "biography" of an adolescent, the bibliography on the Scrolls is immense, and Collins demonstrates a deft hand and judicious choices in what to include and what to omit, what to put in the notes, and what to emphasize in the very helpful annotated bibliographies at the end of each chapter. Sometimes a few more details would have been helpful. For example, giving the standard name and number of a text such as "A Dying Messiah" would have allowed the nonspecialist to search it out in a translation; even the specialist would sometimes appreciate a hint of where to follow up some brief remark (e.g., Collins notes on 109 that the controversial reading of *yolid* in 1QSa "has been affirmed more recently on the basis of computer enhancement"—Where? By whom?). Occasionally it does seem that personal interests have tipped the scale in a certain direction. For example, in the chapter on the Scrolls and Judaism, issues related to "Apocalyptic Judaism" are given over ten pages, while "The Scrolls and Liturgy" gets less than a full page (but now I am showing my own bias!). In his survey of archaeology, Collins acknowledges that it is "unfortunate" that de Vaux did not live to publish his findings in full, but little is made of the fact that after sixty years some of the archaeological finds (including coins, pottery, textiles) are still not published; perhaps Collins does not give this lacuna the priority that some other scholars do. Part of the distinctiveness of the book and its appeal are the personal touches, anecdotes, and asides that reflect Collins's own involvement with many of the characters and incidents over the years. His extended treatment of the difficult and complicated role played by John Strugnell, particularly in the late 1980s and the critical time of transition in 1990–1991, is intrinsic to the biography and handled with great sensitivity; I was less convinced of the necessity to rehash the Wise-Eisenman episode.

There is no scarcity of other topics that could have been included. For example, Collins uses the chapter on the Scrolls and Judaism to treat many key texts (Temple Scroll, 4QMMT) that are pertinent to the study of halakah and legal systems but says little about the reception of the Scrolls within the Jewish world, for example, in yeshivas versus Reform seminaries. I would have been interested to know if Collins thinks the Scrolls have played any significant role in the development and shape of the Jewish-Christian dialogue in the years since their discovery. Although in the preface (xiii–xiv) Collins provocatively raises questions about the ambiguous role of the social media, this topic is not taken up at any length. But it is good when the reader comes to the end of a book and wants more. Perhaps in the future Collins himself can be prevailed upon to return to some of these issues and to share yet more from his years of study and personal investment in the saga of the Scrolls.

JUDAISM: RABBINIC AND MEDIEVAL

The Mishnaic Sotah Ritual: Temple, Gender, and Midrash, by Ishay Rosen-Zvi, Supplements to the Journal for the Study of Judaism 160, Leiden: Brill, 2012. Pp. viii + 293. Hardcover. €123.00. ISBN 9789004210493.

Aaron Koller, Yeshiva University, New York, New York

This book is an English translation of a Hebrew study published in 2008 that bore the title *The Ritual That Never Was* (הטקס שלא היה).[1] The claim implicit in the book's original title, that the ritual of the *sotah* as described in Mishnah Sotah was never actually practiced, is an important part of the argument of the present book but explicitly the topic of only one chapter. The English title, *The Mishnaic Sotah*

---

    1. Yishai Rosen-Zvi, הטקס שלא היה: מקדש, מדרש ומגדר במסכת סוטה (Jerusalem: Magnes, 2008).

Ritual, bland as it may be, does better reflect the topic of the book, since Rosen-Zvi discusses many aspects of the ritual as described in the Mishnah. Still, referring to a ritual as by the text in which it is described (in this case, Mishnaic) rather than by the culture in which it was practiced (as would have been the case had this been called "the Roman-era Jewish Sotah ritual") already presupposes that what we are dealing with is a textualized, and perforce imaginary, ritual rather than a description of something that took place.

The book is divided into two sections of eight chapters (four in each section), preceded by an introduction and followed by an afterword. In the introduction Rosen-Zvi argues that many contemporary studies of rabbinic literature and culture that focus on gender issues and the body in general are important but are no longer furthering research agendas (10–11), since the conclusions of such studies are predictable and the results redundant. On the other hand, old-fashioned philology, an approach quite different from Foucauldian cultural studies,[2] has its own problems, both theoretical and practical, also discussed by Rosen-Zvi (12–13). Rosen-Zvi says that his study will combine the two approaches and the two methodologies, and indeed the rest of the book bears this out.[3]

The first section is called "Textual Studies." Chapter 1 focuses on m. Soṭah 1:2, which introduces us to the concepts of *qinnuy* and *setira*. The Torah itself does not specify any legalistic warning prior to the *soṭah* ritual. The Mishnah takes for granted, however, that such a warning (*qinnuy*) is needed and that this warning be followed by the wife's suspicious seclusion with another man (*setira*). As Rosen-Zvi shows, there are differences between the Bavli and the Yerushalmi relating to this issue; the Yerushalmi asserts that *qinnuy* is a laudable response on the part of the husband to earlier suspicious behavior by the wife; the Bavli, on the other hand, criticizes any husband who employs *qinnuy*. Rosen-Zvi argues that in the Bavli alone there is reflection on the fact that, if *qinnuy* is applied, women's movement in the public sphere is severely curtailed. The Bavli therefore frowns upon the use of this tactic. Chapter 1 is different from the following chapters in that it uses the Mishnah as a starting point, but its conclusions do not relate so much to the Mishnah as much as to the broad range of rabbinic literature (as well as Ben Sira and, briefly, later Hellenistic Jewish texts) on the topic of *qinnuy*.

Chapter 2 then moves to the topic of the "threat" given to the woman by the priest at the temple. By comparing the threat as given in the Mishnah with parallels in the Tosefta and the Sifre, Rosen-Zvi clearly shows that something is strikingly absent in the Mishnah: the possibility of the woman's innocence.

---

2. The term "Foucauldian" here is not synecdoche; Foucault himself makes a few appearances in the second half of the book (see below).

3. Because this book has been in print in Hebrew since 2008, there have already been some reviews. Of those I have seen, the most important discussion of methodology is Moshe Simon-Shoshan, "Between Philology and Foucault: New Syntheses in Contemporary Mishnah Studies," *AJS Review* 32 (2008): 251–62.

Relatedly, in the Mishnah as analyzed here, the purpose of the "threat" is not to get the woman to say "I will not drink"—which is something like pleading "no contest," in that it is not an admission of guilt but carried the same penalty as such an admission—but to get her to confess to her sins. What is striking about this is that the Mishnah seems to take for granted that which in the Torah the ritual is supposed to be investigating: her guilt. The possibility that the woman is innocent is one that is simply not entertained by the Mishnah.

This point is further elaborated in chapter 3, which discusses what is supposed to be the part of the ritual that prepares the woman for the *actual* ritual, the drinking. M. Soṭah 1:5–6, discussed here, describe how the priest stripped the woman and otherwise prepared her body for the drinking, but as Rosen-Zvi demonstrates, far from being preparatory, these steps themselves constitute a large part of the punishment—and the chapter is therefore titled "The Humiliation." Much of the novelty of this punishment is the spectacle inherent within it; according to the Amora Rava, men *may* watch the procedure and women *must*. Rosen-Zvi observes repeatedly that this runs counter to other, well-entrenched principles of rabbinic legal and ethical thinking about punishment (as seen, for instance, in capital punishment, now much discussed in the literature). All this makes the rabbinic ritual of the *soṭah* not just jarring to the modern reader but extraordinary within the rabbinic world as well.

Chapter 4 deals with the death of the *soṭah*. Again, that this is taken for granted is much of the point: "The Mishnah's narration of the *soṭah*'s death … completely ignor[es] the possibility that the ritual will not prove the wife guilty. This is particularly striking because the Mishnah is allegedly conducting an investigation whose purpose is solely to determine whether the *soṭah* had sinned or not." The second half of the chapter deals with the notion introduced in the Mishnah of the woman's previously accumulated "merit" buying her time before the punishment—in other words, a suspended sentence. Rosen-Zvi shows that this was not an attempt to explain the supposed inefficacy of the ritual or a covert way of protesting it, but is rather a stand-in for the possibility of a verdict of innocence. The Mishnah is so convinced that no *soṭah* can be innocent that it offers only two possibilities as to the results of the ritual: immediate punishment because of unmitigated guilt, or suspended punishment because of guilt with the presence of "merit." Thus, some women may walk away from the ritual seemingly unscathed, but this is only temporary.

With chapter 5 we move into section 2: "Contextualizations." We begin with the Tosefta here, which has a long list of *middah ke-neged middah* ("measure for measure") pronouncements about the adulterous *soṭah*. These include, "she adorned her face for him; therefore her face turns yellow.… she wore a belt for him; therefore the priest takes a rope of wicker and ties it above her breasts.… she gave him wine in cups; therefore a priest gives her the water of bitterness in a clay vessel." Rosen-Zvi persuasively develops the argument that the sin described is not the sex itself but the aggressive initiative taken by the woman; the punishment, in which the active party is the male priest, is designed to correct that. "Feminine pro-activeness is replaced by a masculine one, and the sexual act returns to its proper form—a masculine initiative met with feminine passivity" (139). Also included in this chapter is a perceptive discussion of how the *middah ke-neged middah* is usually deployed in rabbinic thought and how this case differs: "In all other instances, 'measure for measure' reiterates divine justice revealed in Scripture. Here, the text sets out to explain certain acts performed within a rabbinic ritual, not Scripture, by presenting them as a reenactment of the sinful gestures that triggered these punitive measures" (151).

Chapter 6 turns to the topic of history, finally tackling head on the question of whether the Mishnaic *soṭah* ritual was every actually practiced. Rosen-Zvi surveys the evidence from elsewhere in rabbinic literature (m. ʿEduyot 5:6 [Karkamit]; m. Yoma 3:10 [Helena's gift]; m. Sotah 9:9 [discontinuation of the ritual]) for the *soṭah* in practice, and observes that in no case is it practiced as the Mishnah here prescribes. In other words, there is evidence that the *soṭah* ritual was practiced in Second Temple times, but not the way the Mishnah describes it. Rosen-Zvi is also unconvinced by earlier claims by towering scholars such as J. N. Epstein that within our Mishnah there is an "early Mishnah." Instead, building on the analysis by Yochanan Breuer, Rosen-Zvi argues that, since the ritual is narrated with perfective verbs rather than participles, it is prescriptive rather than descriptive.[4]

Rosen-Zvi then moves on to argue that, not only was the ritual as described never practiced, but it was a consciously literary creation, in the sense that it is not the result of haphazard interpretations, inheritances, and influences but a systematic, unified ritual created in the *bet midrash* with certain goals and ideologies consciously in mind.

The focus of the book shifts in chapter 7. Having argued previously that the Mishnaic ritual is a consciously edited, systematically constructed ritual, Rosen-Zvi now turns to search for the source for the ideas animating this ritual. He finds the source to be Ezekiel's two descriptions of Jerusalem as an adulteress, with the vicious punishments inflicted on her as a result: Ezek 16 and 23. The chapter begins with an insightful analysis of these two chapters emphasizing the common patterns that structure both of them. The discussion here is rich, and I will emphasize that even readers with limited interest in the Mishnaic *soṭah* ritual will benefit from Rosen-Zvi's analysis of the biblical texts here. One central argument is that the search for real-life contexts in which the descriptions in these texts belong is midguided; "Ezekiel's eclecticism ... creates a hyper-punishment that humiliates, mutilates and kills its subject" (202).[5] Because the Ezekiel passages are not based on anything in real life, Rosen-Zvi argues that it would be a mistake to see

---

4. See Yochanan Breuer, "פעל ובינוני בתיאורי טקס במשנה," *Tarbiz* 56 (1987): 299–326.

5. See b. Sanhedrin 45a for the suggestion that a convicted criminal should be both humiliated and executed and the rejection of this possibility based on the principle of ואהבת לרעך כמוך.

the Mishnaic *soṭah* ritual as *also* reflecting the same underlying tradition. Instead, "the Mishnaic punishment is based *directly* on the prophetic texts" (208).

Concluding this chapter is a very interesting discussion of the Roman arena. According to Rosen-Zvi, the violent and vindictive descriptions of Ezekiel were "resurrected in the Roman arena"; the Mishnah takes the textual basis in Ezekiel and maps it onto the cultural framework of the Roman arena, producing a ritual with elements normally banned in the rabbinic world: "humiliation, mimesis, public exposure, injury, torture and revenge" (223).

Finally, chapter 8 moves to offer a cohesive interpretation of the Mishnaic *soṭah* ritual based on the previous seven chapters. "The ritual serves a textual locus for analyzing and publicizing the threats inherent to womankind and for portraying an ideal, non-seductive woman" (225). Marriage is not a major part of the ritual, and the husband and children of the *soṭah* are not major players, since "the ritual addresses all women ... since the problem it purports to solve is not adultery but seduction" (231). In the next section, Rosen-Zvi moves to consider the theoretically vexed question of "textual rituals," wondering aloud how constructing a literary ritual is meant to affect real life. "We may read Mishnah Sotah as a ritual devised to instill in the hearts of its audience awareness of the dangers dormant in women by presenting a 'well-managed woman,' utterly neutralized and exposed" (236). An afterword deals with the question of "the temple in the Mishnah."

There are many theses, claims, and arguments in the book worthy of further discussion, but rather than tackling any of the details I will conclude with a note about the subject of the study itself. One may be tempted to see something "Neusnerian" in Rosen-Zvi's approach. Rather than dealing with "rabbinic thought," he focuses on just one text and therefore may seem to adopt a documentary approach. Furthermore, he rejects a diachronic understanding of the Mishnah's composition, insisting instead on reading it as synchronically unified.

In part, this is true, but Rosen-Zvi is more sophisticated and nuanced in his analysis. He makes no broad claims about the Mishnah as a whole (until the afterword) but rather focuses on the description of one ritual within the Mishnah. He also is not dealing with "Tractate Sotah" as a whole—a tractate that contains numerous issues that come up "by the way"; Rosen-Zvi is focused only on the description of the *soṭah* ritual within m. Sotah. This book should certainly be taken as an opportunity to continue to evaluate these core questions, and more, in Mishnah research.

Finally, the translation is quite good, although I note a number of small issues in the translation and a small number of typographical issues that can be fixed for future printings: "polemic" rather than "controversy" for the polysemic פולמוס; a comment on page 15 assumes that the title of the book is still *The Ritual That Never Was*; "proximilty" for "proximity" (91); the mistaken "Scripture" (93 n. 116); "4–48" for "46–48" (top of the chart on 185); "Sotah" for "Yoma" (last line of 240).

In sum, this is an excellent, and challenging, book. The author is comfortable with both the fundamental tools of philology and the questions and methodologies of contemporary cultural studies. It is a major contribution to the study of rabbinic literature and a contribution to biblical studies as well.

Tertullian, On Idolatry and Mishnah Avodah Zarah: Questioning the Parting of the Ways between Christians and Jews, by Stéphanie E. Binder. Jewish and Christian Perspectives 22. Leiden: Brill, 2012. Pp. ix + 258. Cloth. $149.00. ISBN 9789004234789.

Michael Rosenberg, Hebrew College, Newton Centre, Massachusetts

When a field of research is riven into two (or more) camps over some fundamental issue, it creates a methodological question for any study in the field. How does an author argue her thesis in a way that can offer something to readers who may disagree with the author's stance vis-à-vis that larger question without becoming paralyzed by the need to provide caveats and alternative explanations at every juncture in the argument? In the study of rabbinic texts and the derivation of history from them, there are a number of such foundational questions, not least of which is the matter of what we can assume about the nature and extent of rabbinic "influence" in late antiquity. To oversimplify the argument: Do we take a minimalist view, seeing no clear evidence for rabbinic influence beyond the very limited personal circles of the rabbis themselves during this period, or should we assume that later history, as well as the testimonies and implications of rabbinic literature itself, likely suggest a relatively broad circle of influence? Any study involving rabbinic texts of this period, whether an intellectual history into some particular topic, a political history, or even a textual analysis and commentary, will inevitably come up against this scholarly dividing line.

In the case of Stéphanie E. Binder's *Tertullian, On Idolatry and Mishnah Avodah Zarah*, the need to address this historiographical question is particularly acute. Binder argues that the similarities between the two works named in the title of her book confirm the findings of scholars who argue for real interactions between the Christian and Jewish communities in Carthage and that elements that "seem Jewish" in Tertullian's work reflect real knowledge of and influence from Jews rather than "chance" (217). Binder states her position on the core methodological point at the outset: "The predominance and extensive influence of the rabbis, as leaders of the main stream within Judaism in the second and third centuries is taken for granted in the present study.... obviously I must concede that a comparison based on the hypothesis that the rabbinical movement was weak in Tertullian's time would lead to different conclusions" (2). In so doing, Binder follows what has become standard practice in the field, positioning herself clearly on one side of the debate and then proceeding to present her study in that context.[1]

---

1. It is worth noting, though, that Binder seems especially convinced of her own scholarly position and dismissive of her interlocutors. Thus, for example, Binder cites Seth

The book is divided into three parts, followed by a number of appendices. In effect, each part of the book narrows the scope of inquiry, beginning with the widest context and narrowing successively. Part 1 addresses scholarly conclusions about the Christian (ch. 1) and Jewish (ch. 2) communities in Carthage, a review of the scholarly debate about the "Parting of the Ways" (ch. 3), and a review of scholarship regarding possible Jewish influence on Tertullian's texts (ch. 4).

Part 2 focuses almost entirely on scholarship on Tertullian specifically. In chapter 5, Binder addresses Tertullian's relationship to Montanism. She maintains that "Montanism was neither a heresy, nor an entity separated from the Church" (56), in large part because "at least in Tertullian's time, there was no definite general character to the Church" (60). This is important to Binder's presentation of Tertullian as an independent thinker willing to deploy any strategy useful to his larger mission of spreading Christianity, rather than as a heretic engaged in some mission against the church. Chapter 6 compares Tertullian's ideas about idolatry to those of other contemporary Christian authors. Binder argues that Tertullian indeed uses similar language and examples as is found in other fathers but that he often comes to unique conclusions and clearly has different goals based on his social setting. Chapter 7 is similar to chapter 6, doing for Tertullian's place in a Greco-Roman context what the previous chapter did for his Christian context. Binder shows that Tertullian's use of Greco-Roman philosophy is typical of his general method, namely, a willingness to make use of any logical or rhetorical method that furthers his goal of spreading Christianity, regardless of its source. She also notes—though it is not clear how this relates to her larger thesis—the particularly close connection between Tertullian and the thought of Seneca. Finally, in chapter 8 Binder considers "the Jews' involvement" in the Greco-Roman world. Citing a variety of sources, often from different locales and historical moments, she presents a number of different theories as to the extent of openness towards "Hellenistic culture," though it is not fully clear which of these she endorses.

Part 3 is the heart of the book, composed primarily of her comparison of the two works named in the title of the book (ch. 9). She compares the rulings and instruction of the Mishnah (and other rabbinic works) and Tertullian's *On Idolatry* on a number of topics, including the observance of idolatrous festivals, commensaltiy, Roman entertainment, and commerce. She is careful in her comparison to note both commonality and difference between these two corpora. In chapter 10 she summarizes and makes explicit the historical conclusions she derives from this comparison and the historical context provided by parts 1 and 2.

Schwartz, E. Goodenough, Shaye J. D. Cohen, and Daniel Boyarin as proponents of the "modern view among scholars" (by which she means something like historical minimalism, but which is in fact Binder's composite of multiple methodologies that do not in fact require each other) (174 n. 189), then writes that "the opponents to this theory … are too numerous to draw an exhaustive list" (174 n. 190). Is this to imply that the four authors mentioned in the previous note represent such an exhaustive list?

Binder's extensive treatment of the state of Tertullian research in part 2 is certainly helpful for someone, such as this reviewer, whose background is primarily in the rabbinic texts and eager for context. Parts 1 and 2 are a useful introduction to Tertullian for a nonspecialist, though at times it would be aided by clearer guideposts regarding the relationship between the context in these sections and her larger argument. Her insistence on the complexity of Tertullian's writings and the inherent dangers in extrapolating anything about Tertullian's thinking from one local passage seems an appropriate firewall against simplistic readings that fail to take into account Tertullian's polemical and rhetorical tendencies. In particular, she reminds us that Tertullian's reputation for "hatred of the Jews" fails to take into account a host of passages in which he (relatively) praises Judaism (201).

Perhaps most striking about Binder's actual comparison is that, despite the title of the work, Binder makes extensive use of rabbinic texts other than the Mishnah in her study. Thus, she writes:

> I adopt the view that the Tosefta is constituted of passages which were elaborated at the same time as the mishnaic ones…. That is why parallel … passages from the Tosefta are taken into account … as elements shedding light on … the text of Mishnah…. As for the treatises of the Talmudim … they must be dealt with carefully … even when [the Babylonian Talmud] quotes the ideas of rabbis who are supposed to be contemporaries of Tertullian…. scholars are divided as to how far these quotations genuinely reflect the original thoughts of the rabbis. That is why quotations from the Babylonian Talmud will be used only rarely and with all due caution. (115)

Binder is indeed right to be cautious about the use of these other sources, but she often invokes them—and especially the Babylonian Talmud—in ways that nonetheless elide the significant gap in time, location, and political setting between these works. For example, referring to a passage from the Babylonian Talmud (Avodah Zarah 2b–3a), she writes that "since the passage is referred to as a *baraita*, it must therefore be no later than Tertullian's time" (84). In this case, the only parallels to the text are also Babylonian and/or late (and if there were earlier or Palestinian parallels, it would be good to cite those rather than the Babylonian version), making such a claim difficult to maintain. Similarly, Binder cites the story of Rabbi Abbahu and Rav Safra (b. Avodah Zarah 4a) in which the latter is claimed to be more expert in biblical interpretation because, as a Palestinian rabbi, he must reply to *minim* (whatever that oft-discussed word means in this context) and their biblical interpretations, whereas the Babylonian Rav Safra has no such debates, as "an example of what could have taken place in Carthage as well, where the African Christian community might have asked the rabbis to arbitrate exegetical disputes" (198). But there is no reason to assume that this story reflects anything like the reality of Christian communities in Carthage, when it is far more likely to reflect rabbinic projection of themselves as the ultimate arbiters of biblical interpretation. This overly broad use of rabbinic sources to think about second- and third-century North African Christian-Jewish interactions is distinct from, but related to, Binder's assumptions about rabbinic influence, in that both tend to lump together all Jews of late antiquity into one basically coherent religious group.

In the end, Binder's study, rooted in an approach to rabbinic texts so different from my own, makes me wonder about—and long for—approaches that, while still offering interesting conclusions dependent on one's methodological assumptions, also are explicit about the ways in which the study can be useful to scholars who do not share those assumptions (as is the case for this particular reader of Binder's book). Such an approach would benefit not only Binder's study but the study of rabbinic literature in general.

The Challenge of Received Tradition: Dilemmas of Interpretation in Radak's Biblical Commentaries, by Naomi Grunhaus. Oxford: Oxford University Press, 2013. Pp. xvi + 258. Cloth. $74.00. ISBN 9780199858408.

David H. Aaron, Hebrew Union College-Jewish Institute of Religion, Jerusalem, Israel

David Kimhi's place in the pantheon of medieval Hebrew grammarians is quite secure. Although not known for being especially innovative, he did provide all subsequent generations of Hebraists, Jewish and Christian alike, with a synthesis of the dominant methods of Hebrew philology as derived from Jonah ibn Janah's (d. ca. 1050) magisterial grammars, syntactic and lexical studies, as well as those counted among ibn Janah's intellectual disciples. Kimhi's role as a Bible commentator has significance predominantly because of its paradoxical nature in the history of Jewish exegesis. Kimhi managed to harmonize attitudes toward Scripture that had previously been considered stridently dissonant. It is this conundrum that occupies Naomi Grunhaus in the study at hand. Radak, the acronym by which Kimhi is also known (1160–1235), managed to bridge intellectually and emotionally the rationalist and traditionalist modalities as they had been developed in personalities as divergent as Rashi in Provence (1040–1105) and Abraham ibn Ezra, who contributed as both an exegete, grammarian, poet, and philosopher.[1]

Radak was deeply schooled in the rationalist approach to the study of Hebrew philology and assertively supported the philosophy of Maimonides when French Jews assailed the *Guide of the Perplexed* (1190) as heretical at the beginning of the thirteenth century. Even so, he regularly drew upon traditional midrashic solutions contained in the Babylonian Talmud and midrashic anthologies to elucidate

---

1. The proposed dates of Ibn Ezra's life have shifted repeatedly over the past century. One can find everything from 1089 to 1093 for a birth year and 1164 to 1167 as the year of his death. Moreover, exactly where he died is uncertain. One reads of England, France, and even back in Calahorra, Spain.

biblical verses. These distinct approaches had been judged antithetical when Saadiah Gaon's asserted that rationalism—as practiced by the Greeks and their Arab intellectual heirs—should dominate Jewish approaches to biblical interpretation and matters of theology. Midrash was seen as decidedly antirationalist and nonphilosophical. The *darshan* draws upon imaginative scenarios and a quirky, home-grown "logic. While midrash engages a rational formalism, it is without the principles of logical necessity that typify the syllogistic reasoning espoused by Aristotle in his collected works, *Organon*.[2]

The rationalism of medieval Spanish grammarians, which is so directly reflected in Radak's own philological works, stands in great contrast to the mindset of the northern French schools of exegesis, most strongly associated with Rashi and his disciples. Radak, Grunhaus suggests, was at the crossroads of these schools of thought, geographically in the French coastal city of Narbonne (the Languedoc region, close to what is commonly called "Provence") and intellectually. He would embrace both as if they presented no tension whatsoever. Why or how he could arrive at this position drives the study at hand.

The Challenge of Received Tradition has six chapters framed by an introduction, conclusion, appendix, and very comprehensive bibliography. Each of the internal chapters endeavors to elucidate typological framings of Radak's use of classical rabbinic literature. While there is value added through each chapter, little can be done to answer how Radak managed psychologically and intellectually to harmonize such conflicting approaches to Scriptures. In effect, Grunhaus provides the reader with a comprehensive analysis of the typologies of Radak's commentaries, but the sum of the parts does not exceed the conclusions offered by any single typology alone. The documents are simply not extensive enough to permit the scholar to transcend the paucity of Kimhi's philosophically reflective writings.

The introduction presents an array of historical concerns, treating each briefly (rarely more than two or three paragraphs). I was left wondering who Grunhaus imagined her target audience to be. The intellectual history behind Radak's own development is cursory, yet Grunhaus offers a definition of the most basic technical terms, *peshat* and *derash*, as would be expected of an introductory study. Those coming from outside medieval studies are not provided an adequate stage for grasping the drama that underlies Radak's fusion of rationalism and traditionalism. Intellectual antecedents are mentioned cursorily. There is no treatment of the history of place or the Jewish social structure in which Radak developed, except to note that Kimhi, unlike so many of the Jewish intellectuals of Spain before him, grew up in peaceful circumstances. Grunhaus provides a minimal sense of how

---

2. For a general survey of the hermeneutic principles in midrashic literature (the *middot*), see my "Language and Midrash," in *Encyclopedia of Midrash: Biblical Interpretation in Formative Judaism* (ed. Jacob Neusner and Alan Avery-Peck; 2 vols.; Leiden: Brill, 2005), 1:400–411.

Jewish, Christian, and Muslim hermeneutics involved a cross-fertilization of ideas both before and during Kimhi's life.

Chapter 1, "Statements of Principles and Methodology," explains that there is no systematic elucidation of Radak's methodological principles in his biblical commentaries.[3] Consequently the scholar must reconstruct Kimhi's attitudes on the basis of comments pertaining to an array of unrelated biblical passages. When introducing his commentary to Joshua and (later) on to Ps 119, Radak indicates a commitment to rationalism but expresses an equal desire to satisfy those enamored with traditional midrashic exegesis. The conclusion of the chapter is that Radak draws upon traditional rabbinic thinking when it serves him well but also that there is no way to establish just why he relates to midrash in some contexts and not others.

The next four chapters focus more intensely on typologies Grunhaus observes in Radak's commentaries. They are loosely dependent upon Ezra Tzion Melamed's still unparalleled study, *Mefarshey Hamiqra* (1978), which is acknowledged in passing (7). Chapter 2, "Rabbinic Interpretation as a 'Necessity,'" surveys those passages that bring midrashic or talmudic materials into a commentary as a dominant exegetical component. Not surprisingly, the embrace of talmudic discourse is particularly common in the context of halakic concerns, but halakah is hardly a dominant feature of Radak's commentaries, given that he did not leave us writings on the pentateuchal books beyond Genesis.

Chapter 3 treats what Grunhaus labels "Polarized Comments." They entail instances when Radak "juxtaposes two alternative interpretations dealing with the same biblical wording ... where one is a *peshat* interpretation and the other is rabbinic" (55). Grunhaus considers one of her more significant contributions to be the realization that Radak's use of tradition, specifically midrashic material, "demonstrates that northern French exegetes influenced [him] far more than scholars had previously thought. From Rashi, Radak appears to have learned the importance of including midrashic-type interpretations as an integral component in his commentary" (58). This thesis first appears in chapter 2, where Grunhaus judges Radak's methods as having been more "sophisticated" than Rashi's by virtue of his awareness of the Spanish grammarians, but still dependent upon him (40). Besides Rashi, it is nearly impossible to establish who might have influenced Radak toward his egalitarian exegetical practice. Radak hardly ever mentions other twelfth-century exegetes who freely combined use of rabbinic teachings with *peshat*. In a word, Radak's integration of rabbinic tradition is labeled correctly by Grunhaus "idiosyncratic" (40); his commentaries deny us greater insight.

In chapter 4, "Further Observations on Radak's Use of Rabbinic Interpretations," Grunhaus offers further reflections on a more subtle type of interpretive

---

3. Radak left us commentaries on Chronicles, Psalms, the division of the Tanak known as "the Former and Latter Prophets," and, from among the pentateuchal books, only Genesis.

modality that is not "polarized" but instead, "supplementary." In this chapter Grunhaus also shows instances where rabbinic traditions alone are cited to support or expand upon the *peshat* as if the *peshat* were not in itself strongly justifiable. Additionally, Grunhaus wonders with the reader how Radak could have been a supporter of Maimonides without integrating any philosophical thinking into his commentaries (82–83). While reiterating that Radak represents a synthesis of rationalism and talmudism, little can be added beyond description.

Chapter 5, "Challenges to Rabbinic Aggadic Statements," relates to passages in which Radak rejects or questions the validity of an haggadic passage. Grunhaus notes that there are relatively few instances in which Radak actually questions the soundness of haggadic reasoning. Most of the instances deal with the feasibility of a midrashic interpretation at the literal level or with regard to linguistic concerns. Additionally, there are times that he questions the haggadah but without making explicit his reasoning. The majority of instances, sporadic in nature, in which haggadah is questioned, occur among Grunhaus's "polarized comments."

Chapter 6, "Rejection of Rabbinic Legal Statements," draws attention to the same type of modality as has been elucidated regarding haggadic material, but specifically regarding legal material. In the final chapter, labeled "Conclusion," Grunhaus summarizes her findings. The chapter adds very little to what has already been stated in the body of the book. Grunhaus will again note that on the occasions Radak validates a rabbinic tradition in a haggadic context "his approval is almost always based on the tradition's efficacious rendering of a biblical text" (144). I am not sure how Grunhaus can use the word "efficacious" given that such a claim is highly contingent upon the character of the unidentified intended audience. A Maimonidean rationalist would not have found such uses of tradition "efficacious." In the end, we learn very little about what motivated Radak's choices. The notion that he was simply trying to placate those who were "lovers of aggadah"—argued early in this volume (22)—hardly proves convincing. We come no closer to understanding how Radak could have been so insouciant to the compelling arguments put forth by rationalists who judged midrashic exegesis irrelevant to the science of biblical interpretation.

The book ends with an appendix (149–54) called, "An In-Depth Analysis of One of Radak's Comments." The specialist and those familiar with this literature will arrive at this appendix and wonder why the entire volume was not written this way. Here Grunhaus demonstrates erudition and a sensitive reading of a complex exegetical passage regarding the so-called "Second Passover" during Hezekiah's reign (2 Chr 30:2–15). Why is this analysis an after-thought? No extended passage brought into the core narrative receives as thorough an analysis as these verses in Chronicles.

Grunhaus's 2003 dissertation, "The Interplay of *Peshat* and Rabbinic Traditions in the Exegetical Works of Rabbi David Kimhi," was a solid study confirming that she had earned her degree admirably (UMI 3089391). While there are many improvements in this volume, the ten years since have not yielded significant new insights. Ironically, Grunhaus herself has published articles whose conclusions are not well integrated into the present narrative. The question of Rashi's influence on Radak is treated better in a 2003 *JQR* study than it is in this volume. There Grunhaus elucidates a variety of passages in which a direct but surreptitious borrowing by Radak of material in Rashi can be surmised on the basis of marvelously observant readings.

Most of the profound questions about how Radak could live with an integrated approach to biblical exegesis go unanswered in this study not through any fault of Grunhaus but simply because we do not have sufficient evidence to truly reconstruct Radak's mindset. Readers only marginally familiar with Radak's biblical exegesis will undoubtedly gain a sense of his syncretistic exegetical method through this study. Those yearning for more substantive considerations of the intellectual history behind Jewish biblical exegetes will not find here a unique historical contextualization or consistently deep textual analyses. Perhaps Grunhaus will treat us to an entire volume at the level of her appendix—a volume she is undoubtedly able to write. That would be a volume worthy of everyone's attention.

Simeon the Righteous in Rabbinic Literature: A Legend Reinvented, by Amram Tropper. Ancient Judaism and Early Christianity 84. Leiden: Brill, 2013. Pp. viii + 249. Cloth. $149. ISBN 9789004244986.

Joshua Schwartz, Bar-Ilan University, Ramat-Gan, Israel

My first academic encounter with Simeon the Righteous was during the course of my doctoral research on Jewish settlement in Judea after the Bar Kokhba War. While studying the rabbinic sources on *Darom/Daroma* (south), I came across the traditions of the famous encounter between Simeon the Righteous and the young Nazirite who came from the "south" (Sifre Numbers 22; t. Nezirut 4:7; y. Nedarim 1:1, 36d; y. Nazir 1:7, 51c; b. Nedarim 9b–10a; b. Nazir 4b) who had become distraught by seeing his reflection in waters of a well in the South. I foolishly (!) spent a good deal of time poring over maps trying to locate the appropriate well or cistern that would fit the tradition.[1] While the specific location of the south might be important to the tradition, my zealousness at the time was certainly misguided.

Over the years Simeon the Righteous continued to occupy me. Every year my students and I study the geographic background of the Simeon the Righteous tradition (b. Yoma 69a) describing the (very theoretical) encounter of Simeon with Alexander the Great at the anachronistic Roman period site Antipatris. Does this tradition make geographic sense, or does the Josephan parallel (*Ant.*, 11.304–347) in which Simeon is replaced by Jaddus and Antipatris is replaced by

---

1. Published as *Jewish Settlement in Judaea after the Bar-Kochba War until the Arab Conquest* (Jerusalem: Magnes, 1986) (Hebrew). See p. 36 and especially n.15. See also Tropper, *Simeon the Righteous*, pp. 93–94 and n.34.

Saphein, identified with the present-day Mount Scopus, north of the ancient city of Jerusalem, work out better geographically? Both of the issues described above are certainly tangential to Simeon the Righteous. Amram Tropper, however, deals with just about everything relevant to Simeon the Righteous, whether core issue or even tangential, and he does so quite successfully.

In an ideal world it would have been possible to write a biography of Simeon. However, the very concept of rabbinic biography is a contradiction in terms, and no serious scholar would contemplate writing a biography of a figure who appears, for the most part, only in rabbinic literature. On top of that, in the case of Simeon there are actually only a handful of Simeon the Righteous sources in rabbinic literature, these never refer to one another, and only one source mentions a phase of his life, namely, his death. In view of all this, Tropper's goals are different. First, he offers a close reading of the Simeon the Righteous traditions in an attempt to determine how they resonated in ancient times and within their cultural setting. Second, he tries to glimpse behind the rabbinic traditions by investigating the process of the literary formulation that generated them. In doing so he seeks to expose the literary and cultural matrix from which the Simeon traditions emerged. Finally, he seeks to identify texts and ideas of both Jewish and non-Jewish origins that supplied the raw materials and literary inspiration to the authors and editors of the Simeon the Righteous rabbinic traditions. In the process of doing all this, Tropper shows how in reinventing the legend of Simeon the Righteous the rabbis created a distinctive vision of early Second Temple history.

The book contains seven chapters, an introduction, and a conclusion. The introduction explains why it is impossible to write a rabbinic biography and why the author is doing what he is doing. Chapter 1 ("The Rabbinic Traditions") is an overview of the thirteen rabbinic Simeon the Righteous traditions. Of these thirteen, only five will merit in-depth analysis and will serve as the major foci of the book. The other eight assume a much smaller role. The chapter presents an overview of all thirteen traditions in the order in which they appear in the subsequent chapters. The first reaction of the reader to this chapter may well be: only five traditions will be treated in depth?! Is that enough for a book? The answer, as the reader soon discovers, is a resounding yes!

Chapters 2 ("Simeon the Righteous, The Great Assembly of *Avot* and the Rabbinization of Early Second Temple Period Judaism") and 3 ("Simeon the Righteous and the Origins of the World's Three Pillars") deal with the possibly best-known Simeon tradition found in m. Avot 1:2: "Simeon the Righteous was of the remnants of the Great Assembly. He used to say: On three things the world stands: on Torah, on worship, and on the bestowal of kindness." This mishnah is the continuation of m. Avot 1:1, which sketches the history of the transmission of Torah from Moses to Joshua, the elders, and the prophets until the men of the Great Assembly. Simeon and the men of the Great Assembly serve as the continuation of the chain of transmission from biblical times until deep into the Second Temple period and beyond. Chapter 2 discusses the framework of the history of transmission, and chapter 3 the contents of the saying.

In chapter 2 Tropper discusses rabbinic and biblical chains of transmission in general, providing detailed analysis and a hypothetical reconstruction of Avot 1:1–2 based on chains of transmission in Neh 8–10 and on earlier rabbinic ones that preceded Avot 1:1–2. He does this also against the backdrop of relevant Hellenistic material. For the rabbis, Simeon and the men of the Great Assembly established rabbinic Judaism. To top it all off, the image of Simeon in Avot here was apparently connected to the depiction of Simeon the high priest in Ben Sira 50. The study of what many have considered a simple mishnah becomes in Tropper's study an example of the reinvented Simeon legend as well as of the invention of rabbinic Judaism.

Chapter 3, as we mentioned above, examines the meaning and history of the sayings attributed to Simeon the Righteous in m. Avot 1:2. Tropper shows how the attribution to Simeon cannot be historically reliable and then examines m. Avot 1:2 in relation to a similar saying of the second-century sage Rabban Simeon ben Gamaliel: "Rabban Simeon ben Gamaliel says: On three things the world is maintained: on judgment and on truth and on peace (m. Avot 1:18)." Although the two traditions are extremely similar, ultimately Tropper decides against connecting the two traditions and finally postulates a connection between Avot 1:2 and m. Yoma 7:1 that mentions Torah and 'avodah (worship) in relation to the high priest and the temple service of the Day of Atonement. The editor of Avot, according to Tropper, fashioned a wisdom saying that embodied rabbinic values but that could also have been articulated by a high priest in Second Temple times. Can any of this be proven? Obviously not, and there are those who do not agree and who will not agree, but in spite of the rather long-winded series of explanations, Tropper provides here a fascinating new reading and understanding of such a well-known mishnah.

Chapter 4 ("Simeon the Righteous and the Narcissistic Nazirite") continues the theme of Simeon as high priest. Simeon states that in all his days he has only eaten once the penalty offering of a nazirite; generally he would have refused, although he was supposed to have done so (Sifre Numbers 22; t. Nezirut 4:7; y. Nedarim 1,1, 36d; y. Nazir 1,7, 51c; b. Nedarim 9b–10a; b. Nazir 4b). As for the time he did, it relates to the story mentioned above of the nazirite who came from the south and who had been overcome by pangs of narcissism upon seeing his reflection in water. The first thing that Tropper does is to make sense out of the penalty offering. Simeon is not expressing a negative thought but rather a positive one; he declares that only once in his life has he enjoyed the rare treat of eating from a nazirite penalty offering, sacrifices that were rare because they were brought by defiled nazirites, which did not happen too often. As for the story of the nazirite shepherd from the south, Tropper shows how the character was modeled on two narcissistic figures from the past, Narcissus and Absalom. Simeon's positive appraisal of the shepherd nazirite reinterpreted the biblical nazirite in line with Greco-Roman ascetic ideals. Jews in Second Temple times made nazirite vows to subjugate evil impulses just as Greeks made hair offerings in times of distress.

Chapter 5 ("Simeon the Righteous and Alexander the Great") depicts Simeon as a savior of the Jewish people during early Hellenistic times. Much has been written about this tradition and the Josephan parallel (*Ant.* 11.304–347) in terms of almost any aspect imaginable, trying to determine which tradition was preferable. Tropper shows how there are numerous shared elements to the two traditions and that they are not entirely independent creations. It is even possible that the rabbinic tradition is derived somehow from *Jewish Antiquities*, in spite of the differences. Tropper lists seven significant differences between the rabbis and Josephus and then ingeniously shows how the biblical book of Esther and the festival of Purim tie everything together. His analysis is not only brilliant, but it changes the entire focus of scholarship on these traditions, which had seen Daniel as the background and formative influence on the rabbinic Alexander narrative.

Chapter 6 ("Simeon the Righteous and the Temple of Onias") focuses on events surrounding Simeon's death. Talmudic tradition relates that shortly before his death Simeon the Righteous designated a successor to the high priesthood, hoping for a smooth transition in leadership upon his death. However, the transition was not smooth, and the ensuing rift it created led to the construction of a Jewish temple in Egypt, the temple of Onias at Leontopolis. Tropper begins with an analysis of the historical information in Josephus that relates to the temple of Onias both in *Jewish War* (1.31–33; 7.42–432) and *Jewish Antiquities* (12.237–241, 387–388; 13.62–73, 285–287; 20.235–237). Unfortunately, Josephus is anything but clear and not terribly helpful, and his accounts often contradict one another. At best we can learn from Josephus that at some time in the second century BCE a high priest named Onias founded a Jewish temple in Leontopolis.

Josephus, moreover, never links the flight to Egypt of Onias and his activities there with the death of his father Simeon the Righteous. For the rabbis, though, it is a tale of a succession that went wrong because Onias's brother Simeon was jealous of him and sought to prevent the appointment of Onias as originally mandated by their father Simeon the Righteous. After a detailed analysis of the two talmudic traditions (y. Yoma 6:3 43c–d and b. Menahot 109b), Tropper examines them in light of foundation and transition stories in rabbinic literature and reaches the conclusion that the death of Simeon the Righteous was a watershed in the rabbinic rendition of Second Temple period history. Simeon the Righteous represented an age of glory when the temple functioned ideally and miraculously. Upon his death, it all fell apart, including the establishment of a schismatic temple by one of his very own sons. When Simeon the Righteous passed from this world, the miraculous gave way to the mundane.

The last chapter (7: "Simeon the Righteous in Second Temple Chronology") tries to make sense out of the lack of sense in the depiction of Simeon the Righteous in the various sources. When did he live and die? Was it during the days of Alexander the Great or during the Hasmonean period? One tradition even dates him to Roman times (t. Sotah 13:6). It does not help matters that Simeon was such a popular name. The sources, however they are explained, are hardly reliable for historical chronology. Tropper shows how ultimately they represent literary mosaics, as it were, whose components were culled from the vast literary and cultural matrix that encircled the rabbinic sages.

If there is one major point of criticism regarding this book, it is that the title does not do justice to its richness that goes far beyond Simeon the Righteous. Tropper, skillfully using all the numerous and relevant methodologies required for a work of this type, from philology and talmudics to literary, classical, and historical analysis, takes the Simeon the Righteous traditions and not only places them in their cultural context but does so brilliantly, engaging the reader with contexts and analyses that at first seem unusual and unexpected but by the end seemingly prove to be an exact fit. This is a fascinating work and important for all who study the Second Temple period as well as the periods of the Mishnah and Talmud.

The Targumic Toseftot to Ezekiel, by Alinda Damsma. Studies in the Aramaic Interpretation of Scripture. Volume: 13. Leiden: Brill, 2012. Pp. xxiv + 235. Hardcover. €107.00. ISBN 9789004229907.

Lena-Sofia Tiemeyer, University of Aberdeen, Aberdeen, Scotland, U.K.

This monograph, the author's revised doctoral dissertation, is devoted to the Targumic Toseftot to Ezekiel. It provides a translation and a commentary of the pertinent texts (Ezek 1; 28:23; 37) and explores their date and provenance, as well as their historical and social setting. As a whole, Damsma's study falls within the wider field of reception history as it looks at how key passages from the biblical book of Ezekiel have been used in Jewish mystical lore.

After a brief introduction Damsma surveys the manuscript tradition of the Targumic Toseftot to Ezek 1. This particular case is complicated by the physical absence of the key manuscript. Scholars have access only to Moses Gaster's copy of a now-lost manuscript, together with fragments from the Cairo Genizah. Damsma's study is based on the former because it presumably contains the complete version.

Over the next pages Damsma provides the reader with the Aramaic text accompanied by extensive textual notes and her own translation of the text. This critical text edition is a very useful tool for future students and scholars of the text. It also forms the basis for Damsma's ensuing commentary. The next fifty pages contain exactly that: a commentary of the text. Damsma goes systematically through the text line by line and discusses its content in dialogue with rabbinic sources, medieval Jewish commentators, and modern critical scholarship. She investigates the ways in which this Tosefta Targum interacts with and interprets the biblical text of Ezek 1, explores how it differs from other Aramaic Targumim (e.g., Targum Jonathan), and highlights the intertexts and traditions, biblical and rabbinic alike, that it brings into dialogue with the text of Ezek 1.

For instance, Damsma explores the relationship between this Tosefta Targum to Ezek 1 and the *hekhalot* literature. In her lengthy discussion of lines 23–57, which describe the physical dimensions of the חיות, she notes that their gigantic bodily dimensions, as well as the foot-to-head description, are reminiscent of a segment of the *hekhalot* literature called *Shi'ur Qomah*. Appendix D contains a helpful table that compares the order of the body parts described in *Sefer Haqqomah*, b. Ḥag. 13a, MS Gaster, and other manuscripts of the Tosefta Targum.

There are pertinent differences between the two texts. In particular, while the Tosefta Targum describes the appearance of the חיות, the *Shi'ur Qomah* depicts God's body parts. Despite this disparity, however, Damsma argues that the parallels between the two texts must be more than mere coincidence. This poses the pertinent question as to why the Targumic author chose to adopt the material from the *Shi'ur Qomah* in the first place, only in order to then transform it "in such a drastic way that even present-day scholars do not recognize its original source" (36). According to Damsma, the answer lies in the overarching goal of the Tosefta Targum: to satisfy the intended audience's craving for mysticism by giving them a small, "safe" taste of the real thing. Mystical knowledge was only available to learned, male sages. In contrast, laymen (and women) did not have access to it. This "taster" in the Tosefta Targum, argues Damsma, thus aimed to satisfy the curiosity of the latter group of people.

Another of Damsma's important insights concerns anthropomorphism. According to her, the rabbinic literature did not necessarily shun away from portraying God in anthropomorphic terms. On the contrary, the inconsistencies in Targum Onqelos and other rabbinic writings read in the synagogue demonstrate that corporeal presentations of God did not present a systematic theological problem for the rabbis. It is thus unlikely that the corporeal description of God's body found in the *Shi'ur Qomah* constituted a reason for the rabbis to withhold this literature from the synagogue. Rather, the literature was kept away from the masses because of its perceived theurgic power. Damsma concludes that the *Shi'ur Qomah* was known already in the late talmudic period but preserved for the learned elite. It found its way in disguised form into the Babylonian Talmud (b. Ḥag. 13a), a text that the Targumic Toseftot later reworked to fit their own purposes (above).

In other discussions Damsma highlights rather intriguing aspects of rabbinic thinking. For instance, she mentions that, while the Tosefta Targum to Ezek 1:1 mentions the knees of the חיות, other rabbinic sources dealing with the same biblical text take pains to explain that the creatures had no knees (see Ezek 1:7, which states that their legs were straight). As to why the existence of knees was a problem to the rabbis, Damsma highlights that having knees enables a person to sit down, something that contradicts the tradition that only God has a seat in heaven.

Other passages of interest are lines 66–74, which speak of Nebuchadnezzar, and lines 74–83, which deal with Sennacherib, two characters not present in the biblical text of Ezek 1. Both men committed crimes against the people of Israel, and both were punished accordingly. Damsma shows how these lines in the Tosefta Targum draw on extant rabbinic traditions, yet how they also contain unique material. The message of the section as a whole is aimed at the people in the synagogue. On the one hand, it may amuse them to hear about the pathetic fate of the two former tyrants who are now wandering about lost in the darkness.

On the other hand, they are being warned, through the same foreign rulers' fate, of the terrible consequences of seeking to know the secrets of heaven.

Damsma further seeks to establish the place in the synagogue service for the reading of the Tosefta Targum. At key points she discusses the transformation of the Targumic material from being an oral tradition to a tradition committed to writing. She also explores the theological standpoints of the Targumic author. For instance, how does he translate the Hebrew term for "idol" in a way that, on the one hand, indicates that foreigners (in this case Nebuchadnezzar, line 12) believed in them and, on the other hand, to preclude any uncertainty as to the folly of such worship, as well as to assure the audience that idols do not possess any divine power?

In the end of the chapter, Damsma points out that the message of this Tosefta Targum can be even better understood when taking its liturgical *Sitz im Leben* into account. It was traditionally read at Shavuot alongside Exod 19. In this Torah portion, God urges Moses to warn the people of Israel not to ascend Mount Sinai lest they perish. The preemptive reading in the Tosefta Targum of Ezek 1 conveys the same warning, in the sense that it aims to discourage the audience's interest in mysticism. What is offered is a strict glimpse of the heavenly realm, accompanied by warnings uttered to Nebuchadnezzar not to penetrate too deeply into the mysteries of the heavenly realm.

The chapter ends with brief discussions of the text of the Targumic Tosefta to Ezek 1:1 preserved in manuscripts other than Gaster's copy, for instance, in the fragments from the Cairo Genizah, as well as in several Yemenite manuscripts that are preserved in libraries and institutes of higher education scattered around the world. Damsma offers a translation and brief commentary of the relevant manuscripts, and she structures the textual evidence in a table so that interested readers can compare the texts of the various manuscripts. She also discusses the chronological relationships between the different manuscripts and identifies other texts that preserve what may be the same Targumic tradition: the *Arukh Ha-Shalem*, Codex Reuchlinianus, *Maḥzor Vitry*, and MS 7 in the collection of the Montefiore Library.

The next chapter looks at the Tosefta Targum to Ezek 28:13, a text that originally constituted the prophet's lament against the king of Tyre. Its synagogue setting is clear, given that Ezek 28:13ff. at one point constituted the haftarah reading for Gen 3:22. The two texts share the Eden setting and the motif of hubris, in the sense that humans try to be similar to God, their creator. This significantly shorter chapter begins, like the preceding one, with a copy of the Aramaic text (presumably according to Gaster's copy), the author's own translation, a copy and translation of the same text as appearing in Codex Reuchlinianus, a comparison with Targum Jonathan, and a line-by-line commentary on the text. The chapter ends with some remarks about the uncertain date and provenance of the Targumic tradition, yet Damsma tentatively suggests Palestine as its place of origin. Damsma further argues that, as the Targum Tosefta to Ezek 1 dealt with the downfall of a foreign ruler, so does this one. They may both have the same aim, namely, to discourage the synagogue-goers from getting involved with speculations about the *merkabah*.

The slightly longer penultimate chapter is devoted to two Targumic Toseftot to Ezek 37. The first one, paraphrasing Ezek 37:1–14, is preserved to us in the Pentateuch Salonika. The second one, focusing on Ezek 37:1 only, has survived in the aforementioned halakic-liturgical composition *Maḥzor Vitry*. Damsma's discussion of lines 5–6 of the former document is of particular interest. The two lines interact with the rabbinic tradition of the premature exodus of the tribe of Ephraim. Damsma notes the biblical passages that are thought to have given rise to this tradition. Further, in dialogue with key scholarly literature, Damsma suggests that this haggadah is unlikely to have been linked to the vision of the dry bones (Ezek 37) until the Amoraic period. There is thus no connection—as previous scholars have suggested—between this narrative and the Bar Kokhba revolt.

The final chapter, somewhat illogically named "Conclusion," does not summarize the findings of the monograph. Instead, it discusses the dialectal classification, date, provenance, and *Sitz im Leben* on the Targumic Toseftot to Ezekiel. The book ends with seven appendices, all of which provide useful background information for the preceding discussions: (1) "The Targumic Version of the Recovery of the Book of the Torah"; (2) "The Targumic Versions of Deuteronomy 28:36"; (3) "The Order of the Heavens in Rabbinic Literature"; (4) "The Stature of the Godhead in *Sefer Haqqomah* compared with the Stature of the Ḥayyot in b. Ḥag. 13a and in TosTgs. Ezekiel 1:1"; (5) "The Concept of the Macrocosmic Body in the Ancient Near East"; (6) "The Order of the Underworlds in Rabbinic Literature"; (7) "The Aggadah on the Premature Exodus of the Tribe of Ephraim in Rabbinic Literature." There is also a bibliography and an index of sources

This is a well-researched book that sheds new light upon the interpretation of the Targumic Toseftot. The discussions of textual and linguistic problems are sound, and the exegesis of key passages convinces. It is definitely a useful book for scholars interested in the Targumic tradition as a whole and in the chronological and textual relationship between the various extant traditions. At the same time, a reader should not expect a monograph, as this book does not have anything akin to a central thesis. Instead, it reads like a commentary to the various texts. As a result, it is difficult to summarize its findings. The one aspect that stands out is Damsma's discussion of the *Shi'ur Qomah*, emphasized by the extended discussion of the text in appendix E.

GRECO-ROMAN WORLD AND HELLENISM

Cosmology and Fate in Gnosticism and Graeco-Roman Antiquity: Under Pitiless Skies, by Nicola Denzey Lewis. Nag Hammadi and Manichaean Studies 81. Leiden: Brill, 2013. Pp. xiv + 206. Cloth. $140. ISBN 9789004245488.

Timothy Pettipiece, University of Ottawa, Ottawa, Canada

This book (NHMS 81) is a version of the author's 1998 Princeton dissertation on attitudes to Fate in gnostic and other Greco-Roman texts. Chapter 1 reexamines and critiques the old scholarly tropes that gnostics were "cosmic pessimists," while chapter 2 looks at the conceptualization of providence (*pronoia*) in "some" Nag Hammadi texts, especially the treatise *On the Origin of the World* and the *Apocryphon of John*. Chapter 3 deviates into a thorough and refreshing analysis of Pauline language of cosmic malevolence and makes a persuasive case that Paul's rhetoric of liberation can only make sense in this cosmic context. Chapter 4 shifts back to the role of *heimarmene* in the same two Nag Hammadi writings, while chapter 5 makes another deviation into Middle Platonic and Hermetic literature before returning with a double examination of liberation discourses in chapters 6 and 7. The book ends with a study of astral determinism in the more recently published *Gospel of Judas* in chapter 8, before closing with a number of suggestions toward a new understanding of the central issues.

The book as a whole is somewhat disjointed. I can easily imagine a far more linear structure, beginning perhaps with the more contextualizing chapters on past scholarship, moving then to Pauline exegesis and Middle Platonism, before zeroing in on the Nag Hammadi writings in particular. As it stands, however, the central argumentation of Denzey Lewis's monograph is often meandering and difficult to discern. It leaves one with the impression that it is not a monograph at all but a collection of loosely connected studies. Unfortunately, this disjointedness is not the only, or even the most significant, of the book's problems.

Let's start with the title itself. On a superficial level, I cannot understand why *Under Pitiless Skies* is the subtitle, since in common practice a suitably evocative phrase such as this typically precedes a more technical subtitle. More significant is the vagueness of the book's main moniker: *Cosmology and Fate in Gnosticism and Graeco-Roman Antiquity*. There is a widespread tendency in recent scholarly publications to market very specific studies under broad ambiguous titles. This book is no exception to that trend. While the reader might expect to embark on a wide ranging examination of cosmology and the question of fate in a wide range of "gnostic" and Greco-Roman literature—the territory that the title stakes out—instead the work presents a series of technical studies limited to a very small group of sources. This leads us to the second problem.

The selection of source material seems entirely arbitrary. As Denzey Lewis states in her introductory chapter, she has deliberately limited her focus to texts "I personally find most compelling" (7) and "what I find to be interesting" (8), without really justifying this very limiting decision. At the same time, she deliberately excludes Bardaisan's important discussion of Fate (8 n. 14) and dismisses as "tedious" treatments of the subject by patristic authors such as Methodius, Origen, and Clement (8). Proto-orthodox authors do make an appearance later in the book, but almost as an afterthought. This immediately undermines her ability to provide a broad contextualization of the central question—a context that itself is extremely opaque. After all, what exactly is meant by "Graeco-Roman Antiquity"? Technically this ought to include sources from Homeric times to late antiquity, when in fact the book's actual focus is almost exclusively on the second century CE, in the "apogee of the intellectual Renaissance that was the Second

Sophistic" (7). Yet even within this limited focus, Denzey Lewis does not exploit the full range of available sources. No mention is made, for instance, of the Greek novels (especially Achilles Tatius), some of which are intensely preoccupied with enslavement to Fate and were themselves products of this so-called Renaissance.

Also surprising is the book's use of the term *Gnosticism*. If the seemingly endless cycle of debates over the validity of the term "gnostic" has achieved anything, surely it has at least resulted in the jettisoning of the term *Gnosticism*, since few scholars in the field would now speak of Nag Hammadi literature as representing any kind of –ism. Denzey Lewis herself acknowledges the "increasingly controversial and problematic rubric 'Gnosticism,'" yet nonetheless uses it in an often inconsistent and unqualified fashion—sometimes occurring in quotation marks, sometimes not.

Setting these general considerations aside, what of the book's argumentation itself? To the degree that it can actually be discerned, Denzey Lewis goes to great lengths to distance herself from European predecessors such as Jonas, Nock, Murray, and Reitzenstein, insisting that the way in which these scholars characterized the later empire's cosmic pessimism is "a purely academic invention" (22) and seeks (ironically enough) to liberate "Gnosticism from the Burden of 'Cosmic Enslavement'" (24). The phenomenon of "cosmic pessimism" is seemingly so elusive that Denzey Lewis cannot decide if it exists or not. Even though she introduces positive evidence of perceived cosmic enslavement from the ancient sources, she later denies its existence. For example, in chapter 2 she states unequivocally that both the author of the *Apocryphon of John* and *On the Origin of the World* did hold notions of "cosmic enslavement" and sought to explain the "evil or 'chaos' of the present age" (51). In chapter 4, which is in many ways a continuation of chapter 2, she cites and discusses at length the very passage from the long version of the *Apocryphon of John* that clearly states that "fate" (*heimarmene*) is an enslaving power and "lord of all" (94). Finally, in chapter 5 Numenius is said to have introduced cosmic pessimism into the Platonic tradition (111) and that in the *Hermetica* "we can and do find occasions of such language" (113), as in the *Poimandres* 15, which explains how "mankind is affected by mortality because he is subject to fate; thus, although man is above the cosmic framework, he became a slave within it" (alluded to on 116). In spite of this, Denzey Lewis claims that nowhere in Middle Platonic and Hermetic thought "do we find a single author who considered himself to be enslaved by *heimarmene's* influence" (126).

How can the concept of cosmic enslavement be a modern scholarly invention and still be found explicitly stated in so many of the ancient sources? As a solution to this manufactured paradox, Denzey Lewis seeks to locate a "social context" in which to situate this attitude—again, she supposes, "if indeed one were to accept that any such thing existed" (28). The result is a reductionist postmodern conception of the "constructed 'Other'" (28) rooted in differentiating sexual norms (100–101). Therefore, in Denzey Lewis's analysis, any language from the texts that invokes an enslavement to fate is nothing more than a "discourse" about alterity and sex—the two core obsessions of postmodernist critique. As she says, the "rhetoric of 'enslavement to fate' ... exists solely within the context of insider/ outsider discourse" (85). In her view, it is nothing more than a dead rhetorical trope (92).

To be fair, I can certainly accept the suggestion that the ancient authors in question used the language of enslaving Fate to differentiate themselves from their rivals, even to underline what they saw as normative sexual values—this surely speaks to the texts' enduring appeal within later Egyptian monastic circles—but this does not automatically mean that the authors did not also *believe* in the harsh reality of enslaving Fate. How could they not? After all, if they were seeking salvation, surely that entails salvation from something other than their own self-serving rhetoric. Yet Denzey Lewis claims that "at no point ... does the rhetoric of 'enslaving fate' exist within the context of people feeling themselves to be enslaved" (101). Why would it? These particular authors (like Paul before them) are writing from the perspective of having been saved. Why, then, should we expect them to describe themselves as *still* enslaved? They have already found the answer and are offering it to others. The passage from Hans Jonas's *The Gnostic Religion* (254–55), which Denzey Lewis spends so much time and energy trying to refute, is meant as a general characterization of the late antique attitude to the oppression of heavens that the "gnostics" sought to overcome, *not* as a definition of the "gnostic" position. As Jonas also wrote: "The total gnostic view is neither pessimistic nor optimistic, but eschatological: if the world is bad, there is the goodness of the outer-worldly God; if the world is a prison, there is an alternative to it; if man is a prisoner of the world, there is salvation from it and a power that saves" (*The Gnostic Religion*, 261).

Denzey Lewis rightly criticizes earlier scholarly caricatures of ancient astrology as symptomatic of a late antique intellectual decline. Many early twentieth-century commentators chafed at the idea that the ancients could actually believe in an oppressive cosmic hierarchy. Yet her central argument, that "enslaving fate is merely a rhetorical stance against religious interlopers or competitors who offered competing religious or spiritual options" (137), leads her into similarly dismissive territory. The language of cosmic enslavement is simply "an ideological position" (137); no one could have *actually* bought into it. In fact, I see in her book each of the methodological shortcomings she attributes to her predecessors in the "Conclusions" (184). First, she states that scholars have tended to rely on an academic "line of transmission" for their interpretations, yet most of the work she seems to take seriously comes from fellow alumni/alumnae of the Ivy League. Almost no attention is paid to thirty years of French Canadian scholarship from Université Laval's Projet Nag Hammadi. Second, she claims that earlier scholars "tended to use sources inaccurately," whereas her selection of material is completely arbitrary and often incorrectly transcribed (see below). Finally, she suggests that prior generations used a "biased hermeneutical framework," even though her own interpretive frame is narrowly postmodernist in its orientation.

While the lack of a clear structure and argument in the book is frustrating, more distressing is the careless manner in which it transcribes and references ancient texts. On a general level, primary texts are rendered in a very inconsistent way. For example, sometimes Greek terms are transliterated, sometimes they are not. Often the original language is woven into the main English text and the translation put in brackets, sometimes the reverse. The Latin titles of ancient sources are sometimes rendered in the traditional way (e.g., *De Platone et eius dogmate*, 33), sometimes not (e.g., *de Facie Lunae*, 42).

More specifically, while all scholarly publications contain a least a few typos, here we find numerous inexplicable mistakes, many of which occur in clusters and cause me to wonder if parts of the book were ever proofread. For instance, titles are sometimes misidentified, as in the reference made to a nonexistent treatise of Athenagoras called *Legatio ad Graecas* (*Embassy to Greek Women*) (35), when the *Legatio pro christianis* (*Plea for Christians*) is intended. As interesting as it would be to have a treatise such as this, it is the result of a confusion with Tatian's *Oratio ad Graecos* (not *Graecas!*) mentioned on the same page. Latin passages are especially poorly rendered, as when Apuleius is said to have "considered fate *divinem legem*" (33), a grammatically impossible substitute for *divinam legem*. Additional transcription errors from Apuleius are found (139), as well as from the Hermetic *Asclepius* (117). Greek, too, gets misconstrued, as when a Greek text of Plato's *Timaeus* is wrongly transcribed and referenced (116). But most surprisingly, numerous errors in transcription of the Greek New Testament are present, again in a cluster (Gal 4:8 on 59; Rom 7:25 on 70; 1 Cor 15:40 on 73; 1 Cor 2:13 on 76). Surely these passages more than others would normally be checked before publication, since they are likely ones with which the readership is most familiar. Coptic texts also contain occasional errors in transcription (see 45, 132) and referencing (86), but here there is a degree of inconsistency commonplace in Nag Hammadi studies. In general, scholars tend to treat the Coptic texts from Nag Hammadi simply as surrogates for supposed Greek originals. As a result, Greek loanwords in the texts are regularly transcribed as Greek, when in fact they are a naturalized part of Coptic vocabulary and should be rendered as such.

I am not trying to be unduly harsh, but errors such as these should not be present in a scholarly publication, especially one in such a distinguished and important series as NHMS. Clearly, more care should have been taken reviewing the manuscript and proofs, although perhaps this in endemic to the increased imperative for authors themselves to provide "camera-ready" copy. A qualified (or at least more qualified) proofreader with even a basic knowledge of the field and its sources language could have spotted most if not all of these mistakes—especially something like Dodd's "*BIble* [sic] *and the Greeks* (113).

The back cover of the book states that Nicola Denzey Lewis "dismisses Hans Jonas's mischaracterization of second-century Gnosticism as a philosophically-orientated religious movement built on the perception of the cosmos as negative or enslaving." Indeed, she does dismiss it, but she does not disprove it. If anything, the evidence she assembles, as eclectic and self-selecting as it is, only reinforces this characterization and in fact broadens it as an essential framework in which much of second-century Christianity ought to be understood. It seems to me that the real contribution of her study is to reveal the degree to which early Christian ideas of salvation, redemption, sin, and even baptism, which so often seem amorphous and opaque, come into focus when viewed against the background of a widespread perception of cosmic enslavement. There are glimpses of this potential, as in chapter 6's intriguing analysis of Christ as a "Star-God" (136) and chapter 7's reading of proto-orthodox authors as cosmic pessimists, but it never really comes into focus. If the study had been more structured and incorporated a wider range of materials, as it briefly does when chapter 6 takes a comparative look at Greco-Roman savior gods, something groundbreaking and significant could have been achieved.

Crucifixion in Antiquity: An Inquiry into the Background and Significance of the New Testament Terminology of Crucifixion, by Gunnar Samuelsson. 2nd edition. Wissenschaftliche Untersuchungen Zum Neuen Testament 2/310. Tübingen: Mohr Siebeck, 2013. Pp. xxxii + 364. Paper. €79.00. ISBN 9783161525087

John Granger Cook, LaGrange College, LaGrange, Georgia

The external examiner of Gunnar Samuelsson's dissertation, Erkki Koskenniemi, was dramatic in his opening statement when he noted, "If he is right, then the contributions to all big lexica/encyclopedias do not agree with ancient sources and should therefore be rewritten or revised." He then warned,

> However, this is also where it gets dangerous. This book is going to be read, and it will be scrutinized very carefully. If it is graded/received well, then the respondent has made church history. But there is also an alternative. Everyone, who has studied classical philology around the same time as I, knows that there are two versions of a certain text, an older and a newer one, and that one should always take the older, "weil die neuere zu nichts taugt" (because the newer is suitable for nothing), as a German philologist once said.[1]

There are strong reasons for rejecting Samuelsson's call in this excellent monograph, which is a revision of his dissertation, to rewrite the lexical definitions of "suspension" words such as σταυρός and ἀνασταυροῦν and to give up the claim that there was a Roman concept of crucifixion before Jesus' time (21).

The first chapter (1–35) is a brief survey of previous investigations of crucifixion. Samuelsson defines crucifixion using four markers of the execution that he takes over from Heinz-Wolfgang Kuhn: "suspension," "completed or intended execution," "with or without a crossbeam," and "an extended death struggle" (19,

---

1. I thank K. Appel for this translation of Erkki Koskenniemi's opening statement at the defense on 21 May 2010, and I thank Professor Koskenniemi for making the statement available to me.

29). His intention is to exclude impalement, postmortem suspension, and hanging (28–29; see also 149, 175, 197). He calls his methodology "minimalistic," which is an attempt "to strip down the information of each text to its explicit features" (30) and not, for example, to read the form of Jesus' death into ancient texts. Semantically, instead of using one word to understand a Greek word, Samuelsson seeks to establish a "range of meaning" of a word through its usage (32–35).

Next Samuelsson surveys Greek literature from Homer until the turn of the first century (37–150). He stops there because "Christianity and its texts were becoming influential" (37). This is a rather mysterious claim, since he includes sections on Josephus, Philo, Plutarch, Appian, and Chariton, and he often quotes texts from Lucian (see the index s.v. [343]). His conclusions are apodictic: "none of the verbs means 'to crucify' and none of the nouns means 'cross'" (147). Samuelsson suggests that the vagueness of the terminology may imply that there was no defined punishment of crucifixion in the time prior to Jesus (147). For example, ἀνασταυροῦν commonly is used "with suspension of corpses, whole or in parts, and impaling" (144), while ἀνασκολοπίζειν is used primarily for the "suspension of corpses" and in some cases for "executionary, ante-mortem, suspensions" (144). The use of nails does indicate that impaling is not the punishment (145). Further, κρεμαννύναι is "almost useless as an indicator of crucifixion" (145). Samuelsson then makes the assumption that if a text does not explicitly contain *all* four markers mentioned by Kuhn, then almost every ancient text must be excluded. These are left: Herodotus 7.33.1, 9.120.4, 9.122.1 (προσδιαπασσαλεύειν and προσπασσαλεύειν are used), Diodorus Siculus 20.54.7 (does not use ἀνασταυροῦν or ἀνασκολοπίζειν), and the crucifixion stories in Chariton (3.4.18, 4.2.6–7, etc.). Josephus, Plutarch, and Appian are "left out. Their suspensions cannot, with any degree of probability, be labeled as crucifixions" (149–50). Whether this minimalistic (and atomistic) assumption is justified will be further discussed below. One need only consider a text such as Josephus, *A.J.* 13.380: ἑστιώμενος γὰρ ἐν ἀπόπτῳ μετὰ τῶν παλλακίδων ἀνασταυρῶσαι προσέταξεν αὐτῶν ὡς ὀκτακοσίους, τοὺς δὲ παῖδας αὐτῶν καὶ τὰς γυναῖκας ἔτι ζώντων παρὰ τὰς ἐκείνων ὄψεις ἀπέσφαττεν. Here it is clearly true that Alexander Jannaeus's victims were suspended alive and that the "suspensions appear to be executions" (103). One can conclude with a high degree of probability that this text is a depiction of crucifixion. Samuelsson's minimalistic interpretation in this example is too skeptical and renders his conclusions about terminology and the practice of crucifixion before the Common Era inherently questionable.

Samuelsson reviews Latin literature from "the advent of Classical language" up until the second century CE (151–207). His terminological conclusions (202) are that "*crux* refers to a suspension tool in a higher degree than σταυρός." *Crucifigere* does not only mean "to crucify" but "to attach in some way to a vertical torture device." "It is … difficult to uphold the notion that *crux* simply refers to the standing pole while *patibulum* refers to the crossbeam. *Crux* is the primary designation for a vertical suspension or torture tool. The primary designations for a carried torture device are *patibulum* and *furca*." However, although *patibulum* refers "generally to a beam, preferably horizontal, often used in connection with punishments," it only becomes "crossbeam" in Christian theology, and *crux* "did not mean cross before Jesus" (202). Samuelsson never proves that the verb *crucifigere* does not mean "crucify." Although Plautus uses *crux* in a sense that is close to "cross" (†) it refers to a variety of devices (203–4; see 172 and the discussion of *Most.* 359–360). Given his terminological conclusions and assumption about a text having to have the four characteristics mentioned above, only one text survives Samuelsson's sifter (206): Seneca, *Dial.* 1.3.9–10. Thus "there was no defined punishment called crucifixion before the execution of Jesus" (205). Several examples will indicate problems in Samuelsson's approach. In Seneca, *Ep.* 101.10–14, the philosopher describes an impalement (189–191, 203), according to Samuelsson. This is not correct, however, because Seneca envisions Maecenas eking out a miserable death while suspended stretched out on a *patibulum* (*patibulo pendere districtum*) and not the immediate death that a lengthwise impalement implies. In his interpretation of the usage of *patibulum*, Samuelsson neglects to use the fundamental work of Paolo Gatti (*Thesaurus Linguae Latinae* X/1.706.48–708.30 s.v. *patibulum*), only mentioning its existence in a footnote (286 n. 109). This results in the following key errors. For Plautus, *Carb.* frag. 2 (*patibulum ferat per urbem, deinde adfigatur cruci*; let him/her carry the *patibulum* [horizontal bar] through the city, then let him/her be fastened to the *crux* [vertical beam, in this usage]), Samuelsson unjustifiably assumes that the *patibulum* might be a separate punishment (174) instead of the horizontal bar that an individual carries before being attached to the vertical pole (*crux*, in this case). From a later text, Firmicus Maternus, *Mathesis* 6.31.58 (*patibulo subfixus in crucem tollitur*; fastened to the *patibulum*, he/she is raised onto the *crux* [vertical beam]), it is clear that individuals were attached to crosses while tied or nailed to their *patibula* (e.g., Seneca, *Ep.* 101.12 above). This is confirmed very clearly by representations of crucifixion from the ancient world (two graffiti by pagans and one by a Christian magician) that show *tau*-shaped crosses (see, e.g., my "Roman Crucifixions: From the Second Punic War to Constantine," *ZNW* 104 [2013]: 1–32, esp. 14 [the Pereire gem], 18 [the Palatine graffito], 23 [the Puteoli graffito]) and by the many texts that describe individuals suspended on *patibula*. In his reconstruction of the *lex Puteolana* (Augustan era), Samuelsson argues that *si in cruc(em) / patibul agere volet* should be reconstructed as "if he wants to bring the slave to a cross or *patibulum*" [201]). This is a philological impossibility due to the fact that in classical Latin no author ever writes that an individual was taken to a *patibulum*. One carries a *patibulum*, never a *crux*, in classical Latin texts. Better-grounded work in the Latin terminology would provide a better understanding of σταυρός when used in texts prior to the Common Era that describe Roman executions.

 Samuelsson then surveys the Old Testament and early Jewish literature (209–36) using David W. Chapman's key monograph, *Ancient Jewish and Christian Perceptions of Crucifixion* (WUNT 2/224, Tübingen, 2008). His conclusions about terminology (תלה [*talah*] and κρεμαννύναι) in the Old Testament is that the words refer to "some kind of unknown form of public execution — or unknown form of suspension of corpses" (234). No "suspension accounts can be labeled crucifixions in a traditional sense" in the Old Testament (235).

His chapter on the New Testament (237–60) displays similar minimalistic conclusions. The "gospel authors offer a series of brief and more or less non-informative reports" (257), and the "texts do not reveal what carrying a σταυρός actually is" (257–258). The Gospels "do not support the carrying of a crossbeam to a waiting pole" (296). Jesus' execution is not an impalement or hanging, and according to John nails were used (20:25 and perhaps Luke 24:39).

Samuelsson (ch. 6: 261–307) then argues against scholars who have attempted to list many characteristics that define crucifixion in the ancient world (e.g., scourging, attachment to a cross beam [*patibulum*], suspension and attachment to cross beam and standing pole, a *sedile* [294]). For Samuelsson, only these characteristics can be assumed: a public suspension, the object is a living or dead person, the victims were slaves or unfree individuals, the suspension tool could be "nearly anything," and the victim was sometimes "scourged or otherwise tortured" before suspension (295). Most of the events that the scholars label as "crucifixions" should be relabeled as "suspensions" (296). He gives an extremely skeptical interpretation of the calcaneum transfixed by a nail (297–98) and denies that the heel bone is "proof of crucifixion." This conclusion is a *reductio ad absurdum* of Samuelsson's methodology and indicates a misunderstanding of historical probability. The Puteoli graffito, for example, depicts a woman, Alkimilla, whose two ankles are attached on either side of the vertical pole (for images, see the reference in my "Roman Crucifixions," 23, and the original publication by Margherita Guarducci, "Iscrizioni greche e latine in una *taberna* a Pozzuoli," in *Acta of the Fifth International Congress of Greek and Latin Epigraphy, Cambridge 1967* [Oxford, 1971], 219–23, pl. 23b), just as in the case of Jeḥohanan ben Ḥagkol. In addition, she is seated on a small *sedile* (for which Samuelsson claims there is no textual evidence [295], although later Christian authors are witnesses to its existence, e.g., Tertullian, *Nat.* 1.12.4). Terminologically, Samuelsson (277 and 309) concludes that σταυρός means a pole placed in the ground but not a cross (†). Here Samuelsson passes over two fundamental pieces of evidence used by BDAG: Lucian, *Jud. voc.* 12 (which he only mentions on 278 in a reference to the lemma in LSJ and which he omits in his quotation from the lemma in BGAD on 276–77) and *Barn.* 9:8. Both authors assume that σταυρός had a *tau* shape, and Artemidorus, *Onir.* 2.53, assumes that it is made from several pieces of wood (see "Roman Crucifixions," 3–4, 12). With regard to the entry for ἀνασταυρόω in BDAG, "always simply *crucify*," Samuelsson argues that of eighteen texts mentioned only Chariton 4.2.6 resembles crucifixion (271–72). His conclusion may be questioned, however, if one is willing to concede that a text such as Josephus, *Bell.* 2.306 (οὓς μάστιξιν προαικισάμενος ἀνεσταύρωσεν), is almost certainly a portrayal of crucifixions despite the absence of an explicit mention of all four markers defined above. The phrase σταυρῷ προσηλῶσαι in *Bell.* 2.308 makes it highly probable that this account is of a set of crucifixions. The word *crux* is "some kind of pole," and *patibulum* is "a pole or a beam in a broad sense." "It could be used as a punishment or torture tool used in connection with *crux* and perhaps also as an equivalent to *crux*" (286). Samuelsson apparently rejects (286) the *OLD*'s definition of *crux*, which is based on the sum of the evidence: "Any wooden frame on which criminals were exposed to die, a cross (sts. also, a stake for impaling)." Seneca, *Dial.* 7.19.3 (cf. *Dial.* 6.20.3), for example, includes a reference to people on *cruces* and further specifies it by noting that those individuals spit on their spectators from their *patibula*. In other words the *cruces* had horizontal bars.

The second edition differs from the first primarily by the addition of material in the sixth chapter with which Samuelsson challenges the characteristics of Roman crucifixion adopted by various scholars (301–7). He adds a paragraph to his original conclusion (309–13) in which he argues that "[*a*]*bsence of proof is not proof of absence*" (313, emphasis original), which means there were punishments during the period studied by Samuelsson that were crucifixions but which left no textual traces.

There are only two clear cases of impalement in Latin literature that describe Roman executions: Seneca, *Ep.* 14.5 (*stipitem* [post] used in a lengthwise impalement, and Seneca distinguishes it from *crux*), and *Dial.* 6.20.3 (Seneca includes *stipes* used in lengthwise impalement as a form of *crux*). Hanging was not a mode of execution in the Republic or the imperium and can be disregarded (see E. Cantarella, *I supplizi capitali in Grecia e a Roma*, Milan 1991, 185 [one among many ancient historians who have come to this conclusion]). One needs to read the Greek texts that describe Roman executions, including the Gospels, using the linguistic precision offered by the Latin texts. When the Gospels describe Jesus (or Simon of Cyrene) carrying a σταυρός, for example, based on Roman usage they mean carrying a *patibulum* (since no classical author ever claims a person carried a *crux*). This is an old result, and there is no clear reason for rejecting it. The immediate corollary to the arguments made here is that we do have a fairly good idea of the shape of the cross on which Jesus was crucified (since it had a *patibulum*). The best word the ancients could find to render *patibulum* into Greek was σταυρός.

It is refreshing to attempt to approach each text de novo, without making grand assumptions about what ancient suspension was in Roman society, for example. However, such an approach ends up in a form of minimalism (better, "skepticism" or "atomistic interpretation" [a phrase of Koskenniemi's]) that is inconsistent with both the nature of language (for which one needs a synchronic or diachronic approach that uses many other texts) and historical probability (that considers the entire Roman practice of crucifixion in antiquity). There is consequently no need for *every* text to mention all four of the markers given above. If an author indicates in a context of execution that a living individual was suspended by a Roman authority, then crucifixion is a justified inference (impalement is extremely rare textually). Samuelsson's neglect of the graffiti (and the gem) is a crucial shortcoming that could be fairly easily rectified, but use of the images would substantially alter his conclusions. His work is not to be ignored, despite the criticisms I have made. It is a valuable contribution to the debate.

Attraction and Danger of Alien Religion: Studies in Early Judaism and Christianity,
by Karl-Gustav Sandelin. Wissenschaftliche Untersuchungen zum Neuen Testament 290. Tübingen: Mohr Siebeck, 2012. Pp. xiv + 270. Hardcover. €94.00. ISBN 9783161517426.

Erich S. Gruen, University of California, Berkeley, Berkeley, California

This volume consists of selective essays previously published, plus two written for the purpose, by the Finnish New Testament scholar Karl-Gustav Sandelin. The selection in general is a judicious one. The papers, although produced over a period of more than two decades, form a coherent unity. All of them deal with the issue of the meaning of pagan cult and cult worship for Christians and Jews of the first century CE. More particularly, eight out of ten essays explore the attitudes of Philo and Paul to participation in "alien religion," the other two taking up the same issue in certain passages from the Gospels and from the Revelation of John.

The first essay (2006) addresses the much-discussed question of how far Jews could go in participating in Greco-Roman religious practices while still remaining Jewish. No definitive answers are possible, but Sandelin performs a service in collecting a number of texts and instances in which borders were ostensibly crossed, such as enrollment of Jews in Greek gymnasia or the contribution by a Jew to a Dionysiac festival, and the divided reactions to such behavior that lack a consistent pattern. The essay constitutes more an assemblage of examples than an effort to provide an overall interpretation.

Sandelin follows with an earlier essay (1991) putting together various comments of Philo on the dangers of idolatry. The piece brings out nicely the diversity of approaches with which Philo exposes and expounds upon this topic: sharp criticisms of myth-makers, reshaping of biblical stories like that of Phinehas, assimilation of idolatry to the passions, allegorical interpretations of biblical narratives such as the golden calf episode, and the ambiguous behavior of Joseph. Sandelin perhaps plays down somewhat the ambiguities in Philo's own position, as for instance his attitude to Greek mythology, which is not purely one-sided. But he rightly sees the philosopher's intense strictures on idolatry as a reflection of temptations felt by Jews of his own society.

Interestingly, and somewhat intriguingly, Sandelin sets in the next place a later essay (2001) that provides a rather different and more nuanced analysis of Philo's attitude toward statues of the gods. Here, as he properly observes, Philo's approach is ambivalent and complex, not straightforwardly hostile. While he denounces the images as idolatrous, he also has praise for Greek artists such as Phidias, and he elaborates on this positive presentation by comparing the artist's creation to God's fashioning of humankind. The metaphor allows Philo to balance his adherence to Jewish aniconic tradition with his admiration for Hellenic artistic achievements. This represents a subtle advance on Sandelin's 1991 article—although he does not acknowledge the fact.

Sandelin shifts gears in the subsequent piece (1995). Here he focuses on a more particular topic, examining a passage in in which Paul warns the Corinthians to shun idolatry and uses the experience of the Hebrews in the desert as a model (1 Cor 10:1–14). Because of Paul's reference to "baptism into Moses," the verses are often taken as alluding to the sacraments and signifying that Corinthian "sacramentalists" were being rebuked for overconfidence, secure in the favor of the sacraments. Sandelin successfully overturns this view by supplying a range of biblical and postbiblical texts to show that the terminology applies regularly to the idolatry and apostasy of the Israelites who had offended God and not to any excessive confidence in divine support. The essay makes its point quite persuasively.

The next piece could perhaps have been omitted without much loss. Published in the same year as the previous item (1995), it makes some of the same points and has the same basic goal. Sandelin narrows the focus still further to emphasize a single verse in the same passage he discussed in the previous essay: 1 Cor 10:7. Here Paul explicitly admonishes against idolatry. Sandelin uses the assertion as a centerpiece to reinforce once again his argument that nothing in the passage alludes to overconfidence stemming from "sacramentalists." In an even closer analysis of the text, Sandelin makes a strong argument that Paul draws on pronouncements from the Hebrew Bible, even reconstructing a possible pre-Pauline text. The latter involves some speculation, but the general argument remains plausible. The essay does not, however, add much to the previous one.

Eight years later (2003) Sandelin turned again to this portion of 1 Corinthians (8:1–11:1) but confronted a somewhat different issue: Is it ever appropriate and acceptable for Christians to partake of food offered to idols? His scrupulous parsing of the texts results in a complex finding. He rejects both the idea that Paul distinguishes between eating at a pagan altar and eating in a temple precinct and the notion that Christian participation in such meals is merely theoretical. He concludes instead that the ban on eating sacrificial food is based not on the food itself (which can be eaten in other circumstances) but on its role as part of the worship of gods, for it could draw the unwary into idolatry. This seems reasonable enough.

Sandelin revisits the subject of Paul's strictures regarding Christian food consumption at a table with idolators in a new essay composed for this volume: "Does Paul Warn the Corinthians Not to Eat Demons?" Here he concentrates on 1 Cor 10:14–22 and the meaning of κοινωνία and κοινωνοί. Sandelin distances himself from those (e.g., Lietzmann) who interpret the phrases as signifying communion with the body and blood of Christ. He argues cogently that nothing in Greco-Roman culture supplies any precedent for the idea of theophagy, that the passage has nothing to do with the Eucharist, and that the context of Pauline statements indicates simply that the apostle warns against participation in pagan sacrificial meals.

The next piece (2005) rehearses material and conclusions that Sandelin had already provided in earlier pieces in the volume and puts them together to draw a comparison between Philo and Paul on the issue of consorting with pagan religion. With regard to Philo, he repeats some of his findings on Jews and Greek gymnasia, on Philo's blending of polytheism with the passions, and on his use of the golden calf and Phinehas episodes to condemn idolatry. With regard to Paul, he returns once more to 1 Cor 8–11. He reiterates his position on the apostle's resistance to Christian participation in formal pagan cultic activities and feasts because of the risk of idolatry and apostasy. Much of this has already been said in previous pieces, but Sandelin uses the occasion not only to draw the threads together but to show the notable parallels between Philo and Paul in encouraging conversion and warning about the hazards of apostasy.

A brief paper (1996) addresses the question of the absence of reference to idolatry in the canonical Gospels. Sandelin examines a few passages that might make indirect allusion to it. He properly doubts that Jesus' famous statement "Give to Caesar what is Caesar's and to God what is God's" alludes to the imperial cult and thus indirectly to idolatry. But he allows the possibility that Jesus' quotation of the Shema may carry such overtones.

The final essay, which was composed for this volume, turns to the Revelation of John and inquires as to whether it, too, struggles with the menace of idolatry. Sandelin investigates references to the "synagogues of Satan" and interprets them neither as Jews nor as Christian sectarians but as signifying the dangers of participation in Hellenistic cult. He does, however, take the "beasts" and "whore of Babylon" in Rev 13 and 17 as representing the Roman Empire or its ruler and suggesting that a major threat lurks in alien religion as exemplified especially by the imperial cult. In this way Sandelin is able to link the Revelation of John to his analyses of Philo and Paul.

The topic treated in this book is an important one, often alluded to but rarely explored in a systematic and comprehensive fashion. Just how Jews and early Christians confronted or adjusted to the practices of pagan cults that surrounded them everywhere in the first century CE is an issue of wide interest not only to scholars of Judaism and Christianity but also to those who conduct research in ancient religions generally. It is very useful to have Professor Sandelin's thoughts on the subject collected in a single volume. But the scope is restricted. The work does not pretend to be a sweeping survey. A large portion of it, in fact, concentrates on just four chapters in 1 Corinthians. Further, inevitably, since the essays were published over a long span of time, they contain a fair degree of repetition. Nevertheless, the author has put his finger on a key matter, with many ramifications, for the field of ancient religion. It will be left to others to investigate those ramifications.

NEW TESTAMENT: GENERAL

Handbook on the New Testament Use of the Old Testament: Exegesis and Interpretation, by G. K. Beale. Grand Rapids: Baker Academic, 2012. Pp. xviii + 173. Paper. $17.99. ISBN 9780801038969.

Pheme Perkins, Boston College, Boston, Massachusetts

This volume is a student's handbook to the New Testament theology in Beale's hefty tome, *New Testament Biblical Theology: The Unfolding of the Old Testa-*

ment in the New (Baker Academic, 2011). Readers unfamiliar with that form of evangelical theologizing may find sections of this slim volume puzzling despite Beale's efforts to incorporate other views of how New Testament writers use the Old Testament. It is a foundational principle of Beale's theological method that most of the New Testament readings of the Old Testament are anticipated there. A coherent biblical theology of salvation history follows from this insistence on a canonical approach. Thus from the outset Beale opposes scholarship that begins with the premise that New Testament authors are using isolated bits of the Old Testament in ways that are divergent from their original meaning(s) and dependent upon Jewish exegesis of the Second Temple period comparable to what has been found at Qumran.

Having introduced his position in the opening pages, Beale then insists that even brief allusions to an Old Testament text are sign-posts to the larger context. Chapter 1 defends against other approaches this maximalist view of the christological interpretation of the Old Testament that "christocentric readings reveal an awareness of the broader OT context and provide satisfying rhetorical and insightful interpretive and theological readings of both the OT and NT contexts" (8–9). Beale then insists that the analogies between New Testament and Old Testament are often marked as such in the context of the Old Testament text itself—if not in a specific passage, the echoes of that passage within the Old Testament canon can be brought in to make the point: "even if there were no such contextual intimations within the book of Isaiah itself, … Isaiah had generally understood the prior biblical revelation about Israel's coming eschatological ruler and David's heir, so that even if messianic nuances were not in his mind … he would not have disapproved of the use made of his words in Rev 3:7" (15). Because the typological methodology is part of a larger program for doing biblical theology, Beale presses the case for expanding its use beyond those actually given in the New Testament itself (25). This form of canon criticism also rules out the possibility of innovative or even contradictory voices within sacred scripture.

Chapter 2 treats the problem of criteria for discerning unmarked citations and allusions to the Old Testament more briefly. Beale largely adapts the criteria advanced by Richard Hays in view of some criticisms of Hays's categories. Finally, in chapter 3 the handbook turns to instructing students in the nuts and bolts of treating this topic. Beale's nine-step program is less dependent upon a particular understanding of biblical theology. Students are told to: (1) identify quotations and allusions, explaining what justifies referring to a passage or phrase as an allusion; (2) analyze the broader New Testament context; (3) analyze both the immediate and broader context of the Old Testament text; (4) survey use of that text in late Judaism; (5) compare the wording of the text in various versions (New Testament, MT, LXX, Targums, early Jewish authors); (6) analyze what text the New Testament author is using; (7) analyze the New Testament author's hermeneutical approach to the Old Testament; (8) analyze the theological approach; (9) analyze how the Old Testament text is being treated rhetorically. Of course, Beale has already tipped his hand on what he thinks a student should come away with at each step. For example, he reminds readers that he considers it more likely that New Testament and early Jewish writers are beginning with the Old Testament text and applying it to their own communities than that the New Testament authors are using early Jewish interpretations of the Old Testament (47).

Chapter 4, the longest in the book, surveys the ways in which the New Testament uses the Old Testament, particularly the categories of prophetic fulfillment, analogy, and typology. Indirect typological fulfillment expands the range of the prophecy–fulfillment schema in the New Testament beyond those instances of directly marked fulfillment (58). Beale further increases the reach of Old Testament texts in shaping the New Testament with such categories as prototype or blueprint as well as listing allusions as "virtually certain," probable, or echo (82). Combining all three versions of the "Synoptic apocalypse" in a single chart demonstrates the saturation of imagery from Dan 7–12. The attempt to make the same case for Isa 49–55 and Paul's letter to the Galatians as evidence for a "second-exodus restoration and new creation" focus in his theology is less persuasive. However, students should find his carefully detailed charts of the relationships between Old Testament texts and the New Testament helpful illustrations of the method.

Chapter 5 returns briefly to Beale's hermeneutical and theological perspectives. A theological claim lies at its core, "the later parts of biblical history function as the broader context for interpreting earlier parts because they all have the same, ultimate divine author" (97). Since Beale's canon-centered perspective on salvation history discounts the extent to which Second Temple Jewish sources such as the Dead Sea Scrolls are decisive for New Testament use of the Old Testament, he provides a brief chapter on the relevance of Jewish backgrounds. Beginning students will find his guide to locating these sources helpful but limited and outdated. Of course, for Roman Catholic and Orthodox students, failure to refer to the scriptural authority of the LXX is problematic. Some failures to "update" resources are inexcusable: the complete LXX Lexicon by T. Muraoka was published in 2009; Lohse's 1964 Hebrew–German edition of the DSS is completely outdated, as is Dupont-Sommer; the F. García Martínez and E. J. C. Tigchelaar, *The Dead Sea Scrolls: Study Edition*, and G. Vermes, *Complete Dead Sea Scrolls*, are sufficient. Students who are going to use English translations of the LXX or either of the two lexica should be alerted to the differences in translation policy between them. Recommending Thackery's Loeb translation of Josephus without pointing to its elements of paraphrase or mentioning the Brill Josephus project is not responsible. The Brill translation has deliberately sought a degree of literalness that facilitates the kind of detailed comparison and search for allusions possible.

The book concludes with a sample largely drawn from Beale's work on Revelation. He presents the use of Isa 22:22 in Rev 3:7, the "key of David," as the sample case. Using this example, Beale is able to argue both for the priority of the Hebrew text as the allusion and to illustrate the ways in which LXX and targumic evidence may point to how the text is developed in Revelation. Finally, the analysis is related to theological issues of Christology, soteriology, ecclesiology, and evangelization.

Although all students will find helpful hints to detailed textual analysis of the ways in which the Old Testament is interpreted and adapted in the New Testament, those not from Beale's evangelical tradition may be perplexed by much of this book. But students and professors who share his theological and hermeneutical assumptions will welcome this new teaching resource.

An Introduction to the New Testament: History, Literature, Theology, by Eugene M. Boring. Louisville: Westminster John Knox, 2012. Pp. xxxiv + 722. Paperback. $50.00. ISBN 9780664255923.

Pheme Perkins, Boston College, Chestnut Hill, Massachusetts

M. Eugene Boring, professor emeritus of New Testament at Brite Divinity School at Texas Christian University, known for his initial work on early Christian prophecy and the formation of the Synoptic tradition, the *Hellenistic Commentary on the New Testament* edited with Klaus Berger and Carsten Colpe, as well as commentaries for seminary students and pastors on Mark, Revelation, 1 Peter, and Matthew, has incorporated a lifetime of research and teaching in this sizable volume. In addition, the author has supplied over half of the excellent black and white photographs from his own collection The subtitle reflects the overall approach: presenting the writings of the New Testament as embedded in the history and literature of their times illuminates their theological significance. The designation "literature" also anticipates Boring's presentation of all the New Testament writings including the epistles and Revelation as "this-worldly narratives that deal with transcendent events and perspectives" (5).

Anyone familiar with Boring's work on the Synoptic Gospels will not be surprised to find him insisting from the outset that students develop into hands-on practitioners of the critical method. He provides detailed summaries of the development of scholarly positions on such debated topics as the Synoptic problem, the compilation of Pauline epistles, pseudepigraphy, and issues of dating and context. The treatment of views contrary to his own allows room for disagreement. For example, Boring considers the Two Document Hypothesis the best working solution to the Synoptic problem. However the nature of the material leaves room for alternatives: "authors/editors were utilizing somewhat unstable versions and editions of both Mark and Q, while interacting with continuing oral tradition. Some documents may not have been composed in their present form all at once but may have gone through more than one edition" (503). In keeping with his stated hands-on learning approach, Boring provides detailed instructions for a tricolor scheme of marking up Synoptic parallels (504–5).

The first five chapters deal with a series of "what is it?" issues. Chapter 1 treats the expression "New Testament," its narrative character, and the relationship of that story to the macro-narrative of the Bible as a whole. Chapter 2 emphasizes the relationship between the New Testament and the community of faith in which it was composed, edited, and transmitted to later generations. Boring rejects the view that the canon originated primarily as a reaction to theological views that the community found unacceptable: "The formation of the canon was not primarily reactive, but proactive, as the church sought for an adequate means to express its own developing faith" (19). Chapter 3 takes readers into the world of textual criticism. Chapter 4 discusses biblical translations from the Septuagint to the NRSV and other contemporary translation projects. Finally, chapter 5 returns to the relationship between the Bible and the church, which has interpreted it through the centuries. *Sola scriptura* is not a principle that should separate the text from the communities of believers who have prayed, theologized, and lived with the text down through the centuries. Boring also provides a brief historical survey of interpretation strategies from reinterpretation within the Old Testament itself up to the varied contemporary hermeneutical lenses students are likely to encounter.

The next four chapters are historical. Chapter 6 surveys the Hellenistic world of the New Testament from the perspective of Hellenization and Roman influences in Syro-Palestine. Chapter 7 provides a fairly standard "Jewish backgrounds" discussion. Boring's treatment of apocalyptic is firmly rooted in the political understanding: "unwilling to surrender Israel's faith in the one true God who is finally the God of justice, unwilling to assign ultimate power to the penultimate unjust powers of this world" (108). Chapter 8, "Jesus within Judaism," surveys the various forms that the "quest for the historical Jesus" has taken since the eighteenth century, followed by Boring's view of what can be known about the historical Jesus. He does not provide arguments for the items in this depiction. Finally, chapter 9 fills in the story of the earliest believers from Jesus' death circa 30 CE to Paul's founding of the church in Corinth circa 50 CE. It includes a stock survey of assorted religious cults and philosophical movements. Deciding to add that dimension of the "religious world" to this chapter leads Boring away from his stated chronological parameters to an unnecessary survey of Gnosticism (158–62).

Although Boring's historical survey has set the stage to begin the discussion of the individual New Testament writings with the Pauline epistles in chapter 10, on Paul's life and the nature of the letters, he treats all of the New Testament letters except 1–3 John before turning to the Gospels. This move matches his identification of four branches of Christianity that emerged from the original Jerusalem church and became evident in Antioch: (1) a traditional Jewish form of Christianity represented by James; (2) a more moderate view represented by Peter; (3) a "Hellenist" group that advocated relaxing requirements for Gentiles represented by Stephen and Philip; and (4) an early effort among Gentiles represented by Paul and Barnabas in Damascus and Cilicia (189). Paul was involved with all four groups. The theology reflected in his earliest epistle, 1 Thessalonians, reflects the years of dialogue in this period. Boring thinks that Paul's basic theological motifs in Christology, soteriology, mission theology, relation to the synagogue, and sacraments emerged prior to the epistles period.

Chapter 11 treats 1 Thessalonians, Philippians, and Philemon as "early Aegean mission." Chapter 12, on the Corinthian correspondence, incorporates an extensive excursus on the composition of 2 Corinthians. Boring defends a five-letter reconstruction that treats 2 Cor 8 as the earliest (254–65). Chapter 13 presents Galatians and Romans together as Paul's last letters. Boring then turns to the letters that derive from the Pauline school associated with Ephesus—Colossians, Ephesians and 2 Thessalonians—in chapters 14 and 15 and the Pastoral Epistles in chapter 16.

Chapter 17 shifts from letters associated with Paul to the adoption of the form in 1 Peter. Relying on the late first- or early second-century tradition of Rome as heir to the traditions of both Peter and Paul, Boring treats Christianity there as a "consolidation of traditions" and shoehorns the nonepistle Hebrews into this chapter. James, Jude and 2 Peter form the topic of chapter 18. Boring thinks that James knew a Pauline letter collection and some version of the sayings tradition employed in the Synoptic Gospels. Though attributed to James, the brother of the Lord, Boring attributes it to an author writing in Rome near the end of the first century. Jude also derives from second- or third-generation Christians in that city, as does 2 Peter somewhat later. Summarizing the picture of Christianity in Rome that emerges from these letters, "a unity without uniformity ... mostly poor Gentiles with strong Jewish roots," leads Boring to the surprising conclusion that material from a collection of Jesus' sayings was known in Rome, "but there is no indication of a connected narrative of Jesus' life until later" (464).

Chapter 19 introduces the basics of Synoptic criticism before readers finally reach a discussion of the Gospel of Mark in chapter 20 on page 507! Chapter 21 summarizes the theology of Mark's Gospel. Chapter 22 treats the Gospel of Matthew. Chapters 23 and 24 discuss the Gospel of Luke and the Acts of the Apostles. Boring sides with those scholars who think that Acts was composed at the end of the first century by an author familiar with not only a Pauline letter collection but 1 Peter, 1 Clement, Hebrews, and the Jewish historian Josephus (579). He details the elaborate parallelism between Peter and Paul in Acts but devotes less space to how Luke anticipates Paul's martyrdom by shaping details of Paul's final journey to and suffering in Jerusalem to echo the story of Jesus in Luke's Gospel.

Finally, Boring lumps the Gospel of John, the Johannine Epistles, and Revelation together in chapters 25–27. The idiosyncratic "letters first" before "Gospel" structure reappears. As "letters" Revelation and the Johannine Epistles are treated before a discussion of the Fourth Gospel concludes this survey of the New Testament writings. For readers with any energy left, Boring adds a brief epilogue on the New Testament as God's word in chapter 28.

Professor Boring provides students with a theological content summary of each book in the New Testament divided by topical section headings much as one finds in the familiar study Bibles. That strategy undoubtedly serves the interests of future pastors and theology students. However, it does mean that the book outlines reflect a sequence of topics rather than rhetorical or literary features. The range of scholarly literature from the early days of biblical criticism up to the present represented in the text, some longer footnotes, and the Suggested Reading at the end of each chapter is stunning. It is not there for show. Boring has digested all of it. In such an ambitious treatment, everyone will find points of disagreement with particular positions that Boring adopts. He often anticipates that possibility and provides the reasons that some scholars hold other positions.

Seminary students who aim to continue in advanced degree programs will be well served by this introduction to the New Testament. Every aspect of critical scholarship turns up in its pages. Boring writes clearly and precisely. However, the length of treatment and level of English is a bit too much for younger undergraduates, most second-career MTS or pastoral ministry students, and the growing population of students from Africa, Korea, and others for whom English is a second or third language. Even for those students able to meet the challenge this book poses, the arrangement invites revolt—or complaints on course evaluations. They come to the introductory course wanting Jesus and the Gospels and perhaps major Pauline epistles along with Revelation. Fortunately, it is possible to take the chapters out of order so that students are not kept waiting until the rushed final weeks of the term to read a Gospel.

Coping with Violence in the New Testament, edited by Pieter G.R. de Villiers and Jan Willem van Henten. Studies in Theology and Religion 16. Leiden: Brill, 2012. Pp. x + 305. Hardcover. $135.00. ISBN 9789004221048.

James Hanson, St. Olaf College, Northfield, Minnesota

According to the preface, this collection of essays, which came out of a conference on violence in the New Testament that took place in Stellenbosch, South Africa, "aims to contribute to the recent scholarly debate about the interconnections between violence and monotheistic religions by analyzing the role of violence in the New Testament as well as by offering some hermeneutical perspectives on violence as it is articulated in the earliest Christian writings" (ix). The scholars represent The Netherlands, Belgium, and South Africa—countries that, as the volume notes, share interesting historical and cultural bonds. While the opening essay does attempt to set the collection in this wider context of the connection between violence and monotheism, for the most part the individual contributions focus on very particular exegetical questions raised by Paul's letters, Jesus and the Gospels, and Revelation.

The collection is divided into three sections: "Introductory Essays," "Case Studies," and an "Epilogue." The first essay, "Religion, Bible and Violence," as noted, deals with the more general issue of the relationship between violence and religion and attempts to arrive at a definition of violence that, it is presumed, will inform the ensuing pieces. Author Jan Willem van Henten, one of the editors of the volume, begins by noting the tension between religion's role in legitimizing or inspiring violence, on the one hand, and the way it can serve as "an important mediating and healing factor, which helps people cope with the

experiences of violence" (4). It is an insightful and potentially framing observation, but van Henten does not develop it. Instead, he offers "a brief and personal
impression of some of the theories about religion and violence that are relevant
for our theme." Included are discussions of René Girard's theories of scapegoating and mimesis, Regina Schwartz's work connecting violence and monotheism,
Mark Juergensmeyer's emphasis on the role that conceptions of "cosmic war"
play in violent actions, and J. Harold Ellens's observations about God as divine
warrior in both Testaments.

Although the opening essay is a helpful discussion of these approaches, the
piece does not serve to frame the volume as effectively as it might; I would suggest
reading the first few sections of the closing essay, "Hermeneutical Perspectives
on Violence in the New Testament" (247–73), by co-editor Peter G. R. de Villiers, which frames the question in terms of the traditional distinction between
the Hebrew Bible's violent nature and the New Testament's emphasis on peace,
nonviolence, and love. De Villiers notes that New Testament scholarship in the
most recent decades has called this deeply entrenched belief into question, beginning with Revelation and its depiction of a vengeful, wrathful God, but extending
also, especially when one defines violence in more than strictly physical terms, to
violent aspects of other writings, including the Gospels and Paul.

The second introductory essay, "Violence in the New Testament and the
Roman Empire: Ambivalence, Othering, Agency," by Jeremy Punt, explores what
the author considers a "neglected factor" in scholarship on the issue: that "the
violent setting of the first century CE influenced and contributed to the shaping of the New Testament documents' appropriation of violence-related issues"
(29). The essay proves helpful by calling attention to different forms of violence,
thus broadening the scope. For example, the very act of determining boundaries
between "insiders" and "outsiders," something fundamental to the founding of
the early church communities, contains within it a form of violence as well as the
seeds of other forms (32–33).

The second, and principal section of the volume presents "case studies" of
violent aspects of and themes in the New Testament. Of the nine essays in this
section, three deal with Paul's letters (one of these with the Pastorals), three treat
questions raised in and by the Gospels, and three address the violent imagery
in Revelation.

Perhaps not surprisingly, the essays on violence in Paul raise some of the
most intriguing questions, since his letters are not the first to come to mind when
the topic is broached. In fact, Andries van Aarde views Rom 12:29 as "Paul's Version of 'Turning the Other Cheek'" (43–68), which for van Aarde is the end result
of a development traceable from 1 Thessalonians, which represents a less-tolerant
Paul, through Galatians, which extends deeds of love to all people (6:10), "until
Paul not only articulates, but also internalizes his own version of Jesus' well-
known expression of 'turning the other cheek' in his last letter (i.e., in Romans)"
(48). Francois Tolmie, on the other hand, more directly addresses the question
of violence in Paul's letter to the Galatians (69–82). He does indeed find that

Paul engages in a "violent rhetoric," largely through the vilification of and threats against his opponents (74–75), but in the end Tolmie seems to let Paul off the hook by suggesting that, in light of the violent context and what was at stake in the conflict, some violent language may have been necessary (82).

In "A Godfighter Becomes a Fighter for God" (83–100), Rob van Houwelingen defends the Pauline authorship of the Pastoral Epistles and attempts to deal with an apparent tension between 1 Tim 1:12–17, in which Paul describes himself as a "godfighter" in the tradition of others who have opposed God (or the gods), and 2 Tim 1:3–5, in which he claims to worship God with a clear conscience, as his ancestors did. The tension is resolved when one realizes, with the New Perspective approach to Paul, that he never did leave his native Judaism; rather, in light of the revelation of Jesus as Messiah, Paul changed from violent to peaceful action on behalf of the God of his ancestors (98–99).

In the first essay dealing explicitly with the Jesus tradition, Ernest van Eck offers "Jesus and Violence: An Ideological-Critical Reading of the Tenants in Mark 12:1–12 and Thomas 65" (101–32). Van Eck argues—quite persuasively—that the parable as found in Mark is likely not the way Jesus told or meant it and that its picture of a violent retribution by an angry God has served to legitimize despotic rule in its reception history. The version in Thomas, which lacks the allegorical dimension, allows us to see that the intent of the parable was to criticize "all kinds of establishment violence" (129): both the tenants' murderous actions and the landowner's attempt to use his honor and status to defend his rights.

Wim J. C. Weren explores "The Use of Violence in Punishing Adultery in Biblical Texts (Deuteronomy 22:13–29 and John 7:53–8:11)" (133–50), concluding that Jesus is essentially faithful to the law of Moses but creates a situation in which it becomes impossible to carry it out.

In "Violence in a Gospel of Love" (151–84), Jan van der Watt and Jacobus Kok raise the provocative question of how a text that speaks of love as the essential quality of the Christian life can also be a "Gospel of violence, filled with language and metaphors of violence" (152). They draw an unflinching portrait of John's more violent dimensions, focusing on the exclusivity of Jesus as the root of the dualism that demonizes the community's opponents. The authors are careful to place this rhetoric in a historical context of powerlessness, but in an abrupt and surprising turn the piece ends up concluding that, since the motives behind the violent rhetoric were not evil—and, in fact, are meant to bring about faith in Jesus and thus eternal salvation—it finally does nothing to diminish the Gospel's emphasis on love and peace.

As noted, the final three essays in the case studies section deal with Revelation. The first, by Paul B. Decock, treats the general question of "Images of War and Creation, of Violence and Non-violence in the Revelation of John" (185–200). Decock raises an intriguing question: How does one square the nonviolent tenor of the early Jesus and his followers with the violence associated with God's final judgment (185)? The answer, he suggests, lies in the distinction between human violence, which no matter its motives must always destroy creation, and divine violence, which defends creation from its deadly enemies (198–99).

The next two pieces address perhaps the most overtly violent chapters of Revelation, 18 and 19, respectively. In "Unmasking and Challenging Evil: Exegetical Perspectives on Violence in Revelation 18" (201–26), de Villiers suggests that, while a surface reading of the chapter might see God's actions as raw vengeance against the enemies of God and the church, a contextual reading—the literary shape of the chapter and its place in the overall message of Revelation—tempers the violent rhetoric: "Though the language is that of retribution, the call to witness is part of and decisively determined by Revelation's larger discourse, which portrays the witness of the community against evil in a non-violent, non-conformist manner" (221). Likewise, in "The Eschatological Battle according to the Book of Revelation: Perspectives on Revelation 19:11–21" (227–44) Tobias Nicklas argues that God's violence should be understood within the broader context of the Hebrew Bible, in which God's violent actions (e.g., in the exodus) are undertaken on behalf of the powerless and marginalized. Further, that the book of Revelation ends with "the grace of our Lord Jesus Christ be with you all" clearly shows "why the book of Revelation may not be misused to justify mercilessness towards dissenters" (244).

As noted at the outset, the volume concludes with de Villiers's very helpful and frank reflections on "Hermeneutical Perspectives on Violence in the New Testament" (247–73). I would have to say that de Villiers, more so than the other contributors, is willing to stare unblinkingly at "The Other Face of Early Christianity" (248). His insightful sections include discussions of violence both inspired by and in the Bible, different forms New Testament violence takes, early Christians as agents of violence and violent discourse, and some reflections on methodology. De Villiers is also keen to point out that in many respects nonviolence remains at the heart of the early Christian witness: Christians are not called to war, for instance, and both Jesus and Paul proffer essentially nonviolent worldviews (266–70). But rather than leave it there, de Villiers comes back to the problem: "Christianity is not merely about people who suffer violence at the and of its persecutors, but also about Christianity itself perpetrating violence in many forms" (273); this recognition is crucial, he concludes, but there remains much to be done, and the stakes are high.

Especially in terms of the questions they raise, these essays represent a helpful contribution to this difficult discussion, and it is certainly the case that the authors take the issue seriously. But I came away from the volume with the sense that in many respects, and perhaps in spite of itself, it represents an *apologia* for the New Testament's violence: it is in the context; Paul gradually comes around to a true, internal nonviolence; the violent rhetoric of Galatians and of the Gospel of John, while not completely justified, is at least mitigated by the life-and-death struggle each faced; the same is true for the violent scenarios portrayed in Revelation; and it is the Gospel writer (Mark), not Jesus, who portrays a violent God in the Wicked Tenants parable. In other words, the authors move too quickly to resolve the very important tensions they uncover, and some of the solutions seem artificial. Is coping with violence in the New Testament a matter of explaining it away? Moreover, given the title of the volume, one might hope for a little more sustained reflection on the hermeneutical issue; even the final chapter represents more of a survey of the problems than a concrete proposal. As de Villiers concludes, "[A]s is clear from what has been written in this volume and elsewhere, much remains to be done" (273).

Finally, the volume also contains a very extensive bibliography on the topic and a very good index of scriptural passages.

Neues aus der Welt der frühen Christen, by Peter Pilhofer. Beiträge zur Wissenschaft vom Alten und Neuen Testament 195. Stuttgart: Kohlhammer, 2011. Pp. xvi + 262. Paper. €39.90. ISBN 9783170218420.

Günter Röhser, Rheinischen Friedrich-Wilhelms-Universität Bonn, Bonn, Germany

Nach den Greifswalder Aufsätzen unter der Überschrift „Die frühen Christen und ihre Welt" (WUNT 145, Tübingen 1995) legt P. hier nun eine Auswahl von Beiträgen aus der Erlanger Zeit unter dem Titel „Neues aus der Welt der frühen Christen" vor. Als Beiträger erscheint auch wieder Jens Börstinghaus (hier neben Jutta Fischer); der Band ist mit 32 instruktiven Schwarz-Weiß-Abbildungen (darunter auch Karten und Zeichnungen) versehen. Die bereits andernorts veröffentlichten Aufsätze sind: (1) P.s Erlanger Antrittsvorlesung „Vom Sinn der neutestamentlichen Wissenschaft", die neben einigen „launigen" und eher allgemeinen Bemerkungen zur Situation des Faches v. a. P.s „lokalgeschichtliche Methode" vorstellt und am Beispiel von Joh 20,28 vor dem Hintergrund des Kaiserkultes für Domitian in Ephesos veranschaulicht. (2) „Die hellenistisch-römische Welt und die neutestamentliche Wissenschaft" bietet inschriftliches Material zu der aus der matthäischen Kindheitsgeschichte bekannten Formel κατ' ὄναρ („im Traum") und formuliert das Programm einer Verzahnung der im Aufsatztitel angesprochenen Bereiche im Hinblick auf Profangeschichte und religiöse Mentalität. (3) „Von Jakobus zu Justin"—mit den Stationen Jak 3,1; Apg 13,1; 19,9; Lukian (Peregrinus Proteus), die Wanderlehrer der Didache und die Schule Justins in Rom sowie bis zu Kelsos—verläuft der Weg, auf dem P. die Bedeutung des Lernens und Lehrens bei den Christen der ersten zwei Jahrhunderte durch öffentliche und private Unterweisung zeigen und damit eine entgegenstehende These von M. Frenschkowski (39) entkräften will. (4) „Das Bild der christlichen Gemeinden in Lukians Peregrinos" setzt sich aus folgenden Elementen zusammen: erstmalige Erwähnung einer christlichen Bücherproduktion (Peregrinos als Verfasser) durch einen paganen Autor, die im 2. Jh. einmalige Wahrnehmung von „Brüderlichkeit als spezifisches Merkmal christlicher Gruppen" (57) durch einen paganen Autor, Kenntnis der Bedeutung des Apostels Paulus für die christlichen Gemeinden, Recherche Lukians bei den Christen—Letztere zugleich „vielleicht ein hinreichender

Grund, nun doch einmal auch nach der historischen Substanz der Christen-
kapitel [in Lukians Peregrinos, G.R.] zu fragen " (61). (5) Der gemeinsam mit
Jutta Fischer verfasste Beitrag „Zwei Thraker an der Ostsee" befasst sich mit der
Inschrift IG X 2,1, Nr. 1020 auf einer Grabstele der Frau Dentoutourmes für
ihren Mann Pyroulas—beide darauf abgebildet in einer seltenen ganzfigurigen
Darstellung und ursprünglich wohl aus dem Strymontal im heutigen Bulga-
rien stammend. Irgendwann zwischen 1885 und 1935 gelangte der Stein von
Thessaloniki (wo er erstmals aufgenommen wurde) in die evangelische Kirche
von Gristow (Vorpommern). Zu beachten ist die Korrektur an der Thessalo-
niki-Monographie von C. vom Brocke (236 Anm. 43; das Geschlecht von D.
betreffend). Die Abbildung auf der Grabstele (228) kann übrigens (worauf die
Verf. nicht hinweisen) als Veranschaulichung zu 1Kor 11,2–16 dienen (vgl. 199
und G. Theißen, Psychologische Aspekte paulinischer Theologie, Göttingen
1983, 162ff.).

Die folgenden Aufsätze werden in diesem Band zum ersten Mal veröffentlicht:
(1) „The Early Christian Community of Smyrna" ist der einzige englischsprachige Beitrag in diesem Buch. Darin befasst sich P. mit den Erwähnungen Smyrnas
im Neuen Testament und den Apostolischen Vätern und trägt die (wenigen)
Daten aus der Offenbarung des Johannes, den Ignatius- und den Polykarpbriefen
zur Geschichte dieser Gemeinde zusammen, die im 2. Jh. die zweitwichtigste der
Welt nach Rom war (35).
(2) Die Titelfrage „Einer der 5984072?" bezieht sich auf die „Zählung der
römischen Bürger durch Kaiser Claudius im Jahr 48 n.Chr." (63) und kommt zu
dem Ergebnis, dass Paulus nicht zu ihnen gehörte und „das römische Bürgerrecht
nicht besessen hat" (75). Der Beitrag beschränkt sich allerdings auf zwei „bisher
vernachlässigte() Faktoren" (63)—nämlich auf die „verschwindend geringe Zahl"
(73) epigraphisch nachgewiesener römischer Bürger aus Kilikien, der Heimat des
Paulus, sowie auf die Argumentationssituation in Phil 1,27–30 und 3,20: Paulus
hätte sich nicht in dieser Weise mit den bedrängten Philippern und ihrer Sehn-
sucht nach dem himmlischen Bürgerrecht solidarisieren können, wenn er aus
der privilegierten Position eines römischen Bürgers heraus geschrieben hätte.—
Nach 69 Anm. 30 soll der Beitrag von J. Börstinghaus zu „Tarsos—Μητρόπολις τῆς
Κιλικίας" (187–205) als Ergänzung dazu verstanden werden. Allerdings befasst
sich dieser v. a. mit den archäologischen, numismatischen und epigraphischen
Zeugnissen für die Bedeutung von Tarsus im 2. und 3. Jh. (mit zahlreichen Abbil-
dungen); für die neutestamentliche Zeit wird lediglich die Bedeutung der ersten
tarsischen Rede des Dion Chrysostomos für das Verständnis von 1Kor 11,2–16
betont in Erinnerung gerufen (197–199).
(3) Der Aufsatz zum römischen Bürgerrecht enthält auch bereits (70 Anm.
34) einen Hinweis auf den später folgenden Beitrag P.s zu der kilikischen Küs-
tenstadt Anemurion und ihrer tausendjährigen Geschichte (samt ausgewählten
Inschriften; 207–226, mit einem Seitenblick auf Paulus 212f).
(4) „Der andere König und sein Reich (Apg 17,7)" beschäftigt sich mit dem
zwiespältigen Verhältnis des Lukas zum römischen Kaiser: Einerseits thematisiert

er offen das Reich dieses Königs Jesus, andererseits meidet er auffällig die politisch und religiös belasteten Begriffe Parusie und Evangelium.

(5) „Wenn es denn vergeblich war ...“ (Gal 3,4) untersucht die wiederholte Rede von der Vergeblichkeit im Galaterbrief und will die—selten gestellte—Frage nach dem „Erfolg“ des Galaterbriefs beantworten—mit dem Ergebnis, ein Erfolg des Paulus sei „die bei weitem wahrscheinlichere Hypothese, wie Texte innerhalb und außerhalb des Neuen Testaments zeigen“ (92)—darunter die Akten des Paulus und der Thekla wegen ihres Bezuges zu Antiochien in Pisidien und Ikonion. Bei diesem Aufsatz fällt besonders die Vorliebe P.'s für ältere Literatur auf, die er ausführlich zitiert (Th. Zahn, H. Schlier, W.M. Ramsay, A. Harnack).

(6) Der Beitrag „Rechtfertigung aus Glauben. Das letzte Wort des Paulus“ ist zweifellos der wichtigste im ganzen Band. Er liefert die in P.s Lehrbuch „Das Neue Testament und seine Welt“, Tübingen 2010, 280 Anm. 17 angekündigte ausführliche Begründung für die bereits dort vertretene Hypothese, der Galaterbrief sei der jüngste und letzte Paulusbrief und erst während der Romreise entstanden. „Als Absendeort käme nach Apg 27,5 Myra in Lykien in Frage“ (107). Doch zuvor wird die nordgalatische Hypothese unterminiert, indem am Beispiel der Hauptorte der drei galatischen Stämme (Pessinus für die Tolistobogier, Ankara für die Tektosagen, Tavion für die Trokmer) gezeigt wird, dass es „selbst in der Landschaft Galatien keine Städte mit kompakt galatischer im Sinne von keltischer Bevölkerung gab“ (95f; als Beleg dafür fügt P. seinem Aufsatz die Inschrift der Kaiserpriester aus Ankara als Anlage bei; diese „wurde abgeschlossen, kurz bevor Paulus zu seiner ersten Missionsreise aufbrach“ [125 Anm. 140]). Dadurch wird das Argument der Anrede in Gal 3,1 („o ihr unverständigen Galater“) stark relativiert. M. E. verliert es jedoch dadurch überhaupt an Bedeutung für die Frage nach den Adressaten. Zudem kann ich nicht erkennen, was dieser Befund zur Datierungsfrage beiträgt. Es bleiben als Argumente lediglich (107–10): Die Angabe der Mitabsender in Gal 1,2 meine eine Gruppe von Reisebegleitern und zeige, dass Paulus keine Mitarbeiter mehr bei sich habe. Ebenso weise der vergebliche Wunsch in 4,20, die Galater besuchen zu können, auf die Situation der Romreise (Gefangenschaft) hin. Schließlich sei der rücksichtslose Ton des Schreibens erst möglich, nachdem jegliche Rücksichtnahme auf die Jerusalemer Judenchristen (wie im Römerbrief) angesichts des Scheiterns der Kollekte überflüssig geworden sei. Der Rezensent würde seinerseits das Argument stärker machen, dass man bestimmte Passagen des Galaterbriefes ohne die Darlegungen des Römerbriefes kaum verstehen kann. Auf jeden Fall ist es diese Hypothese wert, intensiver diskutiert zu werden.

Zu den Höhepunkten in diesem Band gehören zweifellos die beiden exegetisch-theologischen Beiträge von Jens Börstinghaus. Zum Thema „Homosexualität“ bietet er das, was der Untertitel des Beitrags verspricht: Überlegungen zu einer „biblischen Hermeneutik im Zusammenhang einer theologisch-ethischen Beurteilung homosexueller Praxis“ (137). In weit ausgreifenden und sorgfältigen Analysen werden die biblischen und repräsentativen antike Zeugnisse untersucht und anschließend eine vollständige biblisch-hermeneutisch begründete Urteilsbildung vorgelegt.

Abgesehen von einem „Ausrutscher" gegenüber alttestamentlich-jüdischer Geset-
zeskasuistik als bloßem äußerlichen Gebotsgehorsam (164)—mit W. Schrage, der
im Übrigen nach der älteren Auflage seiner „Ethik des Neuen Testaments" zitiert
wird—kann ich allen wesentlichen Aussagen dieses Beitrags voll und ganz zustim-
men. Ich hebe zwei Punkte hervor: Es kann exegetisch kein Zweifel bestehen, dass
Homosexualität in der Bibel „in Bausch und Bogen abgelehnt wird" (165; inst-
ruktiv 170: die gesammelten Ausreden und Relativierungen, um sich vor diesem
Befund zu drücken). Auf der Basis der christlich verstandenen Liebe als letztlich
entscheidendem Kriterium (164), wie es systematisch-ethisch etwa von W. Joest
fruchtbar gemacht wurde und vom Verf. in Auseinandersetzung mit der EKD-Ori-
entierungshilfe „Mit Spannungen leben" von 1996 bewährt wird (174–177), und
unter Berücksichtigung heutiger humanwissenschaftlicher Erkenntnisse gelangt B.
zu einer vollen ethischen Anerkennung und Würdigung von auf Dauer angelegten
homosexuellen Beziehungen—bei gleichzeitiger Zurückweisung der (m. E. etwas
unglücklich) so genannten „Gleichrangigkeitsthese" wegen des in der Homosexualität fehlenden Fortpflanzungsaspekts. „Das Defizit in diesem einen Aspekt aber
sagt allein nichts über die ethische Bewertung im Ganzen aus—diese müßte wieder
auf das Liebesgebot als entscheidendes Kriterium zurückgreifen" (183).

Der zweite Aufsatz (der zugleich das Buch beschließt) stellt eine von P. mit-
getragene Auseinandersetzung mit der—damals vorgeschlagenen, mittlerweile
beschlossenen—Formulierung „bleibende Erwählung Israels" im Grundartikel
der Verfassung der Evangelisch-Lutherischen Kirche in Bayern dar (die jetzt
abgedruckte Fassung der damaligen Stellungnahme wird 239 als „die allein
zitierfähige" bezeichnet). Gegenstand der Kritik ist auch die Metapher von der
„tragenden Wurzel des biblischen Israel", die sich allerdings—anders als die
erstgenannte Formulierung—in der 2012 beschlossenen Änderung der Kirchenverfassung auch nicht mehr wiederfindet (dort ist jetzt einfach vom „biblischen
Gottesvolk Israel" die Rede). Die exegetischen Argumente sind nicht neu, tref-
fen teilweise die damals vorgeschlagene Änderung der Kirchenverfassung nicht
wirklich und sind letztlich in der Zurückweisung der Rede von der bleibenden
Erwählung Israels nach Röm 9–11 auch nicht durchschlagend. Gleichwohl ist die
luzide Argumentation von B. lesenswert und ein wichtiger Beitrag zur theologischen Auseinandersetzung.

Insgesamt entsprechen diese beiden Beiträge von B. am ehesten dem, was der
Rezensent sich unter dem „Sinn der neutestamentlichen Wissenschaft" (Titel von
P.s Antrittsvorlesung) vorstellt.

Die Arbeiten P.s selbst zeigen eine unter heutigen Neutestamentlern kaum
noch anzutreffende Liebe zum historischen Detail sowie eine beinahe skrupulöse
Textgestaltung bis in die letzte Fußnote und die angewandten Rechtschreibregeln
hinein (vgl. Vorwort). Die exegetische oder gar theologische Tragweite der einzelnen Beobachtungen und Untersuchungen—das darf man sagen, ohne dem Verf.
zu nahe zu treten—ist aber sehr unterschiedlich und manches bleibt trotz der
scheinbar mit Fakten gesättigten Ausführungen im Ungewissen. Das gilt gerade
auch für die Einordnung des Galaterbriefes, dessen mögliche Spätdatierung

den Exegeten ja trotzdem nicht der Notwendigkeit eines eigenen theologischen Urteils enthebt—das letztlich nicht von der Reihenfolge der Entstehung der Paulusbriefe abhängig sein kann (vgl. 105f). Immer jedoch erhält man interessantes Hintergrundmaterial aus der Zeit der frühen Christen (samt reichhaltiger Spezialliteratur), das auf die eine oder andere historische oder exegetische Frage ein erhellendes Licht zu werfen vermag.

Der Band schließt mit zwei Indices: zu Stellen und zu Personen, Orten und Sachen.

Light from the East: Papyrologische Kommentare zum Neuen Testament. Akten des internationalen Symposions vom 3.–4. Dezember 2009 am Fachbereich Bibelwissenschaft und Kirchengeschichte der Universität Salzburg, edited by Peter Arzt-Grabner and Christina M. Kreinecker. Philippika—Marburger altertumskundliche Abhandlungen 39. Wiesbaden: Harrassowitz, 2010. Pp. 237. Paper. €48.00. ISBN 9783447062916.

Scott Charlesworth, Pacific Adventist University, Papua, New Guinea

This volume contains papers presented at an international symposium held at the University of Salzburg in December 2009. The introductory essay by Peter Arzt-Grabner ("Papyrologie und Neutestamentliche Wissenschaft: Einige Beispiele aus neueren Papyruseditionen"), one of three PKNT (Papyrologische Kommentare zum Neuen Testament) editors and the driving force behind the commentaries (see http://www.uni-salzburg.at/bwkg/pknt), provides an overview of what papyrology can offer New Testament studies. He begins with a brief history of the relationship between papyrology and New Testament studies (with mention of Deissmann, Moulton and Milligan, Horsley, and Lee). A short survey of recently published New Testament papyri follows. The bulk of the essay is taken up with a comparison of papyrus and Pauline letters. Of roughly 58,000 edited papyri, ostraca, and tablets, about 7,000 are letters. Finding fault with Deissmann's differentiation between "private" letters and "public" epistles, Arzt-Grabner argues that almost any kind of ancient document could take the form of a letter and that private letters became public when published. Moreover, the Pauline letters are not longer and more literary than papyrus letters. The language of papyrus letters covers a spectrum from short messages written in rough Greek to long, private letters in which news, advice, and requests are interspersed with philosophical and abstract musings. One such letter, P.Ammon 1.3, offers a clear parallel to the Pauline letters. Another, P.Oxy. 73.4959, which was dictated to a secretary and then revised by the sender himself, is instructive for the relationship between secretary and author in the Pauline letters. After providing a number of minor philological and interpretative insights gleaned from documentary papyri, Arzt-Grabner closes with positive mention of what the circa 100,000 still-unpublished papyri might reveal.

The two lead papers, which are written by the other PKNT editors (except for Destro), are concerned with methodology and cultural awareness. Adriana

Destro and Mauro Pesce ("The Colour of Words") argue that words lose their original color(s) or meaning(s) apart from the ancient context/s in which they were used. But it is not simply a matter of comparing words as used in Christian and documentary texts. Rather, comparison of words used in different contexts requires "a careful process of interpretation and cultural *mediation*" (28). Drawing on theoretical models and contexts found in ancient sources, Destro and Pesce identify the social and relational context(s) of slavery in the Gospel of John. The household with its masters and slaves is fundamental to John's understanding of the master-disciple relationship. In washing the disciples' feet, Jesus assumes the role of a slave. The tunic, basin, λέντιον (linen cloth), and foot-washing were all elements in the Greco-Roman welcome performed by slaves. So when Jesus adopts the demeanor of a slave, cultural master-disciple roles are inverted. He then invites all of his disciples to take the same servile stance in relation to each other. Other aspects of the slave motif draw on ancient ideas about friendship between slaves and masters and manumission that results, contrary to expectation, in the slave remaining in the house forever.

John Kloppenborg ("Pastoralism, Papyri and the Parable of the Shepherd") insists that interpretative models must be awake to ancient Mediterranean cultural values, social and economic structures, and mechanisms of exchange. He interprets the parable of the shepherd (Luke 15:4–7 par.) using a "carefully constructed model of pastoralism in Mediterranean antiquity," one "that is coherent with modern ethnographies of pastoralism" (52). After discussing various modes of pastoralism, he turns to the papyri. A flock of one hundred sheep was typically managed by a single shepherd. Owners of flocks usually hired shepherds, even when they had relatively few sheep. Small owners pooled their animals into a larger flock under the care of one shepherd. So the shepherd in the parable was probably not the owner of the sheep. Moreover, shepherds were poorly paid and had to replace any animals that went missing. The cost of replacing a ewe was around one month's wages, so the shepherd who left ninety-nine in search of the one may well have been motivated by financial considerations.

There is also some consideration of the Septuagint and papyrology. Christian-Jürgen Gruber ("The Lexical Constancy and Changes in Heb. 7:1–3 Compared to Gen. 14:17–20") looks at the use and modification of the Melchizidek story (Gen 14:17–20) by the author of Hebrews. While certain words that retain their basic meanings are left unchanged, the author replaces ἀναστρέφω with ὑποστρέφω. The papyrological evidence suggests that by the Roman era the meaning of ἀναστρέφω had changed from "to return" to "to behave." As for ὑποστρέφω, it is not attested before the second century CE and always means "to return." Therefore, the author of Hebrews is likely to have made the change in line with current usage, rather than accessing a different septuagintal manuscript. In a brief survey of research, Franz Winter ("Die dokumentarischen Papyri Ägytens und die LXX: Einige Beobachtungen zum Text von 2Kön") notes that the LXX, perhaps because of its voluminous nature, has not yet been thoroughly examined in relation to documentary papyri. As a result, unusual words tend be categorized as neologisms or *voces biblicae.* Among a number of examples is στολιστής, which, in the Ptolemaic papyri, is a high-ranking priest responsible for sacred robes. Rather than being a variation on וַיֵּצֵא לָהֶם הַמַּלְבּוּשׁ ("and he brought out to them the robes") at the end of 1 Kgs 10:22, καὶ ἐξήνεγκεν αὐτοῖς ὁ στολιστής ("and the keeper of the sacred robes brought [them] out to them") is a substitution taken from contemporaneous Greek that explains "the one who is over the wardrobe" (לַאֲשֶׁר עַל־הַמֶּלְתָּחָה) in the first part of the verse. Reference is also made to legal terminology and apparent Semiticisms that have parallels in the papyri.

The remaining essays, which are not discussed in order, are more topical. In a wide-ranging contribution Giovanni Bazzana ("*BASILEIA*—The Concept of Kingship in Light of Documentary Papyri") takes issue with the usual procedure for ascertaining whether the phrase βασιλεία τοῦ θεοῦ can be attributed to Jesus. Instead of searching the Hebrew Bible and the Pseudepigrapha for references to God as a βασιλεύς, a word that occurs very rarely and in a *negative* sense in the Gospels, Bazzana examines the use of both words in documentary papyri. In Ptolemaic papyri βασιλεύς conveys the political and ideological values of Hellenistic kingship. But Augustus, who had appealed to republican traditions during the struggle with Antony and Cleopatra, banned its official use (and, by extension, use of βασιλεία). Bazzana thinks this may account for the absence of βασιλεύς in comparison with βασιλεία in the New Testament. However, Augustus also understood that the concept of divine "kingship" (βασιλεία), when distanced from its embodiment in individual human "kings" (βασιλεῖς), could provide continuity and accommodate change. So Bazzana argues that βασιλεία can mean both "kingship" and "kingdom" in the hypothetical sayings source Q. He then goes on to attribute the two usages to different redactions of Q produced in Galilee at different times (following Kloppenborg and Arnal).

The paper by Joachim Hengstl ("Zum Erfahrungprofil des Apostels Paulus aus rechtshistorische Sicht") is an even more wide-ranging synthesis that draws in particular on Arzt-Grabner's PKNT volume on Philemon. He sets out to show why A. Papathomas (*Juristische Begriffe im ersten Korintherbrief des Paulus*, Vienna, 2009), who argues that in Paul's day legal elements dominated 1 Corinthians, is wrong. Hengstl begins by comparing the backgrounds and experience of Luke and Paul from the standpoint of their language. Luke has an educated knowledge of legal terminology and probably administrative experience in a Greek *polis*. In contrast, the profile of Paul that emerges from his undisputed letters is that of a craftsman who learned Greek from his Greek-speaking environment. Ideas found in apprentice contracts from Egypt appear in Philemon. But apprentices were widely separated, in social terms, from the citizen elites. Therefore, Paul may have been a master of apprentices in a family manufacturing business or factory and so on a par financially with the elites. Familiarity with the formula recommendation letter, which was needed only at higher social levels, may confirm this. At any rate, Paul's accomplished Greek shows that he managed to overcome educational boundaries. How then to explain the lack of strong *legal-specific* concepts in his letters, particularly when both Jews and Romans had pursued him legally? If these were excised by the compilers of Paul's letters, no certain traces of that action can be found. Therefore, like many other people, Paul picked up a *general legal knowledge* from the legal documents produced by scribes. In the same way, the use of general military terms cannot prove that Paul had military experience. Instead, like the Greek papyri, he uses the *koiné* in all of its diversity.

Christina M. Kreinecker ("How Power and Province Communicate: Some Remarks on the Language of the [Non-]conversation between Pilate and Jesus") tackles once again the question of the language(s) of the Galilean Jesus. She proposes that Jesus, an average Galilean, "was *not* able to speak Greek" or, perhaps, very little, certainly "not enough to follow a whole trial in every detail" (177). In a selection of later papyri, legal proceedings appear to have been conducted in Greek, while judgments were pronounced in Latin, a symbol of Roman power. Although Kreinecker has no burden to insist that Jesus was in fact silent, this primary point remains: since the trial was conducted in Greek, the language of the powerful elite, the provincial Jesus would not have been able to follow everything, and this inability might explain his silence. Unfortunately, this conclusion is overly reliant on the work of Mark Chancey, who quantifies and compares lists of texts without examining and analyzing individual texts in detail and context.

The literary-critical paper by Günther Schwab ("Eine echtheitskritische Frage zum Stil und Inhalt von 1Thess 1,5–8") is a by-product of his contribution to research on the PKNT Thessalonian volumes. Comparison is made first to 1 Cor 1:4–9, which has a number of common words and phrases. Schwab argues that these verses may have been added by a redactor to protect Paul from the idea, conveyed by the rest of the letter, that his preaching in Corinth had been ineffectual. But 1 Thess. 1:5–7 is not an interpolation like 1 Cor. 1:4–9. On the basis of a similar structure (arranged around causal particles) and common words in 1 Thess 1:5–7 and Luke 1:1–4, as well as shared echoes of the in-filling Holy Spirit and Lukan world mission, Schwab argues that 1 Thess 1:5–8 and, indeed, all of 1 Thessalonians may be the work of Luke or one of his associates. While the parallels might be dismissed as weak and the result of a shared thought world, Schwab insists that certainty one way or the other will not be possible until the whole book has been examined for affinities to Luke-Acts.

Finally, like Schwab's essay, two other papers are somewhat surprising inclusions in a book about papyrology and the New Testament. Ruth Kritzer ("*Secunda urbis praecipua et patriarchalis basilica*: Paulusverehrung im stetigen Schatten?") responds to the papal finding of 2009 that bone fragments, carbon-dated to the first–second century and found under the altar of the Church of St. Paul Outside the Walls, may belong to the apostle Paul. From the literary evidence, which speaks of a halving or dividing of the remains of *both* apostles in the mid-third century and then deposition in two locations (the aforementioned church and the Lateran), Kritzer ventures that the fragments may come from more than one body. David Martinez ("Epiphany Themes in Christian Liturgies in Papyrus") looks at three hymns on papyrus that illustrate how baptism and Epiphany were commemorated in late antique Egyptian communities. While several papyrus documents are discussed in this study, the late antique and liturgical focus is still somewhat out of place.

The papers in this book provide a good introduction to the purpose and scope of the PKNT project. The PKNT commentaries function as original and innovative supplements to traditional biblical commentaries. As Bazzana notes in his paper, looking at the New Testament through the eyes of documentary papyri "may enrich and sometimes even radically change the traditional understanding of historical and theological issues" (154). If this book can help to alert scholars to the important and growing body of New Testament–related papyrological work, it will have done its job.

Unity and Diversity in the Gospels and Paul: Essays in Honor of Frank J. Matera, edited by Christopher W. Skinner and Kelly R. Iverson. Early Christianity and Its Literature 7. Atlanta: Society of Biblical Literature, 2012. Pp. xxxiv + 359. Paper. $49.95. ISBN 9781589836815.

Lars Kierspel, Trinity College of the Bible and Theological Seminary, Newburgh, Indiana

Concurrent with his retirement from the Catholic University of America in 2012, this collection of essays by friends and colleagues celebrates achievements of New Testament professor Frank J. Matera. After a two-page "Cursus Vitae" and an impressive eighteen-page list of Matera's publications, the book divides into part 1, "Unity and Diversity in the Gospels" (6–145), and part 2, "Unity and Diversity in Paul" (149–324). The following describes each of the fourteen essays.

In "An Enemy of the Gospel? Anti-Paulinism and Intertextuality in the Gospel of Matthew" (7–32), Kelly R. Iverson critiques David C. Sim's thesis that "Matthew openly and savagely attacks Paul and his law-free gospel" (Sim, *The Gospel of Matthew and Christian Judaism* [T&T Clark, 1998], 213). Iverson uses various ways of measuring intentional intertextuality, such as Richard Hays's "seven criteria for the identification of echoes" (12), Manfred Pfister's six parameters for measuring "intertextual intensity" (17), and "ancient media studies" (26) that examine the abilities and limits of a hearer's memory (recall and recognition) in an oral performance. Iverson finds that Sim fails to convince, since his thesis uses only two of Hays's seven criteria, is low on intertextual intensity, and exceeds an audience's ability to detect the allusions to certain texts of Paul's letters.

Francis Moloney examines all seven uses of δικαιοσύνη in the Gospel of Matthew ("Matthew 5:17–18 and the Matthean use of ΔΙΚΑΙΟΣΥΝΗ," 33–54). Taking the salvation-historical perspective of the first δικαιοσύνη text in 3:15 as a narratological key, Moloney finds (with Meier and Deines) that an exclusive notion of "righteousness" in the Gospel as "moral conduct" (so Davies/Allison and Luz) is an overreaction "against possible Pauline interpretations of Matthew" (53). Instead, disciples do the righteousness that Jesus "has already 'fulfilled'" (49). Further, since, in Matthew's realized eschatology (54 n. 69), "heaven and earth" have already "passed away" (5:18) with the death and resurrection of Jesus (37), Jesus consequently "abandons the perfect observance ('not an iota or a dot') of the law in 28:16–20 when he sends his disciples on a mission to all nations" (36).

Jack Dean Kingsbury challenges a messianic understanding of the "Son of Man" title in the Gospel of Mark ("The Christology of Mark and the Son of Man," 55–70). Older redaction-critical approaches imported an outside thesis to the text when they postulated that Mark's Gospel uses a Son of Man Christology in the second half of the book to correct a portrait of Jesus as a divine man in the first half. In contrast, Kingsbury makes six narrative-critical observations that identify the titles "Christ" and "Son of God" as the christological emphasis of the Gospel.

John R. Donahue examines echoes of the "lure of wealth" (Mark 4:19) in the rest of the Gospel ("The Lure of Wealth: Does Mark have a Social Gospel?" 71–93). Beside shorter notes on Mark 4:19, 10:1–10, 10:13–16, 7:1–13 (Corban) and 12:38–44 (scribes devour houses of widows), he discusses extensively the rich man and his question about eternal life (10:17–31), also "the longest narrative on the failure of the word in Mark" (74–75). Donahue concludes that, while "social justice is not the primary concern of Mark's Gospel, the text offers seeds that can grow into reflection on the seduction and dangers of the quest for wealth that are so much a part of our modern society" (92).

Paul J. Achtemeier writes a sermon-like reflection about "Jesus and the Human Condition in Mark's Gospel: Divine Grace and the Shattering Of Human Illusions" (95–108). He shows how Mark uses techniques of sandwiching, irony, and subtlety to shatter human pretensions to do good in the religious sphere (e.g., 3:1–6; 11:15–19), the political sphere (15:1–5; 12:1–12), and the personal sphere (the failures of the disciples). Mark contrasts such "complete human failure" with the "good news [that] Christ is grace.... It is God's faithfulness and grace that save, not one's ability to be faithful to him or to be just, or good, or righteous human beings" (105).

William S. Kurz examines "Paul's Witness to Biblical Monotheism as Isaiah's Servant in Acts" (109–127). The essay is actually more broadly conceived than the title expresses. Kurz walks the reader through selected texts of the whole book of Isaiah and comments on quotations of and possible allusions to it in Luke and Acts. The use of early chapters such as Isa 7:14 LXX (Mary's virginity), of the servant songs of Isa 40–55 in particular (explicitly quoted in Acts 8:32–33), and even of the last chapter Isa 66 (quoted in Acts 7:49–50) demonstrate how LXX Isaiah constitutes a key context for understanding Luke-Acts. But the reinterpretation is equally important: While Isaiah envisions a mission according to which all nations come *to Jerusalem* (centripetal), "Acts, on the contrary, presents believers going out *from Jerusalem* in a centrifugal movement to the ends of the earth" (113; also 122, 125).

John P. Meier seeks to answer the question if the parables in the Gospel of Thomas are dependent or independent of the Synoptic tradition ("The Parable of the Wicked Tenants in the Vineyard: Is the Gospel of Thomas Independent of the Synoptics?" 129–45). After reviewing scholarship on both sides, Meier compares and contrasts the parable of the Wicked Tenants in all four accounts (Mark 12:1–11; Matt 21:33–43; Luke 20:9–18; Gos. Thom. 65–66). He highlights four redactional changes in Luke's version "that are most clearly mirrored in Thomas" and concludes that "Gos. Thom. 65–66 … is an intriguing example of the *Rezeptionsgeschichte* of the Synoptic Gospels in the second century c.e." (144).

Part 2, "Unity and Diversity in Paul," opens with Matt Whitlock's "From the Acts of the Apostles to Paul: Shaking off the Muffled Majesty of Impersonal Authorship" (149–71). Whitlock's goal is to "construct a bridge" between the Paul of Acts and that of the uncontested letters (152). Armed with the methodologies of Mikhail Bakhtin for Acts and the "non-Christian philosopher" (160 n. 29) Alain Badiou for Paul's letters, Whitlock examines Acts 2:1–41, 14:8–18, and 1 Thess 1:1–10. He finds that Luke's Paul shares with the apostle's own letters not "simply *content*, but *the act* of interpretation, personal interpretation of God events, more specifically, God's event in Jesus" (169, emphasis original).

Michael J. Gorman analyzes "Cruciformity according to Jesus and Paul" (173–201). Specifically, Gorman identifies key words and concepts from Mark's passion predictions in Paul's letters (e.g., Mark 8:31–9:1 [Χριστός, πάσχω, παρρησία, εὐαγγέλιον, κερδαίνω] and Phil 1 [Χριστός, πάσχω, παρρησία, εὐαγγέλιον, κέρδος]; Mark 9:30–37 [child] and 1 Cor 1:25–27 ["weakness"]; Mark 10:32–45 [power language; δοῦλος] and Phil 2:6–11 [δοῦλος]; 1 Thess 2:5–9). Thus, "Jesus and Paul agree that passion-shaped discipleship, or participatory cruciformity, consists of cross-shaped (1) witness to the gospel, (2) hospitality to the weak, and (3) power as loving service" (200).

In "Galatians 3:10: A 'Newer Perspective' on an Omitted Premise" (203–223), Andrew Das argues against the "New Perspective" for an omitted but implied assumption in Gal 3:10: the people under the law do not obey the law *perfectly*. While Dunn, Wright, and Hays would find the requirement of perfect obedience "a ridiculous caricature of Judaism" (R. Hays, 215), Das seeks to show (1) that this is exactly the context of Deut 27–30 (Gal 3:10 quotes Deut 27:26; see the emphasis on "all" commandments in 27:10 LXX; 28:1, 15; 31:12; 32:46) and (2) that the "gracious elements in Second Temple Judaism [i.e., election, animal sacrifice] are all understood by Paul in terms of Christ" (216). Paul "divorces God's blessing from Sinai's legislation" (221), since "Christ represents the beginning of a new era in history, the dawning of a 'new creation' (6:15)" (222). Thus, Das's "Newer Perspective" agrees with the "New Perspective" in that God's grace and mercy were familiar concepts in Second Temple Judaism, but it sides with the traditional view when it finds perfect obedience a requirement of the Sinaitic law, which, after Christ's sacrifice, no longer has any provision for human failure.

Luke T. Johnson explores Paul's complex use of the term "body" (σῶμα) in 1 Corinthians and how it constantly intersects with the term "Spirit" (πνεῦμα) ("The Body in Question: The Social Complexities of Resurrection," 225–47). Specifically, he tracks Paul's view (1) of the Christian assembly in 12:12 as "a bodily expression of the risen Jesus" (233; see also 8:12; 2:16), (2) of the intersection of sexuality, body language, and spirituality in 6:12–20, and (3) of the corporate dimension of meals (10:16; 11:29). Against the modern alienation of our human essence and of the Holy Spirit from our individual and social somatic condition, Johnson highlights the significance of (Jesus') past and (our) future bodily resurrection for the present (239).

In "Faith, Christ, and Paul's Theology of Salvation History" (249–71), Sherri Brown briefly summarizes the recent history of the debate regarding the phrase "faith of Christ" and agrees with proponents of a subjective genitive, such as Frank Matera. She then integrates that meaning of the phrase into a salvation-historical sketch, illustrated with the help of a chiasm (understood here merely as a visual aid): history moves from the glory of God before creation (2 Cor 4:6) to God's glory at the end (1 Thess 2:12), "with the Christ event as the crucial turning point (Rom 3:22–23) that moves creation in history back toward God" (266).

Raymond F. Collins compares the use of "coming" (παρουσία) in 1 Thessalonians with that of "appearing" (ἐπιφάνεια) in the Pastoral epistles ("From ΠΑΡΟΥΣΙΑ to ΕΠΙΦΑΝΕΙΑ: The Transformation of a Pauline Motif," 273–99). Both terms are used in eschatological contexts (see "hope" and "glory" in 1 Thess 2:19 and Tit 2:13) and appear in secular contexts for gods as well as for the Roman emperor (282–84, 295–98). Yet, while "both terms are used in Hellenism to refer to similar events, they are not simply interchangeable. Each has its respective connotations" (295), just as ancient Greece and Asia do not offer identical historical circumstances (297).

Christopher W. Skinner studies the subject of "Virtue in the New Testament: The Legacies of Paul and John in Comparative Perspective" (301–24). Beginning with a reference to the four "cardinal" virtues of prudence, justice, fortitude, and temperance, which Ambrose derived from Luke's four beatitudes (Luke 6:20–22), Skinner examines "the writings attributed to Paul and John in order to pinpoint specific teachings that may have impacted subsequent discussions of Christian virtue" (304). He finds in the Johannine imperative to "love one another" (John 13:34–35; 15:12–13; 1 John 2:10–11; 3:11; 4:7) a nonsectarian call to service and sacrifice. Approaching Paul's letters from Gorman's notion of "cruciformity" (316), Skinner comments on Gal 5:16–26 and 1 Cor 13:1–13 (318–23) before summarizing the shared common ground between John and Paul: "love as the highest virtue" is the "work of God," expressed in "sacrifice and service" (323). He finishes with a quote from Frank Matera: the "'indicative of salvation' grounds the 'moral imperative'" (324).

The titles for the two parts do not always match the contents. Thus, the first essay on Matthew and Paul and the last essay on Isaiah and Acts examine matters beyond the Gospels, and only Meier's essay explores the unity and diversity between a parallel account in the Synoptic Gospels. In the second half, only Collins's essay takes on diversity between Paul's letters. Three essays compare Paul's letters with the Gospels (Iverson, Gorman, Skinner), which merits a separate section in the book. Most authors mention Matera's contributions and influence on their work, but apart from short citations and praise, they do so without much interaction with his "12 books" and "65 articles, essays, or chapters" (xii).

This volume rewards the reader with a feast of essays on the Gospels and on Paul! The authors address knotty exegetical and theological issues as well as contemporary concerns and engage with current discussions in their fields. They employ a variety of methods, from ancient media studies to modern literary theory, from historical-critical tools to narrative criticism. Many authors, if not all of them, seem to be of Catholic orientation. But that does not predict the results of their research. Frank Matera is to be congratulated for inspiring such a legacy of scholarship.

Caiaphas the High Priest, by Adele Reinhartz. Studies on Personalities of the New Testament. Minneapolis: Fortress, 2013. Pp. x + 254. Paper. $39.00. ISBN 9780800699406.

Thomas Bergholz, Takaka, New Zealand

Interestingly, in a very short time two major and voluminous studies were published about one of the most infamous persons in the New Testament: Caiaphas, the high priest of Jerusalem during the time of the death of Jesus Christ. Rainer Metzner published his study *Kaiphas der Hohepriester jenes Jahres* in 2010, and he followed a twofold approach in trying to paint a more or less coherent picture of Caiaphas out of the relevant sources both from the New Testament and from those outside the New Testament canon and by reviewing Caiaphas's depiction throughout two thousand years of (mostly Western Christian) reception in art, literature, and theology. Facing the major difficulty that we do not have much (some might say, not any at all!) serious and/or extent material about Caiaphas besides the New Testament, Metzner tried to mine as much information as possible from our general knowledge of Jewish history of the two hundred years before and after the death of Jesus Christ, especially by reexamining our knowledge of the Sadducees, the (Herodian) temple, the political and religious positions of the Sanhedrin, and the interactions of the high priest(s) with the Romans. For example, we actually can draw some interesting conclusions about Caiaphas's life and political actions from the fact that he was possibly the longest-serving high priest during the time of the Second Temple and definitely the longest serving in post-Maccabean history—but everything is of course pure deduction. In short, Metzner's book was well researched and a good read in both parts, but his first (historical) part could not convince completely because it was highly speculative.

Of course, Adele Reinhartz faces the same basic difficulty, as she states already on page 3 of her introduction: "The well-defined scholarly portrait of the high priest was disintegrating before my very eyes." But even if we would have more concrete knowledge about Caiaphas, this would and could not change the fact that almost everything we assume we know about Caiaphas is based on fiction and imagination, not on facts. This verdict includes most scholarly works about Caiaphas as well as his depiction in Christian art from the first illuminated manuscripts to the latest movies and plays from the twenty-first century: "What

the scholarly and artistic depiction of Caiaphas have in common is imagination."
This statement by itself does not pan every scholarly attempt from the beginning;
Reinhartz is just reminding us that the work of the historian and the work of the
novelist share some basics: they both try to depict a coherent picture of characters
and situations, which can be done only by imagination. Referring to Collingwood
and Hayden White, Reinhartz states that not only fictional but also historical
events must be narrated following a "plot," a word we usually link with fiction, not
historiography. But Reinhartz's definition of a coherent narrative plot ("a plausible story line in which events are linked by cause and effect," 179) is of course
also valid for any historiographical treatise. This very honest and open theoretical
approach is, in my eyes, an advantage of Reinhartz's book over Metzner's: not only
is her much shorter chapter 1 more adequate than his in accordance to the very
limited sources, but to me her approach looks a little bit more honest about the
historiographical process itself as a process of reconstruction and imagination.

Reinhartz's book consists of nine chapters after the introduction. Chapter 1
sets "Caiaphas in Context," that is, his historical context of the first century CE.
Outside the New Testament, Caiaphas is mentioned only twice, by Josephus, who
does not deliver any material about Caiaphas's almost twenty years in service but
only records his appointment in the year 18 and his dismissal in 36 or 37. This
said, Reinhartz begins her investigation by establishing as many historical facts as
possible from nonbiblical sources about the duties and the service of a high priest
during the first decades of the first century.

The following six chapters, 2–7, follow Caiaphas as he is depicted and imagined through the centuries, from the postwar New Testament scriptures of the
late first century to the postwar images of Caiaphas on stage and screen in the late
twentieth century. Chapter 8 is some kind of reprise of chapter 1, where Reinhartz
tries to write her own "history" of Caiaphas and where she draws the conclusion
that most of the events and details we assume to know about Caiaphas are completely fictitious from the start. This begins already in the New Testament: chapter
2 looks into the New Testament and its depiction of Caiaphas, which is obviously
already an imaginative one, ruled by its dramatic and literary role in the passion
plot as devised by Mark (or his source). Chapter 3 goes after the nonbiblical sources
of the first centuries: the Apocrypha and the church fathers. Obviously their picture of Caiaphas was completely overruled by allegorical exegesis (Caiaphas as
the prototype of the anti-Christian archvillain) and stereotypical role models. In
the next chapter Reinhartz turns toward the truly fictional depictions of Caiaphas in literature. But unlike Metzner, with his broader historical approach, she
only mentions a single author from the time between the church fathers and the
twentieth century: Dante Alighieri (Oscar Wilde is mentioned only very briefly).
She then continues with various authors of the early and mid twentieth century
(e.g., Kazantzakis, Mailer, Saramago, Graves, Bulgakov). Two of them attract her
special attention: Dorothy Sayers with her famous BBC radio play cycle "The
Man Born to Be King" (1942/43) and Sholem Asch's novel *The Nazarene* (1939),
because, as Reinhartz concludes, for the first time those two authors unfold a dif-

ferent Caiaphas to the broader audience: a political and religious leader who tried
to find a way in a most difficult situation of colonial tyranny and internal unrest.

Chapter 5 has a broader historical approach as it follows "Caiaphas on Stage"
from medieval mystery and passion plays to the (in)famous Oberammergau play.
Reinhartz immerses quite deeply in the development of the Oberammergau script
during the twentieth century, especially during the last two decades, since the
nineteenth-century script of Weis-Daisenberger had undergone a substantial
revision by Christian Stückl in order to expel anti-Semitism and to ensure more
historical accuracy, as in showing Jesus' Jewishness. In the next chapter Reinhartz
changes her method slightly. Now when talking about Jesus in the movies, she
does not discuss the work of a single author or director but follows a more theme-
oriented approach. As with Oberammergau, Reinhartz finds an obvious line
distinguishing the movies from the first half of the twentieth century from those
of the post-Holocaust era, where she can confirm strong revisions of scripts and
role models. Chapter 7 is Reinhartz's discussion with twentieth-century scholars about the role of the Sanhedrin, the priests and the high priest in particular,
during the times of the trial of Jesus of Nazareth. As already said, in the following chapter Reinhartz reprises the initial theme: some kind of historiographical
reconstruction of Caiaphas the high priest based on the sources and evaluations of
the previous chapters. But having eliminated almost all sources as bearing no historical evidence for Caiaphas's actions whatsoever, this result is obvious but also
rather disappointing: "In the end there is no clear evidence for his [Caiaphas's]
direct or even indirect involvement in the events leading to Jesus' death" (179).
"In other words the sources resist coherence." This does not necessarily mean that
the historian is not allowed to fill the gaps with assumptions and imagination to
create a coherent plot. But it does mean that we have to admit what we are doing
by using assumptions and imagination: "The narrative constructed in many of
these historiographical works, while presented as evidence-based and coherent,
is in fact neither." On that behalf Reinhartz's book is a strong reminder for most
of us when dealing with the New Testament: as we cannot avoid imagination, we
have to be clear when reconstructing history by historiography.

Chapter 9 "Face to Face with Caiaphas," follows a double thread. First there
is the question of the visual depiction of Caiaphas in Christian and Western art;
then there is the author's very personal encounter—face to face—with the Caiaphas of the reformed Oberammergau play in 2010. As we learned so much about
scholarly and popular imagination in this book, this private and emotional conclusion seems to me the proper and worthy outcome of the study.

Adele Reinhartz's monograph about the most famous Jewish high priest is
exactly what she describes as the basic task of every scholarly historiography:
coherent, plausible, and honest about the role of imagination in the narrative she
constructs. In my opinion, from now on this book will be a *Standardwerk* (must-
read) on that topic, the quest for the historical Caiaphas.

Miracle Discourse in the New Testament, edited by Duane F. Watson. Atlanta: Society of Biblical Literature, 2012. Pp. x + 277. Paperback/hardcover. $36.95/$51.95. ISBN 9781589831186/9781589837881.

Susanne Luther, Johannes Gutenberg-Universität, Mainz, Germany

This volume comprises an updated version of the papers presented at the 2001 SBL Annual Meeting in the "Rhetoric and the New Testament" section focusing on the rhetorical function of miracles in the New Testament and interacting with Wendy J. Cotter's *The Miracles of Greco-Roman Antiquity* (London: Routledge, 1999). An essay on the Pauline Epistles as well as a response to the methodology of sociorhetorical analysis, an approach developed by Vernon K. Robbins and employed in several of the papers, were added for the publication. In her response to the papers Cotter addresses the desiderata of the approaches, which cover the synoptic Gospels, John, Acts, the Pauline Epistles, and Revelation.

The first essay, Vernon K. Robbins's "Sociorhetorical Interpretation of Miracle Discourse in the Synoptic Gospels" (17–84), examines the Synoptic miracle discourse from the perspective of sociorhetorical analysis. Based on his previous work, miracle discourse is considered one of the six first-century Christian rhetorolects (alongside wisdom, prophetic, apocalyptic, precreation, and priestly), each of which is identifiable by a distinctive combination of topics, themes, and reasoning and allows for specific assertions and strategies of argumentation. The New Testament miracle rhetorolect presents itself primarily as inductive narrative, proceeding from case (e.g., a person in need) to result (e.g., the healing action of Jesus or his followers) without including argumentation or deductive reasoning and featuring topoi related to "human personal afflictions, ailments, and crises" (83). Despite the primarily epideictic function of the New Testament miracle rhetorolect, sociorhetorical analysis offers the potential to disclose aspects of inferential, argumentative miracle discourse. By blending two or more rhetorolects and by thus combining miracle discourse with distinctive cultural and conceptual networks of discourse beyond the miracle rhetorolect, the text enables the recipient to draw inferences about the miracle narrative. Thus miracle discourse moves beyond its narrated base: the multiple blending of different rhetorolects "creates ever-widening networks of reasoning about Jesus as a miracle worker" (43) and transforms the miracle rhetorolect into an early Christian wisdom rhetorolect, which focuses on the topos of faith and stresses God's power in intervening in the sphere of human life.

As opposed to the broad category of "miracle discourse" suggested by Robbins, L. Gregory Bloomquist's "The Role of Argumentation in the Miracles Stories of Luke-Acts: Toward a Fuller Identification of Miracle Discourse for Use in Sociorhetorical Interpretation" (85–124) introduces a specification of two types of miracle discourse and analyzes their function in the argumentation of Luke-Acts. He argues that sociorhetorical analysis, focusing on the specific use of argumentation, topoi, and social and cultural texture of discourses, demands a precise distinction between different rhetorical functions of the pluriform category of "miracle discourse." Therefore, Bloomquist distinguishes between "thaumaturgical" and magic/"gnostic-manipulationist" miracle discourse: the former uses inductive, paradigmatic argumentation (rhetography), the latter deductive, enthymematic argumentation (rhetology). Bloomquist analyzes the miracle discourse in Luke-Acts (based on Luke 5:1–11; Acts 3:1–10; Luke 8:22–39) according to these two categories and their interweaving within the narrative. He draws the conclusion that miracles in Luke-Acts can be characterized as primarily thaumaturgical, as "[t]haumaturgical miracle discourse ... challenges logico-cultural perceptions and logical argumentative explanations ... by leaving various questions and by omitting rationales and conclusions" (122). Thus miracle narratives "do not so much contain argumentation as they *are* argumentation" (123); like parables they remain open to interpretation by the recipients and (unlike the argumentation in gnostic-manipulationist discourse) have the potential to challenge or question cultural rules and concepts. This tendency in Luke-Acts of fostering the thaumaturgical character of miracle stories proves that at least in this literary corpus "one form of rhetorical discourse—thaumaturgical miracle discourse—is ideologically used against another—gnostic-manipulationist miracle discourse—in order to achieve an ideological result" (124).

In "*Res Gestae Divi Christi*: Miracles, Early Christian Heroes, and the Discourse of Power in Acts" (125–73) Todd Penner criticizes that scholars have tended to distance the miracles in Acts from the miracles in the ancient world, thus overlooking the power these Lukan narratives have—like other ancient miracle accounts in political use—in conveying ideology and cultural concepts. He instead suggests a reassessment of the sociorhetorical function of the miracle discourse in Acts, which "must be read and understood in light of ancient perceptions of miracle stories as those intersect with conceptions and images of power in the Roman world" (169), in order to situate them appropriately within their sociocultural context. Within the context of ancient miracle discourse, Penner identifies two main functions of the miracles in Acts: (1) the apostles are authenticated and their power in word and deed emphasized; they are characterized as superior in deeds and ethos to other ancient miracle-workers; and (2) the early Christian claim to Roman space is marked in that the apostles preach and perform miracles in public Roman space and thereby lay claim to the subjects of the Roman emperor by changing their loyalty through conversion. Penner especially focuses on the work of Luke as author: "the narrative itself—both the process of composition and final rhetorical construction—cannot be viewed as an innocuous by-product: it is the medium of power for Lukan discourse, the vehicle by which the culturally complex negotiation of power is manifested and carried out for and over the reader" (149). Hence, the narrative structure of the miracles in Acts reveals the interrelation of culture, politics and literature and mirrors the power struggle between early Christianity and the Roman Empire in the first century.

Gail R. O'Day, in "Miracle Discourse in the Gospel of John" (175–88), examines the interrelation between miracle accounts and key theological themes and arguments, along with the meaning created through this literary interaction. Especially in the Gospel of John the miracle accounts and the narratives in which they are embedded interpret each other: key Johannine themes create meaning in miracle accounts, and (references to) miracles are embedded within narrative arguments. On the basis of a close reading of John 2:1–11, O'Day presents rhetorical strategies through which Johannine topics and motifs are embedded within the miracle discourse: the characters' direct speech and the narrator's explicit commentary. She then refers to strategies through which the miracle discourse becomes embedded within the Johannine Gospel account: through cross-referencing and self-referentiality and through the use of vocabulary or themes of the miraculous in other discourses. Just as the miracle discourse is embedded within the general rhetoric of the Gospel, so, for example, the lack of exorcisms in John may be explained by the reception of the topic of conflict between good and evil in more general arguments in the Gospel.

Duane F. Watson writes on "Miracle Discourse in the Pauline Epistles: The Role of Resurrection and Rhetoric" (189–96) and examines the use and function of miracle discourse in the Pauline Epistles. While miracle discourse does not occur at all in the disputed Pauline Epistles, it is used in a very limited way in the argumentation of the undisputed Pauline Epistles in order to defend Paul's apostolate (2 Cor 12:11–12) or the gospel (Gal 3:1–5) or to legitimize the Gentile mission (Rom 15:17–19). Although Paul mentions his miracle-working indirectly in the context of referring to his preaching (1 Thess 1:4–5; 1 Cor 2:4–5), a miracle discourse cannot be found in his argumentation, as "[r]eference to miracles did not help him address theological and ethical issues, nor were miracle accounts a formal part of a Greco-Roman rhetor's training and arsenal or commonly experienced in public rhetoric" (196). Paul makes no mention of Jesus' miracles, which Watson attributes to the fact that this might have been "rhetorically effective in the initial proclamation of the gospel, but not in letters where Paul addresses specific exigencies" (193). Moreover, Jesus' miracles were superseded by the miracle of the resurrection, which in turn figures prominently in the proclamation of Paul.

In "Toward a Sociorhetorical Taxonomy of Divine Intervention: Miracle Discourse in the Revelation of John" (197–210) David A. deSilva seeks to "identify how and where John invokes the 'themes, topics, reasonings and argumentations' constitutive of miracle discourse in Revelation, and to analyze the rhetorical use to which he puts them" (197). According to Robbins's definition, a miracle discourse presupposes that God's intervention in the world is a response to human need in contexts of danger or suffering; Jesus is regarded as the mediator; and preconditions are prayer, trust and so on. Although Revelation is primarily concerned with God's intervention in the world, it does not have any significant miracle discourse according to Robbins's definition, as the book addresses a specific situation of conflict and focuses on God's intervening judgment. Marvels, wonders, and divine intervention in Revelation foster the rhetorical goals of apocalyptic, prophetic, or suffering-death discourse, not of miracle discourse. This leads deSilva to challenge the boundaries of miracle discourse as set by the definition of sociorhetorical analysis.

In "Miracle Discourse in the New Testament: A Response" (211–23), Wendy J. Cotter responds to the essays collected in the volume. She challenges Robbins's narrow definition of the categories of prophetic, priestly, apocalyptic, and miracle discourse and suggests that his classification needs to be expanded to be applied adequately to the ancient context. Moreover, she criticizes his focus on the role of faith and on the power of Jesus in the New Testament miracle discourse, which is based on later theological reflection rather than on the original predication of the miracle accounts. Cotter affirms Bloomquist's distinction between thaumaturgical and gnostic-manipulationist discourse but adds for consideration that this differentiation would not have been obvious to anyone in the first century. She also questions his disregard of the literary context and the nature of the miracle account. Cotter praises Penner's approach to interpret the rhetorical function of the miracle discourse in contending with Roman imperial propaganda, but she adds that "miracle stories also function to affirm a way of life and a perception of others that would have been challenging to that day"— they promote a social vision of unity and equality (219). Cotter also praises O'Day's and Watson's contributions and stresses that these approaches open up new ways of analyzing miracle discourse. With regard to deSilva's contribution, Cotter strongly supports his final request to redefine and extend the boundaries of early Christian miracle discourse.

The final contribution is Davina C. Lopez's response, "Miraculous Methodologies: Critical Reflections on 'Ancient Miracle Discourse' Discourse" (225–48). Lopez lists three positive aspects about rhetorical-critical analysis: (1) the focus of analysis is no longer on the question of historicity and verifiability of miracle accounts or on personal belief; (2) the important role of power and ideology within and conveyed through the narrative are recognized; and (3) the comparison with the ancient context discloses the tropes the New Testament authors could adopt in order to successfully proclaim their message to a world that was familiar with miracle discourse. She adds three concerns: (1) the problematic distinction between magic and miracle; (2) the lack of recognition of the importance of power dynamics in miracle stories within the ancient context; and (3) the indistinct and constructivist definition of the term *miracle discourse*.

Building on the manifold important and well-justified aspects of praise and critique propounded in the responses by Wendy Cotter and Davina Lopez, the following issues concerning the sociorhetorical methodology and current research into miracle stories may be added. (1) The reader is presented with a series of case studies that apply the methodology set out by rhetorical—more specifically, sociorhetorical—analysis to concrete New Testament texts from the vantage point of "miracle discourse." These "test runs" of a methodology, which claim to "investigate ... form, source, tradition, redaction, history, and theology, not as individual elements, but as interactive elements in miracle discourse" (3) and hence promise a comprehensive hermeneutical reading of the texts, explore the viability and practicability of the approach. On the one hand, in the analyses of several New Testament text corpora the approach in general is proved viable and important and should receive further consideration in New Testament exegesis; negative findings resulting from the analyses of some corpora, on the other hand, initiated the suggestion of new perspectives of possible enhancement and diversification of the methodology and their submission for further discussion. The reader is invited to join into this process of elaborating the sociorhetorical methodology.

(2) Although the presuppositions concerning the definition of "miracle" and "magic" prove highly problematic, the New Testament text studies propounded at the 2001 SBL Annual Meeting and made accessible to the public in the present volume lead the way into current research into miracle stories: the approaches to the text represent a specific mode of studying miracle texts that does not intend to specify the historicity of the miracle accounts through rationalistic or mythological interpretation and that does not use form- or redaction-critical methods in order to expound (apologetically) their existence within the New Testament writings. The studies instead analyze and interpret the literary presentation of early Christian miracle accounts, their form and function as well as their effects on the reader. Thus the literariness is the central focus of the analysis, which is considered within the conventions of ancient rhetoric and the worldview of antiquity.

In the Footsteps of Judas and Other Defectors: The Gospels, Acts, and Johannine Letters, Apostasy in the New Testament Communities 1, by B. J. Oropeza. Eugene, OR: Cascade, 2011. Pp. xviii + 303. Paper, $35.00.

Markus Oehler, University of Vienna, Vienna, Austria

Dieser erste Teil eines mittlerweile auf drei Bände angewachsenen Überblicks zum Phänomen der Apostasie von B. J. Oropeza widmet sich den Evangelien und Johannesbriefen. In den beiden anderen Bänden untersucht der Vf. die Paulusbriefe inkl. der Deuteropaulinen (*Jews, Gentiles, and the Opponents of Paul,* 2012, siehe dazu J. Oryshak in RBL 06/2013) sowie abschließend die katholischen Briefe und die Apokalypse (*Churches under Siege of Persecution and Assimilation,* 2012). Oropeza baut damit auf seiner einschlägigen Untersuchung zu Paulus auf (*Paul and Apostasy. Eschatology, Perserverance, and Falling Away in the Corinthian Congregation* [WUNT 2/115], Tübingen: Mohr Siebeck, 2000), in der der Vf. u.a. sozialanthropologische und rhetorische Ansätze aufnahm und sich ausführlich mit 1Kor 10,1–13 beschäftigte. Drei Fragestellungen sind dem Autor in diesem nun großen Überblick vor allem wichtig (5–6): Welche Gemeinden stehen hinter den Texten? Wie beschäftigen sie sich mit dem Phänomen von Abweichung und Apostasie? Und was wird als deren Konsequenz festgehalten?

In einer knappen Einleitung (1–9) definiert Oropeza Apostasie folgendermaßen: „The phenomenon that occurs when a religious follower or a group of followers turn away from or otherwise repudiate the central beliefs and practices

they once embraced in a respective religious community" (1). Neben "apostasy"
gehe es dann aber auch um "defection", während "dissidents or so-called heretics"
(2) eigentlich etwas anderes seien, da sie ja in der jeweiligen Gruppe verbleiben
würden. Dennoch werden sie in dem vorliegenden Band auch sehr ausführlich
diskutiert. Deutlich wird hier schon, dass der Zugang zu dem gewählten Thema
breiter ist, als es der Titel des Buches sowie der Reihe erwarten lässt. Das hat
vor allem zur Folge, dass praktisch alle Texte des Neuen Testaments, die sich
in irgendeiner Weise mit anderen Positionen auseinandersetzen oder Gruppen
erkennen lassen, die von den Ansichten der jeweiligen Autoren abweichen, unter
dem Stichwort „Apostasie" diskutiert werden können und zum großen Teil vom
Vf. auch werden. Die Aufgabe, die sich der Vf. damit gestellt hat, ist hinsichtlich
der Textmenge dementsprechend groß. Zugleich ist eine intensive Beschäftigung
mit den einzelnen Texten dann auch nicht mehr möglich, wenngleich an einzelnen Punkten durchaus anregende Perspektiven eröffnet werden.

Der breite Zugriff führt dazu, dass die Begrifflichkeit schwammig wird.
Schon die Einleitung lässt kritische Fragen auftauchen: Die Definition von Apostasie nimmt zwar Bezug auf soziologische Ansätze, diese werden aber weder
ausführlicher dargestellt noch werden die differierenden Modelle diskutiert.
Der griechisch-römische Umgang mit religiöser Devianz, aber auch die jüdische
Perspektive (z.B. jene der Qumrantexte) werden beinahe vollständig ignoriert.
Vor allem aber wird schon durch die Begrifflichkeit suggeriert, dass es so etwas
wie eine Abweichung von einer Norm im frühen Christentum gegeben hätte. So
formuliert Oropeza etwa: „We might be able to observe whether the apostasy is
subjective and relative to claims of the New Testament authors, or whether there
are some objective and universal aspects to the claims" (6).

In den Einzelerörterungen setzt der Vf. mit dem Markusevangelium ein
(11–47), das ohne eine ausführlichere Beschäftigung mit anderen Positionen auf
die zweite Hälfte der 60er Jahre datiert wird, verfasst durch einen Judenchristen in Rom. Die Gemeinde habe die Neronische Verfolgung eben überstanden
und daraus seien nun spezifische Probleme erwachsen. Dementsprechend sei das
Evangelium sowohl an jene gerichtet, die der staatlichen Repression standgehal-
ten hätten, als auch an jene, die untreu geworden wären und denen Markus eine
Rückkehr ermöglichen wolle (16). Es folgt eine Beschäftigung mit zahlreichen
Textpassagen aus dem Markusevangelium, u.a. ausführlicher mit dem Sämann-
gleichnis und seiner Deutung (Mk 4,1–9.13–20). Immer wieder verweist der
Vf. darauf, dass Mk daran gelegen ist, den *lapsi*—übrigens fehlt eine Auseinan-
dersetzung mit der altkirchlichen Diskussion dieses Problems – den Weg zur
Wiedereingliederung in die Gemeinde zu weisen. Dass es keinen einzige Text bei
Markus gibt, der dieses Thema dann auch tatsächlich behandelt, geschweige denn
neben den negativen Beispielen (Petrus, die Jünger bei der Festnahme usw.) auch
nur eines der Rückkehr berichtet wird—bei Petrus hätte das ja durchaus nahe
gelegen – irritiert den Vf. allerdings nicht. Auch dass Sätze wie Mk 8,35 „Wer sein
Leben erretten will, wird es verlieren …" nicht dazu angetan sind, eventuellen
Rückkehrern noch viel Hoffnung zu machen, wird nicht diskutiert. Für erwägens-

wert halte ich hingegen, die Perspektive der überstandenen Verfolgungen in die Interpretation des Mk-Ev mit einzubeziehen, freilich braucht es dazu keine zeitliche und örtliche Nähe zur Neronischen Verfolgung. Der Kontext des römischen Imperiums mit seinem politischen und religiösen Anspruch, gerade auch unter dem Eindruck des Judäischen Krieges, ist für die Leidensparänese eine wesentliche Begründung, die wohl tatsächlich auch aus der Perspektive überstandener Verfolgungen neu gelesen werden kann.

Oropeza setzt mit dem Matthäusevangelium fort (48–97), als dessen Adressaten und Adressatinnen er mehrere Gemeinden um 80 in einem städtischen Kontext ansieht. Die Untersuchung setzt hier mit der Diskussion um das Gesetz ein: Matthäus richte sich gegen extreme Paulinisten (51), stehe aber auch im Konflikt mit einzelnen Synagogen (54). Die Verfolgung gehe hier nun von Judäern aus, nicht von den römischen Behörden. Zugleich warne der Vf. die Leiter der Gemeinden davor, diese in die Irre zu führen. Kap. 24 wird relativ ausführlich behandelt: Der Vf. unterscheidet zwischen „false prophets", die als „inauthentic Christ-followers" mit „spurious faith" (85) die Gemeinde bedrohen, und tatsächlichen Apostaten aus der Gemeinde. In diesem Kontext gehe es Matthäus vor allem darum, die Jesuanische Interpretation des Gesetzes als unbedingt verbindlich festzumachen (96).

Das Lukasevangelium wie die Apostelgeschichte (98–159) ordnet der Vf. dem Paulusbegleiter Lukas zu. Die Bücher seien zwischen 70 und 90 nicht für eine Gemeinde, sondern für ein breiteres Publikum geschrieben worden (102). Noch ausführlicher als zuvor beschäftigt sich der Vf. hier mit dem Verhältnis zum Judentum, u.a. im Blick auf Act 28, in einem kleinen Exkurs auch mit dem Thema „Prädestination" (114–17). In diesem Abschnitt zum lukanischen Doppelwerk findet sich auch die ausführlichste Beschäftigung mit Judas (143–50), der als warnendes Beispiel für das Schicksal von Apostaten gelten soll. Apostasie als Folge von Verfolgung spiele bei Lukas eine geringere Rolle, ethische Motive seien entscheidender. Dass die Geschichte vom verlorenen Sohn (Lk 15) auch für christliche Apostaten gedacht ist, wird als Interpretationsmöglichkeit angedeutet (159), aber nicht weiter verfolgt.

Den Abschluss bildet die Beschäftigung mit dem Johannesevangelium und den Briefen (160–228). Der Vf. rekonstruiert aus den Texten verschiedene Formen von Apostasie (163–64): Die „Juden", Judenchristen, die in der Synagoge verblieben, die „Welt", Apostaten im eigentlichen Sinn (1Joh 2,19), Anhänger von Johannes dem Täufer, die anderen Schafe (Joh 10,16) bzw. Griechen (Joh 12,20–22) und schließlich die Petrinischen Gemeinden (Joh 21). Die entsprechenden Texte werden im Folgenden behandelt. Dabei versteht der Vf. etwa jene, die Jesus töten wollen (Joh 8,59; 10,31–39), als Judenchristen, die sich von der Gemeinde abgewandt hätten (vgl. 8,31–47), allerdings ohne Diskussion anderer Interpretationsansätze. Wenig überzeugend ist die Interpretation von Joh 15,1–6 als Warnung vor dem Abfall aufgrund von Verfolgung (199–208), in der das Motiv des Fruchtbringens nicht einmal angesprochen wird. Eine Bestimmung der Gegner in den Joh-Briefen wird ausdrücklich offen gelassen (209), umso ausführlicher werden die unterschiedlichen Aussagen zur Sündlosigkeit im 1. Johannesbrief diskutiert (215–25).

Nach einer knappen Zusammenfassung, die die wesentlichen Ergebnisse wiederholt, schließen Literaturverzeichnis, Stellen-, Autoren- und Sachregister das Buch ab.

Die Abhandlung lässt eine intensive Lektüre der neutestamentlichen Texte erkennen, die für die Fragestellung sehr großzügig herangezogen werden. Vieles liest sich als paraphrastische Neuformulierung der Textaussagen, neue Interpretationsansätze werden relativ unvermittelt und ohne ausführliche Begründung eingebracht. Manche sind durchaus anregend und man wünschte sich eine intensivere Darstellung, die aber nicht Anliegen des Verfassers ist. Die einschlägige Forschungsdiskussion wird nur an sehr ausgewählten Punkten herangezogen, in der Regel trägt der Vf. seine Thesen vor, ohne sie in den kritischen Diskurs einzubetten. Ihm geht es um den großen Überblick, den dieses Buch und auch die weiteren Bände tatsächlich bieten. Für einen Einstieg in das Thema finden Leser und Leserinnen hier erste Anhaltspunkte, die allerdings mit Vorbehalt hinsichtlich der begrifflichen Bestimmung, der historischen Einordnung und mancher interpretatorischer Ansätze zu lesen sind.

The New Testament: A Historical and Theological Introduction, by Donald A. Hagner. Grand Rapids: Baker Academic, 2012. Pp. xxiv + 872. Hardcover. $49.99. ISBN 9780801039317.

Nils Neumann, Institut für Evangelische Theologie, Universität Kassel, Kassel, Germany

Als „historische und theologische Einleitung" („historical and theological Introduction"), so der Untertitel, verbindet Donald A. Hagners Buch „The New Testament" die Lehrbuchgattungen der „Einleitung" und der „Theologie der neutestamentlichen Schriften" zu einem umfassenden Gesamtwerk.

Das Anfangskapitel (3–12) gibt Auskunft über die hermeneutischen Grundüberzeugungen des Verfassers und trägt dadurch erheblich zur Nachvollziehbarkeit der folgenden Gedankengänge bei. So versteht Hagner die Bibel als Gottes Gabe an die Kirche, als vom Heiligen Geist inspirierte Schrift, die kanonische Autorität besitzt und den Glaubenden ihr Heil bezeugt (3). Er sieht zwar die Notwendigkeit, die biblischen Texte mit den Mitteln historischer Forschung zu erkunden (5), verwehrt sich aber gegen eine überzogene historische Kritik, die sich zuvorderst für den Zweifel an der in den Texten dargestellten Sache stark macht. Solche „radikale Kritik" sei deswegen unsachgemäß, weil die Bibel als Buch für Gläubige und nicht für Zweifler geschrieben worden sei (10). Es müsse der biblischen Wissenschaft darum gehen, die vom Autor intendierte Bedeutung der neutestamentlichen Aussagen aufzuzeigen (9). Dabei könne Argumentation jedoch stets nur als Abwägung von Plausibilitäten geschehen. Leitprinzip soll dem Verfasser eine Hermeneutik des Vertrauens sein (9–10).

Diesem Auftakt folgen die Darstellungen zu den Einleitungsfragen und zu den theologischen Hauptgedanken der neutestamentlichen Schriften. Hagners Ausführungen zeichnen sich durchgehend durch sehr gute Erklärungen aus, die nicht nur Ergebnisse bündeln sondern auch Denkvoraussetzungen und Begründungszusammenhänge der Themenkomplexe und Einzelfragen für Studierende verständlich vermitteln. Im Großen und Ganzen folgt die Struktur des Werkes der Abfolge von Schriften im Neuen Testament. Diese wird aber durch thematische Exkurse ergänzt, die nicht im engeren Sinne zur Einleitung oder Theologie gehören aber den Studierenden das Verständnis erleichtern. So äußert sich der Verfasser am Anfang des Werkes zum Schriftcharakter des Neuen Testaments und seiner Bedeutung für die Kirche (3–12), zur Bedeutung des Alten Testaments für das Verständnis des Neuen (13–28), zur Welt, aus der die Schriften stammen (29–55); außerdem gibt es derartige Kapitel mit Hintergrundinformationen u.a. zu den Themen Jesusforschung (83–104), Form- und Redaktionsgeschichte (117–30), Synoptisches Problem (131–53), Leben und Denken des Paulus (345–54), „Frühkatholizismus" (605–13), Textgeschichte und -Kritik (783–802) und Entstehung des Kanons (803–23).

Jedes der Kapitel zu den neutestamentlichen Schriften diskutiert die üblichen Einleitungsfragen und stellt die theologischen Hauptgedanken der Schrift vor. Wer sich über Hagners Erklärungen hinaus noch weiter informieren möchte, wird durch die ausführlichen Bibliographien am Ende jedes Kapitels in die Lage dazu versetzt, eigenständig weiterzulesen und zu forschen.

Im Hinblick auf die Theologie der Schriften bietet das Lehrbuch durchweg sehr verständliche Darstellungen. Aus der großen Fülle der behandelten Themen können an dieser Stelle nur wenige exemplarisch genannt werden: Hagner führt Studierende ein in das „Messiasgeheimnis" des Markusevangeliums (177), die fünf großen Jesusreden des Matthäusevangeliums (197), die Zuwendung Jesu zu den Armen und Schwachen bei Lukas (242), die „Ich-Bin"-Christologie des Johannesevangeliums (285), die Rechtfertigung aus Glauben als theologischen Leitgedanken des Paulus (383), u.v.m. Auf diese Weise werden Studierende, die Hagners Lehrbuch benutzen, solide über die theologischen Charakteristika jeder einzelnen neutestamentlichen Schrift informiert.

In den Diskussionen der Einleitungsfragen wird Hagenr nicht müde, zu betonen, dass es immer nur um das Abwägen von Plausibilitäten gehen kann, so dass vorgebliche Beweise oder falsche Sicherheiten bei diesen Problemfeldern fehl am Platze sind. So müssen am Ende stets Wahrhscheinlichkeitsurteile gefällt werden. Hagners Herangehensweise ist dadurch sehr transparent und wissenschaftlich redlich. Der Autor weist fortwährend auf den Ermessensspielraum der Forschenden hin.

Er selbst nutzt diesen Ermessensspielraum jedoch sehr weitgehend zugunsten von konservativen Positionen aus. Konkret äußert sich dies in frühen Datierungen, traditionellen Verfasserangaben und in der Betonung der historischen Kontinuität. Die Grundannahme von der starken Kontinuität zwischen dem historischen Jesus und den neutestamentlichen Schriften spiegelt sich auch im Aufriss des Gesamtwerks: Zuerst werden die Evangelien vorgestellt, später dann die Briefe des Paulus. Nach Hagners Logik ist dies nicht nur die kanonische sondern vor allem auch die historisch adäquate Abfolge.

Die beschriebene Grundannahme führt u.a. zu den folgenden Thesen: Die mündliche Tradition ist von hoher Zuverlässigkeit (105–6): Durch das Stilmittel des Parallelismus Membrorum versetzt Jesus seine Jünger in die Lage, seine Lehre wortgetreu weiterzutradieren (111); er erwählt sich zwölf Apostel, damit diese die Aufgabe der Tradenten übernehmen (113). Auf den Apostel Petrus geht dann das Markusevangelium zurück; Markus hat als Dolmetscher Petri dessen Überlieferung niedergeschrieben (170–71). Das Matthäusevangelium wiederum enthält solches Material, das von dem Jünger Matthäus gesammelt und weitergegeben wurde (216). Lukas versteht sich selbst als Historiker (228); bei ihm handelt es sich um den in Kol 4,14 erwähnten Arzt. In der Apostelgeschichte reflektieren die Wir-Passagen seine eigenen Erlebnisse (245–46). Wahrscheinlich ist der Autor des Johannesevangeliums der Zebedaide und Apostel, der sich selbst in der Figur des Lieblingsjüngers in seine Schrift integriert (272). Damit ist in den Evangelien des Neuen Testaments ein hoher Grad von Kontinuität zur Botschaft Jesu gegeben. Ähnlich verhält es sich nach Hagner auch für Paulus: In seinen Briefen findet der Verfasser zahlreiche Anspielungen auf Aussprüche Jesu (357). Neben den allgemein als genuin paulinisch geltenden Briefen Gal, 1Thess, 1–2Kor, Röm, Phil und Phlm schreibt Hagner Paulus auch noch 2Thess (465) und Kol (572) zu. Abweichungen im Stil und in der theologischen Argumentation erklärt er teilweise damit, dass Paulus hier einen Sekretär beschäftigt und ihm ein hohes Maß an Freiheit eingeräumt haben könnte (z.B. 572). Der Eph hingegen stammt wahrscheinlicher von einem Paulusschüler (600).

Dass Hagner durchweg auch die jeweiligen Gegenpositionen einschließlich ihrer Vorzüge referiert, muss auf seine konservativen Studierenden am Fuller Theological Seminary durchaus provokativ wirken. Für mich, der ich in der Tradition der protestantischen Exegese des 20. Jahrhunderts an einer deutschen Universität ausgebildet wurde, lesen sich die vorgetragenen Schlussfolgen hingegen befremdlich. Diesbezüglich schlägt der von Hagner so sehr betonte Ermessensspielraum deutlich zu Buche: Ich hätte vielfach genauso argumentiert, dabei jedoch die Reihenfolge der referierten Positionen umgekehrt und dann schlussendlich für eine liberale Interpretation votiert.

Kompakte Darstellungen bündeln in Merk-Boxen die zentralen Informationen aus jedem Kapitel. Diese Boxen sind didaktisch hilfreich, wenn Studierende sich einen schnellen ersten Einblick verschaffen wollen, doch laufen sie u.U. Hagners Interesse der Offenheit und des Abwägens zuwider, wenn sie bei den Leserinnen und Lesern des Buchs den Eindruck erwecken sollten, es gebe eben doch die Sicherheiten, gegen die sich der Autor zu Recht immer wieder stark macht.

Insgesamt nötigt Hagners Theologische Einleitung damit zur hermeneutischen Reflexion. Und wenn nur das der Effekt ist, den das Buch bei liberalen Lesenden hervorruft, dann ist damit auch schon ein gutes Ziel erreicht. Woher kommt die Wahrheit, die Autorität, die Verbindlichkeit der neutestamentlichen Texte? Basieren diese auf historischer Faktizität oder auf der Kanonizität der Schriften bzw. auf kirchlicher Bestätigung? Konservative und auch liberale Lesende, denen diese hermeneutischen Fragen am Herzen liegen, werden an Hagners umfassendem Werk sicher Freude haben.

NEW TESTAMENT AND CHRISTIAN ORIGINS

Self-Designations and Group Identity in the New Testament, by Paul Trebilco. Cambridge: Cambridge University Press, 2012. Pp. xii + 375. Hardcover. £60.00. ISBN 9781107012998.

B. J. Oropeza, Azusa Pacific University, Azusa, California

"How would various 'Christian' groups have answered the question, 'Who are we?'" This is one of the opening questions that Paul Trebilco raises in his study that explores seven important self-designations used by earliest Christians: "brothers and sisters" (ἀδέλφοί) "the believers" (e.g., οἱ πιστοί), "saints" (ἅγιοι), "the assembly" (ἡ ἐκκλησία), "disciples" (μαθηταί), "the Way" (ἡ ὁδός), and "Christian" (Χριστιανός). The book aims to shed light on the "identity, self-understanding, and character" of early Christian communities in the New Testament period (1). This is an important endeavor because self-designations, whether originating from insiders or outsiders, impact a group's behavior and the way it perceives itself.

In the introduction (ch. 1), Trebilco identifies the terms under consideration and criteria for selecting them. Due to limitations on the size of the study, he considers only the self-designations that are most frequently found in New Testament texts. He adds "the Way" because, even though it appears only in Acts, he considers it an early self-designation of significance. Likewise, he selects the term "Christian," which appears only three times in the New Testament, because of its obvious ongoing prominence. He also engages with the notions of social dialect and "shared repertoire" of group language, insider and outsider designations, and representative examples of how early Christians formulated their own social dialects. A Gentile convert who would enter the community of Christ, for example, would have to learn the content and dialect of the Septuagint to make sense of insider language used by the community. Trebilco then concludes with his task in this work: "In the chapters that follow, as well as discussing usage and origin, I will seek to understand how self-designations function in a particular community and to determine what role a self-designation plays in a particular social context" (15).

In chapter 2, the term "brothers and sisters" (ἀδέλφοί), which is said to be the most commonly used self-designation in the New Testament, has both Jewish and Greco-Roman predecessors. For Trebilco, its metaphorical use is exemplified by sources such as Vettius Valens, who associates it with members of a religious sect, and Epictetus, who in Stoic parlance affirms all as αδέλφοί. Trebilco then draws attention to Israel's scriptures, in particular the Deuteronomic use of αδέλφοί in which Israel is viewed as "a people of brothers" (e.g., Deut 15:2–12; 22:1–4). Trebilco suggests that the New Testament use of αδέλφοί is most influenced by language attributed to Jesus, who taught his disciples to perceive themselves as family members (Mark 3:31–35; Matt 12:46–50; Luke 8:19–21). The term was used exclusively as an insider designation and was conducive to community meetings that took place in houses. In the letters of Paul, the apostle grounds the term in the idea of Jesus as the firstborn child (Rom 8:29), and the early Christians, who are being conformed to the image of God's son, thus become brothers and sisters in the family of God's children. Among other New Testament authors, Luke is said to stress the term afer the outcome of the meeting in Jerusalem (Acts 15): Gentile Christians have become full αδέλφοί with Jewish Christians.

In chapter 3 Trebilco informs us that term "believers" highlights the importance of faith in the early Christian communities. It became a prominent self-designation because believing was one of the central characteristics of the movement. Faith, though sometimes present in Jewish and Greco-Roman religious writings, was a defining marker for the Christ-followers. Gentile-Christian usage of the term is said to be derived from the threefold prong of Jesus' own teachings on faith, Jewish-Christian language, and reflections on Isa 28:16. The πιστ- terms stand out especially in Pauline, Johannine, and Lukan writings and provide a general unifying feature in New Testament corpus. The importance of this designation also may be seen in its converse: early Christian groups identified outsiders as "nonbelievers" (άπιστοι).

In chapter 4 Trebilco examines οἱ ἅγιοι. Normally heavenly beings are designated as "holy ones" in the MT, LXX, Pseudepigrapha, and Qumran (but Trebilco notes exceptions in Pss 34MT, 73LXX, 82LXX, and Wisd 18). Daniel 7 provides a unique portrayal of holy ones as angelic beings in heaven who represent faithful Israelites on earth. The identification of οἱ ἅγιοι as humans, then, was rare in the oldest Jewish traditions, and what was reserved as a future label for earth-dwellers in 1 Enoch became for early Christians a present self-designation of privilege. In fulfillment of the new era, the early Christians are now set apart for God as saints through the resurrection of Jesus. For Treblico, the term started with Jewish Christians in Jerusalem (see Rom 15:25–26; cf. 1 Cor 16:1; 2 Cor 8:4; 9:1). Only rarely does οἱ ἅγιοι still identify angels in the New Testament (Eph 1:18; 2:19; Jude 14); its meaning as angels ceases perhaps as a way to avoid confusion for the early Christians. The significance of the term in New Testament letters is that, especially for Paul, Gentiles are now incorporated into the holy people of God along with Israel.

Chapter 5 expounds on the church or "assembly" (ἐκκλησία), which is viewed as a collective identity in continuity with Israel as God's people and who are identified after the Hebrew term קהל (e.g., Deut 23:2; 1 Chr 28:8; Neh 13:1; Mic 2:5; cf. 1QM 4.9–10). Trebilco maintains that the ἐκκλησία of Jesus originated in Jerusalem with the Hellenistic-Jewish Christians who are first mentioned in Acts 6:1

(cf. Gal. 1:22), and the Septuagint provided their background for the designation. The term developed in a way that distinguished this assembly from other Jewish groups that were designated as συναγωγή rather than ἐκκλησία. For Trebilco, συναγωγή was being used by "'non-Christian' Jews of *their* 'gathering', with the meaning of both 'the community which gathers' and 'the building in which they gather'" (193). In the New Testament James and the author of Hebrews use both ἐκκλησία and συναγωγή, suggesting that not all early Christians used ἐκκλησία as a technical term, and whereas ἐπισυναγωγή in Heb 10:25 seems to distinguish between the Christian gathering and Jewish συναγωγή, Jas 2:2 does not make a differentiation. The earliest Christian assemblies, moreover, did not claim that members of the συναγωγή no longer belonged to God's people.

In chapter 6 Trebilco affirms that the historical Jesus used the Aramaic term *talmîdayyā'* to designate his disciples, which the Evangelists translated as μαθηταί. This designation has a broad meaning indicating either an adherent to a teaching or a follower of a movement, but with Jesus it highlights a more particular meaning of radical commitment in which his itinerant followers leave "their homes and livelihoods, risking hostility and loss" (245; cf. 219). Trebilco suggests the designation fell into disuse after the resurrection, with Paul and other New Testament writers who had difficulty applying it to the Christians of their time, so they preferred other terms of allegiance to Christ. The Gospel writers, however, retained μαθηταί and encouraged their readers and auditors to use it.

Trebilco continues in the next chapter to claim that early Jewish followers of Christ in Palestine designated themselves as "The Way" in relation to Isa 40:3, a passage associated with John the Baptist's preparation of the way for the coming Messiah. In this passage, "The way of the Lord" is viewed as a path God will travel when leading the restored people back to Zion after exile. Trebilco suggests from Isa 40–55 that it was very likely the Christian community "found its own place in these prophecies in the image of the highway on which God leads his people to salvation.... 'the Way', prepared by John, had been undertaken and completed by Jesus. It was the Way of Jesus, the Way of salvation, on which they were now walking. They could call themselves by this term" (266). This self-designation, however, did not become suitable for the expansion of the movement in the Greco-Roman world. Hence, it did not persist because it was not distinct enough and became too confusing to Gentile converts who were not as familiar with the biblical background behind the term.

The final self-designation Trebilco explores is "Christian." Unlike the other terms, it emerged from outsiders using the language beginning in Antioch (Acts 11:26), and it designated those who had faith in Jesus as the Christ. A trajectory of non-Christian use of the designation for identifying early Christians runs from Herod Agrippa II (Acts 26:28; ca. 57–59 CE) to the people of Rome (ca. 64 CE), to people in north Asia Minor (1 Pet 4:16; 70–90 CE), to Josephus in Rome (ca. 93/94 CE), to people in various cities addressed by Ignatius (ca. 105–110), and to Pliny in Bithynia-Pontus when writing to emperor Trajan in Rome (ca. 111–12).

The early Christians, then, used Χριστιανός as an "outward-facing" identification marker when conversing with outsiders.

Among other things, the conclusion summarizes the way the self-designations were used, the origins of the terms, insider and outsider language, and Christian language in relation to Israel's scriptures and Greco-Roman contexts. The monograph also contains a large bibliography, a selected author index, and subject and text indices.

Trebilco's scholarly monograph provides a helpful niche in New Testament studies by delineating some of the most important emergent Christian designations. The work is engaging, clearly written, and interacts with a number of secondary sources. His list of designations, however, is not exhaustive, as he candidly admits. One wonders if the study could have been improved with the inclusion of terms such "the elect," "beloved," "children of God," and "body of Christ." Such terms may have been more relevant and useful than a detailed study on "the Way."

Although Trebilco's study is balanced and well-informed, some of his conclusions may be more convincing to his readers than others. His explanation that early Hellenistic Jewish-Christians developed the term ἐκκλησία from "the Assembly of Yahweh" in the LXX is certainly possible. However, there is no stress made on the alternative that ἐκκλησία may have been derived from the apocalyptic idea of a holy assembly that would arise in the last days (Joel 2:16). Although the term normally does not appear in apocalyptic settings in the LXX, the main time it does is quite significant. Both Luke and Paul reference the passage in Joel in relation to Christian conversion by calling on the name of the Lord, and the passage is associated with the last days (Acts 2:17–22; 9:14; 22:16; Rom 10:9–13; 1 Cor 1:2; cf. Joel 2:28–32 [3:1–5]). The text of Joel, then, would seem to be influential for early Christian self-identity, and perhaps it influenced the movement's self-perception as an end-time ἐκκλησία anticipated in the prophetic discourse.

Moreover, it seems that more emphasis should have been placed by Trebilco on ἐκκλησία in the Greco-Roman sense of a civic assembly (he addresses the issue much too briefly on pages 165–66). For example, Paul's prescripts, where he most consistently uses the term ἐκκλησία, bear a striking resemblance to prescripts of letters attributed to Demosthenes (whether authentic or pseudonym), in which the ἐκκλησία in the city of Athens are the recipients being addressed. Since most of the New Testament letters are addressed to predominantly Gentile audiences, Greco-Roman uses of the term would seem to be highly relevant, especially if the sender or recipients understood the ἐκκλησία of Christ as an alternative assembly to political gatherings. An approach that embraces not only Jewish but also Greco-Roman predecessors for ἐκκλησία might shed further light on the term's usage in the New Testament.

Despite these quibbles, Trebilco's work provides a great resource for the study of ancient Christian self-designations that the reader will want to consult repeatedly.

JESUS

'Is This Not the Carpenter?': The Question of the Historicity of the Figure of Jesus,
edited by Thomas L. Thompson and Thomas S. Verenna. Copenhagen International Seminar. Sheffield: Equinox, 2012. Pp. viii + 280. Hardcover. $110.00.
ISBN 9781845539863.

James F. McGrath, Butler University, Indianapolis, Indiana

In certain circles outside of the academy, the view that there was no historical
figure of Jesus is surprisingly popular. The volume *'Is This Not the Carpenter?':*
The Question of the Historicity of the Figure of Jesus brings together scholarly contributions from a range of fields and with a range of viewpoints on that topic. It
includes some good arguments for the historicity of Jesus as well as some good
illustrations of what is problematic about the attempt of those outside the relevant fields to dismiss those arguments.

The introduction by the editors, Thompson and Verenna, engages in an exercise in parallelomania, which seems to them to allow one to jump from a reference
to Jesus being a carpenter to Hephaestus the god of craftsmen to an equation of
the two—with this called a conclusion to an "exegetical excursion" with no indication that the authors are joking (7). They go on to claim that "New Testament
scholarship has avoided direct questions regarding the historicity of Jesus" (7), a
statement that is obviously false. The figure of Jesus has probably been subjected
to more skeptical analysis than any other figure in history. Even after such scrutiny, most historians agree on the authenticity of at least some pieces of evidence
for him having said and done particular things and having died in a particular
way. To suggest that all of the sifting through evidence that has taken place reflects
an avoidance of the question of Jesus' historicity is baffling. There is no evidence
for the existence of any human being from the past apart from the evidence that
she or he said, built, conquered, or otherwise did this or that. The authors point
to the multiplicity of interpretations of Jesus as though it had some bearing on
his historicity. To scholars in the field, the numerous diverse proposals about how
Jesus is best understood simply indicate that Jesus is a focus of intense scholarly
study. Attempts by academics to find something worthy of publication by coming
up with new interpretations of the data is not evidence of the nonhistoricity of the
figure of Jesus.

Thompson's background is in the study of the Hebrew Bible, and this seems to
be reflected in the statement that "[a] historical Jesus is a hypothetical derivative of
scholarship. It is no more a fact than is an equally hypothetical historical Moses or
David" (10). This ignores the differences between the latter figures, mentioned in
texts many centuries after their supposed time, and the figure of Jesus, mentioned
in letters by an individual who had met Jesus' brother within a few years of his
death. The authors regularly assume what they need to prove. Having dismissed
the entire enterprise of historical criticism, the authors continue (immediately
after the words just quoted) by simply asserting that "New Testament literature

was written with literary, allegorical and, indeed, theological and mythic purpose, rather than as an account of historical events," and therefore "there is significant need, not to speak of warrant, to doubt the historicity of its figures to the extent that such figures owe their substance to such literature" (10–11). The widely used literary approach to the New Testament has been popular in some religious circles as a way of avoiding historical issues, but here it is suggested that its application somehow disproves the historicity of figures, simply by virtue of the fact that they appear in literature. In most institutions of higher education, students have explained to them early on that historical and literary approaches, while not irrelevant to one another, are not mutually interchangeable and do not perform the same functions. It is not clear to me how Verenna, much less Thompson, could have managed to miss this basic point at some point in their studies.

Chapter 1, by Jim West, focuses on the trend in the study of the ancient Levant often referred to as "minimalism." As West points out, minimalism is "the *supposition* that the biblical text cannot rightly or honestly be mined for historical reconstructions of ancient Israel or earliest Christianity. The underlying assumption here is that the biblical text is not historically oriented" (27). West goes on to point out that this in no wise leads to the conclusion that there was no ancient Israel and no historical Jesus (28). It rather emphasizes that the theological and other interests of the ancient authors were such that it hamstrings any attempt to use them for historical purposes. West suggests that the biblical authors were themselves "minimalists" and that to use their theological texts for historical purposes distorts their theological message (30–31).

Chapter 2, by Roland Boer, looks at the historical contexts of Ludwig Feuerbach, David Strauss, and Bruno Bauer, whose skeptical approach to the Bible had detrimental effects upon their careers. The chapter will help those interested in the history of biblical interpretation to appreciate how the social and political contexts of pioneers in the field shaped their thinking. Unfortunately, rather than adequately tackling the important issue of academic freedom and how religious institutions have continued to censor and dismiss those who engage in mainstream scholarly study down to the present day, Boer speaks simply in terms of skeptical scholars' "acceptance in the academy" even though it does not seem to be the *secular* academy that is typically the problem (53).

Chapter 3, by Lester Grabbe, looks at the references to Jesus outside the New Testament. Since Grabbe is a scholar whose research has focused on ancient Judaism and its sources, it is not at all surprising that he finds the case for the consensus of historians, that there was a historical Jesus of Nazareth, to be persuasive. Although he wrote almost a century after Jesus is supposed to have died, Tacitus often had good sources and seems not to have derived his knowledge from Christian sources, Josephus, or Pliny (58–59). Tacitus, it is pointed out, is the only Roman source to mention Pilate, and thus he shows himself particularly well-informed about the relevant region and period. Suetonius and Pliny the Younger, on the other hand, do not provide clear signs of having independent sources of information. Since Origen indicates that Josephus mentioned Jesus but did not

regard him as the Christ, this confirms the consensus view that there was an original reference to Jesus by Josephus behind the later Testimonium Flavianum as
redacted by Christians (62). Grabbe also discusses the evidence from Agapius and
Michael the Syrian as possible independent testimony to the original form of the
Testimonium. Later rabbinic material is judged unlikely to contain independent
evidence. Thus Grabbe concludes that we have two sources, Tacitus and Josephus,
who wrote independently of both the New Testament and one another, who can
serve as "a vital check on the Christian sources" (68). What these sources provide
is "minimal but nevertheless significant" (69). Among the things confirmed is that
Jesus existed.

Chapter 4, by Niels Peter Lemche, makes one wish there were more chapters
like Grabbe's. Lemche writes, "Historical-critical scholarship usually stops being
critical when it does become really historical. Just try to question the historicity of Jesus in front of a group of New Testament scholars!" (74). This quip is
nothing more than an insult that backfires on Lemche, as becomes clear if we substitute biologists and evolution into his statement. Being critical does not mean
entertaining fringe viewpoints that have offered only incoherent and unpersuasive "challenges" to mainstream scholarship. Indeed, Lemche indicates elsewhere
in his essay that he is something of a mirror image of such antiscience critics
of evolution, as, for instance, when he describes archaeologist William Dever as
"conservative" and suggests that his religious background is to blame for his views
(75). The chapter in fact has almost nothing to do with the historical Jesus.

Emanuel Pfoh begins chapter 5 with a refreshing caveat, in which the author
recognizes that he writes as an outsider to the field of New Testament studies.
Pfoh mentions more than once that his exploration of Jesus as a figure of myth
and cultural memory is irrelevant to the question of Jesus' historicity and is simply
a different approach entirely. However, his conclusion seems to backtrack on these
points, when he says that "[w]e may write many histories and socio-anthropo-
logical treatises on early Christianity, but we cannot write any about a concrete
historical Jesus" (92). While it has since Bultmann often seemed better simply
to set aside historical debates about Jesus and to focus instead on early Christian
thought, that aim has been driven by a theological desire to avoid the ever-shift-
ing sands of historical uncertainty. It is odd to see that stance now embraced by
those whose aim is quite the opposite of Bultmann's. It may perhaps be easier to
study early Christianity than the historical figure of Jesus. But not necessarily so.
Whether we can know anything about realities in early Christian communities
likewise depends on the trustworthiness or otherwise of textual sources and the
historical-critical study thereof. Consequently, it is not clear that dismissing the
possibility of knowledge about a historical Jesus, while hoping for knowledge of a
historical early Christianity, would actually fare significantly better.

Part 2 of the book begins with chapter 6, by Robert Price, who is always entertaining (if also frustrating) to read. Bald assertions, such as that there is not merely
a paucity of information about a historical Jesus in Paul's letters but "no such material," pepper his work (95). His chapter asks whether an early date for Paul's letters

is essential for mythicism to be plausible, and it is as telling as it is amusing that his conclusion appears to be that *no* particular dating of any of the evidence would in any way be incompatible with mythicism. One can be forgiven for wondering whether this shows that the mythicist stance in fact has nothing whatsoever to do with evidence. This impression is reinforced when notions of Marcionite original versions of texts, as proposed by Couchoud, are simply accepted without evidence or argument (100, 113, 116). Price lays out a list of twenty-two characteristics of mythical figures, some of which fit both historical and purely mythical figures, some of which do not fit Jesus, and some of which match up with later Christian sources but not our earliest ones (108–9). He also fails to notice that his principle that legends grow rather than shrink has the potential to undercut his entire argument (112).

Chapter 7, by Mogens Müller, offers the opposite viewpoint to Price's, namely, that "Paul is the oldest witness to the transformation of the historical person, that is, Jesus of Nazareth, into a heavenly savior" (118). Müller makes a number of important points, including that parallels cannot merely be assumed to indicate sources and that the presence of a mythologized figure in our sources does not mean there was no historical figure at the root of the tradition. A significant portion of the chapter is then dedicated to surveying precisely those few instances of Paul citing Jesus' words that Price claimed do not exist. Müller suggests that the letter genre must have been deemed inappropriate for extensive presentation of Jesus' teaching, since the pseudonymous Petrine epistles do not offer fabricated Jesus' teaching to support their message, despite claiming special eyewitness authority. We would have expected a pseudepigrapher to offer such material if the epistolary genre were deemed well-suited to presenting it (127).

Chapter 8, by Thomas Verenna, tries to find alternative interpretations for those texts in Paul's letters that are most naturally understood as referring to an actual historical human being Jesus, in service of the unconventional argument that "Paul did not believe his Jesus was ever historical in the first place" but was rather derived entirely from Jewish Scripture and thought to be a purely celestial figure (132). Verenna attempts to justify the wedge he inserts between Paul and the Gospels in terms of Paul not having been a Christian, but a Jew, and Judaism therefore being his appropriate interpretative milieu (136). But the New Testament Gospels are not "Christian" in the same sense that Paul is not and are equally Jewish. They are also closer in time to Paul than the rabbis who are offered as an alternative matrix. Moreover, the attempt to use mimesis to argue against historicity is undermined by Paul himself, who expresses his own sense of calling in language drawn from earlier texts. Paul doing so in no way demonstrates his own ahistoricity. Verenna claims that there was an expectation of a crucified Messiah in pre-Christian Judaism (140), and points to Ps 22 and Isa 50–53, which are alluded to by both Paul and Mark, as evidence. Verenna also claims that the archons who crucified Jesus must have been spiritual entities working in a celestial realm, and neither human figures nor spiritual ones working through human agents. He also claims that the death of Jesus was no more literal than Paul's own death together with Christ. He then goes on to use Paul's allegorical treatment of Genesis as though it justified treating Paul's own statements as likewise allegorical (150–51). Treating the reference to Jesus as having been "born of a woman" as a reference to the Hagar/Sarah allegory—without Paul specifying which of the two women Jesus was born from—does not make more sense than other possible interpretations. Finally, that an author engages in allegorical interpretation does not automatically make such a one a *composer* of allegories, much less exclusively such.

Chapter 9, by James Crossley, is on a much more mainstream scholarly topic. Crossley indicates that he does not enjoy the role of defender of the consensus but makes the very important point that not all challenges to established consensuses deserve to carry the day (183–84). Crossley engages the attempts by conservative scholars to rehabilitate the Gospel of John as a source of knowledge about the historical Jesus. Crossley nuances his defense of the traditional view well, making the case in dialogue with Anderson, Bauckham, and others that the Synoptic Gospels are closer to the historical reality, and thus John's differences weaken its claim to provide historical information. Even in those instances where a plausible case can be made for the Gospel of John providing independent historical data, it is a case that could scarcely be made without first having the Synoptics. Crossley also tackles the claim that the author of the Fourth Gospel was an eyewitness, writing, "Even if we were to accept that an eyewitness wrote John's Gospel, it seems to me that we would have a highly creative eyewitness who wrote creative fiction concerning Jesus" (175).

Chapter 10, by Thomas Thompson, explores the possibility that Mark 1:12–13 echoes an ancient mythic theme. In the process, he illustrates well the pitfalls involved in venturing from one's field of expertise into another. Thompson seems to confuse John the Baptist with Jesus, when on page 188 he attributes the saying in Matt 3:9 to the latter. Further, while the chapter itself offers a fascinating intertextual exploration between the temptation narrative and earlier texts, one has to wonder why Thompson considers his treatment of this story, which few if any would claim is historical, germane to the question of Jesus' historicity. As many other contributors to the volume point out, it is not the presence of myth or symbolic storytelling that demonstrates ahistoricity; it is the absence of anything that can be shown to be historical. Nevertheless, considered apart from the volume's supposed aim of exploring "the question of the historicity of Jesus," the chapter is fascinating, as Thompson's knowledge of the Hebrew Bible and the ancient Near East allows him to explore many fascinating points of intersection between those sources and stories about Jesus.

Chapter 11, by Ingrid Hjelm, explores details of Luke's Gospel through their intertextual relationship with texts from the Hebrew Bible. Beginning with a comparison of Matthew's and Luke's genealogies, and continuing by way of Solomon, Hjelm finds there to be important echoes of earlier traditions about relations between the northern and southern kingdoms, which add particular resonances to the parable of the Good Samaritan. The sophistication of Luke's treatment of the Jewish Scriptures in weaving his own narrative leads Hjelm to raise the possibility that the author might have been a Hellenized Jew rather than a Gentile, as tends to be assumed.

Chapter 12, by Joshua Sabih, focuses on Isa in the Qur'an, making the case that treating this figure simply as another iteration of Jesus, and an inferior one when it comes to historicity, reflects only one possible approach to the material. Sabih argues that, rather than representing a poor reflection of the historical Jesus, Isa in the Qur'an represents a conscious rejection of the Christian Jesus and his deliberate transformation into an Islamic figure. This can be seen in particular in the Qur'an's deliberate choice of a different name than any of those used in that time for Jesus, including among Arabic-speaking Christians. Although possible relationships of the Quranic form of the name to earlier Jewish or Mandaean forms are mentioned in the chapter, the question of possible linguistic derivations has yet to be resolved satisfactorily. Sabih's chapter, however, emphasizes that the reason for the different name is ultimately the aim of offering an alternative to the Jesus of Christian beliefs and sources.

Chapter 13, by K. L. Noll, makes readers glad they persisted until the end of the book. Noll offers a fascinating look at the early Jesus movement from a Darwinian perspective, in terms of the concept of memes proposed by Richard Dawkins. He focuses significant attention on the incompatible conclusions of Thomas Thompson and Richard Bauckham regarding the nature of the Gospels and their depictions of Jesus. Noll recognizes that Thompson overreaches in his claim that the presence of common motifs demonstrate Jesus' ahistoricity (246). Noll goes on to suggest, making comparisons with the hadiths about Muhammad, which were invented in an Islamic context, that the attribution of teaching to Jesus in the Gospels is actually an attempt to bolster the teaching of Paul and other early Christians by connecting it with Jesus. There is a great deal within the chapter that is not only insightful but pithy, memorable, and quotable, suggesting that Noll has taken the message of memes to heart not only in relation to the historical questions he investigated but also how he writes about them.

Whether this Darwinian approach to early Christian origins will prove persuasive in most of its details, and particularly in Noll's version, which claims that little if anything of the "DNA" of Jesus' own teaching and ideas managed to propagate to those after him, remains to be seen. But it is a fascinating approach, and one that suggests a take-away message from this volume as a whole. Much that is found within its pages is either not really germane to the question of the historical Jesus or fails to do justice to the relevant evidence. From the rest, the overall conclusion is that (1) there is good reason to think there was a historical Jesus, and (2) we can say almost nothing about him with a high degree of confidence. So, while some of the authors of this book have tried to revive an older meme about a purely mythical Jesus (and, from an opposing perspective, Bauckham and others have tried to revive a meme about eyewitness testimony), it may prove to be a Bultmannian meme that has the features best suited to thriving in the environment of the academy.

Portraits of Jesus: Studies in Christology, edited by Francis J. Moloney, Susan E. Myers. Wissenschaftliche Untersuchungen zum Neuen Testament 2/321. Tübingen: Mohr Siebeck, 2012. Pp. xx + 460. Paper. €89.00. ISBN 9783161517952. SDB

Francis J. Moloney, SDB, Australian Catholic University, Melbourne, Australia

Harold W. Attridge, former Dean of Yale Divinity School, currently the Sterling Professor at the University, is honored by this collection of studies authored by a number of grateful colleagues and former students from his earlier presence at the University of Notre Dame and from Yale Divinity School. The volume responds to its title as a variety of "portraits" are analyzed: Jesus in Gospel literature, Jesus in Paul, Jesus in prayer and liturgy, and Jesus in other early Christian literature. Attridge's broad interest in early Christianity is fittingly celebrated.

The section on the Gospels opens with essays from George L. Parsenios and Joshua Ezra Burns that deal with rhetorical possibilities in the Gospel of John. Parsenios claims that the Johannine Jesus uses *sententious* speech, a maxim that expresses a broadly held truth in a brief and pointed style (e.g., John 3:31: "He who comes from above is above all; he who is of the earth belongs to the earth"), common in Latin rhetoric. He traces its use in Quintilian and Tacitus. However similar the use of this rhetoric might be, John uses it is a way that differs somewhat from other classical examples. While Jesus' *sententiae* may reinforce the distance between Jesus and his world from others, as "no words are able to explain the mystery of the incarnation" (26), he also offers a bridge to cross the gap: faith in Jesus.

Burns finds Jesus' words in John 5:17: "My Father is still working, and I also am working," not primarily a reflection of Jewish reflection upon Jesus' taking over a role allowed only to God in Jewish thought, as is generally claimed. He suggests it is a form of Jewish ironic humor. The Johannine Jesus is poking fun at his Jewish interlocutors, who have misunderstood his actions and claims across verses 1–17, and is out-Jewishing the Jews, a critique of Jewish tradition, but no less Jewish in its formulation.

Stephen P. Ahearne-Kroll draws attention to a wealth of hidden Scriptural references in the Gospel of Mark that heighten the sense of the divine presence in Jesus' messianic sonship, realized only through suffering.

Jeremy F. Hultin examines the many situations in the Gospel of Mark where Jesus' command to silence about his possible messianic status is disobeyed. He suggests that this motif arises from a situation in early Christianity that needed to indicate that Jesus did all he could to keep his miraculous deeds, the milling crowds, and his messianic identity unknown. He, therefore, was not to be blamed for putting religious and political leaders in an impossible situation where that had to act against him and his followers. That blame belongs to others, who were disobedient to Jesus' commands to secrecy.

The Roman world forms the background for the study of Timothy Luckritz Marquis, who draws parallels between a crucified Roman, Gavius (with help from Cicero's *Verrine Orations*), the murder of Germanicus (as reported, largely, by Tacitus and Suetonius), and the crucifixion of Jesus, ironically presented in the Gospels as a coronation-execution, with serious social, political, and religious consequences.

Stephen Davis's fascinating study begins with the well-known story of Jesus and the birds that opens the Infancy Gospel of Thomas. Through an analysis of a remarkable breadth of parallels, he shows that "bird stories" enabled the readers of the Gospel of Thomas to recall their own experience of childhood and locate the child Jesus in that "site of memory," but at the same time make the link with the use of birds in ritual activities that granted humans access to divine power.

The opening essay in the Pauline section is Gregory E. Sterling's fine study of possible Philonic background to the Pauline idea of "the image of God," as it is found in 1 Cor 15:44b–49, 2 Cor 3:7–4:4, Rom 8:29–30 and some christological hymns (Col 1:15; Phil 2:6; Heb 1:3). He traces Philo's interpretation of Gen 1:27 and 2:7, suggesting that Philo and Paul share an exegetical tradition that enabled Paul to present Jesus Christ as the "image" of God and the believer as the "image of the image."

Judith M. Gundry makes a strong case for 1 Cor 7:4 on the blessedness of remaining a widow as a Pauline use of the Jesus tradition found in Luke 23:29 and 20:33–36. An equally strong case is made in Emma Wasserman's reflections on Paul's apparent lack of concern about nonexistent "gods" in 8:1–13 (see v. 4) coupled with his warnings on the dangers of eating at the tables of idols in 10:25–11:1. She suggests that he uses traditional anthropomorphic polemic against "the gods" (see Deut 32, Jer 10; Isa 40–48 [a high God and lesser gods]) and then expropriates Greek philosophical traditions about the metaphysics of causality. Paul is intellectually eclectic "and produces a synthesis that conforms to no single idea" (227).

Thomas H. Tobin unravels Paul's use of pre-Pauline christological traditions in Rom 3:21–26 in an enlightening exposition of this crucial articulation of God's redemption of all who believe in Christ, through the forgiveness of all sins that have been committed in the period of God's patience. His carefully articulated argument attempts to establish the content of the earlier Christian confession and Paul's modification of it. Tobin's temporal setting of the importance of what God does *now*, manifesting righteousness apart from the law, is a helpful contribution to never-ending debates about this crucial Pauline passage.

Paul Bradshaw's rich study of Jesus in early Christian liturgical texts shows that there was a variety of prayerful approaches to Jesus, especially in doxologies. Prayers were often addressed to Jesus without reference to the Father, and it was not until the fourth century, as "orthodox" doctrine became more firm, that prayer was normally offered to the Father, through the Son, and in the Spirit. Susan E. Myers supports Bradshaw's more general study with a detailed analysis of the various prayer "forms" and circumstances in the novelistic Acts of Thomas.

Josef Jungmann's claim that prayers are addressed to Jesus only after the rise of Arianism in the fourth century neglects important evidence that points to a different, and more vibrant, prayerful approach to Jesus, at least in early Syriac-speaking Christianity, well before the rise of Arianism.

Beginning with the current Maronite baptismal rite, Bryan D. Spinks traces images of Christ across early Syriac Christianity, represented by the Odes of Solomon, the Acts of Thomas, the Hymns of Ephrem, and the writings of Jacob of Serugh, recently recovered by Sebastian Brock. He shows that, while the current Maronite rite is contemporary, its use of images of branding sheep, putting on a robe of glory, and the font as a womb is "handing on a tradition" that is deeply embedded in ancient Syriac baptismal traditions.

Two studies of the Letter to the Hebrews open the final section on portraits of Jesus in other early Christian literature. Joshua D. Garroway provocatively suggests that Hebrews' presentation of Jesus as the self-sacrificing high priest after the order of Melchizedek is deliberate post-Pauline explanation of the *hilastērion* of Rom 3:25, indicating how both Jews and Gentiles could become children of Abraham. The new people served by Christ are the people of Abraham because he serves them as priest after the order of Abraham. It would be interesting to know whether Thomas Tobin's reading of Rom 3:21–26 (235–43) would countenance such a suggestion.

Candida R. Moss argues cogently against accepted opinion that Heb 1:1–4 was originally independent of the document as a whole. Structurally and theologically it serves as a genuine "prologue," introducing the reader to the themes delivered at greater length in the document: "The themes of kinship, sacrifice and superiority are all found here, but most important the centre of the chiastic structure (see 324–25) focuses upon the obedient word of the Son" (332).

Daniel C. Harlow argues that there is no charge of illegitimacy aimed against Jesus in John 8:41 but that Origen's interpretation of John 8:41, in both his *Against Celsus* and his earlier *Commentary on John*, reflects the polemical recasting of Matthew's infancy narrative that may have been part of rival disputes in cosmopolitan Caesarea. Jesus was born of an adulterous relationship between Mary and a Roman soldier, Panthera; he learned magic in Egypt, where his mother had fled to escape shame.

Providing the reader with text-critical background and possible thematic (if not literal) deliberate links with the Gospel narratives, Richard I. Pervo argues that the Acts of Paul presents Paul, in considerable detail, as a Christ figure.

In a dense essay (especially for the uninitiated) Dylan M. Burns surveys traces of what he chooses to call "Jesus' reincarnations" (although tempted to regard the tendency as "born again") across very early Jewish Christian literature (Elchasites, Ebionites, and the Pseudo-Clementine literature). He regards this theme as very early, most likely from the second century, and suggests that it has also had an influence upon the use of the same theme for the various incarnations of Seth. There is evidence for reincarnation in some Manichean literature, but this appears to have developed independently.

The final essay, from Michael Peppard, is a delightful study of the use of the image of Jesus as an "apprentice," from John 5:19, and Athanasius's use of the further image of "the imperial statue." Both of these images were used in the fourth-century debates that surrounded the question of the Father-Son relationship. Their ongoing effectiveness, however, has dissipated, so that they have now been "archived."

This is a challenging book. Harry Attridge has excelled in so many areas of specialization that we lesser scholars can only look on in awe. One thing that I missed, so common in Festschriften, was an exhaustive list of Professor Attridge's publications. It would have made sense of the breadth of material covered by the studies in the volume. There are places in this collection where I sense a return to "paralellomania," but that may be my problem. The current interest in "empire" is also occasionally present in a way that may not please some. Every essay is well-researched, well-written, well-documented, full of interest and information. Not everything will interest everyone, but there are important contributions in these essays that deserve the attention of all who work in early Christianity. Whatever the interest may be (Synoptics, John, Paul, Hebrews, Syriac Christianity, early patristics, and gnostic Christianity), it is represented and skillfully discussed by the contributors. All are part of Harry Attridge's prodigious armory!

Soundings in the Religion of Jesus: Perspectives and Methods in Jewish and Christian Scholarship, edited by Bruce Chilton, Anthony Le Donne, and Jacob Neusner. Minneapolis: Fortress, 2012. Pp. xx + 268. Paper. $49.00. ISBN 9780800698010.

Benjamin I. Simpson, Dallas Theological Seminary, Houston, Texas

Chilton, Le Donne, and Neusner have assembled a team of Jewish and Christian scholars to investigate Jesus' Jewishness in order to contribute to the dialogue between Judaism and Christianity. The value of this volume is the diverse perspectives represented. Because of the makeup of the group, tensions inevitably enter the discussion; it is here that the reader will have his or her assumptions challenged. If one is open to the dialogue, with a goal of mutual understanding, there is a pay-off. One gains a greater appreciation of one's own heritage as well as an appreciation of different perspectives.

The book is divided into four distinct parts. In the first, "The New Testament Jesus and Exclusionary Boundaries," contributors show how the Gospels present Jesus' own boundaries. Leonard Greenspoon investigates how English translations omit Jewish characteristics from texts, specifically how translators approach οἱ Ἰουδαῖοι. Within the context of the New Testament, the term suggests opposition to Christianity. A modern reader may construe the term to mean all Jews, but the author may refer to the Jewish leadership. In this respect, the translation has lost exegetical accuracy. A literal translation of a routine first-century term may be offensive to a modern reader. The job of the translator is to portray the text as faithfully as possible; however, this should be done with an eye on how the reader may construe the translation.

In the second essay Joel N. Lohr argues that Matt 25:31–46, Jesus' parable of the sheep and goats, reflects a Jewish worldview. The binary division between two groups along with God as the judge and eschatological punishment as the final judgment reflects a Jewish outlook. However, the object of this judgment is "the nations," excluding Israel. The teaching might create embarrassment for Christians by suggesting that some may achieve eschatological reward apart from faith through good deeds (however, see Rom 2:12–16, 26). The origin of the saying remains debatable, but the saying highlights a growing distance between the Matthean community and the Jewish context.

In "A Dogmatic Jesus," Anne Lapidus Lerner looks at Jesus' interaction with the Syro-Phoenician woman in Mark 7:24–30 (Matt 15:21–28). She highlights Jesus' harsh response and concludes that the woman, with her quick-witted response to Jesus' initial denigration, is the heroine of the story. In contrast, Jesus makes no attempt to heal the daughter and insults the woman. Even more insulting is that, when Jesus relents, he expends no effort in healing the girl. Lerner's reading may shock some conservative Christians. Jesus' statement stands in stark contrast with other interactions between him and Gentiles. In my view, a more plausible reading might be that Jesus made the statement for rhetorical effect; this is more clearly seen in the Matthean account. By reflecting an attitude within the culture and then commending the woman's faith, Jesus challenges the cultural attitude. While we might debate Jesus' intention, he made the statement. In addition, the disciples' assent to the cultural script is often overlooked (Matt 15:23).

The second part of the book, "Early Jewish and Gentile Perspectives on Jesus," addresses how early communities viewed Jesus. First Michael J. Cook analyzes the distribution of the Jewish opponents throughout Mark's Gospel. Cook argues that Mark reveals two conflicts between Jesus and various Jewish groups: Jerusalem Jewish leaders criticizing Jesus' actions against the temple and Galilean Pharisees who differed with Jesus concerning purity and divorce. By projecting the Galilean groups toward the conclusion of the Gospel and retrojecting the Jerusalem leadership toward the front of the Gospel, Mark describes a homogeneous Jewish group. Cook goes too far, I think, when he says that Mark cannot be trusted historically because of this editorial move. It is clear that Jesus would have elicited many different responses, but Mark as a storyteller presented the one germane to his narrative.

Donald Senior discusses the Jewish backdrop of Matthew's Gospel, a community of Jewish Christians. Even in the midst of the growing tension of the dominant Jewish groups and a growing number of gentile Christians, the Matthean community can appreciate the Jewish context of Jesus' message. The author of Matthew provides a Jewish perspective on Jesus' mission and dispute over the law. The author's description of Jesus in exalted terms portrays his theological interest, but the Jewish backdrop creates a helpful perspective for us to understand Jesus. Senior concludes: "When all is said and done the fundamental difference between contemporary Judaism and Christianity is not a dispute about the Jewish character of the historical Jesus but the ultimate identity and mission attributed to Jesus by orthodox Christian faith" (94).

In the last essay in this section, Eyal Regev notes that Mark presented two accusations against Jesus: his action against the temple, and that he is a false messiah. Regev argues that the first is historically plausible, while the second is not. He argues that the messianic accusation fits with Mark's editorial intent; however,

Dunn points out that Jesus' status would have been a point of popular speculation (see Mark 6:14–15; 8:28–29; pp. 168–69). The rest of Regev's essay hellpfully situates Jesus' temple action with the Jewish and Roman responses. By investigating the worldviews of each character, we can see what motivates his or her actions. Jesus' protest against moral impurity, particularly in regard to illicit financial gain, drives his protest against the temple. However, it is against illicit financial gain, not the temple per se. The temple leadership interpreted Jesus' protest as an offense to their purity. Pilate, along with the Roman government, would have interpreted Jesus' action as a threat against the empire, since the government sanctioned the temple and elected its leadership.

Part 3 shifts from looking at ancient texts to discussing Jesus research before and after German National Socialism. Thus Anthony Le Donne argues that the normal three-phase scheme of historical Jesus research, following Albert Schweitzer's research, distorts and obscures a great deal of Jesus research prior to the Enlightenment and during the so-called "No Quest" phase. In his later response Dunn criticizes Le Donne's position for ignoring the critical tools developed after the Enlightenment (179). However, Le Donne's thesis situates historical Jesus research within the larger Jewish-Christian dialogue and merits closer inspection. Not only does this help us read early debates between Christians and Jews; it helps clarify our own historical perspective following the Holocaust.

Dagmar Winter argues that a distinguishing mark of "Third Quest" research is situating Jesus within Second Temple Judaism, unlike previous research, which sought an image of Jesus that was dissimilar to Judaism. Winter shows four motives for creating a dissimilar Jesus: anti-Semitism, projecting Christian theological concerns onto Jesus and his opponents, portraying Jesus as a genius within Judaism and thus setting him apart from Judaism, and understanding Jesus primarily in christological terms and thus setting him apart from humanity. Winter's thesis describes most sound historical work on Jesus today but raises the question of Jesus' relationship to early Christianity.

Gerd Theissen reflects on his own theological education in Germany after the Second World War. He shows that, even though the motive might be different, the New Quest highlights a Jesus distinct from Judaism in the same manner as National Socialistic German Christians. Even though Bultmann rejected discrimination of Jesus and the dejudaization of Christianity, he argued for demythologization, which situated Jesus within Judaism but deemphasized Jesus' Jewishness for Christianity. The New Questers followed this model by showing how Jesus transcended Judaism. Theissen states: "Therefore, they interpreted his conflicts *within* Judaism as conflicts *with* Judaism" (148). Theissen situates Jesus within Judaism by comparing structures within Judaism, various groups, and forms of expression.

The fourth part concludes the book. James D. G. Dunn responds to each of the essays, raising helpful questions and observations. Amy-Jill Levine makes several observations for a fruitful Jewish-Christian dialogue, namely, that we should expect differences but put forward mutual respect. Bruce Chilton and Jacob

Neusner conclude the volume by showing the commitment of both Judaism and Christianity to the Hebrew Bible even though they read it differently.

In short, this is a helpful volume. The significant question that confronts each contributor is Jesus' relationship with Judaism, on the one hand, and Christianity, on the other. It is interesting to see how each responds. As Levine concludes, this is not the center of the dialogue, but it is a center. The editors and contributors are to be commended. Not only does the volume instruct; it models how the dialogue can proceed.

Jesus in Continuum, edited by Tom Holmén. Wissenschaftliche Untersuchungen zum Neuen Testament 289. Tübingen: Mohr Siebeck, 2012. Pp. xxvi + 492. Hardcover. €129.00. ISBN 9783161506833.

Sarah E. Rollens, University of Alabama, Tuscaloosa, Alabama

For those frustrated with the many portraits of Jesus that have emerged in the last several decades of historical Jesus scholarship, this collection hopes to offer a new way forward. Editor Tom Holmén challenges scholars to look anew at how the concept of difference helps us understand the historical Jesus—not just how Jesus differed from features of his contemporary milieu but also how he differed from later Christianity. This method, which he has introduced in previous publications, is coined the "continuum" approach. The present volume is laid out as a series of case studies in which each contributor asks how a dimension of Jesus is different from Judaism or the Greco-Roman world and then how it differs from later Christianity. There is, however, no assumption of a systematic development: "Jesus may have adhered to or departed from early Judaism, and again, early Christianity may have adhered to or departed from the Jesuanic proclamation.... The continuum approach thus challenges scholars to explain 'why'" (x). In his own contribution, he examines the theoretical implications of using "difference" as a heuristic category. His goal is to find a way to understand this as more than a criterion of authenticity. This is a badly needed contribution, for Jesus' dissimilarity, once a popular indicator of the authenticity of his words and deeds, has been roundly critiqued for creating a Jesus who bears no connection to his environment. Holmén uses the continuum method to probe Jesus' teachings on love, sinners, fasting, and divorce, demonstrating that one learns different things depending on whether one compares these features to Judaism or to later Christianity. In particular, early Christians were well aware that they could not reproduce every part of Jesus in their lives: "Jesus' identity, recognized and upheld by his followers, was such that he could not be followed in all things" (40).

After Holmén's opening essay, Gerd Theissen sets out to use the continuum framework to rethink the "universal" and "radical" character of Jesus, eschewing the old criterion of dissimilarity and working instead with contextual plausibility. Within Judaism, he proposes, Jesus was seen as a "liberal Jew" who universalized the message of Judaism to make it applicable to non-Jews, while within Christianity he became "radical Jew" who focused on "elements that distinguished Jews from non-Jews" (44). Universalizing, Theissen argues, is evident in Jesus' teachings and activities, which were presented in such a way that they broke down barriers between Jews and Gentiles. Later Christians were the ones who took these universalizing tendencies out of their Jewish contexts. In fact, this was a strategy for survival. As he explains, "the first Christians developed and radicalized precisely those Jewish features that were hard to accept in the pagan world" (53), such as nationalized messianism or ethical stipulations only applicable to Jews. Following scholars of the cognitive science of religion such as Pascal Boyer, Theissen ends with an intriguing proposal, that the counterintuitive nature of these dimensions (universalism and radicalism) might account for early Christianity's spread: the strange or radical ideas in Jesus' teachings are smuggled in by the familiar and universal dimensions.

Michael F. Bird then examines the relationship between Jesus' teachings about salvation and the Gentiles and the later deliberate effort by early Christians to target Gentiles for conversion. The question Christians eventually had to grapple with was, "what kind of Gentile could be admitted to the group?" Relying strongly on Luke-Acts, Bird focuses on Greek-speaking and Aramaic-speaking Christians; the former especially opened conversion to non-Jews and linked the movement with Paul. Rather than hiving these groups off from one another, Bird sees them as representative of intra-community debates, complete with "cross-fertilization" (76) about how best to achieve successful missionizing. Against the older perspective that saw the Gentile mission as a late development, Bird argues that it actually emerged rather early and that there were several different groups involved, sometimes cooperating, sometimes competing. Jesus himself was "open to receiving Gentiles when they exhibited faith in Israel's God" (80). Even so, Jesus did not anticipate supersessionism—he hoped Israel would be integrally involved in the mission to Gentiles—but his teachings were the "germinal roots" (86) for the Gentile mission.

James G. Crossley follows with an exploration of why Jesus is remembered to have observed purity laws but later Christians did not, invoking socioeconomic explanation to account for this development. Jesus shows no evidence of compromising the basics of food laws; his issues were with the interpretation of some purity practices. By looking at analogies in forms of social banditry (a problematic term, he admits), he observes that many revolutionary actions in the time of Jesus were rooted in socioeconomic circumstances that led people (e.g., John of Gischala and Jesus who burned Tiberias) to reinterpret the law for their own agendas. Jesus' "expanded" purity codes show concern for "people who could not or would not observe them" (105), otherwise classed as "sinners." This concern, moreover, provides space for the inclusion of Gentiles; as more Gentiles accrued to the group, probably with varying levels of commitment, food laws would have become even more lax to the point of "not bothering" (108).

The late Marvin Meyer deals with "[o]ne of the most enigmatic, elusive, and fascinating figures in the entire biblical narrative" (115), Judas Iscariot. He begins by outlining the ways that Judas is progressively maligned over time in early Christian literature, which stands in stark contrast to the generally positive depiction in the Gospel of Judas, then wonders how this transformation came about. It results, he argues, from the general tendency by Christians to shift the blame for Jesus' death from Romans to Jews, as Christians struggled with the cognitive dissonance of living in the Roman world. He suggests that "the role of Judas the betrayer, whose very name recalls the world for 'Jew', is meant to address the same issue" (128), deflecting the blame from the Romans. The Gospel of Judas's Christology, he concludes, further underscores that the passion narrative was not originally the key to all early Christian understandings of Jesus.

In a curious contribution, Riemer Roukema assesses the treatment of "gnostic" and "catholic" Christianities in the popular works of Elaine Pagels and Bart Ehrman. By obliging the Synoptic Gospels to represent "mainstream" or "catholic" Christianity, he compares their ideas to representations of gnostic Christianity, such as the Gospel of Judas and the Gospel of Thomas. He concludes that it is easier to imagine a trajectory from the historical Jesus to "catholic" Christianity than it is to "gnostic" Christianity, suggesting that "catholic" Christianity stands in stronger continuity with Jesus. It is not especially clear, however, why one should consider "mainstream" or "catholic" Christianity to be a coherent entity in such an early time period (or ever, for that matter, given the constant contestation of so many aspects of Christianity throughout history).

Four essays examine Jesus' relation to outsiders. Darrell L. Bock wonders what precisely Jesus did to get himself in trouble and uses a synthetic approach instead of focusing on disconnected sayings or units. He assesses a few "minor" irritants that may have contributed to Jesus' predicament: association with tax-collectors and sinners, Sabbath and healing controversies, and the like. The "major" irritants are familiar: the cleansing of the temple, the threat of future judgment directed at Jewish leaders, and the reorienting of the Passover meal to be about Jesus' own significance. While many of these individual features can be found among Jesus' contemporaries, this particular configuration of irritants points to Jesus' "uniqueness" (208) and hence the reason for his fate. James H. Charlesworth speculates about Jesus' attitudes toward his enemies, based on the "genius" he cultivated to extend the love ethic, which had roots in Jewish teachings but was deployed rather differently by Jesus. André Gagné gives a sociological analysis of the insider/outsider rhetoric in Jesus' teachings. In his examples, Mark and Thomas, Jesus is remembered as cultivating a sectarian identity similar to that present at Qumran, but he seems to have departed from this somewhat by his willingness to extend teachings to outsiders. Mary J. Marshall explores ancient hospitality codes and how Jesus' teachings fit with them. Both Jewish authors and Greco-Roman authors share a concern for hospitality toward strangers, although the former often tie it to religious duty and righteousness. The historical Jesus, she argues, relied on hospitality during his travels and should be understood, in many meal scenes, as a guest who promoted "radical inclusiveness" (321). Early Christians tried to extend this emphasis on hospitality when missionaries went about their work but clearly ran into trouble, as illustrated by the New Testament epistles.

Some of the essays examine very broad themes, such as Mary Ann Beavis's contribution, which probes Jesus in his utopian context, looking both to Jewish utopia ideals and those that eventually surface in Paul's letters. Guiding her analysis is Doron Mendels's list of seventeen features that Hellenistic utopias and the Essenes have in common. She finds most of these to be present in Paul's letters. Jesus' utopian ideals came to expression in the (rather nebulous) kingdom of God, which she argues was "anti-political": it "deliberately downplayed explicitly nationalistic, restorationist, and particularist overtones and aspirations" (163) and was rather an ideology that endorsed God as a universal king.

Other contributions are narrowly focused, such as John S. Kloppenborg's treatment of the measure-for-measure aphorism (Q 6:38c//Mark 4:24//Clem. 13.2), a saying attributed to Jesus that bears strong resemblance to routine agricultural transactions well-attested in documentary papyri. In fact, "Greco-Egyptian agricultural loans ... offer the closest conceptual and verbal parallels to the measure-for-measure aphorism" (258). The saying as it was originally formulated is noteworthy because it is framed from the lender's perspective rather than the borrower's, perhaps indicating that, if the saying is authentic, then Jesus extended his message beyond those who were most economically disadvantaged. At the very least, the different ways the saying was used by later authors shows the creativity of the earliest authors for making the aphorism serve their own ends.

Setting his sights on Jesus' identity, Michael Labahn examines how Jesus was remembered as "God's envoy of eschatological transformation" (265) who did miraculous deeds. Extraordinary deeds, he argues, seem likely to be historical, although we only have access to them through narrative, so his main interest is in the way they preserve "meaning behind memory" (289). By surveying Jewish literature, Labahn finds that God himself is usually depicted as the agent of miraculous events, suggesting that Jesus probably understood God as working though him to do extraordinary deeds. Later Christians reworked the stories to make Jesus himself the focal point so as to serve their own social interests and identity formation. "An agent can make a career," Labahn surmises, "that leads him from being an agent to becoming a powerful character upon which people place their own hopes" (295).

Stanley Porter tackles the lofty topic of resurrection. He shows first that the Jewish precedents for resurrection are not as explicit as many believe, whereas the Greco-Roman ones are actually more developed that many (such as N.T. Wright, a frequent interlocutor in this essay) acknowledge. Paul moves beyond the underdeveloped ideas of resurrection in Jewish and Greco-Roman texts, giving new attention to the physical body and the individual experience, inter alia. Porter concludes that there is sufficient evidence to suppose that Jesus made some sort of prediction about his resurrection, although he comments only briefly on the event itself. Heikki Räisänen likewise analyzes a thorny topic, one that often makes theologians uncomfortable: Jesus and hell. In Jewish discourse, notions of hell are strongly correlated to insider-outsider language and often function to ensure insiders that their enemies will be punished. Early Christian discourse preserves the notion of future punishment but goes much further with these ideas, as in such vivid texts as Revelation and Apocalypse of Peter. In this matrix and by using some of the traditional criteria of authenticity, Räisänen concludes that it would have been normal for Jesus to speak about torment upon death, even hell. "How responsible theology should deal with it" (383) is left for theologians.

Markus Tiwald and Christopher Tuckett ask questions about Jesus' continuity with central features of Judaism: Torah/temple and the Sabbath, respectively. Tiwald counters others who have claimed that Jesus, Paul, and early Christians opposed these aspects of Judaism, finding that even their ostensible criticisms of temple and Torah fit perfectly well *within* contemporary Jewish discourse. Jesus himself reinterpreted these aspects insofar as they played a role in his eschatological expectations of the kingdom. Jesus and Paul sorted out their ideas on a familiar playing field: they "remained Jews and we participants in an inner-Jewish discourse: the quest for the correct interpretation of God's will" (408). Tuckett takes the opportunity to look broadly at the concept of Sabbath in Jewish and Christian texts, lest the analysis get bogged down in "whether Jesus did perform 'work' on the Sabbath" (411). He begins with the reminder that Jewish observance of the Sabbath was about more than the routine avoidance of work. Although he admits that there is nothing "startlingly new" (411) here, the essay is a fine way to cap off the volume by demonstrating that even some of the most studied topics can benefit from a fresh methodology. There is little evidence to suggest that the earliest Christians challenged Sabbath observance from outset, but, of course, they later developed distinctive practices. What can be discerned about Jesus' attitude toward the Sabbath is tricky; Tuckett finds that Jesus may have been openly "indifferent" (440) to Sabbath law. Sabbath controversies, however, seem related to Jesus' authority, so the issue is "exploited to focus and to sharpen this challenge by Jesus to his contemporaries about the nature and status of his activity" (442-43).

This is an enjoyable collection to read because most contributors follow the general framework of examining a feature of the historical Jesus in his context and tracing its continuities and discontinuities with what came before and after. Thus, one looks forward to how the comparison will play out in each essay. Moreover, the methodology is provocative within historical Jesus scholarship, which has for too long been wedded to the predictable routine of first outlining the historical context of Second Temple Judaism, then applying the so-called criteria of authenticity to collect the authentic teachings and deeds of Jesus, and finally stitching them all back together in a grand portrait of Jesus—rarely being phased by the fact that despite the agreed-upon criteria, we were still ending up with a multitude of (sometimes incompatible) Jesuses.

If there is a tension in this collection, it is that while the goal of the volume seems to be to fundamentally reassess the way we think about historical Jesus methodology, many contributors are still found relying on some of the traditional criteria of authenticity. Moreover, despite the innovative nature of the continuum approach, there are a number of unquestioned, and hence rather traditional, assumptions throughout these essays: several essays are still looking for what made Jesus unique or what he did to set later events in motion (Crossley rebuts this view in his essay: "we should not simply assume that Jesus caused everything that followed" [89]); some still assume Paul's writings alone are sufficient representatives of the early church; and some are remarkably confident in the historical reliability of Acts for the decades after Jesus' death. Finally, it is worth mentioning that Holmén wants to settle on finding "one Jesus" (x) to account for movement along each continuum—one can imagine how fruitful his methodology would be even without such an interest.

Happily though, many of contributors themselves reflect on the methodology of the volume. Crossley, for instance, recognizes that there could very well be a "strong discontinuity" (89) between Jesus and how Christians understood him, so relying too strongly on a continuum might be misleading. Perhaps one of the wisest assessments is found in Porter's essay, which contains a crucial caution:

> One of the results of this investigation is to illustrate that … creating disjunctions between Greco-Roman and Jewish or even Jewish and Christian perspectives runs the risk of distorting the evidence in a number of ways. One of the ways is in terms of creating false views of the relationships of these "worlds". There were not Greco-Roman and Jewish worlds, in the sense that they were equally viable alternatives. Nor was there a religious versus a pagan world, or a Christian and a non-Christian world. The Greco-Roman world was a world of religious cults, various people groups, and intertwined cultures. (343)

Many of the contributors are likewise careful to demonstrate that the ideas in Jewish, Christian, and Greco-Roman texts frequently overlap. In all, there are many thought-provoking essays here that challenge us to rethink how we have assessed data for the historical Jesus. Holmén's volume has made a determined and welcomed effort to push the conversation forward, and it is a must-read for students of the historical Jesus.

The Political Aims of Jesus, by Douglas E. Oakman. Minneapolis: Fortress, 2012. Pp. xvi + 192. Paper. $26.00. ISBN 9780800638474.

Tobias Hägerland, Lund University, Lund, Sweden

Ever since the days of his doctoral work, the outcome of which was published as *Jesus and the Economic Questions of His Day* (1986), Douglas Oakman has concentrated his research efforts on the task of gaining a more profound understanding of how the historical Jesus' activities and sayings relate to first-century Galilean taxation policies and the impact of these policies on the peasant class. His latest contribution in this regard is *The Political Aims of Jesus.* The title pays homage to Hermann Samuel Reimarus, whose portrait adorns one of the first pages of the volume, and to his epoch-making *Von dem Zwecke Jesu und seiner Jünger* (1778). Oakman sympathizes with Reimarus's view of a Jesus whose aims were intrinsically political, only to be quickly spiritualized and depoliticized after his death, but he notes that social-scientific research and recent progress in historical Jesus studies necessitate a reevaluation and modification of some of the points that Reimarus made.

Oakman begins by reviewing historical Jesus scholarship from Reimarus via the classic studies of Schweitzer, Wrede, Käsemann, and others up to the recent works of Crossan, Horsley, and Meier, with special attention to how different scholars have paid attention to Jesus' political message—or failed to do so. His overview leads him to conclude that, whereas many have indeed touched on the topic, "their views remain still a bit too diffuse or off the mark regarding Jesus' political agenda in first-century Galilean context" (15). One problem, according to Oakman, is that all previous studies tend to depict Jesus as the prophetic leader of a movement; another shortcoming is their failure to view him from the perspective of peasant culture in Herodian Galilee. Accordingly, there is much more to be said, and Oakman sets out to do so with the help of a method that is based on the conviction that the parables and the earliest stratum of Q provide the best source material. This material will be assessed from a rhetorical point of view, placed within a peasant context, and interpreted through the lens of social-scientific theory.

The second chapter introduces the theoretical framework to be deployed in the study. Oakman uses social-scientific models of power relationships in agrarian societies in order to understand the political conflicts between the ruling elite and peasant villagers in first-century Galilee. The monetization and commercialization of local economies, excessive taxation, increasing debts on the part of tenant farmers, and social unrest are seen to exist in a vicious circle that, as Oakman convincingly points out, could not easily be broken through collective revolt. Instead, the pressured conditions of peasants under debt and heavy taxation would have induced more subtle strategies of resistance, such as tax evasion by various means, such as being dishonest about one's produce and family size. As is demonstrated further on in the book, this sociopolitical context forms a plausible backdrop of several of Jesus' parables.

Jesus comes to the center of the stage in the third and fourth chapters. Jesus was a peasant child who found a trade as a simple craftsman. Being a "peasant theologian," Jesus was not concerned with apocalyptic imagination or the interpretation of Scripture but with immediate and concrete needs. He spoke metaphorically of the presence of God as Father and King. God's kingdom (or "the Power," as is Oakman's preferred term) meant for Jesus both that God is the ultimate patron and that peasants have the right to own their land and its produce. By socializing with the destitute as well as with the society's upper strata, Jesus became a broker of the Power, one who worked to replace the Herodian patronage of exploitation with another patronage that favored the poor. After a detailed section on the functions of money in Gospel traditions, Oakman turns to some of Jesus' parables and shows their concern with peasants struggling under the unfair conditions of a monetized agrarian society. He furthermore suggests that the "sinners" who famously joined in Jesus' meals were debtors and that the point of arranging meals where both debtors and tax collectors participated may have been to negotiate between the two groups and thus to broker tax relief. The concern for debt cancellation is also evidenced, Oakman argues, by the plea for forgiveness of debts (not sins!) in the prayer of Jesus. In fact, all of the earliest Q material can be read as expressive of Jesus' tax resistance (105–9). With such a subversive political agenda, which at times was overtly expressed, it is not surprising that Jesus was finally executed as a bandit, as a practitioner of sedition.

The gradual replacement of Jesus' political program with early Christian religion is traced in the fifth chapter. His original message of tax relief and debt cancellation gave way, according to Oakman, to two levels of "interpretation." The first level, evidenced by Q^2, Paul, and Mark, interprets Jesus within an eschatological, apocalyptic framework; the second level, represented by the deutero-Pauline and Pastoral letters, again replaces eschatology with a cosmic mythology in which Jesus attains quasi-divine status. Jesus is depoliticized and his legacy almost entirely repressed or forgotten. Oakman sums up, in the sixth and final chapter, at which points his reconstruction agrees with or differs from that of Reimarus. Especially noteworthy here is Oakman's conclusion that Jesus was in no way the leader of any messianic movement. The book concludes with a "Postscientific Postscript" that draws out the study's implications for contemporary thought and action and three appendices.

I learned a lot about the social context of early first-century Galilee from reading this book, but I find most of its arguments and claims about the historical Jesus unpersuasive. No doubt the fundamental reason for this is Oakman's complete rejection of any influence of "Judean apocalyptic expectations" on Jesus. Whereas he holds that "a persuasive body of recent scholarship has undermined this position (decisively, in my opinion) through more precise analysis of the early Jesus traditions" (71), I think the exact opposite to be the case: the nonapocalyptic Jesus seems to me a peculiar construct that is being embraced only by a minority of North American scholars and that has been refuted many times, perhaps most definitively in Dale Allison's *Constructing Jesus: Memory, Imagination, and History* (2010). Oakman's insistence that Jesus' message was devoid of any eschatological aspects and dealt solely with this-worldly concerns is dependent on a number of exegetical and historical positions that I—with the vast majority of scholars, I dare say—find highly unlikely: for example, that Jesus' view of God differed essentially from John the Baptist's (81, 146), that the prayer "deliver us from [the] evil [one]" is a plea not to be forced to face an evil judge in court (100), that there was no group of the Twelve in Jesus' lifetime (145–46), that Jesus' campaign against taxation policies can explain the crucifixion (111), and that upon the death of Jesus all his followers (except the author of Revelation) replaced his political aims with spiritualized and apocalyptic notions that evince no continuity at all with the historical Jesus (119–29). It is also prompted by a conviction that "[p]easants are oriented to the very day, 'daily bread,' usually not more than to the next harvest, and rarely to some distant or future utopia" (76), which is a statement that at the very least needs some qualification.

Oakman places much confidence in the stratification of Q, claiming that the wisdom aphorisms of Q^1 provide the best access to the historical Jesus, with later compositional layers obscuring the original picture by interpreting Jesus in prophetic and apocalyptic terms. While such a scenario is possible, the assertion that "Q^1 seems too close to Jesus' worldly wisdom and political praxis to be called an interpretation" (71) can hardly stand up against the insights represented by a recent wave of publications on social memory in historical Jesus research. For example, the reasoning in Anthony Le Donne's *Historical Jesus: What Can We Know and How Can We Know It?* (2011) cautions strongly against the notion of the "uninterpreted past" being available through any source, however pristine its origin.

In the end, the merit of Oakman's book is to have highlighted a topic neglected by many Jesus scholars, including myself. Issues of tenancy, taxation, and debts are recurrent in the Gospel tradition, and it is not implausible that Jesus' view of the kingdom grew partly out of them. On the other hand, Jesus' stance toward these issues has to be integrated within a broader reconstruction that allows for multiple dimensions: wisdom *and* apocalypticism, "worldly" politics *and* transcendent belief, subtle resistance *and* revolutionary messianism. One must be careful not to project the dichotomies seemingly taken for granted in a present-day liberal Protestant setting onto the thought world of first-century popular Judaism. The result of a more nuanced approach might not be a Jesus who "shines like a beacon out of the murky past" (137), but at least a historically credible Jesus.

SYNOPTIC GOSPELS

The Rhetoric of Interruption: Speech-Making, Turn-Taking, and Rule-Breaking in Luke-Acts and Ancient Greek Narrative, by Daniel Lynwood Smith. Beihefte zur Zeitschrift für die neutestamentliche Wissenschaft und die Kunde der älteren Kirche 193. Berlin: de Gruyter, 2012. Pp. xiv + 337. Paper. $140. ISBN 9783110296426.

Alex Damm, Wilfrid Laurier University, Waterloo, Ontario, Canada

In his monograph *The Rhetoric of Interruption*, a revision of his doctoral thesis, Daniel Lynwood Smith seeks to determine how authors of Greek historiography use the rhetorical device of interruption, in order to provide a plausible context for assessing the meaning and function of such interruption in Luke-Acts. In his first chapter Smith documents scholarly awareness that in Luke's Gospel and the book of Acts certain characters in the narrative intentionally *interrupt*, usually in protest, the speech (any speech, whether small-scale or a full-blown speech [5]) of characters such as Jesus and Paul. The problem in literature to date, explains

Smith, is that scholars have neither defined this Lukan technique clearly enough nor explored the extent or purposes for which Luke employs it, leaving us without a thorough knowledge of its significance in the Gospel and Acts. Smith aims to repair this ambiguity and so help us understand what precisely counts as interruption and, most importantly, how it rhetorically functions in Luke-Acts.

To do this, Smith's study unfolds in two broad parts. In the first part (chs. 1–4), Smith examines the ancient literary context of Luke-Acts to gauge the functions of intentional interruption. He begins by examining how ancient rhetoric *defines* interruption (ch. 1). Observing that rhetorical treatises, for instance by Aristotle and Quintilian, lack discussion of intentional interruption, Smith turns to modern dialogue analysis and finds that the most precise and realistic meaning of interruption is "violation of a speaking turn ... [or in other words] the presence of a claim of interruption, and the identity of the one(s) interrupting" (17).

Following this definition, Smith explores the literary or rhetorical *function* or *use* of interruption in narratives that most closely approximate the genre of Luke's Gospel and Acts, especially Greek historiographical texts. In chapter 2 Smith examines the *Iliad* and *Odyssey* of Homer, as well as later historiography, for example, the work of Polybius, discovering not only that interruption serves several roles (to show the status of the interrupting party; to attack the speaking party; to encourage the speaking party) but also that these roles are often shaped by a speaker's rhetorical *context,* for instance, a speech's genre, its audience, and the contents of its surrounding narrative. In chapter 3 Smith studies interruption in specifically Greek Jewish historiography, from Septuagint speeches in 1 and 2 Kingdoms to the *Jewish War* and *Jewish Antiquities* of Josephus. Here he again finds varied roles and contexts of interruption and also presciently observes "instances where audiences appeared to be reacting to the specific *content* of a discourse, rather than reacting generally against the speaker" (165, emphasis added). Finally, Smith turns to the literary genre that some have supposed best parallels Luke-Acts, the Greek novel (e.g., Chariton's *Callirhoe*), and finds similar functions of interruption, sometimes during characters' conversations. From his review of Greek literature, Smith concludes that very often interruption expresses not simply one character's hostility or disagreement with another's speech but also "tends to mark significant conflicts, conflicts that fuel the entire plot" (249).

The second part of Smith's study (chs. 5–6) asks, in light of the historiographical conventions to which Luke was exposed, whether and to what extent he uses such rhetorical interruption. In chapter 5 Smith begins by carefully showing that on the most widely held source hypothesis, the Two-Document Hypothesis, Luke appears to have composed much interruption himself, not simply inheriting it from sources such as Mark's Gospel or Q. Strikingly, occurrences of interruption (which are numerous, as for example in Luke 4:28, 9:34, 11:27, 11:37, 16:14 and 21:5) tend to be the province of nonbelieving Jewish characters with whom Jesus and his followers engage. One good illustration is Luke 4:28, in which Jesus' announcement of his mission at Capernaum is interrupted by other Jews who, "filled with rage … got up [and] drove him out of the town" (194–98). More striking for Smith is Luke's use of such interruption, for given its positions in the midst of Jesus's preaching, it works not simply to show conflict but also to "highlight the proclamation of God's saving action through Jesus Christ and the availability of this salvation to all" (247). Interruption is, then, an all-important attention-drawing mechanism. In chapter 6 Smith observes that interruption functions similarly in the book of Acts (e.g., in Acts 4:1). Both in its accentuation of Jewish hostility to the gospel and in its accentuation of the gospel itself, interruption is a mechanism for drawing our attention to places where Luke wants it to be. In his summary (ch. 7) Smith contends that on a general level the form and function of interruption in Luke-Acts call to mind that in earlier Greek texts. On a more precise level, however, there are "unique aspects of Luke's use of interruption: his unusual form of marking interruption (by focusing on the hearers rather than the speakers), his [high] frequency of interruption … and his tendency to mark rejection and acceptance of certain discourse content by means of intentional interruption" (249).

Smith's monograph is an impressive debut for this young biblical scholar, for it shows numerous virtues of historical- and rhetorical-critical scholarship at its best. For one, Smith discusses key terms such as *interruption* fully and with precision (e.g., 17–24). Such precision matters, for Smith's attention to nuance helps him discover Luke's distinct accent upon interruption of speakers in the midst of people *listening*, a nuance that in turn becomes essential in Luke's drawing attention specifically to Jewish *reactions* to Jesus's gospel and its emphasis on both Jewish and Gentile salvation (see, e.g., 242). For another, he reviews the literature on his topic quite thoroughly, evident in his numerous engagements with German scholarship (ch. 1). Smith also grounds his study of rhetorical interruption in an impressively wide swath of Greek literature, paying close attention to primary sources and to key Greek terms employed in interruption (e.g., 29, 155–56). Further, while he creates thorough taxonomies of ancient data to help show patterns in interruption (e.g., 113, 246, 252–99), he is not afraid to show how Luke departs from such patterns; it is proof of Smith's exegetical skill and confidence that he can elucidate both common and novel features of interruption in Luke-Acts. What is more, Smith's very focus on rhetorical interruption is wise: while many exegetes might regard interruption as a sort of distraction or anomaly, Smith pays close attention to it and in doing so breaks new ground, showing how one of Luke's heretofore neglected techniques draws attention to Jesus's gospel.

What might Smith develop in this work? There is not much to say here, but let me briefly suggest a few points. First, it might yield fruit to revisit ancient rhetorical theory with an eye on interruptions. There are places beyond those noted by Smith (239 n. 136), such as Quintilian's *Institutio Oratoria* 9.2.2, where we can detect, through use of a search tool such as the Perseus Digital Library, some discussion of interruption in ancient rhetoric; there might be clues for instance in texts such as Cicero's *On the Ideal Orator* and the *Rhetoric for Herrenius*. Revisiting these Latin sources could help flesh out how ancients understood interruptive speech. Second and related, it might help to examine Latin histori-ography in some measure, since Greek and Latin traditions had cross-fertilized and fused with each other by the first century CE. To his credit, Smith has done a thorough investigation, and Latin historiography might require a separate study; I only suggest it here as a possible avenue for future research. Third, there are a few places (such as on 215–16) where further recourse to ancient discussion of speech structure (prologue, statement of facts, proofs, and conclusion) and con-text could underwrite our knowledge of interruption. Finally, it might be worth further consulting work by Dennis MacDonald with regard to Luke's possible *imitatio* of Homer (see 123 n. 11). I say this because MacDonald's proposals for imitation are quite sophisticated, grounded not just in parallels between texts but also in other measures of plausible source use (see MacDonald, ed., *Mimesis and Intertextuality in Antiquity and Early Christianity* [2001]). If Smith were to incorporate MacDonald's proposal, he might be able to add nuance in describing Lukan interruption, while still acknowledging that *imitatio* of Homer remains just a possibility. Let these suggestions, however, not take away from the fact that Smith has composed a clear and careful study of Luke's rhetorical use of interrup-tion. Any further comments on his work would only interrupt keen students of New Testament rhetoric in their consultation of his book, a model of scholarship that I strongly commend.

Luke: A Commentary, by John T. Carroll. New Testament Library. Louis-ville: Westminster John Knox, 2012. Pp. xl + 554. Hardcover. $50.00. ISBN 9780664221065.

Daniel L. Smith, Saint Louis University, St. Louis, Missouri

In this latest installment of the New Testament Library series, John T. Carroll offers an insightful, coherent commentary on the Gospel of Luke. While he con-centrates primarily on the Lukan narrative, Carroll is quick to admit that his focus is not restricted to the Gospel's first-century readers and listeners. He also wants to highlight "the religious-ethical vision" of Luke's narrative for modern readers, encouraging his twenty-first-century audience to join him in engaging the challenge that Luke's Gospel presents to readers sharing his social location and economic status.

Carroll is the Harriet Robertson Fitts Memorial Professor of New Testament at Union Presbyterian Seminary, and he also forms part of the editorial board for the New Testament Library series. For the most part, Carroll's commentary aligns well with the stated goals of the series: "providing fresh translations based on the best available ancient manuscripts, critical portrayals of the historical world in which the books were created, careful attention to their literary design, and a theologically perceptive exposition of the biblical text." Of these four aims, Carroll ably fulfills the first, adequately treats the second, and excels in the third and fourth. Throughout the commentary Carroll zooms in on Luke's depiction of Jesus as a prophetic messiah engaged in a threefold ministry of liberation or release: from sin, from indebtedness, and from demonic oppression (e.g., 111).

Carroll provides a new translation, which has come to be standard for many commentary series. What is less common is that he constructs his own Greek text to translate into English. Most notably, he frequently follows shorter readings (or "Western noninterpolations," as labeled by Westcott and Hort) in the later chapters of the Gospel (see his treatment of Luke 22:19b–20; 24:3, 6, 12, 36, 40, 51–52). Although he has clearly devoted attention to the particulars of the Greek text, he has given equal attention to the nuance of his English rendition. His lively translation is faithful to the sense of the Greek, yet he avoids wooden renderings of some of Luke's more cumbersome borrowings from the Septuagint.

Although Carroll does pay attention to the historical context, he does not dwell on historical questions. For example, he does not try to solve the problem of conflicting chronology in regard to the final meal of Jesus and whether or not it is a Passover meal. Instead, a footnote dismisses the question: "Whatever the complexities and complications of early Christian traditions and their long history of interpretation…, in Luke this final meal of Jesus with the Twelve *is* the Passover" (432 n. 4, emphasis original). Carroll's commentary does not get bogged down in such details. While other commentaries might insert an excursus at such a point, Carroll limits his use of the excursus, including only four short digressions: "Parallel Birth Announcements—Mary and Zechariah" (43–44), "Women in Luke's Narrative" (248–49), "Poverty and Wealth in Luke's Gospel" (374–77), and "The Reign of God and the Roman Empire in Luke's Gospel" (398–404).

What Carroll does offer is a fresh "literary reading, a narrative reading that pays attention to sequence" (7). He divides the Gospel into eight narrative segments: 1:1–4; 1:5–2:52; 3:1–4:13; 4:14–9:50; 9:51–19:27; 19:28–21:38; 22:1–23:56; 24:1–53. Instead of giving verse-by-verse commentary, Carroll works with larger units of text, tracing literary connections between different verses and passages. Thus, he begins each narrative segment with a review of the previous segment, followed by an introduction to the first subsection of the larger segment, then the English translation (with any necessary textual notes), and, finally, a treatment of each subunit of anywhere from one to sixteen verses. At each level Carroll points to connections between different verses (including catchwords and common motifs), between different passages within Luke's Gospel, between passages in Luke and other Synoptic Gospels (redaction criticism), between passages in Luke and in Acts (always assuming the unity of the two works), and between Lukan passages and other sources (employing the language of intertextuality).

These approaches are not entirely innovative. One of Carroll's primary conversation partners is Joel Green, with whom Carroll co-authored *The Death of Jesus in Early Christianity* (Hendrickson, 1995). Like Green's NICNT commentary (1997), Carroll's commentary is a literary and theological reading of the Third Gospel. While Carroll's contribution may not supplant Green's, his newer and more up-to-date commentary supports and extends Green's move toward literary readings of Luke in its final, canonical form.

While Carroll's commentary has its shortcomings, they are few and far between. His commentary is obviously the product of great erudition, but the limited number of footnotes may prove frustrating to some scholarly readers (or, alternately, encouraging to lay readers). Some might think he notes too many examples of intertextuality; others, too few. His positions on date of composition (75–95 CE) and genre ("apologetic historiography") are relatively uncontroversial. I found only three errors in an otherwise impressively proofread text: "identify-shaping" should be "identity-shaping" (5); "Elijah" should be "Elisha" (second line of 163); and, in Luke 19:13, the soon-to-be king gave his ten slaves ten minas, or one mina each; he did *not* give them "each ten minas" (378). Unfortunately, Carroll also perpetuates the common but mistaken belief that "Cadbury coined the hyphenated expression Luke–Acts in the 1920s" (9). Actually, as Gregory Sterling has pointed out, Benjamin Bacon frequently used the famous hyphenated compound in *An Introduction to the New Testament* (Macmillan, 1900).

Readers looking for commentary on one particular verse may occasionally be disappointed, but Carroll generally offers sound guidance regarding the meaning(s) of larger units of discourse. Furthermore, running headers make it easy to find a given passage, and Carroll has compiled an impressively detailed set of indices. In addition to a full index of scripture citations (and citations from other ancient sources), the commentary includes a massive "Index of Subjects and Authors" (525–54). This user-friendly addition also includes Greek words with parenthetical English glosses.

Even if Carroll does not break new ground with this commentary, his cohesive and fresh interpretation of Luke's narrative calls for attention both within the academy and without. Those working within a seminary setting will especially appreciate the three "basic questions" of Luke's first audiences that Carroll raises and returns to, again and again:

> Who are we as a people in the light of recurrent conflict within synagogues and increasingly Gentile membership? How is Israel's story—how are its Scriptures, its hopes, its future—still ours to claim? And with the embarrassment of our founder (Jesus) and his prominent successor (Paul) put to death through Roman judicial process, what place do we have in the Roman social world? (4)

In addition to treating the portrayal of Jews in Luke's Gospel, illuminating intertextual connections with the Septuagint, and proposing a Lukan "demotion of the Roman emperor" (49; cf. 383), Carroll directly addresses contemporary ethical concerns of Luke's narrative about Jesus. In a footnote to his discussion of Mary's Magnificat, Carroll warns that "Mary's Song does not cultivate passive spectators" (52 n. 16). Neither does Carroll's commentary.

Abject Bodies in the Gospel of Mark, by Manuel Villalobos Mendoza. The Bible
in the Modern World 45. Sheffield: Sheffield Phoenix, 2012. Pp. x + 210. Cloth.
$80.00. ISBN 9781907534546.

Greg Carey, Lancaster Theological Seminary, Lancaster, Pennsylvania

Abject Bodies in the Gospel of Mark at once challenges, entertains, surprises, and
confounds. On its surface this book advances sustained, coherent interpretations
of several neglected characters from Mark's passion narrative, and of Jesus as well,
that attend to gender, exclusion, and debasement. Ordinarily, one reviews such
a book by rehearsing its arguments and assessing their merits. But this book is
different, and it invites a distinctive sort of review. Heavily influenced by Judith
Butler and her work on gender, embodiment, and performance, this project is
best assessed as a performance in its own right: What does it look like when one
reads Mark's passion narrative from a specific history and identity and from a
specific theoretical perspective? Villalobos Mendoza does advance arguments,
highly textured ones, but the value of his study lies closer to the possibilities it
opens than to the persuasiveness of its logic.

   Villalobos Mendoza draws upon rich theoretical and methodological
resources: Butler's gender analysis, queer theory, autobiographical criticism, postcolonial and liberationist hermeneutics, social-scientific assessments of purity in
ancient Mediterranean cultures, and narrative analysis. Villalobos Mendoza helpfully boils things down to a distinct vantage point: *muchos lados,* or many sides,
of exclusion. His character assessments repeatedly begin with autobiographical
reflection. Villalobos Mendoza recounts unforgettable scenes from his own experience growing up *del otro lado* (literally, "from the other side," or queer) in a
Mexican village and as a member of the Mexican diaspora in the United States.
We meet a woman who was forced to allow a man to work her land as punishment for her "manly" behavior, along with a young woman whose husband beats
her to death for being too outspoken. These particular stories ground Villalobos
Mendoza's interpretations of the woman who anoints Jesus (14:3–9) and of the
slave girl who confronts Peter in the courtyard (14:66–72): he sees both characters as transgressing normative gender codes. Moreover, both characters perform
gospel work: the woman who anoints Jesus challenges the disciples' allegiance to
the poor and to persons marginalized by society, while the slave girl calls forth
Peter's confession of allegiance to Jesus.

   Space prohibits thorough summary and assessment of each of this book's
distinctive interpretations; therefore, I have chosen the man who carries water
(14:13–16) as a case study in Villalobos Mendoza's variegated approach. We begin
with a story from the author's childhood. A young man nicknamed Nachito was
seen carrying water on his head like a woman, a mistake that cost him a beating
from his uncle. After years of harassment, including enforced visits to prostitutes
to demonstrate his *machismo,* Nachito narrowly survived his own suicide attempt
and eventually moved to a big city.

Nachito's story empowers Villalobos Mendoza's reading of Mark 14:13–16 even as it opens the path to objection. When the disciples ask about Jesus' Passover plans, Jesus sends two into the city, telling them they will meet a man carrying a jar of water. Villalobos Mendoza, agreeing with some but not all commentators, reasons by analogy. Carrying water did count as women's work in Mark's world as well as in Nachito's. For this reason Villalobos Mendoza perceives in the man, whom he names Nachito *el machito*, as transgressing conventional gender norms. Indeed, Nachito *el machito*'s queer behavior suggests a dubious reputation for his master and his household. In sending his disciples to meet this man, Jesus opens discipleship to all persons, regardless of whether they fit into normative Greco-Roman expectations. Indeed, Jesus establishes a new household consisting of precisely such persons (85). The link between Villalobos's personal experience and his striking interpretation could hardly be more explicit: "for those of us who have been punished, excluded, tormented in useless therapies, obligated to go to our prostitute sisters, and forced to learn how to do our gender correctly, the story of Nachito *el machito* is a sign of hope and redemption" (75).

This autobiographical reflection indicates Judith Butler's influence. Throughout the book Villalobos Mendoza makes the most effective use of auto-biographical criticism I have yet encountered. Moreover, his take on the man with the water jar takes account of narrative criticism (characterization) and engages debates concerning gender and household in Greco-Roman society. Villalobos Mendoza draws upon the Nachito's reception in Coptic Christianity. He also advances a remarkable argument concerning Matthean redaction: Does Matthew's omission of the water-jar detail reflect Matthew's aversion to the man's gender performance?

This is a powerful, compelling interpretation, yet it invites vexing questions. Villalobos Mendoza maintains that Matthew avoids "incorrect" gender perfor-mances (75), observing that where Luke's Jesus speaks of two men sharing the same bed (17:13), Matthew locates them in a field (24:40). It is a brilliant obser-vation, but is Villalobos Mendoza aware that interpreters such as Theodore W. Jennings Jr. and Tat-siong Benny Liew have noted Matthew's inclusion of sexual and gender "others" ("Mistaken Identities but Model Faith: Rereading the Cen-turion, the Chap, and the Christ in Matthew 8:5–13," *JBL* [2004]: 467–94)? Villalobos Mendoza claims that Matthew "typically adds to the details found in Mark's Gospel" (76), but the exact opposite tends to be the case. Perhaps due to his own life experience, Villalobos Mendoza perhaps overstates the rigidity of gen-dered behaviors and spaces. Yes, water carrying may have been women's work. But for a population that included many more men than women, what was perceived as a "woman shortage," one easily imagines that men often performed "women's" tasks. Would it not be helpful if Mark featured explicit remarks such as John 4:9, in which both the woman and the narrator indicate the unusual nature of Jesus' request for water? Villalobos Mendoza counts gender boundaries among those assumptions that need no comment.

Throughout the book Villalobos Mendoza advances remarkable arguments for his interpretation, and his readings are often extremely attractive, but that hardly means he will persuade most readers. In one instance he writes, "The only thing we can be sure of is that Nachito's gender performance [i.e., carrying water] was against the notion of masculinity and manhood" (81). Villalobos Mendoza may feel sure of this, but I do not know how many others will share his confidence.

Villalobos Mendoza turns his attention to Jesus' abject body in chapters 4–5. Jesus identifies with, even touches, other abject bodies, at once rendering himself one with them and challenging the cultural conventions that debase some for the benefit of others. When Jesus distributes his broken body, his action recalls that he has supplied bread for the hungry. However, when we turn to the passion account the work grows at once more predictable and more tendentious. To be sure, the torture and crucifixion of a naked man, subjected to the gaze of his tormentors and a crowd, implies sexualized humiliation. How much more is there to be said? Villalobos Mendoza compares Mark to a "photographer" who "seems to take delight and pleasure in overexposing Jesus' penetrable body to our eyes, ears and thoughts" (142). Mark repeatedly employs the verb "crucify" in 15:24–27, so that "Mark does not leave too many details to our imagination" (143). I find this reading completely unconvincing. The author of Mark could easily have dramatized the violence perpetrated against Jesus' body, just as Mel Gibson and countless others have. Instead, the Gospel insists upon the reality of Jesus' crucifixion without elaborating its horror—a horror any ancient audience might well have imagined for themselves. I do not believe my personal prudishness or piety explains my dissatisfaction with the characterization of Jesus among the thieves as "a kind of *ménage à trois* sexual encounter" (147). At the same time, Villalobos Mendoza offers a brilliant and sympathetic reflection concerning how their own gazing implicates the women who follow Jesus (15:40–41) in the sexual violence in the public spectacle (149–52).

This daring study began as a Garrett Evangelical Theological Seminary doctoral dissertation, directed by Osvaldo Vena. While it transgresses the genre's conventions in many ways, its most remarkable departure occurs in the final chapter, an epistle from the author, along with others who live *del otro lado*, to the Markan community. The epistle voices the many sides of exclusion and oppression against which Villalobos Mendoza performs his reading of Mark, and it even offers a "little apocalypse" of its own.

At several points in the book Villalobos Mendoza anticipates his work will face rejection. If we review this book as "exegesis" in the conventional sense, it will surprise and enlighten us at some points and baffle us at others. I should note that the book suffers from poor copy editing. However, Villalobos Mendoza characterizes the project as a "confession" (16). I would call it a performance: a disciplined and improvisational rendering that aims to foster life in a world determined to consign millions to death. Taken as performance, this book merits careful study and reflection as a model of transgressive, contextual, and autobiographical reading.

Reading the Gospels Wisely: A Narrative and Theological Introduction, by Jonathan T. Pennington. Grand Rapids: Baker Academic, 2012. Pp. xiv + 268. Paper. $24.99. ISBN 9780801039379.

Cornelis Bennema, Wales Evangelical School of Theology, Bridgend, U. K.

Jonathan Pennington presents a comprehensive hermeneutic for the canonical Gospels by paying attention to its historical, theological, and aretological dimensions. He mainly critiques modernist (read "reductionist") approaches to the Gospels in order to advocate a return to premodern readings, while endorsing some postmodern insights. Pennington writes clearly and persuasively and structures the book in three parts. Using the building metaphor of Matt 7:24–27, Pennington lays an expansive foundation in part 1 (chs. 1–8), constructs the house in part 2 (chs. 9–10), and starts to live in the Gospels house in part 3 (chs. 11–12). A Scripture and author index closes the book, but a bibliography would have been helpful. While I appreciate the work, I disperse my critical comments in the summaries of the individual chapters and finish with a concluding evaluation.

In chapter 1 Pennington surveys the earliest use of the term "gospel" and its origins, then suggests that the "gospel," rooted in the eschatological vision of Isa 40–66, is the message about the restoration of God's kingdom or reign in the person of Jesus. In chapter 2 Pennington turns to the issue of the Gospel genre. While accepting Richard Burridge's position of viewing the Gospels as ancient Greco-Roman *bioi*, Pennington contends that we must go beyond it to a more comprehensive understanding of the Gospels, including the Gospel genre's dependence on the narrative models in the Hebrew Bible, its unique kerygmatic message, and its ethical or transformative nature. Pennington then offers a comprehensive definition of the canonical Gospels as the *"theological, historical, and aretological (virtue-forming) biographical narratives that retell the story and proclaim the significance of Jesus Christ, who through the power of the Spirit is the Restorer of God's reign"* (35, emphasis original). Chapter 3 deals with the issue of *why* we need the Gospels (if we already have Paul) and chapter 4 with the issue of having *four* Gospels. These last two chapters were unexciting, since they offered no new argument or insights; perhaps Pennington felt compelled to cover this ground lest he be criticized for the gaps.

In the more interesting and substantial chapter 5, Pennington deals with the difficult relationship between history and theology. After discussing the various positions (theology versus history; theology through history; theology and history), Pennington concludes that historical criticism is in crisis, drawing attention to a growing movement that is returning to the use of premodern approaches to *theological* interpretation of Scripture. Drawing on the work of Richard Bauckham, Pennington suggests that the category of "testimony," combined with a hermeneutic of trust (rather than one of suspicion, as is common in many historical-critical approaches), is the way forward for reading the Gospels as both history and theology. This chapter will perhaps raise most questions from the reader. For example, without denying the demise of the supremacy of historical criticism, Pennington fails to notice the fresh impetus in historical Jesus studies from scholars such as Chris Keith, Anthony Le Donne, Rafael Rodríquez, and Dale Allison. Moreover, while Pennington admits that not all testimonies are equally good, he does not suggest criteria for distinguishing between them. Finally, I have to ask if Pennington's proposed balancing act—to walk the sharp knife edge of truth without losing out on either history or theology—is realistic. Besides the varying scholarly opinions on where the balance lies, at the individual level, one's understanding of how this truth looks like might change or develop.

In chapters 6–7 Pennington lays the hermeneutical foundation for reading the Gospels "wisely." First he proposes a threefold approach to reading a text (see fig. 1 on 112): (1) a historical "behind the text" approach; (2) a literary "in the text" approach; (3) a theological "in front of the text" approach. This reading process relates to various spectra, including human and divine authorial intent, surface meaning and bonus meaning, mechanics and art, and letter and spirit. For example, according to Pennington, the theological or "in front of the text" reading of the text deals with the divine authorial intention, which goes beyond the human authorial intention, thus creating "bonus" and "spiritual" meaning. Second, while acknowledging the value of authorial intent, Pennington also shows its limitations and argues that meaning is (continually) created in the fusion of the two horizons between the authoritative text and the particular situatedness of the reader. While the text is stable and normative, it is also open, resulting in polyvalent meanings or understandings of the text. At the same time, Pennington draws on speech-act theory to stress that biblical texts are not simply disseminating information (locution) but also call for action and response (illocution) with the intent to transform (perlocution). Third, according to Pennington, "*the most important and determinative aspect of reading Holy Scripture well is not our method or theory but our posture and our goal*" (137, emphasis original), by which he means reading the Bible as Holy Scripture and the obedience to live and love according to its teachings. Chapter 8 concludes part 1, summarizing the findings of the previous chapters and stressing that we should read the Gospels as testimony, that is, as a blending of fact and interpretation, recognizing its theological and transformational purpose. Such reading should lead to an encounter with God (because Scripture is God's speech acts) and consequently a personal application to Christian life and obedience. Pennington summarizes the twofold goal in reading the Gospels as (i) revelation (the Gospels reveal who God is in Jesus) and (ii) identification (the Gospels invite the reader to emulate some and avoid other characters in the stories).

In part 2, comprising chapters 9–10, Pennington moves to the practical matter of reading the Gospels wisely, or the building of the house (on the "rock" of part 1). Having spent considerable time on laying a strong foundation (chs. 1–8 take up almost 65 percent of the book's space), Pennington is now ready to swiftly put up the walls and roof. Drawing on theories of story, including the focus on plot development, he proposes an eight-step narrative model for reading the Gospels: (1) isolate the pericope; (2) read the story multiple times; (3) identify the setting and the characters; (4) observe the story (this step involves grammatical-historical work); (5) isolate the different scenes (i.e., break a story into smaller units); (6) analyze the narrative by tracing the "arc" of the plot—the rising tension, climax, resolution, following action/lessons; (7) consider the wider concentric hermeneutical circles (acts, cycles, literary structures, entire Gospel, entire canon); (8) summarize the pericope. Pennington demonstrates his method on the pericope of Luke 7:1–10.

Pennington starts to live in his Gospel house in part 3. In chapter 11 he groups the eight steps of his above-mentioned reading strategy under step 1, "Reading Actively," in order to add two further steps. Step 2, "Articulating the Revelation and Identification," harks back to the twofold goal of reading the Gospels in chapter 8: (1) articulating the revelation of God in Christ; (2) identifying the character traits to be emulated or avoided. This will enable the reader to apply and subsequently to preach/teach the Gospel narrative. Pennington describes the latter activity as step 3, "Using Framing Questions to Form a Message," where he pays attention to the fallen condition, the redemptive solution, and virtue formation. In the final chapter, Pennington makes a twofold argument—historical and canonical/theological—for the priority and preeminence of the Gospels. In his view, the Gospels are the "canon within the canon" in that they should guide and direct one's overall reading of Scripture. With the Old Testament Scriptures on the one side and the rest of the New Testament writings on the other, the Gospels hold both a privileged place and a controlling position. Among the various implications that Pennington explores, I highlight the centrality of the Gospels for doing "biblical theology." While some practice biblical theology by tracing themes or trajectories throughout biblical history and others examine the contributions of the individual biblical writings toward the whole (and Pennington sees both approaches as valid), Pennington imagines a theological reading of the Bible by starting with the Gospels and reading the other writings through the lens of the Gospels.

In the final analysis, Pennington has produced an excellent, refreshing introduction for those who are interested in the Gospels. He competently discusses the various hermeneutical issues and perspectives in Gospel studies, admirably guides the reader towards a holistic or "wise" reading of the Gospels, and passionately pleads with the reader to seek not just information but also transformation. This book will undoubtedly find a wide acceptance in "confessional" institutions, but I fear it will not fare as well in the "secular" university, where many (still) approach the Gospels exclusively as a historical text, setting aside (or even discarding) its theological and aretological dimensions. An example of this latter approach is found in Dale Martin's *New Testament History and Literature* (see http://www.bookreviews.org/pdf/8502_9313.pdf for my review). Although the two books are on opposite ends of the spectrum, both should be considered in both academic environments in order to stimulate fruitful dialogue. May the reader decide who the wise builder is!

Jesus of Nazareth: Background, Witnesses, and Significance, by Gerald L. Borchert. Macon, Ga.: Mercer University Press, 2011. Pp. xviii + 258 Paper $25.00. ISBN 9780881462661.

Chris L. de Wet, University of South Africa, Pretoria, South Africa

Gerald Borchert's *Jesus of Nazareth* presents biblical scholars with yet another introduction to the Gospels and the life of Jesus. It is a textbook commissioned by Mercer University Press, according to the author, with the purpose of dealing with the introductory issues of the canonical Gospels. In the very first pages of reading the book it becomes clear, however, that it is written for a moderate conservative and evangelical audience, specifically seminary students or students studying at confessional university faculties or divinity schools. The book is written in a colloquial style and comes across as very pedagogical, with a "friendly quiz" already present in the very first pages. The quiz asks the reader to identify geographical areas in Palestine (the map is not of the best quality). The book is also in constant dialogue with modern Christian spirituality and ecclesiastical leadership: "The life and extended ministry of Jesus continues to be the foundation of the church and is crucial to the heart and motivating impetus of every follower of the one whom his disciples appropriately called 'Lord'" (6). The book is also written in a very conventional manner. It starts with discussing background issues in part 1, with part 2 being devoted to discussions of the Gospels as "testimonies" and a chapter on noncanonical Gospel material, part 3 dealing with Gospel methodology and part 4 conclusions regarding the significance and importance of Jesus.

The first chapter typically deals with historical developments from the fourth century BCE to the second CE, commencing with the movements of Alexander the Great, then the Maccabean revolt, the Hasmonean and Herodian dynasties, and the Roman rule in Palestine up to the Bar Khokhba revolt. All of these historical developments are framed within the "fullness of time" scheme (cf. Gal 4:4). Chapter 2 focuses on the formation of first-century Judaism and, again conventionally, discusses issues such as climate, geography, and religio-political groups such as the Pharisees and Sadducees. Up to this point the approach of the book is historical-grammatical, with very little material on recent critical scholarly developments such as the problematization of Christian Judaism and the so-called "parting of the ways," the complex issues of ethnicity and gender, and so on. While the book is not meant to be a guide to the "background" of the Gospels, it discusses in length some historical developments (e.g., the Herodian dynasty) but neglects issues such as patriarchy, gender, and alterity in ancient society. Reading this part of the book challenges the teacher of biblical studies to ask what is more important to include in an introduction with spatial limitations. Borchert prefers not to take the road less traveled and remains conventional in the introduction. At this point the reader would also be acutely aware of homiletic jolts in the text, some that seem so problematic (and perhaps offensive to nonconservatives such as this reviewer) that the author must defend himself from seeming anti-Semitic

(46–47): "Please do not think I am advocating an anti-Semitic approach to the Gospels. I love Israel and have taught in Jerusalem.... I am neither anti-Jewish nor anti-Muslim. I am pro-Jesus and his genuine way of understanding the intentions of God both for believers and for those in the world who doubt him."

Part 2 then examines the canonical Gospels themselves, and the reading is quite narrative and descriptive (as is most of the book, which is certainly a strength, since it is written for an audience of beginners to the study of Jesus). After a brief discussion of the genre of the Gospels, which Borchert calls "testimonies" (probably to emphasize the veracity and factuality of the accounts, which is important to the author) each Gospel is treated per chapter. The discussions of the Gospels are also conventional. Chapter 3 discusses Mark, with the usual emphases on the messianic secret and suffering messiah motifs, and Borchert also emphasizes the motif of the resurrection in Mark by concluding that both the first and last pages of the Gospel are probably missing, the last pages no doubt to him being resurrection accounts. In chapter 4 Matthew is treated as "the witness of Matthew to Jesus as Emmanuel (God with us) and the fulfillment of Old Testament prophecies." The typical Judaistic background of Matthew is constantly highlighted, especially in dialogue with Hebrew Bible traditions. Borchert's discussion of Matthew can be described as highly basilocentric: centered on the kingdom traditions and Jesus as king. In chapter 5 the Gospel of Luke is examined, with a rather helpful précis of its scholarly reception history, and thereafter discussions focused around issues of Jesus as one who *cares*, especially for the "hurting and dispossessed." The chapter on Luke and the one on John are probably the best sections in the book. Borchert describes Jesus' journey in Luke as a path of caring for the poor and those who are suffering, again common motifs in most studies on Luke. The chapter on John is quite extensive and in turn more focused on early Christian Christology than historical issues per se. Borchert traces the movements of Jesus around Judaistic festival cycles and other traditions, and does so quite well. Up to this point the discussions of the Gospels are done in a narrative fashion, and the information is complete for the introductory purposes of the book.

It is in chapter 7 that the book departs to an extent from its conventionality and moves to discuss the noncanonical Gospels, interestingly referred to by Borchert as "rejected witnesses," a phrase already hinting at the direction the chapter will take. There is an underlying polemic present in this chapter, as if Borchert has to defend the canonical Gospels from the "rejected" witnesses, and the evangelical rhetoric of the book is perhaps most potent in this chapter. In short, the departure from its conventionality is only supplemented with disappointing and highly problematic statements. The chapter is riddled with rather patronizing and simply erroneous statements, for instance in the discussion of the famous Gospel of Thomas logion 114 (178–79; where all females are to be made male), Borchert does not hesitate to point out the contrast of this Gospel's views on women with what he calls the "egalitarian" views of Paul (!) and then even citing Gal 3:28 (!!). Borchert seems to be ignorant of early Christian gender rhetoric, since both Gal 3:28 and Thom. 114 imply an androgynism—they in fact say exactly the same thing, Paul is only implicit and the Gospel of Thomas explicit (see J. N. Vorster, "Androgyny and Early Christianity," *R&T* 15/1–2 [2008]: 97–132). Borchert concludes that "it [is] patently clear why none of them are part of the New Testament canon. They present portraits of Jesus that assert a theology that is partly at odds with or completely opposed to the life and teaching of Jesus in the canonical Gospels" (189). He promotes them as "interesting reading" (190) but not adept to what he calls the "the true measure of the authentic Jesus." Chapter 7 is certainly the most problematic.

Part 3 discusses methodological issues in the study of the Gospels, with explanations of orality, textual analysis, source analysis, form analysis, redaction analysis (also historical Jesus research here), narrative analysis, and sociological analysis (Borchert deliberately avoids the term "criticism"). Part 4 examines some of the more controversial theological issues such as the virgin birth and Jesus as messiah as well as a more devotional conclusion to the study of the character that is Jesus and his significance for church life and worship today. I will discuss the strengths and weaknesses of these chapters in summary below.

What is there, then, to say of Borchert's *Jesus of Nazareth*? As a conventional historical–grammatical introduction to the Gospels for an evangelical beginners audience (seminary students, pastors, and even church Bible schools), it does achieve its purpose. The narrative style of writing is helpful, and the oft-surfacing homiletic interludes and subtle polemic may find consonance with the conservative reader. Its personal and pedagogical style is admirable and does not damage the academic standard of the textbook. The treatment of Luke and John stand out in the book (despite the disastrous chapter on the noncanonical Gospels), and most of the important historical data necessary for an introductory textbook is present. In short, Borchert does succeed in taking his conservative readers "back to basics," and the book would give an undergraduate student at seminary a sufficient historical background and textual sensitivity.

However, I do not recommend the book for a more critical audience. While reading the book one may constantly ask: Is there really a need for yet another historical-grammatical introduction to the Gospels and the Jesus-tradition? As an introduction, it cannot be compared with the monumental studies of Theissen, Sanders, Meier, Crossan, and Levine, to name but a few, yet it does not incorporate recent scholarly developments at all (unlike David DeSilva's *An Introduction to the New Testament* [InterVarsity Press, 2004] or Achtemeier, Green, and Thompson's *Introducing the New Testament* [Eerdmans, 2001]). Along with strong competition from the scholars and books mentioned above, this book also exhibits several highly problematic lacunae. First, it still reads as if historical-grammatical critique is at the foreground. This is not necessarily a problem—an author has the liberty to use a method he or she is comfortable with. However, is an introduction to the study of Jesus and the Gospels in the twenty-first century really possible without seriously being in dialogue with historical Jesus scholarship or social-scientific analyses? Notwithstanding these two highly influential developments in the field, Borchert also writes as if the cultural- and feminist-critical turn in biblical and early Christian scholarship never occurred (part 3 exhibits almost nothing of this), not even to mention postcolonial and ethnicity studies (despite several references in the book to the works of Richard Horsley). This review is therefore a mixed one: Borchert's book does hold value for a very specific reading audience and does a good job of revitalizing some basics with regard to the study of Jesus, despite its conventionality. But then, with all the competition from studies on Jesus out there, can a book introducing Jesus and the Gospels really afford to simply restate issues found in much older textbooks and totally neglect new ground-breaking alternative methodologies central to the study of Jesus and the Gospels?

Management and the Gospel: Luke's Radical Message for the First and Twenty-First Centuries, by Bruno Dyck. New York: Palgrave Macmillan, 2013. Pp. xvi + 302. Hardcover. $110.00. ISBN 9781137280886.

Jack Barentsen, Evangelische Theologische Faculteit, Leuven, Belgium

Bruno Dyck is a well-known management author (e.g., his co-authored book *Management: Current Practices and New Directions* in 2010) who contributes regularly to top management journals, often critically comparing current management theory with biblical texts and principles. *Management and the Gospel* is his first book-length treatment. It is a welcome interdisciplinary study that bridges biblical studies and management theory.

Within biblical studies, the book enhances the social-scientific study of Scripture by combining modern management theory with scholarly perspectives on first-century economic practices for an in-depth reading of the Gospel of Luke. In the process, it offers building blocks for constructing a theology of work and economics, of vital interest to today's spiritual leaders. Within management theory, research into "spiritual leadership" for business or politics has become mainstream, and Dyck's project deepens that research by a study of a primary Christian text.

Dyck presents his study as a successor to Weber's analysis of the Protestant work ethic. Weber proposed that Protestantism led to individualism because of its emphasis on personal salvation and to materialism because it saw wealth as God's blessing. However, Weber also believed that these dynamics began to lead a life apart from religion and that such soulless prosperity could not be sustained long term; eventually "new prophets" and "a rebirth of old ideals" would be called for. Dyck signals that such a "theological turn" is taking place today in management literature and proposes to analyze one of the Gospels to reconnect his own discipline with essential spiritual sources.

Dyck, professor of management and organization theory at the Asper School of Business (University of Manitoba, Winnipeg, Canada) surprisingly spends five out of six parts of the book dealing with biblical data from Luke. Two appendices carefully document his research method. Dyck had five biblical scholars indicate break points in the bare text of the Jerusalem journey narrative; he evaluated the results statistically and concluded that the narrative contained six narrative cycles structured as chiasms. Next he conducted a study where thirty students noted parallels between passages from the first three cycles and passages from the last three cycles (the passages were listed randomly in two parallel columns). The statistical analysis of their results overwhelmingly supported the parallels that a chiastic structure would lead one to expect. This statistical approach is unusual within biblical studies, but it is an interesting way to study the reception of narrative features, even if it measures the reception by twenty-first-century U.S. students instead of by first-century city dwellers in the Roman Empire.

How does Dyck handle the study of Luke in the main text? Part 1 begins with a helpful overview of the book. Next, the broad literary structure of Luke is introduced in order to specify the journey narrative (9:51–19:40) as the main focus. Luke is also situated in the biblical story, from creation to fall to salvation to kingdom, with Luke belonging to the third part. Most important, part 1 introduces the cultural background of first-century management. Roman expansion required taxation and urbanization to funnel resources to Rome, which led to an increase in absentee landlords, estate managers, and rural exploitation. Perhaps as much as 8 percent of Galilee's population could be seen as parallel to today's professional managers (21–22). These professionals managed an *oikos*, which refers not simply to a household as the center of consumption (as it is today) but to the primary first-century organization for producing goods and services. Since *oikos* has traditionally been translated as "house" or "household," modern readers have often been blind to the management dimensions in the biblical text (24).

Part 2 explores this first-century management concept and the way it influences two key parables. Discussions of management date back to Aristotle, who distinguished three basic dimensions. The first is *oikonomia*, or the managing of relationship *within* organizations: the typical household relationships of husband-wife, parents-children, and master-slave. The second dimension is *chrematistics*, or the managing of money. Aristotle divided this into natural versus unnatural chrematistics, or sustenance economics where money was used to sustain the normal social and societal functions of an *oikos* versus acquisitive economics where money was used to make more money and to generate wealth. Aristotle was critical of acquisitive economics, but by the time of the first century this form predominated. The third dimension is *patronage versus benefaction*, or the managing of relationships between organizations. The classic Greek understanding of benefaction, where benefits were bestowed "without strings attached," was gradually replaced by the Roman understanding of patronage, which established relationships of obligation and dependency from client to patron, often widening the gap between poor and rich. Dyck depends on biblical scholars such as Neyrey, deSilva and Kloppenborg to provide the basis for his social-cultural understanding; although work from scholars such as Danker, Harrison, and Joubert on benefaction is absent, the nature of Dyck's study does not require it.

These concepts are then applied to the parables of the shrewd manager (16:1–8) and of the ten pounds (19:12–27). The shrewd manager was commended because he scattered his master's resources to reduce the gap between rich and poor, accruing honor for his master as benefactor. In the parable of the pounds, the master and the two slaves who made money represent the worst of acquisitive patronage, while the real hero of the story is the third slave/manager, who refuses to exploit his fellow countrymen.

Parts 3 and 4 explore whether the three dimensions of first-century management are supported by the rest of Luke's journey narrative (51–82) and by Luke's overall message (focusing on salvation, the kingdom of God, and the Holy Spirit, 83–120). Each part contains three chapters of ten or eleven pages each, surveying a dozen passages or more. These passages are often categorized according to context, actor, or some other aspect, then discussed in groups. Some major commentaries or exegetical studies are referenced, but the discussion necessarily skims the text in search of confirmation and explanation of the key management dimensions. For instance, the chapter on household relationships surveys several passages about the husband-wife relationship, eight passages on the parent-child, and five on the master-slave relationship, which results in five short lists and one full-page chart. This may be a helpful survey by way of illustration, but it is impossible to engage these passages with sufficient depth to prove the point.

This results in sometimes questionable interpretations, such as Dyck's conclusion after discussing parent-child relationships that we are encouraged "to consider alternative *oikoi* structures and systems for providing goods and services" (57) and that "adult children are encouraged to leave the security of their parent's *oikos* and to become members of new forms of *oikos* that include marginalized societal members" (63). Elsewhere Dyck reinterprets the parable of the wicked tenants (20:9–19) as referring to legitimate resistance against an absentee landlord but that the use of violence (i.e., mistreating the slave delegates) is unjust. The priests are angered by this parable, because they resist the implication that they themselves are the oppressive landowners (59–62). Dyck does not appear to recognize that this first-century economic dimension does not exclude the more traditional interpretation that the parable blames the priests for killing the son rather than for being exploitative landlords. One wonders if the focus on first-century *oikos* and patronage practices has become so dominant as to blind Dyck to other contexts, such as the context of Jewish Scripture and history.

Dyck frequently highlights the countercultural nature of Jesus' message, as if first-century culture was always focused on acquisitive economics and exploitation. However, Dyck cites Aristotle and Seneca as similar critics, while the Hebrew prophetic tradition is not mentioned as a possible source for Jesus' criticism. Thus, even in his critique Jesus acted contextually appropriate, by siding with the majority of poor and the marginalized people—something that Dyck overlooks. Still, his main argument holds up, that Jesus often challenged people to resist conventional, exploitative systems and "to choose radical alternative forms of goods and service producing organizations that include people at the margins of society" that would be less materialistic and less individualistic than much of today's management (73).

Part 5 moves towards an application of the findings by suggesting that Luke used a four-phase model that helps us to put these principles in practice. The four phases are: problem recognition, action response, changed way of seeing, and institutional change (126). Dyck claims that these four phases can be identified in each of the six cycles of Luke's chiastic journey narrative. Even with three chapters devoted to the exposition, the analyses remain too superficial to convince; with a bit of creativity, a different order of these phases can occasionally be suggested.

Finally, in part 6 the book turns to parallels with modern management theory. A plethora of theories pass review, again subdivided according to the three first-century dimensions of management. We read snippets from organization theory, Maslow's hierarchy of needs, and situational leadership. Basic economic theory (self-interest or altruism?), axioms of finance, and accounting principles pass review. Also, the four Ps of marketing, supply chain management, and business strategy are touched upon. With each theory reviewed, an example from business case studies is presented, although the connection is not always clear. Thus, Dyck often suggests interesting applications of "kingdom of God principles" to modern management theory, although it is often only enough to pique one's interest for further exploration.

This study is a delightful and sometimes frustrating analysis of Luke's journey narrative with a view toward modern management applications. Its interdisciplinary nature is its prime contribution but at the same time its greatest crucial risk. For the biblical scholar it is too superficial and too much management; for the management scholar it is too religious and too ancient. Still, biblical scholars can benefit by considering not just the alternative approaches to the biblical text but also how biblical studies can connect with modern disciplines to create powerful perspectives on Christian practice today, a task that biblical scholars cannot simply relegate to other scholars and practitioners. On the other hand, management scholars can benefit by recognizing that all management is based upon basic religious presuppositions and principles and that a study of these principles is absolutely necessary to work toward ethically responsible management, something that is direly needed in today's world.

The book is a well-produced hardcover edition with endnotes and appropriate indexes for easy study. Unfortunately, the print is very small (what would count as footnotes in many books) and the price out of most people's range. This work is well worth consulting by both theologians and management scholars, so we wait for it to appear in a more affordable paperback edition. [Editor's note: A paperback version was published after this review was submitted.]

Matthean Sets of Parables, by Peter Yaw Oppong-Kumi. Wissenschaftliche Untersuchungen zum Neuen Testament 2/340. Tübingen: Mohr Siebeck, 2013. Pp. xiv + 421. Paper. €89.00. ISBN 9783161517303.

J. R. C. Cousland, University of British Columbia, Vancouver, B.C., Canada

Recent years have seen a resurgence of works devoted to aspects of Matthew's parables (Olmstead, Lybaek, Münch, Ewherido), and Peter Yaw Oppong-Kumi's substantial monograph continues this welcome trend. His volume is especially welcome since it includes careful and detailed examinations of many of Matthew's narrative parables and reopens the question of whether Matthew had a distinct parable theory of his own.

As the title of his work suggests, Oppong-Kumi addresses the "Matthean sets of parables." By these he means three distinct clusters of parables found at Matt 13:3–52; 21:28–22:14; and 24:42–25:30. Though some of the parables in these clusters have antecedents in Mark's Gospel, Oppong-Kumi argues that the redactor of Matthew has consciously and deliberately put his own compositional stamp on them. Further, although these parable sets are spread out over the second half of the Gospel, Oppong-Kumi contends that they display notable affinities in their plot, function, and message.

To illustrate these affinities, Oppong-Kumi adopts an eclectic methodology that emphasizes rhetoric and narrative; this approach enables him to establish that the parable sets address the acceptance or repudiation of Jesus and his gospel. Though they do it in a variety of ways, the interconnected narratives of the parable sets illustrate "the story of the people's response to the message of the dawning Kingdom of Heaven" (368).

Central to this conception is Oppong-Kumi's argument that, contra Kingsbury, Luz, and others, Matthew does in fact have a parable theory of his own, which is expressed in Matt 13:11–13: "To you it has been given to know the secrets of the kingdom of heaven, but to them it has not been given. For to those who have, more will be given, and they will have an abundance; but from those who have nothing, even what they have will be taken away. The reason I speak to them in parables is that 'seeing they do not perceive, and hearing they do not listen, nor do they understand.'" Oppong-Kumi claims that in its essentials this parabolic conception is fundamentally different from Mark's theory; it reveals that Matthew's parables are essentially "audience-oriented" and that they are intended to emphasize the response of Jesus' audiences to him and to his message. Nor does this parable theory apply exclusively to Matt 13; it pertains to all the Gospel's parables and parable sets.

Oppong-Kumi opens his examination with the set of parables found in Matt 13, the Parable Discourse (13:3–52). Instead of considering all seven parables in detail, Oppong-Kumi provides a lengthy, general overview of the chapter, followed by a detailed account of two "sample" parables contained in the discourse: the Mustard Seed and the Buried Treasure parables. When chapter 13 is approached as a whole—"narratively, rhetorically, structurally, and theologically"

(133)—it emerges as a coherent literary unit that consistently confronts the parables' auditors with the question: "Will you accept or reject Jesus and his message of the approaching Kingdom of Heaven?" In keeping with the pattern outlined in 13:11–13, the people of Israel are represented as consistently failing to grasp Jesus' parables, whereas the disciples gain a deepened understanding of the mysteries of the kingdom of heaven. Matthew 13 is thus a "turning point" (though different from the "turning point" envisioned by Kingsbury) and marks the movement of the people away from Jesus, as well as a concomitant growth in the disciples' understanding.

The second set of parables (21:28–22:14) shifts from an audience of the Jewish people and the disciples to one consisting of the Jewish leaders. Here Oppong-Kumi elects to consider in detail the three parables making up the set: the Two Sons (including its well-known textual problems), the Wicked Tenants, and the Wedding Feast. This second set displays the same thematic coherence that was apparent in the first parable set. On the basis of the three parables' form, vocabulary, and theology, Oppong-Kumi shows that Matthew has consciously crafted them into a more coherent entity. All three parables make use of invitational motifs to highlight the choice that Jesus' message of the kingdom presents to his hearers. Moreover, in this parabolic set Jesus repeatedly warns the Jewish leaders about the future and pronounces judgment on their actions. The new *ethnos* of believers (21:43) is also faced with the threat of coming judgment.

This prospect of judgment anticipates the theme of the third and final set of parables, those that deal with the parousia and the consummation of the ages (24:42–25:30). For this set Oppong-Kumi sets out to establish the context and structure of the discourse in chapters 24 and 25. As was the case with the two preceding sets, he determines that the individual parables have largely been structured as a single unit and that they display notable commonalities of vocabulary and theme. In addition to judgment itself, these themes include the coming of the Son of Man, the delay and uncertain time of his coming, and the prospect of being caught unprepared. Oppong-Kumi takes only one of the parables as a "sample" parable—The Wise and Foolish Virgins, which he sees as encapsulating the overall message of 24:3–25:46, as demonstrated by its focus on the Son of Man's unexpected arrival and the judgment to follow.

As a whole, Oppong-Kumi's findings suggest that Matthew has adopted a coherent strategy in assembling the parabolic sets and in linking them internally and externally. The result is a distinct narrative arc that describes the outworking of salvation as it affects the auditors of the parables, either negatively or positively. In addition, the parables serve as commentaries on Matthew's narrative about Jesus and function rhetorically to urge the Gospel's own audiences to respond favorably to him and his message. To illustrate these narrative arcs, Oppong-Kumi includes a helpful appendix with six diagrams charting the internal structure of the three parable sets, as well as the disposition of the sets within the Gospel as a whole.

The value of looking at parables as sets in Matthew is considerable. Oppong-Kumi's detailed arguments help to establish that the individual parables have indeed been fashioned to complement each other in their message and that they tend to present a coherent overall argument. Further, his recognition that there is an underlying narrative character to Matthew's parables provides a strong corrective to many of the atomistic approaches that have tended to isolate the parables from the tenor of the Gospel as a whole. Oppong-Kumi's contention that these parable groupings are informed and united by Matthew's understanding of salvation history is very largely convincing. Much more than is the case with many of Luke's parables, Matthew's have a pronounced teleological and eschatological character that meshes well with a salvation-historical perspective, especially given the fact that many of these parables display an underlying dualism that readily lends itself to this perspective.

Oppong-Kumi's attempt to isolate Matt 13:11–13 as the core of Matthew's own theory of Parables is suggestive but may not convince everyone. Nevertheless, it is certainly worthy of note that there are echoes of 13:12 in 21:43, where these echoes are redeployed to judge the Jewish leaders. That this formula should be prominent in two of the parable sets indicates that its underlying idea is sympathetic to Matthew, even if it may not of itself constitute a parable theory.

Slightly more problematic is the fact that the conception of the work seems arbitrary in some respects. First of all, the parameters of Oppong-Kumi's "parable sets" are open to question. While the limits of the first two sets make sense, his decision to include chapter 24 in his third set seems anomalous, seeing that it contains only one parable: the Faithful or Unfaithful Servant (24:45–51). Oppong-Kumi indicates that the focus of the chapter is on "the context and structure of the *discourse*" (285, emphasis added), which seems to presuppose that the eschatological discourse and third parabolic set are somehow identical. The result is that the nonparabolic passages in 24:1–44 are given an inordinate amount of attention and the parousia parables receive short shrift. Seemingly as arbitrary is the failure to explain why the two parables in the community discourse (ch. 18), which are thematically related, should be defined as "single" parables (1–2, 354). Couldn't they be considered a set as well?

Second, Oppong-Kumi remarks that, given the number of parables he discusses, it was not possible for him to consider all of them in detail—hence the expedient he adopts of providing detailed examinations of "sample parables" taken from each set. One wonders, though, whether he could not have included all the parables if he had opted to treat them in somewhat less detail. Nor is it always clear why he has favored one "sample parable" over another. In the case of the first parable set, for instance, one might have supposed that the Parable of the Sower was a more apt "sample parable" than the Mustard Seed; Oppong-Kumi's "parable theory" is sandwiched right between the parable and its interpretation, and the Sower is the very first parable *qua* parable that Jesus presents to the Jewish people. Moreover, in light of the accompanying interpretation, Matthew indicates that it is closely linked with salvation-historical themes. So why has it been overlooked in favor of a short parable without an express interpretation?

These are minor complaints, however. Peter Yaw Oppong-Kumi has produced a timely volume that consistently challenges scholars to examine Matthew's
use of parables afresh.

The Disciples according to Mark: Markan Redaction in Current Debate, by C. Clifton Black. 2nd edition. Grand Rapids: Eerdmans, 2012. Pp. xviii + 403. Paper.
$45.00. ISBN 9780802827982.

Michael Kok, University of Sheffield, Sheffield, United Kingdom

C. Clifton Black's revised doctoral dissertation put forward a significant challenge
to the application of redaction criticism to Mark, and in this new edition he has
included an afterword that addresses the academic reception of his thesis since
it was published in 1989. The essence of his critique boils down to the question
of how the method can attain verifiable results with regard to Mark when redaction critics neither possess this Gospel's direct literary precursors nor agree on
the hypothetical sources available to its author, leading to the proliferation of
mutually exclusive deductions about Mark's individual contribution to the Jesus
tradition (2). The situation is markedly different for the other Synoptic Gospels,
as scholars, on the assumption of Markan priority, can at least make inferences
about the changes introduced in Matthew or Luke by comparing pericopes in the
Synoptic triple tradition.

Chapter 1 outlines the historical roots and methodology of *Redaktionsgeschichte*. Despite the problem that the traditions available to Mark are no longer
extant, Black summarizes the criteria set out by Robert Stein (see "The Proper
Methodology for Ascertaining a Markan Redaction History" *NovT* 13 [1971]:
181–98) for detecting the Evangelist's editorial hand in the selection, arrangement,
modification, omission, or invention of material for the Gospel as well as in the
Markan seams, insertions, summaries, introduction, conclusion, vocabulary, and
christological titles (22–31). Black notes only that the criterion of vocabulary can
be broadened to literary style and that redaction critics often call attention to the
ways in which Mark arranges the material in the service of key theological themes
(32). A major part of Black's investigation revolves around how faithful redaction
critics have been to implementing these criteria and whether their results necessarily follow from them.

In order to evaluate the validity of the method, Black narrows the parameters to a particular case study concerning Mark's treatment of the disciples
in chapter 2. Black identifies three divergent interpretations championed by
redaction critics: the type 1 "conservative position" upholds Mark's fidelity to
the tradition and positive attitude toward the disciples, the type 2 "mediate
position" offers a nuanced assessment of Mark's handling of pre-Markan traditions and complex portrayal of the disciples, and the type 3 "liberal position"
insists upon Mark's freedom to develop or create new material and to polemi-
cize against the disciples (46–59). Since the labels "conservative" or "liberal"

can carry political or theological connotations not intended by Black, perhaps it would have been better to characterize types 1 and 3 on the basis of how "restrained" or "free" the redactor is judged to have been with respect to the traditions he or she inherited. Even so, in chapters 3–6 Black performs a critical analysis of the three positions on his taxonomy as represented by Robert Paul Meye, Ernest Best, and Theodore Weeden.

According to Black's findings, not all of Stein's criteria are of equal value to Meye, Best, and Weeden. Nevertheless, they agree on the importance of Mark's modifications as uncovered via a comparison with the other Synoptists, literary arrangement, conclusion, and vocabulary or style as evidence of redaction. Indeed, each places particular emphasis on one of these four criteria (192). Black, however, exposes methodological flaws and internal inconsistencies in their work. For example, the differences between Markan passages and their Synoptic parallels may reveal Matthean or Lukan rather than Markan redaction (79, 115, 154). Notwithstanding the form-critical axiom that the pre-Markan pericopes circulated independently, Black is skeptical that we can know whether it is the redactor or a pre-Markan tradent who linked pericopes and imposed structure on the oral tradition (85–86, 119–20). Black observes that the usage in Mark of some of the terms labeled as redactional in the studies under review hardly exceeds that of the other Gospels and adds that the frequency of a term falls short of proof that it is redactional as opposed to the Evangelist fancying a term found in a source (93–95, 130–31, 167). Further, their readings are as much guided by their discernment of major themes in Mark, such as Jesus as the teacher par excellence of a messianic διδαχή (Meye) or a conflict over a θεῖος ἀνήρ Christology (Weeden), which is not a strictly redaction-critical criterion. Lest his case get dismissed for its focus on three exegetes, Black finds similar weaknesses and circular argumentation in the efforts of James Crichton Little, Lloyd Gaston, Charles Joseph Reedy, William Oliver Walker, Edgar John Pryke, and David Barrett Peabody to refine the methodology of redaction criticism in chapter 7.

In chapter 8 Black reviews why redaction criticism became the dominant approach to Mark in spite of its flaws. Redaction criticism, with its stress on the theologies of the individual Gospels, filled in a gap left by the waning confidence in the possibility of reconstructing the historical Jesus behind the texts or in locating a unified theological center in the biblical theology movement. Black accepts the positive contributions of redaction criticism in supplying a comprehensive method for studying the prehistory and final form of the Gospels, recovering the role of the Evangelists as creative authors, and accentuating the theological dimensions of the Gospels. Yet the liabilities inherent in the method include the speculative attempt to delineate the Evangelist's editorial activity when we do not have access to Mark's sources, the fallacious equation of major themes present in Mark with Markan redaction, and the tendency toward "methodological imperialism" in trying to solve all sorts of literary and sociohistorical questions (267–76). As a way forward, Black proposes a model of synthetic biblical interpretation in which a close reading of the literary text is primary and from which scholars may branch out into historical criticism, tradition criticism, authorial-theological criticism, or reader-response criticism. It should be noted that Black believes that a holistic reading of Mark that takes into account the successes and failures of the disciples best supports the qualified positive reading of the disciples that is characteristic of the type 2 "mediate" position (291).

Readers will appreciate the afterword of this new edition for its delightful prose, engagement with the critical reviews, and updated survey of scholarship on the Markan disciples. In his subsequent correspondence with the late Ernest Best, Black rebuts some of Best's counterarguments as well as concedes some of his own mistakes and statistical errors. Moreover, Black recognizes that the "conservative," "mediate," and "liberal" positions on the Markan disciples are alive and well; a new book could be written with types 1 to 3 represented by the recent monographs of Suzanne Watts Henderson, Cédric Fisher, and Mary Ann Tolbert (328). Another valuable observation is that the hegemony of redaction criticism in the mid-twentieth century has given way to a plurality of methodological approaches and, further, that the mediate position has become the majority opinion among scholars studying Mark from different angles. Black sees in this some validation for his model in which a position established from a close reading of the text receives additional confirmation from a variety of methodological approaches (330).

In my judgment, Black has largely succeeded in demonstrating the subjectivity and circularity of redaction criticism when there are no sources to act as controls. There may be limited cases where scholars can point out probable examples of Markan editorial activity, such as the explanatory asides that clarify Jewish customs presupposed in the controversy narratives for the benefit of non-Jewish members in Mark's audience (see 7:3–4), but the wide-scale effort to separate Markan redaction from the tradition may not be feasible. Yet to the extent that redaction criticism flowed into composition and narrative criticism, there may be room to ask questions about the authorial-theological agenda reflected in the inclusion and arrangement of the material in Mark. The redaction-critical method cannot be entirely faulted for the discrepant results on the Markan disciples reached by its practitioners; it is the Evangelist who allowed positive and negative features about the disciples to stand in tension and chose to wrap up the story on an open-ended note instead of narrating the reunion of the disciples with the risen one in Galilee. The reader may thus legitimately fill in the gaps in the narrative in different ways. Even so, since Markan redaction cannot be detected with certainty and a preserved tradition may be as significant to the Evangelist as a minor editorial change, I agree with Black that only a close reading of Mark as a literary whole can resolve the enigma of the Markan disciples.

Parallel Gospels: A Synopsis of Early Christian Writing, by Zeba A. Crook. New York: Oxford University Press, 2011. Pp. xlvi + 320. Hardcover. $39.95. ISBN 9780199739417

Mark Goodacre, Duke University, Durham, North Carolina

Zeba Crook's *Parallel Gospels* combines a lot of hard work with several interesting innovations to produce a new kind of English-language synopsis of the Gospels. The book is clearly intended as a rival to Throckmorton's *Gospel Parallels*,[1] the title of which is clearly echoed. Crook deploys a "source language translation" (i.e., literal, nonidiomatic rendition) that helps the reader to see as many of the actual agreements in the Greek as possible, agreements that are sometimes obscured in "target language translation" synopses such as Throckmorton's.

There is undoubtedly a market for this kind of book. Theology and Religion courses that incorporate the teaching of Greek for undergraduates are a dying phenomenon, and the major Greek Synopses of the Gospels, such as Huck-Greeven and Aland, are now seen as tools for the specialists.[2] American liberal arts students taking courses on the New Testament are highly unlikely to have studied Greek. A good English-language synopsis is just what they need, ideal for the weeks in New Testament introduction that explore the Gospels and especially the Synoptic Problem.

The essential ethos of Crook's synopsis is right. There are drawbacks to using synopses that match up parallels in English that are not actually present in Greek, and there is always the potential for the same Greek in different Gospels to be translated differently. There are false positives, false negatives, and a false sense of security for the student relying on this translated text.

Moreover, the strongest feature of Crook's *Parallel Gospels* is the addition of seventeen "Synoptic Study Guides," which are distributed evenly across the work, pausing at appropriate moments to consider key data sets (Triple Tradition, Double Tradition, etc.) as well as key theories (Two-Source, Griesbach, and Farrer). It is particularly encouraging to see alternative theories being explained clearly and treated fairly. Given the nesting of these essays in the midst of the presentation of the data, the student is encouraged to take the primary evidence seriously while thinking about explanations for it. This is an innovation—Crook is here reversing the normal order, where synopsis excerpts are used to illustrate

---

1. Burton Hamilton Throckmorton, *Gospel Parallels: A Synopsis of the First Three Gospels with Alternative Readings from the Manuscripts and Noncanonical Parallels* (Nashville: Nelson, 1979).

2. Albert Huck, *Synopsis of the First Three Gospels*, 13th edition, fundamentally revised by Heinrich Greeven (Tübingen: Mohr Siebeck, 1981); Kurt Aland, *Synopsis Quattuor Evangeliorum* (Editio quindecima revisa; Stuttgart: Deutsche Bibelgesellschaft, 1996, 1997, 2001).

particular arguments in the secondary literature. Now, instead, the synopsis is primary and the theories secondary.

In spite of its significant advances and advantages, however, there are several difficulties with Crook's *Parallel Gospels* that are sufficiently great to cause concern about its use in the classroom. The first and immediate difficulty with the synopsis is that the parallels are not aligned at the word level. Given the wooden, word-for-word translation, it is surprising that there is no attempt to line up the parallels on the word-level in the Synopsis. This is a fundamental element of good Synopsis construction, and it obtains not only in the major Greek Synopses currently in use (Huck-Greeven, Aland) but also in Throckmorton's English synopsis. Parallel words and phrases frequently fall on different lines in Crook's synopsis, detracting from the essential symmetry that is at the heart of sound synopsis construction. To take one among many examples, Pericope 184 (Matt 18:1–5 // Mark 9:33–37 // Luke 9:46–48) has "young-child" on one line in Matthew, the line above it in Mark, and straddling both lines in Luke; "receives me" occurs on one line in Matthew, the line below it in Luke, and straddling the two in Mark.

The difficulty in part is with the typesetting of the synopsis, which is always left-aligned. There are never any spaces entered in the middle of a line to show where a word is present in one Gospel but absent in another. The student herself is left to work out what goes where, and this detracts from one of the joys of a good synopsis, which should aim to present synoptic agreements and disagreements visually. It is true that on the block level Crook's arrangement allows the student to see where the substantive parallels lie, but if we are to encourage students to fall in love with the intricacies of synoptic agreements and disagreements, word alignment is essential. The student who has been asked to color the synopsis will have a much harder time with Crook than with Throckmorton.[3]

The curious decision to avoid word alignment in the synopsis is in some tension with one of its chief goals: to provide a word-for-word Greek to English "source translation" that facilitates ease of comparison. This element of the synopsis is in some senses its major contribution, its key difference from other English synopses that rely on already-existing translations. Crook's reasoning is sound—it is a laudable goal to try to map one English word to one Greek word so that the reader who lacks Greek can see how the texts are related. In practice, though, the strategy leads to serious problems with clarity and readability, the very issues that are essential in presenting a synopsis to new students.

Crook's key decision is bold but flawed. He attempts to translate the same Greek word, every time it occurs, with the same English equivalent, regardless of case or context. This is "rendition" rather than translation, a word-for-word mapping rather than a clear, contextually coherent translation. It leads to literal

3. On the benefits of coloring the Synopsis for introductory students, see my *The Synoptic Problem: A Way through the Maze* (London: T&T Clark, 2001), 33–35.

translations that are so unreadable that the synopsis has to employ clarificatory words and phrases in square brackets.

The point is easiest to explain by illustrating it. In Pericope 66 (Matt 9:1–8 // Mark 2:1–12 // Luke 5:17–26), Crook's version of Mark 2:7 reads as follows:

> "What this talks [=Why does this man speak] thus? He-blasphemes; what [=who] is-able to-excuse sins if no [=except] the one god?"

The τίς interrogative here means "Why," not "What," so there is no benefit in having the confusing "What" in the main translation. The same is true of "what [=who]." Further, εἰ μή clearly means "except" here, and the translation "if no" makes no sense at all. The whole verse could therefore be translated in line with Crook's square bracket clarifications, and without the clunky translations, as: "Why does this man speak thus? He blasphemes; who is able to forgive sins except one, God?" The issue is one of clarity. The target audience for the book is the student beginning to familiarize herself with the synopsis and with elements in Synoptic scholarship. Navigating through these clunky renditions only makes the job more difficult, more off-putting.

A particular difficulty is the attempt to translate prepositions uniformly throughout, regardless of case, so, for example, Jesus is baptized "under [=by] John" (Pericope 21, Mark 1:9 // Matt 3:13, but separated by two lines in the Synopsis). But ὑπό with genitive is always "by" and not "under," and rendering it "under" is just confusing. Sometimes even the clarificatory, square-bracketed correct translation is absent, as when in Mark 1:14 (Pericope 24), the translation is "So with the to-be-delivered [=arrest] of John, Jesus went into the Galilee." The preposition μετά with the accusative is always "after" and not "with," and this passage is universally translated, "*after* the arrest of John" and not "with" it, whatever that would mean. This uniform translation of prepositions without paying attention to case is an unnecessary and complicating factor in a synopsis aimed at the introductory student.

The danger, moreover, is that these clunky renditions might be misread by the enthusiastic beginner as preserving "what the original Greek really says," offering something of a hostage to fortune. It is, of course, important to consider how best to communicate with the reader who has no Greek, but there is also a case for encouraging that reader to appreciate the limitations of working with English translation and using that as an invitation to study Greek.

This issue may not be the most serious drawback with Crook's *Parallel Gospels*. One of its most striking features is the introduction, for the first time in a Gospel synopsis, of the reconstructed text of Q.[4] On one level, this could be seen

---

4. James M. Robinson, Paul Hoffmann, and John S. Kloppenborg, *The Critical Edition of Q: Synopsis including the Gospels of Matthew and Luke, Mark and Thomas with English, German, and French translations of Q and Thomas* (Minneapolis: Fortress, 2000). Of course,

as a useful and interesting way of introducing new students to the reconstruction of Q, illustrating how it is done, on the basis of analysis of comparisons between Matthew and Luke. The difficulty, however, is that the presence of Q limits the usefulness of the synopsis in a fundamental way by foreclosing one of the key issues in Synoptic Problem research, which is one of the reasons for consulting a synopsis in the first place. Instead of acting as a tool for students to investigate and test the Q hypothesis, the actual printing of the reconstructed text of Q inevitably gives Q a tangibility, a concrete presence that makes it harder to encourage students to examine the hypothesis. It is an issue of what one is trying to achieve in constructing a synopsis. The strong synopsis facilitates good comparison between the Synoptic Gospels, enabling the student to assess competing hypotheses. To integrate one of the solutions to the Synoptic Problem into the presentation of the data can only hinder that aim. It is clear that Crook sees the integration of Q into the synopsis as a feature, even a selling point, but it is difficult to see how the move can facilitate fair and balanced assessment of the synoptic evidence. The issue relates to how data is presented and the importance of differentiating between getting to grips with the data and finding solutions to the problem.

There is a related practical and pedagogical issue. The introduction of Q turns intuitive two-column double tradition into a three-column presentation. It turns intuitive three-column triple tradition into a four-column presentation. Not only does this reduce the simplicity of the layout, thinning out the columns and crowding the page, which is a shame in a synopsis that is designed to appeal to undergraduate students, but also it makes it still more difficult to color the synopsis. It is greatly fortuitous that there are three Synoptic Gospels and three primary colors and that the combinations between them make coloring both intuitive and fun. Coloring a four-column synopsis introduces all sorts of problems. Would one leave Q white? Would one color in-line with the coloring of Matthew and Luke so that one could see how the wording of Q had been reconstructed? Either way, the addition of Q into the synopsis looks a gift horse in the mouth—three Synoptics, three primary colors.

There is a further related problem about using this synopsis in teaching. Pure triple tradition is here still in three columns, so one has the link there between triple and three columns. But pure double tradition is also in three columns, Matthew, Q, and Luke, so it is less straightforward to explain how "triple" and "double" work. This might sound like an overly simple point, but Crook's own Synoptic Study Guides forefront the discussions of "triple tradition" and "double tradition" only to miss the opportunity to illustrate how these work in simple synopsis.

---

the International Q Project themselves use a synopsis of Matthew and Luke (with additions sometimes from Mark and Thomas) in order to illustrate the derivation of their reconstruction of Q. However, this is natural in a work that is all about the reconstruction of the hypothetical document. In the synopsis proper, still more the introductory synopsis, Q is one possible result of the analysis and not an element in the presentation of the evidence itself.

A new Gospel synopsis provides those with an interest in the study of the Synoptics a fresh opportunity to assess how to present the evidence, how to teach the Synoptic Problem, and how to assess the strengths and weaknesses in traditional approaches. While Crook's *Parallel Gospels* offers a welcome stimulus to think about the presentation, the understanding, and the teaching of the issues, it falls short in several key ways. Its word-for-word renditions can be clunky and confusing, its lack of word alignment deprives us of an elegant means of visualizing agreements and disagreements, and its integration of a Synoptic theory into the presentation of the data confuses problem and solution. Lest this seem too harsh, it is worth remembering that Aland's Synopsis is currently in its fifteenth edition, and Huck-Greeven is a world apart from Huck-Lietzmann and other iterations of the same. In time, Crook's *Parallel Gospels* might still take its place alongside the great teaching tools, with its first edition regarded as a useful stepping stone to later, revised versions that ironed out these problems. For the present, though, trying out new ideas helps us to realize where some of the older ideas worked a little better.

Mark, by Mary Ann Beavis. Paideia Commentaries on the New Testament. Grand Rapids: Baker Academic, 2011. Pp. xviii + 302. Paper. $30.00. ISBN 9780801034374.

Jeff Jay, St. Norbert College, De Pere, Wisconsin

Mary Ann Beavis distinguishes her book from other commentaries on Mark by her sustained focus on classroom needs, which is in keeping with the purpose of Baker Academic's aptly titled Paideia series. Beavis specifies her target audience as teachers and their upper-division undergraduate or lower-division graduate students in religious or theological studies in colleges or seminaries (ix, 28). Teachers who order this book for their students will find their classrooms enriched.

In the introduction (3–29) Beavis details vital issues for reading Mark in light of its literary and historical contexts. Students will learn of this text's rise to prominence as the earliest extant Gospel and of the emerging understanding in form and redaction criticisms that this Gospel, rather than conveying the story of the historical Jesus, reflects the concerns of its author and his community (3–5). Beavis judiciously examines Papias and other traditions about Mark as well as potential references to him in the New Testament. She appropriately dates the Gospel near the Roman defeat of Jerusalem in 70. As for the Gospel's setting, Beavis leans toward Rome, although she rightly recognizes the limited evidence and clearly presents the arguments in favor of Galilee or southern Syria (6–11).

Beavis is excellent at introducing these subjects, because, while she makes her own interpretive decisions clear, she always does so in a way that leaves students room to consider all the major scholarly alternatives for themselves. This is true in her treatment of genre, where she explains why genre matters in the process of reading and argues that "gospel" in 1:1 is not to be understood as a generic designation. She focuses on biography and Mark's affinities with biblical narratives, while gesturing toward the Hellenistic novel, the Homeric epic, and ancient drama as other plausible suggestions for Mark's genre (14–16). She details several important literary features, including parataxis, the historical present, hyperbole, intercalation, the omniscient narrator, individual and collective characterization, and setting (17–21). She also highlights "major themes" in Mark, including Christology, discipleship, the portrayal of Jews and Judaism, "apocalyptic epistemology," suffering, and the use of scripture, which are all well chosen eye-openers for students (22–24).

Also among preliminaries is the question of Mark's audience, which, Beavis argues, anticipates persecution, is familiar with figures such as Isaiah, David, Moses, and Elijah, knows the Jewish scriptures, accepts the existence of otherworldly beings such as angels and Satan, affirms the world-wide mission, and expects the imminent appearance of God's kingdom (12–14). This is a good characterization of the ideal (or authorial) audience. But teachers will need to prompt students to question the varying degrees to which Mark's earliest recipients may or may not correspond in reality to the authorial ideal, a distinction that Beavis overlooks.

Structure is the last of the preparatory issues Beavis addresses (25–28). She reiterates the approach of her earlier work (*Mark's Audience: The Literary and Social Context of Mark 4:1–34* [JSNTSup 33; Sheffield: Sheffield Academic Press, 1989]). She argues that Mark's structure reflects that of ancient drama, particularly Greek tragedy. Although I find it problematic (see below), Beavis ascertains five acts with an epilogue and prologue as well as four "teaching scenes" or "interludes," which, like the chorus, clarify the division between acts:

Prologue: John and Jesus (1:1–13)
Transition: Summary of the Good News (1:14–15)
Act One: Jesus in Galilee (1:16–3:35)
Interlude: Teaching in Parables (4:1–34)
Act Two: Beyond Galilee (4:35–6:56)
Interlude: Teaching on Ritual and Moral Purity (7:1–23)
Act Three: Mission in Gentile Regions (7:24–9:29)
Interlude: Teaching on the Way to Jerusalem (9:30–10:52)
Act Four: Opposition in Jerusalem (11:1–12:44)
Interlude: Teaching on the End Times (13:1–37)
Act Five: Passion Narrative (14:1–15:47)
Epilogue: Women at the Empty Tomb (16:1–8).

Beavis devotes one chapter to each of the units in this proposed outline. Like all the commentaries in this series (x), each chapter is divided into three sections.

(1) In "Introductory Matters" Beavis fine-tunes structural divisions and explains the rhetorical and literary features of the particular section under treat-

ment. Notable here is that Beavis continues to correlate aspects of Mark's Gospel with ancient tragic drama. For example, she likens the prologue in 1:1–13 to the monologues at the start of plays, which function to inform viewers of the drama's back-story (30). Beavis takes every opportunity to underline how elements of tragic drama punctuate Mark's Gospel, which is replete with reversals and partial recognitions (8:27–30; 9:2–8 [121–22, 135, 139]) and even a *hyporchēma*, the joyful scene immediately preceding the dénouement (11:1–11 [168]). Beavis thus impresses upon students the dramatic nature of this text in a way that (pedagogically speaking) has the potential to be highly impactful.

(2) Beavis is at her best in "Tracing the Narrative Flow." These sections of the book will prove most useful to students who are ready for interpreting Mark with a commentary-style book in hand. She offers her own translations by which she attempts "to capture the colloquial and vivid quality of Mark's style" in gender-inclusive language. She expressively renders terms in ways that are instructive for students who do not know Greek (e.g., "rule" or "reign" for *basileia* or "good news" for *euangelion*) (21). Beavis also helpfully indicates the many literary allusions and parallels in Mark, especially to biblical and early Jewish literature. To cite one among many instances, Beavis underlines how the stories of both John and Jesus intersect with those of Elijah and Elisha (Mark 1:2–8, 12–13, 40–45 [33–35, 38, 54–57]; 6:34–44 [105–7]; 9:2–13 [134–38]). She sensibly treats long-standing issues of interpretation (e.g., the meaning of "the son of man" [59], the interpretation of parables [74–77], and the ending of the Gospel at 16:8 and subsequent expansions [239–49]). Beavis, moreover, has an especially acute eye for the ways each text recalls or anticipates other Markan episodes by the repetition of words or themes, foreshadowing, and prophecy.

(3) In "Theological Issues" Beavis discusses a wide range of topics bearing on the significance of Mark in contemporary perspective. Beavis, for instance, encourages students to compare Mark's Christology with developments in later creeds (40–41), to think suspiciously about anti-Judaic biases (86, 185–86) and the potentially harmful valorization of suffering and servanthood (160–64), to consider the homiletic elaborations by later Christians such as Augustine and Bonhoeffer (141–42, 236), or to envision Christian life as a dichotomy between "mountaintop" and more "challenging" life experiences (140–42).

On the whole, these sections on theology lack the methodological rigor and clarity that characterize the literary and historical parts of the commentary. What, after all, does it mean to think about Mark "theologically"? Beavis does not answer this question, and her discussions leave students without a strong sense of the various (often conflicting) ways an ancient text like Mark might intersect with contemporary concerns, presenting as she does a grab-bag of the history of reception, critical Marxist or feminist readings, positive retrievals, and even slightly simplistic life applications.

Another problem that impacts the overall success of the book is Beavis's proposed structure. The correlation of these divisions with the acts of drama is problematic because Mark's Gospel lacks the structural feature by which it is

possible to divide dramas into episodes. It is the choral ode that clarifies the start
and close of an episode, and in the tragedies the chorus is distinct in its lyri-
cal meters, antiphonal arrangement, and delivery, which her "teaching scenes"
(Beavis's stand-ins for the chorus) lack. How could Mark compose, or narratees
perceive, acts without a clearly identifiable intervening chorus? Beavis sets aside
Mark's authorial intent as irrelevant in this regard (note her caveat: "whether
the author intended it or not" [26]), but this undermines what is otherwise her
literary-historical approach to interpreting Mark.

Beavis's proposed structure is also problematic on inner-exegetical grounds.
It eschews, for example, the coherence of the journey to Jerusalem (8:27–10:45),
which is enclosed by two stories wherein Jesus heals blind men (8:22–27; 10:46–
52). Also uniting this section are references to "the road" (8:27; 9:33; 10:17, 32),
the passion predictions (8:31; 9:31; 10:32–33), and instruction focused on the
need for followers to live a life of sacrifice and servanthood (8:34–38; 9:33–37;
10:17–31, 41–45). It is important for students to interpret this as a discrete rhetorical unit, which Beavis herself recognizes only in passing (25), and so the
commentary will fail them in this regard.

Criticism of this proposed structure applies to the structure of the commentary as a whole, because Beavis's outline of Mark mirrors the subsequent chapter
divisions. The shortcomings Beavis's structure may have are thus replicated on a
large scale and further reinforce what students will (or will not) see. Nonetheless,
this work will contribute to the task of making classrooms where students are
studying Mark into vital learning environments because even works with which
one disagrees foster the give and take of critical dialogue and the conflict of interpretations, which are what make for educational excellence.

JOHN

John among the Other Gospels: The Reception of the Fourth Gospel in the Extra-
canonical Gospels, by Lorne R. Zelyck. Wissenschaftliche Untersuchungen zum
Neuen Testament 2/347. Tübingen: Mohr Siebeck, 2013. Pp. xvi + 262. Paper.
€69.00. ISBN 9783161523991.

Jason Sturdevant, North Carolina State University, Raleigh, North Carolina

More and more scholars of the New Testament and early Christianity are turning to the area of reception and interpretation history of New Testament texts.
In this book, a revised version of his doctoral thesis at Cambridge (2012), Zelyck
aims to contribute to this growing area by providing a comprehensive study
regarding whether and in what ways the Fourth Gospel influenced the noncanonical Gospels, namely, those reasonably presumed written in the second
to third centuries CE. In so doing, Zelyck presents a case for a more rigorous
and cautious method for examining the relationship between ancient texts and
for challenging the frequently assumed distinctions among diverse Christian

communities (Valentinian, gnostic, "orthodox," and others) in the first three centuries. The work is aimed primarily at those working on questions of the reception of the New Testament in early Christianity. Since many of the texts surveyed (e.g., the Gospel of Thomas or the Gospel of Mary) have played key roles in scholarly reconstructions of early Christianity, however, the study is also relevant for those who are engaged in such work, as Zelyck's observations and conclusions frequently challenge the results of that project.

In the two introductory chapters Zelyck sets the boundaries for his study. In chapter 1 he prudently begins with a definition of what he means by a "Gospel," which he identifies as a third-person account of the life, deeds, and/or teachings of the adult Jesus (see 5–6). To provide further boundaries, he limits himself to Gospels believed to have been written in the second and third centuries and examines only Gospels extant in Greek or Coptic. He then divides the Gospels within this range into several subgenres: narrative Gospels, sayings Gospels, and dialogue/discourse Gospels. This provides the major categories for the study.

The second chapter then allows Zelyck to define and defend his method in analyzing these Gospels. The entire study depends on finding parallels between these Gospels and the Fourth Gospel. This task is not unproblematic, since (1) there may be false positives due to scribes harmonizing the language of different texts or from the influence of a Synoptic parallel to the Fourth Gospel; (2) there may also be false negatives, since the authors of these Gospels may have had different manuscripts of the Fourth Gospel than are extant; (3) one must compare Coptic texts to the Fourth Gospel for verbal parallels via Coptic translations of the Fourth Gospel; and (4) the dating of various texts (including the Fourth Gospel) is imprecise at best. For these reasons, Zelyck opts for a provisional use of three headings: probable use, plausible use, and possible use. He also identifies various criteria for determining parallels: common terminology, presence of uniquely Johannine terminology, cumulative evidence, contextual similarities (in the narrative), evidence of "purposeful alteration of the FG," and the presence of "traditional interpretation" of the Fourth Gospel (17–19). On the whole, when identifying parallels, Zelyck prefers to eliminate unnecessary hypotheses of intermediate sources between the Fourth Gospel and a noncanonical Gospel or arguments for a shared source when a simpler explanation may account for the evidence (though sometimes such hypotheses are seen as quite helpful). Lastly, it should be noted that the work takes a stance of provisional reservation about *how* any author came to know of the Fourth Gospel (14), a move that enables Zelyck to present a case of *potential* influence without getting bogged in the quest to reconstruct a great deal of early Christianity—yet a decision with which not every reader will be satisfied.

The next three chapters cover the narrative Gospels: the Egerton Gospel, the Gospel of Peter, and P. Oxy. 840. Zelyck follows the same pattern for chapters on the sayings Gospels (Thomas and Philip) and the dialogue/discourse Gospels (e.g., the Gospel of the Savior and the Gospel of Mary). For each work, Zelyck begins with an overview of the work itself (helpful for those unfamiliar with the contents of the Gospels as well as their origins), then turns to prior treatments of the relationship of each Gospel to the canonical Gospels. Typically Zelyck notes prior discussions of a Gospel with the Fourth Gospel, but in several places Zelyck is the first to offer a substantive discussion of any possible relationship. From there, his treatment varies depending on the source. With some, he can trace parallels with the Fourth Gospel as the narrative unfolds; with others, especially the discourse-driven works, he divides the treatment into probable, plausible, and possible parallels. No matter the work, however, he not only discusses parallels but provides helpful tables to chart the parallels, which invites the reader to engage in one's own analysis of the evidence. When Zelyck does identify probable and plausible influence, he also notes the variations between the Fourth Gospel and the author's interpretation or use of the Fourth Gospel, which allows him to note important exegetical methods and ideological elements of various noncanonical Gospels. For example, in examining the Gospel of Philip, Zelyck claims that the author adopts Johannine passages (e.g., John 8:32, 34) to bolster the work's authority but in so doing also adapts those passages to reflect his own ideology that overrides the meaning of these passages within the Fourth Gospel. At the end of each chapter, Zelyck provides a summary of the evidence and submits his conclusions, which on the whole are cautious and conservative, regarding the probability of influence from the Fourth Gospel.

Zelyck concludes his study by noting the most important results of his investigation. First, he places the works surveyed into three categories: probably influenced by the Fourth Gospel (Gosp. Savior, Egerton Gospel, Gosp. Philip, Sophia of Jesus Christ), plausibly influenced (Gosp. Peter, Gosp. Thomas, Gosp. Mary), and possibly influenced (Dialogue of the Savior, Thomas the Contender, Gosp. Judas, P. Oxy. 840). These categories allow him to make some broader observations about influence, namely, that "proto-orthodox" works (and narratives at that) tend to reveal the most influence, while gnostic and Thomasine works (generally in dialogue or discourse form) show the least. Furthermore, Zelyck notes that the dating of these various texts appears to have no impact on the influence of the Fourth Gospel, as the evidence shows no "significant correlation between an extra-canonical Gospel's date of composition and the influence of the FG" (196). His study has also shown the various ways the Fourth Gospel appears in these texts: by short quotes, exegesis, and parallels long and short. Finally, the analysis leads Zelyck to conclude that the authors of these noncanonical Gospels interpreted the Fourth Gospel in ways similar to other Christian authors of their time (e.g., Irenaeus, Origen, or Tertullian), leading to the need for reevaluating the provenance and contexts of many of the texts covered in the book. What does not appear from his analysis, as he notes, is anything relevant about the interpretation of the Fourth Gospel on its own.

This study makes several contributions, not only in terms of the analysis and results summarized above, but also in terms of exemplifying a meticulous attention to detail and the virtues of a focused scope and method. The method is well defined and generally useful, keeping the author from making too great of claims for the evidence. Though at times the prose and analysis can be plodding, the writing is nevertheless deliberate. The tables used to present parallels between noncanonical Gospels and the Fourth Gospel are quite helpful, allowing readers to see how Zelyck comes to his conclusions, if not coming to those same conclusions themselves. Also, even though the chapters could be read as stand-alone treatments of specific texts, as the book progresses Zelyck effortlessly connects discussions in later chapters to those made earlier on, which leaves the impression of a unified treatment on the whole. Additionally, the bibliography is remarkably up to date for a revised doctoral thesis, as Zelyck interacts with works published as recently as 2012. In his interaction, finally, with several notable figures in the field, Zelyck finds that important balance between finding his own voice without unfairly dismissing the contributions of his predecessors.

Zelyck manages to remain both incisive and reserved in his observations, evidencing several virtues of critical scholarship. Nevertheless, at times his reserve keeps him from making stronger claims than he might. For example, when discussing the Book of Thomas the Contender, after several comparisons of texts that would dismiss any relation between it and the Fourth Gospel, he concludes "it is only possibly that he was influenced by the Fourth Gospel, since many of these parallels are quite weak." One wishes at points like these that Zelyck would be somewhat more strident. This reserve runs through the book and so pervades the work that one struggles to find an overarching thesis. Indeed, the book feels at points more like an exploration than an argument. Based on his conclusion, Zelyck believes he has presented a case throughout the book, yet it remains implicit, left to the reader to discern. Again, Zelyck's care and caution (so different from many of his interlocutors) is laudable, yet he risks turning the work's greatest strength into something of a liability by not stating clearly enough the conclusions at which he hopes his readers will arrive.

Yet these shortcomings do not overshadow this industrious and illuminating study. Zelyck has shone light on an important piece of the puzzle that is the reception of New Testament texts by their earliest readers. Moreover, even if some disagree with his readings, the attention to detail and the care of his exegesis require that his readings be taken seriously.

John, Qumran, and the Dead Sea Scrolls: Sixty Years of Discovery and Debate, edited by Mary L. Coloe and Tom Thatcher. Early Judaism and Its Literature 32. Atlanta: Society of Biblical Literature, 2011. Pp. xv + 228. Paper. $28.95. ISBN 9781589835467.

Jörg Frey, University of Zurich, Zurich, Switzerland

The volume under review is the documentation of a panel discussion held at the SBL Annual Meeting 2007 in San Diego on the occasion of the sixtieth anniversary of the Qumran discoveries, which was organized by the SBL John, Jesus, and History Group, in collaboration with the SBL Johannine Literature Section. The two editors represent these two groups: Mary Coloe the Johannine Literature

section and Tom Thatcher the John, Jesus, and History Group. The concept and
agenda of the panel was, however, strongly determined by the latter group, with
Paul Anderson as the introductory speaker. The present reviewer was also a part
of the panel but by then had decided not to contribute to the present volume.

Due to its origin, the volume does not aim at a comprehensive overview but
combines three quite different accounts of research with six case studies as to
how the Dead Sea Scrolls can be "applied to" Johannine texts. The program of the
whole is most clearly set out in the overviews by Anderson and James H. Charlesworth, so their tendency must be critically discussed in light of present Qumran
and Johannine scholarship. The six case studies are of quite different scope, range,
and quality and will be discussed in due course. A few final remarks on the methodology of comparison will be appropriate in concluding the review.

In the introductory "Preface" (vii–x), the editors state that the Scrolls "have
played no significant role in discussions of the Johannine literature over the past
several decades" (vii). I am not so sure whether this is true. At least the magisterial
commentary by Raymond E. Brown and also the second edition of C. K. Barrett's
commentary did consider the Scrolls quite intensely, although Barrett finally concluded that the Scrolls did influence but not revolutionize Johannine scholarship.
Admittedly, after the 1970s the stagnation in the publication of the Scrolls led to
a decrease of interest among exegetes, and the very specialized views of recent
Qumran scholarship are still barely known to "normal" exegetes. Furthermore,
the awareness of the methodological problems in relating Qumran and Johannine
texts has grown, so that more recent research has generally become more cautious
against monolithic history of religions views. Of course, it would be a worthwhile
endeavor to link Qumran scholarship in its present state of the art with Johannine
scholarship, but it must be clearly stated that the present volume does not fulfill
this desideratum, and in some of its contributions it seems to be rather stuck in
older and outdated views of relating John with the Qumran Scrolls.

1. THREE DIFFERENT SURVEYS OF RESEARCH AND THE MAIN ASPECTS OF THE
DEBATE

In her sober survey of the last decade of Qumran scholarship (3–14), eminent Qumran specialist Eileen Schuller nicely lists some of the most important
insights of recent Qumran research: It is (1) the publication of almost all remaining texts of the corpus, (2) a substantial rethinking of the core documents such as
the Community Rule (S), the War Rule (M) or the Hymns Scroll (H), which are
now available not only in one Cave 1 manuscript but in a larger number of fragmentary manuscripts that may allow one to reconsider their redactional history
and character on a new material basis, and (3) the application of new methods,
such as social-scientific approaches or ritual studies. Schuller makes no claims for
the relevance of the Scrolls in Johannine studies. Her essay is a merely Qumranis-
tic overview that does not enter the Johannine field.

It is quite different with Paul Anderson, who is not a Qumran scholar but
quite busy in the Johannine discussion and one of the organizers of the John, Jesus,

and History Group. Anderson's "John and Qumran: Discovery and Interpretation over Sixty Years" (15–50) is the most extensive contribution in the volume, providing a rich account of sixty years of relating John and Qumran, quite well informed in scholarship, however partly showing a tendency that deserves at least critical discussion.

It may be useful to know that already in the very early phase after the Qumran discovery scholars utilized the Scrolls not only for reconstructing an alternative milieu of the Johannine language within Palestinian Judaism (in contrast to the Gnosticism that Rudolf Bultmann had suggested as John's background). Some early authors (e.g., W. F. Albright) even concluded that John, when located within a Palestinian Jewish context, might be more reliable historically in some details or even generally. Of course, Qumran scholarship has become much more cautious here, but it seems that these early views still appear attractive for some Johannine scholars: Anderson seems to share that initial optimism and phrases with strong rhetorical pathos: "The way that the scrolls illuminate the ministries of Jesus and John the Baptizer, and also the Fourth Gospel, has been highly significant" (20). The Scrolls, the Baptizer, Jesus and the Fourth Gospel—the line suggested here presupposes the historical validity of the calling narratives in John 1 and the relationship between Qumran or the Scrolls and John the Baptist. Recent research has seriously challenged both these assumptions.

In his review of the history of relating John and Qumran, Anderson claims, again with a bold rhetoric, that Qumran scholarship has replaced most of the presuppositions of Johannine interpretation before 1947, that is, especially of Bultmann's views. This is partly true, but the different aspects must be critically assessed: Anderson mentions (1) the view that John was primarily Hellenistic, not Jewish, and therefore distanced from Jesus and his world, (2) the view that "agency" belonged to a wider Gnostic redeemer myth from which the Johannine discourses are to be explained, (3) the view that Johannine religious forms were non-Jewish rather than Jewish-Christian, (4) the view that the Logos motif comes from Hellenistic speculation, and (5) the view of a somewhat monolithic (normative) Jewish messianism. Against these (partly generalizing) propositions of earlier scholarship, Anderson claims that the Scrolls have demonstrated or led scholars to acknowledge (1) that Johannine dualism is perfectly at home within Palestinian Judaism, (2) that agency is closer to the šālîaḥ motif rooted within the Mosaic prophet agency typology of Deut 18, (3) that the Jesus movement in its individuation from Judaism is illuminated by Qumran sectarianism, (4) that John's Christology is fundamentally Jewish, based on Gen 1 and Prov 8, and (5) the diversity of messianic expectations.

The claims mentioned here deserve a detailed assessment. In my view, not all of them are equally correct. Admittedly, the diversity of messianism in Second Temple times is a very clear insight from the Qumran discoveries, and the basically Jewish background of Johannine Christology was in fact rediscovered under the impact of Qumran studies, even though this background is illuminated by scriptural allusions and parallels in various Jewish texts rather than by direct Qumran parallels. The three other claims, however, should be considered more closely. As recent scholarship, especially by D. E. Aune, R. J. Bauckham, and also by the present reviewer, has demonstrated, the parallels between dualistic motifs in John and the (variegated types of) dualisms in the Scrolls cannot be explained by a direct Qumran influence on the Evangelist or his community but draw on different elements of scriptural and early Jewish tradition that are utilized and combined in the language and composition of the Fourth Gospel. The fact that the early Jesus movement reflects some kind of "individuation" or individual religious "decision" is in a more general manner paralleled in early Jewish "factionalism" of the post-Maccabean period and also by a broader tendency toward individual religious options in the Hellenistic world (e.g., in philosophy, mystery cults), but certainly no direct impact of Qumran sectarianism. Further, the character and background of the Johannine view of the "agency" of Jesus is at least debated in present Johannine scholarship. The pattern of Moses and Deut 18 is one of the options, but this is certainly not predominantly Qumranic but also present in Samaritanism and in other early Jewish texts. Anderson's claim is true insofar the gnostic redeemer myth has faded away in the scholarship of the last decades, but this is neither new nor predominantly due to a Qumranic pattern that could have served as a substitute pattern.

In the main part of his paper (19–31) Anderson enumerates several attempts of relating John and Qumran, from the admittedly overexaggerated theories of Dupont-Sommer, Allegro, Wilson, and later Thiering to the more cautious views of recent scholarship. With obvious sympathy he refers to the assumption of a historical link between the Baptizer and Qumran, which (if John 1 is historically trustworthy) might then also lead to a link between the Beloved Disciple as a disciple of the Baptizer and thus under the influence of Qumran (20–21). Anderson reports the bold views of John Ashton and James Charlesworth that the Evangelist was thoroughly shaped by Qumran dualism and probably a former Essene and the even more daring view held by Brian Capper that the Evangelist "was an Essene" (22). The milestones of the John and Qumran discussion are enumerated: (1) in the 1950s, early studies by Kuhn, Burrows, Brown, and Albright identifying impressive parallels; (2) the important collection of essays edited by Charlesworth in 1972 discussing a number of themes by way of comparison; (3) important later articles by Charlesworth, Joseph Fitzmyer, and Daniel Harrington in the 1990s; and (4) some further, more critical studies that pointed to significant differences, such as by Bauckham and Aune. On these studies, however, Anderson comments that even differences "may reflect intertraditional contact" (31). This is a quite tendentious claim that is not further substantiated. Differences may, of course, imply the rejection of some views known to an author, but this is not necessarily the case. They can also simply show that the relationship is not very close. Anderson's sympathy, however, is obviously with those authors who argue for a close relationship between Qumran and John that is said to explain the thoroughly Jewish character of Johannine dualism and Christology.

Anderson finally browses through a number of significant topics that allow for a comparison. These include creation, dualism, pneumatology, the community dynamics, Scripture and its interpretation, the Baptizer's ministry, archaeological and topographical details, the teacher of righteousness and opposed figures, christological titles, and the Two Ways and their implication. A more detailed comparison in those fields is certainly commendable, but I suspect it will not reveal compelling arguments for any direct dependence of John on Qumran but rather show interesting and sometimes important analogous phenomena, contextualizations, and so on. The close connection that Anderson proposes with respect to the aspect of dualism or to the connection of the Baptizer with Qumran is, in my view, no longer tenable. In the final part of his piece, Anderson also admits that similarities are no longer necessarily to be interpreted as evidence for firsthand contacts, but again he adds an unsubstantiated affirmation: "although some early contact likely existed" (50). Here I must again put a question mark. Anderson's survey is in some decisive points far too uncritical and still strongly dependent on earlier, exaggerated views like those of Ashton, Charlesworth, and others reckoning with a direct dependence between John and Qumran or at least with early contacts between Qumran and John the Baptist and thus with an ongoing tradition into the Jesus movement.

The concluding essay, James Charlesworth's "The Fourth Evangelist and the Dead Sea Scrolls: Assessing Trends over Nearly Sixty Years" (161–82) is also a kind of research survey. It was held as a public lecture and is thus shaped by a somewhat popularizing rhetoric that does not help to advance the scholarly discourse. Moreover, there are some overlaps with Anderson's essay, so that I can discuss Charlesworth's view quite briefly here. In numerous quotations from other scholars Charlesworth emphasizes how Qumran, in his view, has revolutionized Johannine research. Some of the aspects are in fact remarkable; others appear rather insignificant. It is true that Qumran has helped scholars to recognize the Jewish background of John, and numerous details in John can confirm this. On the other hand, the view that the Johannine language is preformed by the dualistic language in Qumran cannot be maintained. Even if there are some similarities with the Treatise on the Two Spirits, this text is also unique in the context of the Scrolls and possibly did not originate within the community but in a sapiential precursor movement. Moreover, some of the "technical terms" emphasized by Charlesworth as an argument for a direct influence are not uniquely Qumran sectarian but also attested elsewhere in presectarian texts such as the Aramaic Visions of Amram or in other contemporary and later Jewish and early Christian documents.

2. "Application" in Five Case Studies

Turning now to the six application essays, I can be briefer and focus rather on Johannine scholarship. In general, the character and scope of the essays is quite different, and the relevance of the findings is often rather limited.

The contribution by Hannah K. Harrington, a specialist in Jewish purity and also in the Dead Sea Scrolls, on "Purification in the Fourth Gospel in Light of Qumran" (117–38) is a sober case study of how the Scrolls can be utilized. In contrast with older views holding that John is far away from all kinds of water rituals and eager to look for a replacement of Jewish purity, Harrington browses through Qumran purification texts and other early Jewish texts demonstrating how in early Judaism water (rites) could be associated with new life, atonement, revelation, and even the eschaton or the eschatological purification. Based on that survey, she concludes that the hints of water purification in John are not un-Jewish nor an empty ritual that merely needed replacement. In fact, the Scrolls and other Jewish texts already show that a metaphorical meaning of water purification had been developing, which is also visible in John. The innovative aspect is, of course, that purification comes to fruition in the person and work of Jesus, but the language and concepts of purification and their metaphorization are quite Jewish.

Another commendable example of the utilization of the Scrolls is given by the eminent Qumran specialist Loren T. Stuckenbruck in "'Protect Them from the Evil One' (John 17:15): Light from the Dead Sea Scrolls" (139–60). In order to illuminate Jesus' prayer in John 17:15, Stuckenbruck draws a comprehensive sketch of early Jewish apotropaic prayers from the Scrolls and other writings, thus demonstrating that the view of the Fourth Gospel that the world is under the dominion of the evil one, the "ruler of this world," is conceivable in the context of contemporary Jewish piety. The vast variety of texts now accessible helps illuminate the background of these views and also their reframing in the light of Jesus' death.

George J. Brooke, another distinguished Qumran expert, is also well aware of the methodological problems of relating John and Qumran, and he explains them quite clearly in the exposition of his contribution on "Luke, John, and the Dead Sea Scrolls" (69–92). His essay focuses on motifs or traditions common to Luke and John and tries to explore whether these common elements can receive some explanation from Qumran texts. Here the discussion enters the difficult and highly debated field of John and the Synoptics, especially John and Luke. Brooke presupposes that John is independent from Luke, while both rely on common traditions that are then developed differently in the two Gospels. Without being able to enter this discussion here, it must be stated that the matter is quite complicated and that the view that John is dependent on Luke has won more supporters in the past decades of scholarship.

Brooke discusses three motifs, (a) the 153 fish in John 21:11 (a story paralleled by Luke 5), (b) the Sons of Light mentioned in Luke 16:8 and John 12:35–36, and (c) the "Son of God" mentioned in Luke 1:32–35 and more prominently in John, now illuminated by the famous "Son of God" text 4Q246. The explanatory value of the parallels, however, is quite limited, and the analogies seem to be somewhat far-fetched. It is true that the title "Son of God" is primarily rooted in Judaism, and the parallel between 4Q246 and Luke 1:32–35 has often been noted. But it is questionable whether the Aramaic text, related either to a messianic figure or (in Brooke's view) to the claims of an opposed figure such as Antiochus IV Epiphanes, is able to illustrate the argument on Jesus' alleged blasphemy in John 10. The term "Sons of Light" is by no means uniquely Qumranic, so that the usage in Luke and John (only once in each Gospel) does not receive much elucidation from the Qumran parallels. Further, the reference to the Commentary on Genesis (4Q252) and its view that Noah's ark came to rest on Mount Ararat 153 days after the beginning of the flood—the number 153 is not even mentioned in the Qumran text—hardly provides an explanation for the number of the 153 fish in John 21:11. Brooke's suggestion that an early tradition with the 153 fish was later used in Luke, where the number of the fish and other elements were removed, is also far from being convincing. It is still more probable that the author of John 21 used Luke's story (either from tradition or from the Gospel), so that the insertion of the number 153 must be explained otherwise—if it will ever be explained.

In concluding his essay, Brooke mentions a number of further points of contact between Luke and John—Jacob traditions, the focus on the temple, and so on—and in all those contexts there is some Qumran material that might be adduced to illuminate the respective backgrounds. It remains doubtful, however, whether the material can also prove a common tradition between Luke and John.

John Ashton has been one of the more influential Johannine scholars of the last three decades. He is not only well-known for the daring view that the author of the Fourth Gospel "had dualism in his bones" (quoted in the present volume by Anderson, 21) but also for his conviction that John is in fact a kind of an apocalypse in reversed form. This means that the Fourth Gospel is a revelatory writing, in a way comparable with apocalyptic writings and including a number of elements of the apocalyptic worldview. This is, in my opinion, a quite interesting interpretation of the Johannine Christology (and will be discussed extensively in a forthcoming volume put together in honor of John Ashton and edited by Chris Rowland and Catrin Williams at Oxford University Press). In the present context, the question is only: Do the Qumran texts contribute to that view, and do we need them?

In his study "'Mystery' in the Dead Sea Scrolls and the Fourth Gospel" (53–68), Ashton focuses on the term and motif of the *rāz nihyeh* known already from 1QS XI but much more extensively now from the sapiential texts (1/4QMysteries; 1/4QInstruction) that became fully accessible only in the 1990s. The term, which is difficult to translate ("mystery to come," "mystery of being"), refers to a hidden mystery, an order of creation and history, including the eschatological visitation, that is, a kind of wisdom that cannot be obtained by all humans but only by a small group of elect or the knowledgeable who are exhorted to consider or meditate on that mystery. Ashton discusses the Qumran material, but without considering that the two wisdom texts mentioned are probably not specifically Qumran sectarian compositions but composed in pre-Qumran sapiential circles. In any case, 1QS XI shows that the term was also known and used within the community.

When reading John against this background, the Johannine community appears as a group similarly based on a hidden or higher wisdom (i.e., the revelation of Christ). But the simple analogy of two "revelation-based" groups is rather unspecific. The same is true for the aspect that the Qumranites and the Johannine group use the term "truth" for their special revelation and the loose analogies between the Johannine Logos (as creational power) and the Qumran view that all being and history is predestined by the creator. For Ashton these rather vague analogies show that the Qumran sectarians and the Johannine group lived according to a revealed mystery and were, thus, both "apocalyptic" (but only in a very unspecific manner). However, Ashton does not consider appropriately the distinction between Qumran sectarian and nonsectarian or presectarian texts, nor does he draw the analogies in a sufficiently specific manner so as to substantiate a closer connection between John and Qumran. In the end, the superficial comparison provides not more than a confirmation for the view that John and the Qumranites lived according to a revealed "mystery" and were thus, in Ashton's terminology, "apocalyptic."

Brian Capper's "John, Qumran, and Virtuoso Religion" (93–116) is, in my view, the most problematic essay in the collection. It shows where uncontrolled speculation can lead to. Based on his earlier work on the communion of goods in Essenism and the Primitive Community, Capper wants to utilize the concepts of "religious order" versus "sect," classifying the Essenes not as a sect but as a religious order still in touch with the mainstream religion. This is based on Josephus's note that the Essenes sent dedicative gifts to the temple. In his whole argument, Capper fully draws on Josephus's description of the Essenes, uncritically linking this with different Qumran texts, including the Temple Scroll, which is most probably a pre-sectarian text. He not only takes Josephus's number of four thousand Essenes in Judea as a historically accurate number but wants to interpret it in view of the mere number of male celibate Essenes, to which several thousand families of the second order should be added. In the end, large parts of Herodian Judea are members of the religious order of the Essenes or connected to it. Based on a passage from the Temple Scroll (11QTemp 46.13–18), he conjectures that also the villages of Bethany and Bethphage were Essene villages, so that Jesus' friends there, Lazarus and his sisters, whom Jesus loved, had been Essenes, and the relationship between Jesus and the Beloved Disciple is the relationship of two brothers of the same religious order. … I stop my renarration of this kind of "science fiction"—the essay is far away from any kind of sound scholarship, both in the field of Qumran and in Johannine studies, and reminds one of certain types of Qumran "fantasy" literature.

3. Methodological Conclusions

The present book is only in some of its parts on the level of current scholarship, and it is remarkable that Qumran specialists such as Stuckenbruck and Schuller did a much better job than "mere" New Testament scholars like Anderson and Ashton. In working with the Qumran texts, there is a need for methodological sobriety, and the desire to find "parallels" or even support for some historical or exegetical viewpoints easily leads to a lack of caution or an overinterpretation of the fragmentary evidence. Doing sound history of religions work is one of the most difficult tasks in scholarship, and dealing with Qumran is not an easy field for Johannine scholars.

This does not mean that the Qumran texts are not valuable for exegesis. The opposite is the case, and I share the view of the editors of the present book that the treasure of the Qumran discoveries has not yet fully come to fruition in biblical exegesis. But it may lie at a different place than most exegetes have hitherto thought. Given the present state of the art in Qumran studies (as described by Eileen Schuller), we can now see that the Qumran corpus is not a mere "library of some Jewish sect" but represents a wide spectrum of the literary production of Second Temple Judaism of almost three centuries. Thus, the questions are no longer about the relationship between New Testament authors or groups with "the Essenes" or the Qumran "sect," nor should the primary interest be in discovering direct "influences" on the New Testament texts. In his thoughtful introduction to his essay in the present book, George Brooke confirms "that the discoveries in the Qumran library are indeed significant for the better understanding of many aspects of the New Testament texts. … However, the relationship between the two bodies of texts is not a simple or straightforward one" (69).

Simply collecting parallels (a symptom called "parallelomania") is futile and misleading. Instead, every parallel deserves cautious interpretation, considering its own original context, the possible ways of transmission, the nature of the suggested analogies, their possible reasons, and alternative explanations. Reading the New Testament texts in their contemporary Jewish context also calls for a broader perspective that includes not only the Scrolls but, as a matter of course, the Septuagint and all the "intertestamental" literature (partly transmitted in translations). We have to consider the texts from the Jewish Diaspora as well, Josephus and Philo, and also the early rabbinic texts, and we must not ignore the field of non-Jewish texts and genres from the Hellenistic-Roman world. Only by such a wide range of research is it possible to decide reasonably on the background of a certain New Testament motif and its underlying concepts.

In such a wide textual framework, Qumran texts are a very valuable source, not for establishing direct links between the Johannine community or the Evangelist and Essenism or the Qumran sectarians, but for putting Johannine ideas or phrases in their Jewish (and other) contexts and to elaborate their profile as precisely as possible. The older views as represented by Albright, Charlesworth, or Ashton (let alone the speculations uttered by Capper) cannot be upheld any longer. All suggestions of any direct historical influence of Qumran or Qumranites, converted Essenes, and the like on the Johannine language, community, or authors remain speculative, but the interpretation of the texts gains depth, if the Johannine exegetes are well-informed about the problems and contexts of the documents from the corpus and their wider Jewish world. In more recent exegetical studies, the pendulum of scholarship has already swung back from a one-sided Jewish contextualization toward a more appropriate (and sometimes again one-sided) consideration of other, non-Jewish, Hellenistic-Roman contexts. Only the integration of both perspectives, at best in interdisciplinary cooperation, will finally lead to a balanced view.

This does not mean that Qumran might not have revolutionized Johannine scholarship, but it would be unwise to merely celebrate the revolution or even stay drunk from the sweet wine of celebrations without proceeding to utilize the new insights for a sober interpretation.

ACTS

Acts: A Commentary, by Richard I. Pervo. Hermeneia. Minneapolis: Fortress, 2009. Pp. xxxvi + 812. Hardcover. $85.00. ISBN 9780800660451.

Don Garlington, Toronto, Ontario, Canada

Professor Richard Pervo's magisterial commentary on Acts is the successor of the previous contribution of Hans Conzelmann to the Hermeneia series. Organizationally, as per custom, the work engages issues of introduction, which is followed by a meticulous and extensively documented exegesis of the Greek text, interspersed with numerous excurses on specialized topics.

As for the date of composition, Pervo maintains that Acts was written circa 115 by "an anonymous author whose perspective was that of Ephesus or its general environs," with the consequence that "the actual author was not a companion of Paul" (5).

The assessment of the language and style of Acts is that its author could write in "middlebrow *Koine* Greek." His greatest facility was the ability to write "like the Bible," that is, to imitate the language of the LXX (7–8). The quality of the Greek improves on occasions such as when Paul addresses the audience in Athens (Acts 17) and defends himself before Agrippa (Acts 26). "These examples also show that, although he can deploy a few optatives and Attic idioms, Luke had difficulty when attempting to write good Greek periods. His literary ambition exceeded his ability" (8). Even so, Pervo terms the author "a competent writer" (11) with "considerable skills" (18). The sources of the composition are said to be the LXX, Mark, a collection of Paul's letters, and some of Josephus's writings. As for Paul, Luke is aware of the use of his letters in church life (15:23–29; 18:27), but he does not associate Paul with this form. "This fact reflects not simply the reluctance of ancient authors to list their sources but more specifically the controversial status of the epistles when Luke wrote. If one of his intentions was to provide a framework for understanding the epistles, he was very successful" (12). That Luke drew on Josephus is a postulation, because the former shares some of latter's understandings and interests. All in all, the author of Acts is the master of his sources, the identification of which has two principle values: the one is the secondary project of utilizing Acts to uncover early Christian history; the other is the negative value of revealing how much of the composition is the creation of the author and how freely he used the sources at his disposal (14).

The genre of the document, as Pervo acknowledges, is "one of the most hotly contested topics in the study of Acts" (14), with two issues driving the controversy. The first is formal: unlike Luke's Gospel, which can be compared with the other Gospels and a variety of biographical texts, Acts is without peers in the New

Testament. "The quest for form," maintains Pervo, "involves the identification of comparable texts. Genre involves expectations and standards" (14). The second is generated by the first: defense of the historical accuracy of Acts long propelled the desire to classify it as historiography. Pervo asserts that this "circular argument" has now been pierced. Vis-à-vis conservative scholars of the stripe of Colin Hemer and Ben Witherington, who claim a high level of accuracy for the composition, he maintains that New Testament scholarship generally has taken a step or two back from that position and has subjected the objectivity of ancient historians to sharp qualification. It is even possible to say that *because* Acts is representative of historiography, one should not expect it to be factual. In a nutshell, "The question of accuracy cannot be resolved by appeal to genre, nor does the identification of genre resolve the debate about accuracy" (15). Nevertheless, "Acts is a history. The author has produced a coherent story in conformity with a plan, and his subject includes historical persons, places, and events" (15). However, Pervo is quick to qualify that judgments about the historical accuracy of particular passages and statements depend on the results of historical criticism, which can often do no more than identify varying degrees of probability, which is a cumulative enterprise. In any event, Acts gains from a comparison with "biblical historiography," a phrase referring not to genre but to ways of narrating history originating in the LXX. Luke thus writes from a "Deuteronomic" viewpoint. It is in keeping with this biblical tradition that the technique of "omniscient narration and its companion anonymous authorship" is derived. For this reason, "Luke's style can be biblical, and his technique of presenting history through the lives of a succession of great leaders can be referred to biblical models" (15). Acts, accordingly, derives inspiration from such sources as the Old Testament Elijah and Elisha cycles and the books of Maccabees.

Given the above considerations, Acts is regarded as a "popular work" in line with other "ancient popular writers." Consequently, "[u]nrestrained by the conventions governing elite literature, popular writers were able to blend genres and create new ones." Pervo thus endorses C. K. Barrett's appraisal of Acts: "The form of the romance is popular history, and that is the kind of history that Acts is." Such a literary identification means that "Luke's achievement as a historian lies more in his success at creating history than in recording it. With his considerable skills this author fashioned what became and has remained the normative story of Christian origins." The book's "major impetus" was, therefore, not history but "the content of the canonical Gospels." "When he turned to writing Acts, Luke did not discard the hat of an evangelist"(18).

Pervo's accounting for "the unity/ies of Luke and Acts" calls to mind that studies of both documents face two challenges: to account for their similarities, including their interrelationships, and their differences. Pervo himself opts for a kind of unity in diversity: "Although the second volume continues the first, it tells a different story with different methods and some different themes" (19). Nevertheless, "The continuity of salvation history is a governing theme that integrates the two volumes" (20).

The general purpose of Acts is taken to be "legitimating narrative." "Narrative" is the function: making a case by telling a story or stories, rather than by means of a treatise or dialogue. "Legitimating" serves to express the object of the work, whether construed more narrowly as the legitimacy of Pauline Christianity or more generally as the claim of the Jesus-movement to possess the "Israelite heritage" (21). In contrast to the ostensible addressees of ancient formal apologies (outsiders), Luke/Acts speaks to insiders or believers in Jesus rather than polytheists or Jews who did not accept Christian claims. "The purpose is to explain and defend a body that has existed for some time and whose identity has been challenged rather than, for example, to nurture a young and fragile body grappling to discover its identity" (22).

As for the theology of Acts, Pervo rejects the older assumption that its teaching is to be discovered in the numerous speeches of the book. Rather, "Acts is a narrative, and its theology must be recovered from the narrative rather than from the embedded speeches" (22). Nevertheless, it is conceded that many of the themes and concepts of the speeches do remain important: "One could not construct a valid summary of Lucan theology by attending to the narrative alone, for the speeches explain why and how the story happened. The speeches are the components of the narrative" (22). In terms of its central content, Luke's theology "appropriated more than a little from Paul," because Torah-observance is viewed an inadequate means of salvation, making the law "soteriologically irrelevant" (23). Luke speaks of justification by faith (13:38–39) as the result of grace (15:11), but because the choice between two competing soteriological systems—one based on the Torah and the other on faith—was no longer relevant, the Pauline opposition of faith to works appeared to Luke to be antinomian; he prefers to view δικαιοσύνη as "just behavior" rather than "justification" (23). Related to this stance is Luke's position à propos the crucifixion, "which is not an ultimate and paradoxical apocalyptic act of God but a tragic and revelatory act reversed by the resurrection." The Lukan "theology of the cross," if it is that, is expressed through continuities: the continued rejection of God's prophets by God's people and Jesus' continuation of his ministry to seek and save the lost. "For Luke, Paul's breathtaking interpretation of the crucifixion was unduly conducive to dualism and actively promoted the discontinuity Luke wished to rebut" (23). Pervo acknowledges, however, that this subject has generated considerable controversy. There are, in point of fact, arguments for a Lukan "theology of the cross" entailing a harmonization with Pauline thought and a presumed consensus of nascent Christianity (23 n. 144). Accompanying crucifixion is resurrection. In a manner similar to but not identical with that of Paul, Luke understood the resurrection as the defeat of Satan. Naturally, no consideration of the theology of Acts would be complete without the role of the Spirit: "The importance of the Spirit in Acts is a pervasive and palpable testimony to the presence of the Pauline legacy. The gift of the Spirit serves both as a means for portraying continuity, signaled by the quotation from Joel in Peter's Pentecost sermon, and as an (unwelcome) indicator of discontinuity" (23). For Pervo, Luke's appeal to the Spirit as the principal mode of legitimating Christianity is essentially charismatic. Acts does not seek to justify the acceptance of Gentiles by appeal to Scripture or other formal norms: it is the Spirit who validated their acceptance. Other aspects of the theology of Acts include the providence of God, early Christian leaders who assume the role of a θεῖος ἀνήρ, ecclesiology, and eschatology. The essence of the last-mentioned is the resurrection: the parousia and judgment are but components of resurrection rather than events subsequent to it.

In terms of an overall assessment of the commentary, one may wince at the suggestion that Luke had difficulty when attempting to write good Greek periods and that his literary ambition exceeded his ability (8). One need only take on board the quality of language that heads both the Gospel (1:1-4) and Acts (1:1-3), not to mention, as Pervo acknowledges, Acts 17. In all likelihood, Luke adopted a LXX type of writing style for the sake of a wider reading audience. On the theological level, it is entirely questionable that the "Pauline opposition of faith to works" appeared to be "antinomian" to Luke, who prefers to view δικαιοσύνη as "just behavior" rather than "justification" (23). After all, it is Paul who writes that "the doers of the law will be justified" (Rom 2:13; cf. 4:20–22). Additionally, scholars of a conservative stripe will question Pervo's postulations pertaining to the dating of Acts to circa 115 (5), its genre as a form of popular historical novel or popular apologetic history (14–16), and his questioning of the traditional outlook that Luke/Acts is a purposeful two-volume work, the former paving the way for the latter, à la: "Luke does not require Acts"; "The unities of Luke and Acts are questions to be pursued rather than presuppositions to be exploited" (19); "This commentary does not presume that the author planned and executed his books in advance" (20). An even larger problem for more traditional readers will be Pervo's skepticism and, at times, out-and-out rejection of the historical veracity of Acts (see, e.g., 19 [a number of the speeches are composed by the author], 58, 59 [the narrative of Pentecost "collapses at the slightest breeze … a confusion worthy of Babel"], 76 ["The narrator takes no pains to establish theological realism: Peter propounds early Christian doctrine"], 115, 239, 302 [12:18-23 raises "moral questions for modern readers"], 331 ["a Lucan invention"], 334 ["the unhistorical character of the mission speeches in Acts"], 519 ["he (Luke) is less interested in genuine synthesis than in making other views conform to his own"], 538 ["If Agabus were a historical person who prophesied in this situation, his character has been obliterated by the author's pen], 685, 688 ["the narrator has painted himself into a corner"], 689 ["'They all live happily ever after' is a fine ending, but it is not the only possibility, and one that is out of favor at present, in both its fictional and nonfictional manifestations"]). The premise of these proposals is, again, that "Luke's achievement as a historian lies more in his success at creating history than in recording it" (18).

Notwithstanding these several reservations, Pervo's tendencies do not preclude the reader from deriving numerous insights from the commentary, which excels as a paradigm of painstaking linguistic analysis combined with historical awareness and expert handling of syntactical and text-critical issues. In short, the work deserves a prominent place on a New Testament scholar's bookshelf and will remain a standard for many years to come.

Peter and Cornelius: A Story of Conversion and Mission, by Nguyen vanThanh. American Society of Missiology Monograph Series. Eugene, Ore.: Pickwick, 2012. Pp. xvi + 193. Paper. $23.00. ISBN 9781610978484.

Sean A. Adams, University of Edinburgh, Edinburgh, United Kingdom

This work represents a detailed reading of the Peter–Cornelius episode with a formal narratological framework. In chapter 1 Nguyen provides the rationale for viewing Acts 10:1–11:18 as a unit by applying "dramatic criteria" and "literary (or stylistic) criteria" (1). In doing so Nguyen concludes that the story of Peter and Cornelius is an "independent narrative episode." One might question the use of the term "independent," as it is clear that the author of Acts bases his account on the earlier narrative, particularly in the reader's knowledge of Peter. "Discrete" may have been a better choice. Overall, this chapter justifies the boundaries of the Peter–Cornelius narrative, although this division is not so controversial a claim as to warrant an extended discussion.

Chapter 2 evaluates the narrative discourse of the Peter–Cornelius episode. Nguyen begins with an overview of narrative transaction, discussing the nature of real and implied author, narrator, narratee, and implied and real reader. This section is fairly elementary and could easily be skipped by someone with a basic understanding of narrative criticism. The remainder of the chapter analyzes the discourse structure of the six episodic scenes (as divided by Nguyen). In these sections Nguyen provides a close narrative reading, identifying changes in location, time, and narrator and outlining the underlying structure of the episode.

The setting of the Peter–Cornelius episode is the focus of chapter 3. In particular, Nguyen focuses on three aspects of setting—spatial, temporal, social-cultural—arguing that a close investigation of the narrative settings will "heighten the interest and tension of the plot of the story" (54). In each of these categories Nguyen provides an exhaustive list of words that deal with geographical, geopolitical, topographical, or architectural space, movement, time references, and social-cultural and religious boundary markers. Overall, Nguyen comes to the conclusion that the different settings developed in the Peter–Cornelius episode are "highly charged with symbolism and theological significance" (81). Though this conclusion is based on his description of the narrative, the metaphorical component (i.e., multiple interpretive layers) is also emic to the text (e.g., the use of unclean food as a symbol for Gentiles), so Nguyen's conclusion identifies a textual component. This identification is not a new argument for Acts scholars, though Nguyen provides a more nuanced theoretical rationale for its inclusion.

The next chapter maps out the plot of Acts 10:1–11:18, fitting it into the quinary plot structure of exposition, complication, climax, resolution, and final solution. Here Nguyen identifies the existence of these five stages in Acts 10:1–48, noting that the final four are repeated in Acts 11:1–18. The final part of this chapter looks at the role of the Peter–Cornelius episode in the council of Acts 15. For Nguyen, Acts 10:1–11:18 "played a significant role in the final decision of accepting Gentiles into the church without first requiring them to become Jews" (104). In the Jerusalem council it "provided an irrefutable test case of God's approval and acceptance" (104). Nguyen is no doubt right when he claims that Acts 15 helps in understanding the full role of the Peter–Cornelius episode. It would have been helpful, however, if he identified which components of his claim were original contributions and how his study supports or challenges previous scholarship.

Chapter 5 evaluates the characters in this episode and is primarily descriptive. Here Nguyen identifies the manner by which the main and secondary characters are portrayed by the author and how they may have been perceived by early readers. This chapter, although modeling an important aspect of a narrative approach, did not provide substantial fresh insight into the text. Two aspects were particularly lacking. First, there was insufficient discussion of the interpretive payoff of such an investigation—why is this important, and how does it change our reading? Second, there was very little connection between the characterization of Peter in this passage to how Peter has been presented previously in Luke and Acts. Both of these are important considerations for a discussion of character in a selected passage in Acts.

The penultimate chapter looks at the theological significance and implications of the passage. Although the first half of the chapter goes through the traditional trope of identifying the number of occurrences of particular words and titles for God, Jesus, and the Holy Spirit, the second half of the chapter provides the main contribution. Here Nguyen shows how particular characters in the Peter–Cornelius episode model for the reader appropriate responses to the conversion of the Gentiles. These characters exemplify the proper way the gospel is to be preached by Christians and to be received by people wishing to convert to Christianity.

The concluding chapter adequately summarizes the contents of the work and so provides a synopsis of the study as a whole. Overall, this work is generally easy to read and is accompanied, particularly in chapter 2, with helpful figures with which Nguyen visually illustrates his point. Moreover there is a glossary (appendix B) in which technical narrative-critical terms are defined. Both of these make the book accessible to readers with little to no knowledge of narrative criticism.

The book's main contribution to New Testament scholarship is its modeling of a close, narrative reading of a biblical text. As such, it would be a useful text for students (especially undergraduates) to read to get a sense of the amount of data that a close reading of the text can provide. The stated aim in the introduction—"to contribute to the understanding and interpretation of the Peter and Cornelius episode as a narrative text" (xiv)—is modest, and in that regard Nguyen has succeeded in showing the episode's narrative quality in great detail. As to its contribution to Acts scholarship in particular, the work had greater potential than it delivered. Though Nguyen does provide a detailed reading of the text, his ultimate conclusion—that the author of Acts is a competent writer who employed varied modes of characterization and narrative repetition to encourage the reader to adopt the perspective of the ideal reader—is not substantially original. There were, however, a few times in which Nguyen highlighted an alternative reading from Codex Bezae that provided a fresh understanding to some narrative elements.

One aspect that would have benefited this work would have been greater engagement with other scholars and their positions, especially those who engage with narrative components of the text (e.g., L. Alexander, F. S. Spencer, M. Slee-man). Throughout the monograph Nguyen provides his own reading of the text; however, he rarely interacts with other scholars in the main text. There are references to other works/scholars in the footnotes, but these are primarily used for identifying similar positions or theoretical underpinnings. A good example of where this interaction could have been employed is Nguyen's division of the narrative into six scenes (52). Although he acknowledges that a number of scholars hold divergent positions, Nguyen does not explain the shortcomings of their theories and why his is to be preferred. Such critical engagement with scholarship would have allowed this book to make a much greater contribution to biblical scholarship.

Another addition that would have improved the work would have been greater engagement with the rest of Luke-Acts. Although Nguyen made occasional reference to other Luke and Acts passages, there is very little expansion to texts outwith Acts 10:1–11:18. It is likely that Nguyen was using this episode as a test case to show Luke's writing ability (and it is a good text for that); however, there were times when the reader was left wondering if other passages in Acts could have supported his conclusions or suggested other readings. For example, when discussing Peter's characterization (116–23), Nguyen does not outline the reader's current understanding/perception of Peter up to that point in the Acts narrative; rather, he focuses almost exclusively on the passage in focus. Since Nguyen is an author who is sensitive to narrative development and the role of managing reader expectations (as was exhibited in his discussion), it is surprising that he did not acknowledge this, as it would have helped him to highlight the unique contributions of the episode.

Overall, Nguyen provides a detailed reading of Acts 10:1–11:18 employing technical narrative-critical methodology that will be of use to anyone studying this passage. Moreover, his work provides a practical example for students looking to understand how a narrative approach can be applied to a biblical text. However, the usefulness of this monograph will be limited by the deficiencies outlined in the foregoing paragraphs.

Baptism in the Spirit: Luke-Acts and the Dunn Debate, by William P. Atkinson. Eugene, Oreg.: Pickwick, 2011. Pp. x + 154. Paper. $19.00. ISBN 9781608999712.

Lars Kierspel, Shiloh University, Kalona, Iowa

Intended "for my fellow Pentecostals" (1), William Atkinson, "a Pentecostal minister in Essex, England and Associate Research Fellow at the London School of

Theology" (backcover), wrote a short defense of "the Pentecostal doctrine of *subsequence*," which he defines as "a charismatic empowering for Christian service distinct from and thus, potentially, chronologically subsequent to initial regeneration faith in Christ" (3). Yet, this explicit apologetic motif does not translate into a predictable selection of easy prooftexts. Atkinson chooses, instead, to defend this doctrine by critically tracing the debate surrounding James Dunn's *Baptism in the Holy Spirit* (1970), the major challenge of Pentecostal pneumatology in the last forty years.

After an introduction, chapter 1 ("The Dunn Debate and Its Inception," 1–25) lays out the six arguments of Dunn's work that support his conclusion: (1) the anointing of Jesus in the Jordan (Luke 3) is not a second experience of the Spirit (after the first one in Luke 1:35 and 2:40, 52) as equipment for ministry but "the beginning of the messianic era" (9); (2) the experience of Pentecost in Acts 2 is not a paradigm for Christians because the recipients of the Spirit in Jerusalem were pre-Christians who stood at a "watershed in salvation-history, the beginning of the new age and new covenant" (10); (3) similarly, the Samaritans' response to Philip's preaching (Acts 8) was defective, and they "were not Christians until they received the Spirit" (12); (4) likewise, Paul did not convert on day one (Acts 9:3–6) and receive the Spirit on day three (9:9–18); rather, his conversion "must be regarded as a process lasting for the three days" (13); (5) Cornelius was not "regenerate prior to Peter's sermon"; only upon hearing and trusting Peter's words about faith and forgiveness did he actually convert and receive the Spirit (Acts 10:43–44) (13); and (6) the Ephesians were baptized "into John's baptism" (Acts 19:3) and therefore non-Christians; hence their water baptism by Paul and reception of the Holy Spirit cannot be considered biblical support for the doctrine of subsequence. Atkinson briefly traces Dunn's later contributions to the discussion (articles from 1993, 1998, 2010) and introduces the main Pentecostal debaters (Roger Stronstad, Howard Ervin, David Petts, James Shelton, Robert Menzies), one of whom converted to Dunn's position (Max Turner).

Chapter 2 continues with "Pentecostal Criticisms of Dunn" (26–65). In general, Roger Stronstad (*The Charismatic Theology of St. Luke*, 1984) finds that Dunn read Luke's theology through the lens of Paul. In particular, Stronstad interprets Jesus' baptism in Luke 3 with the help of Luke 4:16–30 and the fulfillment of Isa 61:1–2, saying that "the gift of the Spirit to Jesus ... is vocational" (29; Stronstad, 45). Such an understanding, then, also applies to the parallel event at Pentecost.

In his dissertation "Luke and the Spirit" (Cambridge, 1980), Max Turner offered a "lengthy rebuttal" regarding Dunn's view of the Samaritan episode in Acts 8. Neither Philip's ministry nor the Samaritan faith were deficient in any way. The later reception of the Spirit through Peter's mediation is, therefore, clear evidence of an experience subsequent to that of conversion-initiation. Turner does refer to Acts 8:16 as an "awkward explanation," indicating that Luke "cannot have believed the Samaritan episode was typical at all" (35; Turner, 162).

Howard Ervin, *Conversion-Initiation* (1984), also highlights that the Samaritans and Paul received the Spirit as believers, therefore subsequent to conversion.

Furthermore, "Luke's genitive absolute ... in Acts 19:6 indicates the sequential rather than the parenthetic, nature of Paul's laying on of hands, contrary to Dunn's claim" (41). Yet Atkinson himself counters Ervin at this point: "to argue that Luke presented the placing of Paul's hands on them as something *other* than a part of their whole initiation procedure is implausible" (41). One wonders if that does not also apply to the Samaritans' reception of the Holy Spirit.

In his ThM thesis (Nottingham, 1987), David Petts understood, with Dunn, that conversion is not complete without the reception of the Spirit, yet to receive the Spirit is neither the same as receiving forgiveness (Acts 10:43–44) nor is it confined to a conversion experience. With reference to Acts 1:8, Petts claims, in Atkinsons words, that "Dunn has seriously underestimated the connection in Luke's mind between receiving the Spirit and missionary enabling" (43). Furthermore, whatever we are to make of the aorist participle in Acts 19:6, the experience of the Ephesians suggests "that it is at least *possible* to believe without receiving the Spirit" (44; Petts, 74).

Robert Menzies's main thesis is evident from the title of his published dissertation: *The Development of Early Christian Pneumatology* (Sheffield, 1991): Luke's view of the Spirit cannot simply be identified with that of Mark, Q, or Paul (47). Atkinson is critical of Menzies's use of Jewish background material for interpreting Luke 3 (49–52), but he praises as a "highly important contribution to the discussion" (53) Menzies's discussion regarding Luke's citation of Joel 2:28–32a in Acts 2:17–21. Menzies argues here as follows: the additions in Acts 2:18 to LXX Joel 3:1 of μου (in τοὺς δούλους μου) and καὶ προφητεύσουσιν in Acts 2:18 show that at Pentecost the Spirit was given to those who were already servants, that is, Christians, and "first and foremost for prophetic enablement" (53).

Lastly, Atkinson turns to two arguments in Max Turner's *Power from on High* (Sheffield, 1996) that indicate Turner's move toward Dunn's position in contrast to his 1980 dissertation. First, Turner reads the phrase βαπτίσει ἐν πνεύματι ἁγίῳ καὶ πυρι in Luke 3:16 as a hendiadys in which "fire" refers to a form of cleansing, thus indicating that "the Spirit of prophecy is simultaneously the soteriological Spirit." Atkinson counters, among other reasons, with Old Testament prophecies of the Spirit's future arrival that associate "the coming Spirit with rain on thirsty ground, not to cleanse the ground but to bring fresh life and growth (Isa 32:15; 44:3; Ezek 39:29; Joel 2:28 [cf. 2:23])" (59). Second, Turner identifies Acts 2:38 as programmatic for all of Acts, implying that the norm for conversions is that the Spirit will be received "as part and parcel" of that experience (60; Turner, 398). Here Atkinson points to Acts 1:8, which shows the need of the Spirit for the mission of the church, as confirmed by Acts 4:31.

In chapter 3, "Pentecostal Alternatives to Dunn" (66–91), Atkinson asks three questions in pursuit of a fuller Lukan pneumatology. First (66), "[I]f it was possibly subsequent to conversion, was reception of the Spirit for Luke attached to Christian initiation at all?" Following Turner, Atkinson derives the norm from Acts 2:38–39 and Paul's question in Acts 19:3 ("Into what, then, were you baptized?"), according to which the reception of the Spirit falls together with the "baptismal initiation into Christian discipleship" (68). The incidents in Acts 8 and 19 of believers without the Spirit are an "anomaly that called for immediate corrective response from the church" (68).

Second, if, contrary to Dunn, the reception of the Spirit is unrelated to "new covenant life and forgiveness of sin" (69), what is the purpose of it? Here Atkinson rejects Menzies's more narrow description of the Spirit's role as the "Spirit of prophecy" (73) and defends Stronstad's broader view according to which the Spirit equips with power (Acts 2:41; 4:31), prophecy (understood as "'invasive' speeches of worship, witness, and judgment," 72; Acts 2:4; 4:8–12; 13:11), wisdom, and faith (Acts 6:3, 5; 11:24).

Finally, Atkinson argues against Turner's "soteriological Spirit" by showing that "Luke recognized and wrote of direct activities in people's lives, prior to their reception of the Spirit, that he would understand as the Spirit's work" (81; e.g., Luke 1:35, 80; 9:1; Acts 9:12; 10:30).

In chapter 4, "Luke-Acts in Its Canonical Context" (92–122), Atkinson examines the discussion on baptism in the Spirit with regard to two test cases from Paul and John. (1) He defends Dunn's soteriological reading of 1 Cor 12:13 against Pentecostal alternatives by Ervin and Petts. In fact, most Pentecostal New Testament scholars support Dunn's view of Pauline pneumatology (e.g., Rom 8:9). On the other side, Atkinson exposes the "scant evidence" (105) upon which Dunn calls out that "crude" Pentecostal view that seemingly dismisses Paul by saying that "conversion is a matter of receiving Christ and Spirit-baptism of receiving the Spirit" (104). Atkinson resolves the resulting tension between Rom 8:9 and Paul's question in Acts 19:2 by saying that the latter text reflects "the linguistic preferences of Luke, not of the epistolary Paul." (2) In John 20:22 Jesus breathed on the disciples and said "Receive the Holy Spirit." While for Dunn this is indeed a separate insufflation of the Holy Spirit prior to Pentecost, yet unique to the first apostles, Atkinson counters that "there is nothing essentially unrepeatable in salvation history or church history about the disciples' lives between their recorded Spirit reception (John 20:22) and their unrecorded Paraclete reception" (114). In Pentecostal pneumatology, John 20:22 then becomes, in fact, *the* piece of evidence for biblical "Spirit reception language of two distinct experiences" (118). While Paul focuses on the first experience of the Spirit in conversion, Luke highlights the second experience of enablement and equipment.

In the final chapter, "Baptism in the Spirit Today" (123–38), Atkinson finishes with a summary of the previous chapters, followed by "Practical Implications" for Pentecostals (127–38). Tying the latter part to specific texts from the book of Acts, Atkinson challenges readers to apply the promise of power to Christians today (Acts 1:8), to include the baptism of the Spirit in Pentecostal evangelism (2:38), to seek the fullness of the Spirit in prayer and for the purpose of missions (4:23–31), to seek *"ongoing evidence"* (133, emphasis original) of the Spirit beyond any initial experience (6:3–7:60), to look and pray for charismatic evidence of the Spirit beyond speaking in tongues (8:14–17), to cross boundaries of people groups and orderliness where the Spirit leads (10:44–47), and to pray for and teach Christians that are not filled with the Spirit (19:1–6).

Atkinson's review of the Dunn debate is studious and challenging for both sides. Although writing for Pentecostals and ultimately critical of Dunn's views, Atkinson is neither too shy to reject weak Pentecostal arguments nor too biased to affirm evidence that favors one of Dunn's exegetical conclusions. Dunn's qualification of the Samaritans' faith as defective in Acts 8 is flawed, and Atkinson rightly so exposes that weakness. Still, important questions remain, some of which might be the following:

(1) Most critical for the Pentecostal case is the insistence that the gift of the Holy Spirit is unrelated to the gift of salvation. Atkinson tries to walk on a tight rope when he associates baptism in the Spirit with baptismal initiation, on the hand, but then disassociates it from any soteriological significance, on the other, and defines the experience exclusively as "charismatic and missionary" (125). However, Luke never connects the baptisms in the Spirit in Acts 8, 10, and 19 with any ministerial purpose. While the apostles at Pentecost do indeed "speak of the mighty deeds of God" (2:11, 14–36, 38–40), the Samaritans, Cornelius, and the Ephesians are never shown to engage in mission work or any other kind of ministry. Why, then, does Luke go to such length to mention the details of receiving the Spirit in these incidents?

Furthermore, a rigid division between a salvific and missional significance cannot make sense of Peter's discovery when he saw that the Roman centurion received the gift of the Holy Spirit. The parallel to Pentecost compels Peter to conclude that God "made no distinction between us [Jews] and them [Gentiles], cleansing their hearts by faith" (15:9), an insight that in turn makes Gentiles now eligible for water baptism (10:47). Further, upon hearing Peter's report of Cornelius receiving the Spirit, the circumcised in Jerusalem "quieted down and glorified God, saying, 'Well, then, God has granted to the Gentiles also the repentance *that leads* to life'" (11:18). As baptism is not identical with faith, these texts also do not necessarily equate baptism in the Spirit with repentance. But that does not make it unnecessary for salvation. Rather, the reception of the Spirit by the Gentiles reveals a core content of salvation as Luke defines it: Gentile participation in the promises for Israel.

Atkinson points to the working of the Spirit in the lives of people prior to their conversion as evidence that the "reception of the Spirit" is no "soteriological necessity" (89). But as the filling of the Spirit is not the same as the initial baptism of the Spirit, so the Spirit's preparatory work in an unbeliever does not replace the actual reception of the Spirit. Atkinson works too much with a concordance and too little with the context.

(2) If Luke views baptism in the Spirit as part of an *initiatory* experience, and if the chronologically subsequent examples of it in Acts 8 and 19 are an "anomaly" in Lukan pneumatology (68), then the question arises if a "doctrine of subsequence" (3, 19) should be based on abnormal exceptions to the rule. Does that not turn the Lukan proportion of things upside down? Theologizing

from narrative particulars is difficult exactly for that reason: the reported incident might be unusual and deviates from the norm. Atkinson has done nothing
to address this hermeneutical question. Yet if exceptions may establish the rule
(instead of proving it), then why should Cornelius's example (Acts 10:47–48) not
teach us a "doctrine of precedence": baptism in the Spirit should precede the baptism of water? If such reasoning may be disqualified as a hasty generalization,
Atkinson still needs to justify why that would not also be true for the "doctrine
of subsequence."

(3) Atkinson rightly observes that the anomalous cases in Samaria and Ephesus "called for an immediate corrective response from the church (Acts 8:15;
19:2–6)" (68). That is still imprecise, because the church at large did not have the
authority to impart the Spirit. Obviously, Philip's ministry among the Samaritans
only went so far and required the ministry of Peter for the baptism in the Spirit.
Likewise, it was not Timothy or Luke who aided the Ephesians in their baptism
in the Spirit but Paul, the chosen agent of God's mission to the Gentiles. In Luke's
narrative and purpose, then, no one other than one of the twelve apostles and
Paul have the authority to baptize anyone in the Spirit. Now, if these events in the
book of Acts have no salvation-historical limits, the question emerges: Who today
would have apostolic authority to confer this special enablement of the Spirit?
Unless Atkinson adopts a system of apostolic succession that identifies leaders
of authority equal to Peter and Paul, he needs to explain why such power moved
from divinely appointed individuals in the early church to "the church" today.

Atkinson's book eases access to a discussion that spans several decades and
that has filled already many volumes with arguments and rejoinders. His concise
and detailed descriptions quickly plow a path to important points of disagreement.
But an apologetic discussion written for insiders is prone to overlook significant
weaknesses of the preferred position, and this one is no exception.

PAUL AND THE PAULINE EPISTLES

*Christ among the Messiahs: Christ Language in Paul and Messiah Language in
Ancient Judaism,* by Matthew V. Novenson. Oxford: Oxford University Press,
2012. Pp. xiv + 239. Hardcover. $74.00. ISBN 9780199844579.

Nijay K. Gupta, Eastern University, St. Davids, Pennsylvania

It has become a nearly settled matter among Pauline interpreters in the present
state of scholarship that the apostle Paul treats the word "Christ" as a name and
not a title. If such a presumption is correct, Paul intends no particular messianic
meaning or content when he uses the word "Christ."

Matthew Novenson, Lecturer in New Testament and Christian Origins at the
University of Edinburgh, challenges this scholarly consensus in a published version of his doctoral dissertation (Princeton Theological Seminary). With a close
study of the historical and literary context of Paul's use of "Christ language" (with

attention to relevant matters in semiotics and onomastics), Novenson argues that Paul's language about Jesus is not as anomalous as it appears to some scholars. Indeed, when all the historical and literary pieces are assembled properly, Paul's Christ language fits quite comfortably as a sensible, albeit creative, instance of "messiah language" in early Judaism.

Three points are remarkable with this purpose and scholarly conversation in view. First, Novenson makes his case(s) against the scholarly consensus convincingly. Second, he writes clearly while navigating convoluted and complex historical and methodological territory. Finally, he executes his full-scale assault against the consensus view in under two hundred pages. Whether or not one finally agrees with the full assemblage of Novenson's arguments, it is quite easy to commend this monograph as a well-reasoned study that models careful scholarship for doctoral students.

Novenson's messianic study includes five chapters sandwiched between the introduction and conclusion. The first content chapter is a history of the study of Paul's Christology. One might imagine that it would be difficult to choose the most important studies. Novenson limits his discussion to the contributions and perspectives of scholars such as F. C. Baur, William Wrede, Adolf Deissmann, Wilhelm Bousset, Albert Schweitzer, W. D. Davies, Nils Dahl, Werner Kramer, E. P. Sanders, Lloyd Gaston, Martin Hengel, N. T. Wright, Andrew Chester, Magnus Zetterholm, and Dieter Zeller. In a helpfully reflective tour through the progress and movement of Pauline Christology, Novenson urges that, while (post–E. P. Sanders) Pauline scholars are currently convinced that Paul is best read within the diversity of early Jewish thought, "on the question of the meaning of *christos* they nevertheless perpetuate the old *religionsgeschichtliche* thesis that Paul is revising, transcending, or otherwise moving beyond the messianic faith of the earliest Jesus movement" (32).

In the second main chapter of the book Novenson engages in the convoluted problem regarding how many scholars presume or argue that, so diverse was the perspective on the messiah in the first century, that the word *Christos* is indeterminate and nearly meaningless. While scholars of a few generations ago once referred to a kind of "messianic idea" within common Judaism, most scholars today are extremely skeptical of this concept. Without wanting to turn the clock back to a "messianic idea" mentality, Novenson argues, quite reasonably, that just because there was no "messianic idea," it can hardly be the case that "messiah language" was devoid of meaning altogether.

Novenson appeals to "messiah language" in early Judaism as a "socio-linguistic phenomenon" whereby "competent members of a linguistic community" could engage in discussions of the messiah with some sense of shared meaning (see 47). Novenson argues that the evidence within early Jewish "messiah texts" establishes the Old Testament/ Hebrew Bible/LXX as the anchor to these conversations that provided a shared set of resources for mutual understanding. While each early Jewish writer engages in "messiah language" from his own communal vantage point, Novenson notes that the same Old Testament texts continue to reappear in such discussions: Gen 49:10; Num 24:17; 2 Sam 7:12–13; Isa 11:1–12; Amos 9:11;

Dan 7:13–14. It is hard to believe, then, that, despite the diversity of perspectives, any writer in this period can be accused of engaging meaninglessly in "messiah language," especially when writers such as Paul also appeal to the same texts that stimulated other Jews.

Perhaps the most important and insightful chapter of the book is the third one: "Names, Titles, and Other Possibilities." While, as noted above, Novenson is intent on disabusing scholars of the assumption that Paul treated *Christos* as a name and not a title, he does not actually conclude that it is a title either. First, regarding the possibility of "Jesus Christ" being a double name, Novenson points out that this would be an exception to Paul's normal practice of using a single name for a person (see 80–81). However, neither does he use titles with names except in the cases of Aretas, Phoebe, and Erastus.

Novenson finds the most reasonable onomastic category for Paul's use of *Christos* to be that of an "honorific": a second term used in conjunction with a personal name in recognition of a public figure. He notes well-known examples such as "Alexander *the Great*" and "Antiochus *Epiphanes*." How is an honorific different from a title? Novenson illustrates this using the example of Bar Kokhba. This is not a name ("Shimon bar Kosiba"). Neither is it a true "title," as his own preferred title was "prince over Israel." Thus, it is best conceived of as an honorific: "It is assumed, not given at birth; its laudatory force is immediately evident, but it is not predicated of its bearer; and it can stand in for the personal name of its bearer" (92). As is true for Bar Kokhba, honorifics were attributed to leaders especially in view of "military exploits or accession to power" (93). While Novenson's categorization of "honorific" sometimes comes across a bit slippery or intangible, this solution to the onomastic *Christos* problem for Paul would help to make sense of both the frequency of its use (as if it were a name), yet allow it to retain some true messianic meaning.

In the fourth chapter Novenson turns to the Pauline letters for close study. His concern here is with "Christ Phrases in Paul." He situates his discussion around Nils Dahl's fourfold argument that Paul's *Christos* language is nontitular because (1) *Christos* always refers to Jesus and never used as a general term, (2) *Christos* is never used as a predicate (as in "Jesus is the Christ"), (3) genitive terms of significance are never added to *Christos* (such as "the Christ of God"), and (4) the form "Jesus 'the' Christ" (with the definite article appearing before *Christos*) is not found in the earliest undisputed letters.

Before addressing these four matters, Novenson points out that the regular alternation of "Jesus Christ" and "Christ Jesus" should not be taken as a strike against *Christos* being a title, nor considered evidence that it is treated as a proper name. From his own study, Novenson notes that "Real double personal names have a fixed word order" (101). As for Dahl's first concern, Novenson points back to his discussion in the previous two chapters that, just because a term approximates a "name," it does not follow that it has lost its titular or honorific meaning. Second, Novenson identifies places where Paul *does* predicate messiahship (e.g., Gal 3:16; 1 Cor 10:4). However, Dahl seems to desire something more direct.

Novenson admits that Paul writes no such thing, but it can hardly be assumed he never preached such a thing. Rather, his *letters* do not mention this. Third, Novenson observes that even the genitive phrase "Christ of God" *does* appear in Paul (1 Cor 3:23), but perhaps not with the meaning Dahl intends. Fourth, Novenson provides a helpful discussion of the proper use of the article, such that even had Paul used the formula Dahl would have wanted, it is unclear how such wording would offer a decisive conclusion.

In the final main chapter of the monograph, "Christ Passages in Paul," Novenson explores nine texts that he believes leads to the conclusion that Paul participates in discourses involving "messiah language" and that "fit" how other contemporary Jews talked about the messiah: Gal 3:16; 1 Cor 15:20–28; 2 Cor 1:21–22; Rom 9:1–5; Rom 15:3, 9; 15:7–12; 1 Cor 1:23; 2 Cor 5:16–17; Rom 1:3–4. I believe his case is best proven by his appeals to 2 Cor 1:21–22 and Rom 1:3–4. I did not find particularly profitable his discussion of Rom 15:3, 9 (connecting Jesus Christ to the Davidic persona of the Pauline quotation from Ps 68). In any case, given the overwhelming number of times Paul engages with the same "messianic texts" that we find other Jews citing (especially passages associated with David), it becomes increasingly clear that, while Paul was making radical claims about Jesus, he *does* seem to be entering into the same conversational stream that Novenson calls "messiah language in ancient Judaism."

The merits of this monograph are obviously many. Novenson has mounted a full-scale attack against a near-consensus view that Paul's use of *Christos* is not loaded with messianic meaning. He amasses linguistic and semiotic swords, historical bows and arrows, and the sturdy shield of logic and common sense. All doctoral students write their dissertations (with fear and trembling) hoping to make a lasting impact on their discipline; Novenson can breathe a sigh of satisfaction and relief, I believe, and rest assured that his case will have a very good hearing due to its cogency.

As with any major argument pressed within such a short space of writing, weaknesses are sure to arise. I will note a few. First of all, regarding his sociolinguistic alternative to the older "messianic idea" (ch. 2), I was disappointed that Novenson did not attempt, seemingly at all, to construct even the broadest idea of how common Judaism of the first century thought about the messiah. Even if the messianic texts of early Judaism demonstrate wide diversity, can we not establish even the broadest level of agreement? Or perhaps two or three common profiles? The impression that Novenson gives is that first-century Jews did talk together about the messiah ("messiah language"), but we cannot expect any of them to hold any ideas in common. I find this hard to believe, but Novenson is certainly not alone in this assumption.

One small lacuna that I noticed was in regard to the discussion of the use of the article in Paul's Christ language. Novenson does a fine enough job demonstrating that Dahl's assumptions about the use of the article are inaccurate, but I was surprised that Novenson did not make appeal to the insightful work of Stephen Levinsohn in his *Discourse Features of New Testament Greek*.

Finally, I was surprised that Novenson's last chapter did not include a discussion of 1 Cor 15:3–8 that seems to bear that kind of messianic creedal formalism that is reminiscent of texts such as Luke 24:46–47 (with its traditional ordering and appeal to Jewish Scripture in a general sense).

Now, at the end of it all, Novenson has made a compelling case even with these very minor lacunae and shortcomings. Thus, I believe whenever Dahl is appealed to in the presumption that Paul did not mean "messiah" when he referred to "Christ," I do not doubt that Novenson's name will be invoked as a responsible voice of critique that encourages interpreters of Paul to revisit how the apostle actually wrote and thought about Jesus Christ.

Temple Purity in 1–2 Corinthians, by Yulin Liu. Wissenschaftliche Untersuchungen zum Neuen Testament 2/343. Tübingen: Mohr Siebeck, 2013. Pp. xvi + 281. Paper. €69.00. ISBN 9783161523809.

S. Aaron Son, Southwestern Baptist Theological Seminary, Fort Worth, Texas

Numerous books have been published on Paul's use of the temple and cultic images within the last ten to fifteen years. Not surprisingly, most of these books focus on 1 and 2 Corinthians and attempt to understand Paul's usage in comparison with or contrast to various views of the temple evidenced in Second Temple Jewish literature. Yulin Liu's book, which is a slightly revised version of his doctoral dissertation, also focuses on a specific topic: temple purity in 1 and 2 Corinthians. Liu, however, attempts to understand Paul's concept not only against a Jewish background but also against its Greco-Roman background.

Liu develops his argument in each chapter as follows. In the first chapter, which serves as the introduction, he stresses the importance of temple purity for understanding Paul's teachings in 1 and 2 Corinthians, then poses a question on "how the Jewish converts and the Gentile converts are [were] able to understand Paul's concern for temple purity respectively" (10), a question that he endeavors to answer in the rest of the book.

Chapter 2 examines various Jewish views of temple purity. Liu first calls attention to numerous immersion pools (*miqvaoth*) discovered in Jerusalem and in Qumran, which must have been used for purification, and to some ancient texts that mention water purification (36–38). He then briefly describes the significance, history, and structure of the Jerusalem temple (39–46) and surveys a wide range of Second Temple Jewish literature (47–68). From this investigation, he concludes that the concept of purity is closely linked with the temple and that ritual purity was a common practice among the Jewish people (38, 46, 68).

In chapter 3 Liu seeks to determine how temple purity was perceived by the Greeks and Romans. He first discusses the role of temples in the Greco-Roman world, then focuses on three specific temples, those of Apollo, Isis, and Asklepios, all of which had their counterparts in Corinth. Based on this research, Liu asserts that both the Greeks and the Romans considered temples as the houses of gods and as a representation of identity, power of cohesion, patronage of common-wealth, and communal value (88). Moreover, they had temple purity in mind when they regularly cleansed cultic statues and temple interior and required wor-shipers to be purified before entering a temple. Although Greeks and Romans did not have "one temple" idea like the Jews, they definitely had concerns for temple purity (105).

Chapter 4 deals with passages in 1 Corinthians in which Liu thinks the idea of temple purity underlies. He first argues that Paul's warning against partisanship in 1 Cor 3 is based on his conception of partisanship as a source of defilement. To support this argument, Liu translates φθείρω (3:17), which is normally translated "destroy," as "defile" or "corrupt" (122–23), then interprets Paul's teaching in light of Korah's rebellion against Aaron and Moses described in Num 16. He thinks that Paul emulates Moses in speaking of partisanship as the rebellion against God and as the reason for defilement of the community (126). In this sense, partisan-ship affects the corporate unity and pollutes the spiritual temple. Paul therefore recommends that partisanship be stopped and different parties be united so that the temple's purity can be restored (127).

Liu thinks that temple purity underlies Paul's warning against the incestuous man in 1 Cor 5, even though no explicit reference is made to the temple or temple purity. He asserts that incest was regarded as a serious sin deserving punishment in both the Jewish and the Greco-Roman worlds. Paul also considers incest as a serious sin that affects the entire church. As the yeast can affect the whole lump of the unleavened bread, the incestuous man can pollute the entire church. For this reason, Paul recommends that the incestuous man be excommunicated and removed from the table fellowship so that the purity of the temple-community can be maintained (145).

An explicit reference to the temple occurs in 1 Cor 6 in the context of Paul's warning against prostitution. Liu interprets prostitution as an act of "image-muti-lation" (165–73). In the ancient world, the mutilation of the divine image was related to the temple's sacrilege, and it meant the removal of the deity's power and the disavowal of his sovereignty. When a believer whose body is the temple of the Spirit and a member of the body of Christ joins himself to a prostitute, therefore, he is dismantling Christ's body and profaning "the temple-body" (145).

Liu alleges that temple purity also lies in the background of Paul's teaching on intermarriage and divorce in 1 Cor 7. He thinks that Paul's instructions are intended for those who regarded the unbelieving partners in marriage as a threat to the purity of the temple-community and thus embraced divorce. To them, Paul states that individual purity is not marred by living with an unbelieving partner; rather, the witness of a believing partner can bring a sanctifying influence to his or her unbelieving partner and their children (191).

Chapter 5 analyzes 2 Cor 6:14–7:1, in which Paul makes an explicit refer-ence to the temple and cites or alludes to many Old Testament passages. After a careful examination of these passages in light of the history of Israel and the social context of the Roman patron-client relationship, Liu concludes that "Paul interweaves the prophetic visions from Isaiah and Ezekiel in his quotation and switched [switches] the exile return from Israel to the temple-community" (214). He thinks that Paul "merges the concept of the Israel remnant with that of the new eschatological temple to identify the community" (213) and thus combines "the overarching theme of restoration and reconstruction of Israel in the prophetic vision" with his "ecclesiology to convey the purification and progressive construction of the temple-community" (208).

In the final chapter (ch. 6), which serves as the conclusion of the book, Liu provides a brief summary of each chapter and reaffirms his view that the believers in Corinth were familiar with the idea of temple purity; thus "Paul's message of temple purity was able to reach his audience, whether Jewish or gentile, without difficulty" (234). He also confirms that "to maintain the purity of the new temple is likened to a dynamic building process of defining the communal boundary and vocation" (234).

Undoubtedly, this is a well-researched and most comprehensive work on temple purity in 1 and 2 Corinthians. It provides an excellent survey of the Jewish and the Greco-Roman literature on the subject and offers a very intriguing analysis of relevant passages. Of course, not everyone will agree on every point Liu proposes, but no one can easily dismiss his claim that temple purity was a concern not only for the Jews but also for the Greeks and the Romans and that the believers in Corinth, regardless of their ethnic background, had some preknowledge when they heard Paul's message about temple purity. How this preknowledge affected their understanding of Paul's message, which is deeply rooted in the Old Testament and much influenced by early Christian tradition, is, however, a matter that needs further discussion.

Liu's use of sources is careful and his exegesis coherent. Nevertheless, they present some problems. Due to the limitation of space, only a couple of major problems will be mentioned. First, Liu's strong desire to find similarities among various sources sometimes causes him to ignore or overlook their vast conceptual differences. For instance, he supports Paul's "temple-body" concept in 1 Cor 6:19 by citing Philo's view of the body as the temple of the soul (155) and the Stoic idea of the universe and the state as a unified body (156–58). Paul, however, never designates the body as the temple of the soul and would never accept the Hellenistic view of the body as entanglement of the soul. Second, Liu's exegesis involves many assumptions and lacks solid textual connections. For example, his interpretation of partisanship in 1 Cor 3 in light of Korah's rebellion against Moses and prostitution in 1 Cor 6 in light of image mutilation is a mere conjecture and has no clear textual basis. There might be some conceptual similarities, but nothing in the text warrants such connections. Likewise, the evidences that Liu presents for temple purity in 1 Cor 5 and 7 are too weak. The idea of purity or holiness may be present, but the attempt to relate incest and intermarriage to temple purity is unwarranted textually or contextually. If this kind of approach is allowed, one can easily find temple purity in other passages. For example, Paul's instructions on eating food offered to idols (1 Cor 8), his warning against idolatry (1 Cor 10), and his advice on discerning the body of Christ (1 Cor 11) would be good candidates. The problems mentioned above, however, do not diminish the importance of Liu's otherwise fine work and the contribution it has made.

1 and 2 Corinthians, edited by Yung Suk Kim. Texts @ Contexts. Minneapolis: Fortress, 2013. Pp. xx + 201. Cloth. $49.00. ISBN 9780800699352.

Matthew R. Malcolm, Trinity Theological College, Perth, Western Australia

This volume is part of a series that emphasizes the need to consider not only the contexts of the biblical texts, but also the contexts of interpreters:

> Contextual readings of the Bible are an attempt to redress the previous long-standing and grave imbalance that says that there is a kind of "plain," unaligned biblical criticism that is somehow "normative," and that there is another, distinct kind of biblical criticism aligned with some social location. (x)

> [A] book series focusing specifically on contextual multiple readings for specific topics, of specific biblical books, would be timely. (xii)

> Our contributors were asked, decidedly, to be responsibly non-objective. (xiii)

All the chapters are written in English, and most of the contributors have studied or worked in the United States; nevertheless, they represent distinctive reading contexts from across the globe and across society. The volume is divided into three parts: "Identity," "Ritual," and "Community."

The opening chapter in part 1 is "Identity and the Embodiment of Privilege in Corinth," by Love L. Sechrest. This is, to my mind, one of the strongest chapters in the volume. Sechrest discerns in first-century Corinthian disdain for Pauline leadership a resonance with modern disdain for "black and brown bodies as humble, cheap, and disposable" (10). Sechrest insightfully opposes "[d]isembodied constructions of Christian identity … in modern discourse about Christian theology," arguing that Paul's countercultural leadership affirms the embodied ministry of low-status, nonprivileged ministers. The exegetical discussion in this essay is careful, conversant with relevant scholarship, and largely persuasive. The consideration of issues of race, privilege, embodied ministry, and suffering proves greatly helpful in illuminating both textual and modern horizons.

Chapter 2 continues the focus on "identity" with Jeremy Punt's "Identity and Human Dignity amid Power and Liminality in 1 Corinthians 7:17–24." Punt sees a "make the best of one's life situation" reading of this passage as problematized by the "flesh-and-blood" reading context of modern South Africa. Such a consideration is indeed useful in returning to the passage with fresh questions. Punt suggests that, rather than positively justifying the status quo of societal standing, Paul may be heard as holding that social standings are irrelevant to one's calling in the *ekklesia* and therefore may be maintained, while being recognized as nonessential. Punt insightfully notes, however, that in authorizing this subversive perspective, Paul is himself exercising authority that he expects to be respected.

The part of the book that relates to "identity" is rounded off with "An Intercultural Latino Reading of Paul: The Example of 1 Corinthians 9:19–23," by Efrain Agosto. This chapter presents a hermeneutically informed awareness of the value of "otherness" in interpretation. Agosto suggests that U.S. Latinos and Latinas find this awareness heightened on account of their social and linguistic situation. This readiness to operate as "others" in everyday life resonates with, and illuminates, Paul's ministry example in 1 Cor 9. This is highly useful, although I wonder whether the "liberation" agenda consciously set by this contextualized reading sometimes skews the context of the letter's first recipients. For example, the "weak" of 1 Cor 8 are read as the economically weak who had "little or no access to 'meat offered to idols'" (60). This reading is at odds with most readings of the chapter (including that of another essay in this volume), given that it seems that the "weak" of 1 Cor 8 are precisely those who are in danger of being lured to eat meat offered to idols.

Part 2 of the volume (on ritual) begins with "2 Corinthians 7:1 against the Backdrop of African Purification Rites," by J. Ayodeji Adewuya. This essay continues the volume's explicitly contextualized readings of select passages by reading 1 Cor 7 in the light of African perspectives on "cleansing, the idea of pollution, and the fear of God" (67). The positive payoff of this approach is that it can offer new illumination of themes that might otherwise be missed or downplayed. The danger of this approach is, again, that it might simplify the nuanced "otherness" of the first-century context. For example, I wonder whether the apparently direct link between personal "uncleanness" and "sin" in the reading context is quite equivalent to first-century Judaism. But this tension is not ignored, and in this and other essays there is an attempt to give considered attention to both horizons. The positive illumination provided by the reading context in this essay includes the perspective that "the behavior of the individual determines what happens to all. As such, one may say that sin is not a private matter" (70). Adewuya has helpfully detected and amplified a resonance here between the African cultures in question and the cultures represented in the Corinthian correspondence.

Chapter 5, by Menghun Goh, is "The Issue of Eidōlothyta: An Inter(con)textual Interpretation of 1 Corinthians 8:1–11:1 and Chinese Ancestor Veneration." Another valuable element of consciously contextual readings is highlighted in this essay, in which an instinct that a cultural behavior (ancestor veneration) might find fresh acceptance drives a rereading of the biblical text. As this volume illustrates, different cultures and reading situations will approach the texts with different instincts, suggesting a range of fresh readings to be tried. Like the previous chapter, this essay finds a resonance between the reading situation and the first-century context, specifically, "the nondualistic worldview in the ancient world." This is indeed enlightening, and while not all will be convinced by Goh's attempt to reconfigure ancestor veneration as "iconic," the critique of the limitations of Anglo scholarship is worth hearing.

Chapter 6 rounds off the focus on "ritual" with Ma. Marilou S. Ibita's "A Conversation with the Story of the Lord's Supper in 1 Corinthians 11:17–34: Engaging the Scripture Text and the Filipino Christians' Context." This essay illustrates well the value of the broader enterprise. Ibita rightly points out that a resonant context may "augment" one's sensitivity to the text itself. I find that this is indeed the case in this instance, as Filipino meal traditions are considered alongside the Corinthian practice of the Lord's Supper. This results in giving attention to an interesting rereading of 11:17–22, such that the greedy are admonished for failing to open their houses to all of their brothers and sisters. This is let down a little by incomplete formatting (there is no shading in the table), but is genuinely interesting and worthy of consideration. In fact, I find that despite—or perhaps *because*—the subsequent application to the Filipino situation is so particularly located, it is remarkably penetrating and transferable.

Part 3 ("community") opens with chapter 7: "Pauline Theological Counseling of Love in the Language of the Zhuangzi: A Reading of Love In 1 Corinthians in a Chinese Philosophical Context," by K .K. Yeo. Yeo is well published, including on the Corinthian correspondence, and is one of the most established scholarly contributors to the volume. Here Yeo attempts "to read 1 Corinthians through the eyes of the *Zhuangzi* (the philosopher's work goes by his name), noting the kind of intertextual relationship that can exist between the two documents for a reader of both classics" (118). In contrast to the previous essay, I did not find the intertextual echoes to be especially illuminating beyond their possible interest to those engaged with Zhuangzi.

Chapter 8 is "Reading 1 Corinthians 11:1–16 through Habits and Hijabs in the United States," by Janelle Peters. As in chapter 6, this chapter explores a possible rereading of a passage of 1 Corinthians in the light of concerns and insights raised by a particular reading context. Here it is that of religious veil-wearers in the United States. Rather than seeing Paul's insistence on headcoverings as a concession to culture, Peters sees it as an egalitarian instinct: "Paul uses veiling to blur class distinctions" (129). The danger identified above, in which the interests of the reading context might constrain one's reading of the first-century context, is also relevant here. To me it seems that Peters's proposal relies on evidence that is speculative (about the pervasive religious influence of Roman priestly headcoverings) and narrow (excluding Jewish backgrounds).

The third part of the book is rounded off with chapter 9: "What Queer Hermeneutics Can Do for Us in Spain: The Case of 1 Corinthians 6:1–9," by Luis Menéndez Antuña. Despite the mention of 1 Cor 6:1–9 in the title, the passage is not really the focus of the essay. Indeed, it is a chapter on hermeneutics rather than on any particular biblical passage. Having said that, it is a very interesting exploration of a Spanish queer reading context. Antuña aims to explore the ways in which the scriptures have been used in the context of a "culture war" over marriage. This issue is of major contemporary significance, so Antuña's insights about oversimplifications by both the Catholic Church (e.g.. 153) and the Spanish state (e.g.. 155) are well worth considering. I find his critiques quite penetrating, as he argues that both "the church and the state envision the homoerotic, and the sexual realm for that matter, as always referring to static identities" (157). The reader is thus sensitized for a fresh reading of the biblical material, although such a fresh reading is not to be found here.

One finds in this volume, then, both the promise and the hazards of an approach in which the reading context is intentionally foregrounded. This approach seems to hold the most promise when a resonance between cultural horizons enables augmented sensitivity to features of the "other." It is most hazardous when the commitments of a reading context flatten first-century nuances. Overall, as an Australian biblical scholar, I found the volume to be worthwhile in helping me to approach the texts with fresh questions and perspectives.

Celebrating Paul: Festschrift in Honor of Jerome Murphy-O'Connor, O.P., and Joseph A. Fitzmyer, S.J., edited by Peter Spitaler. Catholic Biblical Quarterly Monograph Series 48. Washington, D.C: Catholic Biblical Association of America, 2011. Pp. xxviii + 439. Paper. $25.00. ISBN 0915170477.

Nijay K. Gupta, Eastern University, St. Davids, Pennsylvania

Celebrating Paul is a Festschrift honoring Catholic scholars Joseph Fitzmyer and Jerome Murphy-O'Connor (now deceased) together, both highly respected in New Testament studies for their many contributions, especially in Pauline studies. A note in the editor's preface explains that the title of this volume was inspired by Pope Benedict XVI's "proclamation commemorating the second millennium of the birth of the Apostle Paul beginning June 29, 2008 and ending June 29, 2009" (xviii). Villanova University began the Jubilee Year with a symposium honoring Murphy-O'Connor and Fitzmyer (September 9–10, 2008).

Peter Spitaler's preface also contains short academic biographies of both honorees, but I was particularly interested in the personal statements made by one of the essay contributors, Robert Jewett, at the beginning of his chapter on Rom 13 and its context:

> The two colleagues being honored in this volume demonstrate a self-critical spirit that has served as a model for many of us. Jerome Murphy-O'Connor's fearless and fair-minded weighing of evidence encouraged me to follow my own judgment in controversial aspects of biblical history and interpretation. Joseph Fitzmyer's exhaustive catalogues and analyses of scholarly investigations, including numerous items written outside of the North Atlantic arena, were invaluable resources in my study of Romans. I have cited their work in hundreds of footnotes over the last several decades. (265)

I am sure many New Testament scholars, including myself, would offer the same kind of sentiments regarding the contributions of these two men.

In the more than four-hundred pages of the monograph, there are nineteen chapters. Fitzmyer and Murphy-O'Connor each offer their own contribution.

Fitzmyer presents a broad snapshot of "The Significance of the Pauline Writings" as a whole, recognizing in Paul's uncontested letters ten different "effects" of the Christ-event: justification, salvation, reconciliation, expiation, redemption, freedom, sanctification, transformation, new creation, and glorification. While Fitzmyer has clearly chosen ten key results of the work of Christ according to Paul, I found his brief discussions of the *sources* of these metaphors and ideas too one-sided. For example, when it comes to "transformation," Fitzmyer traces this idea to "Greco-Roman mythology," where shape-shifting is a rather normal occurrence. Be that as it may, when Paul refers to transformation with "unveiled faces" (2 Cor 3:18), he seems to be drawing from Old Testament imagery. Later Fitzmyer links "glorification" with God's *kabod* in the Old Testament. This is almost certainly a key association, but it should not exclude the very Greco-Roman identification of *doxa* with the social value of honor. Nevertheless, one can hardly deny the importance of the concepts Fitzmyer identifies as central to Paul's theology.

Murphy-O'Connor focuses on a single verse (1 Cor 11:19) in the second essay, entitled, "Divisions are Necessary." This verse has perplexed interpreters because it appears that, in a letter so focused on unity, Paul appears here to promote divisions. Finding most commentators' exegetical explanations wanting, Murphy-O'Connor tries to develop an idea found in Thiselton's commentary, that the phrase "divisions are necessary" is Paul's redeployment of a Corinthian slogan. Murphy-O'Connor argues that the Corinthians probably promoted a very general maxim ("There must be divisions in order that those who are tired and tested may be recognized"), and Paul added "among you" in order to focus the spotlight on their own acts of immorality and competitiveness. While I am not as confident as Murphy-O'Connor that Pauline redaction of Corinthian slogans are as easily identifiable as he suggests, his rhetorical reading of this verse in light of 1 Corinthians as a whole is quite convincing.

Most of the contributors chose to focus their essays on Romans. Mark Nanos ("Paul and the Jewish Tradition: The Ideology of the *Shema*"), working with Paul's interpretation of the Shema, adumbrates how Paul conceived of the inclusion of Gentiles into the people of God (as Gentiles, not proselytes) as a sensible eschatological result of the work of the one living God over all humanity. Stanley Stowers ("Paul's Four Discourses about Sin") reads Romans very differently than scholars such as Nanos, who focus on the Jewish background and context of Paul. When it comes to Paul's discussion of sin, Stowers finds the "thought world" of Hellenistic moral psychology more plausible regarding Romans than the common appeals to Paul's apocalyptic "sin as [cosmic] power" viewpoint. I find Stowers's case highly dubious, however, especially in light of Paul's frequent association between sin and Adam and sin and the Jewish law.

Jan Lambrecht ("Ecocentric or Anthropocentric? A Reading of Romans 8:18–25") reexamines a key text used in recent years to give theological attention to ecological concerns. Lambrecht ultimately finds an "ecocentric" view of Rom 8:18–25 an overcompensation, as Paul did not view the world as having significance apart from humanity: "most likely it exists for human beings" (185). Ekkehard

Stegemann ("'Set Apart for the Gospel': (Romans 1:1)" explores how Paul intro-
duces himself and explains his gospel to the Romans. Brendan Byrne ("Adam,
Christ, and the Law in Romans 5–8") draws attention to Paul's discussion of the
Jewish law in chapters related primarily to righteousness and Christian obedience.
Paul is trying to convince the Torah-sympathetic Romans that the Spirit will guide
them through their new life morally and that the Torah should be set on the Adam
side of the Adam-Christ equation, as it cannot lead to righteousness. Gregory
Tatum offers a remarkably different reading of Romans in his own chapter ("'To
the Jew First' (Romans 1:16): Paul's Defense of Jewish Privilege in Romans"), where
Paul appears to Tatum to be quite sympathetic to the Torah-observant Christians.
Tatum discourages interpreters from reading Romans with Galatians in mind (as
a comparative text). Rather, underscoring the *differences* between the two letters,
Tatum sees Paul blaming the flesh for the problem of sin and extending a place of
respect and honor for the Torah and other "privileges" that God gave to Israel.

   In Jean-Noël Aletti's essay ("Interpreting Romans 11:14: What Is at Stake?"),
attention is paid to the word *parazēloun* and Paul's desire to provoke Israel to jealousy as a key part of the wider plan to bring the nations to Christ. Robert Jewett
("Reinterpreting Romans 13 within Its Broader Context") attempts to read Rom
13 in view of two polarized politics attitudes toward Rome among Christians:
zealot desire for the subversion of the state, or unqualified support for imperial
leadership. Making connections to the problems of pride and greed found in Rom
1:18–32 as well as Rom 7, Jewett argues cogently that Paul encourages respect
toward governing authorities with a view toward the loving God who stands over
them, the deity made known to them in the crucified Christ.

   It is no wonder that so many essay contributors chose to write on Romans, as
Fitzmyer has influenced the study of Romans in numerous writings, particularly
with his Anchor-Yale commentary (1993). Fitzmyer also wrote, more recently,
the 1 Corinthians volume for the Anchor-Yale series, but Murphy-O'Connor has
left a stronger mark on the study of that epistle (see Thomas Martin, "Augustine's
Pauline Method: 1 Corinthians 11:2–16 as a Case Study").

   Another group of contributors examine broader themes in the study of Paul.
James Dunn ("In Search of the Historical Paul") sets the apostle within his early
Jewish context and briefly explores his role as messenger and proclaimer of Jesus
Christ. Also paying very close to attention to Paul's first-century context, Helmut
Koester ("Nomos, Agapē, and Charismata in Paul's Writings") attempts to read
Paul's *nomos* language in light of how Hellenistic diaspora Jews tended to asso-
ciate the Jewish "law" with both the "law of nature" (Philo) as well as "existing
Roman political and social order" (see 234). From this perspective, Paul's rejec-
tion of the "law" would relate to a wider circle of ideas than simply Jewish Torah.
Alternatively, Paul was promoting the unifying and sanctifying guidance of love
and the gifts of the Spirit. While I think one can learn much from Koester's positive conclusions about Paul's ethics, I am unconvinced that writers such as Philo
supply the best contextual clues for making sense of Paul's *nomos*-language.

   David Aune ("Paul, Ritual Purity, and the Ritual Baths South of the Temple

Mount [Acts 21:15–28]") offers a close look at historical evidence for how the rites of the Nazirite vows would have taken place in Paul's time. Paul's view of his former life of Judaism is a matter taken up by William Campbell ("'I Rate All Things as Loss': Paul's Puzzling Accounting System. Judaism as Loss or the Re-evaluating of All Things in Christ?"). Campbell makes the important case (especially in view of Phil 3:2–8) that Paul's main point was *not* to undermine Jewish values but to reject any sense of worth outside of Christ.

John Pilch tries to analyze Paul from a sociological perspective in his contribution ("Paul, Change Agent: Model for the Twenty-First Century"). While there are some advantages to viewing Paul as someone who "functions as a communication link between two or more social entities" with a view toward applying "innovation-decisions," I doubt that many readers will find convincing Pilch's argument that Paul's ministry was focused on Hellenized Jews among Gentiles rather than Gentiles themselves (see Nanos's essay as a nice counterperspective to Pilch's argument).

While the subject of Adam is a rather frequent occurrence among the essays in this volume (see especially Stowers and Byrne), Pheme Perkins's essay is a broader and more synthetic discussion of this primal figure ("Adam and Christ in the Pauline Epistles"). She proves herself to be a minimalist by arguing that there is no good reason to import an Adamic "back-story" every time one finds Paul comparing Adam and Christ. If it is true that the Adam-Christ discourses are contingent and not consistently part of a wider theological narrative, Perkins urges that, while Adam-Christology is present in Paul's letters, it hardly generates any real insight. Perkins has made a strong case for her "contingent" view with regard to texts such as 1 Cor 15:20–22 and Rom 5:12–19, but how might the landscape change if texts such as Rom 1:18–32 and Rom 7 are included, where Adam may be present (with a story behind him) more allusively?

Frank Matera offers a sustained discussion of ethics ("Living in the Newness of Life: Paul's Understanding of the Moral Life"). Matera appeals to the Bultmannian paradigm of the indicative (of salvation) and the imperative (of behavior and obedience). Looking at Rom 6–8 in particular, he underscores the Pauline imagery of baptism as death to self as one is buried in baptism into the death of Christ. Matera also points to the importance of the Spirit for Paul vis-à-vis the life of obedience to God in Christ. He concludes with three theological implications: Pauline ethics is Trinitarian, sacramental, and Spirit-empowered (see 167–68).

If there is one weakness to this Festschrift as a whole, it is in the arrangement of the essays. There was no clear ordering to them, and I would have appreciated a division of the essays into section groupings (perhaps splitting those on Romans/1 Corinthians from those on broader themes). This organizational matter notwithstanding, each of the essays in this volume proved stimulating and was carefully written. The variety in subject matter, while sometimes overwhelming, offered a salutary reminder of the broad impact on Pauline studies of the work of Fitzmyer and Murphy-O'Connor. The honorees' contributions to scholarship have, indeed, made a lasting impact.

Keys to Galatians: Collected Essays, by Jerome Murphy-O'Connor. Collegeville, Minn.: Liturgical Press, 2012. Pp. xvi + 194. Paper. $24.95. ISBN 9780814680704.

Frank J. Matera, The Catholic University of America, Washington, D.C.

A collection of the essays that a scholar has already published in journals and books is usually of little interest. On the one hand, such collections tend to lack thematic unity and inevitably appear self-serving. On the other, they offer readers dated material that many of them have already read. But there are exceptions to this rule, this volume being one of them.

For nearly half a century, Jerome Murphy-O'Connor of the École Biblique in Jerusalem was one of the foremost interpreters of Paul. While he is probably best known for books such as *Paul: A Critical Life* and *St. Paul's Corinth: Texts and Archaeology,* he consistently provided the scholarly community with a number of rigorously academic articles, especially but not exclusively in *Revue biblique.* The publication of some of his most significant articles dealing with Saint Paul's letter to the Galatians, then, is an event worthy of note, especially now that Murphy-O'Connor has passed on.

Six of the ten essays published in this collection originally appeared in *Revue biblique,* the other four in *Catholic Biblical Quarterly, Zeitschrift für die neutestamentliche Wissenchaft, Communion et Réunion: Mélanges Jean-Marie Roger Tillard,* and *Christian Origins: Worship, Belief and Society; The Milltown Institute and the Irish Biblical Millenium Conference.* Although all of these essays appear in their original form, Murphy-O'Connor added an interesting postscript to each in which he engaged those who responded in some way to the original essay or in which he reinforced and fine-tuned his argument on the basis of new material that became available to him. While some of the postscripts are tedious at times, and while Murphy-O'Connor's "take no prisoners" approach can be startling, these postscripts are interesting because they show the scholar at work. In them, we see someone who read the field and seriously interacted with those who opposed as well as supported the theses he proposed. All scholars, especially aspiring young scholars, can learn from this methodology.

These essays tend to focus on those issues the commentators of Galatians have overlooked or have not been able to arrive at a consensus. They look for clues and hints that others have missed. Thus it may appear that the author is dealing with insignificant issues, but on further reflection it becomes apparent how important these issues are for understanding the situation that led to Galatians.

The larger picture that emerges from these studies can be summarized in this way. Paul wrote the letter to the Galatians *before* the great conference at Jerusalem. The audience to whom he wrote was a community composed of house churches in Pessinus (north Galatia). Although the letter is addressed to the Galatians, it was in fact directed to the Judaizers, the only ones who would have been able to appreciate its complex argumentation when it was read aloud. These Judaizers did not come from Jerusalem, as is usually thought. Rather, they arrived from the church at Antioch in Syria, the community that originally sent Paul on mission to the

Gentiles but had now retreated to the position espoused by those who had come to Antioch from James. The Antioch incident and Paul's letter to the Galatians, then, mark a decisive change in his understanding of the gospel, which becomes apparent in his radical rejection of the law and the new Christology of the crucified Messiah that he develops, for the first time, in the letter to the Galatians.

In the first essay, "Mission in Galatia, Macedonia, and Arabia before the Jerusalem Conference," Murphy-O'Connor investigates three studies of Pauline chronology. Then, building on the work of two of them (Lüdemann and Jewett), he uses the "hint" embodied in Gal 2:7 to argue "that prior to the Jerusalem Conference of AD 51 he [Paul] had evangelized Galatia, Macedonia, and Achaia" (21). The second essay ("Paul in Arabia: Gal 1:17") deals with the period immediately after Paul's call. Why happened during this time? After reviewing the historical situation, Murphy-O'Connor maintains that the only plausible explanation for the reaction of King Aretas to Paul is that Paul went to Arabia (Nabatean territory) to make his first converts among the Gentiles, this indicating that from the beginning Paul was convinced that his mission was to the Gentiles. In a third essay ("The Names for Jerusalem in Galatians [1:17–18; 4:25–26]"), Murphy-O'Connor investigates the two forms of the Greek name for Jerusalem that appear only in Galatians and concludes that, while Paul was more comfortable with the Semitic form *Ierousalēm*, he also uses the Greek form *Hierosolyma* in Galatians because it would have been more familiar to the intruders from Antioch.

All of these essays are subtle, leading readers down surprising and unexpected paths. For example, the fourth essay ("To Run in Vain [Gal 2.2]") interprets the text of Gal 2:2 ("lest I should run or had run in vain") in light of the rhetorical device of *concessio,* so that the text gives the impression "that the Jerusalem leaders were exactly what the intruders in Galatia said they were because he [Paul] could go on to say that they agreed with Paul rather than with the intruders" (58). In "Nationalism and Church Policy: Reflections on Galatians 2:9," Murphy-O'Connor examines the political situation of the day and James's nationalistic concerns to explain why he sided with Paul at Jerusalem about circumcision but not at Antioch when it came to food laws.

The sixth essay of this collection ("Galatians 2:15–16a: Whose Common Ground?") prepares the way for the final one ("The Origins of Paul's Christology: From Thessalonians to Galatians"). In the essay on Gal 2:15–16a Murphy-O'Connor shows how Paul arrived at the conclusions stated in this text and argues that in this text Paul "attributes to Christian Jews a theological position *that they should have defended,* not the one they actually maintained" (81). The position that Paul arrives at in this text is the ground for his Christology, which is presented in the last essay, which traces the movement from Paul's Christology in 1 Thessalonians (a Christology that nearly anyone in the early church could have articulated) to the radically new Christology of the crucified Messiah in Galatians.

The seventh ("The Irrevocable Will: Gal 3:15") and ninth ("The Unwritten Law of Christ [Gal 6:2]") essays take up two problems that commentators have struggled with: Paul's reference to a will that cannot be revoked and the phrase "the law of Christ." Taking its starting point from a text of Lucian's *Disowned*, which Ramsay first noted, this essay argues that in the case of a testator who conferred his goods on his adopted son, this was an irrevocable will *in the estimation* of the general populace, even though the will could legally be revoked. As for "the law of Christ," Murphy's O'Connor views it as an unwritten, living law, namely, "the law which is Christ," which ought to guide believers.

Finally, in an essay that shows his attention to detail ("Galatians 4:13–14 and the Recipients of Galatians"), Murphy-O'Connor takes up the question of who were the Galatians. Noting that the text of Gal 4:13–14 presupposes a single community rather than a number of widespread geographical communities, he employs this text to argue against the south Galatian hypothesis and even the standard version of the north Galatian hypothesis, which views the recipients as inhabitants of multiple cities. In Murphy-O'Connor's view, the letter was sent to a single city, Pessinus, where the community was composed of multiple house churches.

One will not agree with all of Murphy-O'Connor's conclusions. For example, I find his thesis that the intruders came from Antioch intriguing but not convincing, and I find his use of *concessio* for interpreting Gal 2:2 too subtle. I am, however, intrigued by his insight that Gal 4:13–14 points to a single community, and I find the argument that the mission to Galatia occurred before the council convincing. As one reads through these essays, one stands in admiration of the author's knowledge of the historical and geographical background of the Pauline material as well as his mastery of the secondary literature. Thus, even though readers may not agree with all of his conclusions and hypotheses, those who are intent on investigating Galatians will do well to wrestle with these essays.

Emerging Leadership in the Pauline Mission: A Social Identity Perspective on Local Leadership Development in Corinth and Ephesus, by Jack Barentsen. Princeton Theological Monograph Series. Eugene: Pickwick, 2011. Pp. xviii + 378. Paper. $44.00. ISBN 9781610972444.

Jan G. van der Watt, Radboud University Nijmegen, Nijmegen, The Netherlands

Emerging Leadership in the Pauline Mission is an award-winning publication analyzing the phenomenon of (organizational) leadership in several Pauline texts related to Corinth and Ephesus. One of the major strengths of the book is the effort Barentsen makes to illustrate that leadership in Paul's situation was not a stagnant phenomenon but a dynamic group phenomenon that was adapted from situation to situation and from time to time. Barentsen is interested in identifying leadership patterns in certain Pauline communities as well as how Paul and these communities influenced the development of these patterns. Barentsen situates his study within the history of Pauline scholarship of local church leadership and develops it by using the theory of social-identity formation.

The book is divided into nine chapters preceded by an introduction and preface and concluded by the bibliography and several useful indexes (author, subject, Scripture). Although Barentsen does not divide the book in two sections, the material is presented in this way. The first three chapters mainly deal with introductory historical and theoretical issues, while the last chapter, of course, offers concluding remarks, also spelling out the implications of this study. The remaining five chapters (4–8) focus on specific Pauline texts exegetically analyzed in light of the nature of leadership that are presented in these different texts.

Barentsen positions himself in the introduction. First, he points out that traditionally New Testament leadership studies focused mainly on church office, which often led to a defense of denominational leadership structures. However, more recent focus on the social dimensions of the text opened readers' eyes to the diversity of leadership structures, people, situations, and so on, which questions the idea of finding universal norms for leadership in the New Testament, something that more than often happens in so-called studies on "biblical leadership." Rather Barentsen prefers to approach the dynamics of leadership from a group (social) perspective, taking into account aspects such as the social interaction between members of the group, the different positions taken within the group, roles played in the group, the social situation faced, and the kind of leadership that is chosen in response to different situations.

Second, Barentsen acknowledges the necessity of working with a clear chronological and geographical range if one wants to follow the patterns of development of leadership within a specific group. He defines his geographical range to be the Pauline communities at Corinth and Ephesus as two of the major locations of Paul's Aegean ministry. These two communities are the recipients of several Pauline letters, such as the Corinthian correspondence, the Letter to the Ephesians, and 1–2 Timothy. Barentsen's position that the latter documents (Ephesians and 1–2 Timothy) are indeed Pauline moves against the majority opinion, and he recognizes that. He offers arguments for his position, but it goes without saying that he will not convince the majority. This poses one of the major problems of the book, since the construct he makes of leadership and leadership development in these Pauline communities is based on his reading of the relevant Pauline letters within their respective situations. Any change in the time, situation, author, or addressees of the letters will by default influence any structural development proposed based on these letters. In short, since Barentsen's theory works with interrelatedness and development, a different view on these letters could lead to different positions. A positive is that Barentsen is aware of this, and with his fine exegetical abilities he does take off some of the sharper sides of the problem.

Third, Barentsen explains and defends his use of the social-identity model of leadership, focusing on the social positions of the members of a group relative to one another, as well as of the leader within the group. The social and psychological processes underpinning structural developments are presented in a clear and accessible way.

In chapter 2 Barentsen reviews the history of scholarship on church leadership, starting with figures such as Hatch, Harnack, Lightfoot, and Holtzmann. He aptly points out that denominational ideology plays an important role in leadership discussions. Here he rightly alerts us about the tendency of scholars to interpret biblical material in a way that suits their specific perspectives. Three terms dominate in these recent discussions—leadership, authority, and office—and these also determines the agenda of research and consequent results. Since the 1980s anthropological approaches shifted the focus to the ancient household as the framework for Pauline churches and leadership, while the role of elders and practices in the synagogue and patronage as social phenomena influenced the practice of leadership. He sees his own work in line with these developments.

Chapter 3 explains how the social-identity model of leadership works. Henri Tajfel (1919–1982) initiated the social-identity theory. This perspective, as part of social-scientific criticism, is a hermeneutical tool that is applied along with rhetorical, narratological, and literary criticism. The model is here presented in two stages. (1) The first stage presents the concept of social identity, referring to the person's sense of "us," belonging to a particular group. The social-identity narrative within a particular group provides cohesion by forming social identities often through comparison, leading to stereotypes. (2) The second stage presents leadership as the ability to manage social identity and embed people within that identity. Leaders are seen as more prototypical than other members of the group and are thus expected to represent the group identity and embed others within that identity. They consequently become more and more charismatic, allowing them to facilitate the process of succession. Barentsen points out that succession is often neglected in leadership studies and gives due attention to this phenomenon. It is commendable that Barentsen indeed develops this aspect of leadership and is one of the very positive contributions of this book.

Barentsen applies this method in a consistent way to all the documents he discusses, and by doing so the results he gets from the different letters gain validity. The saying is true, however, that you only get the answers to the questions your method allows you to ask and that you only observe what your methods allows you to see. Since Barentsen applies his method in such a consistent way, critique against much of what is done should not be aimed at him but at the theorists of the method itself.

Without going into detail, I often wondered whether the conclusions were too easily made and positions too easily taken, without giving due attention to some other major views on the interpretation of a particular text. It is not a matter that attention is not paid, but the point here is that it could have been given more frequently. Some of the issues involved are more complex , and sometimes the perspective chosen is not the only or even the best one but fits the theory. This has to my mind more to do with the nature of this social method than with the exegetical skills of Bartentsen, which should be commended. In any case, his overall thesis makes sense and seems plausible.

Chapters 4 to 8 deal with the respective Pauline letters (1 and 2 Corinthians, Ephesians, and 1 and 2 Timothy). The pattern of discussing the different letters is more or less the same, although the contents not, since Barentsen follows the development of Pauline thought on leadership throughout these different documents. Each chapter starts with an introduction to the particular letter and situates it within Paul's ministry. With the aid of the social-identity model, relevant aspects of the particular texts are studied in the light of the leadership material they offer. Initially the processes of social identification are surveyed, followed by looking at the role of the leader in the community, focusing on both local as well as Pauline leadership. This allows Barentsen to describe the processes of leadership emergence, maintenance, and succession, leading to a description of the patterns of leadership.

In these latter descriptions of the leadership material in the different letters, the diverse developments related to the role and function of leadership in the Pauline communities are highlighted. For instance, in chapter 4, dealing with 1 Corinthians, Bartentsen shows how the local leadership became divided due to the development of subgroups. Many aspects of the group were threatened, even their participation in the Eucharist. The problem, according to Barentsen, had a lot to do with a more Jewish vision of social identity, which sidelined Paul, leading to a lost tearful letter. Negotiations restored the situation and confirmed Paul's position as founding apostle of the congregation. Moving to the letter to Ephesus, it becomes apparent that Paul's stature and charismatic position within the community grew, also because of his successful negotiations with Corinth. In this case the picture is one of a more stable subgroup of leadership that maintained the unity and cohesion in the community and allowed Paul to write to the church from prison. They indeed lived out Paul's vision of Christian identity in opposition to competing Jewish and Greco-Roman identities. The leadership narrative, however, continues. Nearing the end of his ministry, Paul instructed Timothy how to maintain local leadership by keeping it aligned with God's mission with the church. Timothy is encouraged to provide a positive model of leadership within the competing Jewish and Greco-Roman settings. This assumed the presence of a functioning subgroup of leaders, working together. In 2 Timothy Paul, based on his own status as leader, ensures succession of local leadership through the mediation of Timothy.

The conclusions in chapter 9 provide the reader with a comparison of leadership patters that developed. It is also pointed out that, although Paul functioned within whatever cultural forms of leadership that were on offer, he consistently offered a pattern of leadership focusing on self-sacrifice for the community in service of the gospel. In this way he aligned leadership with the beliefs and values of Christian social identity. Although situations differed, this golden line was woven into every situation. Similar patterns of collegial leadership were developed, although earlier patters are more concerned with leadership emergence and later patterns with leadership maintenance and succession. Paul's ability to facilitate succession is the result of communities ascribing a charismatic leadership position to Paul. Barentsen concludes that Paul indeed attempted to establish some uniform leadership patterns for his churches, based on consistent sustenance of the communication of Paul's gospel in each community in alignment with other churches in the Pauline network. In this way he promoted uniform patterns as a cross-cultural norm with the aim of promoting future stability and cohesion. Barentsen questions whether Paul intended historical structures to serve as cross-cultural norms. Leadership patterns evident in the discussed Pauline letters should not be ahistorically applied to today's situation.

Judged from the perspective of leadership studies that are linked to biblical material, Barentsen's work must be highly commented. Although not the first one, he shows that leadership studies that want to make leadership patterns of important biblical figures such as Moses, Paul, or even Jesus normative for yesterday, today, and tomorrow do not take the nature of the text or the social dynamics of the text seriously. In this sense his work will certainly challenge researchers to deal with greater nuance and care when it comes to issues such as leadership and the Bible. A last remark should be made. Barentsen's emphasis on the requirement of a leader to also lead or at least guide the process of succession should be noted. This is an issue that should receive more attention in future.

Reading this book was educational and enjoyable. Although there are smaller exegetical issues that need further discussion or clarification (I may say, as usual), I recommend this book as a must to anyone who wants to study leadership in the New Testament, scholar, student, and interested reader alike.

Canonizing Paul: Ancient Editorial Practice and the Corpus Paulinum, by Eric W. Scherbenske. New York: Oxford University Press, 2013. Pp. xiv + 383. Cloth. $74.00. ISBN 9780199917341.

David Trobisch, Springfield, Missouri

The book is a revised version of a dissertation accepted by the University of North Carolina at Chapel Hill and written under the advisement of Bart Ehrman. The 236 pages of narrative are supported by 106 pages of notes and by a 38-page bibliography.

After a brief methodological introduction, Scherbenske sets out to describe editorial practices in antiquity using observations gleaned from the transmission of the works of Homer and Hippocrates. He then interprets three historical editions of the *Corpus Paulinum*: (1) the edition of Marcion, (2) the Euthalian edition as documented in Codex Coislinianus, and (3) a revision of the Vulgate present in Codex Fuldensis. Scherbenske makes a passionate plea not only to focus on the history of a text but also to take the history of its editions into account. The diverse editorial features "demonstrate the profound effect an editor could have on Pauline traditions and, as a result, their interpretations" (236).

The title of the book might be easily misunderstood. The book does not focus on the history of the canon, nor is it interested in a discussion of discrepancies between the historical Paul and the literary Paul as indicated in the editorial concept of the editions that Scherbenske analyzed. Except for Marcion's edition, the other two editions discussed in the book are clearly products of very late antiquity and describe practices typical for the Middle Ages rather than those of antiquity. Scherbenske, however, does not assert that the three editions discussed are representative among the numerous editions that have circulated in the manuscript tradition. They resemble "case studies" (9) that will inform future research.

The book aptly reports the history of research on these three editions of the Pauline corpus, and it will be of great help to those who have not studied Marcion's edition, the Euthalian Recension, or the competing editions of the corpus in Latin manuscripts. The summaries about editorial practices in antiquity (16–70) will be helpful to interpreters interested in the practice of writing for publication in antiquity and in the challenges of authors and publishers attempting to protect the copyright and deal with forgeries.

Although Marcion's edition (71–115) has not survived in manuscript form, some of its editorial features can still be reconstructed, including the editorial frame described in the selection and arrangement of writings and in the introductory paragraphs to the letters. Together with Ulrich Schmid, Scherbenske supports the view that Marcion did not rewrite the Pauline text to accommodate his own theology, as claimed by the second- and third-century heresiologists. Rather, "Marcion sought to reestablish what he thought was the original," and he formulated his interpretation through editorial additions or, as Scherbenske phrases it, through "paratextual materials" (115). Marcion, therefore, might be better understood being a collector and publisher rather than an editor or forger. The discussion of Nils Dahl's position concerning the Marcionite origin of specific editorial additions in the appendix (237–42) is most insightful.

The Euthalian edition of Paul's letters (116–174) comprises a prologue to the collection of Paul's letters, introductions to each individual letter, chapter headings, a list of citations, an account of Paul's martyrdom, and a description of Paul's travels (118). Although the origin and authorship is obscure (usually placed at the end of the fourth century [120]), the pedagogical focus of the edition is apparent. The colometric arrangement of the text—one of its distinctive characteristics—may have been designed to guide reading "for private catechetical study or public liturgical worship" (174). The specific manuscript chosen for studying this edition is majuscule H (015), commonly dated to the sixth century, parts of which are held at Mount Athos, Kiev, St. Petersburg, Moscow, Paris, Torino, and Washington, D.C.

The last chapter (175–229) describes just one codex, the so-called Codex Fuldensis, a collection of elements of numerous editions that was completed by Victor of Capua in May of 546. The revision of the text of the letters of Paul from the Vulgate is introduced with a prologue to the collection, and it contains the Marcionite prologues to the individual letters, *capitula* to the letters drawn from diverse sources, a concordance often attributed to Pelagian circles, and the letter to the Laodiceans (175). Whereas the edition of Marcion and the Euthalian edition are clearly publications, the Codex Fuldensis with its scholarly compilation from other published sources is an author's copy that exists only as a single original. Its value for the discussion of editions therefore lies more in its documentation of earlier publications and in offering us the opportunity to watch an editor at work. Nevertheless, this manuscript allows Scherbenske also to reflect on the methodological problems of his approach. Under the heading "The Vulgate Text, Codex Fuldensis, and Editorial Hermeneutics," he uses prooftexts (1Cor 15:38; Rom 5:12; 6:16; 5:14) to test his approach when investigating "the possible relationship between interpretive concerns and the text transmitted" (211). It is here where many of the threads are brought together and where the author showcases what it means to use editorial interests of manuscripts, older editions, and the intention of implied biblical authors to revise a translation. Specialists in translation studies might appreciate this discourse. I would have loved to see a discussion of Matthias Klinghardt's numerous articles on Marcion or of my *Die Entstehung der Paulusbriefsammlung* (1989), which would have supported the author's case. But considering the enormous breadth of material covered in this work, omissions are unavoidable.

The outcome of this study is formulated in modest terms: the goal was to create a stronger interest in "those spaces before, after, and around the text of ancient manuscripts" and to stop focusing on textual changes alone "as the locus of textual manipulation" (236). In this sense, Scherbenske supports a new direction of textual criticism that tries to understand the history of the New Testament as the history of an edition rather than the history of a disembodied text. I commend him for this approach, and I hope this book will encourage colleagues also to engage in this new line of study.

Studying Paul's Letters: Contemporary Perspectives and Methods, edited by Joseph A. Marchal. Minneapolis: Fortress, 2012. Pp. xiv + 233. Paper. $32.00. ISBN 9780800698188.

Brian J. Robinson, Fuller Theological Seminary, Pasadena, California

Readers familiar with the work of Joseph A. Marchal know him to be insightful, creative, and often provocative. In *Studying Paul's Letters: Contemporary Perspectives and Methods*, Marchal lives up to this reputation by bringing together ten respected scholars in order to identify the presence and effect of ideologies within the Pauline corpus and Greco-Roman world as well as how contemporary ideologies influence the reader. The contributors do not simply present introductory material but guide both novice readers and seasoned scholars to examine the presuppositions and tendencies that inform their own choice of methodology and, in turn, shape how they read and appropriate Paul's letters (6). To this end, the chapters do not pit the various methods against one another, nor do they represent exhaustive treatments of each method. Rather, they are a "good faith" effort to demonstrate how each method illuminates different aspects of the text and also of readers as they engage the text (10–11). Marchal hopes that, by foregrounding discussions of method and why readers approach the text the way they do, readers will "become more accountable not only for their perspective or approach but also for the results" (8). This concern for accountability, or understanding the ethical implications of how one reads Paul's letters, is one of the book's most provocative and important contributions. It also lays bare the question of why one reads Paul's letters and the influence that motivation has on the reading process.

In the opening chapter, "Historical Approaches: Which Past? Whose Past?" Melanie Johnson-Debaufre explores ways in which tradition influences how a reader constructs history and how that history then shapes the interpretation of Paul's letters (14–15). For example, readers within the Christian tradition have often anachronistically read 1 Thessalonians as if Paul were a "Christian" who stood outside the Jewish tradition; this reading has more to do with contemporary frameworks than it does with evidence from Thessalonians or first-century Thessalonica (23–29). This chapter plays a crucial role in the book's overall project because it problematizes the objectivity of historical criticism, which can create the illusion of neutralizing the influence of the reader's perspective. Only after a reader has let go of "objective" interpretations can one be honest about the influence of one's own perspective.

The next four chapters engage topics more familiar from introductions to method, yet each chapter moves beyond obvious points of contact with the text. For example, the chapter on economics discusses not only instances where Paul explicitly mentions money but also texts that reveal the underlying, often unstated, social structures that reinforce economic practices. At times these chapters also address how the application of the methods reveals aspects of the reader's perspective and how that influences the conclusions drawn from the text. Todd Penner's and Davina C. Lopez's "Rhetorical Approaches: Introducing the Art of Persuasion" focuses not on the obvious rhetorical features of Paul's arguments but on "moving beyond surface appearances of textual rhetoric" in order to uncover how texts can reinscribe ideologies through subtle uses of language and cultural codes (46). Penner and Lopez also address the ethical implications of uncritically adopting arguments and concepts found in a text because these argument and concepts often bring forward assumptions about people and society that are no longer appropriate (42).

In a similar vein, Laura S. Nasrallah, in "Spatial Perspectives: Space and Archeology in Roman Philippi," argues that ideology shapes and is reinforced by how a society organizes people in physical spaces (56–58). So as Paul exhorts the Philippians to mimic Christ, who voluntarily moves between the forms of God and a slave, he simultaneously confronts the ideologies and physical spaces of Roman Philippi, which keep the higher social groups separate from the most oppressed (68–69).

Likewise, Peter Oakes, in "Economic Approaches: Scarce Resources," not only provides a general introduction to how texts provide information about the diverse economic situations within a community but also discusses how economics shape a society through the allocation of resources (77–81). He then applies this understanding to argue that the commands in Rom 12 evidence a social structure that focuses resources toward those who represent the lower socioeconomic positions instead of the head of the household, which would have been the norm in Greco-Roman society (85–88).

In "Visual Perspectives: Imag(ing) the Big Pauline Picture," Davina C. Lopez argues that images should not only be used to confirm concepts already identified from texts but also allowed to raise their own questions and present their own perspectives on reality (100–101). The decision by some readers to favor texts demonstrates a preference that skews the way those texts are read by controlling the background against which they are understood (104). Lopez leverages this control of background to show that even establishing the background against which a text is read is a choice motivated by the reader, not the text, and has ethical consequences (113–14).

The final six chapters model how foregrounding perspective can produce startling new insights from familiar texts. Cynthia Briggs Kittredge, in "Feminist Approaches: Rethinking History and Resisting Ideologies," begins with a lucid discussion of the historical reconstruction undertaken by first- and second-wave feminist criticism (120–25). She then applies ideological criticism to demonstrate how the language of freedom in Rom 8:14–39 simultaneously transcends and reinscribes kyriarchal structures that undermine the very freedom and equality the passage espouses (125–31). Kittredge's chapter also includes a brief treatment of ideological criticism that addresses the interplay between language and power that is foundational for every chapter in the book (125–27).

Pamela Eisenbaum's "Jewish Perspectives: A Jewish Apostle to the Gentiles" argues that, by adopting a post-Holocaust perspective, one can uncover anti-Semitic assumptions in interpretations of Paul's letters. This allows her to reread Paul as offering salvation through Christ only to Gentiles without questioning the efficacy of the Jewish covenants. Her discussion offers not only a forceful presentation of the "radical new perspective" (136-40) but also a concise treatment of Paul's "apocalyptic orientation," which lends considerable support to her argument (141).

Likewise, in "African American Approaches: Rehumanizing the Reader against Racism and Reading through Experience," Demetrius K. Williams addresses how assumptions about slavery reinforce reading Onesimus as Philemon's slave. Williams begins by describing how early African American readings of the Bible self-consciously adopted an interpretive strategy that rehumanized the African American community in opposition to the dehumanizing narratives presented by society (157–59). This part of Williams's chapter essentially provides a historical precedent for the type of interpretive accountability Marchal hopes the entire volume will engender. Williams goes on to argue that incorporating experiences is valid and necessary for interpretation, since traditional readings are themselves informed by the experiences of previous interpreters. To demonstrate this point, Williams uses Allen D. Callahan's rereading of the relationship between

Onesimus and Philemon, which showed that reading Onesimus as Philemon's runaway slave was equally based on the interpreter's experience and assumptions.

Sze-Kar Wan, in "Asain American Perspectives: Ambivalence of the Model Minority and Perpetual Foreigner," takes a slightly different approach by finding a "prototype" for the Asian American experience in the dynamics between Paul and the Jerusalem church. Wan discusses how some Asian Americans adopted a stance of ambivalence, simultaneously rejecting the dominant culture while also seeking inclusion within it, to their role as a model minority. He then argues that Galatians presents Paul in a similar tension with the apostles in Jerusalem as he attempts to validate his ministry to Gentiles.

The final two chapters adopt perspectives that are more theoretical and are therefore able to provide important discussions about the interplay between language and perception. Jeremy Punt, in "Postcolonial Approaches: Negotiating Empires Then and Now," provides an excellent introduction to postcolonial criticism that describes the way marginalized groups respond to the ideological narratives of empires through various forms of resistance and adoption (191–97). Punt then applies this dynamic to 1 Thessalonians to show how Paul's language both undermines Caesar's claims to authority while simultaneously adopting imperial strategies to assert his own authority over the community in Thessalonica (199–205). One of the chapter's most important contributions to the volume is Punt's demonstrations that contemporary readers need not choose between abandoning Paul's writing because he reinscribes oppressive imperial narratives or uncritically adopting those narratives. Instead, Punt provides the reader a way to understand how Paul's language functioned in a particular context and points toward how contemporary readers can more critically accept or reject various parts of Paul's arguments.

The final chapter, Marchal's "Queer Approaches: Improper Relations with Pauline Letters," focuses on the instability, or queerness, in Paul's writing and how it provides readers a way to renegotiate some of the troubling uses of biblical language and arguments already highlighted throughout the previous chapters. Marchal reviews the historical-contextual approach and the apologist-affirmative approaches that represent two standard means of countering arguments that use Scripture to affirm heteronormativity (214–17). Although acknowledging their value, Marchal argues that these arguments both fall into the trap of attempting to normalize, or naturalize, performative aspects of identity that, by their very nature, are continually being reappraised and relabeled. Undermining the idea of normalization represents Marchal's goal in order to make the reader more accountable for how she or he reads and applies the text (218, 224).

The authors of this volume should be lauded not only for the depth and clarity of their contributions but also for their seeking to represent a model for biblical studies on the other side of historical criticism. There are, however, a few questions I wish to pose in the hopes of sharpening the project as a whole. On a structural level, I wonder why Marchal's chapter comes last. His work most clearly embodies the book's stated focus on deconstructing normalizing readings and demonstrating the ethical implications of particular readings. Although the volume coheres, the difference between Marchal's chapter and introduction and the rest of the chapters is palpable. This tension is exactly what the volume is meant to address, but I wonder if it would be profitable to use Marchal's chapter as a framework for the book as a whole instead of just another perspective among many. Also, although Eisenbaum presents a solid articulation of the "radical new perspective" as set against a "Lutheran" reading of Paul, I wonder if her chapter would be more illuminating if she had set her reading alongside other readings from the new perspective that attempt to take Paul's Judaism seriously but still understand Jews as requiring salvation through Christ (e.g., Wright, Gaventa, Dunn). In fact, her chapter does not mention these arguments at all, and there are no references to them in her bibliography. The effect is that her chapter appears to present the "correct" reading of Paul, which stands in some tension with the approach of the volume as a whole. Finally, although the chapter on rhetoric by Penner and Lopez addresses the presence and power of ideologies, their discussion does not mention rhetorical approaches that utilize ancient forms of rhetoric such as those by Stanley K. Stowers or Robert Jewett. Granted, attempting to survey the vast array of rhetorical approaches would require its own volume, but if these chapters are meant to introduce students to the field of Pauline scholarship, then it deserves a mention.

Studying Paul's Letters not only offers useful introductions to some of the most important developments and methods within Pauline studies; it also succeeds in creating a space for students and scholars to examine carefully how ideology not only shaped the production of these texts but also guides how they are currently read. Some of its assumptions about the nature and function of language and Scripture may not be accepted by each reader, but that should not prevent the volume from being a useful resource in studying and teaching the Pauline corpus.

The Authentic Letters of Paul: A New Reading of Paul's Rhetoric and Meaning, by Arthur J. Dewey, Roy W. Hoover, Lane C. McGaughy, and Daryl D. Schmidt. Salem, Ore.: Polebridge, 2010. Pp. xvi + 270. Paper. $27. ISBN 9781598150193.

Nijay K. Gupta, Northeastern Seminary, Rochester, New York

The Authentic Letters of Paul is a new translation of the undisputed letters of Paul with some additional introductory, explanatory, and reference material. This translation is called the "Scholars Version Paul" (SVP) by the editors. As the introduction makes clear, the purpose of the new translation is to recover the "voiceprint of Paul" that has been lost over the years and has been "distorted by the cacophony of later voices that have attempted to speak in his name" (1). What the cohort of translators has agreed to do in this work is to decanonize Paul, so to speak, and allow him to be read, known, and understood on his own terms within his sociohistorical context. Thus, three important choices were made in the re-presentation of the writings of Paul. First, the "authentic" writings were separated from those deemed pseudonymous. Second, the authentic letters were arranged according to the historical progression of their authorship (1 Thessalonians as the hypothetical initial extant correspondence). Third, the translators present the letters, where necessary, in their "fragmentary condition" (see xi).

The SVP itself aims at a "dynamic equivalent translation" conformed to North American English. In their own words:

> We have not attempted to create a new Paul. Rather, we have tried to translate Paul dynamically. We do not present a literal, wooden rendering. We aim to express what Paul meant in clear North American English. We have sought a dynamic equivalence of Greek to English in order to communicate the meaning Paul wanted to convey (6).

In order to get a flavor for this translation, it may be useful to read two familiar Pauline texts in the SVP:

> Paul, slave of God's Anointed, Jesus—summoned as an envoy [and] appointed to announce God's world-changing news, which was anticipated by the prophets in holy scriptures. This news is about the "son of God"—who was physically descended from David, appointed and empowered as "son of God," in accordance with the spirit of holiness, from the time of his resurrection from the dead—Jesus, the Anointed, our lord. Through him I have received the gracious favor of my calling to promote in his name the obedience that comes from a confident reliance upon God among all the world's nations. (Rom 1:1–5)

> I appeal to all of you to think in the same way that the Anointed Jesus did, who
> Although he was born in the image of God,
> did not regard "being like God"
> as something to use for his own advantage,
> but rid himself of such vain pretension
> and accepted a servant's lot.
> Since he was born like all human beings
> and proved to belong to humankind,
> he recognized his true status
> and became trustfully obedient all the way to death,
> even to death by crucifixion.
> That is why God raised him higher than anyone
> and awarded him the title that is above all others,
> So that on hearing the name "Jesus,"
> every knee should bend,
> above the earth, on the earth, and under the earth,
> and every tongue declare: "Jesus the Anointed is lord!"
> to the majestic honor of God, our great Benefactor. (Phil 2:5–11)

Given the translational approach attempted by the committee here, their word and phrase choices are often appealing and illuminating. For example, calling Paul an "envoy" (*apostolos*) is a very reasonable interpretation and substitution for "apostle." Similarly, calling the *euangelion* of God his "world-changing news" is a sensible gloss that carries the essential meaning, drawing out not simply its personal orientation (with a view toward individual conversion) but the cosmological and communal aspects as well. "Christ" becomes "the Anointed," translating the term in light of its original meaning, rather than a name only. Perhaps one of the more noticeable translational choices was the rendering of *pater* as "Benefactor," no doubt an attempt to communicate the social dimension of the value of this word in light of Paul's Greco-Roman context. Another observable choice: *ethnē* is translated as "nations," never as "Gentiles."

As a *translation*, the SVP offers a nice, fresh English translation of the letters the editors wished to publish. Most of the word and phrase choices of the committee demonstrate careful thought and consideration. However, sometimes it seems that the choices were driven more by their own theology than a straightforward translation. For example, *ta einai isa theo* (Phil 2:3) is translated as "being like God," which does not seem to be a sensible representation of *isa*. Even if one were disinclined to support a reading that made Paul's Jesus "equal" to God (as in most translations), retaining the "equality" language would still fit with an anti-imperial reading where some emperors claimed *isotheos*—equality with God (see Plato, *Republic* 360c).

At other times the translation can be found to be inconsistent. For example, sometimes *pater* is translated as "Creator and Benefactor" (1 Thess 1:1; Gal 1:1; 1 Cor 1:1; 2 Cor 1:1), with Philemon *pater* (for God) is translated lowercase "creator and benefactor" (3), and in Philippians *pater* is translated as "our great Benefactor" (with no reference to "Creator"; Phil 1:2; so also Rom 1:7). Was this intentional? Was it a "consistency-check" problem? Another concern I have with *not* translating *pater* as "father" (in reference to God) is the challenge readers would have connecting the "sonship" of Jesus to God the *pater* in Paul's thought. This is quite clear in Greek but would be opaque in the SVP. The Pauline use of kinship language is a prominent feature of his writings. Even the SVP (wisely) retains the fictive kinship language in Rom 8:29: "God provided for those who are called, and God decided in advance that they would take on the form of God's "son", so that he would be "the first" among many brothers and sister." (I am not sure why the SVP regularly puts sonship language for Jesus in quotes, since I would assume readers would not need a special signal that this is unique language.) If the SVP preserves this familial dimension of Paul's communal rhetoric, I cannot comprehend why they would choose to render *adelphos* as "friends" (so, e.g., 1 Thess 1:4; 4:1; Gal 3:15; 5:13; 6:18; Phil 3:1; Rom 1:13; 7:1).

While this is a problem for translations in general that aim for maximum comprehension or "readability," this raises a serious question about when a translation goes too far in breaking down biblical language that should be treated as irreducible. For example, this is relevant to the SVP regarding the Pauline language of sin (*hamartia* and its cognates). Can Paul's concept of all people "under sin" (*hyph' hamartian einai*) be adequately conveyed by saying all people are "prone to wrongdoing" (SVP Rom 3:9)? Or can "sin" (*hamartia*) be sufficiently described as or limited to "the corrupting seduction of power" (SVP Rom 5:12)? Or the "law of sin" as "being ruled by seductive corruption" (SVP Rom 8:2)? The SVP takes an entirely different angle when translating 2 Cor 5:21 (NRSV: "For our sake he made him to be sin who knew no sin, so that in him we might become the righteousness of God"): "[It's as if] God took him, a coin in mint condition, and treated him as if he were [a] coin that has lost its value for our benefit so that through him we might be recast into the coinage of God's integrity" (SVP). Here the concept of "sin" is understood in terms of loss of value. Is that sufficient to convey how Paul understood the work of Christ with regard to the problem of *hamartia*?

The same problem exists with holiness language in the SVP. In 1 Cor 1:30, *hagiasmos* is translated "integrity" (NRSV "holiness"). However, the translators accept the use of the language of "consecrated" when it comes to *hagiazo* in 1 Cor 7:14. At the end of the epistle there is no "holy kiss," but the request that believers "should embrace one another" (16:20). Can Paul's holiness language be dispensed with in this way and still present "the authentic Paul"?

Once one removes key Pauline theological platforms such as the "fatherhood" of God (which goes with the "sonship" of Jesus), the siblingship of the Pauline community members, and the holiness language of identity, ethos, ethics, and spiritual experience, then translations such as we find with the SVP begin to feel unmoored from Paul's Jewish heritage and context.

Now I want to address two ideological concerns of this new translation of Paul. First, I wish to examine the project's desire to (re)capture the real Paul. While it is somewhat subtle in the introduction, the work as a whole implies that traditional translations obscure and burden the real Paul with ecclesial teachings, doctrinal jargon, and theological embellishment. However, their own "new" approach brings to my mind the same concerns that Jesus scholars have inherited from Schweizer: recognition that the temptation is almost overwhelming to mold Jesus (or Paul, in our case) into one's own desired image. I found this concern come to the forefront in the SVP's detection of interpolations. For example, it is no wonder Colossians and Ephesians are not acceptably "authentic" if the SVP treats Rom 13:1–7 as an interpolation (see 252). Similarly, it is easy to treat 1 Cor 14:33b–38 as an interpolation (*with* text-critical evidence) if 1 Cor 11:2–16 is also considered an interpolation (with *no* extant text-critical evidence). The SVP approach appears to have a kind of circular reasoning. The SVP determines what appears authentically Pauline, cuts out what does not, and then uses that retained material to further refine what is genuine. Leaving the interpolations *in* would apparently seem to make for too complex and contradictory of a person. However, I had hoped the long and winding history of Jesus studies would have proven that real people in history are very complex. A few years back I co-wrote an article with a colleague. Our "voiceprints" were not consecutive but interwoven. Now, just a handful of years later, I could not go back through our article and pull out my own contributions. It surprises me, then, that the SVP can detect interpolations (in most cases with no external evidence) so deftly.

Second, I wish to address the matter of how the SVP partitions the authentic and inauthentic letters. While the SVP does acknowledge that the methodological issues in determining authenticity are challenging, they take a "structure" approach, allowing those letters that follow "Paul's unique changes to the conventional form of personal letters" as genuine. However, this approach does not take into consideration Paul's use of a letter-secretary, or the possibility of a co-worker writing the letter or writing with his genuine authorization (as many scholars believe to be true regarding Timothy's association with Colossians, for example). A rigid "structure"-based approach may seem "objective," but, again, one can hardly think Paul felt constricted by his own approach to letter-writing as demonstrated in 1 Thessalonians or Romans. After all, not only did he already adapt the traditional letter form in many ways (as the SVP acknowledges), but he even did so along the way as demonstrated in Galatians' missing introductory thanksgiving.

It has been said, and I concur, that translation of New Testament texts should happen freshly as readers are born into new contexts. In many ways, the SVP offers a satisfying rethinking of how to express concepts in Paul's undisputed letters. I welcome many of these efforts and commend the editors for their careful thought. However, if I were able to consult with them along the way, I would have pressed for (1) more consistency in their translation across these letters, (2) the retention of key Pauline concepts and vocabulary (especially regarding kinship and holiness), and (3) a more thorough and balanced argument for why these letters in particular represent Paul in the most genuine manner.

From Typology to Doxology: Paul's Use of Isaiah and Job in Romans 11:34–35, by Andrew David Naselli. Eugene, Ore.: Pickwick, 2012. Pp. xii + 201. Paper. $24.00. ISBN 9781610977692.

Robert Foster, Madonna University, Livonia, Michigan

The topic of what used to be called "the New Testament interpretation of the Old Testament" has of late become increasingly specialized. Entries in this genre rarely attempt to span the entire New Testament corpus but often limit themselves to single authors or even specific passages. The advantage of this approach is that it permits focused, intensive investigation of problematic or interesting passages. Andrew David Naselli's *From Typology to Doxology* provides a clear example of this development, focusing on the appearance of Isa 40:13 and Job 41:3 in Rom 11:34–35. The book was originally a dissertation completed under D. A. Carson of Trinity Evangelical Divinity School.

In the first chapter Naselli points out that, despite a flood of literature on biblical interpretation in the New Testament, Rom 11:34–35 has been unjustly overlooked. He aims to remedy this situation by providing a comprehensive examination of the passage and its scriptural precedents.

Chapters 2–4 place Rom 11:34–35, Isa 40:13, and Job 41:3 in their respective contexts, which for Naselli means the canonical books in which they appear. In each case he examines the unifying theme (whose existence he never doubts), the immediate literary context, and, finally, the relevant verses themselves. He argues that the main theme of Romans is "the gospel in its salvation historical context for Jews and Gentiles" (11). Chapters 9–11 vindicate God's righteousness by demonstrating that "God has kept and will keep his covenantal promises to Israel" (13). These chapters conclude with the doxology in 11:33–36. Naselli demonstrates that it is carefully crafted, showing no evidence of independent existence prior to Paul's authorship of these verses. His analysis of the passage is sensible and convincing.

Turning to the Old Testament, he summarizes the message of Isaiah as, "People should trust the Holy One of Israel because he is the incomparable King and Savior." The argument of chapter 40 is that God both desires and is able to comfort his people in exile and that his people should trust him to do so (51, 53, 54). Verse 13 asserts that no one gives God advice, thereby underscoring his unrivaled wisdom (62).

"Trust" also features in the theme of Job, which Naselli states as, "People should respond to innocent, unexplained suffering by trusting God because he is supremely wise, sovereign, just, and good" (77). The book's climax occurs in the theophany of 38:1–42:6, significant for its theological principles (e.g., God is too small in Job's eyes [84]). The text quoted by Paul, 42:2–3, provides a lesson on humility and divine ownership (88–89).

In chapter 5 Naselli takes up textual issues. He is probably correct that the questions arising here do not bear on his conclusions with respect to Rom 11. However, a few things should be noted. The antiquity and unity of the Masoretic Text is presupposed throughout, a surprising assumption given current scholarship. Further, there is no indication that the Göttingen volumes of the Septuagint were consulted.

From here the investigation moves to the relevant uses of Isa 40:13 and Job 41:3 in Jewish literature. Naselli finds some interesting parallels but concludes that the results show only some similarities and differences between Paul and other interpreters.

With chapter 7 Naselli arrives at the heart of his study. In it he presents his understanding of Paul's warrant for using Isa 40:13 and Job 41:3. From a variety of possible rationales (he lays out ten), Naselli selects two that are mutually reinforcing. First, Paul interprets these passages *canonically*, meaning that they are interpreted in light of the entire canon as the ultimate literary context. Further, he interprets them *typologically*, meaning that New Testament persons, events, and institutions repeat with greater profundity an Old Testament model. According to Naselli, Paul does not merely actualize language from Isa 40:13 and Job 41:3 because they were for his contemporaries a recognizable and religiously potent way to evoke God's infinite wisdom. Instead, Paul goes beyond this to develop a salvation-historical argument that brings into Romans the redemptive themes that are latent in the antecedent verses and determined by their contextual relations as components of both a discrete biblical book and a complete biblical canon.

Naselli justifies this typological connection by positing a sevenfold pattern shared by Isaiah, Job, and Romans. He argues that Isa 40 and Rom 11 (and, mutatis mutandis, Job) presuppose the following sequence of events: (1) Israel has experienced God's blessing; (2) God strips Israel of this blessing; restoration seems impossible; (3) Israel questions God's righteousness; (4) Israel receives a difficult revelation that does not provide all the desired answers but indicates the prominent role of Gentiles; (5) Israel must repent of its flawed view of God and trust him; (6) Israel will experience a restored and even greater relationship with God in an unexpected way; (7) this salvific plan shows God's wisdom, kindness, and severity (133). (Additional though minor parallels buttress the case.) Therefore, Naselli concludes, Rom 11 typologically fulfills Isa 40 "by repeating the Old Testament situation at a deeper, climactic level in salvation history" (134).

Chapter 8 assesses "Paul's Theological Use of Isa 40:13 and Job 41:3a in Rom 11:34–35." Despite this title, the chapter focuses on Naselli's theological interpretation of his text for contemporary believers. A concluding chapter summarizes the book. There follows a full bibliography but no index.

As an argument that Rom 11:34–35 gains depth from the themes present in Isaiah and Job, this book is a success. The rich texture of Paul's closing doxology incorporates theological threads that Naselli identifies in the precursor texts: God is transcendent; he answers to no one; humanity's proper response is humble praise. Isaiah and Job evoke the paradox of God's self–revelation and transcendence in powerful ways, and the rhetorical effect of Rom 11:34–35 increases profoundly when this is realized. Furthermore, throughout the book the secondary sources are thoroughly researched and the argument clearly written.

Unfortunately, Naselli sets the bar too high for himself and comes up short. He repeatedly argues *not* that the immediate context of Isa 40:13 and Job 41:3 will enrich our understanding of Rom 11 but that the full context of the entire book of Isaiah and the full context of the entire book of Job are *necessary* for understanding the references in Rom 11:34–35 (39, 61–62, 63, 87, 89). He claims to demonstrate that Paul interprets Isaiah and Job canonically (!) and typologically in a very precise sense, so that the pattern of divine interaction with and through Isaiah and Job are climatically fulfilled in Paul's own day. This much stronger thesis encounters two significant obstacles.

First, many of the supposed connections work because of their relatively high level of abstraction. For example, Naselli claims that in both Isa 40 and Rom 11 God's revelation includes "the prominent role of Gentiles with reference to Israelites" (132–33). What does this mean? That Isa 40 and Rom 11 present analogous ways in which Israel and the Gentiles interact, such that the relationship in Isa 40 anticipates their interconnection in Rom 11 as type to antitype? But in Isa 40 the Gentiles are vain nothings (vv. 15–17), idolaters (implied in vv. 18–20) whose leaders will be scotched in a single day (vv. 23–24). How does this relate to the salvation-through-jealousy program of Rom 11:11–24, which if it has any scriptural antecedent derives from Deuteronomy rather than Isaiah? Based on what Naselli asserts elsewhere, he may want to respond that the proper context for interpreting Isa 40 is the entire book of Isaiah. But this requires an argument, and none is provided. Without one, why interpret Isa 40 in light of the positive portrayal of Gentile salvation in, for example, Isa 2, or the Servant Songs—both still a far cry from Rom 11—rather than, say, "They shall lick the dust of your feet ... and I will make your oppressors eat their own flesh" (Isa 49:23, 26)? When the texts are read closely, the typological connection becomes strained.

This imprecision points to a second reason why Naselli's argument is not as strong as it might be: it lacks focus. Naselli explicitly demurs from offering a guiding thesis (2 n. 3), and the effects of this decision are significant.

Chapter 3, "Isaiah 40:13 in Context," presents a tour of the entire book of Isaiah, identifying theological themes that summarize all sixty-six chapters. Although Naselli narrows the discussion down to Isa 40 and finally 40:13, he leaves the reader wondering where exactly all of this fits into Rom 11:34–35. Naselli provides only the assurance that when Paul quotes a single verse, he presupposes the entire book (61–62). This astounding claim is never justified. The actual argument for the typological analogy between Isa 40 and Rom 11 in chapter 7 does not help. There is almost no overlap between "the theme of Isaiah" or "the argument of Isa 40" in chapter 3 and the seven-stage sequence of events supposedly demonstrating the typology in chapter 7. I wonder if a clear thesis that controlled the contents of each chapter might not have tightened the argument at this point.

The situation is the similar with Job. Naselli repeats his claim that the reference to a single verse invokes the entire book (89–90). Even if established, this claim does not explain the need for an eight-page summary of the entire drama— presented as an in-character paraphrase (64–72)—or an extended discussion of the identity of Leviathan (81–83), who does not reappear in the analysis of Rom 11:34–35.

Except for Naselli's statement that his monograph unfolds as he wrote it, it is difficult to understand why these issues should eclipse more urgent ones: What evidence suggests that Paul reads Isaiah or Job as discrete books in their entirety? What evidence suggests that he reads discrete scriptural books *canonically*? Why suppose that when Paul refers to a specific verse he evokes entire books, and if so, how do we know that he evokes the themes abstracted by Naselli? Does the argument establish only the effect of the Old Testament on Paul's understanding of salvation history, or does it reveal a scriptural interpretation that functions at the communicative level of the epistolary rhetoric? If the latter (implied on p. 141 but not argued for), how could Paul's audience have tracked his meaning? Without a thesis-driven argument, marginal topics garner prolonged attention while substantive methodological problems are sidestepped.

The challenge of interpreting how Paul read, reflected on, performed, and deployed the Scriptures of Israel continues to demand ever-more specialized attention from scholars. Naselli's contribution reflects the necessary depth of investigation now required to advance our understanding of the dialogue occurring between Paul and his forbearers. When read according to its accomplishments rather than its more ambitious goals, it shows that Isaiah, Job, and Paul share not a typological connection but a theological vision: God is God; we are not.

Individual and Community in Paul's Letter to the Romans, by Ben C. Dunson. Wissenschaftliche Untersuchungen zum Neuen Testament 2/332. Tübingen: Mohr Siebeck, 2012. Pp. xii + 217. Paper. €59.00. ISBN 9783161520570.

Jason Weaver, Catholic University of America,Chicago, Illinois

Dunson's enlightening monograph on the individual and community in Paul's letter to the Romans highlights the necessity of a critical examination of the individual in Paul's letters and how the individual exists with regard to community. Dunson proposes that much of the recent scholarship regarding Pauline theology disregards the role of the individual and instead focuses on the concern for communities in Paul's thought. He believes that this blatant disregard of the individual has been detrimental to understanding Pauline theology as well as to understanding Pauline community. The purpose of this monograph is to show how the individual and the community belong together in Paul's theology. For Paul there is no individual outside of community, and there can be no community without the individuals who form it.

In order to defend his point that the individual and community in Paul are interrelated, Dunson begins by examining the shift in Pauline scholarship from an individual focus to a communal focus. He then examines the debate concerning the individual in the writings of Bultmann and Käsemann. In order to exemplify the understanding of the individual in Paul's time, he then examines the discourses of Epictetus. Dunson then proceeds with a typology of the individual in Paul's letter to the Romans. Finally, he attempts to synthesize his understanding of the individual and community in Paul's thinking.

In chapter 1 Dunson addresses the shift in the interpretation of Paul's letters from a focus on the individual to a concern for the communities. He argues that within recent scholarship the argument is made that Paul has no conception of the individual whatsoever. Dunson highlights three strands of scholarship that challenge the traditional individual approach: social-scientific anti-individualism, anti-individualism in the wake of the New Perspective, and apocalyptic anti-individualism. All three of the these strands of scholarship focus on the community in which the individual plays very little to no role as the central point of Paul's thinking. The overall argument of his book is to show that the antithesis of the individual and community in Paul's letters is unwarranted. Dunson proposes that some scholars suggest that any discussion of the individual is too modern. However, through his examination of one of Paul's contemporaries, Epictetus, Dunson shows that this claim is not accurate.

Dunson proceeds to examine the debate between Bultmann and Käsemann in chapter 2. His examination of these two preeminent scholars is both thorough

and critical. In this chapter he successfully examines the theological and hermeneutical constraints that lead each scholar to arrive at his conclusions regarding
Pauline theology. For Bultmann the starting point is anthropology; for Käsemann
it is cosmology. Dunson rightfully points out that the result of Käsemann's debate
with his former teacher is the shift in Pauline scholarship away from the individual as a key element in Paul's thought.

Chapter 3 is a crucial part to Dunson's overall thesis. Here he looks at the discourses of Epictetus to see if the general scholarly apprehension toward speaking
about the individual in Paul's letters is warranted. Contrary to much of scholarship, Dunson's point is that the individual does play a key role in Paul's thinking,
and he is critical of scholarship that claims that any thought toward the individual
is too modern. His examination of a Pauline contemporary sheds light on the fact
that thinkers in the first-century world had a sense of the individual. He presents
how the entirety of Epictetus's ethical discourse is focused primarily on the individual. This does not, however, discount communal responsibility. Dunson clearly
shows how, according to Epictetus, social relations are dictated by one's self-pres-
ervation. His examination of Epictetus correctly demonstrates that the individual
and the communal are not antithetical in the minds of first-century thinkers.

Dunson gets to the heart of his discussion of the individual and community
in chapters 4 and 5. In them he outlines a typology of the Pauline individual in
Romans. His purpose is to counter the argument that within Pauline literature
there is only one understanding of the individual. Instead, he argues that there
are many "individuals" within the Pauline corpus. In identifying the individual
in Romans, Dunson will also address how the individual fits within Paul's communal framework. His point is that communal concerns help shape how Paul
understands the individual.

Dunson begins constructing his typology of Pauline individuals in chapter 4
by outlining the first four types of individuals found in Paul's letter to the Romans.
First is the "characteristic" individual identified by a belief in soteriological privilege based on covenantal protection. Second is the "generic" individual. Paul's
purpose in using this individual is to highlight that there is no covenantal privilege,
in order to generalize the human condition. Third is the "binary" individual. This
individual, according to Dunson, "captures the remnants of Paul's main ways of
ordering the universe according to an oppositional system of classification" (128).
Finally, Dunson remarks on the "exemplary" individual, identified in Romans as
Abraham. Dunson is correct in suggesting that the individual shapes Paul's vision.
Therefore, in order to understand the Pauline letters, one must understand the
Pauline individuals.

Dunson turns to the second part of his typology in chapter 5. What separates
this chapter from chapter 4 is that Dunson now identifies where the communal
element becomes prominent. Here he astutely discusses how the individual is situated within the community. Again, he addresses four types of individuals. First
is the "representative" individual, whom he identifies as Adam and Christ. Second
is the "negative exemplary" individual for whom Paul uses himself as the model.

This individual presents a negative example to be avoided. Third is the "somatic" individual. Here Dunson reaches the most crucial part of his thesis (166–71). It is also here that he is the most successful. The "somatic" individual is the individual within the body (see Rom 12:1). Dunson rightly suggests that for Paul there is a melding of the individual and the community. His most crucial point comes when he states, *"There is no Pauline individual who is not also a somatic, or bodily integrated, individual, just as there is no body without individual members"* (169). His entire examination of the individual and community in Romans builds to this point, and it is clear from his presentation that both the individual and community are crucial elements of Pauline theology. The final type is the "particular" individual marked by the real flesh-and-blood persons mentioned in Rom 16.

Chapter 6 serves as a synthesis of what Dunson has presented in this monograph. He points to the fact that his purpose is to show that an integration of individual and community is not foreign to Paul. He uses the final chapter to highlight differences between Epictetus and Paul. However, he is correct in noting that, although there are contrasts, the examination of Epictetus is vital for an understanding of how Paul would have understood the individual.

Dunson states in chapter 6 that his work seeks to "explicate the necessary relationship between Pauline individuals and community, and in so doing to provide resources for a theological understanding of the relation between the individual and community in the broader Pauline corpus" (180). His work succeeds in its purpose. Dunson's fresh perspective on the individual in the Pauline corpus is a much-needed reexamination of the individual in Paul. His thesis and methodology are clear and well executed. Many of his critical points are thoroughly defended and bring attention to the need to reexamine long-held beliefs regarding Pauline theology with regard to the individual. In his thoughtful examination of the discourses of Epictetus he correctly highlights the need for Pauline scholars to examine Paul with his contemporaries. Overall, scholars will benefit from Dunson's approach and methodology.

Some scholars may question whether his selective typology overlooks elements that may take away from his thesis. It may also be possible to argue that this is not how the Pauline individual is represented in the entirety of the Pauline corpus. Although it would require a much lengthier monograph, the reader is left to ponder if we can apply this typology to the broader Pauline corpus. Is this how Paul understands the individual and community throughout? One small critique regarding Dunson's typology is whether or not the discussions regarding the "binary" individual and "particular" individual are necessary. I understand Dunson's desire to be as thorough as possible in his discussion of the Pauline individual. However, I am not convinced that these discussions add to his overall thesis. Ben Dunson's work is an excellent addition to the field of Pauline theology. His critiques require that Pauline scholarship reevaluate the way we have understood the individual and the community in Paul.

Jews, Gentiles, and the Opponents of Paul: The Pauline Letters, by B. J. Oropeza. Apostasy in the New Testament Communities 2. Eugene, Ore.: Cascade, 2012. Pp. xviii + 405. Paper. $47.00. ISBN 9781610972901.

Joseph Oryshak, York University, Toronto, Ontario, Canada

This book represents the second of a three-volume series regarding apostasy within New Testament communities. In particular, this volume focuses on apostasy within the Pauline letters. Within the introduction Oropeza defines apostasy as "a phenomena that occurs when a religious follower or group turns away from, or otherwise repudiates, the central beliefs and practices they once embraced in a respective religious community"(1). The purpose of this volume is to offer a better understanding of the nature and consequence of apostasy among Pauline Christians and those who interacted with them (ix, 1).

Chapter 1 (3–36) is an analysis of Galatians. In this chapter Oropeza tackles the issue of whether Paul was a Jewish apostate (4–9) and the nature of the opponents working against him in Galatia (9–32). In regard to Paul's self-identity, Oropeza concludes that it is likely that Paul was perceived as an apostate by mainstream Jewish communities (5–7). Nevertheless, he also notes that Paul saw himself as continuing the mission of the Isaianic Servant (Christ), thus placing himself firmly within Judaism (7–9). In the second section of this chapter, Oropeza categorizes Paul's Galatian opponents as Jewish-Christians who insisted on Torah observance for all Gentile converts (15). In addition, he asserts that Paul believed that following these opponents would lead to apostasy because their gospel nullified the redemptive work of Jesus' death, leading to a fall from grace and loss of salvation (28, 30–31, 33).

Chapter 2 (36–65) examines Paul's correspondence with the Thessalonians. Oropeza begins this chapter by dating both letters to 51 CE and argues for authentic Pauline authorship of 2 Thessalonians (37). Since Oropeza believes that both epistles were likely written a few months apart from each other, he reads both together as addressing the same situation in Thessalonica (37). This chapter shows that this community was largely made up of Gentiles (40) and that Paul feared that outsider societal pressure (39–45) and vice (46–54) might lead members within this group to commit apostasy. This chapter concludes with a discussion of Paul warning the Thessalonians of Christian apostates who would appear during the eschaton (54–58) and the observation that Paul's main concern was to insulate his community from vice, which, if unchecked, leads to apostasy (64–65).

Chapter 3 (66–111) discusses 1 Corinthians. In providing context, Oropeza notes that this group was primarily made up of Gentile converts (67) and that the major issues facing them were factionalism (66–72, 88–102) and immoral conduct (73–88). In addition, this chapter asserts that Paul argued against the Corinthian concept of a spiritual resurrection and urged them to stay loyal to his gospel, or else they would jeopardize their eschatological salvation (105–8). Oropeza also notes that the Pauline concept of "election" is corporate and that, although the Corinthian community would receive salvation, an individual could lose "elect" status through his or her conduct (72–73). Lastly, it is observed that those who cause others to commit apostasy will be punished as apostates themselves (73–76).

Chapter 4 (112–134) is a survey of 2 Corinthians. Oropeza prefaces this chapter with the assertion that, despite the possible composite nature of this letter, Paul is addressing the same opposition throughout (112–113). Next, he theorizes that these opponents were Jewish-Christians who were slandering Paul's leadership (113–17, 119). Oropeza continues on to show that Paul believed that his opponents were false Christian teachers (118) and that, if the Corinthians were to follow them, they would lapse into apostasy, losing God's grace and salvation (120–29). The chapter then moves into a discussion of the hardships endured by Paul. The apostle presented these adversities as evidence of the truth of his gospel, thus providing a counterargument to the slanders of his opponents (130–33). Oropeza concludes with the observation that the opponents in 2 Corinthians were not the same as those in Galatia and that they may not have been from Jerusalem (133–34).

Chapter 5 (135–203) presents a comprehensive analysis of Romans. Oropeza dates this letter to circa 57 CE and notes that Paul had never visited this community (135). Oropeza asserts that Paul's motives in writing this letter were to garner support for his upcoming Spanish mission (135), to dispel any negative rumors that had circulated about him (135–36), and to settle the possible issue of table fellowship, which based on past experience (Corinth) may cause some controversy during his forthcoming visit (136–44). Oropeza also asserts that this epistle is relevant to his study because it provides the reader with Paul's general thoughts on apostasy (136, 166). In his analysis of Romans, Oropeza discusses the Pauline concept of righteousness and obedience to faith (144–51), the importance of doing works (152–60), defeating sin (160–65), divine foreknowledge and predestination (166–75), and the fate of unbelieving Israel (175–99). This chapter concludes with Oropeza noting that Paul believed that an apostate can be restored to salvation regardless of his or her past associations (201).

Chapter 6 (204–223) addresses the situation that lies behind Philippians. Oropeza begins by stating that this letter was written to encourage this Gentile community to remain strong in the face of general harassment from Hellenistic outsiders (204–8). He then discusses Paul' opponents mentioned in Phil 1:15–18 (208–11) and the "enemies of the cross" found in 3:17–19 (212–14). Lastly, this chapter addresses Paul's warning that the Philippians must resist apostasy in the form of vice in order to ensure their salvation (214–23).

Chapters 7 and 8 focus on the epistles to the Ephesians and Colossians, respectively. Regarding Ephesians (224–42), Oropeza argues that this letter is communal and that it was likely meant to be circulated around Western Asia Minor (224–25). It is theorized that this letter was written to promote unity (225) and ethical behavior (226–27, 235–38) and to dissuade this Gentile community from lapsing back into preconversion practices, which would lead to apostasy (227–35, 238–40). In examining Colossians (243–59), Oropeza asserts that this community faced opposition in the form of a Jewish sect similar to the Essenes (243–52), in particular one persuasive individual who is described as worshiping angels, practicing asceticism, and adhering to Jewish customs (252–55). Although the situation does not appear to be as dire as in Galatians (245), Paul does attempt to encourage this community to remain strong in their faith and to refrain from acting immorally (256–58).

In the final chapter of this book (260–308), Oropeza provides an analysis of the Pastoral Epistles, which he dates to shortly after Paul's martyrdom (ca. 64 CE) (260, 298). He also argues that these letters were written by a single author, a colleague of Paul's, and that they address the same themes, thus allowing them to be read together (260–61). Next Oropeza asserts that one of the main purposes of these epistles is to combat an opposition made up of Christian apostates who were disrupting Pauline communities in Ephesus and Crete (260–64). The following five observations are made: the author calls for the expulsion of all ardent apostates (268–72); these apostates were coercing wealthy widows (272–78); the author reassures his audience that the community will survive despite any opposition (279–91); the opposition discussed were likely Hellenistic Christians who used the Torah, Jewish traditions, and a "misdirected" concept of the resurrection to support their teachings (293–99); and those who deserted Paul during his arrest were not considered apostates (302–6). Oropeza concludes by noting that, by the time that these letters were written, there were many Christian groups in competition with each other (308).

This book represents a very intriguing study of the Pauline letters. Its main strength lies in its detailed analysis of the theology contained within these epistles. Oropeza makes a concerted effort to base his arguments on his own interpretation and understanding of early Christian texts, producing a work that is clear, concise, and easy to comprehend. This approach also provides the reader with a detailed textual exposition of the Pauline concepts of salvation, grace, election, predestination, foreknowledge, faith, and truth. In addition, Oropeza also offers a fine explanation of the Pauline position on the relations between Jews and Gentiles and the importance of proper moral conduct. This text would make a great resource for anyone wishing to gain a better understanding of Pauline theology.

Regarding Oropeza's study of apostasy within the Pauline letters, several methodological issues should be noted.[1] First, Oropeza's categorization of apostasy may be too broad. Although he offers a very narrow definition for apostasy at the beginning of this volume, as one reads on one notices that he generally categorizes any behavior or thought that the Pauline author denounces as relating to apostasy. Given that, during Paul's career it is likely that there was no set doctrine of beliefs or practices, it seems very probable that he would have often

---

1. Any critiques of methodology are based solely on the information presented in this volume. It is very possible that the issues raised in this review are addressed in volumes 1 or 3 of this series.

have to correct his communities due to a lack of a unified ecclesiastical structure. A correction in the form of a threat of losing salvation may have been a rhetorical strategy used by Paul to maintain control, not an indication that the group he was addressing was in danger of committing apostasy. Oropeza's broad categorization of apostasy becomes apparent as he spends one-fifth of this volume discussing Romans. Oropeza concedes that Paul had never visited this community (135–36, 199) and that there was probably no crisis being addressed (136, 199). This calls into question whether Romans is actually addressing the phenomena of apostasy and Oropeza's categorization of this concept.

Second, Oropeza does not critically discuss whether Paul would have been considered a Christian apostate. He does mention this idea within the conclusion (311); however, throughout this entire volume it is assumed that the Synoptic authors and the Jerusalem church were aligned with Paul under the traditional category of orthodox Christianity. From a historical perspective, this approach makes the assumption that Paul and the early Christians had a set doctrine of beliefs and practices, which they used to define themselves. Such an assumption anachronistically asserts a unity and a level of doctrinal development that may not have existed in early Christianity until the end of first century. This assumption allows Oropeza to use the Synoptic Gospels to interpret various passages in the Pauline corpus, a hermeneutical technique that may assign a concept anachronistically back into Paul's undisputed letters. Such an approach may be valid, but it does require an argument as to why it is being utilized.

Third, Oropeza does not question the historicity of the Synoptic writings and uses them to help elucidate Paul's thoughts and the context behind the various epistles. In particular, Acts is used as a historically reliable account of Paul's career. From a historical perspective, since the historicity of these texts is debatable, information from them should not be used without a detailed explanation as to why it is reliable.

Fourth, Oropeza shows a tendency to favor a conservative approach in regard to dating and assigning plausible authorship to the Pauline letters. Although he does acknowledge the scholarly debates regarding the backgrounds of the deutero-Pauline and the Pastoral Epistles, he still assigns them a relatively early dating and direct connection to Paul. This type of approach allows Oropeza to use the entire Pauline corpus to interpret a particular passage in any one of Paul's letters, since they are all connected to the apostle. From a historical perspective, this approach runs the risk of anachronistically reading a concept developed later in the first century back into one of the authentic Pauline letters. In addition, the deutero-Pauline epistles may represent documents that were written to address issues facing Pauline communities' years after the death of the apostle. It is possible that these letters show how different Pauline communities confronted and addressed their adversaries towards the later part of the first century and not how Paul dealt with opposition during his career.

In sum, *Jews, Gentiles and the Opponents of Paul* offers a detailed and conservatively oriented discussion of Pauline theology and opposition. It represents a useful counterpart to some of the more liberal studies examining the various forms of early Christianity.

GENERAL EPISTLES AND HEBREWS

Joshua Typology in the New Testament, by Richard Ounsworth. Wissenschaftliche Untersuchungen zum Neuen Testament 2/328. Tübingen: Mohr Siebeck, 2012. Pp. xii + 214. Paper. €54.00. ISBN 9783161519321.

J. Cornelis de Vos, University of Münster, Münster, Germany

Joshua Typology in the New Testament is the fruit of a doctoral thesis by Richard Joseph Ounsworth, O.P., at the Theological Faculty of the University of Oxford. To put my cards on the table from the start, I enjoyed reading this monograph and found it a marvelous book with very clear, straightforward, and convincing argumentation.

Ounsworth's suggestion is that "a greater sense of unity of the Letter to the Hebrews can be achieved by inferring from the Letter a typological relationship between Joshua the son of Nun and Jesus" (1). By means of this Joshua-Jesus typology he is able to connect Heb 3–4, in which Joshua is explicitly referred to (Heb 4:8); Heb 11, in which there is a deliberate "Joshua-Shaped Gap in Israel's History"; and the middle part of Hebrews dealing with Christ as high priest who passes beyond the veil and enters the heavenly sanctuary. Ounsworth succeeds in using Joshua-Jesus typology in a heuristic way even for the middle section, without disregarding the well-known fact that chapters 6–10 draw heavily upon the imagery of the Day of Atonement (Lev 16), the heavenly model of the sanctuary shown to Moses by God (Exod 25:40), the figure of the (high) priest Melchizedek (Gen 14; Ps 110:4), and the new covenant (Jer 31).

In short, the argument is as follows: Joshua, who together with Caleb believed the promise of God in contrast to the rest of the wilderness generation, including Moses and Aaron (Exod 17; Num 14; 20), was able to bring the next generation of believing Israelites into the promised land. However, Joshua was not able to bring them into God's rest. This task fell to Jesus, who bore the same name in Greek as the Old Testament Joshua (Ἰησοῦς) and who entered this rest of God, opening the way for the believers to follow him into the heavenly realm. Thus Jesus both resembles Joshua and surpasses Joshua. For Heb 11, the positive counterpart of Heb 3–4, Ounsworth makes clear that Joshua and the passing of the Jordan are deliberate omissions. The Jordan represents the barrier and boundary into the promised land. However, Heb 11 is not about the entrance into the physical promised land but about the entrance into the transcendent "promised land," that is, heaven. The entrance to heaven is the veil through which Jesus passes (Heb 6–10; see esp. 6:19–20; 9:1–14; 10:19–20). The veil is thus a typological representation of the Jordan. It is worth noting that the crossing of the Jordan is mentioned neither in Heb 3–4 nor in Heb 11. For the duration of the Letter to the Hebrews, the

Israelites remain "on the threshold of the promised land," which is equivalent with the threshold of heaven for the addressees. Only Jesus, as a pioneer and perfecter of faith (Heb 12:1–2)—recalling Joshua as a pioneer and believer in Num 13–14—crosses "the Jordan." The sacrificial death of Jesus is for believers that which enables them to pass through the veil into heaven. It must be remembered also that this time for the Hebrews was imbued with a feeling of imminent end of days.

It is clear from the summary above that the imagery of Hebrews and its message is produced by an intermingling of typological references and deliberately ambivalent concepts. The danger of such an interpretation is obvious: Where are the criteria found in a more objectively reproducible method, such as, for example, the historical-critical method? Ounsworth is fully aware of this threat and therefore exposits his presuppositions and his methods in a highly nuanced way; he points not only to the strengths but also to the weaknesses of his method.

Of great importance, of course, is the definition of typology. In the introductory chapter Ounsworth pleads for what he calls an *ontic typology*. Both type and antitype are considered to be real in Hebrews. This pertains not only to what is referred to as the horizontal typology of Joshua-Jesus as historical personalities but also to the vertical typology of heaven and earth. The earthly temple is real —as opposed to the Platonic concepts— simply because it is an *Abbild* of the heavenly *Urbild*. The connex of typology is the isomorphic correspondence of events, person, places, and practices. Ounsworth then dwells on the much-debated question of the qualitative relationship between the typological elements. For example, is the second element better or higher than the first? In vertical typology the heavenly element is, of course, higher. For horizontal typology in general, the only relationship that is always true is that of divine providence and guidance. This means in relation to Joshua and Jesus that God guided the people of Israel under the leadership of Joshua to the promised land just as he guided the believers of Hebrews under the leadership of Jesus to heaven.

The monograph has a clear structure. After the "Introduction" (ch. 1), Ounsworth gives a broad exposition of "The Typological Interpretation of the Old Testament in Hebrews" (ch. 2). These thorough and systematic chapters are followed by three chapters providing a detailed typological exegesis of three core texts: "Joshua as a Type of Christ in Hebrews 3 and 4" (ch. 3); "Hebrews 11 and the Joshua-Shaped Gap in Israel's History" (ch. 4); "Passing beyond the Veil" (ch. 5). In the last chapter, "Conclusion and Prospects" (ch. 6), Ounsworth not only gives a review of his study; he also deals with the problem that lurks when using typological exegesis: the problem of supersessionism. He ends with theological prospects educing from his kind of analysis. The book concludes with a bibliography and three indices: of ancient sources, of modern authors, and—also very useful—of subjects.

What I would like to call Ounsworth's method of synthesis is also noteworthy. First of all, he does not separate horizontal, historical typology from vertical, cosmological typology. By doing this he is able to overcome the alleged disunity in the book of Hebrews. Progress in "Heilsgeschichte" is at the same time a march toward heaven. Second, Ounsworth claims that the typological resemblances are not to be exhausted and that more typologies can merge in Hebrews. Caleb, for example, the other believer in Num 13–14 next to Joshua, does not occur in Hebrews, and when Jesus passes through the veil into heaven, this alludes not only to crossing the Jordan but also to the high priest passing through the veil on the Day of Atonement (Lev 16) and to Moses' vision of the heavenly sanctuary (Exod 25:40). Jesus being a high priest alludes not only to the high priest of Lev 16 but also to Melchizedek in Gen 14 (there "priest"). Ounsworth connects the disappearance of the first tent with the earthly temple and the old covenant and the appearance of the second tent with the heavenly temple and the new covenant (Heb 8–9). When Jesus enters the heavenly temple, he simultaneously inaugurates the new covenant and the heavenly temple. As Ounsworth stresses, this is not supersessionism. The former, earthly element is real because it is intertwined with the latter, heavenly element. However, now at the end of times, the former and the earthly are *surpassed, not superseded*. Third, words can have ambivalent references. When the addresses of Heb 4:8 read Ἰησοῦς, they primarily assume it speaks of Jesus. However, this presumption will prove erroneous as they realize that it is about Joshua. This connection between Joshua and Jesus is intended for anyone reading Heb 4:8.

This brings me to the concept of the addressees in Ounsworth's monograph. Ounsworth focuses on the intended audience because through the pragmatic intentions of the text the readers become more extant than the anonymous author. Ounsworth has chosen from the range of potential readers the ideal readers for his analyses, that is, readers who understand the intentions of the author, including all the typological and intertextual allusions. This presupposition might not be far beyond the truth: Hebrews makes the impression that it is meant for an intelligent audience well-versed in the Bible.

Notwithstanding the enormous achievement Ounsworth has made with his monograph, I have some points of critique. First of all, the title *Joshua Typology in the New Testament* is misleading. Ounsworth deals almost exclusively with the Letter to the Hebrews. Reference to other parts of the New Testament are found only in the first two chapters. Second, it would have been more comfortable for readers to add English translations to the Greek, Latin, German, and French quotations. Third, it is, of course, impossible for a monograph that deals with almost the whole Letter to the Hebrews to list all relevant literature. However, there are some gaps, particularly with regard to non-English literature.[1]

---

1. For example, Karl-Heinrich Ostmeyer, "Typologie und Typos: Analyse eines Schwierigen Verhältnisses," *NTS* 46 (2000): 112–31; Bryan J. Whitfield, "The Three Joshuas of Hebrews 3 and 4," *Perspectives in Religious Studies* 37 (2010): 21–35. See also Samuel Bénétreau, "Le Repos du Pèlerin (Hébreux 3,7–4,11)," *ETR* 78 (2003): 203–23; Sebastian Fuhrmann, *Vergeben und Vergessen: Christologie und Neuer Bund im Hebräerbrief* (WUNT 113; Neukirchen-Vluyn: Neukirchener, 2006); Paul-Gerhard Müller, *Christos Ἀρχηγός:*

However, my critique may not extenuate my enthusiasm about Ounsworth's work. I can heartily recommend this ingenious, well-readable book about a complicated matter that deserves to be read by many others.

Pioneer and Perfecter of Faith: Jesus' Faith as the Climax of Israel's History in the Epistle to the Hebrews, by Christopher A. Richardson. Wissenschaftliche Untersuchungen zum Neuen Testament 2/338. Tübingen: Mohr Siebeck, 2012. Pp. xii + 280. Paper. €69.00. ISBN 9783161503979.

Philip Church, Laidlaw College, Auckland, New Zealand

In light of the ongoing debate in Pauline studies over whether the genitive in the phrase πίστις Χριστοῦ is subjective or objective, Christopher Richardson set out to let the voice of Hebrews be heard on the faith/faithfulness of Jesus. He notes that Heb 2:13 places the words "I will trust in him" in the mouth of Jesus, that Heb 2:17 ascribes the adjective "faithful" (πιστός) to Jesus, and that Heb 12:1 refers to him as "the pioneer and perfecter of faith" (τῆς πίστεως ἀρχηγὸς καὶ τελειωτής). Another impetus for Richardson's work is the claim by Lenski, Spicq, Ellingworth, and Vanhoye that Hebrews nowhere refers to Christ as a "believer." The book is a revision of Richardson's 2009 Aberdeen PhD thesis, supervised by Francis Watson.

In chapter 1 Richardson introduces his study and embarks on discussions of typology and rhetoric. He defines typology as "identifying correspondences or analogies between a person, place, event, or institution in the past (*type*) and another in the present (*antitype*)" (7–8). On rhetoric, he discusses the features of Greco-Roman rhetoric dating back to Aristotle and argues that, while Hebrews contains features of both deliberative and epideictic rhetoric, the "epideictic or encomiastic genre governs Heb. 11.1–12.3" (11). This chapter of Hebrews rehearses the lives of faithful people from Israel's past so as to enable the readers to understand the superior faith of Jesus. These people are typological anticipations of Christ, whose faith/faithfulness was superior to theirs. Thus, the author uses typology to present an encomium to Jesus.

Chapter 2 is an exegetical treatment of those texts in Hebrews that refer to or imply the faith/faithfulness of Jesus: 2:13, 17; 3:1–6; 4:15; 5:7–8; 10:5–7; 12:2. The treatment extends over ninety pages, around 40 percent of the book. Richardson clearly establishes that faithfulness can be attributed to Jesus, and while there is a degree of complex argumentation, he does establish his case well. He also argues that it was at Golgotha that Christ's faith/faithfulness is supremely seen. This is

---

Der Religionsgeschichtliche und theologische Hintergrund einer neutestamentlichen Christusprädikation (Europäische Hochschulschriften. Theologie 28: Bern: Lang, 1973); Christian Rose, "Verheißung und Erfüllung: Zum Verständnis von ἐπαγγελία im Hebräerbrief," *BZ* 33 (1989): 60–80, 178–91.

especially the case with the treatment of Heb 5:7–8, where Richardson argues, against the prevailing consensus, that these verses refer not to Gethsemane but Golgotha (74–81).[1] The chapter concludes with a discussion of the words "pioneer and perfecter" (ἀρχηγὸς καὶ τελειωτής) in Heb 12:1–3, with the former word indicating that Jesus is "the exemplary leader/model of steadfast confidence, who also elicits the faith that is required of his people" (99), and the latter indicating that the faith of Jesus is "qualitatively distinct and superior to the faith of other exemplars" (101).

Chapter 3 is an introduction to Hebr 11 (actually 11:1–12:3). Richardson sets the chapter in the wider context of 10:19–12:29, which he then narrows to 10:32–12:17. He then concentrates on 11:1–12:3, which, he argues, is an encomium to Jesus. He discusses literary parallels to Heb 11 in other literature from the Second Temple period and later (Wisdom, Sirach, 1, 2, and 4 Maccabees, 4 Ezra, Acts 7, CD, Philo, and 1 Clement), and while he sees some similarities with this material, especially with Sirach, he finds that Heb 11, written by "an author with a Hellenistic-Jewish background, high education and Christian commitment" (149), displays closer affinities with Aristotelian rhetoric; he thus argues that it is an encomium written "to magnify the person *and faith* of Christ" (165, emphasis original). On page 150 he lists the structure and subject matter of an encomium, and on 160 he shows how most of this structure is reflected in Heb 11:1–12:3.

Chapter 4 is the book's main contribution. Here Richardson sets out to establish that, in the encomiastic structure of the chapter, the individuals listed in Heb 11 act as the "ancestors" of Jesus, typologically anticipating his faithfulness, which is discussed in 12:1–3. By including 12:1–3 (rightly, in my opinion) with Heb 11, Richardson is able to present a christological reading of the chapter pointing to Christ rather than the more usual ecclesiological reading, where it is seen to encourage the faith and endurance of the readers. Chapter 5 is a brief conclusion reiterating the main points of the work.

Certainly Richardson has written a valuable study, particularly in chapter 4, where he shows convincingly how the individuals listed anticipate the superior faith/faithfulness of Christ. The chapter contains many important exegetical insights (as indeed does ch. 2). However, three questions arise for me.

First, Richardson's analysis of the structure of Heb 11 as an encomium seems somewhat overstated. Given that the so-called encomium contains forty-three verses, it seems unbalanced to have thirty-five of these devoted to the "ancestors" and only three devoted to the person being honored. Of course, since he is the subject of all of Hebrews, "Jesus does not need to be mentioned" (161) in Heb 11, but Richardson's brief discussion of this—his comparison on the encomium

---

1. An earlier version of this material was published as Christopher A. Richardson, "The Passion: Reconsidering Hebrews 5:7–8," in *A Cloud of Witnesses: The Theology of Hebrews in Its Ancient Contexts* (ed. Richard Bauckham et al.; LNTS 387; London: T&T Clark, 2008), 51–67.

form with Heb 11 is "meant only to emphasize the *points of contact*" (160)—still leaves me wondering about the appropriateness of the analysis and whether it has been imposed on the chapter by the reader rather than being an integral part of an author's argument. Given the importance of the LXX in Hebrews, I wonder whether some of the other texts Richardson lists (Wisdom, Sirach, Maccabees) might have been more significant background than Aristotle, especially since the comparison with the encomium does not quite work.

Second, Richardson's exegetical work on Heb 11 compares the details recounted about each of the ancestors to highlight typological correspondences with Jesus. While the chapter contains many significant insights, some of the correspondences seem a bit forced. For example, he glosses μετατίθημι with "taken up" (174 n. 26) and makes considerable capital on the exaltation of Enoch as a type of Christ, who was also exalted. But μετατίθημι does not really have the sense of "taken up" (despite the ESV translation of Heb 11:5); rather, the sense is "transferred" or "changed" (see BDAG). In the light of the considerable Enoch speculation in middle Judaism, the New Testament treats him with remarkable reticence and nowhere uses the language of exaltation with reference to him.

Third, in a long footnote on page 217 Richardson takes issue with Carl Mosser, who argues that Rahab is the rhetorical climax of Heb 11.[2] Of course, for Richardson Jesus is the rhetorical climax (12:1–3). Richardson is right, to be sure, but Mosser is not wrong. Richardson critiques Mosser for prioritizing ecclesiology over Christology, but surely that is precisely what Hebrews does. Hebrews is not a dispassionate christological treatise; it is an urgently written word of exhortation (13:22), written to encourage the readers to faithfully endure as Jesus did, as also the ancestors (deliberative rather than epideictic rhetoric!). There are correspondences between Heb 11:1–40 and 12:1–3, as Richardson has convincingly argued, but there are also correspondences between Heb 11 and Heb 13. These were not part of Richardson's thesis, but some attention to them would show that, as always in Hebrews, Christology is put to the service of ecclesiology. The exhortations of Hebrews have priority and the theology serves the exhortation.

I also noted a few minor issues. On pages 8–9 Richardson claims that the former tent and means of worship were "copies and shadows of the true, permanent realities in heaven." A glance at BDAG and LSJ (and the NRSV) will show that the semantic range of ὑπόδειγμα does not include "copy," although this sense persists with reference to Heb 8:5 and 9:23. In his discussion of Hebrew words Richardson uses BDB, even though it is over one hundred years old and has been superseded by *HALOT*. Indeed, the definition he offers of 169) שָׁעָה n. 8) does not appear in *HALOT*. On page 72 he reads Heb 4:2 with the sense that "the message Israel heard was not united with *faith*." There is a complex textual issue in this verse that Richardson overlooks. The preferred reading based on the text adopted

---

2. See Carl Mosser, "Rahab outside the Camp," in *The Epistle to the Hebrews and Christian Theology* (ed. Richard Bauckham et al; Grand Rapids: Eerdmans, 2008), 383–404.

in UBS4 and NA²⁸, as also reflected in the NRSV and NIV 2011, is that those who *heard* the message failed because they were not united in faith with those who *listened* to it. On page 79 ὅς has a grave accent rather than an acute (twice, as also in the previous edition of this part of the work),[3] and on page 159, section 2.3 is printed as section 3.3.

None of these criticisms detract from the valuable contribution Richardson has made to Hebrews scholarship. This is a worthy addition to the WUNT series and a fine contribution to the scholarly discussion of Hebrews. Ultimately, though, it has little to say to the debate in Pauline studies over πίστις Χριστοῦ. While Richardson did not set out to solve that issue, he does remain skeptical of the subjective reading of the expression (225 n. 3).

The Centrality of Αἱμα (Blood) in the Theology of the Epistle to the Hebrews: An Exegetical and Philological Study, by Hermann V. A. Kuma. Lewiston, N.Y.: Mellen, 2012. Pp. xxvi + 422. Paper. $159.95. ISBN 9780773414617.

James R. Harrison, Sydney College of Divinity, North Ryde, New South Wales, Australia

Hermann V. A. Kuma, who pursued his doctoral studies at the Seventh Day Adventist Seminary (Andrews University, Bierren Springs, Michigan) under Richard Davidson, has published a revised version of his doctoral thesis. The book revisits an infrequently traveled path of New Testament scholarship since the famous encounter of the Welsh scholar C. H. Dodd with the Antipodean scholar Leon Morris in the middle of the last century. Dodd and Morris faced off on whether "blood" in the New Testament signified "death" or "life." Arguably, Morris nudged of Dodd in a close photo finish, proposing that that αἷμα primarily signified "death," although Morris acknowledged the ambiguity of meaning in Lev 17:11. Kuma, in this most readable monograph, traces comprehensively the scholarly debate regarding blood from 1881 to 2003 (5–81), sweeping across the academic literature and highlighting key scholarly contributions to the understanding of αἷμα in the epistle to the Hebrews. As a result, Kuma justifies the writing of his monograph in the conclusion to his literature review by saying that that "no study has yet appeared which deals with the various issues and numerous passages concerning blood in Hebrews in a systematic and comprehensive way" (79). His work, therefore, represents a very helpful contribution to scholarship on Hebrews and, more generally, provides indirect insight into other New Testament writers' attitude to the Old Testament sacrificial cultus and its fulfillment in Christ.

The central thesis (245–350, 358–60) is that there is ambiguity, ambivalence, and multivocality in the biblical understanding of blood, positing that for the

---

3. Richardson, "Passion," 56.

writer to the Hebrews blood signifies both life (Heb 10:19) and death. As Kuma sums up the central role of blood in the Scriptures,

> Blood is the medium of approach to God and, as such, it overarches the argumentation in Hebrews. Blood also constitutes the medium of power because it sanctifies, consecrates, purifies, and, by it, the covenant is inaugurated. Furthermore blood effects perfection and brings about decisive purgation resulting in forgiveness. (359)

However, in Kuma's view (347–48, 349–50), a clear weighting of theological interest emerges in the references to blood on the part of the writer to the Hebrews. Notwithstanding the multivalent quality of blood, signifying both life and death, the emphasis of the writer to the Hebrews is decidedly on life:

> Thus, as important as it is, the death of Christ is not the focus of the author of Hebrews. His chief interest is life, which is the result of Christ's death. This first-century author comes across as a brilliant rhetorician whose primary aim is to call attention to the vicarious self-sacrifice of Jesus and all the benefits that accrue from that sacrifice to a community who stand in danger of losing their focus on Christ. (347–48)

The writer to the Hebrews refers to blood twenty-one times, fourteen of these references occurring in Heb 9–10, the crown of the christological and theological argument of the epistle. Indeed, the entire epistle's arguments are framed by allusions and references to Jesus's sacrificial blood (Heb 1:3; 13:20–21). The author of Hebrews adopts an *arumentum ad minore ad maius*, establishing that the blood of Christ represents the "most powerful medium" over its precedents in the Hebrew cultus. The unique self-sacrifice of Christ (1) occurs in his incarnational humanity (flesh and blood, Heb 2:14) because he is the high priest who offers himself as the atoning sacrifice on behalf of the entire human family as opposed to Israel alone; (2) cleanses the conscience in contrast to the Old Testament sacrificial rituals; (3) ratifies an everlasting covenant (Heb 9:15–22; 10:29) as opposed to the temporary Mosaic covenant (Exod 24:4ff.); (4) effects a once-for-all care of humanity as far as its sin in contrast to the incessant sacrifices of the Hebrew cultus; (5) opens up to believers "the power of inalienable life" over death; (6) unveils a rich Christology (incarnate Son in human flesh and blood; high priest; sacrifice for the human race) as much as a powerful soteriology.

Unfortunately for the reader, no updating of the academic scholarship on blood since 2003 has been attempted in this book. Consequently, readers will need to review for themselves the most recent contributions to the debate, including D. M. Moffitt's monograph (*Atonement and the Logic of Resurrection in the Epistle to the Hebrews* [Leiden: Brill, 2011]), as well as his chapter on the same issue in another Brill publication (T. Heicke et al., eds., *Day of Atonement* [Leiden: Brill, 2012], 211–24); Y. Feder's monograph (*Blood Expiation in Hittite and Biblical Ritual* [Atlanta: Society of Biblical Literature, 2011]; (3) S. Niditch's investigation of blood in Zech 9 (*VT* 61 [2011]: 629–25); and an article discussing the tau-robolium in relation to the New Testament (E. M. Cornelius, *Acta Patristica et Byzantina* 18 [2007]: 32–42), among other pieces. Obviously, scholarly interest in this area of study has revived, and Kuma's discussion is a welcome addition to these new books and articles.

Kuma's coverage of the background and understanding of blood in the Old Testament writings (97–174) is very comprehensive, although his small subsec-tion on the ancient Near East (83–96) would now have to be expanded by virtue of the fine study of Y. Feder on Hittite expiatory rituals. Then Kuma proceeds to discuss the wider context of blood in the New Testament world (175–219), focus-ing on the Apocrypha, Pseudepigrapha, the Qumran literature, Philo, Josephus, rabbinic literature, and the Greco-Roman world. The author is clearly much more at home in the literature of Second Temple Judaism than the Greco-Roman con-text, with the former being covered thoroughly in a most effective discussion. In the latter (215–19), however, Kuma makes a fleeting reference to the mystery reli-gions and then exclusively focuses on the taurobolium, which is largely carried by a long source extract from Peristephan. But the practice of these sacrificial rituals, as Kuma is well aware (218 n. 139), dominated the second to fourth centuries CE and have limited (if any) relevance to the context of Hebrews. There is more help-ful contemporary evidence that could have been referred to in this section. Three examples will suffice.

First, there are the inscriptions of the Acts of the Arval Brethren at Rome, the ancient priestly college in the city's foundation myths supposedly opened by Romulus, which recount in elaborate detail the sacrificial offerings made to the Julio-Claudian rulers and subsequent imperial dynasties on particular days (J. Scheid, *Commentarii Fratrum Arvalium Qui Supersunt: Les copies épigraphiques des protocoles annuels de la confrérie Arvalae [21 AV.—304 AP. J.-C.]* [Rome: École Française de Rome, 1998). Second, there are the various festival calendars, includ-ing one at an Italian temple of Augustus (the Feriale Cumanum: *CIL* X. 8375) recounting the prayers and sacrifices offered to Augustus. Third, at Ankara in Roman Galatia, in the Sebasteion of Augustus, where the *Res Gestae* was inscribed in Greek and Latin, an inscription lists the gifts, festivals, and sacrifices offered by the Galatian imperial priests at the sanctuary (S. Mitchell and D. French, eds., *From Augustus to the End of the Third Century AD* [vol. 1 of *The Greek and Latin Inscriptions of Ankara [Ancyra]* [Munich: Beck, 2012], 138–50). Further grist to the mill could be added by searching the inscriptions of the imperial priests in provincial Asia (G. Frija, *Les Prêtres des empereurs: Le culte impérial civique dans la province romaine d'Asie* [Rennes: Presses Universitaires de Rennes, 2012]), the corpus of which can now be searched on the Internet site-by-site, with original texts and French translations (prêtres civiques.org/). In other words, if the origi-nal destination of Hebrews was Rome, as several recent Hebrews commentators argue, the writer's emphasis on the superior sacrifice of Jesus as the Son of God, the high priest over a new household, would have resonated with both Jewish and Roman audiences.

Last, in his discussion of the αἷμα passages in Hebrews (245–345), Kuma adopts the same structure throughout: providing the original Greek text and translating it, outlining in each case the exegetical considerations, and discussing the significance of the αἷμα reference(s) in each pericope. This section is insightfully done, and there is much to be learned here. There is only one disappointment: there is no brief discussion of the historical context of the epistle, as much as we can discern it, from the internal evidence and the (hypothetical) reconstruction of its audience and destination. Instead, we are only presented an overview of Hebrews and its rhetorical structure (245–52).

Certainly it is true to say, as P. O'Brien has recently observed (*The Epistle to the Hebrews* [Grand Rapids: Eerdmans, 2010], 15), that few exegetical decisions hang on the precise geographic location of the epistle. Nonetheless, a (hypothetical) Roman audience, under heavy but not mortal persecution (Heb 12:3) and tempted to compromise (10:32–34), would make sense in the pre-Neronian persecution period (see Tacitus, *Annals* 15.44) where increasing opposition from many quarters became increasingly apparent during 60–64 CE (Heb 11:26; 13:13). The virulent anti-Semitism of the Roman intelligentsia in the mid-50s probably posed as many problems for the Roman believers as their Jewish brethren at one level, living in the capital of an idolatrous empire, with its priestly sacrificial system in honor of the Roman ruler. What relevance, if any, did this have for the writer's presentation of the superior high priesthood of Jesus in the order of Melchizedek and the surpassing excellence of his blood offered on behalf of his dependents? Whatever one makes of this (entirely) speculative reconstruction, it would have been stimulating to know Kuma's reconstruction of the epistle's context, whatever that might be, as part of his fine exegetical exposition.

Kuma's expert and insightful coverage of the motif of "blood" deserves a wide readership among Hebrews scholars, and the monograph should be included in seminary and university libraries, as well as in private libraries.

The Greening of Hebrews? Ecological Readings in the Letter to the Hebrews, by Jeffrey S. Lamp. Eugene, Ore.: Pickwick 2012. Pp. xii + 134. Paper. $18.00. ISBN 9781610976558.

Amy L. B. Peeler, Wheaton College, Wheaton, Illinois

Utilizing the work of Norm C. Habel and composed for the meetings of the Consultation on Ecological Hermeneutics of the Society of Biblical Literature, the essays in *The Greening of Hebrews?* aim to "hear a suppressed voice, the voice of Earth, in, through, or even against the text" (3). Three criteria allow Jeffrey S. Lamp to recover this voice. The sections using suspicion acknowledge the inherent anthropocentrism in the biblical text and its subsequent interpretation. The method of identification allows readers to "come to grips with their kinship with Earth in order to become more sensitive to the voice of Earth" (6). Finally, the act of retrieval determines what Earth might say from a given passage. Hebrews provides an excellent test case for this methodology because of its reputation of a spiritualized book that focuses on the heavenly realities rather than their earthly "shadows." Lamp queries if his ecological perspective might challenge such a reputation of the letter.

Lamp's study of the book unfolds through seven exegetical chapters, book-ended with analysis of the christological assertions of Heb 1 and 2. In these two chapters he presents the framing argument of his book, "creational Christology," in three key moments. The incarnation shows that God has taken on the stuff of earth, thereby enduing it with worth. The resurrection "is the point of contact that brings together human beings and Earth in an eschatological framework that does not abandon the present order to an inevitable doom, but rather gives place for Earth to speak to use about how we might evidence this eschatology in our present care for creation" (79). Finally, the ascension shows that a piece of Earth, a human, reigns in heaven and "anticipates a time when heaven and Earth will be brought together as a dwelling place for God and human beings (Rev 21–22)" (115).

In between these focused christological chapters, Lamp engages the perspective of sacrificed animals (ch. 3) and the land (ch. 4), attends to the pneumatological (ch. 5) and liturgical (ch. 7) aspects of the text in light of ecology, and takes on the frequent question of the presence of an escapist eschatology in Hebrews (ch. 6).

A hermeneutic of suspicion allows him to ask honest and legitimate questions of the letter that might either be ruled as off limits or simply ignored in more traditional analyses. For example, the appeal to Israel's sacrificial cult throughout Hebrews prompts Lamp to ask: "Why is the almighty God of the universe so interested in articulating meticulous directions for cutting up birds?" and "is all this detail really intrinsic to the logic of reality?" (21) Surely these are modern questions that the first-century audience familiar with sacrifice would not have posed. Nevertheless, Lamp's articulation of them is a pointed way to remind readers of their distance from the text and the challenge of putting oneself into the same perspective as the author and his original audience. Refusal to domesticate the text also allows Lamp to highlight just how radical the argument of Hebrews would have sounded. It does not question the people's obedience with regard to the cult, as did the prophets, but questions the intrinsic value of the cult itself (27). Hence, Lamp's suspicion helps to recover the challenge of the text for the present and the past.

Lamp's consistent appeal to Hebrews' use of the Old Testament provides another methodological benefit of the book. In many instances he utilizes the context of the passage the author of Hebrews cites in order to recover an ecologically powerful reading. Lamp has good knowledge of both Testaments, as evidenced in his appeals to psalms that lead him to other psalms and then back to Genesis, an interconnected view of Scripture that he persuasively argues the original readers and certainly later interpreters of the church possessed.

In addition to these large arguments of the text, Lamp provides several enlightening insights along the way. In his discussion about Christ's sacrifice and that of animals, he shows how Christ literally provides redemption for them. Because Christ's sacrifice is final, according to the author of Hebrews, all the animals that would be sacrificed no longer need to be. They have, in reality, been "saved." (22). Drawing from this point, he includes a poetic re-presentation of classic creeds from Andrew Linzey, which affirms the beauty and value of all God's creation (35–36). In his analysis of Heb 1, Lamp suggests that, just as creation can reveal the wisdom of God, so also can creation teach about the Son who is the wisdom of God and the agent of creation (17). When thinking about the status of Abraham and his descendants as resident aliens, Lamp points out a more positive implication of that idea, that as visitors readers could think of Earth as a "host country," one that deserves "appreciation for the hospitality of earth" (82).

The latter point highlights one final positive contribution of the book. Lamp is writing so that his readers might be encouraged to think seriously not just about Hebrews but about "the conduct of faithful human living on planet Earth" (118). Hence, his work, in a final assessment, is aimed at *praxis*, and he seeks to provide readings of the text that will promote such action.

I was left wondering, however, if Hebrews as Lamp reads it really provides much motivation for this kind of response. He had hoped that an ecological reading of the letter might call into question its escapist reputation, but his results of that hope are, at best, ambiguous. On several occasions throughout the book Lamp casts Hebrews as indifferent to the concerns of the Earth. It is Lamp's reading—sometimes cast as in opposition to the author—that recovers the voice of creation. For example, at the conclusion to his chapter on the pneumatology of Hebrews, wherein he argues that the author of Hebrews focused largely on the Spirit of Christ and the redemption secured for human beings, all he can claim for Hebrews is that "it is not inimical to an Earth-friendly reading as the surface features of its rhetoric first suggests" (68), hardly a ringing endorsement. In the chapter on Heb 2, Lamp shows how Ps 104 proclaims God and the Son as "both creator and sustainer of the universe," yet that "the argumentation of Hebrews was not concerned with this message has been made abundantly clear" (112). This depends, however, on how one reads allusions to Scripture. Could not the author intend just the type of argument Lamp proposes through his echoes and allusions to Ps 104?

On the other hand, several times Lamp misses the opportunity to show the positive ecological implications of Hebrews. Most apparent in this regard are his frequent appeals to Rom 8, surely a powerful text that affirms the connectedness of all creation and its future redemption, but these are instances in which Lamp could have appealed to Hebrews. Hebrews also believes that creation will be redeemed in Christ because his salvific work reinstates him as the heir of *all things*, not just humans (1:2, 13; 2:8–9). If creation is reoriented under the authority of Christ, this allows for a certain kind of redemption, a powerful ecological hint arising from Hebrews itself.

While I would love to pass this book on to those who still question the value of environmentalism (as Lamp catalogues on p. 19), I wonder if fronting his discussions with the tone and content of suspicion may ostracize just those who most need to hear his message. But for those who already are comfortable with such criticism of the text, Lamp opens eyes and ears to places where Hebrews— and, in my opinion, even more than Lamp allows—supports a reading that encourages a positive view of the Earth as an object of divine care and concern, a co-beneficiary of the redemption of Christ, and a recipient of present acts that anticipate the eschatological fulfillment (116).

NEW TESTAMENT AND BIBLICAL THEOLOGY

The Spirit and Christ in the New Testament and Christian Theology: Essays in Honor of Max Turner, edited by I. Howard Marshall, Volker Rabens, and Cornelis Bennema. Grand Rapids: Eerdmans, 2012. Pp. xx + 367. Paper. $60.00. ISBN 9780802867537.

James P. Sweeney, Winebrenner Theological Seminary, Findlay, Ohio

Martin Maximillian Barnaby (Max) Turner was formerly Professor of New Testament at the London School of Theology. Upon his retirement in 2011 he was awarded the title of Emeritus Professor. He is well-known for his contributions to New Testament studies. His interests encompass linguistics, interpretation, lexicography, and New Testament theology. Two of his specific foci have been New Testament pneumatology and Ephesians. The present Festschrift consists of a collection of twenty essays presented to Turner in commemoration of his sixty-fifth birthday. The contributors focus on two principal themes, both of which are of interest to him: pneumatology and Christology. The introduction of the volume provides details regarding the list of contributors (viii–xii), abbreviations (xiii), the editors' foreword (xiv–xv), and Steve Walton's "An Introduction to Max Turner" (xvi–xx). The aforementioned twenty essays follow (1–355). The volume closes with three appendages: "List of Publications by Max Turner" (356–60), "List of Published PhD Dissertations by Max Turner's Research Students" (361–62), and an "Index of Authors" (363–67). The following comments will provide a brief sketch of the content of the essays.

In the initial essay, "'The Lord, the Giver of Life': The Gift of the Spirit as Both Life-Giving and Empowering," James D. G. Dunn focuses on the theme of the Spirit as "the giver of life." Dunn maintains that the life involved is neither passive nor unconscious. Rather, it is "vitality, a life that liberates, energizes, empowers, and expresses itself in a variety of forms all indicative of the fact that the Spirit is *life!*" (17, emphasis original). In the next essay, "The Spirit, Simeon, and the Songs of the Servant," John R. Levison teases out thematic connections between Luke 2:25–35 and Isa 40–55. Following this Steve Walton pursues the question, "Whose Spirit? The Promise and the Promiser in Luke 12:12." In it he examines the promise of Luke 12:12 against the parallel of 21:14–15, similar Old Testament and postbiblical promises, and the backdrop of Acts 2:33.

Robert P. Menzies addresses the Lukan theme of persecuted prophets in "The Persecuted Prophets: A Mirror Image of Luke's Spirit-Inspired Church." He notes in the light of Luke 10:1–16 and 2:17–21 that Luke has crafted his narrative "to challenge his church to consider the nature of their prophetic calling" (69). Joel B. Green focuses on Lukan soteriology in "'Was It Not Necessary for the Messiah to Suffer These Things and Enter into His Glory?': The Significance of Jesus' Death for Luke's Soteriology." Green maintains that Luke 22:19–20 and Acts 20:28 indicate some interest in Jesus' substitutionary death. He further contends that the soteriological significance of Jesus' death should be pursued along a humiliation/ exaltation model. Luke's narrative invites approaches to atonement models not predetermined by Markan or Pauline categories.

The following two essays are devoted to Johannine themes. In "The Giving of the Spirit in John 19–20: Another Round," Cornelis Bennema examines John 20:22. He takes issues with the widely held view that the giving of the Spirit refers to a singular event (20:22, fulfilling 7:39 and 16:7). In contrast, Bennema maintains that it is a process that runs parallel to and in step with the process of Jesus' glorification. It involves three steps: the cross (19:30), Jesus' resurrection (20:22), and Pentecost (Acts 2 in fulfillment of John 16:7). D. A. Carson thereafter pursues the question, "Is Faith in Christ without Evidence Superior Faith? A Re-examination of John 20:29." Carson contends that the implied contrast in the two lines of 20:29 is not so much between inferior and superior faith as between "the grounds of faith that were possible for the first generation of believers and the grounds of faith needed by subsequent generations" (114). The means by which the latter is fulfilled is indicated in 20:30–31.

Conrad Gempf's essay focuses on Acts 18:24–19:7: "Apollos and the Ephesian Disciples: Befores and Afters." Gempf likens the narratives about Apollos (18:24–28) and Ephesian disciples (19:1–7) to the pattern of healing stories, which supply resources for understanding the "before" state with the "after" state of both.

Pneumatic themes in Paul's writings are the subjects of the next two essays. Volker Rabens examines "Power from In Between: The Relational Experience of the Holy Spirit and Spiritual Gifts in Paul's Churches." He notes that the work of the Spirit in Paul's churches was a communal experience. It also had a "private" dimension. It served "the edification of the individual *and* the community" (155, emphasis original). Desta Heliso examines "Divine Spirit and Human Spirit in Paul in the Light of Stoic and Biblical-Jewish Perspectives." Heliso maintains in the light of Stoic, biblical-Jewish traditions, and Pauline usage (Rom 8:16; 1 Cor 2:11) that Paul's *pneuma* language refers not to two different entities but to "Christ residing in the believer as and through the *life-giving Spirit*" (176, emphasis original).

The next two essays examine issues related to the later letters of the Pauline corpus. Chris Tilling looks at "Ephesians and Divine-Christology." He initially reviews and critiques a sampling of recent christological discussion related to Ephesians vis-à-vis divine-Christology (Bauckham, Hurtado, Fee, Dunn). He then offers what he characterizes as a fresh analysis of the Christology of Ephesians summarized under five parallel points organized under the rubric of God language and Christ language. Tilling maintains a divine Christology in Ephesians, albeit a relational one. Robert W. Wall focuses on "Salvation's Bath by the Spirit: A Study of Titus 3:5b–6 in Its Canonical Setting." Wall purposes that the Pastoral Epistles were added to the ten-letter collection as a guide to using the Pauline corpus as Scripture. He then offers an exegesis of 3:5b–6 and outlines its canonical effect.

Steve Motyer addresses the neglected topic of pneumatology in Hebrews with "The Spirit in Hebrews: No Longer Forgotten?" He proposes that the recipients of Hebrews were a group of Jewish Christians who still belonged to the synagogue but also met with messianic believers to exercise gifts of the Spirit. They were being tempted by the renewed threat of persecution to slip back into Judaism. At the heart of this merging back was "*a separation between Jesus as Christ and the Holy Spirit, the giver of the gifts they enjoy*" (215, emphasis original). Motyer examines successively Heb 2:1–4; 6:4; 3:7; 10:15; 9:8; and 9:15 in the light of this proposed setting and maintains that the author of Hebrews argues that "the Holy Spirit now comes only with Christ the Son of God." The recipients therefore "cannot keep their charismatic gifts just as Jews, no longer attached to Jesus" (227)

John Christopher Thomas offers "New Jerusalem and the Conversion of the Nations: An Exercise in Pneumatic Discernment (Rev. 21:1–22:5)." He contends that the conversion of the nations is a major theme in Revelation. He notes that the evidence for this is both subtle and explicit. His reading attempts to allow for tension between the prospect of inclusion of the nations and warnings of exclusion. These seemingly disparate emphases, he suggests, "would serve to form the hearers as they seek to offer faithful witness to a hostile world" (245).

Richard Bauckham addresses the question, "Moses as 'God' in Philo of Alexandria: A Precedent for Christology?" Bauckham notes that Philo's use of *theos* in connection to Moses is based on the Pentateuch's lone usage in Exod 7:1 LXX. Philo's references are therefore exegetical. That Philo does not use *theos* in reference to humans outside of eleven references to this passage, "where he takes up a specific scriptural usage and gives it a special meaning, actually suggests that Jews would be very wary of using god-language of human beings" (264). Bauckham hence finds no precedent in Philo's use of *theos* in relation to Moses for the attribution of divine nature or status to Jesus.

In "Jesus and the Spirit in Biblical and Theological Perspective: Messianic Empowering, Saving Wisdom, and the Limits of Biblical Theology," Mark L. Strauss initially provides brief summaries of the role of the Spirit in Jesus' ministry in the Synoptic Gospels, with focus on Luke, and the Gospel of John. The common feature he finds in the four Gospels regarding Jesus' relationship to the Spirit is that the Spirit functions as the essential empowering and revelatory agent for Jesus to accomplish his messianic task (272). Following this, Strauss undertakes to bridge biblical and systematic theology in exploring the role of the Spirit in relation to the humanity and deity of the incarnate Christ. He notes that this question cannot be answered through exegesis alone, for the texts of the Gospels were not intended to answer the issues that arise from philosophical and theological questions about the incarnation. In this regard, biblical theology must give way to philosophical and speculative theology.

Anthony N. S. Lane offers an essay on "Cyril of Alexandria and the Incarnation." Lane notes that Cyril reduces the various issues related to the incarnation to a simple point: the human being Jesus is the Word who was made flesh. One must not speak of Jesus *and* the Word because Jesus is the Word made flesh. Lane notes that Cyril's anathemas expose the weak point of Nestorius's Christology. Lane suggests that they are also important for contemporary christological reflection, namely, "the need to ensure that underneath the complex language of many contemporary Christologies there lies indeed the core belief that in Christ 'the Word became flesh'" (302).

Veli-Matti Kärkkäinen examines the relationship between the Spirit and justification in "'By the Washing of Regeneration and Renewal in the Holy Spirit': Towards a Pneumatological Theology of Justification." He seeks to revise and reconceptualize the traditional Protestant/Lutheran doctrine of justification by recasting it against the backdrop of a robust pneumatological and Trinitarian framework. In Kärkkäinen's model there is "real" participation for believers in the life of the triune God through the work of the Holy Spirit as the faithful Creator justifies himself and renews creation.

Graham McFarlane's "Towards a Theology of Togetherness—Life through the Spirit" offers reflections on a theology of human togetherness or at-one-ment in the context of global lack-of-human-togetherness (sin). In so doing McFarlane reflects on the ongoing reconciling role of the Spirit in the work of Christ on the cross in contemporary context. The Spirit's role in atonement includes believers' reception of power to become children of God, enablement to live by the law of the Spirit of life in Christ Jesus, gifts, a realizable eschaton, and the gift of true forgiveness.

André Munzinger provides the final essay: "Creative Reason and the Spirit: Identifying, Evaluating, and Developing Paradigms of Pneumatology." In it Munzinger sketches an interpretive paradigm that brings together the differing emphases of pneumatic creativity and reasonable reflection. He offers a way forward in adopting a paradigmatic approach to philosophical methodologies that differentiates among being, subjectivity, and language. Munzinger maintains that all three dimensions need to be drawn on together in a synchronic method of correlation.

The editors have collected a wide range of interesting essays on the subjects of pneumatology and Christology and, in some instances, the relationship between the two. As is typical in a Festschrift, the quality, detail, and insightfulness of the contributions vary considerably. In the present volume, the contributors provide a broad range of exegetical and theological insights. Some of the essays, given the constraints of space, are too ambitious in objective. Many, however, provide helpful contributions to contemporary scholarly discussion. Others are more suggestive in nature. Given the growing contemporary scholarly interest in pneumatology in biblical and theological studies and the ongoing interest in

Christology, this collection will be a useful resource for scholars working in either or both areas. Religious, theological, and seminary libraries will doubtlessly want add it to their inventory. Altogether, it is a fitting tribute to Max Turner, who has contributed creatively to both subjects—especially pneumatology—for more than three decades.

Scripture and Tradition: What the Bible Really Says, by Edith M. Humphrey. Acadia Studies in Bible and Theology. Grand Rapids: Baker Academic, 2013. Pp. x + 182. Paper. $19.99. ISBN 9780801039836.

Richard S. Briggs, St John's College, Durham University, Durham, U.K.

This is an elegant book about Christian reading practices that identify themselves from *within* the "Great Tradition," by which Humphrey means the theological consensus of the early creeds and councils. I think the subtitle is slightly unhelpful, for reasons I shall come to, and the title itself needs to be heard as a lightly polemical response to the notion of "scripture *or* tradition." It is not irrelevant to the project of this book that its author recounts her own journey through differing traditions within Christian faith, notably from the Salvation Army, then Anglicans, and now the Eastern Orthodox Church. To her credit, she makes no attempt to disguise this personal background. To my mind, it raises a very interesting question about what forms of argument make sense within each tradition. But first, what Edith Humphrey really says ...

The introduction orients the reader to the question of tradition and indeed to various traditions concerning what role tradition plays. To evangelicals, Humphrey says that everyone has a tradition, even if they think all they do is appeal to scripture. The Catholic (i.e., Roman) church at least offers clear articulations of the links between written and oral tradition and explicitly affirms that tradition has its part to play in (or with or alongside) the reading of scripture. In the context of Anglican and Wesleyan attempts to clarify the authoritative sources of Christian teaching, in three-fold or four-fold models of stools or quadrilaterals, Humphrey explores the slippage that often takes place as the formal elements of the model (scripture, tradition, reason, experience) get realigned in practice. In the face of such a crowd of competing frameworks, Humphrey's goal is expressed in the form of a question: "What does the Bible *really* say about tradition?" (22).

The first of the six chapters to follow is then a fairly straightforward study of "tradition" in the New Testament, focusing on the noun *paradosis* and the verb *paradidōmi.* Humphrey laments the absence of an English verb "to tradition," though this does not stop her coining such a term for frequent use through the book. What makes this chapter interesting is its simple but revealing focus on the ways in which English translations handle these terms. They typically obscure the relevant Greek words and offer circumlocutions, whenever "tradition" is intended in a positive sense (thus "teachings" or things "passed on'). On the other hand, they leave the translation as "tradition" whenever it is intended in a negative sense (thus Mark 7, as a parade example, where most translations still talk of the "traditions" that Jesus opposes). A secondary focus of this chapter is then the several references within the New Testament to the traditions that constitute the heart of Christian teaching as it is passed on from Jesus through the apostles to all the saints.

Chapter 2 is titled "Deadly Traditions" but actually takes a while to arrive at the focus on what can go wrong with tradition. Initially it is a rehearsal of the point that the stories that make up scripture (the Old Testament, in the first instance) were themselves passed down in traditions that exercised various degrees of creative interpretation as they passed the material along. By the time we arrive at the New Testament, we arrive at the Pharisaic/rabbinic traditions, on the one hand, and Jesus and Paul weighing in strongly against them, on the other, opposing certain kinds of tradition. Humphrey is then concerned to point out that what is being opposed here, the "deadly traditions" of her title, are those interpretations that make the text itself the goal rather than the pursuit of God. She then develops the further claim that within the New Testament itself one does not in fact find that written communication is valued more highly than other forms of communication. As a result, it is a mistake, she argues, to see "tradition" as an oral (and lesser) counterpart to the reliable written word. Rather, traditions are both oral and written, and they are essential to anyone's access to the real goal: God (or God in Christ, depending on the specific focus).

Chapter 3, "The Apostles, the Word, and the Letter," goes over similar ground but with a particular focus on how the apostles within the New Testament orient themselves to their own role in the tradition and again to the question of how they in turn relate the oral and written tradition. Particular focal points here include aspects of Galatians that certainly sound, at least to Protestant ears, as if Paul is an apostle of the direct word from the Lord rather than beholden to any tradition. By contrast, says Humphrey, the real issue is "about discerning the difference between living and dead tradition." (83) Likewise, 2 Pet 1 is read as witness to the living tradition of God's word both spoken and written. (72)

The sequel to the argument thus far is clearly the need to address the question of how to tell the difference between tradition that leads to life, or God, and tradition that needs to be rejected in the name of God. In fact, Humphrey delays this key topic to chapter 6 and inserts here two further chapters that do not obviously contribute to the specific focal questions of the book. First is a study of "The Blessed Delivery: Receiving in Both Directions." I read this as a study intended to head off any concern that tradition is an authoritarian top-down phenomenon. Instead, Humphrey emphasizes that God is both gift and giver in and among God's people and that the tradition is thus passed down both "from above" and "from below." The pay-off at the end of the chapter is that "[t]he proclamation of God's Word and the handing down of our family ways are matters that call not for shrill voices demanding equal rights but for faithfulness and humility, as God calls on us to exercise these within the company of the Church"

(108). The next chapter seems to range even more widely from the key topic, exploring "Tradition as God's Personal Gift": the personal God who gives God's self to God's people. A passing illustration probably serves best to anchor the relevance of this to the book as a whole: Humphrey compares learning a piano "in theory" (from a book) to learning a piano by way of lessons from a piano tutor who plays and models how to play. Although this chapter does not entirely draw this together into the argument, the point is clear: God may have given a book to the church, but this in itself would be to no avail if God were not personally present to "tutor" the church.

So we come to chapter 6: "Holy Tradition versus Human Traditions," with its subtitle, "Discerning the Difference Today." This opens with a recap of the interweaving of scripture and tradition that has been the focus thus far and sets the reader up to explore how change can take place within a tradition that is itself part of the revelation of God. Humphrey offers four "hard cases" to explore her thesis that "some traditions undergo change or modification ... [that may be] theological in nature" (137–38). The four "mutable" cases are: (1) the LXX rendition of Isa 6:9–10 as taken up in the Gospels, (2) the question of whether the New Testament enjoins upon Christians the keeping of a Sabbath (to which Humphrey answers no, although allows that the Sabbath makes something of a reappearance in the fourth century), (3) the notorious case of the rationale for the decree of the council of Jerusalem in Acts 15, which she reads, perhaps too briefly, as a short-term compromise not intended to be binding in perpetuity, and (4) the practice of invoking or addressing the Holy Spirit in prayer, in which different traditions have read the scriptural evidence in divergent ways. The overall argument here is that attention to scripture is the key in all cases. Then Humphrey turns to four debated matters today (at least among those who are attempting to submit their theological judgments to scripture): (1) women's head coverings in worship, a little oddly, (2) celibacy for clergy, (3) changes to Trinitarian formulae (thus "Creator–Redeemer–Sustainer" instead of "Father–Son–Spirit" as one obvious example, which Humphrey opposes), and (4) whether gender-inclusive translations, for instance, distort the text so as to mitigate against christological readings of Old Testament passages such as Ps 1. In all eight of these cases, the point is that there is theological work to be done in assessing what may or may not change: cultural change is never a good enough reason to jettison tradition.

A brief conclusion talks about the rule of faith, "reading with the fathers," and starts to point toward the "Great Tradition." Humphrey closes with a celebratory emphasis on the challenges and joys of inhabiting and negotiating tradition in the life of the church.

This is a serious book about a topic of ecclesial significance. Its slim format and at certain points its brevity of discussion should not disguise the weighty agenda: Humphrey wishes to mediate the riches of tradition to those she thinks may set it aside too quickly and default just to scripture. On the whole, this is a compelling presentation, though one that is set forth in somewhat insistent personal terms, at times appearing to serve as a kind of a testimony to Humphrey's pilgrimage into the Orthodox Church. I have two (related) questions for further consideration.

First, there is an underlying oddity about a book that seeks to work from "what the Bible really says" in service of an argument that the appropriate ecclesial configuration of scripture and tradition is not one that is based on scripture, pure and simple. In other words, this feels very much like a Protestant argument for an Orthodox position. At the risk of simplification, it is as if Humphrey's own view has changed in substance but retains the form of thinking that what counts as a good argument is "what the Bible really says." Conversion to Orthodoxy from elsewhere presumably involves a commitment to accepting that its realignment of priorities downgrades the typically Protestant argument that one asks first what scripture says. From the new vantage point, one would not anticipate any form of unmediated access to the Word of God in Scripture that is not via the Church's own tradition and office in the first place. Admittedly I speak as an (Anglican) outsider here, but the point, as I see it, is that what counts as the appropriate form of a theological argument is different across the different traditions that Humphrey has inhabited. Thus my first question: If this book were to set forth Humphrey's own convictions about the topic in a manner coherent with its own perspective, would it not proceed rather differently via a dogmatic and/or ecclesial account of what role the Orthodox tradition accords scripture and why, in light of which one might then go on to frame certain exegetical and interpretive questions?

The second question is a corollary. Humphrey's interlocutors, interestingly enough, are not biblical scholars all that often, though without a doubt she is fully aware of standard critical discussion among biblical scholars at every turn. Instead, she interacts lightly with some Catholic and Orthodox scholars, occasionally others, on the questions of framing the scripture/tradition issue. The result is a little unsatisfactory. For example, de Lubac's *L'Ecriture dans la Tradition* is mentioned twice but nothing else by him, while the wide-ranging considerations of Joseph Ratzinger (Pope Benedict XVI) are noted only in one brief footnote. It is as if Humphrey has attempted to engineer a discussion of scripture and tradition from the text up, whereas this is in fact a conversation already well-established, especially among the twentieth-century Catholic theologians mentioned. Arguably, at least, a more explicit joining of this conversation would have allowed the book either to go further and deeper or perhaps to clarify the extent to which one's conclusions might always be tradition-specific. Instead, complex questions of the criteria for assessing variant traditions are left somewhat underexplored. To take one example, where does Humphrey's argument intend to leave those of us in traditions that are not Orthodox but that do not start straightforwardly from scripture alone? All in all, it is unclear.

Nevertheless, there is much to appreciate here, and one may hope that Humphrey will return to these issues in further dialogue in the future.

Holy War in the Bible: Christian Morality and an Old Testament Problem, edited by Heath A. Thomas, Jeremy Evans, and Paul Copan. Downers Grove, Ill.: Inter-Varsity Press, 2013. Pp. 352. Paper. $26.00. ISBN 9780830839957.

Guenther ("Gene") Haas, Redeemer University College, Ancaster, Ontario, Canada

In the introductory chapter of this volume the authors note that "The 'holy wars' of the Old Testament stand in many ways as a theological crux in the goal of a right interpretation of Holy Scripture" (1). The challenge for biblical interpreters is what to make of biblical texts that present a God who commands ruthless warfare that sometimes includes genocidal extermination of people groups and that seem to support coercion and even violence against the enemies of the Christian faith, whether these are nations or communities. One's understanding of these biblical texts of divine warfare shapes one's theological perspective on the salvific movement of God and the missional calling of the church.

Chapter 1 introduces the volume as a whole. Geth Allison and Reid Powell rightly note that the issue demands an interdisciplinary approach. Thus this volume contains contributions by academics from a variety of perspectives: biblical, theological, ethical, philosophical, and historical. All problematic aspects of this matter are not resolved in this work, but the contributors do provide insights on the interpretation, ethical applications, and contextual applications on divine warfare in Scripture. This is especially helpful in the light of a history of misinterpretation and faulty appropriation by Christians and churches.

In chapter 2 Douglas Earl refutes the widely held belief that the "holy war" texts in Joshua were used to justify the Christian Crusades of the eleventh through the thirteenth centuries and subsequent colonialism and militarism of "Christian" nations. Through careful examination of the *Bible Moralisée* and *Glossa Ordinaria,* two influential medieval works of interpretation and application of biblical texts, Earl demonstrates that Joshua was primarily read in terms of a typology of the church (influenced by Origen's spiritual reading), not to support crusades. In addition, his investigation of the primary crusade texts, especially sermons, reveals that Joshua plays no role in promoting crusade. Rather, recurring appeal is made to the Maccabbeean revolt to support the call to sacrifice and even to martyrdom in the summons to liberate and reestablish what was captured by pagans. A survey of medieval texts also demonstrates that the book of Joshua is not used to support just-war theory.

Part 2 of the book consists of two chapters dealing with "Old Testament Perspectives." Stephen Chapman points out that the term "holy war" is not found anywhere in the Bible. He suggests that "Yahweh war" and "divine war" are more appropriate phrases to describe the ban (*ḥērem*) and divinely sanctioned warfare. God is the ultimate warrior who commands Israel to destroy idolatrous peoples so that his people may live in undivided devotion to their God. The goal of this periodic and limited warfare is peace, which is the thrust of Israel's history and which reaches fulfillment in the redemptive work of Christ.

In chapter 4 Heath Thomas briefly examines the response to the divine warrior as found in the Writings. Heath finds statements both of celebration that God fights on behalf of his people for justice and righteousness and of lament when God acts against his people for their injustice and idolatry. While both are prayerful expressions of faith in God's goodness and fidelity to his covenant, the latter allows for a spirituality that engages difficult issues and directs them to God.

Part 3 deals with "New Testament Perspectives." Each of the two chapters examines the use of warfare imagery in a New Testament book: Ephesians and Revelation. Through the detailed examination of such imagery, Timothy Gombis (Ephesians) and Alan Bandy (Revelation) show that these books portray God's warfare in the new covenant as directed against the spiritual powers opposed to, and even persecuting, Christ's church. The goal is to assure believers that they can find confidence and peace in the divine victory. To be part of the new humanity in Christ means participating in the rule and victory of God. Gombis unfolds the narrative emphasis in Ephesians that Christians have their participation in God's victory over the cosmic powers of evil through the death and resurrection of Christ. Bandy expounds the central theme of Revelation as God's vindication of persecuted Christians. God responds to their pleas for justice by promising the future retributive justice of Christ, the divine warrior, against these enemies. Both chapters argue that neither book provides any justification for militant Christian social action nor for the use of political power to achieve the victory of God. Christians embody and participate in this victory through lives of love and discipleship according to the sacrificial pattern of Christ, while patiently enduring hardship and trusting in God's justice.

Part 4, "Biblical-Theological Perspectives," offers two chapters that use a comprehensive biblical theology to situate divine warfare in the biblical metanarrative of redemption. In chapter 7 David Lamb surveys biblical passages from Exodus to Acts to argue that the motivations for Yahweh's warfare are always presented as compassion and anger. Yahweh responds in compassion to the cries of his oppressed people (e.g., in Exodus, Judges, Psalms, Isaiah), and he wages war in anger against the oppressors. This makes God's warfare not only less problematic but even worthy of praise and thanksgiving. In chapter 8 Douglas Earl deals directly with the ethical and theological difficulties of "the ban" (ḥērem) in Joshua. This poses a particular challenge for biblical theology in the light of the claim that the Old Testament biblical narrative of redemption finds it fulfillment in Christ's kingdom of love. Earl argues that the various occurrences of ḥērem in the Old Testament need not be interpreted as reports of literal genocides. Rather, the three main contexts in which ḥērem appears (Deuteronomic materials, Joshua, and the prophetic writings) suggest that it invokes separation from the idolatrous world and dedication to YHWH. Earl presents two other reasons for reading the ḥērem texts as symbolic/ existential/rhetorical rather than as literal/ontological/ historical: similar ḥērem imagery is found in other ancient Near Eastern texts, and the eschatological purpose of the biblical texts indicates the ultimate fate of the nations. The application of these texts for believers is not a report of, or call to, warfare but rather exhortation to faithfulness before God by radical separation from idolatry, mission to those facing judgment, and worship in response to Christ's redemption.

Part 5, "Ethical and Philosophical Perspectives," contains four chapters that present various attempts to harmonize divine warfare in the Old Testament with Christian morality. Daniel Heimbach finds in the Old Testament Yahweh wars a crusade ethic with clear conditions, criteria, and practices that God alone can authorize and initiate. Thus, there could never be divinely sanctioned war enacted by human initiative. Chapter 10, by Paul Copan and Matthew Flannagan, is devoted to refuting the argument by Raymond Bradley that ḥērem is inconsistent with Christian theism, especially the notion of a morally upright God. The authors respond with a hyperbolic interpretation of the ḥērem texts rather than a literal one, refuting Bradley's claim that God (ever) commands the slaughter of innocent civilians. In his chapter on "The Prophets' Call for Peace-Making Practices" Glen Stassen draws heavily from Norman Gottwald's *All the Kingdoms of the Earth* to highlight two ethical imperatives from the prophetic writings, that war is a sign of God's judgment on the unjust practices by one or both of the participants and that God calls his people is to just peace-making. This chapter is a puzzling part of the book for two reasons: Stassen does not deal with ḥērem in the Old Testament, and his material is focused on promoting his notion of the prophetic call to "just peace-making." In chapter 12 Robert Stewart presents a philosophical response to the (implied) argument of the New Atheists against belief in a God who commands genocide. While he surveys other possible rejoinders, Stewart devotes most of the chapter to an inerrantist Christian response that takes the biblical accounts of ḥērem as historical. He concludes by pointing out that the selective and caricatured use by the New Atheists of biblical and theological material does not undermine the Christian belief based on the whole of the Bible, that God is holy, trustworthy, and loving.

Part 6, "Theological Perspectives," contains two essays. In "The Unholy Notion of Holy War," Murray Rae argues for Christian pacifism by appealing to early church fathers and councils and by refuting the just-war arguments of Reinhold Niebuhr, Karl Barth, and Oliver O'Donovan. Rae concludes by appealing in a rather cursory manner to the traditional New Testament pacifist texts to reject any use of military action to oppose evil. It is also puzzling why this essay is included, since Stassen's essay is focused on endorsing pacifism, and his only treatment of ḥērem is to summarily dismiss it as part of the inferior Old Testament ethic. In the final chapter, "'Holy War' and the New Atheism," Stephen Williams argues that the New Atheists' problem with "holy war" in the Bible is ultimately their problem with God. Thus, the only adequate response is to present and defend the comprehensive portrait of the character and actions of the biblical God.

The volume ends with a chapter of concluding observations by two of the editors to the question, "Where do we go from here?" First, they note that philosophical/ethical considerations require careful distinctions: between descriptive and the prescriptive claims, and between historically specific, and normative absolute, values/obligations. Further work in this area requires not only a clear conception of different notions of justice but also a biblical account of divine justice resulting from God's self-disclosure through actions in the world. Concerning biblical and theological considerations, the editors note the importance of understanding the varieties of warfare within specific contexts as well as within the biblical metanarrative. Further biblical research should explore and relate the two biblical themes of God's judgment on rebellious people and the divine mercy toward and even suffering with those under divine judgment.

This volume serves as a valuable resource for dealing with this difficult issue of *ḥērem* in Scripture. First, some common misconceptions are corrected: there are no appeals to "holy war" in the crusades and later colonialism; the practice of *ḥērem* in the biblical narrative is limited; and divine warfare is sometimes practiced against idolatrous and corrupt Israel itself. Second, the fact that this issue is engaged by authors in various disciplines recognizes that it must be dealt with from various perspectives: biblical interpretation, narrative analysis, systematic theology, philosophy, apologetics, and ethics. It is not simply a matter of how the biblical narratives of *ḥērem* are interpreted but also of how such divinely commanded acts fit with redemptive history culminating in Christ and of our understanding of a God who commands such acts. Divine warfare also bears upon our understanding of Christian ethics and the challenge of Christian apologetics today. Third, the contributions are not confined to the literalistic interpretations characteristic of the evangelical world. While some may find the range of contributions too narrow for their liking, there is some a clear attempt to broaden the conversation.

While there are some weak points to this volume—two chapters that do not directly engage the issue of *ḥērem* and the absence of a chapter in which divine warfare is discussed by a proponent of just-war theory—the book serves as a valuable resource on this difficult issue. While the authors do not all agree on the interpretations and applications of the texts, and while this volume is not the final word on the matter, it has definitely advanced the discussion.

From Jesus to the New Testament: Early Christian Theology and the Origin of the New Testament Canon, by Jens Schröter. Translated by Wayne Coppins. Baylor–Mohr Siebeck Studies in Early Christianity. Waco, Tex.: Baylor University Press, 2013. Pp. xiv + 417. Cloth. $59.95. ISBN 9781602588226.

Lee Martin McDonald, Acadia University, Wolfville, Nova Scotia, Canada

Jens Schröter has produced a helpful examination of the origin of the New Testament canon, tracing its origins back to Jesus himself and the early interpretations of his teachings and deeds. This volume was originally published in German as *Von Jesus zum Neuen Testament* (2007) and subsequently translated into English as the inaugural volume of the Baylor–Mohr Siebeck Studies in Early Christianity series. Schröter offers a framework for understanding the various historical and theological processes that led to the formation of the New Testament canon, attempting to connect them to Jesus himself, followed by Paul as an early interpreter of the gospel about Jesus and its implications, and Luke's Doppelwerk as a whole that bridged the witness of Jesus to the early church through the apostles. Schröter clarifies the criteria employed in the selection and deselection of books in the New Testament corpus that he says is also the foundation for a New Testament theology.

The volume is divided into four parts. Part 1 (chs. 1–4) is a sophisticated examination of the nature of history and how historical inquiry can be understood in light of the biblical claims of God's activity in history. For Schröter, Christian faith must be investigated by the same standards and methodologies that apply to all fields of historical inquiry, but he argues that this alone cannot account for the New Testament story about Jesus. Part 2 (chs. 5–11) focuses on an interpretation of Jesus that is commensurate with a careful critical-historical examination of his life, but also in keeping with the New Testament proclamation of him. Paul's interpretation of Jesus using metaphors fit within the already-acknowledged understanding of Jesus and the gospel about him. Finally, Luke presents a salvation-historical understanding of the origins of the church in relation to the history of Israel and the activity of God. Part 3 (chs. 12–14) deals with canonical formation that connects Schröter's prior discussions of Jesus, Paul, and Luke-Acts to a rationale for the emergence of the New Testament canon. Finally, part 4 (chs. 15–16) concludes with summary of the challenges of constructing a New Testament theology and a discussion of the criteria that led to the formation of the New Testament, the foundation of that theology.

More specifically, Schröter investigates the Christian traditions about Jesus and the early church's proclamation about him through modern historical understanding. He contends that any inquiry of Jesus and the traditions about him must be involved in historical-critical investigations involving memory, recollection, and historical fact, as well as in a theological understanding of God's activity in Jesus that he sometimes calls "myth." The myth designation does not deny the reality of the activity of God in the story of Jesus the Christ but distinguishes it from other categories of *historical* inquiry. The combination of both approaches are necessary for understanding the life, death, and resurrection of Jesus (49–70). The faith that maintains that Jesus lived in history cannot be separated from historical-critical inquiry, but that alone does not establish the reality of Jesus' life and fate. "If one nevertheless asks about the events under the conditions of the historical-critical consciousness, then one must remain conscious of the fact that such an approach also does not get to the reality behind the events" (69). Like others, Schröter contends that the significance and interpretation of the activity of God in the life and activity of Jesus cannot be understood solely by historical-critical inquiry alone, but what remains cannot be classified as a historical "science." Rather, it is something beyond the scope of both history and science as we now know it. I question here, however, whether Schröter has made that case for modern scholars. His use of "science" and "myth" may be more confusing to

English-speaking readers than to those more familiar with Gustav Droysen, Paul Ricoeur, and Rudolf Bultmann. Schröter's later discussion of this (130–31) makes it clearer that by "myth" he refers to the *interpretive* element in historical inquiry rather than concluding whether something is true or false. He understands that the epistimological presuppositions of interpreters of the Jesus tradition always color their conclusions about the events they are investigating (73).

Schröter follows this with an examination of the biblical tradition of Jesus (chs. 5–6), opting not for the usual Mark and Q hypothesis as the original sources for that tradition but rather, like Dunn and Herder, appealing to the oral tradition that circulated among the earliest Christians and found its way into the *freely constructed* Gospel narratives (75–76). Because Christianity claims to be a faith rooted in a historical person who lived and died in a specific time and geographical location, Schröter insists that Jesus' story must be subjected to historical-critical examination. He adds that archaeological evidence also helps identify the context in which Jesus lived as a historical person (95ff.). The theological interests of the church, however, must accompany any historical-critical inquiry of Jesus traditions. He does not believe the church's message about Jesus can be effectively evaluated apart from the conviction of their authors that in the life, death, and resurrection of Jesus the activity of God is also present. However, Christian proclamation cannot be understood without historical-critical inquiry as well, and this "mixture" of history and theology is essential for a realistic picture of Jesus as he actually was.

Schröter contends that the primary sources for investigating the historical Jesus are the Synoptic Gospels, although he acknowledges that the Gospel of John also offers independent and useful historical information (96 n. 4). While non-canonical writings, especially the apocryphal Gospels, do have some benefit in understanding the Jesus tradition, he concludes that their value is often overestimated (96). He also makes clear that the writing of history is not necessarily a reconstruction of the past but rather "history" written from the perspective and values of the writer (98–99). Also, contrary to earlier studies that concentrated on the sayings of Jesus and often ignored their narrative contexts, the sayings of Jesus in the Gospels are better understood in their *narrative* presentations and cannot be adequately understood apart from that historical context (130–32).

In chapters 7 and 8 Schröter defends that there was only one gospel presented in the early church, explaining that the divisions in the early church came in relation to the application of that gospel to concrete situations, as in the understanding of the function of the law in Jewish and Gentile Christian contexts. Galatians 2:16 is a pivotal text for him in which he argues that, while there were divisions in earliest Christianity on the importance of the law, the gospel was the same. Schröter begins with Pokorny's 1985 arguments to contend that there was only one Christology despite its different applications in emerging situations (Gentile Christianity). This Christology can also be seen in the metaphorical language of Paul as a means of clarifying the gospel to contemporary developments in early Christianity (ch. 9). He concludes his focus on the

Christology of early Christianity with a discussion of Luke's understanding of how salvation history is rooted in the promises of God to Israel and how Luke connects those traditions with the gospel and all the apostles and the extension of the salvation of Israel going also to Gentiles through faith in Jesus the Christ (chs. 10–11). Despite how Acts seems to exclude Jews from that salvation as a result of the hardening of their hearts (Acts 13:46; 18:6; 28:26–28), Luke does not exclude Jewish participation, and even in Acts it was only temporary (so Paul, Rom 11), and even after such declarations Paul continued to evangelize Jews (227–46). These chapters provide the background for understanding subsequently how Acts serves as a bridge that ties the whole of the New Testament canon together (chs. 12–15), focusing on God's salvation to Jews and Gentiles in light of the promises to God to Israel.

The third and fourth parts of this study (chs. 12–16) are at the heart of Schröter's enterprise and focus on the selectivity of the books that reflect the story of Jesus. He prefaces this by observing that the notion of canon initially had to do with a *regula*/rule/canon of faith and not with a specific collection of sacred books (fourth century) and that there were other Christian books read by the early Christians that were not eventually included in the binding texts that make up the New Testament canon. He rightly claims that it is "self-evident" that the "New Testament texts did not yet possess their status as texts that were binding for the Christian church at the time of their emergence, but obtained this in a lengthy process" (331). The Gospels, he claims, eventually formed a four-Gospel collection by the second and third centuries, and the Acts of the Apostles formed the connection that bridged the witness of Jesus with the writings of Paul (formed late first century or early second) and the rest of the apostles.

For Schröter, the teaching of Jesus was the "impulse" for the New Testament canon (250–57) and underscores that he was the undisputed authority of the early church whose words were often understood as "scripture" (e.g., 1 Tim 5:18; 1 Cor 9:14; Did. 13.2) and that the New Testament takes its origin in the words and narratives of Jesus, including his fate (death, resurrection, exaltation). Schröter is also aware that for a couple of centuries other books were read in the churches along with the New Testament writings, but at their core were the canonical Gospels and letters attributed to Paul. Schröter notes the many challenges in discovering the "original" historical Jesus or the "original text" of the New Testament and rightly observes that until the invention of the printing press there could be no universal text acknowledged by all. There was no "original New Testament," but what we have is an agreement on the parameters of the message of and about Jesus (ch. 12). While acknowledging the considerable diversity in the New Testament canon (340), Schröter suggests that the diversity in the New Testament canon is due in part because the canon came into existence largely by exclusion of heretical texts rather than by a formal fixation of canonical texts (344).

The criteria employed for distinguishing between canonical and noncanonical writings in antiquity included the notion of heresy, namely, that which did not cohere with what had been handed on in the churches (Irenaeus), but also whether a writing had been forged (Origen and Eusebius). Authenticity alone, however, did not make the case for canonicity, since the writings of neither Clement of Rome nor Ignatius were heretical or forged (304–13). Schröter also observes that the canonical Gospels were always listed in the later lists of canonical books, but the so-called noncanonical Gospels were never in those lists. The parameters of the acceptable books in the canon was guided by a broad agreement on the witness of and about Jesus. The earliest theology of the church was rooted in a Jesus tradition that influenced its decisions about what books constituted their binding collection.

Schröter claims that what accounts for the various New Testament books is that the witness of Jesus is *best* preserved in them: a *historical* Jesus who lived and died among humanity (contrary to Docetism) and was exalted. He also emphasizes the importance of the apostolic heritage (writings believed to be produced by an apostle or someone close to an apostle) and the commitment of the New Testament authors to the scriptures of Israel, the Christian Old Testament. Those second-century heresies that ignored or dispised the Jewish heritage and its scriptures (Marcion and Gnosticism) or emphasized new prophecies (Montanism), were excluded because they were out of step with the inherited tradition of the church that is rooted in the witness of Jesus (ch. 16). Early Christian heresies denied the humanity and suffering of Jesus and the church's relationship with the history of Israel and its sacred scriptures. Schröter contends that there never could be a New Testament without an Old Testament!

Schröter is well informed about the notion of history and its development in modern times, although some may disagree with his notion of history as a "science," and his understanding of an appropriate hermeneutical approach for interpreting the biblical message needs further clarification. I am uncomfortable using the language of "science" in regard to historical investigations of the New Testament, since the limitations of that inquiry have long been known and are often at odds with modern scientific research despite a number of methodological overlaps.

Schröter is conversant with contemporary biblical scholarship, including traditional German scholarship, such as we see in his references to F. C. Baur, Strauss, Harnack, Wrede, Schweitzer, Bultmann, and many others. His bibliography reflects an awareness of contemporary scholarship in the overlapping fields that he investigates, and he shows considerable awareness of the ancient sources as well. He argues well against positions that are no longer useful in historical Jesus studies, New Testament theology, and canon formation issues and offers helpful guidance and resources for future research in those fields. No other book, to my knowledge, describes the relationship between the early witness of Jesus, canon formation, and the theology of the New Testament. While each major section of this book could easily become an extended volume in itself, bringing them all together is a special talent. In sum, this an excellent book that should lead to a fair amount of rewriting of both historical Jesus and canon formation books!

EARLY CHRISTIANITY AND EARLY CHRISTIAN LITERATURE

Das frühe Christentum und die Stadt, edited by Bendemann, Reinhard von, and Markus Tiwald. Beiträge zur Wissenschaft vom Alten und Neuen Testament 198. Stuttgart: Kohlhammer, 2012. Pp. 256. Paper. €39.90. ISBN 9783170220737.

Stephan Witetschek, Ludwig-Maximilians-Universität München, Munich, Germany

It has become a piece of common wisdom that Christianity, although originating from a rural movement, spread throughout the Roman world mostly as a city religion. This should quite naturally prompt New Testament scholars from highly urbanized Western societies to recognize the city as a worthy topic of research—parallels between urban religious situations in the first and in the twenty-first century are obvious. It is due to this reflection that New Testament scholars living and working in the Ruhr region in northwestern Germany ("Die Megalopolis des Ruhrgebietes," 7) have focused two conferences (in 2010 and 2011) on the city as the habitat of early Christianity. The papers given at these two conferences are now published in this volume.

In the introduction (9–42), the two editors enter into a critical dialogue with Max Weber's conception of a "city" (Stadt) and with its reception among sociologists and historians. They suggest an approach to the phenomenon of ancient cities (including the distinction between city and countryside) along several parameters, such as the geographical position, the political constitution, social structures, economy, buildings (contrary to the "definite" state we encounter on excavation sites, ancient cities, too, were constantly subject to change and rebuilding), defense, dependence on supra-urban authorities, legal status, availability of technology, access to education and health care, religion, and, finally, the idea of *urbanitas.* In all this complexity it becomes clear that to speak of a "city" carries with it a broad range of connotations and implications.

The article by Reinhard von Bendemann ("Jesus und die Stadt im Markusevangelium," 43–68) goes back to the beginning, to Jesus' activity in and around Galilee *as narrated by Mark.* Von Bendemann argues that, although much of the narrative is situated in rural regions, Mark, writing for an urban audience, proposes a positive view of cities (the Decapolis, the area of Tyre and Sidon, or Jerusalem) as places of revelation and proclamation. In this sense, cities are "agents of meaning."

Rainer Riesner ("Zwischen Tempel und Obergemach—Jerusalem als erste messianische Stadtgemeinde," 69–91) offers an overview of the Jewish-Christian community in Jerusalem before 70 CE. Based on a rather optimistic reading of Acts together with scattered traditions (mainly preserved by Eusebius) and on Qumran parallels, he describes it as an Essene-like community whose traditions are found, among others, in Luke's special material and in 2 Cor 6:14–7:1.

Thomas Söding ("Apostel gegen Apostel: Ein Unfall im antiochenischen Großstadtverkehr," 92–113) understands the Antiochene incident (Gal 2) as peculiar to an urban setting with a strong Jewish community and a certain level of diversity among Christians. It is, according to Söding, not a conflict between city (Paul) and countryside (Peter) but between two cities, Antioch and Jerusalem.

Kurt Erlemann ("Antiochia und der Hebräerbrief—eine Milieustudie," 114–27) makes the attempt to localize Hebrews with its critical view of the empirical sacrificial cult (among other things) within the theology of the "Hellenists" in Antioch (Acts 6:1–6; 11:19–30), composed in the 60s of the first century. However, he only suggests the *possibility* of an Antiochene context and gathers some arguments *against* a post-70 date for Hebrews, but these indications do not add up to a *positive* argument (the next-to-last sentence: "Und natürlich ist hier nichts zu beweisen" [126]).

With Markus Tiwald ("Frühchristliche Pluralität in Ephesus," 128–45), the focus turns toward another center of early Christianity. Tiwald states that recent research tends to assume a remarkable plurality among the several early Christian groups in Ephesos at the end of the first century. His test case is Revelation and its way of dealing with the Nicolaitans, presumably urban Christians whose more liberal views on social participation were quite the same as Paul's. In this regard, the dividing line is not to be drawn between Jews and Christians but between more "liberal" and more "conservative" views in both Judaism and Christianity, each of which had its place in the setting of a large city such as Ephesos.

Jens-Christian Maschmeyer ("Der Glaube auf dem Marktplatz: Freiheitskämpfe in Korinth," 146–63) takes us one stage further to the next "Pauline" city. He understands the problems discussed in 1 Cor 6–10 as caused by the setting of a Hellenistic/Roman city, yet he mainly elaborates Paul's conception of freedom in rather philosophical terms and then attaches the conclusion: "Die Stadt mit ihrer 'weltanschaulichen' Pluralität wird zum Theologie produzierenden Ort." (162) Does it?

The contribution by Alexander Weihs ("'Gott liebt einen fröhlichen Geber': Zur Strategie und Theologie paulinischer Spendenakquise in Korinth (2Kor 8—9)," 164–88) remains in Corinth. As the title suggests, Weihs gives a thorough analysis of Paul's arguments in 2 Cor 8–9, where the apostle endows the donations he asks for with theological dignity: they are founded in Christ's pro-existence and are a tangible sign of unity with the community in Jerusalem.

Jan Schäfer's paper ("Vom Zentrum zum Zentrum: Die Achse der Apostelgeschichte von Jerusalem nach Rom," 189–207) fits the design of the volume, since it provides some theoretical reflections on the dichotomy of center and periphery and its use for understanding the conception of space in Acts. In his reading, the narrative of Acts traces the move from one center (Jerusalem) to another (Rome) via several cities, that is, centers with their peripheries, where Christian centers (e.g., Ephesos) are established.

Robert Vorholt ("Alle Wege führen nach Rom: Die Hauptstadt im Blickfeld des Paulus," 208–18) is less interested in the city of Rome as such but rather in Paul's missionary strategy as it is expressed in Romans: its focus on Rome follows from Paul's Roman-imperial conception of space.

Quite the same is true for the contribution by Volker Rabens ("'Von Jerusalem aus und rings umher...' (Röm 15,19): Die paulinische Missionsstrategie im Dickicht der Städte," 219–37). He, too, is more interested in Paul and Paul's ideas about his mission, but in the latter part he treats Paul's way of earning his living (by manual labor) as peculiar to a city setting.

Finally, Peter Wick ("Das Paradies in der Stadt: Das himmlische Jerusalem als Ziel der Offenbarung des Johannes," 238–50) discloses the implications of the city imagery in Rev 21–22. He interprets the end of Revelation in dialogue with Gen 1–11, especially with the rather negative assessments of cities in Gen 4:17 and Gen 11: now the place of salvation is the city. This imagery brings him to the question of continuity. In dialogue with Isa 65, he favors an understanding of this "new creation" as a transformation rather than annihilation and substitution. Thus, his contribution provides in fact a theological assessment of the city.

It is not easy to assess the volume as a whole. All the essays come with rich bibliographies. A good number of them are explicitly focused on the topic of the city (esp. von Bendemann, Tiwald, Schäfer, Wick) and are thus very instructive on the theoretical level as well as in the exegesis of concrete texts. Others have a rather loose connection with the topic of the city and appear more interested, for example, in classical research questions about Paul himself than in the significance of city settings for his mission. With regard to the content of the volume, the title can be misleading: all the contributions remain within the New Testament and the first century, hence they study only one section of early Christianity ("Das frühe Christentum"). Notwithstanding this minor criticism, the reader of this volume encounters a broad range of exegetical approaches to the significance of cities in the New Testament—the life setting of Christians marked by enormous diversity, religious and otherwise, both then and now. Thus, this project is a highly commendable piece of contextual exegesis, this time in a modern "Western" society.

The Myth of Persecution: How Early Christians Invented a Story of Martyrdom, by Candida R. Moss. San Francisco: HarperOne, 2013. Pp. 308. Hardcover. $25.99. ISBN 9780062104526.

N. Clayton Croy, Trinity Lutheran Seminary, Columbus, Ohio

Candida Moss, Professor of New Testament and Early Christianity at the University of Notre Dame, has penned a provocative book that is sure to enthuse some readers and enrage others. The thesis is evident in the title, and the topic is one on which Moss is well-qualified to write. She has previously written two academic books on early Christian martyrdom (one being a revision of her Yale dissertation) as well as a raft of scholarly articles.

The book's introduction reveals that the author's concerns are not solely historical. Moss begins with the story of the New Year's Day (2011) bombing of a Coptic Church in Alexandria, Egypt, a violent act that ended the lives of over twenty worshipers and injured nearly a hundred more. Moss notes that the victims were soon declared martyrs and that, rather than turning the other cheek, the Christian community became "militarized," as the incident came to be seen in the context of a two-thousand-year-old religious conflict. Moss's concern is that the rhetoric of persecution "legitimates and condones retributive violence" (3). The foundation of that rhetoric, the "myth," goes far beyond modern attacks against Coptic Christians; it is rooted in a narrative that begins with the early church. But according to Moss, this rhetoric lacks justification, and "the purpose of this book is to show that the foundations for this idea [sustained early Christian persecution] are imaginary" (20).

Chapter 1 examines "Martyrdom before Christianity." The aim here is to refute the notion that martyrdom was peculiar to the Christian faith, and Moss rightly argues that the phenomenon of martyrdom existed long before the term was coined. Although the technical meaning of *martus* as "one who bears witness at the expense of his or her life" may be a Christian innovation, there are clearly precedents in the "noble death" tradition of the classical era and in the heroes of the Maccabean conflict. The similarities here have validity, but Moss overplays them and obscures distinctive Jewish features when she implies borrowing from Plato on the part of 2 Maccabees (50).

Chapter 2 explores "Christian Borrowing of Jewish and Pagan Martyrdom Traditions." Early Christian martyr acts occasionally allude to the Maccabean martyrs and, more rarely, to the example of Socrates, but it is an error to assume, as Moss does, that the presence of intertextual echoes means that narratives ostensibly relating actual events are nothing but "highly stylized rewritings of earlier traditions" (56). Luke has indeed given us a portrait of Jesus' passion in which the central character is more resolute than in Mark. Whether this means that "Luke's heavy-handed editorial work" constitutes overwriting the events with a non-Christian theology of noble death is another question (61). If Luke's aim was to portray Jesus as a second Socrates, he could have made it a lot clearer. Moss similarly analyzes parallels between the Martyrdom of Polycarp and both canonical and classical accounts of death. She acknowledges similarities to Jesus' passion but also finds Greco-Roman philosophical influences. Again, meager evidence is inflated to conclude that "one of the most famous and important Christian martyrdom accounts was dependent on pagan martyrdom for its substance" (66). Other early Christian martyrs are likewise portrayed as "heroes of the classical world [who] were reshaped into soldiers for Christ" (79). Allusions to pagan models occasionally peek above the surface in martyr acts, but echoes of Jesus' passion are far more numerous and more deliberate. Moss's analysis lacks nuance and a sense of proportionality.

Chapter 3 picks up the language of the book's subtitle: "Inventing Martyrs in Early Christianity." Moss begins with the story of Chrysanthus and Daria, saints in the Catholic and Orthodox churches, a story that she characterizes as "romantic, exciting, interesting, and completely untrue" (85). Moss may be overconfident in her dismissal of the account (*National Geographic* aired a program in April 2011 describing the analysis of relics from the tomb of Chrysanthus and Daria that seemed to corroborate the basic fact of their death), but she raises an important issue thereby. The cult of the saints that began in the fourth century gave rise to a large body of hagiography, stories of venerated martyrs that often were of dubious historical value. Moss notes that later Protestants were critical of the cult, especially its traffic in relics and superstition. She helpfully describes the work of John Bolland and his students, who gave birth to critical hagiography (89–91). Without question, the corpus of martyr acts, especially those stemming from the Middle Ages, contains a mixture of history, legend, and piety. In the spirit of the "Bollandists," Moss isolates the six authentic martyr accounts that remain from the church before 250 CE. She is emphatic that "these six accounts are as good as it is going to get" and that "if we cannot trust that these stories preserve the events precisely, then we cannot trust that any martyrdom stories do" (93). Moss is correct that these six accounts are generally judged to be the most reliable ones *from the early period*, but the implication that everything thereafter is legendary chaff is quite mistaken. Persecution from 250 to the early fourth century was even more systematic and widespread, and it is often attested by contemporary or near-contemporary writers.

The bulk of this chapter is devoted to a march through these six accounts, dissecting them for every possible anachronism or inconsistency, real or perceived. The drift of the chapter is clear: even in these six stories we are on shaky ground. But Moss's skepticism is often unwarranted. She says, for example, that "literary flourishes make it impossible for us to imagine that the *Martyrdom of Polycarp* is a historical account of the events as they actually happened" (100). But surely literary flourishes versus historical information is a false dichotomy. The same is true for allusions to the Gospels, alleged anachronisms, and other peculiarities. Some of these are hardly as compelling as Moss thinks; others, even if valid, scarcely require us to dissolve the account into sheer fiction or a "pious fraud" (104). Moss earnestly argues that the Martyrdom of Polycarp was written in the third century (nearly everyone dates it to the 150s or 160s), but the chief merit of this dating is that it serves Moss's thesis by removing the story further away from the events, thus undermining its historical value. In general, the issues that Moss raises in this chapter deserve consideration, but they do not necessarily compel her conclusion. She notes that "there is no early Christian account that has been preserved without emendation" and that "none of the early Christian martyrdom stories is completely historically accurate" (124). Even if one grants both of these claims, the result is by no means a thin residue of legend. Emended texts with occasional inaccuracies may still relate substantially historical events.

Chapter 4 takes up the basic question: "How Persecuted Were the Early Christians?" In contrast to the distorted picture of constant persecution that we get from Christian literature, art, and film, Moss asserts that "Christians were executed as the result of imperial initiatives" for fewer than ten years out of the nearly three hundred from Jesus to Constantine (129). Apart from the fact that someone would have to be omniscient to make this claim authoritatively, the numbers Moss cites misrepresent the lived reality of Christians in the Roman Empire. As Paul Holloway warns, "scholars of early Christianity make a serious mistake when they focus on the 'local and sporadic' nature of early Christian persecution—as if tallying actual deaths allows one to somehow quantify the lived experience of lethal prejudice" (*Coping with Prejudice*, 36). The *threat* to Christians' lives pervaded the first three centuries, with the exception perhaps of the latter part of the third century. Even when martyrdom was not being carried out, all that stood between Christians and the executioner was the lack of a *delator* (an accuser).

Chapter 4 first treats the persecution of Christians by the Jews. In a post-Holocaust world, this is indeed an area to tread lightly, but Moss's minimizing conclusion involves a peculiar word game. She claims that Jews did not persecute Christians in the first century because Christians did not yet exist: "Not only did the name 'Christian' not yet exist, but the *idea* of Christians as a group distinct from the rest of Judaism did not exist in the lifetimes of the apostles" (133, emphasis original). The alleged nonexistence of the name does not reckon seriously with Acts 11:26; 26:28 and 1 Pet 4:16, but more importantly, the fact that Jews might not have viewed Christianity as a religion distinct from Judaism is irrelevant. Persecution can take place *within* a religious group. By Moss's line of reasoning, Pharisees, Sadducees, and Essenes did not exist in the first century either!

More troubling in this chapter is the treatment of Roman sources: Tacitus and Pliny. Tacitus (*Annals* 15.44) records the famous incident of the Great Fire in Rome and Nero's attempt to pin the blame on Christians. Because Tacitus wrote about fifty years after the events, and because Moss finds his use of "Christians" to be anachronistic, she asserts that Tacitus "does not provide evidence for their persecution" (139). There is simply no warrant for this kind of skepticism. The Great Fire, including Nero's persecution of Christians, is accepted by virtually all Roman historians. The persecution is partly corroborated by Suetonius (16.2) as well as 1 Clem. 5–6. The difficulty that Nero poses for Moss's "myth" is an early, large scale, lethal assault on Christians. Even if this was limited to Rome—which appears to be the case—it set a precedent to which later emperors and governors could appeal.

Pliny is harder for Moss to dismiss, since he deals with contemporary issues in his own administration. Trajan's response is notoriously terse and does not directly address every issue that Pliny raised, but the ambiguity does not permit Moss's conclusion that "the climate was hostile, but there was no active persecution" (145). Both Pliny's letter and Trajan's response presuppose that being a Christian was punishable by death. The correspondence does not create a policy but rather clarifies a preexisting practice. Whether it had the force of imperial law would have mattered little to the Christians whom Pliny executed.

Moss moves on to the emperor Decius and later incidents of centrally orchestrated persecution. She notes that these events caused a crisis for the church, both externally with Roman authority and internally in dealing with those who chose exile, relapse, or subterfuge rather than death. Even here Moss wonders if Decius is rightly characterized as a persecutor, given that his legislation may have been politically motivated. But her effort to drive a wedge between intent and result is unsuccessful. Moss's discussion of Decius, Valerian, and Diocletian underscores their political motivation of unifying the empire and tends to exonerate them of religious persecution. She acknowledges that a dichotomy of politics and religion is impossible in antiquity (174), but she still seems to appeal to it when she insists on distinguishing between persecution and prosecution (172). A century or more after the Pliny-Trajan correspondence, the emperors had to know that their actions would chiefly impact Christians and that their political aims entailed religious proscriptions.

Chapter 5 deals with the reasons for Rome's hostility toward Christians. Moss rightly contextualizes the issue by noting that life in antiquity was often brutal and that capital punishment was meted out broadly. Christians were not the only group with whom Rome had issues; there were also the Druids and Bacchants. Rome was suspicious of novelty and secrecy wherever they occurred. The Christians' particular error, however, was their refusal to support the *pax deorum* by honoring the gods of Rome. In this respect, the charge of atheism against Christians is paradoxical but understandable from Rome's point of view. In addition, there were the rumors of cannibalism and incest, which, although groundless, undoubtedly fed the fires of popular resentment.

In chapter 6 Moss examines common misperceptions and half-truths about martyrs: their pacifism, passivity, meekness, altruism, and so on. There are proper clarifications here, combined with some insufficiently discriminate analysis. True, not all Christian martyrs were passive. There were some voluntary martyrs who "outed" themselves to the authorities without coercion. Whether that justifies Moss's assertion that "Christians were eager to die" (196) is debatable. In addition, some martyrs railed against their persecutors, but Moss fails to appreciate fully the distinction between rhetorical, eschatological violence and real, historical violence. She cites the Circumcellions, a fringe group of the schismatic Donatists, as an example of violent Christian martyrs, despite their being roundly condemned by the church fathers. Moss's definition of martyr seems to expand to include persons who will taint the reputation of early Christians and then contract to exclude passive and humble persons who might provide historical evidence for the "myth." Moss asserts that "there was little difference between the behavior of orthodox Christians and the behavior of heretical ones" (213). Are we really to believe that Polycarp and the Circumcellions were cut from the same cloth?

In chapter 7 Moss identifies Eusebius as the architect of the myth. Through a selective and censorial telling of the story of the Christianity, Eusebius created the myth of the persecuted church. According to Moss, his use of the martyrs amounts to a power play; he associates martyrs with the orthodox bishops of his own day and their persecutors with the heretics. But Eusebius lived through the "Great Persecution" under Diocletian. Even if he sometimes employs the rhetorical power of martyrs for the sake of the church, it is hardly the case that the persecution that he himself witnessed or knew of is only a grand, fraudulent myth. Eusebius is a critical, contemporary witness for the events of this period. There is irony in Moss's criticism of Eusebius's method: "he suppresses the voices of those who disagree with him and ignores information that does not fit with his argument" (217). One could change the pronouns in that sentence to the feminine and it would describe Moss to a tee.

Chapter 8 brings the argument back to the contemporary scene. The Left's favorite whipping boys—Glenn Beck, Newt Gingrich, Rush Limbaugh, Ann Coulter, and pro-life bishops—are trotted out. When they express concerns about life and religious liberty, Moss finds the perpetuation of the "myth" of Christian martyrdom. Moss reasserts: "Very few Christians died, and when they did die, it was often because they were seen as politically subversive" (255). Doesn't this sound just a bit like (first minimizing and then) blaming the victims?

Despite the author's considerable erudition, this is a deeply flawed book, a work of revisionist history. One might judge that conservative Christians in the West have sometimes overplayed the persecution card, but they have not created instances of cultural hostility out of whole cloth, and they certainly did not create the "Age of the Martyrs" out of thin air. More important, Moss largely overlooks modern Christianity in the two-thirds world, especially in the Middle East and in Communist states. Here we find not just cultural insensitivity but old-fashioned persecution: arrests, beatings, and decapitations. Exactly one week after the publication of Moss's book, another book came out: *Persecuted: The Global Assault on Christians*, authored by Paul Marshall, Lela Gilbert, and Nina Shea. They document persecution in about forty different countries. Moss's opening story about the bombing of the Coptic Church in Alexandria is part of that reality, but the fact that Moss uses this story to launch a criticism, in effect, of the rhetoric *of the Coptic victims* rather than the actions of the jihadist perpetrators is grotesque.

While conservative Christian rhetoric is sometimes guilty of excesses, this book swings hard in the opposite direction, revising history and denying much of the evidence for early Christian persecution. Modern ideology drives Moss's thesis more than ancient testimony, and the result is a distortion of history more severe than the caricature she wants to expose.

Die Bibel bei den Manichäern und verwandte Studien, edited by Alexander Böhlig, Siegfried G. Richter, and Peter Nagel. Nag Hammadi and Manichaean Studies 80. Leiden: Brill, 2013. Pp. xii + 211. Cloth. $125.00. ISBN 9789004233348.

Jason BeDuhn, Northern Arizona University, Flagstaff, Arizona

Alexander Böhlig's unpublished 1947 University of Münster dissertation has circulated in photocopied form among interested scholars of Manichaeism for decades. The main challenge in making the author's survey and analysis of Manichaean handling of biblical material valuable to biblical studies some sixty-five years after its composition has been met by the editors (with additional contributions by Christoph Markschies), who have supplemented the notes and bibliography to take account of pertinent research in the intervening years. The effort is well-spent, since Böhlig's analysis of Manichaean biblical interpretation remains valid and insightful even though he had a smaller set of data to work from than is now available, and few have ventured into this subject since his pioneering study.

Peter Nagel's introduction (1–17) outlines Böhlig's career and his contributions in several fields of religious studies and intellectual history and provides excellent guidance to the author's other publications closely related to this study. In the four chapters that follow, Böhlig establishes the context of Manichaean contact with biblical traditions, surveys Manichaean use and interpretation of the principal subjects of biblical theology, examines the use of biblical material in three key Manichaean texts from Egypt, and draws conclusions about Manichaean views of Christian scripture and the potential for Manichaean texts to contribute to the study of the New Testament.

In the first chapter, Böhlig establishes the various sources through which Mani (Manichaios), the founder of Manichaeism, would have been exposed to the Judeo-Christian tradition in his Mesopotamian homeland. He sees Mani as the product of a distinct "oriental" Christianity (22ff.), mediated in his case through the Jewish-Christian Elchasaite community in which he was raised, yet also engaged with the surviving Hellenistic culture of the region (29), including the Marcionite tradition. Crucially, Mani was exposed in the first half of the third century to an already-established *textual* Christianity, embodied in such literature as the Diatessaron or other Gospel harmonies and the epistles of Paul. Manichaean discourse on biblical literature included a critique of Christian literature as corrupted and misinterpreted and of Jewish scripture as an invalid source of revelation.

In chapter 2 Böhlig surveys Manichaean citation of the familiar themes of the New Testament, covering such subjects as God, good and evil, humanity and sin, Christ, the Holy Spirit, ethics, and eschatology. For each theme, Böhlig highlights what elements of biblical discourse interested the Manichaeans and how they integrated them into their distinctive doctrines. He notes that Manichaeans used Trinitarian phraseology and believed in God's involvement in creation, aligning them more with mainstream Christianity on these matters than was true of a number of other early Christian sects (36–37). Regarding Manichaean dualism, Böhlig observes that the idea of "the existence of a radical evil" is inherent in New Testament texts (38), including dualities of God and Satan, light and darkness, good and bad trees, good and bad seed, new and old wine, new and old humans, and broad and narrow ways. He provides several examples of Manichaeans citing such passages and images not only in a Western, Christianized context but also in Manichaean texts from Central Asia and China, demonstrating that they do not represent secondary regional adaptations but core resources of the religion from its inception. The discussion of humanity and sin offers perhaps the most intriguing set of observations deserving of further study. As in the alternative readings of creation found in so-called gnostic systems, Manichaeans offered a counter-exegesis of the Genesis account, seeing human beings as concocted by evil as a means of entrapping and dominating divine light (42–43). But this reading of creation does not make human beings per se evil, nor does it correspond to notions of a fall into original sin that make humans the unique source of evil in the world (43–44). Rather, humans are a mixture of good and evil just as everything else in the physical world is, so their internal struggle reflects a conflict throughout the cosmos. Paul's characterization of this internal duality in Rom 7, as well as his image of the old and new human, found repeated citation by Manichaean spokesmen (44–47). This anthropology leads in Manichaeism to an emphasis on the need for God's intervention in human salvation at the expense of free will (46), which Böhlig characterizes in terms of predestination (68, 109), but which is perhaps better captured by the notion of grace. Manichaean Christology shows the special influence of the Gospel of John (perhaps mediated through the Diatessaron), as well as Paul. Christ is a divine being, interconnected with God and sent by him as revealer in merely the *schēma* of humanity (cf. John 1:14; Phil 2:7ff.; 1 Tim 3:16). His ascetic moral code of discipleship served as a template for the life of the Manichaean electi, and his selection of twelve and seventy-two disciples established the template for Manichaean church organization (52). The events of his life were mined for their symbolic value, not least of which was the dualistic conflict suggested by his passion (53–54), and Mani's own life and martyrdom came to be seen in parallel to Christ's (56–57). Eschatology likewise provides another rich subject due further research, as Böhlig demonstrates Manichaean dissemination of Christian scenarios drawn mostly from Matthew and Paul (61–64).

In the third chapter Böhlig surveys some of the major pieces of surviving Coptic Manichaean literature, examining the use of biblical material in each. In a dogmatic-catechetical work such as the Kephalaia, New Testament passages are rarely cited verbatim but form the subtext and provide language and imagery taken up into discussions of theology, creation, cosmology, and religious practice (65–71). Such works as the Sermon on the Great War, found in a homiletic collection, elaborate on the eschatological outlines and themes found in the New Testament (72–75). But it is the hymnic material found in the Psalm-Book where both verbatim quotation and detailed exegesis of the New Testament find fullest expression, and hence Böhlig's closer attention (76–104). While a subset of this material called the Psalms of Heracleides is likely to reflect secondary engagement with a Western, Christian environment, Böhlig counterbalances this by noting the presence of many of the same Christian elements in Central Asian and Chinese Manichaean hymns.

Chapter 4 summarizes Böhlig's conclusions about the Manichaean "Schriftprinzip." Mani did not accord the books of the New Testament full canonical status (indeed, what would constitute such status at a time when the biblical canon was still in formation?), while giving equal weight to a number of noncanonical texts (such as the books of Enoch and the apocryphal Acts). He contended that the original revelation through Jesus had been passed down imperfectly by his disciples and needed to be sifted, verified, and interpreted according to his own personal visionary experiences. In both this theory of corruption and his high regard for Paul, Mani appears to owe something to Marcion. But what about mining Manichaean sources for information helpful to text criticism and canon criticism, given the relatively early date of the Coptic Manichaean texts and their presumed originals? Böhlig offers cautious assessments (107–8), noting the periphrastic quality of the richest resource, the Psalm-Book, yet pointing to the possibilities of this material in the study of Gospel traditions (direct quotation of the Gospel of Thomas has since been demonstrated), reconstruction of the Diatessaron or other harmonies, and the relative regard given at the time to texts later to find themselves on either side of the canonical boundary. He sees greater potential for the material to shed light on the history of biblical theology and interpretation, the evolution and application of key terms and images drawn from New Testament literature (108–9). An extensive register of biblical citations (193–200) will facilitate use of the material collected here in such biblical research. The study concludes with two excurses, on borrowings in Manichaean hymnography from the Old Testament psalms and various lists of Jesus' apostles in Manichaean sources, respectively.

The editors have appended to the author's main study three related articles not already included in the two collections of Böhlig's research, *Mysterion und Wahrheit* (1968) and *Gnosis und Synkretismus* (1989), to which the reader should turn for much else directly relevant to the subject of this book. The first, "Die Bedeutung des CMC für den Manichäismus," outlines the principal issues regarding the origin of the Cologne Mani Codex, and surveys the text for various connections to Christian biblical themes (Mani's apostleship, his relation to the Paraclete, parallels in his life to Jesus', and Jesus as authority behind Mani's teachings). The second, "Synkretismus in der Überlieferung von Manis Passion," gives particular attention to the parallelism that developed between Mani's martyrdom and Christ's passion in Manichaean memory and commemoration. The third, "Der Manichäismus und das Christentum," fittingly closes the volume with a programmatic discussion of Manichaeism as a fundamentally Christian sectarian movement whose remarkable success catapulted it to the status of an independent religion in regions of Asia relatively untouched by competing Christian missions.

Throughout the studies collected in this volume, Böhlig clearly intends to demonstrate the Christian foundations of Manichaeism, even to the point of relegating Zoroastrian, Buddhist, and other elements visible in Manichaean texts to the status of inessential, secondary adaptations. But his exclusive consideration of Christian connections provides at best only one side of a basis on which to assess the religion's historical and ideological antecedents. The New Testament passages Manichaeans cited in support of their ascetic regimen, for instance (59–60), scarcely represent its exclusive source, which in its details shows close affinities to Buddhist, Jain, and Hindu precepts and practices. A similar imbalance of evidence has afflicted most attempts to ascertain a historical pedigree for Mani's religion, up to today, and the subject is in desperate need of more sophisticated models of the genesis of new religious identities against the background of (multiple) older ones. Yet Böhlig effectively establishes that Manichaeism had an organic, not artificial, relation to the Christian tradition and that its core concepts and institutions found inspiration in Christian scripture, rather than being foisted arbitrarily upon it from a fundamentally alien worldview.

Ancient Christian Martyrdom: Diverse Practices, Theologies, and Traditions, by Candida R. Moss. New Haven: Yale University Press, 2012. Pp. xiv + 256. Cloth. $40.00. ISBN 9780300154658.

Jan Willem van Henten, University of Amsterdam, Amsterdam, The Netherlands

The cross-cultural phenomenon of martyrdom is more than two thousand years old but, as contemporary events show time and again, still very much alive. Martyrdom is part of the foundation myth of Christianity. It appeals to the imagination of many because it is a highly ambiguous spectacle with thrilling deadly consequences. Currently the concept of martyrdom itself becomes more and more blurred, also because secular or religious martyrdom plays an important role in current social, political, and ethnic conflicts. Depending on whose side one chooses, martyrs become heroes or icons of the enemy. Points such as these may explain why there is an ongoing stream of studies about martyrdom—not in the least about the beginnings of martyrdom in the Christian tradition. What is new in Candida Moss's book about early Christian martyrdom during the first two centuries CE? First of all, it concerns a fresh and well-presented synthesis of existing scholarship on early Christian martyrdom. Second, the book has a geographical focus, which is new indeed: five regions are discussed together with the key documents that originated in those areas (Asia Minor, Rome, Gaul, North Africa, and Alexandria). A major purpose of this arrangement is to highlight the different articulations of martyrdom in those regions. Third, related to the second point, Moss aims at contextualizing the martyrdoms by linking them to related contemporary documents, social and cultural trends within the specific region, or local key figures from the period involved.

The introductory chapter lays out the set-up of the book. Chapter 2 indicates the importance of the strategy to read martyrdoms in the cultural context of their regional origin. The next five chapters all discuss martyrdom in one particular region. These chapters offer a broad perspective and include documents that deal only partly with martyrdom (e.g., apocryphal Acts of the Apostles) or appear to be relevant in other ways. Building on her own previous work, Moss argues that the old bishop Polycarp may have died a martyr's death sometime in the second century but that the Martyrdom that describes this death must date from the third century. The implication is that the Martyrdom of Polycarp "did not initiate the era of Christian martyrdom" (19). The use of the first-person and eyewitness vocabulary does not necessarily imply that the document is an eyewitness account penned shortly after Polycarp's death. The first-person narrator and the eyewitness vocabulary are strategic tools that validate otherwise unsubstantiated miracles. The sophisticated incorporation of many parallels from the Gospels that associate Polycarp's death with that of Jesus Christ also speaks against the authenticity of the Martyrdom. Nevertheless, Asia Minor is the first region discussed, which suggests that Christian martyrdom did originate in this region. This would mean that Ignatius of Antioch's seven letters are the key documents about the beginning of martyrdom in the Christian tradition, but this is actually far from certain. Moss knows about the complexities of the history of transmission of Ignatius's Letters, and the fact that several scholars argue that the articulation of martyrdom in these letters hardly matches an early date at the beginning of the second century. Nevertheless, she seems to leave the issue of the date open.

Moss's monograph offers a fresh perspective on early Christian martyrdom, and her critical attitude toward the issue of authenticity of some of the key documents should be appreciated. Her elaborate discussion of the Martyrdom of Polycarp is excellent, and her conclusion—based on a historical, literary, and conceptual analysis—that this martyrdom must originate from the third century is persuasive. As a matter of fact, I would have welcomed that she would have applied her rigorous critical approach toward the Martyrdom of Polycarp also to other martyrdoms, such as Ignatius's Letters and the Martyrdom of Pionius. There are close connections between the Martyrdom of Polycarp and the Martyrdom of Pionius (e.g., the focus on martyrological orthopraxy and the function of martyrs as models of the catholic church), which triggers the question what the implications of a third-century date of Polycarp's Martyrdom are for the Martyrdom of Pionius (date after 250 CE). Unfortunately, the latter martyrdom is hardly discussed by Moss because she deals only with the first two centuries.

As already indicated, Moss's regional approach focuses upon the differences among the early Christian martyrdoms. Her discussion of Rome highlights the philosophical martyr. Justin Martyr, not Paul, is the key figure here. Moss argues that Justin's conversion to Christianity "was part of his philosophical quest for the vision of God" (81). In his *Apologies* Justin elaborates the practice of martyrdom in order to point out what it means to be a Christian, and he builds his argument on contemporary philosophical conventions and values. He also defines Christian identity by constructing the Jews as a counterpoint. He claims that only the Christians had martyrs and that the Jews were famous for rejecting and persecuting God's messengers, including Jesus. The Acts of Justin and his Fellow-Martyrs also presents the martyrs as philosophers and implies, therefore, that Christianity was a harmless philosophy. Nevertheless, the martyrs' main opponent, Governor Quintus Iunius Rusticus, instructor of the philosopher-emperor Marcus Aurelius, did not fall for this type of philosophy. His values and ideals function as a contrast to the philosophy of the protagonists of the Christians, with *eusebeia* (the proper attitude toward the emperor/Jesus Christ) as a key word (at least in recension B).

This argument is appealing and even triggers the question whether the author of the Acts aims at depicting Justin beating the Stoic Rusticus, so to speak, "at his own game." I wonder, however, whether the philosophical articulation of martyrdom is unique to the Roman region. As a matter of fact, the contemporaneous Jewish martyrdom 4 Maccabees shows important and intriguing analogies with the philosophical martyrdom connected with Justin, including conventional ideas such as "living in accordance with nature," "living in line with reason," and "appealing to justice." *Eusebeia* is a key word in 4 Maccabees as well, although interpreted from a Jewish perspective. Scholars mostly argue that 4 Maccabees originates from Antioch, some plead for Asia Minor, but nobody, as far as I know, for Rome. So, how should we explain these analogies between the philosophical interpretation of martyrdom in Rome and that in 4 Maccabees, all the more so since Justin stereotypes the Jews as those who reject God's messengers?

Moss interprets the North-African traditions of martyrdom from the perspective of apocalypticism—with a strong focus on the vindication of the martyr and heaven as the place for future judgment—and the appeal to Paul's letters in support of certain community practices. Her discussion of martyrdom in Alexandria concentrates on the deconstruction of the idea that attitudes toward martyrdom can be delineated on doctrinal grounds and the ideal of true martyrdom. For one of the regions the approach of Moss works less well, as she herself acknowledges: the case of Gaul. The names of the martyrs described in the Letter of the Churches of Lyons and Vienne imply that some of them were immigrants from Phrygia and others had Romano-Gallic connections. Nevertheless, the precise context in which this martyrdom originates remains largely unknown. A further complication is that it is unclear to what extent Eusebius, who transmits the letter, adapted the text. Moss argues that external evidence for a persecution of Christians in Gaul in the second century is missing and that the details about the martyrs' arrest are improbable. The highly literary character of the martyrdom, with a strong focus on the details of torture and the degradation of the martyrs' bodies, shows important correspondences with martyrdoms from other regions. The martyrs from Lyons and Vienne do not feel pain, similar to the Maccabean martyrs in 2 and 4 Maccabees, and in this way they triumph over their opponents, who are depicted as beasts and barbarians. The theme of Blandina's role as mother of a Christian family, perhaps a family of martyrs, reminds one of the striking change in the construction of Perpetua's family relations: in light of her upcoming martyrdom, Perpetua moves over from a Roman patriarchal family context to the alternative household of Christ, and she becomes a role model for other Christians. In short, it remains difficult to indicate what would be typical for the configuration of martyrdom in Gaul.

I warmly recommend this book to anyone interested in the topic of ancient martyrdom. Moss's regional approach offers new insights and rightly emphasizes the important differences between the early Christian constructions of martyrdom. By offering a grand but nuanced picture of Christian martyrdom in the first two centuries, it also stimulates one to analyze the correspondences and differences between early Christian and early Jewish martyrdom, which is referred to time and again. One question remains after reading this fascinating book: Would the picture change if the problematic history of transmission of some of the key documents and the important historical and textual problems connected with them—pointed out by Moss—leads to the conclusion that at least some writings in their current form, such as the Letter of the Churches of Lyons and Vienne and the Passion of Perpetua, should be dated later than the usual dates assigned to them? Moss is fully aware of this complication, but drawing the consequences of a Decian or even post-Decian date of some of the key documents may call for another book.

Christ's Resurrection in Early Christianity and the Making of the New Testament, by Markus Vinzent. Farnham, Eng.: Ashgate, 2011. Pp. vi + 276. Paper. $39.95. ISBN 9781409417927.

H. H. Drake Williams III, Tyndale Theological Seminary, Badhoevedorp, The Netherlands

How did the resurrection become a key belief within Christianity? Was it always so important for early Christians, or did it become so much later? In this volume Markus Vinzent considers texts from early Christianity and concludes that the resurrection of Christ was largely nonexistent for the first 140 years of Christianity, except in Paul's writings. It was also not of central importance until the fourth century. Vinzent provocatively claims that interest in Christ's resurrection came about as a result of a declining fascination in the Christian faith. He argues this way clearly in all three chapters of this book. These chapters examine Christian roots from Judaism, the reception of the resurrection within first- and second-century Christian texts, and the place of the resurrection within early Christian liturgy.

Vinzent goes about making his explanation in his first chapter by examining the roots of Christianity from Judaism. He rightly notes the importance of considering the Christian faith from this perspective. He claims that the resurrection is found within later sections of the Old Testament, particularly Isaiah, Ezekiel, and Daniel. Judaism in the time of the first century also had beliefs in the resurrection. Texts such as 2 Maccabees link the resurrection also with martyrdom. The Pharisees claimed confidence in the resurrection, while the Sadducees and Samaritan Jews did not.

When it comes to the understanding of Jesus's resurrection, Vinzent claims that the New Testament and early Christian literature largely see it as "obscure, sometimes entirely abandoned, or survives only as one among other testimonies of God's acting" (44). One way that he comes to this conclusion is by seeing several documents from early Christianity in contradiction with each other. For example, Vinzent sees Paul overturning the importance of the resurrection in the Thessalonian correspondence. While Paul presented the resurrection of Christ in 1 Thessalonians, the letter of 2 Thessalonians seems more interested in salvation through the gospel, the traditions that were taught, and the glory of the Lord Jesus Christ. While the resurrection is clearly presented as being important within the Corinthian epistles, Vinzent concludes that it is overshadowed by other concerns by the time of Clement's writing to the Corinthians in 1 Clement. Other letters such as Colossians or Ephesians switched the focus away from the resurrection of Christ to other matters such as Jesus's death or his incarnation. Vinzent also sees the letters of Hebrews, James, the Epistle of Barnabas, 2 Clement, Shepherd of Hermas, and the Letter of Diognetus containing many critical ideas but lacking Christ's resurrection. While Vinzent finds Johannine literature containing salvation and eternal life, he finds these to be connected with incarnation, revelation, and the communion of love rather than the resurrection of Jesus.

Vinzent's claims should be questioned, however. Must a later writing contain everything that is within an earlier writing to conclude that the earlier subject matter is still important? Would it not be possible that a writer could build upon earlier statements, assuming the importance of what was previously written? This could especially be the case in an epistle such as 1 Clement. In 1 Clem. 47.1 Clement urges the readers to "take up the epistle of the blessed Apostle Paul," thereby using Paul's former letter to inform the current situation. Clement specifically uses 1 Corinthians to build upon when he employs it in 1 Clem. 37.5–38.2; 49.5. When the resurrection is mentioned within 1 Clem. 24–26, the approach of the author is also to build upon 1 Corinthians. Scholars such as A. C. Gregory, A. J. Carlyle, and A. Lindemann, who have identified the presence of the New Testament in 1 Clement, find 1 Clem. 24.1, 4–5 dependent upon 1 Cor 15. This would indicate that the author of 1 Clement built upon the conclusion from 1 Cor. 15 rather than obscuring or abandoning the importance of Christ's resurrection.

Within his second chapter, the longest of the book, Vinzent attempts to show that Paul's viewpoint of the resurrection of Christ was rediscovered. He claims that it was as a result of Marcion that the resurrection came back into interest within Christianity. According to Vinzent, Paul's view of Christianity with the resurrection of Christ had faded over time. Many of the fathers, he claims, "remained reluctant" toward Christ's resurrection and even remained silent about it. The resurrection of Christ became much more prominent in the second half of the second century, thanks to Marcion of Sinope. Vinzent believes that Marcion was the rigorous disciple of Paul who reestablished the importance of the resurrection within Christianity. He promulgated this by advocating for a New Testament.

Two issues are at stake within this section. The first concerns whether the resurrection truly faded and was later rediscovered. The second concerns whether Marcion played the significant role in shaping Christian history that Vinzent claims that he did. Regarding the idea that the resurrection lapsed and was rediscovered, Vinzent makes his case without sufficiently regarding and addressing majority viewpoints. When one is advancing a controversial thesis, it is important to address the majority viewpoint before moving forward, but Vinzent does not do this in several places. For example, he does not address at length the resurrection accounts at the end of the canonical Gospels. Many scholars would date the canonical Gospels from within the period of 50 CE through to the early part of the second century. Most would date the canonical Gospels to a period following the writing of Paul's letters, thereby indicating that resurrection tradition was valuable in other places besides Paul's writing. While Vinzent will address viewpoints of the resurrection from the perspective of the Pharisees and Sadducees, he does not include a section to address the presentation of the resurrection in the canonical Gospels within his book.

Instead, Vinzent provides this controversial statement regarding the canonical Gospels:

> recent scholarship on the reception of the later canonical Gospels and Acts up to Irenaeus (ca. 177/180 AD) shows that neither these texts, nor any of their narratives (the miracles, for example), nor their authors, were ever quoted, acknowledged or referred to by any author prior to Marcion; and even after Marcion, Justin, for example, who clearly knows so-called Gospels, uses only sayings of the Lord, not the Gospels' narratives. (84)

Such a statement undervalues the work that has been accomplished in the reception of the canonical Gospels in recent studies. While Vinzent refers to Gregory and Tuckett's edited volume, *The Reception of the New Testament in the Apostolic Fathers* (Oxford: Oxford University Press, 2005), at times, he does not interact with conclusions made that the writer of the Didache and the Epistle of Barnabas likely knew the Gospel of Matthew. Some acknowledgement of this alternate viewpoint and interaction with it would be appropriate.

Critical to Vinzent's case for a lapse in the resurrection following Paul's letters until the time of Marcion is the dating of several documents. He dates several early Christian documents much later than what the majority of scholarship would. For example, he treats texts such as Ignatius's letters to be dated near 180 CE. These letters contain several sections that speak of the resurrection of Christ. Many scholars date them to 110, but Vinzent chooses to accept a date of 180. He also dates the fragments of Papias late. Traditionally, Papias's fragments are dated 60–130 CE, but Vinzent dates them at 140 or shortly thereafter and claims that they are part of the anti-Marcionite approach at that time. While Papias's fragments do not contain many references to the resurrection of Jesus, they do specifically mention the canonical Gospels of Matthew, Mark, and John. An early dating of Papias's fragments would suggest that the canonical Gospels with their belief in the resurrection of Jesus would have been well before the time of Marcion.

Also suspect is the treatment of the date of several New Testament books, such as the Acts of the Apostles, 1 Peter, and Revelation. These New Testament books were not written by Paul, yet they mention the resurrection of Christ in several places. Acts specifically refers to the resurrection of Jesus Christ in several places (e.g., 1:22; 2:31–32; 4:33; 5:30; 17:18, 32). Vinzent dates this book later than 140 CE and believes that it was influenced by Marcion. There is no interaction with Acts commentators who view the date of Acts much earlier, such as Munck, Conzelmann, Peterson, Marshall, Bock, Bruce, and Barrett.

The resurrection of Jesus Christ is found explicitly within 1 Pet 1:3, 21; 3:21. While Vinzent acknowledges this, he states that 1 Peter sounds as if the letter reflects a pro- or anti-Marcionite stance. Thus, Vinzent dates this letter well into the second century. This again is a minority opinion on 1 Peter, yet there is no substantial interaction with other commentators on 1 Peter such as those by Selwyn, Jobes, Achtemeier, Davids, Michaels, and Elliot, who date this epistle in the first century.

In his treatment of Revelation Vinzent does acknowledge that the resurrection of Christ is present, but he minimizes its importance, stating that other issues about Christ as well as ethics were more important. However, the appearance of the resurrected Jesus who proclaims himself to be alive and resurrected appears at a key point within Revelation in 1:18. The fear expressed by John is countered by Jesus's proclamation of being the first, the last, and the living one. In 1:18 Jesus is the one who was dead and is alive. It is from this basis that John is instructed to write what he has seen, the things that are, and the things that are to be (1:19). The declaration of Christ being raised is a critical basis point, then, for the remainder of Revelation.

Equally suspect is Vinzent's claim that Marcion played a significant role in shaping Christian history, reviving the tradition of Paul and the resurrection of Christ. Others, however, would state that Paul's influence was represented in the writings of other early Christian documents well before Marcion. For example, Polycarp's Letter to the Philippians is known to have a significant amount of Pauline influence. It contains several references to Paul and also to his writing. Some scholars (e.g., Berding) have found that Paul's influence is the most significant one within the Letter to the Philippians. Unlike Vinzent, many recognize Polycarp's Letter to the Philippians to be dated well before Marcion. Some would date the document around 135–137 CE, but others would date the letter as early as 108–109, while others would prefer 110–117. Vinzent provides no substantial interaction with scholars such as Grant, Hartog, Wake, Goodspeed, Andrews, and Ayer, who date Polycarp's letter earlier than Marcion.

Vinzent's third chapter considers the celebration of life and death in the early church. He makes the case that the early church did not emphasize the resurrection in its Sunday observance. He finds Christian observance of Sunday to be much more closely identified with Jewish Sabbath rather than the resurrection of Jesus. In his analysis of Philo and other Jewish literature, he does rightly highlight the continuity with Judaism between the Sabbath and Sunday observance. His consideration of Hippolytus, Justin Martyr, Melito of Sardis, and Origen does also raise the importance of Christ's death in early Christian Sunday observance.

Vinzent is less convincing, however, when he drastically reduces the connection between the resurrection and Sunday observance. Vinzent claims that only three of the many sources that we possess for early Christianity refer to the resurrection as a part of Sunday observance (Ignatius, Magn. 9.1; Barn. 15.9; 1 Apol. 67.7). His handling of Bar. 15.9 particularly seems suspect, however. The passage reads, "Therefore, also we celebrate the eighth day with gladness, for on it Jesus arose from the dead, and appeared, and ascended into heaven" (B. D. Ehrman, *The Apostolic Fathers* [LCL; 2 vols.; Cambridge: Harvard University Press, 2003], 2:71). While this is only one mention of the resurrection, the statement seems to tie the Sunday observance directly to the resurrection. The framework of the

Sabbath may rightly be Jewish, as Vinzent describes, but the addition of the resurrection seems evident from this text.

Vinzent has considered much of early Christian history in a new way. He arrives at a controversial conclusion when he states, "In the first two centuries, however, Christ's Resurrection was soon of little theological importance and influence to the wider Church, except for Paul, and only began to become recognized when Marcion of Sinope made Paul's writings resurface, and when he introduced the Gospel into Christianity" (226). His volume, however, moves too quickly without engaging sufficiently with the opinions of other scholars who hold different stances on the dating of several early Christian texts. Those who are interested in the study of Marcion and unorthodox perspectives in early church history will be particularly interested in Vinzent's book.

Augustine's Manichaean Dilemma, Volume 2: Making a "Catholic" Self, 388–401 C.E., by Jason David BeDuhn. Divinations: Rereading Late Ancient Religion. Philadelphia: University of Pennsylvania Press, 2013. Pp. x + 538. Cloth. $79.95. ISBN 9780812244946.

Timothy Pettipiece, Université d'Ottawa, Ottawa, Ontario, Canada

The late Augustinian scholar Kevin Coyle, to whom this volume is dedicated, would often state that one could not hope to understand Augustine without understanding Manichaeism. In this multivolume work Jason BeDuhn has taken up the ambitious challenge to turn this basic axiom into a nuanced and sophisticated study.

In the previous volume (*Conversion and Apostasy, 373–388 C.E.*), BeDuhn persuasively argued that the young Augustine was primarily motivated by a life-long search for intellectual community. After nearly a decade of affiliation, he eventually abandoned this search among the Manichaeans, who he finally realized were not philosophers, and ultimately decided that his deeply felt need for Ciceronian philosophical kinship could be met within the Neoplatonically inclined Christianity presented to him by Ambrose of Milan. In this second volume BeDuhn unpacks the implications of this decision for Augustine's career as a Christian intellectual, polemicist, and priest, as well as its significance for the construction of his "Catholic self."

BeDuhn prefaces his sequel by carefully justifying his use of the terms "Catholic" and "Nicene" as identifying the Christian community to which Augustine belonged (ix–x). He is careful to point out that this represents only one stream of early Christianity in late fourth-century North Africa—a minority one at that—and by no means refers to the fully formed Catholicism of later centuries, regardless of Augustine's significant contribution to that later tradition.

With that caveat in mind, BeDuhn proceeds to reexamine the fundamental ways in which Manichaean ideas influenced Augustine's own theological development. He deliberately sets out to challenge the oft-repeated notion that, in spite of his formal disassociation from Manichaeism, Augustine's thought continued to bear an inescapable Manichaean imprint (1). Instead, what BeDuhn sees is the various ways in which Augustine sought to push "Nicene" theology into areas that Manichaean teachers had effectively staked as their own (4–5).

Any study of Augustine is burdened by its subject's own theological significance. At the same time, Augustine is one of the most self-conscious and self-consciously revisionist authors from antiquity. As a result, he often remains inscrutable and difficult to pin down. Traditionally, Christian commentators have had so much invested in Augustine theologically that any challenge to the integrity or coherence of his thought is taken as an affront to the consistency of Christian theology as a whole. Yet, all great minds are works in progress, and Augustine's, as BeDuhn illustrates, is no exception.

Throughout the study BeDuhn wrestles with the basic but important question of how to "read" (13–14) Augustine when all we possess is a (rather large) collection of rhetorical performances that may or may not at any given time communicate the full range of his understanding of Christian ideas. Moreover, was that understanding in a constant state of flux, as the "developmental" readings of Augustine would suggest, or was a fully formed "theology" present from the moment of his conversion (13)? In the end, and this is true of all ancient authors, all we have is what Augustine *wrote*; what he actually thought or believed is pure speculation. BeDuhn stakes a middle ground by suggesting that Augustine's commitment to a core of set "Nicene" beliefs was likely continuous, but his understanding of those beliefs changed over time (14–15).

In the decades after his "conversion"—perhaps we should say "realignment"—Augustine was primarily engaged in a project of outreach to his former Manichaean associates, trying desperately at times to convince them to follow him into the light of "Nicene" orthodoxy. It was during this period of prolonged engagement with Manichaean ideas that, BeDuhn argues, Augustine forged his own core theological positions (24–25). For example, central Augustinian ideas about the soul, creation, scripture, free will, and grace were all worked out in an anti-Manichaean context. For BeDuhn, a proper historically rooted understanding of Augustine *must* be based upon a proper reconstruction of his context. Doing so leads to some rather remarkable results. For instance, in chapter 7 BeDuhn discusses Augustine's little-known treatise On Lying (*De mendacio*), which happens to have been written around 395, when Megalius was actively opposing his promotion to the episcopate and accusing him of crypto-Manichaean sympathies. It is also in this particular context that BeDuhn suggests the intriguing possibility that (a version of) *Confessions* books 5–9 may have constituted Augustine's original response to these charges (257) and that this act of self-examination closely resembles Manichaean patterns of public confession. Ironically, however, Augustine would remodel this account into an extended "performance of self" aimed at a specifically Manichaean readership.

Although primarily a type of intellectual history, BeDuhn's book underlines the remarkable degree to which personal encounters with prominent Manichaeans shaped the trajectory of Augustine's thought. In volume 1 we saw how Augustine's disappointing encounter with the Manichaean bishop Faustus helped stimulate his eventual apostasy from the movement, while in volume 2 BeDuhn points to his public debate with the Manichaean teacher Fortunatus in the summer of 392 (120–21) as a turning point in his "Nicene" theological reflection. In that debate Augustine realized the degree to which his lack of a thorough acquaintance with the scriptures was a major liability in his articulation of an effective "Nicene" theology. Until this point he had relied on a small number of biblical catch phrases to justify his philosophical positions (164), which until that time remained his intellectual priority. Yet being exegetically outmatched by Fortunatus led Augustine into a far deeper engagement with the scriptures, especially the writings of Paul (192)—traditionally the most contested portion of the biblical canon. After all, Pauline ideas had certainly made a profound impact on Mani, who in imitation called himself an "apostle of Jesus Christ," as they had done on Marcion a century earlier. What Augustine did was to seek to reclaim this scriptural territory from the Manichaeans who had so efficiently cultivated it (195).

Time and again the modern analysis of early Christian thought has shown that theological positions labeled "mainstream" or "proto-orthodox" most typically emerge in reaction to other alternatives later deemed untenable and "heretical." In this way Christianity consistently displays a reactionary and revisionist tendency. It is defined by the gradual whittling away of theological options until a stable core of beliefs eventually emerges. In this book BeDuhn demonstrates that Augustine participated in this process in a very direct way—defining, reworking, and shaping his theology in response to often-powerful Manichaean ideas.

Therefore, the stereotype that Augustine introduced—consciously or unconsciously—Manichaean ideas into the mainstream can be dismissed as overly simplistic. Rather, the ideas that his exceptionally sharp mind did bequeath to mainstream Christian tradition were forged and tested against a Manichaean anvil. Manichaean thought is not merely a footnote in his biography but a powerful and challenging stimulus against which he would struggle through the course of his career. Ultimately what BeDuhn suggests is not that Augustine gave Manichaean answers to "Catholic" questions but "Catholic" answers to Manichaean dilemmas.

If I have one small criticism of the book, it would be as follows. BeDuhn points out that many modern interpreters of Augustine take his characterizations of Manichaean ideas at face value without considering what Manichaean sources actually say (107–8). For example, he points to the idea of the "two souls" that Augustine misrepresents as a typically Manichaean position (105). Unfortunately, however, more often than not, when contrasting one of Augustine's evolving "Nicene" positions to a Manichaean alternative, BeDuhn very rarely cites Manichaean sources themselves, often appealing to a vague notion of "Manichaean discourse" (see 80, 105, 117, 119, 142, 157, 212, etc.) and relying on his (well-deserved) authority as a Manichaean specialist to support such assertions. In my view, these contrasts would have been far more effective if the Manichaean sources, instead of being relegated to the footnotes, were brought into full view, since as BeDuhn is obviously aware, few of his readers will have had any direct engagement with primary Manichaean literature, and, as he himself emphatically states, "all those who labor in Augustinian studies must come to realize that they cannot understand Manichaeism through Augustine's eyes" (412). After all, as his study also illustrates, even though Manichaeans were never very numerous, they nonetheless made an important contribution to the debates that shaped the development of early Christian discourse and are thus intrinsically worthy of our attention.

Loving the Poor, Saving the Rich: Wealth, Poverty, and Early Christian Formation, by Helen Rhee. Grand Rapids: Baker Academic, 2012. Pp. xx + 279. Paper. $29.99. ISBN 9780801048241.

Michael S. Moore, Arizona State University, Tempe, Arizona

This book attempts "to show how early Christians adopted, appropriated, and transformed the Jewish and Greco-Roman moral teachings of giving and patronage, as well as how they developed their distinctive theology and social understanding of wealth/the wealthy and poverty/the poor" (xiii). A church history professor at Westmont College (Santa Barbara, California), the author insists that "Christian reformulation and practice of wealth and poverty are indispensable for shaping Christian self-definitions *vis-à-vis* the Greco-Roman and Jewish worlds" (xiii). Investigating selected patristic resources with an appreciative eye for their multifacetedness, she nevertheless presumes that these sources usually voice the perspective of the wealthy versus that of the poor—a common presumption among historians of antiquity. Employing a variety of "interdisciplinary tools and resources"—none fully defined or even explained—she reads this selection of early Christian literature from a perspective shaped not by the history of ideas, nor by the canons of comparative anthropology/sociology, nor even by the canons of standardized literary-historical criticism, but simply as a "sociocultural and theological historian" (xvii), whatever *that* is, exactly.

Chapter 1 seeks to do what most researchers try to avoid: summarize the socioeconomic, cultural, and theological context of early Christian literature whenever and wherever these texts interface with anything having to do with the poverty-wealth polarity, focusing the survey on (1) Greco-Roman perceptions of benefaction and patronage, followed by (2) a brief encounter with various understandings of almsgiving preserved within the Hebrew Bible and selected postbiblical texts. Chapter 2 then attempts to examine the poverty-wealth polarity as refracted through various patristic writings, focusing on the presumed impact of what Rhee calls "the eschatological great reversal," that is, that idealistic moment when wealthy Christians en masse leave their old habits and begin to invest in heavenly riches through almsgiving (presuming, apparently, that the message of Paul's sermon in 2 Cor 8–9 eventually receives more-or-less universal acceptance among the majority of those Christians living in North Africa).

Chapter 3 investigates the theology and practice of "redemptive almsgiving" against the context of soteriological developments affecting the North African Christian world as represented by (1) Clement of Alexandria's tractate *Who Is a Rich Man That Is Saved?* (2) Origen's allegorical/spiritualizing writings, (3) Tertullian's understanding of how salvation can become possible for the rich (*contra* Marcion's hyper-asceticism), and (4) the musings on almsgiving as merit/penance preserved in the writings of Cyprian and Lactantius. Chapter 4 focuses on the role played by the wealth-poverty polarity whenever it challenges Christian communities to rethink a whole panoply of eschatological/ soteriological issues, obligatorily highlighting the role(s) enacted by women in the practice of φιλοξενία ("hospitality") and pastoral care for the sick, prisoners, and survivors of the dead.

Chapter 5 is in many ways the most interesting section of the volume, attempting as it does to describe the simultaneous development of the institutionalization of almsgiving alongside the corollary Christianization of patronage. Here the author makes a valiant attempt to illustrate the process by which Christian charity and Hellenistic benefaction fuse together into something approximating a socio-religious singularity, focusing on (1) the role(s) enacted by bishops in creating the institutional structures necessary to exercise social control within the North African church (focusing especially on Cyprian, bishop of Carthage), and (2) the complexities forced upon and to which ecclesiastical leaders eventually assimilate as they transform over time into wealthy landowners. Chapter 6 explores how the positive association of almsgiving becomes an identity marker distinguishing Christians from pagans (and "orthodox" believers from heretics) in the thinking of North African leaders such as Cyprian and Tertullian. Finally, chapter 7 asks what a better understanding of the poverty-wealth polarity in early Christianity might contribute to spark deeper reflection among contemporary Christians presently engaged in sociological, economic, ethical, and theological discourse, particularly those historically associated with "prosperity Pentecostalism" in the global South, a region where "poverty defines the existence of an overwhelming majority of people" (xx).

This is a well-written survey peppered with many interesting ideas. Like Rhee's Fuller dissertation (*Early Christian Literature: Christ and Culture in the Second and Third Centuries* [Routledge, 2005]), it's something of a reportorial tour de force designed to gather together a great deal of material into essays long on summary but short on analysis, particularly textual analysis. This methodological criticism applies most obviously to the extremely shallow concordial analysis laid out in chapter 1, where, unfortunately, no attempt is made even to *recognize*, much less assess, the impact of the literary-historical context against which Tanak originally comes to life. Given the author's stated delimitations, this does not come as a surprise—indeed, how many of our students are as familiar with the Greco-Roman sources as the ancient Semitic sources upon which they so thoroughly, osmotically, and lavishly depend? Yet, it is still disappointing and only serves to reinforce Daniel Snell's challenge to those he labels the "champions of the

Greek miracle" (*Flight and Freedom in the Ancient Near East* [Leiden: Brill, 2001] 135) to rethink their presumptions. This challenge applies to the present study on at least two levels.

First, the poverty-wealth polarity preoccupying this survey is well known to scholars of antiquity to be deeply embedded within the ancient Near Eastern literary world against which Tanak originally takes shape, and failure to recognize this reality automatically misleads readers into thinking not only that its origination is Greco-Roman but that a pan-Hellenistic portrayal of its developmental history is somehow holistically accurate. Bluntly put, such an approach unnecessarily entices readers to begin their investigation of this and many other topics on the proverbial "wrong foot" (see literature cited in M. S. Moore, "Socioeconomic Conflict Motifs in Ancient Near Eastern Epics," in *Wealth Watch: A Study of Socioeconomic Conflict in the Bible* [Pickwick, 2011], 26–99).

Second, the poverty-wealth polarity embedded in the great literature of the ancient Near East significantly shapes the form and substance of Tanak itself, not to mention the Second Temple Hebrew literature that is totally dependent upon it. Shallow concordial surveys like the one laid out on pages 27–32 of the present study not only obscure this truth; they perpetuate the same sort of static pan-Hellenism against which even nineteenth-century luminaries such as F. C. Baur justifiably reacted (*Paulus, der Apostel Jesu Christi: Sein Leben und Wirken, seine Briefen und seine Lehre. Ein Beitrag zu einer kritischen Geschichte des Urchristentums* [Stuttgart: Becher & Müller, 1845]; see further literature cited in M. S. Moore, "Socioeconomic Conflict Motifs in the Hebrew Bible" and "Socioeconomic Conflict Motifs in Early Jewish Texts," *Wealth Watch*, 100–167, 168–201).

Having said this, let it quickly be emphasized that students can learn much about the osmotic impact of the poverty-wealth polarity on the identity of early Christianity from this elegantly written book. Its greatest strength is its encyclopedic grasp of a topic that for far too long has been forced to stand on the periphery of serious attention in New Testament/patristic studies. Its greatest weakness, however, is its unwillingness/inability to exegete actual texts in their literary-historical contexts, thus leaving the impression of authenticity where it often, in fact, does not exist. Still, for beginners unaware of these issues at all, it may well prove to be an enlightening first step.

HISTORY OF INTERPRETATION

Inheriting Abraham: The Legacy of the Patriarch in Judaism, Christianity, and Islam, by Jon D. Levenson. Princeton: Princeton University Press, 2012. Pp. xvi + 244. Cloth. $29.95. ISBN 9780691155692.

Sara Koenig, Seattle Pacific University, Seattle, Washington

In the acknowledgments at the beginning of *Inheriting Abraham: The Legacy of the Patriarch in Judaism, Christianity and Islam*, Jon Levenson avers that he has lectured on this subject for more than three decades. Reading through his thoughtful and extensive treatment of the patriarch, one can certainly see connections with his previous publications on such topics as the Aqedah or Sinai, but this work is in no way redundant. A new dimension of this book is the way that Levenson discusses the relationships between the three faiths mentioned in the subtitle, highlighting the commonalities as well as the differences. When Levenson discusses the Christian and Jewish understandings of Gen 12:3b, for example, he explains that he is concerned to "challenge the convenient dichotomy" (34) between them. Such an impulse runs through the book as Levenson is careful to note connections and overlap. Yet he is also careful not to blur the differences among the faiths. In fact, throughout the book Levenson makes the case that Abraham can only be understood as the father of Judaism, Christianity, and Islam if the distinctions between the three are flattened.

The introduction—"Who Was (and Is) Abraham?"—lays out the structure and central ideas in the book, which will attempt to answer the titular question by starting with the Jewish Bible. Levenson is a careful reader attuned to literary details, but he also utilizes source criticism and theology as he discusses the specific texts. However, as Levenson points out (2), any discussion of Abraham cannot limit itself to Genesis, for three reasons. First, because the text is laconic, it calls for interpretation. Levenson writes concerning Gen 12:10–20 that it is "so compressed and so cryptic that it is susceptible to many interpretations, some diametrically opposite to others" (37). In reference to Gen 22, he explains, "the austerity of the narrative leaves us uncertain, even as it prompts us to fill in the gaps." (75) Second, Levenson points out that within Judaism the Bible is always "bundled" (2) with a rich corpus of interpretation. The postbiblical Abraham found in those interpretations may take on qualities not explicitly described in the text and in some cases the traditions about Abraham overwhelm the textuality. Third, Abraham's relationship to Islam and Christianity can only be seen fully by moving beyond Genesis. Within Islam, Genesis is not part of the canon. Within Christianity, Abraham is read through the lens of Paul (and, at times, a distorted understanding of the Pauline message, as Levenson demonstrates). Therefore, Levenson includes reception history of Abraham, tracing his identity through midrash and Talmud, within the Qur'an and New Testament, and even through the present day.

Chapter 1, "Call and Commission," considers the topic of "chosenness" and its related term, "election." Levenson points out how the tradition of Israel's origin in Gen 12—as a divine promise to a childless ancestor—demonstrates that this is a people whose very existence depends on God's providence and God's willingness to sustain it. Levenson also reads Ezek 16 as a variant tradition about origins, suggesting that if we read the people of Israel as standing for Jerusalem in the text, then the chosen people are a child born of mixed origins, adopted (and married) by God (22). Ezekiel's depiction of Israel coming from the mixed marriage between an Amorite and a Hittite means that chosenness cannot equal racism (23). Still, the text's emphasis on a promised heir coming from Abram's own loins

(Gen 15:4) means that the people of God are not merely a community with a common creed or faith. Levenson explains,

> the people Israel is neither a nationality in the conventional sense nor a church-like body composed of like-minded believers or practitioners of a common set of norms. Having something in common with both of these more familiar identities, it reduces to neither of them. Rather, as the call and commission of Abram already indicate, it is a natural family with a supernatural mandate. (24)

In this same chapter Levenson also treats the common understanding that God's people are chosen for a mission, as he patiently explains varying—and variant—interpretations of the phrase in Gen 12:3b about Abram blessing the families of the earth. Levenson concludes this chapter by dealing with the Christian interpretation of chosenness that equates being chosen (or "elect") with being saved. In particular, he argues that the book of Genesis lacks a notion that Abram's chosenness is contingent on, or even implies, the rejection of others.

In chapter 2, Levenson treats the "Frustrations and Fulfillment" related to childlessness and its eventual end. As he discusses Gen 12:10–20, he places Ramban's interpretation in conversation with that of Assyriologist Barry L. Eichler (38–39). The way Levenson combines interpretations, and utilizes differing methodologies, is part of what makes his work so rich. Levenson also poses a theological question about Abraham that reverberates into the three faiths discussed: "Does faith in God and his promises require in the beneficiaries a stance of quietism and passivity, or does it, rather, require the opposite stance of human initiative and activism to help bring about the promised result?" (38). Obviously, there cannot be a simple or simplistic answer to that question, and Levenson does not attempt such an answer. He will deal with it in more detail in subsequent chapters, particularly as he looks at the reception of Gen 15:6.

Chapter 3 is titled "The Test," and, indeed, the Aqedah can be understood as the single most important test Abraham undergoes. The chapter begins with a close reading of Gen 22, followed by a tour through its reception in Second Temple and rabbinic Judaism (89–99), in Christian interpretations (99–104), and in the Qur'an (104–6). Tucked within these pages are insightful comments on topics such as the association of the Aqedah with Passover and Rosh Hashanah (92–96) and negative implications of typology (103). Levenson concludes the chapter by working through Immanuel Kant's use of the Aqedah as the example of an irrational person believing that an "immoral" command can come from God. He warns that Kant has "abstracted the story not only from the larger web of biblical law and theology but also from the story of Abraham in Genesis" (107). Levenson suggests that Kant's interpretation of Abraham, which locates the story within ethics and not in narrative and theology, is the forerunner for subsequent interpretations of Abraham's actions as villainous or violent. A recent example he gives is Yvonne Sherwood's point that the letters found in the Boston airport, written by the al-Qaeda hijackers of the planes on September 11, 2001, suggested "an allusion to the Abrahamic sacrifice in the Qur'an" (108, referencing Sherwood's "Binding-Unbinding: Divided Responses of Judaism, Christianity, and Islam to the 'Sacrifice' of Abraham's Beloved Son," *JAAR* 72 [2004]: 824). Levenson deals with the assumptions present in such interpretations of Abraham as willing to commit a heinous, immoral act. To those who are concerned that reading Gen 22 could lead to such disastrous real-world results as filicide, he argues that there is a scarcity of attempts to imitate the Aqedah (111). With reference to Islam, he is careful to acknowledge the complexity of 9/11 and the intricate hermeneutics that would be required for someone to draw on the Muslim story of Abraham's near-sacrifice of his unnamed son as a model for contemporary violent behavior (111).

Chapter 4 departs from a pattern of beginning with the Jewish Bible, then discussing implications and interpretations of the texts. Instead, titled "The Rediscovery of God," this chapter traces how the biblical Abraham evolves into a "monotheistic purist" (117) and an iconoclast who refuses to serve false gods (121) in Judaism and Islam. As Levenson puts it, he traces "the process by which Abraham the father of the Jewish people became Abraham the founder, or rediscoverer, of belief in the one true God as well" (139). Levenson points out the "profound philosophical issues lurking behind these seemingly naïve stories" (123), such as God's relationship to physical matter (God exists, but not as an object; God created the universe with its physical laws, etc.). Thus, the postbiblical Abraham is not only a champion of monotheism, but he also becomes a teacher of philosophy, particularly in Josephus's characterization of him in the *Jewish Antiquities*. Different midrashim have Abraham teaching others about God and even converting them into Judaism. Even if these Abrahams bear scant resemblance to the patriarch in Genesis, Levenson shows how they have been shaped into their final forms through the religious traditions that reflect upon him.

Chapter 5, "Torah and Gospel," focuses on the way that Judaism and Christianity respectively understand Abraham to be a model for following the law and walking in faith. It is in the Second Temple period that Abraham is understood as someone who kept the Torah—in whole or in part—even before it was revealed to Israel at Sinai. Throughout the book Levenson has pointed out that interpretations within Judaism do not agree, and the same is true within Christianity. Levenson's explanation of how Paul and James use Gen 15:6 is a salient example of how the New Testament is consistent in insisting that Abraham is a model, even though he models different things (faith and works) in different ways.

"One Abraham or Three?" (ch. 6) returns to a discussion of all three faiths. Levenson begins by describing the recent initiative for interreligious and international cooperation sponsored by the Global Negotiation Project at Harvard University and titled "Abraham's Path." Ultimately Levenson praises the impulse behind the initiative, as it seeks reconciliation in a deeply divided world. Yet he points out that, if Abraham is the one in whom Judaism, Christianity, and Islam find their common ground, some of the distinctive theological positions of the three faiths—such as the Christian belief in a triune God—must be suspended. Levenson addresses Bruce Feiler's popular (and best-selling) work on Abraham and Karl-Josef Kuschel's scholarly treatment of the patriarch. As Levenson goes through their arguments, he explains how some of their assumptions are not accurate. This final chapter of the book culminates with the point Levenson has been making throughout the work, that Abraham is seen quite differently in Judaism, Christianity, and Islam.

It is worth noting that the three faiths mentioned are not given equal amounts of time in the book; Levenson spends more time discussing Judaism than Christianity and less time on Islam than the other two. This is not necessarily a fault because Levenson's work reflects his own religious commitments, but it may be helpful for the reader to know of time.

In Levenson's own words, he is writing for "both general and scholarly readers" (xiii). Throughout the book he strikes a fine balance in addressing both audiences, with the exception of a few places where his argument would benefit from more detailed referents. For example, when Levenson discusses Abram and Sarai's sojourn to Egypt in Gen 12:10–20, he refers to the reputed sexual deviance of the Egyptians elsewhere in the Bible (36). It would be helpful to have a brief reference to Ezek 16 and 23, particularly for those readers who might be unaware of how those chapters describe Egypt. A second example where Levenson's characteristically careful and detailed discussion seems to be missing is in his assertion that in Gen 17:18 Abraham fears that God will kill Ishmael (51). If Levenson is drawing on interpretive traditions to explain Abraham's emotions, it would be helpful to read some referent to that tradition. That leads me to another critique of the book: instead of footnotes, it has endnotes. This seems to be typical of the Princeton University Press, but because Levenson's citations are so rich and thoughtful, it is especially frustrating to have to flip back and forth between the chapters and the endnotes.

Overall, *Inheriting Abraham* is a book to be savored, lingering over the fine points in Levenson's writing. It is a book to be discussed in the classroom (probably at the graduate level, though a colleague of mine used it with undergraduate students) and in religious communities. It is an important book, particularly in our present historical situation, when it is imperative that we understand the differences, as well as the commonalities, among these religions.

Jacob: Unexpected Patriarch, by Yair Zakovitch. New Haven, CT: Yale University Press, 2012. Pp. vii + 206. Cloth. $25.00. ISBN 9780300144260.

Ronald Hendel, University of California, Berkeley, Berkeley, California

Yair Zakovitch, the eminent biblical scholar who retired last year from the Hebrew University, has written a marvelous book about Jacob in the Jewish Lives series by Yale University Press. It is always a challenge to distill serious scholarship into nontechnical and readable prose, and Zakovitch accomplishes this goal admirably. The book is accessible without sacrificing nuance and conceptual complexity.

The idea of writing a "life" of Jacob is fraught with peril. Other biographies in this series include Sarah Bernhardt, Franz Kafka, and the baseball legend Hank Greenberg. Jacob is clearly a figure of a different kind. Zakovitch lays out his approach carefully. He writes, "the unity of the story that begins with Jacob's birth and ends with his death is … largely an illusion, the product of artistic editing." He is concerned, therefore, with a literary life, which has many interpretive and compositional levels. One level of this "life" is the compositional mosaic of the Jacob stories in Genesis. Another level consists of traditions that have been rejected or marginalized in the main narrative but that can be carefully prized out of other texts, an approach that Zakovitch calls "literary archaeology." A third level is the exegetical reception of the life of Jacob by later interpreters. This involves "the free interpretation and adaptation of the ancient texts for contemporary needs [which] is what we call 'midrash.'" Recounting the life of Jacob, in Zakovitch's approach, requires attention to all these levels, which often intertwine. This involves a considerable amount of erudition, literary acuity, and, occasionally, intellectual risk. Zakovitch's book is a fulsome treat in all these respects.

Let me give an example of how Zakovitch pursues his task, from his exposition of Jacob's encounter with God at Penuel (Gen 32). Zakovitch shows that there are overt and covert narrative evaluations of this divine encounter. In the main story, Jacob gains a blessing as a consequence of his physical and violent confrontation with God. Yet even as Jacob identifies his divine adversary in his etiology of Penuel—"For I have seen God face to face"—there is a countervailing tendency "to combat the ancient tradition of a physical struggle." Zakovitch observes that the writer of this verse softens the impact of the encounter by emphasizing its *visual* aspect ("I have *seen* God"), not its physical aspect. This is just one of several interpretive efforts to soften the tradition, this one, remarkably, in the main narrative itself.

This strategy is taken up at the beginning of the chapter, where "angels of God" encounter Jacob. The verb of encounter, *vayifge'u,* could mean a violent encounter, but the text clarifies that it is purely visual encounter: "When he *saw* them, Jacob said, 'This is God's camp.'" Zakovitch suggests that "this writer wanted to deny that such a violent encounter took place, to neutralize the tradition about a struggle with divine beings … by deliberately using the ambiguous verb." This purely visual encounter adopts the same strategy as the etymology of Penuel. Similarly, when Jacob subsequently encounters Esau, he says, "To see your face is like seeing the face of God." This clearly echoes the etymology of Penuel and repeats the emphasis on seeing, not fighting. Zakovitch describes this utterance as a covert reinterpretation of the etymology of Penuel, which "shifted the tradition from the realm of the holy to the profane." Each of these narrative moves softens the effect of the physical encounter with God, moving it toward the purely visual and toward a lesser type of adversary—angels or human.

This interpretive tendency is taken further by other biblical writers. Hosea turns this episode into an encounter with an angel. The angel grants the blessing when Jacob "wept and implored him"—so it is not a violent encounter after all. The

P writer in Gen 35 eliminates the physical encounter completely and has God give Jacob the blessing and new name in a speech at Bethel. The dangerous encounter at Penuel is airbrushed away in favor of God's purely verbal blessing at a different holy site. Hosea and P both agree on this: "At Bethel he found him, and there he would speak with him" (Hos 12:5). (This verse in Hosea may even be a secondary borrowing—what Zakovitch nicely calls the "boomerang effect"—from the P passage.) As Zakovitch explains, these writers "replace the physical struggle with an exchange of words." The interpretations have become the story itself.

As this example shows, this is no simple retelling of the life of Jacob in Genesis. It is a penetrating reading of the Jacob narrative in its biblical versions, and also many postbiblical versions, yielding a multilayered view of Jacob and his interpretive life. It exposes the intertextuality of the Jacob narrative, bringing into focus marginalized traditions, inner-biblical arguments, and the ebb and flow of midrash both within and without the Bible. This book is the result of decades of assiduous literary scholarship. It is a work to be savored, reread, and argued with, like the polymorphous patriarch that is its subject.

History of New Testament Research, Volume 3: From C. H. Dodd to Hans Dieter Betz, by William Baird. Minneapolis: Fortress, 2013. Pp. xx + 775. Cloth. $70.00. ISBN 9780800699185.

Joshua Jay Stigall, Briercrest College and Seminary, Caronport, Saskatchewan, Canada

> When the writers of the New Testament put down their pens, they could not have imagined the amount of industry their works would generate.... To the modern observer, the New Testament appears like a tiny treasure buried under a mountain of scholarly debris. The attempts to uncover its riches has enlisted the arduous labor of scores of persons employing a multitude of methods, like a crowd of excavators using everything from trowels to bulldozers. (Baird 1992, xiii).

So begins the first volume of William Baird's three-volume series on New Testament research. The characterization of New Testament scholarship as a mountain covering a tiny treasure is apt, and the task of charting the pathways up, down, and around that mountain is equally as arduous as the work of the excavators who built it.

It is well documented that Baird's original intent was to present his historical survey in two volumes, but that the project expanded to include a third. Now, after close to thirty years of effort, the series has come to a conclusion. The fruits of his labor now complete, Baird is able to put down his own proverbial pen. As is the case at the completion of all major projects, there are mixed feelings.

On the one hand, completion of the task is admittedly bittersweet for the author as he expresses relief to be finished, "but reluctant to end what has been an exciting adventure" (3). No doubt the task was daunting and, one can guess, often overwhelming.

On the other hand, the readers who have benefited from his judicious and thorough treatment of the history of New Testament research will be disappointed that he will not continue as a guide in this important area. This disappointment is, of course, a high compliment to Baird's deft ability to survey the "crowd of excavators," identify those who have most significantly impacted New Testament scholarship, present their contributions fairly and concisely, and to do so in an engaging manner. Baird's accomplishment is truly astounding, and students and scholars of the New Testament owe him a debt of gratitude.

The final volume of *History of New Testament Research* continues the general focus and format of the first two volumes. Baird's focus continues to be German, British, and North American scholars who employ a predominantly historical-critical methodology. In this volume Baird made an admittedly "arbitrary decision" to further narrow his focus to scholars who, for the most part, were born before 1930, wrote their major works in the twentieth century, and are now retired. While one may critique Baird's focus as too limited, as do several reviewers of volumes 1 and 2, to do this would be unfair. It is impossible in three volumes, let alone one volume, to do justice to New Testament research around the globe. Baird does well to limit his focus to a (more) manageable segment of New Testament research and to leave to others the task of filling out the history on a global scale. He has carved out a niche in the history and filled it very admirably.

The format of volume 3 also generally follows the pattern established for the first two volumes. Divided into three main parts ("The Renaissance of New Testament Criticism," "The Revisiting of Critical Problems," and "Theological and Synthesizing Movements"), the thirteen total chapters, including epilogue, are arranged chronologically. Different from volumes 1 and 2, however, is that Baird no longer categorizes the main parts of his work based on different "eras" of world history. This does not mean, however, that Baird does not situate developments in New Testament research into their cultural context, whether that be the aftermath of World War II, scientific developments, or the "information revolution" that began in the latter half of the twentieth century.

New to the present volume are two features. First is the inclusion of anecdotes of personal encounters with a number of scholars surveyed in this volume. While Baird is reluctant to include these stories (2), their presence is welcome for a number of reasons: the stories have the effect of humanizing several scholars in a way that does not always happen when reading primary texts, and personal anecdotes have the capability of shedding light on the character of scholars in a way the brings to mind Plutarch's admonition that a "trifling incident ... shows more of a person's character" than grand achievements (Plutarch, *Alexander*). As an example, Baird recalls the time Henry Cadbury sat with him at lunch during an SBL meeting in the 1960s and asked the young scholar what he was reading and what Cadbury, himself, should read. This illustrates Cadbury's humility and kind nature.

The second new feature in this volume relating to focus is the inclusion of work carried out collectively. This is a departure from a previous focus on research conducted solely by individuals. In part, this is an inevitable consequence of the significant discovery of source material in the twentieth century, including the Nag Hammadi Codices, the Dead Sea Scrolls, and papyri.

In terms of content, Baird's thoroughness in the first two volumes is evident in the third. Part 1, "The Renaissance of New Testament Criticism," is divided into three chapters. Chapter 1, "The Zenith of Enlightenment Criticism," is exemplified by the work of Taylor, Cadbury, Manson, and Dodd. In all cases, these scholars refined the "methods of the nineteenth century" (52), working with exactness and skill that is commendable. Chapter 2, "The New Biblical Theology," traces the efforts of Barth and Bultmann. These two scholars, especially Bultmann, are deemed the most influential scholars of the twentieth century. Their work "affirmed the importance of the Bible for theology and faith," affirmed the importance of the historical-critical method (Barth was more prone to be skeptical), and set forth the agenda that would occupy New Testament scholars for decades. Chapter 3, "The Bultmann School," is devoted to the influence of Rudolf Bultmann on the history of New Testament scholarship. Scholars such as Käsemann, Bornkamm, and James Robinson, a student of both Barth and Bultmann, carry on the legacy of Bultmann in various ways, even if they depart from their teacher at important points. Baird is clear that these three scholars are not the only influential students of Bultmann. Important figures such as Conzelmann, Koester, and Betz are treated at other sections of volume 3.

Part 2, "The Revisiting of Critical Problems," is divided into five chapters. Chapter 4 deals with "New Discoveries, Archaeology, Textual Criticism" and the source material available to New Testament scholars. The discovery of the Nag Hammadi Codices, the Dead Sea Scrolls, and numerous papyri not only sheds light on religious backgrounds and the textual history of the New Testament but also demands cooperation between scholars, since no individual scholar can master the disciplines necessary for effective research in all these areas. Even more important, however, the discovery of these texts "demonstrate ... a common social concern: the Scrolls lead us into the life of a particular Jewish sect; the new archaeology is concerned with the daily life of ordinary people; textual criticism has become aware of political forces functioning in the shaping of the text" (258). Chapter 5, "Historical Backgrounds: Judaism," is a review of the post–World War II "reassessment of Judaism" in New Testament research (279). The work of scholars such as Jeremias, Black, Davies, Sanders, and Hengel are surveyed in a way that illustrates the "prevailing problem in historical criticism: scholars using the methods do not produce the same results" (324). In this context Jeremias, Black, and Hengel continue "the older view of Judaism as a foil for Christianity," despite the evidence provided by Davies and Sanders (324). In chapter 6, "Developments in Historical Criticism," Baird surveys the rise of "Introductions" via the work of Kümmel and Koester, changes in Gospel research seen in the rise of redaction criticism and the work of Conzelmann and Marx-

sen, and discussions of the so-called Synoptic problem with the revival of the
Griesbach Hypothesis in the work of Farmer and the research on Q exemplified
by Goulder and Kloppenborg. Chapter 7 documents "Confessional Research:
Roman Catholic Scholarship." The focus in this chapter on the work of scholars
such as Schnackenburg, Raymond Brown, and John P. Meier is a welcome expansion from a focus on Protestant scholars. The final chapter in this section, "The
Development of Scholarly Societies," surveys the rise of the Society of Biblical
Literature and the Catholic Biblical Association, as well as more focused groups
such as the Jesus Seminar.

In part 3, "Theological and Synthesizing Movements," Baird discusses "Theological and Hermeneutical Developments" (ch. 9) and "Critical, Exegetical, and
Theological Accomplishments" in Europe (ch. 10) and America (ch. 11). The
focus in chapter 9 is on the work of Cullmann, Knox, Minear, and Bruce. These
scholars all address "the importance of Scripture for the life and thought of the
church" (525). The work of each is an example of the attempt to show how "the
Bible or a biblically oriented theology" might "offer hope" in the "troubled times"
following World War II (475). Both chapters 10 and 11 are somewhat "catch-
all" chapters that speak to the state of New Testament research in the two most
influential geographical centers: Europe as seen in the work of Barrett, Dunn,
and Gerhardsson; America as seen in the work of Schüssler Fiorenza (Harvard),
Martyn, Keck, Furnish (Yale), and Betz (Chicago).

Overall, the third volume of *History of New Testament Research* is an excellent conclusion to a very helpful series. Baird deals with each scholar fairly and
presents the history of New Testament research in a readable and engaging
manner. Readers will no doubt lament gaps in this history, perhaps the most
glaring of which is the paucity of female scholars surveyed in the volume. As
is evident above, only Schüssler Fiorenza is treated in detail, and Baird only
makes brief mention of Adela Yarboro Collins, Beverly Roberts Gaventa, Margaret Mitchell, Judith Lieu, Barbara Aland, and Oda Wischmeyer, each of whom
has made important contributions to the field. It is possible, however, that criticism for this omission should be directed more at the academy than the author
of the volume.

In the end, this volume, as well as the first two, is indispensable for the New
Testament student and scholar. The series provides a survey of the history of our
discipline. The importance of understanding our discipline is well summed up by
Baird himself in the first volume of the series, "Failure to know one's history is a
failure to understand one's identity, a failure that destines one to repeat old mistakes and neglect venerable solutions, to put old wine in new wineskins without
even knowing that it is old" (Baird 1992, xxii).

History of New Testament Research, Volume 3: From C. H. Dodd to Hans Dieter Betz, by William Baird. Minneapolis: Fortress, 2013. Pp. xx + 775. Cloth. $70.00. ISBN 9780800699185.

Benjamin A. Edsall, University of Oxford, Oxford, United Kingdom

This book is the long-awaited third volume in William Baird's highly respected *History of New Testament Research* (vol. 1: *From Deism to Tübingen* [1992]; vol. 2: *From Jonathan Edwards to Rudolf Bultmann* [2003]). Begun in 1984 with a contract for a single volume of around five hundred pages, the project has concluded almost thirty years later with yet another fine contribution.

It should be noted at the outset, as Baird does himself, that this book, for all its size, is not truly a history of New Testament research. "This is a history of NT research in *some* places by *some* scholars" (2). The choice of scholars was largely limited to those born prior to 1930 who operated in North America and Northern Europe (1–2), although this focus does not preclude his interaction with scholarship as recent as 2005 on particular subjects such as the Dead Sea Scrolls. Baird states, "an earlier plan to investigate the multitude of new methods that emerged in the last half of the century had to be abandoned because of lack of space and time. Also, the original plan for Volume 3 included more scholars, but again space and time limitations made this impossible" (1). It seems to me that Baird's choice was made all the more difficult for the lack of hindsight from which his earlier surveys benefitted; in another century or so it will perhaps be clearer what the most important strands of New Testament research are today. In any case, a history of scholarship is never simply a dispassionate history. It is a constructive story we tell to make space for a particular project or study, to explain why a certain work needs to be done or needs to cease. Here Baird tells the story of the enduring value of historical criticism of the New Testament and of its relationship to biblical theology (of various stripes).

The book proceeds in three parts bookended by an introduction and epilogue: part 1 "The Renaissance of New Testament Criticism" (chs. 1–3); part 2 "The Revisiting of Critical Problems" (chs. 4–8); part 3 "Theological and Synthesizing Movements" (chs. 9–11). Each chapter is prefaced by a bit of general historical context and concluded with a "summary" in which Baird draws the various threads together (insofar as that is possible) and offers a few critical remarks. Further, each scholar discussed receives a short biographical treatment, and, where possible, Baird provides personal anecdotes from his own experience.

Chapter 1, "The Zenith of Enlightenment Criticism," covers Vincent Taylor, H. J. Cadbury, and T. W. Manson, culminating with C. H. Dodd. For each of these scholars, as indeed for the rest of the scholars discussed in the volume, Baird addresses the various aspects of their work, focusing on their most well-known contributions, but not excluding some classic chestnuts (e.g., Cadbury's 1933 *JBL* article, "Luke and the Horse-Doctors"). His treatment of Dodd, for instance, begins with his early work on Paul, his classic work on the parables, his argument regarding the "apostolic preaching," and his seminal work on the scriptural "substructure" of the New Testament, but Baird devotes most of the space to Dodd's work on the Fourth Gospel (45–52).

In chapter 2, "The New Biblical Theology," Baird addresses the work of Karl Barth and Rudolf Bultmann. While Baird's previous volume dealt with Bultmann's work on form criticism and *Religionsgeschichte*, the emphasis in this volume is on Bultmann's theological side. Indeed, a concern with theology is a red thread that runs throughout this book. Given the focus of the book on New Testament research, Bultmann receives fuller treatment, and Baird's thorough knowledge of him (and his detractors) is evident. He moves from Bultmann's theology through his hermeneutic of demythologization to his New Testament exegesis. Baird's attention to the theological impetus that drove (or at least enabled) Bultmann's critical work is illuminating.

Bultmann remains in view in the following chapter 3, "The Bultmann School." This chapter covers Ernst Käsemann, Gunther Bornkamm, and James M. Robinson. By placing Bultmann in the title of the chapter and in giving attention to the theological continuities and differences between these scholars and their teacher, Baird illuminates the theological context for their historical scholarship, even where that context involved a deep rift, as in the case of Käsemann.

Part 2 begins with an overview of scholarship on the Nag Hammadi materials, the Dead Sea Scrolls, new archaeological discoveries, and advances in textual criticism (ch. 4: "New Discoveries, Archaeology, Textual Criticism"). While the sections are not quite even—with more space devoted to the Dead Sea Scrolls and textual criticism and fewer resources provided with respect to archaeology—all are in fact helpful summaries and would function as useful reference points for scholars and students alike.

Baird divides chapter 5, "Historical Backgrounds: Judaism," into three sections, with the first section devoted to Joachim Jeremias and Matthew Black as representatives of "the conventional view" of Judaism and the second devoted to W. D. Davies and E. P. Sanders as representatives of the "new perspective." Martin Hengel closes the chapter as a representative of a new take on the conventional view. Additionally, the chapter begins with a short discussion of the increasing availability of Jewish texts through the work of scholars such as George W. E. Nickelsburg, Michael E. Stone, R. H. Charles, and James H. Charlesworth.

Chapter 6, "Developments in Historical Criticism," covers New Testament *Einleitung* scholarship, represented by Werner Kümmel and Helmut Koester (who was also mentioned in chapter 3 on the Bultmann school), the redaction criticism of Hans Conzelmann and Willi Marxen, and the Synoptic problem debate, including William Farmer, Michael Goulder (with Farrer and Goodacre), and a short mention of Christopher Tuckett and Franz Neirynck. In discussing Q scholarship, Baird focuses on John Kloppenborg's work. Throughout the discussion of the Synoptic problem and Q, it becomes clear where Baird's sympathies lie, and it is an unfortunate necessity of a book like this that each view does not get a fully nuanced exposition. As in the previous topical discussions, however,

Baird's treatment provides plenty of references elsewhere and could serve as a useful summary and introduction to the issues.

Rudolf Schnackenburg, Raymond E. Brown, and John P. Meier are featured in chapter 7, on confessional Roman Catholic scholarship. Schnakenburg's work on the Fourth Gospel and New Testament ethics, Raymond Brown's work on the Johannine materials, and John Meier's study on the historical Jesus dominate the discussions about each scholar. Part 2 concludes in chapter 8 with a discussion of the establishment and development of the Society of Biblical Literature (SBL), the Catholic Biblical Association (CBA), and Studiorum Novi Testamenti Societas (SNTS). That chapter closes with a discussion of Robert Funk and the work of the Jesus Seminar.

Part 3 of Baird's work is perhaps where the constraints of space and the absence of clarity afforded by hindsight are felt most keenly, as he moves fully into the latter part of the twentieth century. His discussion of "Theological and Hermeneutical Developments" (ch. 9) focuses on Oscar Cullmann, John Knox, Paul S. Minear, and F. F. Bruce. Chapters 10 and 11 address "Critical, Exegetical, and Theological Accomplishments" in Europe and North America, respectively. European scholarship is here represented by C. K Barrett, James D. G. Dunn, and Birger Gerhardsson, while North America (restricted in practice to the United States) is represented by Elisabeth Schüssler Fiorenza, J. Louis Martyn, Leander Keck, Victor P. Furnish, and, finally, Hans Dieter Betz. Baird's explanation in his introduction that the original plan included more scholars than the final product accounts for the potentially surprising absence of Nils A. Dahl, Krister Stendahl, Wayne Meeks, or David E. Aune, among others. But this is niggling over what is inevitably a subjective (and difficult!) decision, and even the list of omitted scholars reflects this reviewer's scholarly biases and experiences at least as much as Baird's selection reflects his concerns in this volume. Indeed, those scholars included are formidable and influential voices in New Testament studies and well repay Baird's attention.

At times throughout the work Baird resorts simply to listing positions held by a particular scholar (perhaps a necessary quality for a book like this), but he is at his best when he illuminates underlying theological or ideological factors in scholars work, as in his comparison of Sanders and Hengel (310) or his discussion of the foundation for Käsemann's theology (147). Since Baird is the one telling this story of scholarship, it is only to be expected that his editorial comments reveal his own commitments, as in his lament at the perceived lack of suitable preparation in American graduate schools (585) and the encomium for "the venerable tradition of German scholarship" (677).

All in all, Baird's work is a valuable addition to any library and would make an excellent reference work. Scholars and students will learn much in it and will undoubtedly find allies they did not know they had. Baird's topical discussions are well-documented and can serve as helpful introductions for the neophyte in need of a place to start. To be sure, the reader will occasionally (even frequently, perhaps) find herself or himself on the other side of Baird's critical comments, but Baird makes a clear effort to be even-handed in his treatment of all scholars, including those with whom he clearly disagrees.

If there is one principle criticism to make of this work, it is to be laid at the feet of the publisher rather than the author. Given that a book like this is most often used as a reference work, the anemic table of contents (there is no clear indication of which scholars or topical issues are covered in which chapters) and lackluster subject index somewhat inhibits its usefulness for that role.

Even so, this book is a fitting conclusion to three decades of work, and the guild of New Testament scholarship should be grateful for the immense amount of valuable material gathered and analyzed by Baird over the course of his project.

HERMENEUTICS AND METHODS

Expresión literaria del placer en la Biblia hebrea, by Mike van Treek Nilsson. Asociación Bíblica Española 51. Navarra, Spain: Editorial Verbo Divino, 2010. Pp. xxix + 444. Paper. €29.45. ISBN 9788499451121.

César Melgar, Graduate Theological Union, Berkeley, California

The topic of pleasure has often been avoided or discussed from an overly spiritualized standpoint within Christian circles. Recently this approach has been called into question not just by the culture outside of these circles but also within them by scholars, clerics, and lay people. As the need for an open discussion about human sexuality and emotions increases, studies that deal with these topics become more relevant. The present work by Mike van Treek Nilsson, a professor of Hebrew Bible at the Pontificia Universidad Católica de Chile, is an original contribution that explores what the Hebrew Bible describes about pleasure. Although this work is predominantly academic in character, the main questions the author deals with echo the curiosity and concerns raised by faith-based communities. These questions include: "What do the sacred texts speak about pleasure? Is the Bible an instrument to marginalize and punish pleasure? Is pleasure a mortal trap? And what relevant elements can be encountered in the Sacred Scriptures to integrate eroticism and spirituality?" (xx). These questions demonstrate part of the theological background that informs this investigation, and they also implicitly hint at the new perspective the author conveys in this study.

Following a brief introduction, the author discusses the place that pleasure has in contemporary culture and proposes new alternatives that move beyond the spiritualization of this human emotion. After this initial chapter, the work splits in two major parts. Part 1 consists of a lexical study that both establishes the theoretical framework of cognitive linguistics and explores eight Hebrew terms that express the idea of pleasure (רצה, חפץ, ענג, ערב, נעם, עדן, יאל, שׁושׂ). Part 2 applies the concepts explored in part 1 to analyze three narratives where pleasure plays a prominent role in the development of the drama (1 Sam 17:55–21:1; 2 Sam 13:1–22; and Gen 29:1–30:24).

In chapter 2 ("Dominios semánticos"), the author sets the stage for his lexical analysis by defining a semantic field as a web of paradigmatic relations that exist between words and their meaning(s). Some of these semantic relations include: synonym, antonym, and hyponymy (20–21). Chapter 3 ("Análisis Componencial") introduces the concept of componential analysis in order to highlight the complexity of the process that aims at capturing the meaning of words across languages, cultures, and epochs. In this chapter the author recognizes both the merits and shortcomings of doing a componential analysis of a term such as *pleasure* and proposes that this tool should be combined with an analysis of the literature where this expression takes place (33–34), such as the narratives in the Hebrew Bible.

Chapter 4 ("Lingüística Cognitiva") deals with the concept of cognitive linguistics and how humans categorize ideas through mental processes brought about by both physiological and cultural aspects (37–38). This basic categorization of ideas takes place through the creation of metaphors and metonyms, which function not just as forms of poetic expression but as fundamental conduits for the transfer of knowledge (44–45). Chapter 5 introduces the notion of conceptual metaphor ("La metáfora conceptual"). Influenced by the seminal work of George Lakoff and Mark Johnson (see *Metaphors We Live By* [Chicago: University Of Chicago Press, 2003]), the author proposes that conceptual metaphors are omnipresent parts of human experience and that they are useful for the study of language and the expression of emotions (47–48). Chapter 6 deals with the role of conceptual metaphors within the realm of human emotions ("La metáfora y mundo emocional"), and chapter 7 ("Hacia un prototipo del placer") concludes this theoretical section with an analysis of pleasure and physiology. In this chapter the author also creates a hypothetical prototype for an ideal expression of pleasure based on psychological, emotional, and physiological dimensions.

Chapters 8–15 together constitute an analysis of eight Hebrew terms that express the concept of pleasure. In these chapters the author utilizes the tools described in the previous chapters to explore the semantic field of each of these terms throughout the Hebrew Bible. He then uses these findings to demonstrate the different instances where these terms appear as conceptual metaphors. Chapter 16 concludes part 1 of this study by summarizing the metaphorical uses of pleasure in the Hebrew Bible, and it introduces the study of the narratives where the role of pleasure will be explored.

Before delving into the analysis of these narratives, chapter 17 ("Un modelo de análisis narrativo") recounts the author's initial study of these narratives while teaching at the Pontificia Universidad Católica in Chile and at the Université catholique de Louvain. It also describes the theoretical foundation that he uses in interpreting these stories as fictional and intertextual accounts where the narrator describes a world where the reader is invited to participate in the drama as the characters and plot evolve (204).

Chapter 18 ("Traje desastre: 1 Sam 17,55–21,1") analyzes the role of power, pleasure, and affection. In this chapter the author divides these accounts into eight scenes that he analyzes from a narratival standpoint. The scenes demonstrate two contrasting pictures: on the one hand, Saul's desire for power propels him into a belligerent attempt to control and eliminate David; on the other hand, Jonathan's sincere affection and homoerotic desire for David expresses a vision for a mutual relationship (299).

Chapter 19 analyzes the story of Amnon and Tamar ("Espuma en las caderas 2 Sam 13,1–22"). The author proposes that this account demonstrates how in his narcissistic intentions Amnon uses pleasure to fill the void of not having Tamar (333). The problem in this account is not with eroticism per se but with love that moves forward without any restriction in trying to possess the other. The consequence of such action dehumanizes Tamar, and she ends up being just "pechos y caderas."

In chapter 20 ("La mitad del amor: Gn 29,1–30,24") the author studies the role of pleasure and love in the account of Jacob and Rachel. This narrative is broken down into four scenes where these emotions play out in the development of these characters and in their relation to the surrounding context. The chapter concludes with an assessment of how the rivalry between Leah and Rachel influenced the tragic and ephemeral character of some of their kindred, such as Dinah and Joseph.

Van Treek Nilsson has provided a thorough investigation of the topic of pleasure in the Hebrew Bible. The initial chapter ("El placer revisado en la cultura") offers a fruitful contextualization of this topic in today's culture. Also, the development of the theoretical framework of cognitive linguistics and the use of conceptual metaphors provide innovative examples of how these tools can be applied to the field of biblical studies. Likewise, the analysis of the Hebrew terms for pleasure reveals the author's careful work and attention to detail, as he does more than just provide a listing of the different meanings. By demonstrating how these words function in various literary contexts, he has demonstrated that words constitute metaphorical expressions of thought and emotion. Lastly, with the implementation of these linguistic tools into the analysis of the narratives in part 2, the author brings to light his sophistication as a reader. Although his conclusions do not necessarily represent a revolutionary interpretation of these texts, his methodology demonstrates an appreciation of the different traces where the literary richness of the biblical texts appear.

Despite these accomplishments, a few observations are necessary. Van Treek Nilsson starts from the standpoint of trying to answer some of the fundamental questions that Christian circles deal with when talking about pleasure. However, his final product may not necessarily be the most ideal tool to use when trying to answer some of these vexing questions, as the very technical character and length of this work (409 pages) is not conducive to be used outside of the academy. Another aspect that might work against its use is the high cost. At €29,45 ($40), the price might be too high to pay by people within these circles, especially those who are in predominantly Spanish-speaking communities. Lastly, the manuscript would be better served with some editing. Besides some sporadic misspellings (e.g., "hebra" for "hebrea" [202]; "hipotetiza" for "hipotetizar" [388]), the numbering of the chapters in the index and the introduction do not match (cf. xxviii, 443).

Essentially, van Treek Nilsson's contribution is an academic work for scholars who are interested in investigating what the Hebrew Bible has to say about pleasure and how linguistic tools (i.e., conceptual metaphors) can aid in this process. His boldness in writing about a topic often considered taboo is commendable and inspiring for other scholars who try to grapple with some of the social issues that affect their religious communities. This creative and thorough work demonstrates why it was given "la más alta distinción" at the Université catholique de Louvain, and it is a good example of how to integrate multiple interdisciplinary tools to analyze the teachings of the Hebrew Bible.

In the Second Degree: Paratextual Literature in Ancient Near Eastern and Ancient Mediterranean Culture and Its Reflections in Medieval Literature, edited by Philip Alexander, Armin Lange, and Renate Pillinger. Leiden: Brill, 2010. Pp. xiv + 284, Hardcover, $154.00, ISBN 9789004187733.

Anthony Swindell, Saint Saviour's Rectory, Jersey, United Kingdom

The essays that form this collection are based on papers given at a symposium held at the University of Vienna in February 2007 and center broadly on the applicability of the theories of Gérard Genette's study, *Palimpsests: Literature in the Second Degree,* to a range of paratextual literature from the ancient Near East and Mediterranean and medieval Europe. The discussion explores issues that lie at the heart of rewriting as a notion.

A wide range of topics is addressed, and it becomes apparent that the matrix derived from Genette's *Palimpsests* needs to be adjusted in some cases. For example, a number of the contributions stress the multiplicity of "hypotexts" for the "hypertexts" that they consider. Armin Lange in the introduction provides an overview of all the contributions, arguing that "literature in the second degree" addresses the needs of updating and adaptation that cultural memory requires. Invoking Jan Assmann's ideas about the need for cultural memory to be selective, lest (like individual memory) it be overwhelmed by the sheer volume of unsorted material, he considers that Genette's analysis of hypertexts in relation to hypotexts does justice to the way in which the rewritten texts discussed in this volume build on their antecedent base texts, sometimes bidding to replace or erase them, sometimes reasserting the base text's authority in changed cultural conditions. He parses the development of the Book of Watchers in its various renderings as indicative of this process.

Georg Danek, in "The Homeric Epics as Palimpsests," situates Genette's work within the watershed around 1972 when postmodernist and structuralist ideas were giving way to poststructuralism and deconstruction. He sees Genette's book *Palimpsests* as in part an attempt to deal with the challenge that the new emphasis on intertextuality brought to the structuralists' insistence on concentrating on the semiotic integrity of the single text. By taking the parody as the clearest example of deliberate rewriting, Genette was able to formulate a system for classifying "hypertexts" that were dependent unambiguously on an antecedent "hypotext." He finds this model particularly illuminating for the relationship of the Homeric epics on the antecedent epic tradition, even though the hypotext in this case only survives in fragments and in adaptations that already bear the mark of being influenced by the Homeric texts themselves.

Other contributors to the volume express reservations about swallowing the *Palimpsests* approach whole. Philip Alexander warns of the dangers of decontextualizing the rabbinic paratexts from their historical-critical settings. There must be a balance between exploring the phenomenology of rewriting and anchoring specific texts in their historical situation.

Along the way numerous issues are discussed that are relevant to the study of rewriting as a general topic. Thus the balance between the relative importance of "hypotext" and "hypertext" may shift, leaving the supposedly secondary work dominant. In such cases, knowledge of the hypotext may add to appreciation of the hypertext without being indispensible. In some cases the rewritten text has made a bid to eclipse or even to erase the base-text. Then there is that problem raised by the dependence of a hypertext on multiple hypotexts or base-texts.

In part 1, "Ancient Judaism," George J. Brooke examines the "Parabiblical Dead Sea Scrolls" as hypertexts in the Genettian sense. He seems more comfortable with the terminology of "hypertext" itself than with "palimpsest" as a matrix for understanding the rewritten scripture of Qumran. Among the important insights of Brooke's essay are those of the Qumran hypertexts as a form of exegesis that prospered in the precanonical period, to be replaced in the postcanonical period by the commentary; the sense of these hypertexts as more than "literature in the second degree," since in some cases, such as the Temple Scroll, they claim to have prior authority over the hypotext; the idea of the ongoing production of scriptural hypertexts as constitutive of a "rolling corpus"; and the observation that rewriting in this context performs a role in selecting metanarratives, with the community (he conjectures) excluding the Davidic narratives, on account of their association with the Hasmonean kingship project, and concentrating on hypotexts that it found more conducive to its own vision, namely, the Psalms and the Prophets. The latter discussion deserves wide notice, since the part played by hypertexts in selectivity (choosing one biblical hypotext rather than another for rewriting) is something that could be explored on a wide historical canvas. At the end of his essay Brookes argues for the hypertext as mediator of the hypotext, making it available in new cultural situations and thereby forming part of the evidence for the reconstruction of the historical circumstances of the movement "whose identity is expressed in the [Qumran] library." Jacques T. A. G. M. van Ruiten discusses Jubilees as paratextual literature, concentrating on Jub. 15 as a paratext of Gen 17. The main point here is that Jubilees rewrites a significant part of the Pentateuch (Gen 1–Exod 19), imposing its own metanarrative embracing a solar calendar dividing history into forty-nine-year epochs and making circumcision on the right day the sign of the covenant. It is a strong example of a hypertext that respects the hypotext and at the same time transforms the way it is read.

In part 2, "Graeco-Roman World," Annemarie Ambühl looks at how the fifteen Attic tragedies draw on the Homeric epics, which turns out to be a complex example of paratextuality, since these works not only confine themselves to selecting the mythological material handled in Homer but also intertext with the wider literary heritage, which includes poems and tragedies that themselves rework Homer. Most significantly, Ambühl demonstrates the "monopolizing reading" of the *Iliad* by Euripides, in which the playwright focalizes the fall of Troy from the perspective of the defeated and in particular that of the women, even transferring epic values from the Greeks to the Trojans. Troy is transmuted into a transhistorical symbol. George Danek, in his review of the Homeric epics themselves as palimpsests, finds Genette's matrix of the relationship of hypertext to hypotext particularly illuminating, since it takes account of the way in which a rewriting may erase the base text(s) and yet become richer when we realize that it is precisely a rewriting, a hypertext. In the case of Homer, however, the hypotext is largely only reconstructible from the hypertext itself.

In part 3, "Ancient Egypt and the Ancient Near East," Beate Pongratz-Leisten shows how an Old Babylonian text, *Ludlul* (for biblicists an analogue of the book of Job) relies on a mosaic of references to ritual practices and cultural signs such as the names of temple gates, a composite hypotext. Looking at Egyptian priestly literature, Sydney H. Aufrère treats the wall inscriptions in the Horus temple in Edfu as examples of Genettian intertextual play.

In part 4, "Late Classical and Medieval Paratextual Literature," Philip S. Alexander treats the *Eikah Rabbah* as a model for problematizing the roots of midrash, arguing that, in place of the postulate of a monolithic rabbinic tradition, we should envisage a mixture of sources, including the survival of priestly exegesis in the targum, the polemical debate with Christianity in the *forum*, and the folkloric tradition of Palestinian Jewish communities. Felicia Waldman traces the development of the figure of Enoch/Metatron in the Jewish mystical tradition as a merging of the biblical character Enoch with the angelology of the *hekhalot* literature. Kurt Smolak explores three contrasting Latin works of late antiquity and the early Middle Ages that subvert their base texts for polemical purposes. Renate J. Pillinger reveals the influence of the early Christian paratext, the *Acta Pauli et Theclae*, on depictions of the apostle Paul and the Thekla of Acts in Christian art of late antiquity, amounting to evidence of the paratext's informal canonicity. Finally, Assinava L. Miltenova discusses medieval Bulgarian apocalypses that are rewritten in response to shifting historical circumstances.

In *Palimpsests* the vast majority of works mentioned belonged to modern literature. This outstanding collection of essays not only confirms the overall viability of Genette's models for classifying the relationship between "hypotexts" and "hypertexts" in premodern literature but also acts as an extended illustration of their outworking across a formidable range of texts. The discussion also yields concepts that are useful in supplementing the Genettian repertory, in particular that of the "rolling corpus" (ancient texts that were subject to constant amendment and addition by scribes) and that of "archiving," whereby texts are set aside in the canon in favor of others that are of more relevance to the needs of the culture. The latter notion could inform the study of the neglect and rescue of specific biblical stories in the history of formal exegesis and of literary, musical, and iconographic appropriation.

Horizons in Hermeneutics: A Festschrift in Honor of Anthony C. Thiselton, edited by Stanley E. Porter and Matthew R. Malcom. Grand Rapids: Eerdmans, 2013. Pp. xv + 301. Paper. $40. ISBN 9780802869272.

Donald A. Hagner, Fuller Theological Seminary, Pasadena, California

Containing twelve essays by friends and students of Tony Thiselton, this celebratory book is intended by the editors as a "contribution in its own right" to the related fields of hermeneutics and biblical studies. The essayists were asked specifically "to reflect on the impact of Professor Thiselton's work." In addition to an introduction, the editors present a brief summary of the life and work of the honoree, following which is a useful list of his publications.

The essays are organized into three sections entitled "Facing the Other," "Engaging the Other," and "Projecting Possibilities." In Thiselton's language "the other" refers to the text (or person) that is encountered and comes from a horizon different from that of the interpreter.

The first section begins with John Goldingay's "Poetry and Theology in Isaiah 56–66." Goldingay explores the advantages of the various devices of poetry in conveying a complex theology that transcends the capabilities of ordinary prose. Poetry can employ ambiguity and even obscurity in a deliberate way that promotes thinking. The Isaiah text, although poetic, is not a fully decontextualized, "open" text but rather a text that also reflects realities at the time of its writing. Next, Robert Morgan's "Thiselton on Bultmann's *Sachkritik*" brings clarity of understanding to Bultmann's use of *Sachkritik* while at the same time exploring similarities and differences between Bultmann and Thiselton. Morgan shows that, for all their differences, both theologians respect the distinctive horizon of the text and have as their goal a critical historical exegesis that at the same time provides a theological interpretation of the text for modern readers. The third essay in this section is Mark L. Y. Chan's "Experience and the Transfiguration of Tradition in Paul's Hermeneutical Christology." Making use of Gadamer's and Thiselton's stress on the historical situatedness and self-involvement of the interpreter, Chan shows how Paul's experience of the risen Christ caused "a radical reconfiguration of his convictional or narrative world" enabling him to read the Jewish scriptures from a new, christocentric perspective. This transformation, together with its eschatological dimensions, involved an extensive reunderstanding of his inherited Jewish tradition. Matthew R. Malcolm's "*Kerygmatic Rhetoric* in New Testament

Epistles" argues for the existence of a distinctly Christian form of rhetoric arising out of liturgical activities of the early church that centered on the kerygma of
the died-and-risen Messiah. This kerygmatic rhetoric provides the basis of both a
new mindset and ethical exhortation, and it can often be detected in the macro-
structure of the epistles. The final essay in the first section is Richard S. Briggs's
"'The Rock Was Christ': Paul's Reading of Numbers and the Significance of the
Old Testament for Theological Hermeneutics." Briggs wrestles with the special
character and nature of theological hermeneutics by focusing on Paul's quotation
of Numbers in 1 Cor 10:4. General hermeneutics is ill-equipped to handle a text
such as this because of the text's two-Testament structure. It is the Old Testament understood as Christian scripture that constitutes the stumbling block of
general hermeneutics and posits the challenge and importance of theological
hermeneutics.

The section entitled "Engaging the Other" begins with James D. G. Dunn's
"The Earliest Interpreters of the Jesus Tradition: A Study in Early Hermeneutics."
Dunn contrasts the use of the Jesus tradition in the Gospels of John and Thomas,
focusing on their Christologies and the good news they proclaim. He concludes
that the striking differences are due to two different hermeneutical strategies,
John working on the Jesus tradition from the inside, Thomas from the outside,
each using the tradition with the perceived needs of their respective communities in mind. David Parris's "Metaphors, Cognitive Theory, and Jesus' Shortest
Parable" employs cognitive metaphor theory to "Physician, heal thyself" (Luke
4:23). Making use of contextual "frames" and metaphorical "blends," Parris illustrates the interpretive potential of cognitive theory. The third and last essay in
this section is that of Richard H. Bell, "'But We Have the Mind of Christ': Some
Theological and Anthropological Reflections on 1 Corinthians 2:16." Working
toward a "Theology of Mind," Bell argues that by the "mind of Christ" Paul means
that Christians have the "organ of thought" that enables them to access the mind
of God whether through the agency of the transformative word, the Holy Spirit,
or participation in the life of the Trinity. Spiritual Christians are co-creators and
representations of Christ.

The final section of the book, "Projecting Possibilities," contains four essays.
The first is Tom Greggs's "Reading Scripture in a Pluralist World: A Path to
Discovering the Hermeneutics of *Agape*." Greggs draws out the hermeneutical
implications of Thiselton's definition of *agape* as "regard, respect, and concern
for the welfare of others above the interests of the self." The practice of "Scriptural Reasoning," where Muslims, Jews, and Christians meet together to read each
others' scriptures, provides a context in which one can read lovingly, that is, in
humility, and "for the sake of God and of the other," thereby anticipating an era
of eschatological and inter-religious peace. Stephen Fowl's essay on "Scripture
and the Divided Church" argues that arguments and disagreements about the
meaning of scripture need not end in ecclesial division, which contradicts Christ's
teaching about love for others, especially brothers and sisters in the faith, but
even love for one's enemies. Fowl advocates figural interpretations of scriptural

passages, for example, concerning division in Israel and the early church, which will enable Christians to understand and address the various consequences of contemporary division within the church. Stanley E. Porter contributes the third essay in this section, under the title "What Exactly Is Theological Interpretation of Scripture, and Is It Hermeneutically Robust Enough for the Task to Which It Has Been Appointed?" Porter makes his way through the subject by means of the comparison of four authors who have recently written on theological interpretation: Joel B. Green, Daniel J. Treier, Stephen E. Fowl, and J. Todd Billings. After a section in which he examines how these authors define theological interpretation, he provides a preliminary evaluation, then proceeds to the question of whether theological interpretation is a hermeneutic. This involves discussions of the relation to historical criticism, premodern interpretation and the rule of faith, the role of the interpretive community, the role of the Holy Spirit, and the relation between general and special hermeneutics. Porter's answers to the questions in the title: there is no agreement about what theological interpretation is, other than "an undefined and varying set of tendencies or interests"; it is not hermeneutically robust enough to accomplish its task. The final essay in the book, by John B. Thomson, has the unusual title "'Let Us Cook You Your Tea, Vicar!' Church, Hermeneutics, and Postmodernity in the Work of Anthony Thiselton and Stanley Hauerwas," referring to the biweekly practice of children who make tea for the vicar and his staff in the pit village of Doncaster in South Yorkshire. This provides a small example of the many embodied communities and communal traditions that make up the church and display the truthfulness of the gospel in the contemporary postmodern climate. Despite significant differences between Thiselton and Hauerwas enumerated by Thomson, both agree on the importance of the practices of the church as "instantiations of graced life."

This Festschrift succeeds admirably in fulfilling the express desideratum of a contribution in its own right to the fields of hermeneutics and biblical studies. The essays are all of a high quality. Many of them provide further substantiation of the usefulness of Thiselton's basic two horizons paradigm, and many provide examples of its specific application and its fruitfulness in understanding scripture as well as its application. Undoubtedly reflecting my own horizon, I found most profitable the essays by Morgan, Chan, Briggs, Dunn, and Porter. This is not to demean the other essays, which undoubtedly have their own merits. Readers who work their way through these essays will have their hermeneutical sensitivities sharpened. Thiselton fans, of course, will need no encouragement to read these essays.

In all this is a volume that rightly brings honor to its most worthy honoree. Thiselton's skill as a scholar is abundantly apparent here, even if indirectly. At the same time, however, the personal warmth of students, friends, and colleagues is also plainly evident here, and it says very much about Thiselton the man.

Beyond Feminist Biblical Studies, by Deryn Guest. The Bible in the Modern World 47. Sheffield: Sheffield Phoenix, 2012. Pp. xiv + 192. Cloth. $70.00. ISBN 9781907534621.

Amelia Devin Freedman, Merrimack College, North Andover, Massachusetts

Deryn Guest begins *Beyond Feminist Biblical Studies* with the observation that in recent years many academics have adopted the phrase "gender studies" to replace "feminist studies." A corresponding shift in terminology has failed to take place in the field of biblical studies, however. This discrepancy leads Guest to pose the following question: "should feminist biblical criticism and gender criticism coexist … or does the shift to gender criticism move us beyond feminist biblical studies in such a fundamental way that the latter will be entirely superseded?" (xi)

In chapter 1, "Gender Criticism: Remit and Concerns," Guest examines what is meant by "gender criticism" in the wider academy (that is, outside of biblical studies). She defines it as an approach that "queries … the formation of sexed and gender identities in a wide range of contexts, alert to the ways in which these identifies are differently organized and intersected always by issues of race, class, geographical location" (12). Guest argues that most of the work in biblical studies that uses the term "gender" to describe itself is not, in fact, properly gender-critical. Rather, biblical scholars have generally focused their attention "on women, as characters in texts, as readers and interpreters, as the category of people likely to benefit from such readings"; by contrast, a gender-studies approach would have "broaden[ed] the lens, so that the gender of all the characters is included" (25). Second, feminist biblical scholars' work on male characters and masculinity has largely been conducted "in the service of a prioritized focus on women"; a gender-studies approach would have sought to "expose the norms that create, sustain, and police the idea of sex and gender … and the role of compulsory heterosexuality in that process" (26). Third, while feminist biblical scholars have been committed to unmasking "facile attempts to use the Bible as some kind of universal moral guardian," Guest charges, they have paid inadequate attention to "the [contemporary] import of their work … leaving it for interested readers to make connections" (28).

Queer theory is the subject of chapter 2, "Que(e)rying the Agenda: The Impact of Queer Perspectives for Feminist Scholarship." Guest argues that queer theory emerged from feminist studies in the 1980s as a response to the latter's unquestioned "heteronormative standpoint" (52). Guest enumerates four characteristics of queer theoretical work that set it apart from feminist studies. First, it recognized "difference and specificity, opening up a frame of reference to cover a wide range of sexualities" (52). Second, it "address[ed] the limits of feminist theorizing [that took place within] a heteronormative framework" (52). Third, it encouraged a "new antihomophobic theorization of sexualities" (52–53). Fourth, it called attention to "a social context of oppression that prompts the need to 'do something'" (53). Guest suggests that feminist biblical scholars adopt a "queer inspired gender criticism or, better still, genderqueer criticism … [that has the potential to] provide new, rich layers of analysis that have not yet been mined [by feminist studies]" (76).

In chapter 3, "Genderqueer Analysis of the Pornoprophetic Debate," Guest presents a "case study" in which she discusses the prophetic marriage metaphor texts from a genderqueer perspective. She identifies four themes in these texts that a genderqueer analysis might explore fruitfully: "the sexual economy underpinning the marriage metaphor" (105); "men as traitorous whores and the connotations of homoeroticism" (110); "the alternative space of female homoeroticism" (111); and "masculinities, competition and violence" (113). As before, Guest argues that a genderqueer approach calls for political action on the part of the scholar. She writes, "too often the Bible is taken hostage by conservative groups and wielded as an authoritative weapon; the genderqueer critic is aware of … the political import of their work in demonstrating how the Bible is not the easy purveyor of family values it is often thought to be" (114).

Guest explores how analyses of masculinity can add to genderqueer criticism in biblical studies in chapter 4, "The Critical Study of Masculinities and the Hebrew Bible." Here she returns to the prophetic marriage metaphor texts, pursuing the following four goals from CSM analysis: "to remove the invisibility of men as a marked category" (125); "to let the culture-specific constructions and performativities of masculinities in ancient Israel speak for themselves" (128); "to identify hegemonic norms of masculinity and map instances of alternative, subordinated, marginalized masculinities" (131); and "to highlight the constructedness of both sex and gender" (133). Once more, Guest argues that a CSM approach calls for political action on the part of scholars, who should take it upon themselves to demonstrate that "hegemonic masculinity is always open to challenge, resistance, contestation" (135).

The book's provocatively titled conclusion, "From the F-Word to the G-Spot," repeats Guest's call for a move beyond feminist studies to gender studies. She argues that gender studies is important because it allows scholars to challenge "the biblical construction of heterosexuality as an institution, as an apparently divinely sanctioned position … and as an apparatus of heteronormativity" (162). She observes that biblical scholars today are "in the enviable position of being experts on the very texts currently used to uphold and challenge current religion/state policies on adoption, marriage, civil partnerships, who can serve as ministers, and so forth" (163). Guest asserts that this privileged position "obliges us to ask what we can do to ensure that biblical studies embraces equality for all" (164).

Biblical scholars interested in issues of gender, sexuality, and the like will find *Beyond Feminist Biblical Studies* a valuable addition to the discussion. Guest clearly summarizes the progression from feminist studies to gender studies in the wider academy, referring to many important scholarly works in the process. This summary is valuable, since biblical scholars may not be familiar with recent trends in feminist and gender studies in the wider academy. She makes a persuasive case for the benefits of a gender-critical approach. She helpfully identifies areas of the Hebrew Bible that scholars might explore fruitfully from this perspective. For example, she points out that biblical scholarship to date has largely neglected Yahweh's depiction in the prophetic marriage metaphor texts, who, from a gender studies viewpoint, could be described as "an alpha dominant male, stripping, battering and raping his wayward male underlings who … have been imaged as adulterous women" (143). Finally, her argument that biblical scholars have an obligation to speak out on the use of the Bible in contemporary public discourse is both important and timely. One need only look at the recent rhetoric, for example, of the Westboro Baptist Church on "traditional marriage" to see some of the ways in which nonexpert readers in the United States, at least, have misunderstood and/or oversimplified complicated biblical traditions. I agree with Guest that biblical scholars have a duty to counter nonexpert readers' misconceptions when they arise in the public square, especially when they lead to the use of the Bible as a theological and political weapon.

One negative aspect of the book is that Guest's discussions are not based firmly enough in specific biblical texts. Although she talks about the prophetic marriage metaphor texts for large portions of two chapters, these discussions are very general. This is most striking in chapter 3, which she describes as "a practical case study" (5). That description made me expect a close, gender-critical reading of a specific biblical text or texts with which I could follow along, but such a close reading never materialized. A concrete demonstration of the approach she espouses would have strengthened the case that Guest is making with this book.

Between Text and Text: The Hermeneutics of Intertextuality in Ancient Cultures and Their Afterlife in Medieval and Modern Times, edited by Michaela Bauks, Wayne Horowitz, and Armin Lange. Journal of Ancient Judaism Supplements 6. Göttingen: Vandenhoeck & Ruprecht, 2013. Pp. 363. Cloth. €99.99. ISBN 9783525550250.

Geoffrey David Miller, St. Louis University, St. Louis, Missouri

This collection of essays represents the fruits of a 2009 meeting of the "Hermeneutics of Judaism, Christianity, and Islam" group held at the University of Koblenz-Landau. Twenty-one European and Israeli scholars presented papers on the topic of intertextuality, focusing primarily on Jewish, Christian, Hellenistic, and related texts. The essays are classified under three headings: (1) "Methodology," (2) "The Intertextualities of Written and Visual Texts," and (3) "Cultural Memory and Canon."

The essays in part 1 examine methodological issues regarding the study of intertextuality. Michaela Bauks's "Intertextuality in Ancient Literature in Light of Textlinguisitics and Cultural Studies" discusses the many problems with studying intertextuality in ancient texts. "Texts" should be understood very liberally, applying not only to written compositions "but also [to] conventions and discourses of history, culture, art and the dialogical perception of text" (27).

Identifying the original author and the historical provenance of an ancient text is extremely difficult, and modern readers must also be wary of other important factors in their study of intertextuality, such as cultural memory, the impact of canonization on intertextuality, and the effects of tradition and transmission of texts over time. In "Texts, Textual Bilingualism, and the Evolution of Mesopotamian Hermeneutics," Gebhard J. Selz examines the progression of Mesopotamian hermeneutics from the fourth millennium onward. Selz covers a wide range of topics, including the development from concepts to signs, the bilingual nature of Sumerian-Akkadian signs, and the spatio-temporal aspects of texts. Philip Alexander's "A Typology of Intertextual Relations Based on the Manchester-Durham Typology of Anonymous and Pseudepigraphic Jewish Literature of Antiquity" is connected to a larger database project that classifies Jewish texts from 200 BCE to 700 CE by means of a textlinguistic approach. In terms of intertextual relationships, these texts belong to four main groups: metatextuality (implicit and explicit), extensive verbal overlaps (narrative and nonnarrative), borrowings of text-segments and language (quotations, allusions, reuse), and literary models (i.e., genres).

Part 2, on written and visual texts, is subdivided into four sections. The first is "Retelling, Rewriting, and Continuation." In "Tradition and Transmission of Texts and Intertexts in the Hebrew Bible and in Ancient Jewish Literature (Gen 6:1–4)," Markus Risch looks at the intratextual gaps in the story of Gen 6:1–4 as well as the reception history of this passage in early Jewish literature, specifically 1 En. 6–16, Jub. 5:1–10, and 4Q252. These three epi-texts reinterpret the Genesis story in diverse ways, all of which are made possible by the twofold aim of Gen 6:1–4, namely, an account of the limitation of human life (v. 3) and a genealogy of semi-divine beings (v. 4). Jacques T. A. G. M van Ruiten's essay, "Abraham's Death: The Intertextual Relationship between Gen 25:7–10 and *Jub.* 22:1–23:8," illustrates how a phenotext (Jubilees) adapts an earlier genotext (Genesis) for a new context, connecting Abraham more closely to Jacob than the biblical story does. Lautaro Roig Lanzillotta, in "*Gospel of Thomas* Logion 7 Unravelled: An Intertextual Approach to a *locus vexatus*," resurrects the correct but rejected claim that logion 7 of the Gospel of Thomas draws on Plato's tripartition of the soul from his *Republic*. The political and juridical framework of the hypotext (*Republic*) becomes transformed into an anthropological one for the audience of the hypertext (Thomas). Sydney H. Aufrère's "An Attempt to Classify Different Stages of Intertextuality in the Myth of Horus at Edfu" studies intertextuality between the hieroglyphic wall inscriptions and the iconographic reliefs in the temple of Horus at Edfu. This interplay creates an intertexual mythological "take-over by force," which results in a new mythological reading that deviates from the original story of Horus. In "Kabbalistic Elements in Popular Movies," Klaus Davidowicz traces the trope of the Golem in literature and cinema throughout the nineteenth and twentieth centuries. The driving influence behind most of these works has been Yehuda Judel Rosenberg's 1909 folkbook *Miracles of the MaHaRaL of Prague*. Manfred Oeming's "'*In kino veritas*': On the Reception of the Biblical Book of Job in the Context of Recent Cinematography" pursues a similar tack by studying the use of the book of Job in modern film and even YouTube videos. He focuses especially on the reworkings of the story in *Adam's Apples* and *A Serious Man*.

The next section of part 2 considers commentaries and translations. In "Controlling Intertexts and Hierarchies of Echo in Two Thematic Eschatological Commentaries from Qumran," George J. Brooke looks at multiple aspects of intertextuality in two Qumran commentaries: the Florilegium (4Q174) and Catena A (4Q177). Each text exhibits a hierarchy of allusions where the hypertext makes references to earlier authoritative hypotexts (the highest level of intetextuality) but also contains echoes with other literary traditions that may not have been intended (the lowest level). Gilles Dorival offers "Biblical Intratexutality: MT-Numbers and LXX-Numbers: A Case Study," which studies not *inter*textuality but *intra*textuality, examining how the book of Numbers alludes to other parts of the Pentateuch. These inner-biblical links are more numerous in the LXX than in the MT, showing the importance the Greek translators placed on reading the Pentateuch as a contiguous whole. Margaret Dimitrova's "New Testament Quotations in a Medieval Slavonic Manuscript with Commentaries on the Song of Songs" studies the use of New Testament verses in Theodoret of Cyrrhus's *Explanatio* of the Song of Songs. The translator draws on both the Greek text of these biblical quotations as well as their medieval Slavonic translations, preferring the latter over the former.

The third section of part 2 is concerned with quotations and allusions. In "Quotations in the Writings of Aristotle," Martin F. Meyer looks at Aristotelian scientific treatises for clues about text production and orality. Aristotle's references to Plato suggest he was not citing written texts, since he alludes to them paraphrastically, though his reference to his own works show the importance of auxiliary written texts for illustrations and examples. Annette Harder's "Intertextuality as Discourse: The Discussion of Poetry and Poetics among Hellenistic Greek Poets in the Third Century B.C.E." compares poetic works on the Argonauts by Callimachus of Cyrene, Apollonius Rhodius, and Theocritus. The intertextual links among these texts elucidates the authors' understanding of poetics. Lukas Bormann concludes this subsection with "The Colossian Hymn, Wisdom, and Creation," which uses Hebel's allusion paradigm to study Col 1:15–20 and its connections to several wisdom texts: Prov 8:22–23, 26; Job 28:23–24; Sir 24:8–9; Wisd 6:17; 7:26–27. These connections create a relationship among the texts centered around three poles (the Creator, a mediator or agent of God, and creation itself) and adapts sapiential theology to Christology.

The fourth section of part 2 contains only the essay by Andreas Wagner: "Typological, Explicit, and Referential Intertextuality in Texts and Images of the Old Testament and Ancient Israel." Wagner examines prophetic warnings, *kô ʾāmar* formulae, and the motif of the raised arm, arguing that intertextuality is essential for good exegesis, should include images rather than only written texts, and should be studied diachronically but should not be restricted by authorial intent.

Part 3 is devoted to issues of cultural memory and the canon. Wayne Horowitz's "The Astrolabes: An Exercise in Transmission, Canonicity, and Para-Canonicity" considers the transmission of Mesopotamian astronomical texts (the Astrolabes) over many years. Many variations exist among the versions handed down, yet the basic content remains the same, meaning they do not comfortably fit in categories of "canonical" or "noncanonical" but an intermediate one: "para-canonical." In "Reading the Canon Intertextually: The Decentralization of Meaning," Stefan Alkier challenges the common Christian belief that canonicity is the unifying principle of the bible. The canon is not a dogmatic scriptural prison but creates a reading strategy by putting individual texts in relationship with one another, allowing for myriad connections to be drawn among these texts. Felicia Waldman's "Turning the Interpretation of the Text into Text: Written Torah and Oral Torah in Jewish Mysticism" examines kabbalistic interpretations of the Torah, both written and oral. The kabbalistic approach creates an intertextual relationship between these two Torahs in their mystical reading of rabbinic traditions (oral Torah) about the Sinaitic revelation to Moses (written Torah). In "Intertextuality in the Orthodox Slavic Tradition: The Case of Mixed-Content Miscellanies,") Anisava L. Miltenova studies the works collected in South Slavic anthologies, including apocryphal works such as the Life of Adam and Eve. By grouping various texts together, these miscellanies communicate important messages about eschatology, political ideology, and the connection between the Old and New Testaments. Finally, Armin Lange and Zlatko Pleše's "Text between Religious Cultures: Intertextuality in Graeco-Roman Judaism" moves beyond the domain of intra-cultural intertextuality and studies the connections between texts from different cultures. They demonstrate how the Letter of Aristeas and Aristobulus of Alexandria employ two different approaches to the relationship of Jewish and Greek cultures.

Between Text and Text is a thoroughly eclectic collection that contains something for everyone to enjoy. It includes writings both ancient and medieval, biblical and extrabiblical, Greco-Roman and Mesopotamian. Its diversity, however, has one potential drawback. Scholars looking for a clear explanation of how to identify intertextual relationships will find little guidance here, since the volume does not employ a uniform methodology throughout. Part 1 leans toward a more synchronic, reader-oriented approach espoused by Julia Kristeva, but many of the later essays employ a more diachronic, author-oriented approach, especially as articulated by Gerard Genette.

This hermeneutical ambiguity notwithstanding, *Between Text and Text* beautifully illustrates the manifold connections that exist among texts from the ancient world. Readers will learn much about the study of intertextuality from this volume and how European scholars in particular delineate parallels within the biblical corpus and beyond.

Feminist Biblical Interpretation: A Compendium of Critical Commentary on the Books of the Bible and Related Literature, edited by Luise Schottroff and Marie-Theres Wacker. Grand Rapids: Eerdmans, 2012. Pp. xxvi + 1030. Paper. $80.00. ISBN 9780802860972.

Lynn R. Huber, Elon University, Elon, North Carolina

Over a thousand pages in length, *Feminist Biblical Interpretation: A Compendium of Critical Commentary on the Books of the Bible and Related Literature,* edited by Luise Schottroff and Marie-Theres Wacker, is a valuable resource for scholarx interested in the insights of feminist biblical criticism. Originally published in German in 1998 as *Kompendium Feministiche Bibelauslegung,* this is a translation of the second edition from 1999. The volume, as explained in the preface to the first German addition (translated in this volume), continues in the spirit of *The Women's Bible Commentary,* edited by Carol Newsom and Sharon Ringe in 1992, and *Searching the Scriptures,* edited by Elisabeth Schüssler Fiorenza, although the editors suggest that the explicit feminist commitments of the volume's many contributors make it more similar to the latter (xiii). Although most of the contributors are located within the German-speaking world and the original audience was assumed to be Christian, the volume includes a diversity of feminist perspectives, including Jewish feminist perspectives, and occasional voices with roots in the U.S., Latin America, Asia, Africa, and the Middle East. The volume, moreover, covers the breadth of the Catholic canon, including texts from the Apocrypha, and includes a number of early Christian writings, such as Gospel of Mary, Shepherd of Hermas, Gospel of Peter, and Protevangelium of James. In the "Editor's Preface to the American Edition," the editors note that they originally sought to address the "most extensive form of the canon" (xx). However, in retrospect they admit that they failed to recognize the distinct parts of the Orthodox and Ethiopian canons. Still, the compendium is expansive in its offerings, including seventy-six essays. For the most part, essays are fifteen to twenty pages in length, including bibliography. Most bibliographies include works referenced in the essays as well as sections "For Further Reading," which primarily include works published since the first edition. Given the context of the compendium, the bibliographies include numerous works in German, which will be helpful to English-speaking/reading scholars less familiar with these works. Unfortunately, not all of the bibliographies appear to have been updated (e.g., Gen 12–50, Exodus, Deuteronomy, Joshua, books of Samuel, Matthew, John, Galatians), and some are lacking relevant works in English (e.g., Revelation's entry does not include works by Tina Pippin).

One of the most interesting parts of the volume is the editors' candid reflection on the shape of the work over time. Included in three distinct prefaces, this reflection describes the ways that interpretive perspectives and questions can change significantly even over a decade. In the original preface to the volume, for example, the editors articulate the compendium's "conviction that Christian anti-Judaism, Western colonialism, and all forms of racism have to be opposed

at the same time misogyny is" (xiii). However, in a later preface Schottroff and
Wacker note the volume's lack of anticolonial or postcolonial perspectives, things
we might expect in a feminist collection today. Likewise, the editors explain that
feminist conversations about the relationship between "sex" and "gender" have
advanced and became more complicated since the volume's original publication.
They observe that some of the compendium's contributors have since gone on
to engage these categories in more diverse ways (xxi). Given their candor and
insight, I can imagine using these prefaces in a class session devoted to feminist
biblical criticism.

In the most recent preface to the compendium, Schottroff and Wacker
underscore the variety of feminist perspectives in the volume. In fact, the essays
differ widely on how they understand the project of feminist interpretation,
some essays focusing specifically upon passages specific to women, other essays
examining texts in their entirety as a way of getting at issues related to women,
gender, patriarchy, and the like. As with any edited volume, some of the essays are
more successful than others in making their points, although overall the essays
are clearly written. Unfortunately, given the number of essays, it is impossible to
mention each one in this review. Attention to a few of the entries, however, should
give the reader a sense of the compendium's feel.

Among the essays that highlight portions of the text pertaining specifically
to women is the opening essay, "Genesis 1–11: The Primordial History," by Helen
Schüngel-Straumann. In it the author focuses upon gendered imagery in the creation and so-called fall narratives of Gen 2–3, including the ways in which these
texts incorporate ancient Near Eastern goddess imagery, and "male acts of violence" in Gen 4–11 (1–14). Although the content of most of Gen 1–11 is covered in
the essay, the genealogy of chapter 10 and the story of Babel are, interestingly, not
discussed. While not explicitly about gender, these texts arguably have much to
offer a feminist interpretation, providing founding mythologies for patriarchy and
the emergence of difference as expressed in language. Similarly, "Genesis 12–50:
The Story of Israel's Origins as a Women's Story" by Irmtraud Fischer, focuses
upon the stories of women characters in Gen 12–50, challenging the traditional
identification of these narratives as being about the "Patriarchs" (16). Among
the New Testament texts that highlight particular passages related specifically to
women is Habermann's "Gospel of John: Spaces for Women," which commends
the Johannine idea of "loving one another" as a liberating idea for feminists (675).
Claudia Janssen and Regene Lamb's "Gospel of Luke: The Humbled Will Be Lifted
Up" (645–61) and Ivoni Richter Reimer's "Acts of the Apostles: Looking Forward
and Looking Back" (680–97) also highlight the depiction of women in Luke and
Acts, respectively, although the latter also pays some attention to how women are
coupled with men in the narrative (695).

As mentioned above, a number of essays approach their respective texts
in their entirety, offering feminist readings that are more holistic. In "Exodus:
The Meaning of Liberation from 'His' Perspective," Susanne Scholz highlights
the androcentric perspective of the text, a perspective that engages a number of

oppressive structures, including ethnocentrism and class discrimination along with sexism (34). In this vein, Martina S. Gnadt's "Gospel of Matthew: Jewish-Christian Churches in Opposition to the Pax Romana" emphasizes Matthew's theme of resistance against the Roman "fathers" in favor of aligning with the Heavenly Father. Gnadt admits that Matthew is a male-dominated book but stresses that ultimately the text is about an "inclusive community" (620). Luise Schottroff's "1 Corinthians: How Freedom Comes to Be" attends to the letter's entirety, hearing "the voices of many women" even in texts that are seemingly androcentric, such as Paul's teaching on resurrection in 1 Cor 15 (739). Caroline Vander Stichele's essay on 2 Corinthians offers a thorough and subtle reading of the text (which she reads as it is presented in the canon), exploring how it engages in a dualistic thinking that is problematic from a feminist perspective as it contributes to misogyny and sexual asceticism (749). Luzia Sutter Rehmann's treatment of Revelation offers a hybrid approach, first working through the text's narrative and then returning to themes that are of particular interest to feminist interpreters. These themes include the Whore and Bride, the 144,000 Male Virgins, the Woman in Labor, and a focus upon the Earth's mistreatment that Rehmen characterizes as "Creation Spirituality" (922).

Some of the most interesting contributions to this feminist compendium are those that address texts with seemingly little to do with women or gender. Christine Karrer-Grube's essay, titled "Ezra and Nehemiah: The Return of the Others," interrogates the ways in which these texts collapse the "foreign other" with "woman as other" in an effort to reconstitute the community of Judah after the exile (192–206). Similarly, in "Job: Questioning the Book of the Righteous Sufferer," Christl Maier and Silvia Schorer raise provocative questions about the relationship between men's suffering and women's suffering, the latter of which is erased from the text, and the way Job's experience of the Divine decenters humanity within creation (221–39). Sometimes, however, the reader is left wanting a little more attention to the ways in which certain texts, ostensibly having little to do with women or gender, provide insight into issues such as the nature of structural powers and oppression. For instance, Ilse von Loewnenclau's treatment of Daniel seems to have more interest in the apocryphal text of "Susanna," which appears in the Septuagint, than in the Hebrew/Aramaic version of Daniel (361–370).

While the volume makes no excuses for being "woman centered" (xiii), this focus contributes to the volume's somewhat dated feel. At times there seems to be too little attention to the ways in which women's experiences are complicated by race, class, ability, and sexuality, intersections that are highlighted in more recent feminist-critical approaches. For example, while LGBT and queer biblical interpretation is a relatively recent area of biblical studies, it is still surprising to see texts pertaining to same-sex relations glossed over in the volume, especially when these texts reference women's experience in some way. In "Leviticus: The ABC of Creation," Gerburgis Feld specifically addresses Lev 12, 15, 18 and 20, after treating the general themes of purity and sacrifice (51–67). Although she generally discusses Lev 18 and 20, Feld fails to address 18:22 or 20:13, which describe men who "lay with a man as with a woman," important texts in conversations about biblical attitudes toward same-sex relations. In these verses in particular, we see how misogyny serves to link the oppression of women and men who ostensibly act like women. More surprising is Elsa Tamez's relative silence on Rom 1:26 in "Romans: A Feminist Reading." Instead of addressing the text's description of women giving up "natural intercourse for unnatural" as part of what seems to be God's punishment for idolatry, Tamez offers a general and somewhat abstract discussion of violence against women and children as a structural sin of patriarchy (703–5). This failure to explicitly engage how particular texts are employed vis-à-vis debates about homosexuality is a drawback of the volume overall, which fails to include heterosexism among those things feminist interpretation counters. Still, the translation of this volume into English provides biblical scholars, especially those interested in the history of ideological criticisms, an important resource both for examining the variety of the biblical texts, especially in their depictions of women, and for understanding the ways in which our interpretations of these texts are shaped by political and social commitments.

TEXTUAL CRITICISM AND TRANSLATION

Ideology, Culture, and Translation, edited by Scott S. Elliott and Roland Boer. Semeia Studies 69. Atlanta: Society of Biblical Literature, 2012. Pp. viii + 228. Paper. $29.95. ISBN 9781589837058.

Lénart J. de Regt, United Bible Societies, The Hague, The Netherlands

This volume is a collection of essays from the Ideology, Culture, and Translation group of the Society of Biblical Literature. Part 1 is drawn from the session in Boston (2008) and explores the intersection of translation studies and critical theory in biblical studies. Most of part 2 ("Sites in Translation") is drawn from various other sessions of the group, while two papers (Nielsen and Voth) were first presented elsewhere.

Roland Boer ("The Dynamic Equivalence Caper") presents a criticism of dynamic equivalence translation and what he sees as the ideology behind it. He points out that Nida's concept of dynamic equivalence in Bible translation is not new but rather recovers the older practice of paraphrase (adapting the text so that readers understand it). Dynamic equivalence has an instrumental view of form: the form of the text can/should be adapted in order to ensure that the message still comes through in translation. Boer regards dynamic equivalence as a symptom of globalized capitalism that reduces the Bible to a commodity, as if Nida did not recognize and allow for local and cultural variation and indeed specific literary requirements of the local target language. Nida's recommendations to translators in *Bible Translating* (1947; rev. ed., 1961) and *Fascinated by Languages* (2003) prove otherwise. At times Boer's style is derogatory: "Nida is a craftsman first, artist a distant second" (19).

K. Jason Coker ("Translating from This Place: Social Location and Translation") explores the complex relationship between interpretation and the social location of the interpreter and welcomes the recent shift in emphasis from the text and its meaning (how best to translate what the original author/editor wrote) to the translator, who interacts with the text in a specific location and culture. Coker uses Fernando Segovia's concept of cultural studies as a model for Bible translation. Scholarly interpretations of a text would pass as an objective historical and factual reconstruction of the past reality of that text, but in reality these interpretations were subjective, ideological, and social (Eurocentric) constructions. Readers in other social locations, then, should develop their own (partial) perspectives on the biblical text. The emphasis should shift from the text to the translator, who can shape the local readers' perspective. Coker claims that in many if not most cases the translators are not from the local culture but are white Western men (32). However, although this was often the case in the past, this situation no longer applies today.

Scott S. Elliott ("Translation and Narrative: Transfiguring Jesus") looks into the intersection of translation and narrative discourse in relation to Bible translation and literary characters in translation—especially intermedial translation, that is, translation of speech into writing. Thus, the Gospels render in written Greek words Jesus historically spoke in Aramaic or Hebrew, so that even the so-called original text is already a translation. Also, the Gospels themselves already translate Jesus into a character, a literary figure. The characters come to us through narrative and are thus inseparable from discourse and narration. Elliott's definition of translation is very wide; he goes as far as stating that the Gospels invite additional translations and adaptations (such as novels and graphic novels) that appropriate diverse readings of Jesus.

Raj Nadella ("Postcolonialism, Translation, and Colonial Mimicry") focuses on how South Indian nationals as well as missionary translators followed a colonial model of Bible translation during and even after the colonial era. The colonized imitated the colonizers and their mindset. Replacing Western concepts in Bible translations with terms from Sanskrit or other dominant regional languages still amounts to colonialism and suppression of native languages of subaltern communities. Nadella implies that, for example, the concept of predestination should have been translated in Telugu as *karma*, not with a neologism. Biblical texts should be translated into peripheral dialects, valuing local practices of oral communication.

Part 1 concludes with a response to these papers by George Aichele ("The Translator's Dilemma"). In response to Boer, he notes that, while dynamic equivalence is only possible if the translator knows how the original readers understood the text, literal translation has no interest in what the author or any reader ever understood the text to mean but is the manifestation of the text itself (60). But this notion of literal translation almost denies the possibility of any communication; it does not take into account that even an interlinear translation cannot be done without making interpretive decisions and is therefore not as open or as incomprehensible (Aichele's goal, 65) as the source text. Aichele seconds Coker's call to focus on the role of the translator as the one who (re)distributes the meaning of the texts.

In a fascinating chapter (the first of part 2), Virginia Burrus ("Augustine's Bible") revisits the correspondence and dispute between Jerome and Augustine regarding biblical translation, while she dialogues with Naomi Seidman's *Faithful Renderings: Jewish-Christian Difference and the Politics of Translation* (2006). For Augustine, the Septuagint was the manifestation of Scripture precisely as translation and revelation (without displacing the original; *City of God*). Burrus evaluates Augustine's claims for the Greek text and aligns his view of translatability with the views of Philo and particularly Franz Rosenzweig (the Bible is not the Bible until it has been received and made audible in another language).

Alan H. Cadwallader ("Identity Politics and the Revised Version") looks into the revision (1870–1881) of the Authorized Version of the Bible. He describes how the relation between an imperial nation, an established church, nonestablished denominations, and competitive international tensions—UK Nonconformists were admitted, but American Episcopalians were denied an equal role in the revision project—made this project an illustration that translation is about the politics of negotiation over the end translation and the pragmatic obstacles that constantly impinge upon decision making (Umberto Eco). The participation of Nonconformists relied upon their acceptance of the established church's dominant position and terms of reference. Faithfulness in translation was interpreted as literalness, establishing a more accurate Greek text of the New Testament, as well as rigid uniformity (a Greek word was to be rendered uniformly by a single English word; the distinction between the aorist and the perfect was to be preserved).

Jacqueline S. du Toit ("Seeing Is Believing: Children's Bibles as Negotiated Translation") considers the role and significance of the illustrations (visual language) in children's Bibles as child-appropriate renditions of adult translations. (Children's Bibles from the United States or United Kingdom are often translated into South African languages without adapting the illustrations, despite huge differences in target culture.) Du Toit claims that children's Bibles adhere to societal context (values, didactics, and entertainment displayed in the illustrations) rather than textual content. Children's Bibles often aim to serve a dual audience: "the illiterate and semiliterate adult convert" as well as (their) children. Their highly selective adaptation of the source text belies their claim to authority as "translation" of the source text. Du Toit attributes this claim to children's Bibles, but she does not give actual evidence that this is what children's Bibles claim for and of themselves. While titles like *God's Storybook* (Ewald van Rendsburg, 2006) and *My Creation Bible* (Ken Ham, 2006) do make the translators invisible, this does not amount to "a simulation of formal equivalence" (107) to the source text in children's Bibles in general.

Two contributions are devoted to the history of Bible translation in Greenland: Flemming A. J. Nielsen's "The Earliest Greenlandic Bible: A Study of the Ur-Text from 1725" (which includes a fascinating and informative brief history of Greenland and Greenlandic) and Christina Petterson's "Configuring the Language to Convert the People: Translating the Bible in Greenland." Nielsen describes how biblical stories were reshaped and integrated into local oral tradition and how indigenous shamanistic concepts (e.g., "helping spirit") were misunderstood by missionaries when they either used or avoided them in translation. Nielsen and Petterson come to radically different conclusions: while Nielsen sees biblical translation as the major reason why Greenlandic has survived and is now an official language, Petterson considers (much more polemically) that the missionaries colonized the language and society by transforming the language into a written language and by coining new terms or use Danish ones in translation.

Naomi Seidman ("'A Gift for the Jewish People': Einspruch's *Der Bris Khadoshe* as Missionary Translation and Yiddish Literature") first discusses British and Foreign Bible Society translations of the New Testament into Jewish languages intended "to proselytize Jews" (151) and then goes on to assess Einspruch's Yiddish New Testament translation (and its reception), distributed by the Society for Distributing Hebrew Scriptures, and David Stern's *Complete Jewish Bible*. Each in its own way, these translations attempted to be a retroversion rather than only a translation, highlighting the Jewishness of the New Testament itself.

Esteban Voth's ("Masculinidad en la traducción de la Biblia en Latinoamérica") analyzes six Spanish translations in Latin America. An ideology of masculinities (plural: idealized and realistic) is present in most of these translations. Voth makes a plea to revise them and investigates a range of places where the text permits and requires a nonandrocentric translation of key words (*adam, ish, anthropos, aner*: "human being," "humanity," "who," "people") and of references to women. The *Traducción en Lenguaje Actual* (2003) turns out to be the most sensitive to this concern. Among the essays in this volume, Voth's is the only one that focuses positively on how ideological distortions in a translation can actually be corrected.

Matt Waggoner ("Is There Justice in Translation?") draws a parallel between the tower of Babel account (Gen 11) and the modern West: both conflate the universal and the particular—a long narrative of homogenization of humankind and cultural imperialism, in which translation is all too often an assimilator. Much of Waggoner's contribution is actually a response to essays that are not in this volume.

Part 2 concludes with a response from John Eipper. He is struck by a unifying thread in which biblical translators have sought justice *in* but also *through* translation. Mistakes were made, but "we can also picture Poul Egede's work in the bleakness of the Arctic night as no less a search for justice than twenty-first century attempts to eliminate masculine bias in the Spanish New and Old Testaments" (205)—a refreshingly positive statement after the polemical and sharp tone of some of the essays in this volume.

While this volume is an eye-opener to how ideological translation has sometimes been, some of the essays do put biblical translation under sharp scrutiny as soon as it is connected with any missionary activity. Even if we acknowledge that meaning is not objective and stable, meaning still needs to be found, reconstructed, and expressed in an attempt to bridge cross-cultural differences, if we want ancient texts to communicate anything at all. Dynamic equivalence translation, if sometimes too optimistically, has helped to make that possible. Having said that, in a variety of contexts biblical translation has moved on from dynamic equivalence—a development that most of the essays in this volume hardly take into consideration.

Novum Testamentum Graecum Editio Critica Maior, Parallelperikopen: Sonderband zu den synoptischen Evangelien, edited by Holger Strutwolf and Klaus Wachtel. Stuttgart: Deutsche Bibelgesellschaft, 2011. Pp. x + 138. Cloth. €49.00. ISBN 9783438056085.

Thomas J. Kraus, Federal Republic of Germany

The *Editio Critica Maior* is probably *the* current mammoth project of the Institute for New Testament Textual Research in Münster, Germany, though researchers there work on diverse other projects that are not less important. With the publication of its first fascicle in 1997/1998 (James) and the following in 2000 (1–2 Peter), 2003 (1 John), and 2005 (2–3 John) the project had an impressive start. But the speed of publishing further texts of the New Testament slowed down, if not to say it came to a stop since 2005. But such an assessment would be unfair and incorrect. Work continued, of course, and the complexity of specific New Testament texts required fresh reflections on method and outline of the next volumes to come (see http://www.uni-muenster.de/INTF/ECM.html). This can be demonstrated by means of the edition process of the text of Revelation performed by the Institute for Septuagint and Biblical Textual Research at the *Kirchliche Hochschule* in Wuppertal (see http://apokalypse.isbtf.de/de/open).

Consequently, it is a pleasure to hold some results from the brilliant work at the Münster Institute in one's hands, the volume being published in 2011. As the editors write in their preface (vii), the synopsis is "published preparatory to the *Editio Critica Maior* (ECM) of the Synoptic Gospels," and its "critical apparatus is arranged synoptically to facilitate research on the influence of textual parallels on the emergence of variants." Although work on the synopsis had begun in 1997, its completion and publication had to give way to work on the ECM itself. As a side effect to the synopsis, two effective online tools have been developed at Münster. First, manuscripts can be grouped and classified (Manuscript Clusters; http://intf.uni-muenster.de/TT_PP/); second, these findings can be used for studying the genealogy of variants (Find Relatives; http://intf.uni-muenster.de/PreCo/). In addition, the text-critical apparatus of the synopsis has been posted online to allow further analyses of the material (http://intf.uni-muenster.de/PPApparatus/).

The volume is structured as follows: preface (vii–viii), introduction (1*–13*), text and apparatus (1–121), and appendices (i–xvi). Everything apart from the Gospel texts and the apparatus is presented in German *and* English, so that those not familiar with German have the opportunity to understand explanations and headlines by means of the *lingua franca* English. Method and material are presented in the introduction, and we get to know that (1) thirty-eight of the forty-one parallel pericopes selected for the synopsis are taken from the Synoptics, while most of them can be found in all three Gospels. (2) Only three other pericopes are added (two from John and one from 1 Corinthians) to complete the picture for the individual section they relate to. (3) All in all, 154 manuscripts "from at least two Synoptic Gospels" (5*) form the basis of the apparatus, and their variants are supplied in full. Of course, prominent manuscripts are there (P45, P46, P66, and P75 for papyri, 01–05 for majuscules, and, e.g., 1, 13, and 33 for minuscules; for a complete list, see 9*–10*), and the issue of being a witness to all three, to two, or only to one Synoptic Gospel is problematized. (4) The presentation of text and variants follows the outline and layout of the ECM volumes published so far.

Of course, readers should and must know about the text-critical method the Münster Institute applies and be familiar with clustering, classifying, and genealogizing manuscripts that forms the ground for ECM and synopsis alike. The editors do not leave any doubt about that and provide their readers with definitions of the terms "reading," "variant," and "error," and, eventually, with a handy explanation of the sigla and symbols of the critical apparatus (6*–7*); all that is taken from the introduction to the James ECM volume and only slightly modified. The actual treasure trove of the introduction, however, is the presentation of "majority readings differing from the established text" (10*–12*). This chapter ends with an index of pericopes with titles and numbers according to K. Aland, *Synopsis Quattuour Evangeliourum* (13th ed.; Stuttgart: Deutsche Bibelgesellschaft, 1985).

Of course, this small volume only offers a selection of pericopes, and the reviewer himself was rather disappointed not to find exactly the passages he has currently been working on. But this is nothing to blame editors and/or volume for, because a complete synopsis of all the pericopes (see Aland, Synopsis) was never intended.

The presentation of text and variants is, as not expected otherwise, sound and admiringly concise. Readings and variants can be identified and clustered easily. But for those often studying textual variants and manuscripts, the appendices offer the actual gems. The first appendix provides "[v]ariation probably influenced by textual parallels" (i–v). The second helps to identify *lacunae* in the manuscripts utilized for the synopsis and to describe them in more detail as homoioteleuton/homoioarcton, illegible traces, supplements, and nonsensical omissions (vi–viii), while the third lists "[e]rror readings" (ix–xiii). My favorite is appendix 4, with "further information on ↔ entries" (xiv–xvi). For instance, readers get to know about the real extent of a reading, that is, what is actually left off a line before *lacuna* or at the rim of the fragment where material got lost. For Luke 9:27, for example, P45 reads την βασι[and not the complete word. For Matt 13:13 we find επι τον ιορδανην προς τον ιω̄ in a considerable number of minuscules so that readers get to know the way Ἰωάννην was abbreviated by these, while minuscule 1336 shortens the name as ιω(ανν)ην, that is, by contracting the form without ανν.

The synopsis is an indispensable tool. It precedes the ultimate full volumes of the ECM for the Synoptic Gospels (and John and 1 Corinthians) that are expected in the far future, whenever that will be. With the apparatus of at least a major selection of significant manuscripts at hand, scholars and students are enabled to study text-critical issues more easily and appropriately on their own, though the attestation from the early church writers, lectionaries, translations/versions, and, perhaps, from noncontinuous and magical texts (e.g., amulets) are missing here. The members of the Institute for New Testament Textual Research in Münster are to be thanked for their work.

New Testament Textual Criticism: The Application of Thoroughgoing Principles, by J. K. Elliott. Supplements to Novum Testamentum 137. Leiden: Brill, 2010. Pp. xv + 661. Cloth. $259.00. ISBN 9789004189522.

Daniel B. Wallace, Plano, Texas

J. K. Elliott is a household name for anyone who has more than a passing acquaintance with New Testament textual criticism. He is known for his meticulous care in his numerous publications about manuscripts, textual problems, and secondary literature. Elliott sends out once or twice a year articles and book reviews to a list of textual critics. It is always a thick packet (now sent as an email attachment). I know of no one in the discipline who produces more literature of this kind. The quantity, breadth, and depth of such pieces reveal an encyclopedic knowledge of the field. This can be seen in the "Publications by J. K. Elliott" at the back of this work (633–57): by 2010, Elliott had published 29 books, contributed to 63 others, authored 97 articles in refereed journals, and posted 415 book reviews. The great majority of these are directly related to New Testament textual criticism. Even after his recent retirement as Professor of New Testament Textual Criticism at the University of Leeds, his production has continued unabated.

This collection of fifty-seven articles by Elliott, all previously published over a span of forty-one years (1968–2008), is in keeping with Brill's helpful volumes of collected essays by noted textual critics of the New Testament, including Eldon J. Epp, Bart D. Ehrman, and T. C. Skeat. As the subtitle implies, the work lays out under one cover detailed arguments for rigorous eclecticism (a.k.a. thoroughgoing eclecticism, radical eclecticism, consistent eclecticism), the method that focuses far more on internal evidence (both transcriptional and especially intrinsic) than external. The articles are grouped into thirty-one chapters for this book under four headings: "Methodology" (11–49), "Manuscripts" (51–174), "Studies and Praxis" (175–467), and "Reviews of Recent Critical Editions" (469–610). Prior to the essays is prefatory material including original places of publication (xi–xv) and an introduction (1–9) that surveys the book's contents, including a summary of each essay. The book concludes with an appendix (611–61), which features the thirty-second essay (613–31), publications by Elliott, and a brief index of biblical scholars and passages discussed in detail (659–61). One essay that seems out of place is "Is Post-baptismal Sin Forgivable?" (356–58), which addresses an exegetical issue in Heb 6:4–6, sans discussion of any textual problem (even though this passage is listed in the index under biblical references [661], prefaced with the claim, "These references apply only to a major discussion of a text-critical variant").

It is not possible to discuss each chapter, let alone each article, in the space allotted for this review. An overview of each section, with brief discussion of a few of the essays, followed by some critiques and observations will constitute my appraisal.

In the introduction Elliott notes that his views have changed over the years in three important respects: (1) he is no longer confident that determining the wording of the "original" text is an achievable goal of textual criticism, a point he reiterates especially in chapters 30 (e.g., "there is no need nowadays to establish a critical text, because any attempt to create such an 'original' text is an elusive and illusory task" [593]) and 31 (e.g., "the autograph … is irrevocably lost" [595]); (2) he views "text-types" as a problematic term and prefers instead to speak of "text-forms" (7, 601) as the preferred name given to what some are now calling streams of transmission; and (3) he is open to occasional conjectural emendations representing the autographic wording (8), a view in keeping with abandoning the original text as an achievable goal.

Part 1, "Methodology," has three chapters. The first two deal with the text of the New Testament in the second century. *Inter alia*, Elliott suggests that if the goal of textual criticism is no longer to recover the autographic wording, a number of forms of the text are to be rooted in the second century, and we must embrace this diversity as a good thing—perhaps even as *Ausgangstexte* rather than an *Ausgangstext* (22). The third essay in this section, "Thoroughgoing Eclecticism" (41–49), though brief, is programmatic for Elliott's theory. This is the latest general defense of rigorous eclecticism by the author, but also one of the shortest. One could wish for a more substantive essay on this topic (such as "In Defence of Thoroughgoing Eclecticism in New Testament Textual Criticism," *ResQ* 21 [1978]: 95–115; or "The Case for Thoroughgoing Eclecticism," in *Rethinking New Testament Textual Criticism* [ed. D. A. Black; Grand Rapids: Baker, 2002], 101–124), even if such were not as current as the included essay.

Part 2, "Manuscripts," includes eight chapters. The topics range from singular readings in P[45]; the date and origin of Codex Vaticanus (in which Elliott agrees with Skeat that this majuscule, along with Codex Sinaiticus, was probably produced in Caesarea); the relation of Bezae to the early papyri; a complete transcription, with plates, of the Greek-Sahidic majuscule 0205; an industrious and helpful listing of all known continuous-text Greek manuscripts of Acts (612 at the time the original article was written in 1996), listed by Gregory-Aland number, contents, and date; two chapters on the manuscripts of Revelation, including a useful conversion table for Hoskier's numbers; and a four-part essay on recently published papyri.

Part 3, "Studies and Praxis," the largest part of the book, comprises two main sections ("Textual Variation," with two subsections, "Short Studies" and "Longer Studies," with the first essay of the "Longer Studies" ["Mark 1:1–3—A Later Addition to the Gospel?" 235–41] more properly belonging to the former category; and "Exegesis and Textual Criticism"). This section includes sixteen chapters. Several of the titles here seem to border on the trivial to the uninitiated (e.g., "τε in the New Testament"), but every one is relevant and more interesting than the occasionally anodyne headings suggest. For example, the article "καθώς and ὥσπερ in the New Testament" (186–89) in the twelfth chapter, "The Influence of G. D. Kilpatrick" (177–210), targets for special consideration the καθώς clause that begins Mark 1:2. Here Elliott argues that, since καθώς never begins a clause that introduces a quotation in the New Testament, it is likely that it is a continuation of verse 1 and that verses 1–3 form a single sentence (187). If true, this would effectively nullify the view that the opening verse of Mark's Gospel functions as a title. Elliott builds on this argument in his article "Mark and the Teaching of Jesus: An Examination of λόγος and εὐαγγέλιον" (190–98; originally published in 1997) in the same chapter, arguing again that Mark 1:1 is not the title to the book. Curiously, in chapter 14 ("Mark 1:1–3—A Later Addition to the Gospel?"), published originally in 2000, Elliott argues that these three verses are not authentic and were added later, but he does not mention that, if so, this would largely nullify his previous arguments about *Mark's* usage of καθώς and εὐαγγέλιον as indications that verse 1 was not a title to the Gospel.

Among the major textual problems discussed in part 3 are those in Matt 21:28–32; Mark 1:4, 45; the ending of Mark; John 1:18; 1 Cor 13:3; and Heb 2:9. Elliott's treatment of Heb 2:9 (226–32) is a model of lucidity and compelling internal evidence. Here he argues that χωρὶς θεοῦ is the authentic reading instead of χάριτι θεοῦ—that is, that Jesus died "apart from God" instead "by the grace of God." Although the Greek manuscript evidence for this reading is paltry (three late manuscripts), there is overwhelming patristic evidence on its behalf. Further, the internal evidence is strongly on its side—both the usage in Hebrews and the connection to the cry of dereliction from the cross recorded in Matthew and Mark. I am now convinced, based on Elliott's arguments, that χωρὶς θεοῦ is authentic.

Part 4, "Reviews of Recent Critical Editions," includes four chapters. The author assesses the UBS[4]/Nestle-Aland[27] texts, the *Editio Critica Maior* (*ECM*) of the Catholic Epistles, the International Greek New Testament Project (IGNTP) on Luke, and the *Marc Multilingue* Project. Although Elliott had a major role in the IGNT Luke and has a major role in the *Marc Multilingue* Project, he did not mince words in his critiques. In fact, his harshest critiques were for the IGNT (575–94). After a lengthy and fascinating introduction on the history of the IGNTP (575–80), he rehearsed criticisms leveled at the Luke volumes (published in 1984 and 1987) by Barbara Aland, J. Neville Birdsall, José O'Callaghan, C.-B. Amphoux, W. L. Peterson, Tjitze Baarda, and especially Kurt Aland. The criticisms included the use of the *textus receptus* as a base text, prompting Elliott to suggest the more accurate title of *A Thesaurus of Textual Variants in the Greek Text of the Gospel of Luke* (582); sloppy workmanship in the citing of the evidence; the use of the Claremont Profile Method for minuscule selection; and outdated editions of the versions. The criticisms by Kurt Aland occupy eight pages (580–87). Repeatedly throughout this chapter Elliott praised Münster's *ECM* for a variety of features, especially on what should go into an apparatus and how it should be laid out; he also viewed an Anglo-American collaboration with the German institute as vital for the improvement of the IGNT John. A happy postscript to this chapter is that the IGNT John is now being worked on by this very collaboration, with the volumes on the papyri and majuscules already published.

The final chapter, the only one in the appendix, is on "Manuscripts, the Codex and the Canon." An illuminating, detailed survey of the various orders of both Old Testament and New Testament books found in codices, the chapter also offers a treatment of manuscripts that included extracanonical books. Elliott rightly notes that, when modern scholars think about ancient canonicity, the information provided in the manuscripts is often ignored, with the writings of the fathers being exclusively privileged. This chapter provides a necessary antidote to this lacuna. However, Elliott is too quick to opine that Barnabas and the Shepherd of Hermas at the end of Sinaiticus (fourth century) and 1 Clement and 2 Clement at the end of Alexandrinus (fifth century) demand an interpretation that these books were considered canonical by the authorities behind these Bibles (619). This may well be the right interpretation, but it is not the only possibility. Elliott himself provides an analogy with modern printed Bibles that may be apropos: up until the nineteenth century, the King James Version, a Protestant Bible, almost always included the Old Testament Apocrypha *between* the Testaments, even though Protestants have historically rejected the canonical status of such books. The same is true for the Geneva Bible. The position of these Old Testament Apocrypha was the key to understanding: they came *after* the canonical Old Testament books. Analogies, of course, prove nothing, but when coupled with patristic evidence to the effect that both in the East and the West the New Testament canon was effectively closed in the fourth century, they take on weight. Even in the late second and third century, everywhere in the Mediterranean world (with only a few, largely isolated exceptions) the main question about the canon was not whether the list of twenty-seven books should be larger but whether it should be *smaller*. We may not know why some New Testament manuscripts have other books between their covers or lists of other books (such as in Claromontanus), but the unexamined assumption that these manuscripts *must* be evidence of a larger canon is hardly the only viable interpretation.

Several general critiques are in order. First, it has been a longstanding principle of rigorous eclecticism that the autographic text is surely to be found somewhere among the witnesses to the New Testament (see, e.g., George D. Kilpatrick, "Conjectural Emendation in the New Testament," in *New Testament Textual Criticism: Its Significance for Exegesis* [ed. Eldon J. Epp and Gordon D. Fee; Oxford: Clarendon, 1981], 349–60). Yet, as Gordon Fee noted ("Rigorous or Reasoned Eclecticism—Which?" in *Studies in New Testament Language and Text:*

Essays in Honour of George D. Kilpatrick on the Occasion of His Sixty-Fifth Birthday [ed. J. K. Elliott; NovTSup 44; Leiden: Brill, 1976], 183–84, 189 n. 45), rigorous eclecticism logically leads to conjectural emendation. The (former) denial of the need for conjecture is a position that rigorous eclectics held by fiat since they strongly privilege internal evidence over external, even to the point of finding the autographic wording at times in a lone manuscript. The danger of abandoning history altogether by using authorial style to trump *all* manuscript evidence was simply denied. But Elliott has now taken rigorous eclecticism to its logical conclusion and has thus fallen prey to Fee's pointed criticism.

Second, as helpful as Elliott's detailed analyses of grammatical and stylistic features of the New Testament are, he often treats the New Testament in isolation from the LXX, apostolic fathers, and other Hellenistic writers. Elliott insists that Atticisms were a prominent source of corruption while ignoring the equally if not more common Septuagintalisms as a cause of corruption. Coupled with him often making absolute claims based on low-frequency patterns, the author is frequently more confident than the evidence warrants.

Third, Elliott is occasionally inconsistent in his views, even in the articles written since 2000. Perhaps most remarkably, he claims that "Thoroughgoing critics see no reason to resort to conjecture" (44 n. 10), in an article originally published in 2003, yet in one published three years *earlier* he claimed that Mark 1:1–3 is not authentic, even though it is found in all extant witnesses (235–41).

Fourth, even though the author protests the criticism of thoroughgoing eclecticism as a view that largely disregards history and manuscripts (45–46), his treatment of both seems to betray this declaration. It is to be noted that he is not here claiming any revision of his views (this essay was originally published in 2003) but is saying that thoroughgoing eclecticism, in principle has been falsely accused. Yet earlier in the same article (44 n. 8) he notes that C. Landon, on rigorous eclecticism principles, embraced "several readings in Jude that have only meager external attestation"—a view that he seems to reject: "I must now admit that one feels more comfortable with the favored reading if it is not found only in a solitary late minuscule or in only a versional witness." Yet elsewhere, Elliott does regard a single manuscript as occasionally having the autographic reading, and he even goes so far as to propose as autographic a conjecture that has *no* manuscript support. As to history, although he recognizes text-forms, he does not consider them to be particularly relevant to recovering the original wording, since they all developed after 200 CE, that is, after the time when presumably all meaningful variants had come into existence (36, 45, 599). He goes so far as to say that "the Gospel text read in Alexandria in 200 A.D. [*sic*] differs from that read there in 350 A.D. [*sic*]" (597), a view strongly contested by Günther Zuntz, Gordon Fee, Barbara Aland, and others. The fact is that, if we have several decent Alexandrian manuscripts from the second century or on the cusp between the second and third, then the "cult of particular manuscripts" (18; see also 43, 300) which Elliott eschews, is actually a reasonable, historically sensitive position.

Fifth, in light of the strong preference for intrinsic evidence that rigorous eclectics embrace, it is most surprising to read Elliott's recent position of denying that we should even attempt to recover the autographic wording (see, e.g., "the aim of restoring one, original text is impossible" [596]; "inappropriateness of trying to establish one immutable original text" [592]; "something approximating to the autographs is beyond our aspirations" [593]). As Moisés Silva once commented about Eldon Epp's abandonment of this goal, "to retreat from the traditional task of textual criticism is equivalent to shooting ourselves in the foot" ("Response," in *Rethinking New Testament Textual Criticism* [ed. David Alan Black; Grand Rapids: Baker, 2002], 149). This is even truer in the case of rigorous eclectics, since authorial usage is *the* methodological *sine qua non* of the theory. To the extent that the autographs are irrelevant or unobtainable, rigorous eclecticism is invalid.

Scores of typographical infelicities, rather uncharacteristic of any work by Elliott, mar the volume. I counted over 150. Such errata were in all probability mostly due to typesetting almost seven hundred pages of articles that had originally been published elsewhere. Most egregious were three in the original places of publication and a multitude of violations in chapter 20, "The Divine Names in the Corinthian Letters" (325–37). In the former, the titles of three of the articles were absent, all of them reviews of various books of the *Editio Critica Maior* (James; 1 John; and 2 John, 3 John, and Jude are unnamed here [xiv]). In the latter, many of the Greek characters in the *nomina sacra* are written in English characters, and usually consistently so (including N as V, Ω as W, and even Υ once as U!). This chapter alone included more than eighty errata. Although the great majority of these errors are immaterial (but note, e.g., labeling Vaticanus as "02" [600], or Bezae as a *fourth*-century manuscript [602]!), their presence is surprising nonetheless.

On the positive side, Elliott's painstaking attention to detail regarding manuscripts, critical editions, textual problems, and Hellenistic grammar renders this volume a veritable feast of information and insights. Even though he is virtually alone in the rigorous eclectic camp today, his criticisms of the text-critical guild comprise a welcome viewpoint. He has unceasingly criticized reasoned eclecticism for its inconsistencies and lack of coherence in solving textual problems. Most important, he is a careful student of authorial usage, with an enviable knowledge of Koine Greek (and he has mastered the Atticistic writers Moeris and Phrynichus). Although he has been rightly criticized for regarding Atticism as a primary—and often, *the* primary—culprit of textual corruption in the New Testament, his knowledge of the various registers of the Hellenistic language is indeed enviable. Not only textual critics but, more broadly, exegetes, are in his debt.

To sum up: in light of the variety of journals, Festschriften, and multiauthor works that Elliott's articles were originally published in, having these fifty-seven articles in one place is a real time-saver for those interested in textual criticism. Although I had perused many of the articles *in situ*, I had not seen them all. To get Elliott's textual theory worked out in relation to several passages, manuscripts, grammatical constructions, and critical editions, all under one roof, may well become the legacy that thoroughgoing eclecticism needed if it was to influence the next generation of *Neutestamentler*. Unfortunately, the cost of the book is prohibitive, and unless SBL or some other publisher produces a significantly cheaper paperback version, its impact will not be all that the author had hoped.

Das koptisch-sahidische Johannesvangelium sa 506 aus dem Jeremia-Kloster von Sakkara: Mit Textvarianten der Handschriften in Barcelona, Cairo, Dublin, Naqlun, New York, by Karlheinz Schüssler. Arbeiten zur Biblia Coptica 1. Wiesbaden: Harrassowitz, 2013. Pp. xii + 277. Paper. $121.00. ISBN 9783447067355.

Johanna Brankaer, University of Münster, Münster, Germany

This new series, Arbeiten zur Biblia Coptica, is conceived to make available (some of) the texts of the manuscripts enlisted in the Biblia Coptica. The first volume is dedicated to one of the six sahidic manuscripts that have the complete text of John.

The text of the Gospel of John in the edition of the Sahidic New Testament by G. W. Horner is based on more than ninety "manuscripts," none of which have the complete text and many of which only have very short fragments. The text by Horner is a construct, based on fragments from very different contexts and periods. Since the publication of the text by Horner, about one hundred new witnesses have been found, some of which contain the entire text of the fourth Gospel. A new edition of the Sahidic John is being prepared within the context of the International Greek New Testament Project under the direction of D. Parker. Parallel to this critical edition, K. Schüssler prepares the edition of single manuscripts in this new series.

The manuscript sa 506 is a small parchment codex that contains the Acts of the Apostles and the Gospel of John in Sahidic dialect. The text of Acts was edited by H. Thompson in 1932; the Gospel of John was collated by H. Quecke in his edition of PPalau Rib. 183 in 1984. This is the first edition of the Gospel of John based uniquely on this manuscript. Sa 506 belongs to the collection of the Chester Beatty Library in Dublin, where it is known as Cpt. 814 (formerly Ms. B). The Codex was found in the winter of 1924–1925 in an excavation near the Jeremiah Monastery in the vicinity of Sakkara in Egypt. It was hidden with four other codices in a vessel, together with coins from the time of Justinian I (527–565), Justin II (564–578), and Mauritius Tiberius (582–602). These point to a date of origin at the end of the sixth century.

This volume contains a description of the codex with an overview of the different layers of the manuscript and the structure of the text as it is rendered through the use of coronis and obelos. A comparative table allows readers to compare the subdivisions of sa 506 with other Coptic manuscripts of John, some of which are organized according to the "Coptic mode," others to the "Greek mode." Our manuscript shows the structure typical of the Coptic mode.

Schüssler compares the citations of Old Testament texts in the Gospel of John from sa 506 with the Sahidic text of the Old Testament passages (if available) and with the LXX. He also gives an exhaustive list of the characteristics of the language of the manuscript: the numerous corrections made by the scribe, the remaining mistakes (dittography, haplography, the omission of single letters, other omissions, divergent spelling), other orthographic characteristics (monographic spelling, *nomina sacra*), and the spelling of Greek words. He also examines the variants of Greek words, some conspicuous features of the Coptic vocabulary and syntax, the use of prepositions in comparison with the other Sahidic manuscripts, and variant readings with regard to the content in comparison with the Greek text and the other complete Coptic manuscripts. The Greek text of reference is the most recent edition of Nestle-Aland. Readings from individual Greek manuscripts are not taken into consideration.

The main part of the book consists of the edition of the text of John from sa 506. This text is first presented as a continuous text with the subdivisions in chapters and verses of the Fourth Gospel. The continuous text is followed by a transcription of the manuscript with critical signs and notes about the corrections and insertions by the scribe. The variants of the other complete Sahidic codices of John are not dealt with in the apparatus, but they are treated exhaustively in the introduction.

This is not a critical edition of the Sahidic Gospel of John, but it is the edition of a single text that really existed (contrary to the reconstructed text in Horner) and was read around the end of the sixth century. Sa 506 is an important codex, and it is useful to have an accurate rendering of it. It is a shame that this volume contains only one photograph of the manuscript (the first page of John), but it would have been too expensive to integrate more photographic material.

For scholars who are interested in all the aspects of this manuscript, this edition will prove to be a useful tool. Other manuscripts will follow and will allow New Testament scholars as well as Coptic scholars to access individual manuscripts of biblical texts that are important for the reconstruction of Coptic Bible texts, as will be the result of the Coptic John project. It comes in handy that these Coptic manuscripts are not only available in libraries all over the world or through the apparatus of critical editions, but also as a complete text. Therefore, this series seems like a good idea for New Testament textual criticism and for Coptic studies.

VI-4 Ordinis sexti tomus quartus: Novum Testamentum ab Erasmo Recognitum, IV, Epistolae Apostolicae (secunda pars) et Apocalypsis Iohannis, by Desiderius Erasmus. Edited by Andrew J. Brown. Opera Omnia Desiderii Erasmi—Erasmus, Opera Omnia. Leiden: Brill, 2013. Pp. 698. Cloth. $221.00. ISBN 9789004202153.

Jerome A. Lund, Accordance Software, Kviteseid, Norway

Scholars of the text history and exegesis of the Greek and Latin New Testaments will greatly appreciate this volume, which contains Erasmus's edition of the Greek with his Latin translation of 1 Timothy through Revelation. It will serve as an indispensible tool for the writing of serious language-based commentaries of the future. The body of the work consists of the Greek text in the left column and Erasmus's Latin translation of the Greek in the right column, with detailed commentary under the text. The notes in the commentary section in particular comment on the selection of Greek readings available to Erasmus and how his Latin translation differs from the late form of the Latin Vulgate known to him. Brown interacts with the annotations given by Erasmus in his editions; the commentary is Brown's. Erasmus attributes the authorship of the Epistle to the Hebrews to Paul, which he believes was "written" (Greek ἐγράφη; Latin *missa* "sent") from Italy by Timothy (348). The names of the biblical books appear in Latin.

Erasmus made five editions of the Greek New Testament, dated 1516, 1519, 1522, 1527, and 1535. His influence on European vernacular translations was profound. Martin Luther used his second edition as the basis of his translation of the German Bible. Erasmus's third edition served via Robert Etienne's later text as the basis of the English Authorized Version, also known as the KJV. Consequently, students of both the English and German Bibles will find this work of immense value. Greek and Latin textual variants within the different editions are indicated in the first (Greek) and second (Latin) apparatuses of the present volume, where the editions are given letter equivalents in italics: A = 1516 edition; B = 1519 edition; C = 1522 edition; D = 1527 edition; and E = 1535 edition. The third apparatus contains the commentary.

The introduction is meaty. Brown discusses in detail the Greek manuscripts available to Erasmus and his choice of text. Erasmus used only five Greek manuscripts in his first edition of 1516 for the Pauline Epistles (Basle Cod. 1; Basle Cod. 2815; Basle Cod. 2816; Basle Cod. 2817; Bodleian Cod. 2105), three for the General Epistles (Basle Cod. 1; Basle Cod. 2815; Basle Cod. 2816), and one the Apocalypse (Augsburg Cod. 2814). Basle Cod. 2817 served as Erasmus's principle manuscript for the Pauline Epistles, but from Heb 12:18, where Basle Cod. 2817 breaks off, through the end of the General Epistles he used Basle Cod. 2815. In addition, he used emendation and back-translation from Latin as sources for reconstructing what he perceived to be the *Graeca veritas*. For example, he added the words ταῖς ἐν Ἀσίᾳ "which are in Asia" to his Greek text after the words "the seven churches" on the basis of the late form of the Vulgate *quae sunt in Asia* (Rev 1:11). The manuscripts cited in the commentary, including additional ones not recorded above, are listed on page 112.

Erasmus's editions of 1516 and 1519 came under sharp criticism for their omission of words from 1 John 5:7–8 about the three heavenly witnesses (omission in italics: "For there are three who bear witness *in heaven, the Father, the Word, and the Holy Spirit. And these three are one. And there are three who bear witness on earth*: the spirit, the water, and the blood. And these three are one."), which critics perceived as an attack on the doctrine of the Trinity. Erasmus countered that the reading lacked any Greek manuscript support. In his 1522 edition he added the words largely on the basis of Dublin Cod. 61 (Montfortianus). Brown discusses this issue in detail in a long excursus placed as part 2 of the introduction. Brown argues convincingly that the addition of these words in Dublin Cod. 61 were not due to "a conscious act of deceit" nor "part of a conspiracy against Erasmus by his opponents" (110–11). Rather, the manuscript reflects a practice of correcting Greek readings on the basis of the Vulgate, a practice known from other Greek manuscripts written in Europe in the late medieval period. In fact, the manuscript in question may have been written prior to 1516.

The commentary contains copious notes on Erasmus's Greek text and his Latin translation, especially in relation to the Vulgate. For example, the commentary treats the reading "only wise God" found in Erasmus' Greek manuscripts over against the reading "only God" (1 Tim 1:17), the latter reading being that of the Vulgate. Although Erasmus retained the reading "only wise God" in his Greek text and Latin translation, he considered the word "wise" an addition to the text, according to his annotations, first in 1516 as an Arian addition but subsequently as the influence of the phrase "only wise God" from Rom 16:27. Again, his Greek text and Latin translation read "the name of Christ" in 2 Tim 2:19, whereas the Vulgate reads "the name of the Lord." The Vulgate reading, which reading Erasmus himself preferred in his 1527–1535 annotations, has better Greek manuscript support than its competitor. The Textus Receptus, however, retains the reading "the name of Christ." Further, Erasmus translates χαρακτὴρ as *expressa imago* in contrast to the Vulgate *figura*, explaining in his annotations that the Greek word means an image stamped into a wax seal, not just any outward shape as conveyed by *figura* (Heb 1:3). He improved his Latin translation from the first edition, where he rendered ἀρχιερεύς by *sacerdos* in Heb 5:1, by substituting *pontifex* in his subsequent editions. At Heb 10:30 Erasmus adds the word *eum* before *qui dixit* (Vulgate reads *qui dixit*) to make it clearer "that this is knowledge of a person, i.e. of God, and not merely of a fact" (303). In Jas 1:12 Erasmus reads "the Lord" as the subject of the verb "promised," where the Vulgate reads "God." By contrast to both Erasmus and the Vulgate, the Greek codices Sinaiticus, Alexandrinus, and Vaticanus all omit the expressed subject. In 1 Pet 2:20 Erasmus renders κλέος as *laus* ("praise") against the late Vulgate's translation *gratia* ("favor"). Brown remarks that Erasmus suggested the rendering *gloria* ("glory") as an alternative, the reading of the earlier Vulgate. In 1 Pet 2:24 Erasmus replaced the Vulgate's ambiguous *liuore*, which "could mean envy and malice as well as the mark of bruising," with *vibice* "weal" (407). The late form of the Vulgate known to Erasmus read *propitiatorem* ("propitiator") as the translation equivalent of ἱλασμὸν in 1 John 4:10, which rendering "obscures the deeper concept of the Son of God himself becoming the sacrificial offering" (479). Thus Erasmus rendered the term more faithfully as *propitiationem* ("propitiation"), which rendering agrees with the reading of the earlier form of the Vulgate.

A list of abbreviations, indices of Greek and Latin words discussed in the commentary, and an index to the excursus "Codex 61 (Montfortianus) and 1 John 5, 7–8" are found at the back of the volume.

Throughout the text one will see the abbreviation "LB" plus a number in the margin. This is a cross reference to the Leiden edition of Erasmus's *Opera Omnia* printed in 1703–1706. The present volume is part of the Amsterdam edition.

In sum, this present volume should be obtained by every research library as a significant resource for all future investigation of the texts of both the Greek and Latin Bibles. Students of the English and German Bibles will also find this a valuable tool. The commentary provides excellent material for evaluating readings. Writers of future language-based commentaries would be well-rewarded by consulting this volume.

BIBLE AND CULTURE

Sacred Word, Broken Word: Biblical Authority and the Dark Side of Scripture, by Kenton L. Sparks. Grand Rapids: Eerdmans, 2012. Pp. xii + 180. Cloth. $20.00. ISBN 9780802867186.

Hector Avalos, Professor of Religious Studies, Iowa State University

This book is part of a recent trend focusing on ethical problems in the Bible that pose a challenge to biblical authority in the modern world. Examples of such a trend include Paul Copan's *Is God a Moral Monster? Making Sense of the Old Testament God* (2011), Eric A. Seibert's *Disturbing Divine Behavior: Troubling Old Testament Images of God* (2009), and Caryn A. Reeder's *The Enemy in the Household: Family Violence in Deuteronomy and Beyond* (2012).

Genocide, misogyny, and intolerance of other religions are among the few ethical problems in the Bible explored by Kenton L. Sparks, a professor of biblical studies at Eastern University in St. Davids, Pennsylvania, in what can be described as an extended theological meditation. Previously Sparks authored an excellent exploration of ethnic identity in ancient Israel (*Ethnicity and Identity in Ancient Israel: Prolegomena to the Study of Ethnic Sentiments and their Expression in the Hebrew Bible* [Winona Lake, Ind.: Eisenbrauns, 1998]).

At the outset of *Sacred Word* Sparks tells readers that "[t]his is a book written for confessing Christians" (3). At the same time, he appeals to scientific evidence that transcends religious affiliation, as when he rejects a literal interpretation of Gen 1 because the "'red shift' and the decay of radioactive isotopes are as much God's voice as Genesis 1" (135).

The book is divided into thirteen chapters and some "Final Thoughts." The first two chapters summarize what Sparks finds truthful and beautiful in scripture, as well as how the existence of evil bears implications for canonical theology. Sparks seeks to explain the seeming endorsement of unethical acts in the Bible by showing that "the Bible actually stands *within* the fallen order that we seek to understand" (22, emphasis original). That is to say, since the biblical authors are part of a fallen world, so the scripture that they write has aspects of that fallen world inscribed in the text.

Chapter 3 focuses on Christology and a brief critique of those biblical scholars who deny Jesus his humanity. Chapter 4 shows how the various historical and logical contradictions found in scripture can be explained as imperfections reflecting a fallen world. At the same time, Sparks declares that "[t]he ethical problems in Scripture are real" (44).

Chapter 5 begins an exploration of more specific ethical problems, including the genocide of the Canaanites (e.g., Deut 7, 20, Josh 6). Although he does not deny that genocidal sentiments and actions were expressed by biblical authors, Sparks says that, "in spite of this—here I simply assert a dogmatic theological point—we cannot trace the human evil back to God" (49).

Sparks's version of St. Augustine's accommodationist approach to scripture is outlined in chapter 6. For Sparks, "God has adopted the words and viewpoints of finite, fallen human authors as the words and viewpoints of his holy book: The entire Bible is accommodated discourse" (54). Yet, Sparks also argues that the word of God can be found outside (e.g., in nature, science) of scripture (61).

"The Redemption of Scripture: Biblical Examples" is the title of chapter 7, which explores how some biblical authors tried to mitigate ethical problems found in biblical texts. One example is the substitution of Satan for God in 1 Chr 21:1 to avoid attributing to God a census he commanded but for which he later punished Israel in 2 Sam 24.

With chapter 8 Sparks shifts toward a philosophical discussion of epistemology in order to make sense of how we can detect God's voice. He settles on what he denominates as "practical realism," which he calls "the preferable Christian view of human knowledge" (73–74). Practical realism, which is responsive to the work of Richard Rorty and E. D. Hirsch, allows for the idea that scripture "is itself a book of theological discourse that advances the truth, but also stands in need of redemption" (88).

"Sacred Scripture as Ancient Discourse" (ch. 9) lays out hermeneutical rules for understanding God's word. For Sparks, "one must understand the text and then reflect theologically on what is said in light of other biblical texts and in light of God's voice as it speaks to us through tradition, cosmos, experience, and Spirit" (90). In studying Paul, for example, we must "inform ourselves about the historical situation and context of Paul's day insofar as this is feasible" (91).

Chapters 10 through his "Final Thoughts" flesh out his hermeneutics, especially the role of the Spirit, Cosmos, Tradition, and Experience in interpreting the Bible. Sparks is willing to admit that "the author of Deuteronomy *wrongly believed* (as Luther did) that God told his people to slaughter their enemies" (105, emphasis original).

Sparks argues that "Scripture from Genesis through Revelation presents a tolerably coherent story, what one scholar has called a 'theodrama'" (106). However, "our theology should grant priority to Jesus Christ to knowing him, his teachings, and the redemptive character of his resurrection, ascension, and eventual return" (107).

Since Sparks grants that his book is meant for confessing Christians, I will review it from the viewpoint of both a Christian and a secular academic biblical scholar, which is how I identify myself.

From the viewpoint of Christianity, I am uncertain what the book intends to accomplish, especially as Sparks admits that Christianity is very diverse. It seems that the book will simply attract those who already share his theological presuppositions. The book does not present anything that will compel those self-described Christians who do not share his theological presuppositions to change their minds.

For example, Sparks views "the Nicene Creed and Definition of Chalcedon, as foundational for biblical interpretation" (89). This leaves out millions of non-Trinitarian Christians and Jews who see unitarianism as foundational to biblical interpretation.

Sparks also presents his work as "ecumenical" (89), yet it is clear that "ecumenical" is simply a cipher for other Christians who agree with him. By that standard, the Christian Coalition of America is also ecumenical, as it allows Christians, whether Protestant or Catholic, who fight against abortion into their group.

In many other ways, Sparks still harbors a very traditional Christian viewpoint that does not view Judaism as equal to Christianity in its ethical development. So, when comparing Jesus' view of the Sabbath in Mark 2:27 to that in Num 15:32–33, where someone is executed for not observing that sacred day, Sparks says, "it seems to me that the spirit of grace and freedom in the ministry of Jesus is very different from the legalism of Numbers" (108). Yet theologically the Nicene and Chalcedonian creeds view Christ as God, and so that would mean that it is also Christ who approved of the laws demanding the death penalty for violation of the Sabbath (Exod 31:15; Num 15:32–36). Further, who decided that "legalism" is unethical or less desirable for God in the first place?

From a secular academic viewpoint, this sort of theological approach to biblical studies is futile and frankly incomprehensible in the twenty-first century. It is futile because there are no objective means to adjudicate which theological interpretation is correct or valid. Sparks is most perceptive when he remarks that "there is an unavoidable circularity in parsing out where God speaks explicitly in Scripture and where he speaks implicitly" (111).

I would go further and argue that all notions of when God is speaking, whether explicitly or implicitly, are circular. They all devolve into this rationale: "I believe God thinks X because I believe God thinks X." It inevitably becomes an act of self-deification on the believer's part because the believer comes to see himself or herself as speaking for God. So, unlike Newton's laws of gravity or Ohm's Law of electrical current, which can be demonstrated to people of different religious backgrounds, everything Sparks says about God cannot be demonstrated to be anything other than the work of his own imagination or subjective beliefs. That is why Sparks appeal to practical realism is not successful when referents such as "God" are involved. There are no practical methods by which we can ascertain anything about a being that can be perceived by everyone in the same way even when we assume that such a being exists.

I would go much further and argue that all theistic ethics are inherently unethical because, at least from a secular viewpoint, a functional ethical system is one in which all members of a community have at least the same potential ability to verify the information on which their actions are based.

In theistic ethics, some people will claim the privilege to be perceiving God's word correctly, so that ability will not really be distributed evenly to all. It is, therefore, inherently undemocratic. Indeed, Sparks's book would have been improved if there were a more thorough discussion of metaethics, not just epistemology.

To understand why I say projects such as this are incomprehensible in this century, imagine that someone in a classics department in a secular university proposed that we can still understand the mind and motives of Zeus in Homer's *Iliad* and in every other work of ancient Greek literature. If we just "listen hard enough to Zeus's voice," or if we just dogmatically assert that that Zeus is good no matter what Greek texts might say, then we can come to understand why Zeus might have ordered the slaughter of people here or there.

Sparks's view of the value of tradition as a guide to scriptural interpretation also inevitably generates moral relativism. He tells us that "[t]he Christian tradition is not a single authoritative voice so much as a family of closely related traditions that have different but overlapping judgments ... but no single traditions holds all the cards" (127). But how do we know which tradition holds the right card? Such a claim regresses to Sparks's own circular judgment: "I believe tradition X holds the right card because I believe tradition X holds the right card."

Furthermore, we could just as well redefine the family of traditions as consisting of all Abrahamic religions, and then we might also include Islam in our "family" and view Muhammad as the final arbiter of previous biblical interpretation. Or we could include Mormons with their expanded canon in our "family" of traditions.

Yet, Sparks has already explicitly declared at various points that his beliefs are dogmatic. For example, note how he includes the belief that Jesus God is Christ incarnate as one of the "matters of dogmatic theology that I will treat as finally settled" (3). But if no one tradition holds all the cards, then how did he decide that this dogma should be settled? If anyone else can be just as dogmatic about Muhammad being the last prophet, then why choose Sparks's dogmatic beliefs over those of Islamic theologians?

The idea that the Bible bears ethical problems because it is part of a fallen world will not help redeem the Bible from its moral flaws. The whole idea of a fallen world may itself be a flawed idea generated by an author who is as wrong about the world being fallen as Sparks contends the author of Deuteronomy was wrong to believe "that God told his people to slaughter their enemies" (105).

Given these intractable problems, Sparks's book can be seen as another attempt to preserve the value of the Bible in the modern world by whitewashing its ethical problems. It is an instance of what, in *The End of Biblical Studies*

(2007), I termed "bibliolatry" among modern biblical scholars. Bibliolatry entails the belief that the Bible is a superior text to all others even if it has ethical, logical, and historical problems.

Such bibliolatry is apparent when Sparks discusses Deut 22:28–29, which decrees that an unengaged rape victim must marry her rapist. Sparks remarks that "we are all understandably repulsed by what looks like very sick and twisted logic" (39–40). Yet Sparks defends the Bible by saying that "the law actually served a role in defending women's rights" (40). He argues that, "[b]ecause ancient Israelites greatly valued virginity, rape victims tended to remain unmarried and, hence, to become economically vulnerable in a patriarchal world. Given this eventuality, rapists were forced to marry and economically care for their victims.... So, though I freely admit that I am troubled by this law as it stands, the law is 'good' in ways that I would not have expected because my world is so profoundly different from the world of ancient Israel" (40). Sparks cites Jeffrey Tigay (*Deuteronomy* [Philadelphia: Jewish Publication Society, 1996], 208–9) for support, but Tigay actually says something quite the opposite. Tigay notes that, "[a]ccording to the halakah in cases of both seduction and rape, the girl as well as the father has the right to refuse the marriage" (208). In fact, in Exod 22:16 the father can refuse a marriage to a man who seduces his unbetrothed daughter: "If her father utterly refuses to give her to him, he shall pay money equivalent to the marriage present for virgins" (RSV). In light of how Sparks claims that ancient Israelites valued virginity, such a girl might also remain unmarried and be vulnerable. But someone had at least thought of the option to not marry a man if her father refused regardless of the girl's loss of virginity. So, other options for a girl in such circumstances could have been contemplated in the ancient world. Indeed, there is no reason why an ancient society could not have imposed the death penalty on the rapist, then transferred at least part of his family's property to the raped girl's household for her support.

I have argued elsewhere (*Fighting Words: The Origins of Religious Violence* [2005]) that we need to treat ethics in biblical texts just as we treat ethics in any other works of ancient literature. It is a vacuous exercise to pick and choose which atrocities were really ordained by any gods and which were not. We should have a zero-tolerance view of any text or collection of texts that at any time endorses genocide, misogyny, and other atrocities. We always judge ancient texts by modern ethical standards, and the Bible should not be treated differently.

Sparks's book does show that the ethical problems in scripture are increasingly bothering the conscience of biblical scholars who are still affiliated with religious traditions. Whereas the first couple of centuries of modern biblical scholarship focused on issues of historicity and literary analysis, this century of biblical studies may be marked by its ability or inability to address Sparks's own realization that the ethical problems in Scripture are real.

The Bible and the Believer: How to Read the Bible Critically and Religiously, by Marc Zvi Brettler, Peter Enns, and Daniel J. Harrington. Oxford: Oxford University Press, 2012. Pp. x + 210. Hardcover. $27.95. ISBN 9780199863006.

Greg Carey, Lancaster Theological Seminary, Lancaster, Pennsylvania

Emerging from a 2010 symposium at the University of Pennsylvania, this book sets forth contemporary Jewish, Protestant, and Roman Catholic accounts of historical criticism's role in the life of faith. After a collaborative introduction, the volume features one essay by each author, followed by responses from the other two panelists. The essays all speak to the common perception that critical biblical scholarship stands in tension with faith, and each essay draws upon the rich resources of a particular religious tradition for wisdom in answering the question. All three authors agree that historical criticism plays a valuable, in this age indispensable, role in contemporary faith communities. Refreshingly, all three authors likewise agree that historical criticism and academic biblical scholarship in general neither exhaust nor govern the Bible's meaning. Each author writes crisply and clearly, with both wisdom and erudition.

From the outset we should consider what counts as historical criticism for these interpreters. The introduction articulates the sort of "chastened" historical criticism that now seems normative in our field. This historical criticism is less confident than it once was in our ability to uncover layers of tradition from historical events and to tease out a document's source history. It acknowledges critiques against a naïve historical positivism, and it includes insights from literary and social theory. In the end, however, the authors agree that "we can offer reasonable and compelling explanations of an author's meaning or a text's function in the original context," enough to rule out other, inferior, interpretations (6–7). I experience both sympathy and discomfort with this claim.

The book's chief value may lie beyond its stated purpose. The essays indeed make the case that historical scholarship contributes value to faith communities, but I found most compelling how the essays articulate the distinctive preoccupations, limitations, and resources of the traditions they represent.

For example, Brettler denies that Judaism is a "religion of the book" in that the Bible alone does not norm Jewish practice, nor does dogma define Judaism. Most Jews, therefore, have not confronted modernism or evolutionary biology as grave threats to their belief systems. Jews have not typically struggled with biblical literalism, nor have they wrangled over definitions of inspiration. Brettler devotes significant attention to Maimonides's "eighth fundamental principle," that the Torah in its entirety derives from God and is "perfect, pure, holy and true" (34). Brettler both examines rabbinic contradictions of this claim and argues that the Torah itself invites historical-critical approaches.

In the end, Brettler maintains a pragmatic view of the Bible's role in Judaism. In a reading of Ps 114 he notes that contemporary Jewish interpretation tends to minimize the sort of multitiered historical speculation concerning source, form, and redaction that once characterized historical criticism, instead emphasizing the literary and rhetorical dynamics of biblical texts. Brettler holds that the Jewish people possess the authority to determine their own religion and that rabbinic teaching does not so much derive from the Torah as seeks to ground itself in Torah. The Bible's significance is not "confined" to its original meaning(s), but historical criticism enriches the understanding of it (63). He proposes an analogy: the Bible is a key sourcebook that interpreters transform into a textbook.

As Brettler draws upon rabbinic conversations, Harrington fittingly engages recent Catholic teaching on Scripture, what he describes as a well-kept secret (80). Reviewing the progress from the *Divino afflante Spiritu* (1943) and the "Dogmatic Constitution on Divine Revelation" (1965; also known as *Dei Verbum*), to the more recent "The Interpretation of the Bible in the Church" (1993), "The Jewish People and Their Scriptures in the Christian Bible" (2002), and Pope Benedict XVI's *Verbum Domini*, Harrington demonstrates the classic "both ... and" quality that tends to mark Catholic thinking (80). Yes, the Bible reveals divine truth. Yes, Catholic teaching encourages spiritual and typological interpretation. Yes, Catholicism honors historical research. Historical criticism, then, is "indispensable" but "not sufficient" (88), and "spiritual" interpretation may not be alienated from "literal" or historical readings (100). What Catholicism cannot embrace, Harrington maintains, are historical approaches given to undisciplined speculation or bound by naturalistic presuppositions (94–95).

Just as Brettler denies that Judaism is a religion of the book, Harrington maintains that Roman Catholicism is more a religion of a person, Jesus Christ, than a manual for doctrine (85). The Bible's value, then, resides in its capacity to draw people toward salvation, and its trustworthiness resides in that capacity. As a means of understanding the Bible's relationship to its historical particularities, Harrington advances an incarnational model, one basically shared by Enns as well. The larger revelation reveals that God works through specific people and places. Both authors recognize the analogy's limitations, but it basically works like this: we speak of Christ as fully human and fully divine, so we might likewise acknowledge the Bible as "a thoroughly human *and* divine product" (141).

Peter Enns has gained notoriety especially among evangelicals for his insistence that Protestant interpretation should not be governed by abstract theories of inspiration (or "inerrancy") but by the Bible as it is: "The challenge ... is for Protestants to realign their convictions to reflect how their Bible actually behaves and not how they feel it should behave" (149). Enns's essay reflects the specific struggles of evangelicals to come to terms with modernity: he cites *sola scriptura*, the ways in which the Bible's content resists the doctrinal uses that preoccupy Protestants, and the "contentious legacy" of nineteenth-century polemics against evolution and higher criticism as obstacles Protestants must face before "moving forward" (131–40). In the end, Enns suggests that the Bible cannot provide the center of Christian faith (God does), that fear easily derails the dialogue between faith and criticism, and that "[a]n unsettled faith is a maturing faith" (159–60). In other words, Enns does not offer a straightforward program by which Protestants may integrate criticism and faith; rather, he insists that Protestants must embrace intellectual integrity and models a spirit of flexibility and openness.

A second great contribution of the book involves what almost amounts to a sidebar conversation: the matter of figurative reading. Figurative, or typological, interpretations pose significant challenges for ecumenical dialogue. On the one hand, we Christians tend to find Jesus throughout our Old Testament, a practice that leads to misunderstanding not only of Jews and Judaism but of Jesus and his earliest followers. Moreover, we Protestants often show disdain for the spiritual and allegorical exegesis of our ancient and medieval forebears. Protestantism's humanist roots often preclude our awareness of how we indulge in similar practices ourselves. Brettler sets a most generous tone for this conversation when he points out that early Christian typological readings amount to "a continuation of those [typologies] found in the Jewish Hebrew Bible" (62). Whatever the dangers of typological interpretation, all three authors agree that its basic practices were operative among Jews before Christians trained them upon Jesus.

All three authors acknowledge that the word "Bible" refers to diverse collections and arrangements of texts for Jews, Protestants, and Catholics. Harrington advances a compelling case for the value of the Catholic Old Testament, which includes the "so-called Apocrypha" (81–82); beyond that, this matter does not receive the level of reflection it might.

I found much to admire in this volume. It accomplishes exactly what it sets out to do: demonstrating the distinctive ways in which historical scholarship can nourish diverse faith traditions. While not directly engaged with some cutting-edge theoretical developments in biblical interpretation, the authors all demonstrate a winsome combination of humility and self-awareness. Moreover, all three authors honor the wisdom embodied in their own historical traditions. We biblical scholars tend to overlook the ways in which the Bible has been used and understood through the centuries; these authors do not.

It is unfair to ask a book to accomplish things it does not set out to do. Nevertheless, one observes that all three authors are men and that many people would consider them all to be white. We find little in this book regarding ethically and theologically troubling aspects of the Bible or about the diverse social, ethnic, and economic realities of its readers. The authors demonstrate keen self-awareness concerning the interpreter's agency, but they do not seriously engage the challenges of postmodern interpretation or cultural studies approaches. (Enns's quick survey of hermeneutical options mentions Hirsch, Ricoeur, and Gadamer.) I do not suggest that the authors are *obliged* to take up such topics, only that one might imagine very different books from a more diverse array of interpreters—and that difference matters.

I do find myself unsatisfied by one aspect of the book. All three authors identified biblical passages through which they might model how biblical criticism might nourish faith. Brettler takes on Ps 114; Harrington, the call of Moses in Exod 3–4; and Enns, the exodus traditions. Each author advances impressive critical insights. Each speaks powerfully to the religious value of the text. My own judgment, however, is that none of the three examples forcefully demonstrates how historical criticism, as historical criticism, *contributes* to the religious meaning its author articulates. For all this book's formidable virtues, that seems to constitute its primary challenge, and in this detail it may fall short.

The Invention of the Biblical Scholar: A Critical Manifesto, by Stephen D. Moore and Yvonne Sherwood. Minneapolis: Fortress, 2011. Pp. xiv + 138, Paperback, $22, ISBN 9780800697747.

Matthew V. Novenson, University of Edinburgh, Edinburgh, Scotland

The title of Stephen Moore and Yvonne Sherwood's *The Invention of the Biblical Scholar: A Critical Manifesto* promises big things, and the book delivers them. These big things are, first, an account of how biblical studies became the kind of academic discipline that it is, and, second, a proposal for how it might yet become a different kind of discipline altogether. The material included in the book is not entirely new. It had its origins in a panel on the topic "After Theory" in the Reading, Theory, and the Bible Section of the SBL, papers from which subsequently appeared serially in *Biblical Interpretation* in 2010. That material has been revised and focused into monograph form, a form that suits the subject matter well. The book is co-authored in the strong sense: Moore and Sherwood consistently speak in the first-person plural "we," so that whatever philosophical and stylistic differences the two authors may have are not evident to the reader. The argument of the book unfolds as follows.

A brief preface lays out the authors' thesis, which is really bipartite: that modern academic biblical studies, even in its ostensibly postmodern forms, continues to underwrite the Enlightenment Bible project first imagined around the turn of the eighteenth century; and that the discipline can and ought to embrace a more radical turn to philosophy than it has yet done.

Chapter 1 ("Theory and Methodolatry") assesses the status accorded "Theory" in literary studies on the one hand and biblical studies on the other. By Theory Moore and Sherwood mean "a paradoxically expansive yet selective body of work: Russian formalism, French structuralism, semiotics, poststructuralism, deconstruction, Lacanian and post-Lacanian psychoanalytic theory, assorted Marxisms and neo-Marxisms, reader-response criticism and *Rezeptionsästhetik*, "French feminist theory' (more precisely, *écriture féminine*), 'third-wave' feminist theory, gender studies, queer theory, New Historicism, cultural materialism, cultural studies, postcolonial studies, and (academic) postmodernism *tout court*" (3–4), but above all poststructuralism and deconstruction. The authors point out the irony that, while literary studies has for some time been discussing the death of Theory, biblical studies is still in the early stages of converting bits and pieces of Theory into exegete-friendly methodologies.

Chapter 2 ("The Invention of the Biblical Scholar") comprises a selective history of biblical scholarship from the early eighteenth century to the present, not—the authors emphasize—as a self-congratulatory etiological saga but as a demonstration that the discipline remains still in thrall to the anxieties of its Enlightenment forebears. Here Moore and Sherwood lean heavily on Jonathan Sheehan, *The Enlightenment Bible* (Princeton University Press, 2004), in particular the latter's claim that eighteenth-century European intellectuals created a new, nonreligious mode of authority for the Bible, namely, cultural authority. This development allowed, and still allows, the guild of biblical scholars to justify its existence in a modern, secular social context. In particular, Moore and Sherwood argue, biblical scholars made a place for themselves by subtly shifting the angle of approach to the Bible from moral criticism to historical criticism. So whereas eighteenth-century biblical critics such as Pierre Bayle were preoccupied with the ethical problems raised by the contents of the Bible (e.g., the divinely authorized slaughter of the Canaanites), nineteenth-century critics such as Julius Wellhausen turned instead to textual and historical problems (e.g., the sources of the Pentateuch). This shift secured the perennial necessity of the methodological specialist, a disciplinary paradigm that continues unchallenged even by postmodern, Theory-influenced developments in the field.

Chapter 3 ("Onward toward the Past") provides an analysis of the interdisciplinary encounter between the Bible and Theory in two parts: "Theory in the First Wave," which recounts how biblical scholars have ransacked Theory for exegetical methodologies (e.g., feminist exegesis, postcolonial exegesis, Marxian exegesis) and thereby actually shored up the Enlightenment Bible project rather than undermined it; and "Theory in the Second Wave," which explains how secular literary critics and philosophers (e.g., Jacques Derrida, Giorgio Agamben, Stanley Fish) are, surprisingly, once again using the Bible as a resource for posing major moral, aesthetic, and even religious questions. In a hortatory peroration, Moore and Sherwood urge biblical scholars to embrace this recent religious turn in Theory and so join a wider humanistic academic discourse: "We are on the cusp of more significant and more searching engagements between Bible and Theory than before.... We stand to gain this broader academic relevance as biblical scholars by the most unlikely means imaginable. We need to find religion" (130–31).

The Invention of the Biblical Scholar is a well-executed and important book. The authors, both skillful writers of academic prose, are also among our foremost authorities on the dialogue between Bible and Theory, so their "state of the discipline" address deserves to be heeded in all corners of the biblical studies guild. With this book, Moore and Sherwood also make an important contribution to the lively recent discussion of the social history of modern biblical studies (alongside interpreters such as Michael Legaspi, Suzanne Marchand, Dale Martin, and Jonathan Sheehan). Their perceptive assessment of the sometimes clueless absorption of Theory into biblical studies methodology is convincing and indeed disturbing. Their argument that the historicist center of the discipline has silenced potentially damning criticisms from various ideological approaches with the rhetoric of benevolent pluralism ("Let many flowers bloom"), while not unassailable, does identify an embarrassing dynamic in our disciplinary *habitus*. In these and other respects, *The Invention of the Biblical Scholar* has to be considered a very important achievement.

In a book with many impressive strengths, one relatively weak part is the last, shortest part: the manifesto proper, in which Moore and Sherwood offer their prescription for the future of the discipline. In the authors' vision, the future of the Bible lies in its utility as a site or a resource for Theory: "a key site where foundational, but unsustainable, 'modern' separations were made" (128), "a resource for philosophers to think beyond the limits of empiricism, ontology, and metaphysics" (129), "an exceedingly unlikely but extremely productive site where contemporary Theoretical questions ... are hashed out" (130). No doubt the authors are right that the Bible is and will continue to be useful in this way, but they suggest that this turn toward Theory entails a turn away from philology and history, which is by no means necessary. Indeed, some of the very philosophers whom Moore and Sherwood hold up as examples provide counterevidence. Jacob Taubes and Giorgio Agamben, to name two, do a great deal of quite conventional philological and historical work with the Epistle of Paul to the Romans en route to their respective neo-Pauline political philosophies. If, as Moore and Sherwood suggest, the recent obituaries for Theory have been premature, perhaps the same is true of obituaries for historical criticism. Granted, the hegemony of historical criticism in biblical studies has functioned in such a way as to insulate the Bible from more radical moral criticism and to protect the social and economic interests of the guild of biblical scholars. But as Moore and Sherwood point out, we can at least imagine the history of the discipline running differently than it has in fact run. If so, then perhaps this second wave of the encounter between Bible and Theory need not consign philology and historical criticism to the dustbin of history.

RECEPTION HISTORY

Remembering Eden: The Reception History of Genesis 3:22–24, by Peter Thacher Lanfer. Oxford: Oxford University Press, 2012. Pp. x + 256. Hardcover. $74.00. ISBN 9780199926749.

L. Michael Morales, Reformation Bible College, Sanford, Florida

Peter T. Lanfer's *Remembering Eden: The Reception History of Genesis 3:22–24*, a study of the later versions and interpretive traditions of the expulsion narrative, is a welcome contribution to the budding field of reception history. Although a revision of his doctoral dissertation directed by Bill Schniedewind at UCLA, this well-written work, utilizing endnotes, is an enjoyably engaging read.

In the first chapter Lanfer introduces the expulsion narrative and argues that, in spite of its apparent marginality in the Hebrew Bible (Masoretic Text), early Jewish and Christian literature demonstrate interpretations and expansions of themes and motifs, symbols and metaphors, employed by the Hebrew Bible itself—that is, the presumed marginality of the expulsion narrative vanishes when the restraint of "explicit reference" is removed. The interpretations and expansions themselves preserve the specific ideological tensions of their own historical contexts and in turn reveal the dialogue latent within the redacted text of Gen 2–3. Lanfer next delineates his methodological pluralism, whereby he, in line with the approach of Annette Yoshiko Reed (*Fallen Angels and the History of Judaism and Christianity* [Cambridge University Press, 2005]), appropriates gains from source, form, and redaction criticism while nevertheless seeking to understand the significance of the composite text itself (rather than an elusive *Ur-text*). Refreshingly—and this is the boon of reception studies in general—he does not quickly discard as *eisegetical* the contribution to our understanding of a text's meaning by early divergent interpretations.

While not presuming to establish either the text's singular meaning or the author's intent, Lanfer's common-sense course seeks to promote boundaries to a text's meaning, as constrained by its "symbolic capital" identified in part by interpretations of the text. The symbols or motifs then become topics for the ensuing chapters (the tree of life, wisdom, immortality, and the temple), which Lanfer tries to approach more or less chronologically as follows: (1) Masoretic Text; (2) Septuagint; (3) Dead Sea Scrolls; (4) pseudepigrapha; (5) New Testament; (6) rabbinic literature; (7) patristic literature; (8) gnostic texts—and by moving from translation texts to narrative expansions to literary allusions.

Referring to the tree of life as the most salient and problematic motif, chapter 2 rightly argues that, despite the scarcity of explicit citations, the tree of life metaphor and related motifs are ubiquitous. After considering the ancient Near Eastern background to the tree of life, Lanfer suggests that the quest for wisdom from the tree of knowledge in Gen 2–3 presents a polemical response to the ancient Near Eastern analogues, with the tree of life being inserted as an effort to prioritize the cult and covenant (over against an independent pursuit of wisdom). Gilgamesh, for example, "is encouraged to seek wisdom when he loses the plant of life," whereas in the expulsion narrative, "immortality is lost with the acquisition of wisdom (or at least a particular type of illicit wisdom)" (36). This fertile chapter also explores the concepts of the cosmic tree and the "eternal planting," where the attributes of the tree of life are transferred to the righteous community and, in Christian interpretations, to the cross of Jesus, as well as being widely developed as a metaphor for the presence of God.

The third chapter, exploring the wisdom motif, posits a tension between the individual pursuit of wisdom, which Lanfer argues was part of the core Eden narrative (Gen 2–3), and the Deuteronomic ideology of the (polemically inserted) expulsion narrative, which is concerned primarily with covenant and cult. This tension in turn "reflects the cultural tensions between the emerging sapiential schools and those focused on covenant and cult during the Josianic reforms or in early exilic literature such as Jeremiah and Lamentations" (68). Later sapiential interpreters, it is suggested, co-opted the motifs and themes of the expulsion in their own writings so that its polemical role progressively vanished. Along the way, Lanfer covers motifs related to the interpretation of the problem of knowing in the expulsion narrative (including the idea of hubris in the pursuit of wisdom); of the threat of godlikeness in Gen 3:22 (including the role of the Torah, adherence to which allows the righteous a metaphoric return to Eden); and of life as the goal of wisdom and the "way" to the garden.

Chapter 4 examines the motifs associated with immortality, a hope expressed by interpreters as a regaining of access to Eden *via* reversal: the removal of the flaming sword, the opening of the gates, and so on. The great variety of interpretations of immortality—from astral immortality and lengthy blessed life to bodily resurrection in the eschaton—demonstrate the instability of ideas related to this hope. Lanfer further develops here the motif of the "way," which, he writes, "may be most directly connected to the preparation of the 'way of the Lord' in Isaiah and the 'way of life' in Proverbs, though these may ultimately be aligned with the 'way to the Tree of Life' in the expulsion narrative" (126).

The fifth chapter investigates interpretations of the expulsion narrative that affirm the connection—more symbolic than "strictly exegetical," as Lanfer explains—between Eden and the temple. This theme, Lanfer correctly notes, appears in such a variety of materials (archaeology, iconography, texts) and so persistently surfaces in both Jewish and Christian interpretations of the expulsion narrative that the original centrality of the temple in the Eden narrative of Gen 2–3 appears to be a foregone conclusion. The association of Eden and the temple is considered across three main avenues: Eden as an ideal temple, the present temple as Eden, and the future temple as a restored Eden. Throughout these sections Lanfer mines the richness of the Eden–temple connection within the history of interpretation, utilizing helpful subsections, such as on the priestly role of Adam and the dwelling of God as holy mountain.

The concluding chapter rehearses the preceding labors in summary fashion, reaffirming the composite nature of the text—essentially twofold: an older narrative containing only the tree of knowledge and a later editorial frame that inserts the tree of life (in Gen 2:9 and 3:22–24) as well as the expulsion narrative. Lanfer also reiterates his assessment that the dialogical approach to biblical studies he has employed constrains the interpretive possibilities more helpfully than other approaches, such as literary or reader-response criticism.

As already mentioned, *Remembering Eden* is a sound contribution to the field of reception history (and to that of interpretation in general); the comments that follow do not detract from this valuation. To begin, while there is wide consensus in scholarship as to the composite nature of the Eden narrative, some readers will not be entirely convinced that the prioritizing by interpreters of one motif (such as wisdom) over another (such as cult, emphasized by other interpreters) *necessarily* betrays the composite nature of a text. In any case, the interpreters themselves, as Lanfer notes, "do not necessarily choose sides between wisdom and cult/covenant, but the dialogue between the two provides a framework of interpretive restraint" (162), and this constraint—Lanfer's main contribution from my perspective—is valid regardless of one's view of a text's provenance. Returning to the point, is it possibly an anachronism to drive such a wedge between wisdom and covenant (cf. Prov 1:7; 9:10; Ps 111:10; Job 28:28, etc.), especially when one then needs to posit a progressively vanishing polemical role for the expulsion, it being co-opted by later sapiential interpreters? At the least, when one emphasizes that the pursuit of "wisdom" described in Eden is that of *illicit* knowledge (noted by Lanfer, though he does not follow the implications of this adequately), then the "tension" between wisdom and covenant is relieved somewhat.

Moreover, while Gen 3:22–24 is certainly freighted with temple motifs, is this insertion (along with the tree of life in 2:9) really *so* out of place in the Eden narrative—that is, can the temple symbolism of the Eden narrative be restricted to these verses? Gordon J. Wenham, in a landmark essay—curiously absent altogether from Lanfer's footnotes and bibliography—entitled "Sanctuary Symbolism in the Garden of Eden Story" (1986), argued that Eden is a highly symbolic narrative presenting the garden as an archetypal sanctuary. Now while many of Wenham's parallels between the garden and Israel's later tabernacle/temple are to be found within the expulsion text (such as the cherubim and the eastward orientation of the gateway), several important parallels are from other parts of the Eden narrative. For example, the verb used for Yhwh's walking (*hithallēk*) in the garden in Gen 3:8 is used to describe the divine presence in the later tent sanctuaries (see Lev 26:12; Deut 23:15; 2 Sam 7:6–7); the verbs utilized for Adam's work, "to worship and obey" (*lĕʿobdâh ûlĕšāmrâh*) in Gen. 2:15 are used together elsewhere in the Pentateuch only with reference to the Levites' duties in guarding and ministering in the sanctuary (Num 3:7–8; 8:26; 18:5–6); Yhwh's clothing of Adam in Gen 3:21, utilizing *kĕtōnet* and the *hiphil* of *lābaš*, appears to be echoed in Moses' clothing of priests (Exod 28:41; 29:8; 40:14; Lev 8:13); the river flowing through the garden, branching out into four headwaters in Gen 2:10–14 may also be included as temple imagery (Ps 46:5; Ezek 47); the presence of "good gold," along with bdellium and onyx/carnelian stones in Gen 2:12 also connects the garden with the temple—a connection acknowledged by Lanfer (142). Interestingly, Wenham had also connected the tree of the knowledge of good and evil with Israel's later sanctuaries, drawing particularly on D. J. A. Clines's "The Tree of Knowledge and the Law of Yahweh" (1974).

Apart from Lanfer's proposed historical context for the redaction of the garden of Eden narrative, this discussion brings up another question regarding the possible limits of a reception history *merely* of the expulsion narrative per se, namely, is it possible? Given that the expulsion narrative was read by interpreters "canonically," not only within the final form of the Eden narrative, but within that of the Pentateuch, which contains intertextual parallels between the creation account(s) and the tabernacle, is it possible to determine how later interpreters viewed the expulsion account in isolation from the dynamic of its presence within the larger corpus inevitably feeding into its meaning? In *The Tabernacle Pre-figured* (2012), for example, I have argued that the Eden narrative functions within the Pentateuch precisely in order to explain the logic and function of the tabernacle/temple cultus, with the Day of Atonement reversing the movement of expulsion—this latter point militating against Lanfer's assertion that "the Eden narrative as a myth about the origins of sin is a largely Christian concept" (109).

Finally, a point of lesser material, in several places (42, 45, 205 n. 54) Lanfer states that the LXX of Ps 1 interpretively inserts "of life," reading "trees of life"—a puzzling remark I cannot substantiate.

Having registered some issues for consideration with regard to its more theoretical aspects, I close by reaffirming the more sure contribution of Lanfer's stimulating book. *Remembering Eden* convincingly maintains that the history of interpretation should serve to constrain the possible meaning(s) of a text. Perhaps it turns about as fair play: after reading (and often judging) ancient interpreters for so long, they wind up reading (and often judging) us.

The Book of Genesis: A Biography, by Ronald Hendel. Lives of Great Religious Books. Princeton: Princeton University Press, 2012. Pp. xii + 287. Hardcover. $24.95. ISBN 9780691140124.

Bradford A. Anderson, Mater Dei Institute, Dublin City University, Dublin, Ireland

Over the past several decades Ronald Hendel has contributed in substantial ways to the critical study of Genesis,[1] and this rich history of scholarship has laid the groundwork for the present volume: an accessible and enlightening tour through the "life" of Genesis, part of Princeton University Press's sharply presented Lives of Great Religious Books series. Here Hendel's wide-ranging interests are on display, as he not only touches on issues of relevance to traditional biblical scholarship but also draws comfortably from a number of ancillary fields and subject areas that contribute in significant ways to this important study.

Hendel introduces the book by pointing out several issues that inform the larger project, including the notion that the ways in which people have read and understood Genesis throughout history correlate broadly with their notions of reality. As such, the diverse ways in which Genesis has been read can help us trace how understandings of reality have changed over time. This trajectory—"from realism to figuralism and back again" (11)—is important to keep in mind, as it helps give shape to Hendel's biographical sketch.

In chapter 1 ("The Genesis of Genesis") Hendel explores the birth (or births) of Genesis. Here Hendel introduces the reader to literary sources in a section heavily indebted to traditional source criticism, using Gen 6–9 and the Yahwistic and Priestly accounts to illustrate how scholars have identified different sources in the text of Genesis. The chapter then explores the ancient Near Eastern context

---

1. Ronald S. Hendel, *The Epic of the Patriarch: The Jacob Cycle and the Narrative Traditions of Canaan and Israel* (HSM 42; Atlanta: Scholars Press, 1988); idem, *The Text of Genesis 1–11: Textual Studies and Critical Edition* (New York: Oxford University Press, 1998); idem, ed., *Reading Genesis: Ten Methods* (Cambridge: Cambridge University Press, 2010).

out of which Genesis emerged, returning again to the flood narrative as well as the creation accounts of Gen 1–2, highlighting ancient parallels and the distinctive ways in which the biblical authors reshaped older traditions. What emerges is a picture of a book "born from a combination of stories and sources that derived from the traditions of ancient lore," a "plural and complex book, which corresponds to a multifarious world" (44).

The second chapter looks at the beginnings of interpretation, and here Hendel draws on the four assumptions that, according to James Kugel, shaped biblical interpretation in the earliest eras in which these texts were read: that the Bible is cryptic, relevant, perfect, and divine. These assumptions would lead early readers and interpreters to employ figural interpretation, and the two main forms of figural reading that emerge from this are what Hendel refers to as apocalyptic and Platonic, approaches that would function as the dominant reading strategies for centuries to follow.

Chapter 3 ("Apocalyptic Secrets") unpacks in more detail apocalyptic readings of Genesis. The rise of apocalyptic is accompanied by two factors, according to Hendel: the advent of critical crises, beginning with the Babylonian exile, and the increasing availability of sacred texts. Apocalypticism is thus an attempt to provide hope at a time of great difficulty, and the early chapters of Genesis would provide much fodder for this type of interpretation. Drawing on Ezekiel, texts from Qumran, and Pauline material, Hendel traces the use and reuse of the rivers of paradise and various appropriations of Adam, all of which attempt to unlock the apocalyptic secrets embedded in the material of Genesis.

Chapter 4 ("Platonic Worlds") explores the second of Hendel's figural approaches, focusing on the influence of Greek thought in early interpretation of Genesis. Following a brief introduction to Plato, the chapter introduces the reader to the Septuagint, Philo, and Paul, all of which demonstrate Greek influence in unique ways. The chapter concludes with explorations of gnostic appropriations of Genesis, as well as various ascetic uses of Adamic motifs, namely, in relation to issues of corporeality.

In chapter 5 Hendel investigates the liminal space "Between the Figural and the Real," focusing on the late medieval and Reformation eras, when "the figural sense of Genesis became strained and began to break" (110). This chapter focuses on three individuals, with particular attention given to their contributions on Genesis. The first is Rashi, with his focus on the "plain sense" of Scripture. Hendel suggests that Rashi "travels a middle path between the figural and the real, embracing the claims of reason while preserving … the legacy of traditional commentary" (120). The second is Martin Luther, and here attention is given to the convergence of Luther's Renaissance heritage, appeals to the light of reason, the rise of *sola scriptura*, and the concomitant rejection of tradition. Finally, Hendel looks at François Rabelais and the first volume of his comic novel, *Gargantua and Pantagruel*. The mockery and parody of both Genesis and figural thinking that is found in this work demonstrates the way in which figural readings were losing their grip in the advent of modernity.

Chapter 6 continues the conversation with a more topical theme, "Genesis and Science: From the Beginning to Fundamentalism," which follows on nicely from the previous chapter. After some reflections on ancient cosmology and early figural readings, the story jumps to Galileo, where Hendel offers a clear and helpful account of Galileo's views of science and Scripture. Galileo's appeals to figural readings of the text were deemed insufficient in large part, Hendel suggests, because "realism was ascendant," and "the figural interpretation of Scripture was rooted in the figural interpretation of nature" (163). Hendel turns next to Spinoza, recounting how he took Galileo's scientific method and began to employ it with the Bible, paving the way for what would become the historical-critical method. The chapter then offers a concise summary of a number of the debates that would ensue in the pushback to these developments, including various attempts to once again make Genesis compatible with science. In this period, Hendel notes, "Old assumptions were questioned, and new problems, which had previously been unthinkable, became unavoidable" (195).

The final chapter, "Modern Times," looks at the increasingly fragmented use of Genesis in light of the changing perspectives noted in the previous chapter. The highlight of the chapter is Hendel's engagement with three modern writers who used Genesis in various ways and with differing effects. Emily Dickinson's complex relationship with the Bible is illustrated, noting that, while she is aware of the legendary nature of the Genesis material, "she perceives its literary capacity for truth" (215). Franz Kafka's *The Trial* is seen as an example of the author's parabolic use of the Bible. Like Dickinson, Kafka clearly recognized the legendary nature of Genesis; however, his work suggests that these are narratives "that expose greater possibilities," in part because they are stories that are "at the same time impossible, redemptive, and obscure" (229). Finally, Erich Auerbach's reading of Gen 22 not only highlights the literary art of the text but also "points to the complexity of our modern consciousness of history" (239), and in doing so links Genesis to the beginnings of realism.

Hendel concludes that we, like these writers, "live on the far side of tradition" (241). The stories of Genesis can no longer be understood in the ways in which they have been in the past; however, unencumbered by tradition, Genesis is open to new ways of being used and understood, as these writers so ably demonstrate.

This is an enlightening and entertaining volume, one that is accessible and yet steeped in broad learning and critical scholarship. Hendel has chosen to tackle issues that give an expansive picture of the life of Genesis, touching on key figures and important hermeneutical developments that even readers familiar with the history of interpretation of the Bible's first book will no doubt appreciate. Further, his forays into territories less familiar to biblical scholars are insightful and refreshing and will offer an important point of reference for those working with the reception of Genesis.

In spite of these strengths, there are aspects of the volume that left this reader wanting more. For example, one gets the impression reading the volume that, for all intents and purposes, critical biblical studies climaxed with Spinoza. Of course, one cannot be exhaustive in such a study; however, the uninitiated reader will gain little awareness of the methods and approaches that have proliferated in recent decades and that have added in significant ways to the biography of Genesis (one thinks, for example, of the contributions made by feminist readings of Genesis). Further, Hendel makes the case that Genesis can and should be read today "on the far side of tradition," and he gives numerous engaging examples of such readings. Still, Genesis continues to be read as Scripture by Jews and Christians around the world, and, given the religious nature of the material, such continued use of the text seems an aspect of the biography of Genesis that is worth noting. Indeed, the fact that it continues to be read within the traditions is perhaps one of the more fascinating aspects of the life of Genesis, and I found myself wishing for further reflection on how such use might fit within the broader trajectory of Hendel's biographical account.

These quibbles notwithstanding, this is a fascinating and learned account of the life and afterlife of Genesis. Hendel is to be commended on the volume, particularly for its erudition and accessibility. Indeed, one hopes that its readers will pick up Genesis for themselves and so perhaps contribute in new ways to the afterlife of this foundational text that Hendel has so skillfully explored.

Index

REVIEWERS

PUBLISHERS

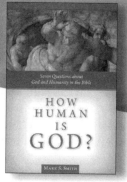

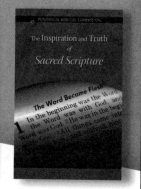